Jordan & Syria

a Lonely Planet travel survival kit

Damien Simonis
Hugh Finlay

Jordan & Syria

3rd edition

Published by
Lonely Planet Publications
Head Office: PO Box 617, Hawthorn, Vic 3122, Australia
Branches: PO Box 2001A, Berkeley, CA 94702, USA
12 Barley Mow Passage, Chiswick, London W4 4PH, UK

Printed by
Pac-Rim Kwartanusa Printing
Printed in Indonesia

Photographs by

Olivier Cirendini, Christine Coste, Hugh Finlay, Tony Howard, Leah McKenzie, Sarah Myers, Damien Simonis, Tony Wheeler

Front cover: Temple of Artemis, Jerash (Olivier Cirendini)
Title page: Statues from Tell Halaf (Christine Coste)
Black & White photography: Preparing *khobz*, p 56 (Sarah Myers); Umm al-Jimal, p 72 (Tony Howard); Wadi Rum, p 98 (Tony Howard); Petra monastery, p 99 (Hugh Finlay); Bedouin camp, p 100 (Tony Howard); Palmyra tetrapylon, p 202 (Leah McKenzie).

First Published
October 1987

This Edition
January 1997

Although the authors and publisher have tried to make the information as accurate as possible, they accept no responsibility for any loss, injury or inconvenience sustained by any person using this book.

National Library of Australia Cataloguing in Publication Data

Simonis, Damien.
Jordan & Syria.

3rd ed.
Includes index.
ISBN 0 86442 427 2.

1. Jordan – Guidebooks. 2. Syria – Guidebooks. I. Title.
(Series: Lonely Planet travel survival kit).

915.6904

Damien Simonis

Damien is a London-based journalist. With a degree in modern languages and several years' newspaper experience on, among others, the *Australian* and the *Age*, he left Australia in 1989. He has worked and travelled widely in Europe, the Middle East and North Africa, and put in several years' hard labour on such London papers as the *Guardian* and the *Independent*. He has worked on Lonely Planet's guides to *Egypt & the Sudan*, *Morocco*, *North Africa* and *Italy*. Damien is currently co-writing Lonely Planet's guide to Spain. He has also contributed to publications in the UK, North America and Australia.

Hugh Finlay

After deciding there must be more to life than civil engineering, Hugh took off around Australia in the mid-70s, working at everything from spray painting to diamond prospecting, before hitting the overland trail. He joined Lonely Planet in 1985 and has co-authored *Kenya* and *East Africa*, and has contributed to other LP guides including *Africa*, *North Africa, India*, *Australia* and *Nepal*. He lives in central Victoria, Australia, with his wife Linda and his daughters Ella and Vera.

From the Authors

From Damien Many people helped make the research and travel in Syria and Jordan just that little bit easier. In London, I am indebted to David Butter and Edmund Blair for allowing me access to the cuttings library of the Middle East Economic Digest.

In Damascus I would like to thank Joseph Sein, Irma van Mil, Peter Poort and Muriel Holstvoogd (all Netherlands) for good company and useful tips. Jeffrey Hayes, of the American Language Center, bent over backwards to help out with information. Thanks also to Ahmed Safadi of Silk Road Tours. In Hama, I owe a particular debt to Bader Tonbur. On the road, Steve Anderson (Aus), Mike Trentham, Charlotte Jordan and Roz Lucas (UK) all contributed information and were willing partners (no arm-twisting ever required) in a beer at the end of a hard day's travelling. David Rossi (Malta) provided valuable information on student permits. To them and others not mentioned here, many thanks.

In Amman, Mohiseen and his merry band at the desk of the Bdeiwi Hotel helped me out with minor customs hassles, and Sami Twal was also most willing to extend aid. Thanks also to Hector Low of the British Council.

Travelling partners I owe thanks to for company and patience are Michelle Byrnes, Felicity Campion (Aus) and, above all, Elisabeth Mead (USA).

A long overdue vote of thanks goes to all

the guys at Lonely Planet London, who have not only gone beyond the call of duty in helping me keep bits of my life ticking over, but have always kept the welcome mat out. The Paris office and their intrepid updaters have also helped me out greatly on this one – *merci beaucoups*.

And to the many other people of Jordan and Syria who did not hesitate to hold out a hand of friendship, *shukran jazeelan*.

From Hugh Thanks to Tony Howard and NOMADS for continued permission to reproduce the Wadi Rum map.

This Book

Hugh Finlay researched and wrote the 1st edition of this book. Damien Simonis updated the 2nd edition and extensively researched and revised this 3rd edition, with assistance from Olivier Cirendini and Christine Coste.

From the Publisher

Susan Noonan edited this book with assistance from Miriam Cannell, Helen Castle, Michelle Glynn, Lindsay Brown and Rachel Scully. Rachael Scott drew and updated the maps with help from Sally Gerdan and Trudi Canavan. Rachael was also responsible for the design and some of the illustrations. Margaret Jung, Indra Kilfoyle, Valerie Tellini and Ann Jeffree provided additional illustrations. Simon Bracken designed the cover and Adam McCrow was responsible for the back-cover cartography. Thanks to Michelle Glynn for translating some of the boxed stories, to Dan Levin for the soft fonts and to Chris Love for the climate charts.

Thank you to Vicky Clayton and Diana Taylor for their information on accommodation for women in Jordan and Syria, and to Peter Ward of Peter Ward Exports for information on bookshops.

We are also very grateful to Olivier Cirendini and Christine Coste, authors of the French edition of this book. Their extensive revisions were most helpful in the preparation of this edition.

Finally, many thanks to Dr Stephen Bourke for contributing the archaeology section, 'Digging up the Past', and to Tony Howard and Diana Taylor for their comprehensive introduction to trekking, 'Trekking in Jordan'.

Thanks

Many thanks to the travellers who used the last edition and wrote to us with helpful hints, useful advice and interesting anecdotes. Your names appear on page 376.

Warning & Request

Things change – prices go up, schedules change, good places go bad and bad places go bankrupt – nothing stays the same. So, if you find things better or worse, recently opened or long since closed, please tell us and help make the next edition even more accurate and useful.

We value all of the feedback we receive from travellers. Julie Young coordinates a small team who read and acknowledge every letter, postcard and email, and ensure that every morsel of information finds its way to the appropriate authors, editors and publishers.

Everyone who writes to us will find their name in the next edition of the appropriate guide and will also receive a free subscription to our quarterly newsletter, *Planet Talk*. The very best contributions will be rewarded with a free Lonely Planet guide.

Excerpts from your correspondence may appear in Updates (which we add to the end pages of reprints); new editions of this guide; in our newsletter, *Planet Talk*; or in the Postcards section of our Web site – so please let us know if you don't want your letter published or your name acknowledged.

Contents

Map Legend

BOUNDARIES

International Boundary
Regional Boundary

ROUTES

Freeway
Highway
Major Road
Unsealed Road or Track
City Road
City Street
Railway
Underground Railway
Tram
Walking Track
Walking Tour
Ferry Route
Cable Car or Chairlift

AREA FEATURES

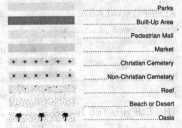

Parks
Built-Up Area
Pedestrian Mall
Market
Christian Cemetery
Non-Christian Cemetery
Reef
Beach or Desert
Oasis

HYDROGRAPHIC FEATURES

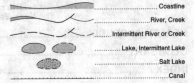

Coastline
River, Creek
Intermittent River or Creek
Lake, Intermittent Lake
Salt Lake
Canal

SYMBOLS

CAPITAL — National Capital
Capital — Regional Capital
CITY — Major City
City — City
Town — Town
Village — Village
Place to Stay, Place to Eat
Cafe, Pub or Bar
Post Office, Telephone
Tourist Information, Bank
Bus Station or Terminal, Bus Stop
Museum, Youth Hostel
Caravan Park, Camping Ground
Church, Cathedral
Mosque, Synagogue
Temple, Parking
Hospital, Police Station
Embassy, Border Crossing
Airport, Airfield
Swimming Pool, Gardens
Shopping Centre, Petrol Station
Winery or Vineyard, Picnic Site
A25 — One Way Street, Route Number
Stately Home, Monument
Castle, Tomb or Mausoleum
Cave, Hut or Shelter
Mountain or Hill, Lookout
Lighthouse, Shipwreck
Pass, Spring
Beach, Surf Beach
Archaeological Site or Ruins
Ancient or City Wall
Cliff or Escarpment, Tunnel
Train Station

Note: not all symbols displayed above appear in this book

Introduction

Lying in the heart of an area as volatile as the Middle East, Jordan and Syria for many people hardly represent the ideal holiday destinations. Indeed, television reports of all the bad news that tends to emerge from here are about as close as most want to come to these two countries.

Given its unflattering media profile – that of a region of barren desert and fanatics bent on revolution – it may come as a surprise that not only is it safe to travel here, but that the local Arab inhabitants are among the most hospitable people in the world. The closest you'll come to being hijacked here is to be dragged off to a café to drink tea and chat for a while.

Certainly, things aren't the same as at home – in many cases they are a whole lot better. Where else can you leave your belongings unattended for hours, safe in the knowledge that they will be there on your return, and where can you wander the streets any time of the day or night without fear for your safety?

With a history of permanent settlement going back some 11,000 years, the number of archaeological and historical sites is enough to satiate even the most avid ruin buff. They run the gamut from relics of Stone Age settlements through the civilisations of the Phoenicians, Greeks, Romans and Byzantines to the more contemporary Muslims, Crusaders, Ottoman Turks and even the British and the French – they have all left their mark. Add to this a few lesser known cultures such as the Nabataeans (builders of the incredible city of Petra) and the Palmyrenes, who at one stage had the audacity to threaten the might of Rome, and you start to get an idea of the diverse influences that have played a part in shaping this region. Everyone from Tutankhamen to Winston Churchill has walked across this stage.

When you've had your fill of history, you can take time out to explore some of the natural wonders on offer: take a camel ride through the incredible desert landscapes of Wadi Rum (one of Lawrence of Arabia's old

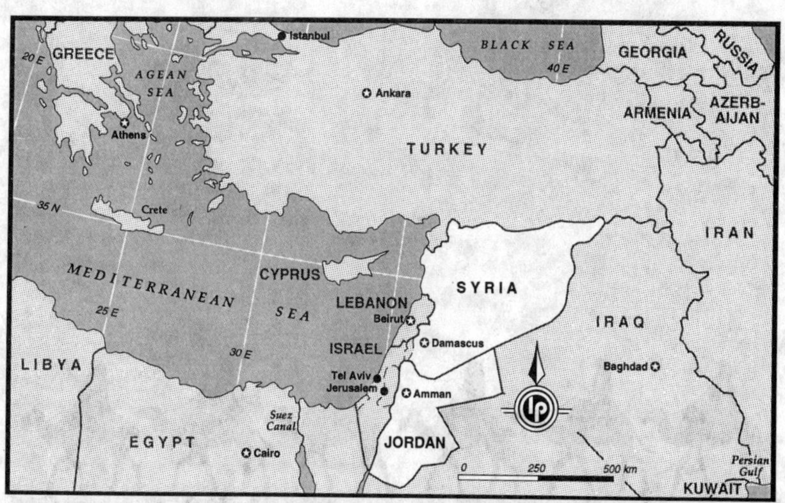

stamping grounds); explore the grandeur of the Euphrates River; don a mask and snorkel and head underwater in the Gulf of Aqaba to see some of the finest coral reefs anywhere; or have a swim, or more precisely, a float, in the saline waters of the Dead Sea – the lowest point on earth.

Jordan and Syria have developed rapidly this century and both offer the facilities to make life comfortable at an affordable price. Accommodation ranges from five star luxury for the well-heeled down to simple but perfectly adequate establishments for the impecunious. Transport is fast and efficient, and modern, air-conditioned buses or trains service all the major centres. When it comes to food, sit down to a formal banquet, or squat around a communal bowl of rice and meat with a Bedouin family in their goat-hair tent and tuck in by hand.

The peace process has given the region's tourism a bit of a boost, and the tour bus has definitely arrived in Jordan and, to a lesser extent, Syria. That said, there remains plenty of elbow room for those seeking to stray from the beaten track. With an open mind, a bit of patience, plenty of time and a taste for something different, the more adventurous traveller will not be disappointed by the Jordan and Syria travel experience.

Facts about the Region

HISTORY

The history of Syria and Jordan is one of invasion and conquest. The region was never strong enough to form an empire itself, and it was for the most part a collection of city-states, but its strategic position ensured that all the great early civilisations passed through here. The Egyptians, Assyrians, Babylonians, Hittites, Greeks, Romans, Arabs, Turks and Crusaders all helped to shape the history of the region. They traded, built cities and fought their wars here, leaving behind rich cultural influences.

Although the modern states of Jordan and Syria are creations of the 20th century, the region they encompass can lay claim to having one of the oldest civilisations in the world. Archaeological finds from Jericho, on the west bank of the Jordan River, have been positively dated at around 9000 BC. They have revealed an extensive village where the inhabitants lived in mud and stone houses and there is evidence of agriculture and animal domestication. Major finds in Syria at Ras Shamra (Ugarit, circa 6600 BC) on the Mediterranean coast and at Mari (circa 4500 BC) on the Euphrates River, show more advanced settlements that would later become sophisticated city-states.

From 3000 BC, the region was settled by the Amorites, a warlike Semitic tribe, and the Canaanites, who mostly inhabited the coastal lowlands. The villages of Syria and Palestine came to the attention of Egypt to the south-west, and the expanding Euphrates Valley empires to the east, around this time.

Sargon of Akkad, a powerful ruler of Mesopotamia from 2334 to 2279 BC, marched to the Mediterranean in search of conquest and natural resources to supply his growing empire. From humble beginnings, he became the greatest ruler in Mesopotamia. It is said that as a baby he was fished from the Euphrates River by a gardener who found him floating in a basket. He was raised as a gardener, but Sargon obviously had greater things in mind. After becoming cup-bearer for the ruler of the city of Kish in northern Sumer, he gathered an army and, with his great military prowess and ability to organise, set about conquering the cities of the south. He went on to become king and the world's first great empire-builder.

Sargon's ascendancy in the Mediterranean area led to the growth of many towns with strong Mesopotamian influence. Trade with Egypt flourished as it, too, needed wood, stone and metal to supply the needs of its rapidly expanding empire. Cities like Jericho and Byblos (in present-day Lebanon) became well established and prospered with this trade.

By about 1700 BC, Palestine was part of the Hyksos Empire of Egypt. The Hyksos were themselves Asiatic invaders and despised in Egypt. The revolt and pursuit of the

Sargon I, King of Sumer and Akkad, ruled over Sumeria, with his kingdom extending to Arabia, Syria and Asia Minor.

Hyksos across Palestine by the Egyptians, under the leadership of Kamose of Thebes, led to a period of expansion of the Egyptian Empire. By 1520 BC, Thutmose I claims to have reached the banks of the Euphrates River, although he was met by stubborn resistance from the local inhabitants and by no means controlled the entire area.

In 1480 BC, a revolt organised by more than 300 Syrian and Palestinian rulers was easily crushed and Egypt was by this time firmly established in Palestine and the southern Syrian region. It would remain so for over a century. In the north, however, the various principalities coalesced to form the Mitanni Empire. They held off all Egyptian attempts at control, helped in part by their invention of the horse-drawn chariot as a weapon of war.

It was the encroachments of the Hittites from the north in about 1365 BC, under the young, ambitious leader Suppiluliumas, that led to the fall of the Mitanni Empire. Despite some half-hearted attempts by the new pharaoh, Tutankhamen, to gain control, by 1330 BC all of Syria was firmly in the hands of the Hittites.

The two powers clashed at the bloody Battle of Kadesh on the Orontes River in Syria around 1300 BC. Militarily it was an indecisive meeting but it dealt the Egyptians a strategic blow and saw them retreat into Palestine. Finally, the two opposing forces signed a treaty of friendship in 1284 BC, which ended a long period of clashes between empires for control of Syria. It left the Egyptians with a turbulent Palestine and the Hittites with Syria and the threat from the rising power of Assyria.

Thus came to an end three prosperous centuries in this part of the Levant. The area was well placed to make the most of trade between Egypt to the south, Mesopotamia to the east and Anatolia to the north. Although suited to the production of olives, grapes, barley and wheat, as well as the raising of livestock, the prosperity of the various cities really depended on the extent to which they controlled the mule and caravan routes. Those very routes is what held the foreign powers' interest in this part of the world.

One of the most important contributions to world history from this period was the development of written scripts. The ancient site of Ugarit in Syria has yielded the oldest alphabet yet known. Until then only Egyptian hieroglyphics and Mesopotamian cuneiform existed. Both required hundreds of symbols that were far too difficult for anyone but the scribes to use. By 1000 BC linear, rather than pictorial scripts, were in general use. It is from these alphabets, developed further in Palestine, that today's scripts are derived.

From about the 13th century BC, Palestine was threatened by an invasion of 'Peoples from the Sea' – possibly the Philistines. The Egyptian Empire was in decline. It had overextended itself and was under threat from Libyan tribes to the west, allowing the raiders from the Aegean to assert themselves and take control of the area. Egyptian influence rapidly dwindled and the Hittite Empire also declined, finally collapsing around 1200 BC. The Philistines settled on the coastal plain of Canaan in an area that came to be known as the Plain of Philistia and from which the name Palestine ('Filasteen' in Arabic) is derived.

The Philistines' ascendancy owed much to their use of iron for weapons and armour, which the Canaanites and Egyptians did not possess. In fact the Iron Age is traditionally given as beginning in the 12th century BC.

At about the same time the east bank of the Jordan River was settled by three other groups: the Edomites in the south, the Moabites to the east of the Dead Sea, and the Ammonites on the edge of the Arabian Desert with their capital at Rabbath Ammon, present-day Amman.

Coming of the Israelites

Much of what we know about the history of this part of the world comes from the books of the Old and, later, New Testaments, which have naturally propelled essentially Jewish history into the foreground.

It was not until the late 11th century BC

that the Philistines were threatened. Led by Moses, the Israelites left Egypt around 1270 BC – the Exodus – and, after the traditional 40 years in the wilderness, they overran the local rulers and settled in the hills of Transjordan (the name used to describe the area east of the Jordan River).

Following the victories of Moses, his successor Joshua led the 12 tribes across the Jordan River and conquered Jericho. The Israelites then suffered a severe defeat at the Battle of Ebenezer in 1050 BC, which saw the Philistines capture the Ark of the Covenant – the symbol of unity of the 12 tribes of Israel. Further disaster came after another major battle when Saul, who had been made king of Israel in 1020 BC, took his own life and left the Israelites without a leader and at the mercy of the Philistines.

Empire of David & Solomon 1000 – 930 BC

The fortunes of Israel took a turn very much for the better when Saul's successor, David, was proclaimed king in 1000 BC. After defeating the Philistines near Jerusalem, he set about regaining the territory of his neighbours east of the Jordan. By the end of his reign in 960 BC, he ruled the principalities of Edom, Moab and Ammon (the city-states of southern Syria) and was paid tribute by the Philistine princes and the tribes as far east as the Euphrates.

After the death of David and the ascent to the throne of his son Solomon, Israel entered its golden age. This period saw great advancements in trade, which extended down the African and Red Sea coasts and into Asia Minor. A visit to Jerusalem by the Queen of Sheba (in present-day Yemen) is evidence that there was also overland trade to the Arabian Peninsula.

A great part of the success of Solomon's rule was derived from his administrative skills which, however, also led to high tax burdens and forced labour. Resentment of these hardships led to a revolt against Solomon, and following his death in 922 BC the united kingdom was divided into the separate kingdoms of Judah in the south and Israel in the north.

The main threat to Israel was the Aramaen state of Damascus, as the two were rivals for the lucrative Syrian and Transjordanian trade. This rivalry led to an alliance between Israel and the Phoenicians when the sixth king of Israel, Omri, married off his son Ahab to the Phoenician princess Jezebel. The defeat of Ahab by Mesha, the King of Moab, is recorded in the famous Mesha Stele (Moabite Stone) found at Dhiban (north of present-day Kerak in Jordan). A short period of relative peace was shattered in 722 BC when the Assyrians under Sargon II devastated Israel and its capital Samaria, deported the citizens and replaced them with settlers from Syria and Babylonia. The northern kingdom of Israel had ceased to exist.

In the south, Judah survived for another century under Assyrian rule until the Babylonian king Nebuchadnezzar overthrew the Assyrians and took control. Rebellions under the last kings of Judah were put down and resulted in the destruction of many Judaean cities and finally the taking of Jerusalem in 597 BC. After the puppet-king installed by the Babylonians also rebelled, Jerusalem was taken for the second time in 587 BC. The Jews were deported en masse to Babylon – the Exile – ending the history of the southern kingdom of Judah.

In 539 BC Cyrus II came to power in Persia and allowed the Jews to return to Palestine. Under Nehemiah they rebuilt the walls of Jerusalem. The next two centuries were a period of calm during which the Jews were able to implement various social reforms.

The Greeks & Romans

In 333 BC Alexander the Great stormed through Syria and Palestine on his way to Egypt. On his death, his newly formed empire was parcelled up among his generals.

In his short reign, Alexander the Great conquered the Middle East from Greece to India initiating an era of Greek territorial monarchies.

Ptolemy I gained Egypt and parts of Syria, while Seleucus established a kingdom in Babylonia.

For the next century, the Seleucids disputed the Ptolemies' claim to Palestine and tried unsuccessfully to oust the Ptolemies before finally succeeding in 198 BC under the leadership of Antiochus III. He then tried to extend his influence westwards but met with the new power of Rome. His army was defeated by the Romans and in 188 BC he was forced to cede all his territories in Asia Minor.

After attacking Egypt the Seleucids, under Antiochus IV, sacked Jerusalem and left the Jews with no alternative but to revolt after virtually banning their religion as well as dedicating the Temple of Jerusalem to Zeus – the supreme god of the ancient Greeks.

Led by Judas Maccabeus of the Hasmonean family, the Jews gradually re-established themselves and by 141 BC were recognised as an independent territory, occupying a large area east of the Jordan River. During the reign of John Hyrcanus and his successors, the boundaries were further extended to cover most of Palestine and Transjordan. On Hyrcanus' death, a squabble between his sons, Aristobolus and Hyrcanus II, led to the intervention of the Romans under Pompey, who took Damascus in 64 BC and Palestine the following year. The Jewish kingdom was now under Roman control and Hyrcanus II was appointed high priest.

All of western Syria and Palestine became the new Roman province of Syria. The most important cities east of the Jordan were organised into a league of 10. The Decapolis, as it was known, was formed as a commercial and military alliance for the advancement of trade, and as protection against the Jews and Nabataeans.

The Parthian kings of Persia and Mesopotamia invaded and occupied most of the province in 40 BC but Mark Antony was able to restore order, albeit with some difficulty. Antipater, minister for Hyrcanus II, was made governor of Judaea and his sons Herod and Phaesal were appointed governors of Jerusalem and Galilee, respectively.

Kingdom of Herod the Great 40 – 4 BC

With the Parthian invasion, the Hasmonean family, now led by Aristobolus' son Antigonus, was able to seize power. Phaesal and Hyrcanus II were captured and Herod escaped to Rome where, on appeal to the senate, he was named king of Israel and returned to Palestine. With Roman help he expelled the Parthians and took Jerusalem in 37 BC in a bloody conflict. Mark Antony had Antigonus executed.

The period of Herod's rule, from 40 BC to 4 BC, was a time of relative peace and prosperity for Palestine. What followed after his death was a period of unrest that led to a Jewish revolt in 66 AD. Nero entrusted the commander Vespasian with the task of restoring order and he effectively subdued Galilee and Judaea. His son Titus captured and virtually destroyed Jerusalem.

The Herodian rulers were a perverse lot. In his later years, Herod the Great suffered from mental instability and became increasingly tyrannical. He murdered his ex-wife Mariamne, and for good measure also murdered many of her family, including her mother, brother, grandfather and her two sons. Fearing plots against him, he also disposed of three of his own sons. He tried at least once to commit suicide but finally died of natural causes. His son, Herod Antipas, had John the Baptist put to death; his sister's grandson, Herod Agrippa I, had St James executed and St Peter imprisoned. The last of the line was Herod Agrippa II, son of Herod Agrippa I, who lived incestuously with his sister Berenice.

In the first century AD, the Apostles – followers of a Jew named Jesus – propagated a new faith: Christianity.

Apart from making the Jewish nation a province, the Romans made remarkably few changes to the Jewish way of life. This leniency led to a second revolt in 132 AD which was put down by Hadrian, who then gave Jerusalem the new name of Aelia Capitolina. Captive Jews were sold into slavery and the religious practices of the survivors were strictly curtailed.

Only about 20 years before, in 106 AD, the Romans had incorporated the loose empire of the Nabataeans, centred on the rock city of Petra, into the Roman orbit. The Nabataeans were unusual in that they retained much of their nomadic character as traders rather than settling down to develop agriculture. In the previous 300 years they had established a fluid control over an area stretching from Damascus to Wejh on the coast of modern Saudi Arabia, and from modern Suez to Wadi Sirhan in the desert of eastern Jordan.

Nabataean strength lay in the control of trade routes and almost exclusive knowledge of desert strongpoints and water supplies. Their greatest economic trump was the trade monopoly they exercised over the difficult route into Arabia Felix, which the Romans attempted without success to penetrate shortly before the birth of Christ. Heavy duties imposed on goods transported on these routes and protection money to keep bandits at bay were the principal source of wealth.

The Nabataeans never really possessed an empire in the common military and administrative sense of the word, but rather a 'zone of influence'. After 106, the Nabataeans lost much of their commercial power and faded into insignificance.

In the 3rd century the Sassanian Persians (or Sassanids), the successors to the Parthians, invaded northern Syria but were repelled by the Syrian prince Odenathus of Palmyra. He was granted the title 'dux orientalis' (commander of the east) by his Roman overlords for his efforts, but died shortly afterwards. Suspected of complicity in his death, his widow, the ambitious Zenobia, assumed the title Augusta and, with her sights set on Rome, invaded western Syria, Palestine and Egypt. In 272, Aurelian destroyed Palmyra and carted Zenobia off to Rome as a prisoner.

With the conversion of the emperor Constantine early in the 4th century, Christianity became the dominant religion. Jerusalem became the site of holy pilgrimage to Christian shrines and this did wonders for the prosperity of the area. During the reign of Justinian from 527 to 565, churches were built in many towns in Palestine and Syria.

This rosy state of affairs was abruptly shattered in the 7th century when the Persians once again descended from the north, taking Damascus and Jerusalem in 614 and eventually Egypt in 616, although Byzantine fortunes were revived when the emperor Heraclius invaded Persia and forced the Persians into a peace agreement. In the south, however, the borders of the empire were being attacked by Arab raiders – no new thing – but these Arabs were ambitious Muslims, followers of Mohammed.

The Advent of Islam

With the Byzantine Empire severely weakened by the Persian invasion and the Aramaen population alienated by Constantinople's domination, the Muslims met with little resistance and in some cases were even welcomed.

In 636 the Muslim armies won a famous victory at the Battle of Yarmouk, which marks the modern border between Jordan and Syria. At the same time Ctesiphon, the Persian capital on the Tigris, also fell. Within 15 years the Sassanian Empire had disappeared and the Arab Muslims had reached the river Oxus on the northern frontier of modern Afghanistan.

In the west, the Byzantine forces never recovered from Yarmouk and could do little but fall back towards Anatolia. Jerusalem fell in 638 and soon after all of Syria was in Muslim hands. Egypt fell shortly after.

Because of its position on the pilgrims' route to Mecca, Syria became the hub of the new Muslim empire which, by the early 8th century, stretched from Spain and across northern Africa and the Middle East to Persia (modern Iran) and India. Mu'awiya, the governor of Damascus, had himself declared the fifth caliph, or successor to Mohammed, in 658 and founded a line, the Omayyads, who would last for about a century. Damascus thus replaced Medina (in present-day Saudi Arabia) as the political capital.

The Omayyad period was one of great achievement and saw the building of monuments such as the Omayyad Mosque in Damascus and the Mosque of Omar and the Dome of the Rock in Jerusalem. The Omayyads' great love of the desert led to the construction of palaces (the so-called Desert Castles east of Amman) where the *caliphs* (successors) could indulge their Bedouin past. Nevertheless, it was also a time of almost unremitting internal struggle, and Damascus found itself constrained to put down numerous revolts in Iraq and Arabia itself.

Omayyad rule was overthrown in 750, when the Abbasids seized power and transferred the caliphate to Baghdad. Syria and Palestine went into a rapid decline as a result; administratively, they were no more than a coastal strip stretching as far inland as Damascus and Jerusalem.

The Abbasids, too, had their share of problems, and by the 900s had lost their grip and been replaced by other families. Imperial control slipped increasingly out of Baghdad's hands and, by 980, all of Palestine and part

OLIVIER CIRENDINI

HUGH FINLAY

HUGH FINLAY

HUGH FINLAY

OLIVIER CIRENDINI

A	B
E	C
D	

A: Desert Patrolman, Wadi Rum (Jordan)
B: Repairing fishing nets (Jordan)
C: Souq stall, Aleppo (Syria)
D: Cinema poster, Amman (Jordan)
E: Enjoying the local tea, *shay* (Syria)

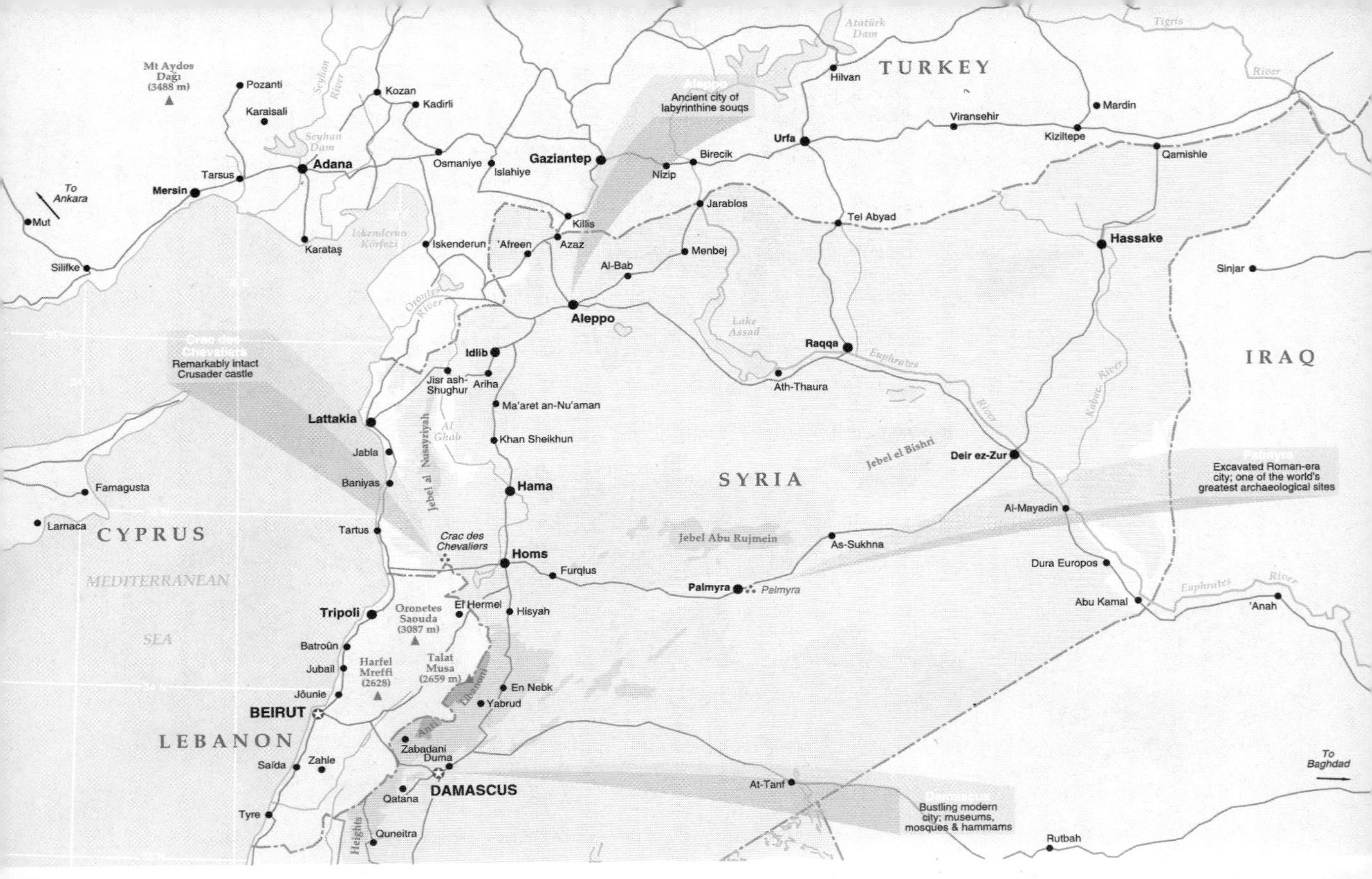

TURKEY
SYRIA
IRAQ
LEBANON
CYPRUS
MEDITERRANEAN
SEA
Aleppo
Ancient city of labyrinthine souqs
Crac des Chevaliers
Remarkably intact Crusader castle
Palmyra
Excavated Roman-era city; one of the world's greatest archaeological sites
Damascus
Bustling modern city; museums, mosques & hammams
Mt Aydos Dağı (3488 m)
Pozanti
Karaisali
Kozan
Kadirli
Seyhan River
Seyhan Dam
Adana
Tarsus
Mersin
To Ankara
Mut
Silifke
Karataş
Iskenderun Körfezi
Osmaniye
Islahiye
Gaziantep
Iskenderun
'Afreen
Killis
Azaz
Nizip
Birecik
Jarablos
Menbej
Al-Bab
Aleppo
Orontes River
Urfa
Hilvan
Atatürk Dam
Viransehir
Kiziltepe
Mardin
Qamishle
Tigris
River
Tel Abyad
Hassake
Sinjar
Lake Assad
Raqqa
Euphrates
Ath-Thaura
Khabur River
River
Idlib
Jisr ash-Shughur
Ariha
Ma'aret an-Nu'aman
Khan Sheikhun
Al Ghab
Jebel al Nasayriyah
Lattakia
Jabla
Baniyas
Hama
Jebel el Bishri
Deir ez-Zur
Al-Mayadin
Famagusta
Larnaca
Tartus
Crac des Chevaliers
Homs
Jebel Abu Rujmein
As-Sukhna
Dura Europos
Furqlus
Palmyra
Palmyra
Euphrates River
Abu Kamal
'Anah
Tripoli
Oronetes Saouda (3087 m)
El Hermel
Hisyah
Batroûn
Jubail
Harfel Mreffi (2628)
Talat Musa (2659 m)
Lebanon
En Nebk
Jôunie
Yabrud
BEIRUT
Anti
Zabadani
Duma
Saïda
Zahle
DAMASCUS
Qatana
At-Tanf
To Baghdad
Tyre
Heights
Quneitra
Rutbah

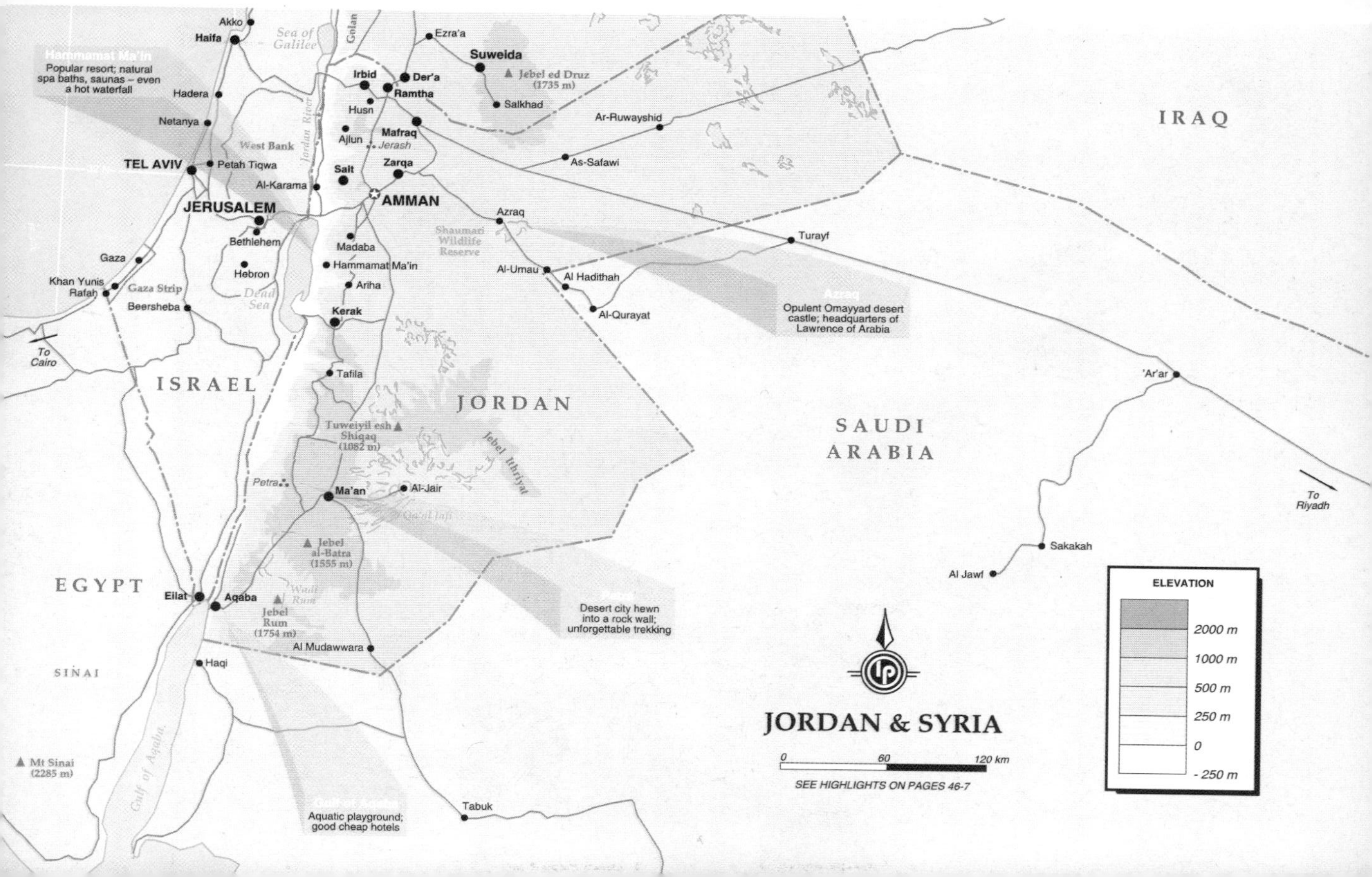
Hammamat Ma'in
Popular resort; natural spa baths, saunas – even a hot waterfall
Azraq
Opulent Omayyad desert castle; headquarters of Lawrence of Arabia
Desert city hewn into a rock wall; unforgettable trekking
Aquatic playground; good cheap hotels
IRAQ
JORDAN
SAUDI ARABIA
ISRAEL
EGYPT
SINAI
Golan
West Bank
Gaza Strip
Sea of Galilee
Jordan River
Dead Sea
Gulf of Aqaba
Akko
Haifa
Hadera
Netanya
TEL AVIV
Petah Tiqwa
JERUSALEM
Bethlehem
Hebron
Gaza
Khan Yunis
Rafah
Beersheba
To Cairo
Al-Karama
Irbid
Husn
Ajlun
Jerash
Salt
Der'a
Ramtha
Mafraq
Zarqa
AMMAN
Madaba
Hammamat Ma'in
Ariha
Kerak
Tafila
Tuweiyil esh Shiqaq (1082 m)
Petra
Ma'an
Al-Jair
Qa'al Jafi
Jebel al-Batra (1555 m)
Wadi Rum
Jebel Rum (1754 m)
Eilat
Aqaba
Al Mudawwara
Haqi
Tabuk
Mt Sinai (2285 m)
Ezra'a
Suweida
Jebel ed Druz (1735 m)
Salkhad
Ar-Ruwayshid
As-Safawi
Azraq
Shaumari Wildlife Reserve
Al-Umau
Al Hadithah
Al-Qurayat
Jebel Ithriyat
Turayf
'Ar'ar
To Riyadh
Sakakah
Al Jawf
ELEVATION
2000 m
1000 m
500 m
250 m
0
- 250 m
JORDAN & SYRIA
0
60
120 km
SEE HIGHLIGHTS ON PAGES 46-7

DAMIEN SIMONIS

Narjilehs (water pipes) for sale at Souq al-Hamadiyyeh in Damascus, Syria.

of Syria (including Damascus) had fallen under Fatimid Cairo's rule. Aleppo and northern Syria and Iraq were controlled by the Hamdanids, a Shiite group.

It was into this vacuum of central power that the Crusaders arrived, and in fact it is unlikely they would have lasted long at all if the Muslim lands had not been so divided. They established four states, the most important being the kingdom of Jerusalem in 1099. Fortresses were built at Kerak, Shobak, Wadi Musa and the island of Far'aon just offshore from Aqaba. In Syria a string of castles, including the well-preserved Crac des Chevaliers, was constructed along the coastal mountain ranges. Their hold was always tenuous as they were a minority and could only survive if the Muslim states remained weak and divided, which in fact they obligingly did until the 12th century.

Nureddin (or Nur ad-Din, literally 'light of the faith'), son of a Turkish tribal ruler, was able to unite all of Syria not held by the Franks and defeat the Crusaders in Egypt. His campaign was completed by Saladin (or Salah ad-Din, literally 'righteousness of the faith'), who overthrew the Fatimid rulers of Egypt in 1171 and recaptured Palestine and most of the inland Crusader strongholds. European rule was restored to the coast for another century with the Third Crusade.

Prosperity returned to Syria with the rule of the Ayyubids, members of Saladin's family, who parcelled up his empire on his death. They were succeeded by the Mamelukes, the freed slave class of Turkish origin that had taken power in Cairo in 1250, just in time to repel the onslaught from the invading Mongol tribes from central Asia in 1260. The victorious Mameluke leader, Baibars I, ruled over a reunited Syria and Egypt until his death in 1277. By the beginning of the 14th century, the Mamelukes had finally managed to rid the Levant of the Crusaders by capturing their last stronghold – the fortified island of Ruad (Arwad) – off the coast of Tartus in Syria.

However, more death and destruction was not far off and in 1401 the Mongol invader Timur (Tamerlaine) sacked Aleppo and Damascus, killing thousands and carting off many of the artisans to central Asia. His new empire lasted for only a few years but the rout sent Mameluke Syria into a decline for the next century.

The Ottoman Turks

By 1516, Palestine and Syria had been occupied by the Ottoman Turks and would stay that way for the next four centuries. Most of the desert areas of modern Syria and Jordan, however, remained the preserve of Bedouin tribes.

Up until the early 19th century, Syria prospered under Turkish rule. Damascus and Aleppo were important market towns for the surrounding desert as well as being stages on the desert trade routes to Persia and stops on the Pilgrimage route to Mecca. Aleppo also became an important trading centre with Europe, and Venetian, English and French merchants established themselves there.

For almost the whole of the 1830s the Egyptians once again gained control, led by Ibrahim Pasha, son of the Egyptian ruler Mohammed Ali. The high taxation and the conscription imposed by Ibrahim were unpopular and the Europeans, fearful that the decline of Ottoman power might cause a crisis in Europe, intervened in 1840 and forced the Egyptians to withdraw.

The Muslim Arabs had accepted Turkish rule and the Ottoman Empire as the political embodiment of Islam, but already in the 19th century groups of Arab intellectuals in Syria and Palestine (many of them influenced by their years of study in Europe) set an Arab reawakening in train. With the Young Turk movement of 1909, imperial power was in the hands of a military group, the harsh policies of which encouraged opposition and the growth of Arab nationalism.

WWI

During WWI, the area of Syria and Jordan was the scene of fierce fighting between the Turks, who had German backing, and the British based in Suez. By the end of 1917, British and Empire troops occupied Jerusalem and, a year later, the rest of Syria. Their successes would have been impossible without the aid of the Arabs, loosely formed into an army under Emir Faisal, son of Hussein, who was Sherif (ruler) of Mecca and had taken up the reins of the Arab nationalist movement in 1914. The enigmatic British colonel, TE Lawrence, better known as Lawrence of Arabia, helped coordinate the Arab Revolt and secure supplies from the Allies under General Allenby's command.

Under the Sykes-Picot agreement of 1916, Syria and Lebanon were to be placed under French Mandate, and Palestine would go to the British. By the Balfour Declaration of 1917, Britain pledged support for the ambiguously phrased 'Jewish homeland'.

In March 1920, Emir Faisal was proclaimed king of Syria but the Allied powers refused to recognise him. At the Conference of San Remo, the Allied Supreme Council confirmed France's mandate over Syria and Lebanon, and the British got Palestine, part of which later became Transjordan (see History in the Facts about Jordan chapter).

Out of this mess emerged the modern states of Syria, Lebanon, Transjordan (subsequently Jordan) and, later, Israel. The path to the creation of the modern independent states of Syria and Jordan from 1920 on is covered in their respective Facts about the Country chapters.

ARTS

Music

Arab music reflects a successful synthesis of indigenous harmony and taste, not to mention instruments, with some traits and instruments of the west. The popular music takes some time to get used to, and for many its attraction remains a mystery. Others however, are eventually caught up in its own particular magic – which is probably a good thing, because you'll hear it in one form or another wherever you go!

In the sands of the Arabian deserts, the Bedouin have long had their own musical traditions, simple but mesmerising. The chanting of men at a distant wedding drifting across the desert on a still night is a haunting sound. Up close, the musical side of the evening's festivities are clearly rooted in ancient traditions. A row of men will, arm in arm, gently sway backwards and forwards engaged in what appears to be an almost trance-like chant. They are singing to and calling a lone woman who, veiled, dances before them with restrained but unmistakable sensuality. One is tempted to conclude that the belly dance, a largely Egyptian genre that has spread to nightclubs throughout the Arab world, is a considerably less demure offshoot of the purer desert art.

The music that you hear in the streets of Damascus and Amman today, however, has precious little to do with timeless desert traditions. The most common and popular style of music today focuses on a star performer backed by anything from a small quartet to a full-blown orchestra. An enormous number of such performers have emerged in countries all over the Arab world. National boundaries do not play a critical role in this sense.

There appears to be a consensus that one of the all-time greats remains a woman known in her homeland as the 'Mother of Egypt' – Umm Kolthoum. She died in 1975, but her voice still resounds from radios and TV sets today. Although to non-Arabs her singing can be difficult to appreciate, she gets virtually unanimous applause from Arabs.

The kind of orchestra that backs such a singer is a curious cross-fertilisation of east and west. Western-style instruments such as violins, the piano and many of the wind and percussion instruments predominate, next to such local species as the *oud* (lute). The sounds that emanate from them are anything but western. There is all the mellifluous seduction of Asia in the backing melodies, the vaguely melancholic, languid tones you would expect from a sun-drenched and heat-exhausted Middle Eastern summer.

Umm Kolthoum owed much of her fame to the fecundity of Egyptian cinema between the world wars and into the 1950s. Her male equivalent was Fareed al-Atrash, also a gifted player of the oud. Although he made his career in Egypt, he was born in the Jebel Druze. Another great of this genre was

Abdel Halim al-Hafez. All are long gone, but their cassettes still sell like hot cakes.

This is not to say that all of the Middle East's popular singers are dead. Lebanon in particular has produced many. If you develop a liking for this kind of music, there are some names to keep an eye out for. Najwa Karam, Fairouz and Magda ar-Rumi are all female Lebanese artists much appreciated throughout Jordan and Syria. A couple from Syria include Mayada al-Hanawi and Asala Nasri. Among male performers is the Aleppo-born Sabah Fakri, as well as Gharib Alami and Walid Tawfiq from Lebanon.

Cassettes & CDs Innumerable cheap tapes of these and an enormous gamut of performers from right across the Middle East and North Africa are available in stalls all over Syria and Jordan. CDs are in shorter supply but do exist. Umm Kolthoum, Fareed al-Atrash, Abdel Halim al-Hafez and Fairouz are among those whose work has been put on to CD. Sabri Moudallal, who performs traditional Syrian chants and hymns, is also available on CD.

Art & Architecture

There is little artistic tradition in the western sense of painting in Syria or Jordan, nor really through most of the Arab world. Rather, the works of art on show here are the great buildings left behind by the early Muslim caliphs and their successors, especially in the cities of Damascus and Aleppo.

This is not to forget the priceless patrimony in ancient and classical sites spread mostly across Syria and to a lesser extent Jordan, some of them thousands of years old. Also, a tradition of, on occasion, magnificent mosaics forms a notable decorative artistic tradition spanning Roman, Byzantine and Islamic times. See also the boxed stories called 'Digging up the Past' and 'Islamic, Byzantine & Military Architecture'.

Figurative Arts That Islam frowns on the depiction of living beings does not mean that everyone took the hint. Long-standing artistic traditions in Asia Minor, Persia and further east, not to mention in Spain and other parts of Europe held for a time by the Muslims (such as Sicily), could not be so completely swept away. While the greatest riches of this kind are largely to be found in illustrated manuscripts mostly coming from Turkey, parts of Iraq and further east, examples can still be seen in Syria and Jordan today. The Omayyad rulers who comprised the first real dynasty after the demise of the Prophet left behind them a series of desert castles (which bear no resemblance at all to the military forts built centuries later during the Crusades) sprinkled across the Syrian and Jordanian deserts. In most of these can be found some traces of frescoes on the wall, but none so extraordinary as in the Qusayr 'Amra in Jordan. Here you find not only kings depicted on the walls but a nude woman bathing – certainly not the kind of thing one might have expected from the earlier austere rulers of Islam.

Of course the Christian presence never completely disappeared from this part of the Levant, and today the most representative artwork of the various Christian communities is to be found in religious works conserved in churches and monasteries.

Literature

Classical Writing The first great literature in Arabic has its source in the heartland of the Arab universe – the Arabian peninsula itself (today made up of Saudi Arabia, Yemen, Oman and the Gulf States).

The Qur'an itself is considered as the finest example of classical Arabic writing. In fact it underwent several transformations before a final version was settled upon, and this is what has come to us today.

Al-Mu'allaqaat, which predates the Qur'an and the advent of Islam, is a collection of some of the earliest Arab poetry and is widely celebrated. Prior to Islam, the poet was regarded by Arabians as having knowledge forbidden to ordinary people, supposedly acquired from the demon. Al-Mu'allaqaat means 'the suspended', and refers to traditions according to which the poems were

Islamic, Byzantine & Military Architecture

Islamic Architecture The earliest construction efforts undertaken by Muslims – more often than not mosques – inherited much from Christian and Graeco-Roman models. The Omayyad Mosque in Damascus was built on the site of a Christian basilica, which itself had been the successor of a Roman temple. With the spread of the Muslim domain, various styles soon developed, each to some extent influenced by local artists' tastes, but increasingly independent of their architectural forbears.

Mosques are generally built around open courtyards, off which lie one or more *iwan* (covered halls). The iwan facing Mecca is the focal point of prayer. A vaulted niche in the wall called the *mihrab* indicates the *kibla* (the direction of Mecca, which Muslims must face when they pray). Of course, other floor-plans are possible. Where a mosque is built around a mausoleum, the main sanctuary of the structure can be found in the centre of the courtyard. The *madrassa*, or theological school-cum-mosque, almost always has at least one iwan – the ideal place for classes.

Islam does not have priests as such, and the closest equivalent is the mosque's sheikh, schooled in Islam and often doubling as the muezzin, who calls the faithful to prayer. At the main Friday prayers in particular, the sheikh gives a *khutba* (sermon) from the *minbar* – the pulpit generally raised above a narrow staircase, better examples of which are ornately decorated.

The mosque also serves as a kind of community centre, and often you'll find groups of children or adults getting lessons (usually in the Qur'an), people in quiet prayer and others simply picnicking in the courtyard or sheltering peacefully from the din of daily life outside.

The minaret (from the word '*manara*', meaning lighthouse) comes in all sorts of shapes and sizes depending on which part of the Arab world you are in. In fact the form of the minaret often gives a lot away about who was behind the mosque's construction. In the east (Iran and beyond, but also in some mosques in Iraq) the minaret is generally a solid looking cylinder wrapped in a sheet of gaily coloured tiles and at times even topped by an onion-shaped dome. That very shape certainly appears in the main domes over many such mosques. Not a style indigenous to Syria or Jordan, you can nevertheless see a couple of fine modern examples in the Iranian-built Shiite mosques in Damascus (see the Damascus chapter). In Turkey, the tapering pencil-shaped minarets represent a clear style on their own, occasionally repeated in various parts of the former Ottoman Empire, especially in Damascus (Takiyyeh as-Sulaymaniyyeh Mosque) and Cairo (the Mosque of Mohammed Ali in the Citadel).

The Omayyad Mosque in Damascus is one of the earliest and grandest of Islam's places of worship. In this case the minarets are square-based, a mark of Omayyad architecture that was carried right across to north Africa and Muslim Spain – where you would be hard-pressed to find any minarets or church bell-towers that were not square based.

Of course, there are plenty of other styles and variations whose elaboration lie well beyond the scope of this brief summary. Most minarets have internal staircases for the muezzin to climb to the top. The advent of the microphone and the loudspeaker saves them the trouble, and has robbed us of a true aural delight. The tinny crackle of the loudspeaker just ain't quite the same.

Decoration of mosques and of many other public buildings is an exercise in geometric virtuosity. As Islam frowns on the artistic representation of living beings, the art of carving complex arabesques of vines, palms and other flora in various deceptive designs merged with a growing tradition of highly intricate decorative calligraphy. The predominantly floral motifs of the Omayyad Mosque's mosaic are among the most stunning of the genre.

Much of the adornment

St Simeon Basilica (Byzantine architecture)

along the top end of walls and on lintels tends to be more or less stylised verses from the Qur'an. The phrase *la illah illa Allah* (there is no god but Allah), appears in a seemingly unlimited variety of designs as an integral part of decoration, fusing religious precept and the very reference to God with the art that exhalts him.

The carved woodwork ceilings in some iwans displays painstaking, again largely geometric, and graceful decoration.

The same guidelines in decoration influenced domestic building as well, and can be seen in some of the grander Ottoman-era residences that have survived principally in Damascus and Aleppo.

Byzantine Architecture The transition from pagan Rome to Christian Byzantium is most evident in the architecture that came in its wake. Scattered across north-western Syria in particular lie the often fully ignored stone block ruins of towns dotted with noble, houses, churches and other civic buildings, some in a remarkable state of preservation. Perhaps the most stunning example is the 5th century basilica complex of St Simeon. Built in the limestone of the area, its series of arches (ranked around what remains of the pillar upon which St Simeon spent much of his ascetic life) are a reminder of the grandeur of imperial church building, at this stage only in its early stages. Scattered around the neighbouring plains and valleys you can find, all constructed in the same stone, a smorgasbord of more modest houses of worship. Generally they were built on a small-scale basilica plan, with the nave running east to west and ending in a semi-circular apse. Along the north and south sides galleries were usually added, and increasingly towers were raised at the end opposite the apse.

The single greatest variation on this theme involved the use of a central dome above a square-based church structure, a decidedly oriental touch that would continue to see widespread use in mosques and other buildings long after Christianity in the region had been reduced to a minority faith. This style predominates in southern Syria and can be seen in Jerash, northern Jordan.

Military Architecture The Byzantine defensive line against Persian attack was dotted with heavy fortifications that still stand. Many were simply adaptations of existing structures, such as that at Halabiyyeh on the Euphrates. Emperor Justinian was responsible for this defensive renovation, and the fortress and church complex at Rasafeh, on a desert crossroads north-west of Halabiyuyeh, is probably the greatest testament to his ultimately vain efforts at reconstituting the vigour of empire.

The medieval Crusades encouraged the flourishing of another kind of construction, more practical in its aims but to the 20th century eye another jewel in the area's architectural crown – the castle. Perhaps the most staggering of these military outposts is the Crac des Chevaliers in Syria, a classic warren of battlements, tortuous passageways and with all the self-contained paraphernalia such an anti-siege machine required – everything from kitchens and dining halls through to chapels and armouries. Most of the string of castles inland from the Mediterranean in Syria, Jordan and Lebanon were erected to formulae already well known throughout Europe by the Crusaders, who thus created a network of outposts, each in visual contact with the next. A few were built by the Arabs and later taken by the Christian knights. In the end, of course, they all fell to the Muslims as the Europeans were gradually and painfully dislodged, and in many cases what you see today owes as much to subsequent refinements as to the original soldierly genius of their engineers. ■

Fortress and church complex, Rasafeh (military architecture)

hung for public view, possibly on the walls of the Ka'aba in Mecca.

Among the better known later poets was Abu Nuwas, faithful companion to the 8th century Baghdad caliph Harun ar-Rashid and a rather debauched fellow. Apart from humorous accounts of court life, he left behind countless odes to the wonders of wine.

Towards the end of the 10th century, Syria became the focal point of one last great flash of classical Arabic poetry. Al-Mutanabbi, born in Al-Kufah and thought of by some as the Shakespeare of the Arabs, spent his youth bragging to local Bedouin that he was a prophet. A direct rival and contemporary was Abu Firas al-Hamdani, born in Aleppo, who wrote a good deal of his poetry while a prisoner in Byzantium. The last of this flowering of poetic genius has come down to us known as the blind 'philosopher of poets and poet of philosophers', Abu al-'Ala al-Ma'ari (973-1057). His writings were marked by a heavy scepticism in the face of the decadent and fragmented society that surrounded him, and he was something of a recluse.

Other great writers of the Arab world that may attract your attention include the medieval Arab world's answer to Marco Polo, Ibn Battuta. Born in Tangier in 1304, he travelled through and wrote a good deal about the Muslim world prior to his death in 1377. For history, Ibn Khaldun (1332-1406), wrote one of the more interesting, if not necessarily startlingly accurate, classical accounts of Arab history. It is most famous for his thoughts on historiography expounded in the *Muqaddamah* (Prolegomena).

On a considerably lighter note are the mixed bag of tales known as *Alf Layla wa Layla* (A Thousand and One Nights). Based initially on a Persian work, the tales were gradually compiled and expanded from the 10th century until well into Mameluke times in Egypt, drawing on sources as far flung as Greece and India. It is probably the best known Arabic work in the west, and several translations have been done. Ibn Battuta and Ibn Khaldun have also been translated, but much classical Arabic poetry remains in the original only.

As the Middle Ages drew to a close and the fractious Arab world came to be dominated by other forces, most notably the Ottoman Turks, Arabic literature too faded, stagnating in a classicist rut dominated by a complex and burdensome poetical inheritance until well into the 19th century.

Contemporary Literature Modern literary genres such as the novel are therefore a relatively new and unexperimented area, with such works only beginning to emerge in the last century or so, largely due to increased contact with Europe and a reawakening of Arab 'national' consciousness in the wake of the Ottoman Empire's putrefaction.

Egyptians (such as Nobel Prize-winning Naguib Mahfouz), Lebanese and, to a lesser extent, Palestinians seem to dominate the Middle Eastern scene. Further to the west, a great deal of Maghreb literature has been produced in French rather than Arabic, although a growing number of writers choose Arabic as their medium. It is also true that many writers from the Middle East itself, particularly Syria and Lebanon, have tended to choose French over Arabic. Arab writers have found less use for English and increasingly those who write in Arabic are becoming known to the west through translation.

Beirut long held centre stage for writers from the Levant, and even today remains something of a publishing centre.

Repression in Syria has tended to hold literary production there at a banal level. The exceptions generally turned first to Beirut and later to exile. The self-taught Zakariya Tamir, who has lived in exile in London since 1978, was born in 1931 and for a time worked for the Ministry of Culture. His work deals with everyday city life, marked by a frustration and despair born of a social oppression that probably explains why he ended up in London. Initially his stories contained a strong realist tone, but from the late 60s his writing turned increasingly to fantasy. For instance, in *Snow at the End of Night* (1961), Tamir deals in a slightly hallucinatory manner with the subject of family dishonour caused by a wayward daughter. Sexual repression is a recurring theme in his early writings, but by 1979, when *The Day on Which Genghis Khan was Angry* appeared, he had moved more clearly into fantastical political allegory.

Walid Ihklasi, born in 1935 in Iskenderun, in the province later ceded to Turkey, sets an even gloomier tone in his four novels and numerous short stories. His family moved to Aleppo and from there he has taken his cues for stories that nearly always revolve around questions of oppression (his first years were lived under the French Mandate). By extension, his characters tend to be lost, lacking in identity in a society and world that increasingly alienates them.

Ghada al-Samman, born in Syria but now living in Beirut, is one of the country's foremost women writers. Much of her work is an angst-ridden ride through constraint and social alienation, with particular attention paid to the plight of women caught between love and traditional bourgeouis values. Civil war in Lebanon has given her plenty of material: see, for example, *Beirut Nightmares* (1975).

Since the early decades of the century, poets from the Middle East have drawn away from classic moulds. Of the avant garde that got particular impetus in Beirut, Syria's Adunis (his real name is Ali Ahmad Said), has made a deep impression. Exiled to Beirut in 1956, his poetry is rich with the evocation of death and renewal, and the latter is the key to his thinking. His writing demonstrates a conviction that a melding of all he sees as positive in the Arab world with the good of other civilisations is necessary to bring the Arab world into the 20th century.

Handicrafts

Some go to Syria and Jordan for the ancient sites and great mosques, others to immerse themselves in Arab society. But for many visitors to this part of the world, it is the markets and the panoply of exotic merchandise that constitute the main attraction.

Of the many goods available, some at least have their roots in Bedouin crafts. The most striking of their work is silver jewellery. Some items are made with old coins, and the more worthwhile pieces are often quite intricately patterned. In some cases, precious or semiprecious stones are worked in: everything from amber to turquoise.

The Bedouin also continue to produce the most colourful textiles. Women's clothing in particular captures the eye with its vivid design and colours, all of which can change from region to region and tribe to tribe.

Another Bedouin speciality is the production of knives – and in certain parts of Jordan they produce them like there is no tomorrow – for the tourists of course.

For the buyer there is plenty more to find in the souqs – see Things to Buy in the Regional Facts for the Visitor chapter.

SOCIETY & CONDUCT

Traditional Culture

Welcome! You could be forgiven for think ing that 'welcome' is about the first word of English learned by the people of Jordan and Syria. At every turn you will hear it, and it seems to leave as many travellers perplexed as enchanted. Behind this simple word and makeshift translation lies a whole series of social codes in the Arab world. It is worth giving a little thought to just what your average Syrian or Jordanian means by it.

One of the most common greetings in Arabic is '*ahlan wa sahlan*'. The root words mean people/family ('*ahl*') and ease ('*sahl*'), so loosely you might say the expression translates as 'be as one of the family and at your ease'. A nice thought, and one that ends up as simply as 'welcome' in English. Among the Arabs it is used to mean anything from 'hello' to 'you're welcome' (after thanks). This at least explains a lot of the 'welcomes' you hear – people are just saying 'hi'!

There is, however, a lot more to it than that. Throughout the Arab world survives a deeply rooted sense of hospitality to strangers. There is little doubt that for many travellers this can be the most attractive aspect of travel in these countries. Equally true, westerners often have trouble in interpreting what is good form in these circumstances – and clearly each case will be different.

The Arab traditions of hospitality are not simply an expression of individual kindliness but are based in the harsh realities of life in the desert and have been virtually codified in social behaviour. As a rule, strangers were given shelter and food as a matter of course (three days seems to have been the mutually recognised limit to the hosts' bounty). Read Wilfred Thesiger's *Arabian Sands* and you will get a good idea of just how inconvenient this rigorously observed code could prove to the providers! In the desert it was not a matter of waiting for an invitation, but virtually an obligation that wayfarers tended to take for granted as a right. To maintain a balanced view of this situation, it should be borne in mind that such wayfarers also ran considerable risks of being attacked by bandits while on the road – one took the good with the bad!

Now there will be few times when the modern traveller will find him or herself in the extreme conditions Thesiger experienced in Arabia, but the code is deeply embedded and extends in some degree to the city as well as the country.

And so we come to another Arabic word that comes out more often than not as 'welcome'. In every daily exchange, people invite each other to drink or eat with them. It is part of the often complex exchange of social niceties. '*Tafaddal*' is the generic word for asking someone to come in (to the house for instance), to invite someone to a drink or to eat. It is usually rendered as 'welcome' in English.

How is one to respond to these invitations? Obviously, where possible, accepting an offer to join people in a meal or a cup of tea can be a wonderful way to learn more about the people and country you are travelling in. You really should take up the occasional offer if you can. Some visitors voice the concern that they feel bad for accepting what is often very generous treatment and giving nothing in return. Small gifts or mementoes are a way around this. Some people travel armed with postcards or distinctive stickpins to distribute to people at appropriate moments.

At times you will find people truly insistent about you joining them, but nine times out of 10 this is not the case. Rather than curtly saying 'no', the way to divert from you any kind of invitation that, for whatever reason, you feel disinclined to follow up, is to refuse politely with your right hand over your heart. You may have to do it several times. This is part of the ritual of polite insistence.

Body Language

Arabs gesticulate a lot in conversation, and some things can be said without uttering a word. Certain expressions also go together with particular gestures.

Jordanians and Syrians often say 'no' by raising the eyebrows and lifting the head up and back. This is often accompanied by a 'tsk tsk' noise and it can be a little off-putting if you're not used to it – don't take it as a snub.

Shaking the head from side to side (as westerners would to say 'no') means 'I don't understand'. Stretching out the hand as if to open a door and giving it a quick flick of the wrist is equivalent to 'what do you want?', 'where are you going?' or 'what is your problem?'.

If an official holds out their hand and draws a line across their palm with the index finger of the other hand, they are not pointing out that they have a long life-line but that they want to see your passport, bus ticket or any other document that may seem relevant at the time.

Guys asking directions should not be surprised to be taken by the arm or hand and led along. It is quite natural for men to hold each other by the hand and, despite what you may think, rarely means anything untoward is happening. Women should obviously be more careful about such helpfulness.

A right hand over your heart means 'no, thanks' when you are offered something. When you've had enough tea, Turkish coffee or anything else to drink, you put your hand over the cup. The polite thing to say is *da'iman* ('always', more or less meaning 'may it ever be thus'). Arabic coffee has its own rituals, see Food in the Regional Facts for the Visitor chapter.

As the left hand is associated with toilet duties it is considered unclean and so you should always use the right hand when giving or receiving something. ■

Adding something non-committal like, 'perhaps another time, in sha'allah (if God wills it)' is a perfectly suitable, ambiguous and, most importantly, inoffensive way to turn down unwanted offers.

In the Home Many families, especially in smaller town and rural areas, remain particularly traditional in terms of divisions within the house. Should you be invited into one, it is worth bearing a few things in mind. As a rule various parts of the house are reserved for men and others for women. This becomes especially apparent when guests appear. Remember that on entering the home it is customary to take of your shoes, for simple reasons of cleanliness.

Given that the most likely reason for you ending up in someone's home is to eat, bear in mind that meals are generally eaten on the floor, everyone gathered around several trays of food shared by all.

Single men invited to eat or stay over at a house will be taken to a room reserved for men or perhaps a mixed dining area. You are a guest, so you will be served. Depending on how conservative your hosts are, you may be directly served by the women or simply observe them bringing food and drink to the men, who then deal with you the guest. The foreign woman will in these circumstances more often than not be treated as an honorary male – not always for honorable reasons. The ambiguity of the situation is worth exploiting however. In the case of a couple, the woman may be welcome to sneak off to hang around with the women and then come back to see how the men's world is getting on. In this sense, the foreign woman can find herself in the unique position of being able to get an impression of home life for both sexes.

More traditional families often divide up into quite a hierarchy at meals too. The grandparents and male head of the house may eat in one circle, the latter's wife and the older children and other women in the family in another, and the small children in yet another. Obviously there are plenty of exceptions to the rule, but it is interesting to observe. Usually, outsiders eat with the head of the household.

Dos & Don'ts

Syrians are conservative when it comes to clothes and are not accustomed to the bizarre ways some tourists dress. Jordanians are more used to the antics of foreigners, but in general the same common-sense rules apply in both countries.

Women should always wear at least knee-length dresses or trousers and tops that keep at least the shoulders covered. More is said on this subject under Women Travellers in the Regional Facts for the Visitor chapter, as well as under Society & Conduct in the Facts about Jordan and Facts about Syria chapters.

Men will generally have no problem walking around in shorts but will be considered a bit eccentric and should expect to get stared at.

To avoid unpleasant scenes, you should dress conservatively if you want to enter a mosque. Some, such as the Omayyad Mosque in Damascus, will provide you with a cloak if they feel you're 'indecent'. On a bad day, men wearing shorts will find they cannot enter, cloak or no cloak. ■

RELIGION

Islam

Islam is the predominant religion in both Jordan and Syria. Muslims are called to prayer five times a day and no matter where you might be, there always seems to be a mosque within earshot. The midday prayers on Friday, when the sheikh of the mosque delivers his weekly sermon, or khutba, are considered the most important.

Islam shares its roots with the great monotheistic faiths that sprang from the unforgiving and harsh soil of the Middle East – Judaism and Christianity – but is considerably younger than both. The holy book of Islam is the Qur'an. Its pages carry many references to the earlier prophets of both the older religions – Adam, Abraham (Ibrahim), Noah, Moses and others – but there the similarities begin to end. Jesus is seen as another in a long line of prophets that ends definitively with Mohammed. The Qur'an is said to be the word of God, communicated to

Mohammed directly in a series of revelations in the early 7th century. For Muslims, Islam can only be the apogee of the monotheistic faiths from which it derives so much. Muslims traditionally attribute a place of great respect to Christians and Jews as *Ahl al-kitab*, the People of the Book. However, the more strident will claim Christianity was a new and improved version of the teachings of the Torah and that Islam was the next logical step and therefore 'superior'. Don't be too surprised if you occasionally find yourself on the receiving end of attempts to convert you!

Mohammed, born into one of the trading families of the Arabian city of Mecca (in present-day Saudi Arabia) in 570 AD, began to receive the revelations in 610 AD, and after a time began imparting the content of Allah's message to the Meccans. The essence of it was a call to submit to God's will ('islam' means submission), but not all Meccans were terribly taken with the idea.

Mohammed gathered quite a following in his campaign against Meccan idolaters and his movement especially appealed to the poorer levels of society. The powerful families became increasingly outraged, and by 622 had made life sufficiently unpleasant for Mohammed and his followers to convince them of the need to flee to Medina, an oasis town some 300 km to the north and now Islam's second most holy city. This migration – the Hijra – marks the beginning of the Islamic calendar, year 1 AH or 622 AD.

In Medina he continued to preach and increased his supporter base. Soon he and his followers began to clash with the Meccans, led by the powerful Quraysh tribe, possibly over trade routes. By 630 they had gained a sufficient following to return and take Mecca. In the two years until his death, many of the surrounding tribes swore allegiance to him and the new faith.

Mecca became the symbolic centre of the religion, containing as it did the Ka'aba, which houses the black stone that long had formed the object of pagan pilgrimage and later was said to have been given to Abraham by the Archangel Gabriel. Mohammed determined that Muslims ('those who submit') should face Mecca when praying outside the city.

Upon his death in 632, the Arab tribes exploded into the Syrian desert, quickly conquering all of what makes up modern Jordan, Syria, Iraq, Lebanon, Israel and the Palestinian occupied territories. By 644 they had taken Egypt and spread into North Africa, and in the following decades they would cross into Spain and for a brief moment reach deep into France.

The initial conquests were carried out under the caliphs, or Companions of Mohammed, of whom there were four. They in turn were followed by the Omayyad dynasty (661-750) in Damascus and then the Abbasid line (749-1258) in the newly built city of Baghdad (in modern Iraq).

In order to live a devout life, the Muslim is expected to carry out at least the Five Pillars of Islam:

Shahada This is the profession of the faith, the basic tenet of Islam: 'There is no God but Allah and Mohammed is his prophet'. It is commonly heard as part of the call to prayer and at other events such as births and deaths. The first half of the sentence has virtually become an exclamation good for any time of life or situation. People can often be heard muttering it to themselves, as if seeking a little strength to get through the trials of the day.

Sala Sometimes written *salat*, this is the obligation of prayer, done ideally five or six times a day when the muezzins call upon the faithful to pray. Although Muslims can pray anywhere, a strong sense of community makes joining together in a *masjid* or *jami'* (mosque) preferable to most. The midday prayers on Friday are usually held in the jami', the main district mosque.

Zakat Alms giving to the poor was, from the start, an essential part of Islamic social teaching, and was later developed in some parts of the Muslim world into various forms of tax to redistribute funds to the needy. The moral obligation towards one's poorer neighbours continues to be emphasised at a personal level, and it is not unusual to find exhortations to give posted up outside some mosques.

Sawm Ramadan, the ninth month of the Muslim calendar, commemorates the revelation of the Qur'an to Mohammed. In a demonstration of the

Muslims' renewal of faith, they are asked to abstain from sex and from letting *anything* pass their lips from dawn to dusk every day of the month. This includes smoking. For more on the fasting month, see Islamic Holidays in the Regional Facts for the Visitor chapter.

Hajj The pinnacle of a devout Muslim's life is the pilgrimage to the holy sites in and around Mecca. Ideally, the pilgrim should go to Mecca in the last month of the year, Zuul-Hijja, and join Muslims from all over the world in the pilgrimage and subsequent feast. The returned pilgrim can be addressed as Hajj, and in simpler villages at least, it is not uncommon to see the word Al-Hajj and simple scenes painted on the walls of houses showing that its inhabitants have made the pilgrimage.

Sunnis & Shiites In its early days, Islam suffered a major schism that divided the faith into two streams: the Sunnis (or Sunnites) and the Shiites.

The power struggle between Ali, the last of the four Companions of Mohammed and his son-in-law, and the Omayyad dynasty in Damascus lay at the heart of the rift that tore asunder the new faith's followers.

The succession to the caliphate had from the first been marked by intrigue and bloodshed. Ali, the father of Mohammed's sole male heirs, lost his struggle and was assassinated, paving the way to the caliphate for the Omayyad leader Mu'awiya. The latter was related to Ali's predecessor, Othman, in whose murder some believed Ali was implicated.

Those who recognised Mu'awiya as caliph (the majority) came to be known as the Sunnis, who would become the orthodox bedrock of Islam. The Shiites, on the other hand, recognise only the successors of Ali. Most of them are known as Twelvers, because they believe in 12 *imams* (religious leaders), the last of whom has been lost from sight, but who will appear some day to create an empire of the true faith. The rest are called Seveners because they believe seven imams will succeed Ali.

The Sunnis later divided into four schools

Islam & the West

Unfortunately, Islam has been much maligned and misunderstood in the west in recent years. Any mention of it usually brings to mind one of two images: the 'barbarity' of some aspects of Islamic law such as flogging, stoning or the amputation of hands; or the so-called fanatics out to terrorise the west.

For many Muslims, however, and particularly for those in the Middle East, Islam is stability in a very unstable world. Many of them are keenly aware that Muslims are seen as a threat by the west and are divided in their own perceptions of western countries. Not without justification, they regard the west's policies, especially towards the Arab world, as aggressive and they often compare its attitudes to them with those of the medieval Crusaders. Despite this view that western culture is dangerous to Muslim values and the growing influence of anti-western religious groups, many Muslims still admire the west. It is common to hear people say they like it, but that they are perplexed by its treatment of them.

If the west is offended by the anti-western rhetoric of the radical minority, the majority of Muslims see the west, especially with its support of Israel, as a direct challenge to their independence.

Although the violence and terrorism associated with the Middle East is often held up by the western media as evidence of blind, religiously inspired blood-thirstiness, the efficient oppression of the Palestinian Arabs by Israeli security forces has until fairly recently barely rated a mention. The sectarian madness of Northern Ireland is rarely portrayed as a symbol of Christian 'barbarism' in the way political violence in the Middle East is summed up as simple Muslim fanaticism. It is worth remembering that while the 'Christian' west tends to view Islam with disdain, if not contempt, Muslims accord Christians great respect as believers in the same God.

Just as the west receives a distorted view of Muslim society, so too are western values misread in Islamic societies. The glamour of the west has lured those able to compete (usually the young, rich and well educated) but for others, it represents the bastion of moral decline.

These misunderstandings have long contributed to a general feeling of unease and distrust between nations of the west and the Muslim world, and often between individuals of those countries. As long as this situation persists, Islam will continue to be seen in the west as a backward and radical force bent on violent change, rather than as simply a code of religious and political behaviour that people choose to apply to their daily lives, and which makes an often difficult life tolerable for them. ■

of religious thought, each lending more or less importance to various aspects of doctrine.

Islamic Customs When a baby is born, the first words uttered to it are the call to prayer. A week later this is followed by a ceremony in which the baby's head is shaved and an animal is sacrificed.

The major event of a boy's childhood is circumcision, which normally takes place sometime between the ages of seven and 12.

Marriage ceremonies are colourful and noisy affairs. One of the customs is for all the males to drive around the streets in convoy making as much ballyhoo as possible. The ceremony usually takes place in either the mosque or the home of the bride or groom. After that the partying goes on until the early hours of the morning, often until sunrise.

Before praying, Muslims must follow certain rituals. They must wash their hands, arms, feet, head and neck in running water before praying. All mosques have a small area set aside for this purpose. If they are not in a mosque and there is no water available, clean sand suffices, and where there is no sand, they must just go through the motions of washing.

Then they must cover the head, face Mecca (all mosques are orientated so that the mihrab, or prayer niche, faces the right way) and follow a set pattern of gestures and genuflections – photos of rows of Muslims kneeling with their heads touching the ground in the direction of Mecca are legion. Out of the mosques, Muslims can pray anywhere, and you regularly see them praying by the side of the road or in the street. Many keep a small prayer rug handy for just such moments.

In everyday life, Muslims are prohibited from drinking alcohol, eating pork (as the animal is considered unclean) and must refrain from fraud, usury, slander and gambling.

Islamic Minorities In Syria, the Shiites and other Muslim minorities, such as the Alawites and Druze, account for about 16% of the population.

The Druze religion is an offshoot of Shiite Islam and was spread in the 11th century by Hamzah ibn Ali and other missionaries from Egypt who followed the Fatimid caliph, Al-Hakim. The group derives its name from one of Hamzah's subordinates, Muhammad Darazi. Darazi had declared Al-Hakim to be the last imam and God in one, but most Egyptians found the bloody ruler to be anything but divine. When he died in mysterious circumstances, Darazi and his companions were forced to flee Egypt.

Most members of the Druze community now live in the mountains of Lebanon, although there are some small Druze towns in the Hauran, the area around the Syria-Jordan border. Their distinctive faith has survived intact mainly because of the secrecy that surrounds it. Not only is conversion to or from the faith prohibited, but only an elite, known as *'uqqal* (knowers), have full access to the religious doctrine, the *hikmeh*. The hikmeh is contained in seven holy books which exist only in handwritten copies. One of the codes it preaches is *taqiyyeh* (caution), under which a believer living among Christians, for example, can outwardly conform to Christian belief while still being a Druze at heart. They believe that God is too sacred to be called by name, is amorphous and will reappear in other incarnations. Although the New Testament and the Qur'an are revered, they read their own scriptures at *khalwas* (meeting houses) on Thursdays.

In Syria, the Alawites, an extreme Shiite sect, are considered by some to be heretics as they worship Ali as a god. They live mostly around Lattakia or in the Hama-Homs area. They are usually found tilling the poorest land or holding down the least skilled jobs in the towns. A smaller group goes by the name of Ismaelis, another splinter Shiite group that believes in seven imams.

Jordan has a 25,000-strong community of non-Arab Sunni Muslims known as Circassians. They fled persecution in Russia in the late 19th century and settled in Turkey,

Syria and Jordan. Intermarriage has made them virtually indistinguishable from their Arab neighbours.

The Chechens are another group of Caucasian origin in Jordan and are similar to the Circassians.

There is also a tiny Shiite minority in Jordan.

Christianity

Statistics on the number of Christians in Jordan and Syria are hard to come by and often wildly contradictory. They are believed to account for about 6% of Jordan's and 13% of Syria's population. There is a bewildering array of churches representing the three major branches of Christianity – Eastern Orthodox, Catholic and Protestant.

Eastern Orthodox This branch of Christianity is represented by the Greek Orthodox, Armenian Orthodox and also the Syrian Orthodox churches.

Greek Orthodox has its liturgy in Arabic and is the mother church of the Jacobites (Syrian Orthodox), who broke away in the 6th century, and the Greek Catholics, who split in the 16th century.

Armenian Orthodox (also known as the Armenian Apostolic Church) has its liturgy in classical Armenian and is seen by many to be the guardian of the Armenian national identity.

Syrian Orthodox uses Syriac, closely related to Aramaic. The patriarch lives in Damascus and the *see* (where the patriarch lives) has jurisdiction over foreign communities such as the Syrian Malankars in Kerala, India, and Syrian Orthodox in the USA.

Coptic Orthodox, with their pope and most coreligionists in Egypt, have a small community in Jordan.

Catholic These churches come under the jurisdiction of Rome and are listed from largest to smallest.

Greek Catholics, or Melchites, come under the authority of the patriarch who resides in Damascus, but his jurisdiction includes the patriarchates of Jerusalem and Alexandria. The church observes the Byzantine tradition, where married clergy are in charge of rural parishes and the diocesan clergy are celibate.

Armenian Catholics form a tightly-knit community. They fled from Turkish massacres in 1894-1896, and 1915-1921 and hold their liturgy in classical Armenian. The patriarch resides in Beirut, and more than half their members are from Aleppo.

Syrian Catholics have Syriac as the main liturgical language although some services are in Arabic. They are found mainly in the north-east of Syria and in Homs, Aleppo and Damascus.

The Maronites trace their origins to St Maron, a monk who lived near Aleppo and died around 410. Their liturgy is in ancient West Syrian, although the commonly used language is Arabic. They are found mainly in Lebanon (about one million), where their patriarch is based, but there are sizable numbers in Aleppo. As with the other Christian groups of the Middle East, the majority live outside their countries of origin: there are estimated to be about three million living in Europe, North and South America, and Australia.

Roman Catholics live in western Syria and Aleppo. Rome recently restored the patriarchate of Jerusalem, and a patriarch was elected there in 1987.

Chaldean Catholics, who have preserved the ancient East Syrian liturgy which they practise in Syriac, are found mainly in eastern Syria, Aleppo and Damascus. Their patriarch resides in Baghdad, the Iraqi capital.

Jews

The small Jewish population still left in Damascus at the beginning of the 1990s is now all but a memory. In an attempt to curry favour with the USA, President Assad promised in early 1992 to ease restrictions and allow Jews to leave the country. This promise he made good on, and most of the few thousand Jews who for years had regularly been wheeled out in spontaneous demonstrations of affection for their president voted with their feet for the USA. It is estimated that only a few hundred remain.

Digging up the Past

What is Archaeology?

If you have ever watched archaeologists on a dig, handling with meticulous care what to the outsider seem little more than discarded rubbish, you may have asked yourself how archaeology works. Contrary to popular portrayals, archaeology is not so much the study of lovingly excavated objects in themselves, as of what they can tell us about the human past.

Questions asked about the past vary with time and place, but many are constant. When did permanent settled life begin, and how? When did complex city-based civilisation arise? If civilisations end suddenly, why? From Graeco-Roman times onwards, more and more written records became available, but relating the written and archaeological record is often far from easy.

Middle Eastern archaeology began around 1830, prompted by a desire to know how the recorded traditions of the Bible related to the archaeological remains discovered in the Bible lands. The results of such comparisons rarely satisfy more than a minority.

Today archaeologists concentrate on questions which lend themselves to more or less unambiguous results. They are better at determining when and how things have happened, but they are less confident about determining why. Ever more sophisticated scientific techniques are employed in the detection and analysis of archaeological remains.

Water Goddess statue (circa 1800 BC), Mari

Multidisciplinary studies have become standard practice. So, for instance, when investigating the first permanent settlements, archaeologists study animal and plant remains, as these provide them with information on foraging patterns and the time of year in which they took place, as birth, migration and harvest patterns have remained nearly constant for the past 10,000 years. Carbon dating gives us an approximate time, osteology a fair idea of the physical condition of the settlers, lithic and bone tool analyses some idea of the technology of settlers, and chemical analysis of flaked stone tools (like obsidian), ground stone bowls (like fine basalt), and stone ornaments (greenstone and carnelian), coupled with shell ornament sourcing (dentalium and cowrie) gives an idea of trade routes and the extent of interregional contact at any given time.

Studying these features across 20 sites should allow a more general picture to emerge, but this is not always so. The more archaeologists explore the past, the harder it becomes to see general laws. They are learning that a variety of paths can lead to the same result. The human past is always fascinating, for like travelling, you are confronted by differing values and ways of doing things, prompting a reassessment of your own culture and achievements – not a bad thing.

Early Exploration

Biblical concerns fuelled the first explorations of Mesopotamia and Palestine, largely ignoring what are today Syria and Jordan. Only after the Napoleonic Wars was any organised exploration of this part of the Levant undertaken.

Depicted here in a lithograph by David Roberts (1839), the Petra monastery commands stunning views of Wadi Musa and Jebel Haroun.

Syria: 1860-1920

Coastal Syria (including Lebanon) became the province of French archaeologists exploring the great cities of the Phoenicians (Lebanese city-states of Tyre, Sidon and Byblos and the Syrian island-state of Arwad), the castled Crusader hinterland of the principalities of Antioch and Tripoli, including Saone (Sahyun) and Crac des Chevaliers (Qala'at al-Hosn) and the many well-preserved Byzantine villages west and south-west of Aleppo, now known by the generic name of the Dead Cities.

The Germans tended to work further north and east, rediscovering the biblical Hittites in their Iron Age city-states of Sam'al (Zinjirli) and Guzana (Tell Halaf). Some of the magnificent material found there can now be seen at the Aleppo National Museum. A British team under Leonard Woolley and a young TE Lawrence worked at the great Bronze and Iron Age centre of Carchemish.

These figures (now in front of the Aleppo Museum) once guarded the temple palace at Tell Hallaf.

Jordan: 1860-1920

Jordan was first explored by a collection of American, French and German surveyors, seeking to emulate the formidable and exemplary (not to say militarily useful) British Survey of Western Palestine. Apart from the discovery in 1868 of the Mesha Stele, raised by King Mesha of Moab, extolling his victories over the Biblical Israelite kings, there was little progress as the Ottoman hold over this territory was unsteady at best, and the locals not terribly partial to foreigners poking around.

Syria: 1920-1960

The border created after WWI between Syria and Turkey has to this day frustrated archaeological research into the Late Bronze Age Mitannian kingdom and the Iron Age Neo-Hittite states straddling the border.

French missions spread throughout their mandate territory over the 20s and 30s, studying Crusader castles, the Dead Cities, Bosra, Apamea and Palmyra among many projects. Americans worked on the Euphrates site of Dura Europos, the British (under Mallowan) at Brak in the Jezira and Atchana (under Woolley) in the Amuq, and the Danes at Hama on the Orontes.

In 1929 Claude Schaeffer made the first great discovery of the interwar period, when he stumbled onto the Late Bronze Age (circa 1500-1200 BC) maritime trading centre of Ugarit north of Lattakia (see the Mediterranean Coast chapter). Four years later Andre Parrot found the fabulously preserved mud-brick palace of the Middle Bronze Age (circa 2000-1700 BC) city-state of Mari, complete with polychrome wall paintings and 20,000 clay tablets.

The events of WWII and the postwar period halted all major work in Syria until the second half of the 50s.

Jordan: 1920-1960

Under cautious British mandatory rule, modest excavation projects got under way from the mid-20s, aimed above all at consolidation of the main standing monuments from the Desert Castles, Crusader Ajlun, Kerak and Shobaq and Roman-Islamic Amman.

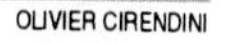

OLIVIER CIRENDINI

HUGH FINLAY

OLIVIER CIRENDINI

DAMIEN SIMONIS

Jordan

Top Left: Petra's *Khazneh* where treasure was supposedly once hidden.
Top Right: In attendance at Petra's supermarket.
Bottom Left: Mosaic featuring map of Palestine, St Georges, Madaba.
Bottom Right: It's a steep climb to the monastery, one of Petra's 'high places'.

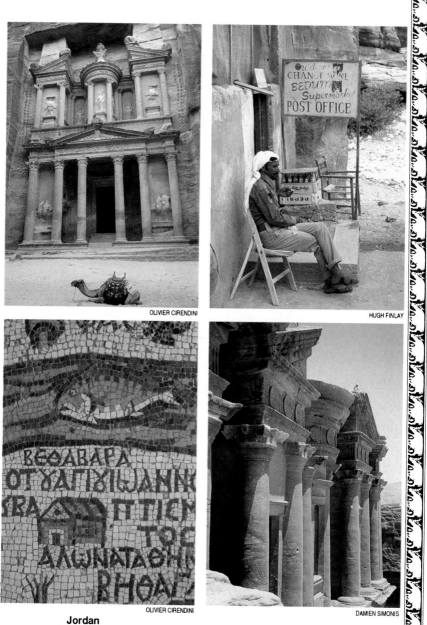

HUGH FINLAY

HUGH FINLAY

DR LEAH MCKENZIE

Syria

Top Left: The full splendour of Bosra's Roman theatre was laid bare only this century.

Top Right: Excavation work, Bosra.

Bottom: The Salon at the Crusader fort Crac des Chevaliers – a fort which accommodated 4000 troops.

Research-oriented projects focused on the large Graeco-Roman cities of the Decapolis. Anglo-American excavations began at Jerash, the best preserved Roman provincial city in the Middle East, and a German team returned to Roman Gadara (modern Umm Qais, west of Irbid).

In the 30's, a Franco-German team began excavations at prehistoric Teleilat Ghassul (3 kms north-east of the Dead Sea), the first great prehistoric site (circa 4000 BC) discovered in Jordan, and the Franciscans began to uncover the remarkable mosaics of Madaba and Mt Nebo, among the best in the Levant.

Unrest in the 30s, WWII and the first Arab-Israeli wars greatly curtailed archaeological work in Jordan for nearly 20 years, although major Canadian-American excavations at Dhibon (south of Amman), and renewed British work at Petra commenced early in the 50s.

Syria: 1960 onwards

With independence, the Syrian Department of Antiquities assumed responsibility for all museums and sights, but foreign teams gradually became more active. A major upsurge in activity began in the 70s with the Euphrates Tabqa Dam project and continuing plans through the 80s for the flooding of the upper Euphrates plain has drawn over 50 projects from 20 countries into the investigation of archaeological remains soon to finish up underwater.

This magnificent Siyagha mosaic can be viewed today at the site of Mt Nebo where the Franciscan brothers have excavated the ruins of a church and monastery. The existence of the church was reported as early as 393 AD.

Most notable here was the German-Dutch work at Habuba Kabira, Tell Qannas and Jebel Aruda, which led to the discovery of a series of Sumerian trading centres that forced a complete reassessment of early Syrian history, and its relationships with the better known Mesopotamian cultures.

The second major development was Italian work (from 1964) at Tell Mardikh, ancient Ebla. The stunning discovery of palace archives (between 20,000 and 30,000 tablet fragments) between 1974-76, and the reconstruction of well-preserved palaces, temples and burial grounds have made Ebla the most spectacular Early Bronze Age site in Syria.

In the 70s, a British team returned to Tell Brak in the Jezira, and another began at Tell Nebi Mend (ancient Qadesh), site of one of the great battles of the ancient world between Egypt and the Hittites. Together they have uncovered archaeological materials that stretch over 5000 years of Syrian history.

Other projects include Belgian work at Qala'at al-Mudiq and Apamea (west of Hama), German-Dutch work in the Jezira, Syrian-Japanese work at Idlib and the stunning Neo-Hittite temple site of 'Ain Dara (north-west of Aleppo), French work at Mari and Bosra, the Polish at Palmyra and Americans along the Euphrates.

In the 1980s, Australian teams started exploration on the Euphrates east of Aleppo, working first at the Middle Bronze Age fortress of Al-Qitar, and now at Jebel Khalid (Hellenistic) and Tell Ahmar (Assyrian/Neo-Hittite).

Overall, the number of teams and participating countries has mushroomed, producing a confusion of riches still to be properly digested.

Jordan: 1960 onwards

The Six-Day War and subsequent unsettled conditions interrupted big projects across the country, the Americans at Heshbon and Bab ad-Dhra, Tell as-Saidiyeh and Pella, British work in and around Petra (notably at prehistoric Al-Beidha), the Germans at Umm Qais, the French at Petra, the Dutch at Deir 'Alla, Australians at Teleilat Ghassul, and the Franciscans at Mt Nebo and Madaba.

Since the mid-70s, there has been an exponential increase in activity each decade.

Major British work in southern Jordan concentrated on the ancient Edomite capital of Buseirah (west of Tafila), whilst investigating the Roman legionary fortress at Udhrah, the Byzantine-Islamic city at Khirbet Faris, continuing work on the Amman Citadel (Ammonite-Islamic), at

Roman column capital from the Civic Complex, Pella

Getting Involved

If you're interested in work on archaeological excavations, plan ahead. No dig director will welcome an enquiry two weeks before a season begins. Many permits and security forms may have to be completed, so allow time for all possible bureaucratic niceties.

Opportunities *are* growing as field project leaders realise the advantages of taking on energetic, motivated amateurs, often willing to pay for the privilege of working on a dig.

When you write to dig directors, tell them what you can do. If you have special skills (photography, draughting), have travelled in the region or worked on other digs (or similar group projects), let them know.

Before you get started, you might like to do a little reading. There are several popular periodicals, including the American *Expedition* and *Archaeology*, the French *Le Monde du Bible* and the German *Antike Welt*.

Archaeological Schools

To get an idea of what is going on and where and when, try some of the following:

Deutsches Evangelisches Institut für Altertumswissenschaft des Heiligen Landes, Zweigstelle Amman,
PO Box 183 11118 Amman, Jordan
American Center for Oriental Research (ACOR)
PO Box 2470, Jebel Amman, Amman 11181, Jordan
British Institute at Amman for Archaeology & History
PO Box 519, Al-Jubeiha, Amman 11941, Jordan
Deutsches Archäologisches Institut
PO Box 11870, Al-Malki, Damascus, Syria
Institut Français d'Archéologie du Proche Orient
PO Box 5348, Amman, Jordan
Institut Français d'Archéologie du Proche Orient
PO Box 3694, Damascus, Syria

The French and Germans have schools in both countries; the Americans and British only in Jordan, although these cover activities in Syria as well.

ACOR is part of the Archaeological Institute of America (AIA). This institution prepares an extensive annual listing of field-work opportunities in the Middle East. Write to the AIA at 135 William St, New York NY 10038.

In Australia, the Near Eastern Archaeology Foundation at the University of Sydney runs a number of volunteer programmes in Jordan, notably at Pella. Write to the Volunteer Coordinator, Near Eastern Archaeology Foundation, SACAH, A14, University of Sydney, Sydney 2006. For Syria, write to the project directors at the University of Melbourne and the Australian National University.

Among universities that send teams to the Middle East are:

Australia	Universities of Melbourne & Sydney Australian National University (Canberra)
Canada	University of Toronto
France	CNRS Lyon & Paris I
Germany	DAI Berlin, Tübingen & Heidelberg
Holland	Universities of Amsterdam & Leiden
Italy	Rome & Turin
Switzerland	University of Bern
UK	Universities of Cambridge, London & Edinburgh
USA	Chicago, UCLA & Yale

Jerash (the North Theatre), in the Eastern Desert, and in the Jordan Valley, most notably at Tell es Saidiyeh.

The American pressure grew steadily in the 70s, but since the early 80s has spread throughout the country taking up projects far too numerous to cite here. Among the most spectacular are the excavations at prehistoric Ain Ghazal (Amman), where a number of 8500 year old life-size plaster statues were discovered and now displayed in a purpose-built museum; the Amman Citadel (on which parts of the monumental Roman Temple of Hercules has recently been re-erected), the Nabataean-Byzantine Petra excavations, featuring a recently discovered Greek manuscript library; Roman-Islamic Aqaba (ancient Ayla) and Umm al-Jimal; and Byzantine-Islamic Madaba (where a fine archaeological park is being developed.

Australian archaeologists have been working in Jordan for 30 years, with particular emphasis on the Jordan Valley – first at prehistoric Teleilat Ghassul (where a temple complex and a stunning wall painting were discovered) and for the past 17 years at Pella of the Decropolis (constantly occupied over the last 10,000 years). Activity has gradually spread to Jerash, the Hawran and south Jordan.

German teams continue to focus on Decapolis cities, mainly Roman-Byzantine Umm Qais (ancient Gadara) several Bronze Age sites (east of Irbid), important early mining sites in the Wadi Feinan region (west of Kerak) and the well-preserved early Neolithic village site of Basta (near Petra).

French work has grown steadily from the 70s, most notably on the stunning Zeus temple and South Gate excavations at Jerash, and projects at prehistoric Abu Hamid (Jordan Valley), the enigmatic Hellenistic mortuary temple site of Araq al Amir (south-west of Amman), and at Petra.

As with Syria, both the number and variety of excavation projects in Jordan have increased exponentially since the middle 70s. Major regional survey projects (American, British, French and German) have mapped large areas of Jordan, and a sophisticated Cultural Resource Management strategy is being developed to balance the needs of tourism with research and conservation.

Dr Stephen Bourke, Department of Archaeology,
University of Sydney

LANGUAGE

Arabic is the official language in Jordan and Syria. English is widely spoken in Jordan and, to a lesser extent, French in Syria, where English is also rapidly gaining ground, but any effort to communicate with the locals in their own language will be well rewarded. No matter how far off the mark your pronunciation or grammar might be, you'll often get the response (usually with a big smile): 'Ah, you speak Arabic very well!'. Greeting Syrian officials, who are often less than helpful, with *salām alaykum* (peace be upon you), will often work wonders.

Learning a few basics for day-to-day travelling doesn't take long at all, but to master the complexities of Arabic would take years of consistent study. The whole issue is complicated by the differences between Classical Arabic ('*Fus-ha*'), its modern descendent MSA (Modern Standard Arabic) and regional dialects. The classical tongue is the language of the Qur'an and Arabic poetry of centuries past. For long it remained static, but in order to survive it had to adapt to change, and the result is more or less MSA, the common language of the press, radio and educated discourse. It is as close to a lingua franca as the Arab world comes, and is generally understood, if not always well spoken, right across the Arab world – from Baghdad to Casablanca. An educated Iraqi would have no trouble shooting the breeze about world politics with a similarly educated Moroccan, but might have considerably more difficulty ordering lunch.

As it happens, the spoken dialects of Syria and Jordan are neither all that far removed from one another, nor are they too distant from MSA. For most outsiders trying to learn Arabic, the most frustrating element nevertheless remains understanding the spoken language (wherever you are). There is virtually no written material to refer to for back up, and acquisition of MSA in the first place is itself a long-term investment. An esoteric argument flows back and forward about the relative merits of learning MSA first (and so perhaps having to wait some time before being able to communicate adequately with people in the street) or a dialect. If all this is giving you a headache now, that will give you some inkling of why so few non-Arabs, or non-Muslims, embark on the study of the language.

Pronunciation

Pronunciation of Arabic can be tongue-tying for someone unfamiliar with the intonation and combination of sounds. Pronounce the transliterated words slowly and clearly.

The following guide should help, but bear in mind that the myriad rules governing pronunciation and vowel use are too extensive to be covered here.

Vowels Technically, there are three long and three short vowels in Arabic. The reality is a little different, with local dialect and varying consonant combinations affecting their pronunciation. This is the case throughout the Arabic-speaking world. More like five short and five long vowels can be identified:

a as the 'a' in 'had'
e as the 'e' in 'bet'
i as the 'i' in 'hit'
o as the 'o' in 'hot'
u as the 'oo' in 'book'

A macron over a vowel indicates that the vowel has a long sound:

ā as the 'a' in 'father'
ī as the 'e' in 'ear', only softer
ū as the 'oo' in 'food'

Combinations Certain combinations of vowels with other vowels or with consonants form new sounds:

aw as the 'ow' in 'how'
ay as the 'i' in 'high'

This last one is tricky, as the pronunciation can slide from one to the other, depending on the word and who is speaking.

Consonants Most of the consonants used in this section are the same as in English.

However, a few of the consonant sounds must be explained in greater detail.

' glottal stop; the sound you hear between the vowels in the expression 'Oh oh!'. It is a closing of the glottis at the back of the throat so that the passage of air is momentarily halted. It can also be pronounced with a slight growl at the back of the throat but it's best to listen to a native speaker to know exactly how the glottal stop is pronounced.

There is another sound in Arabic, called the 'ayn', that is often represented by an opening quote mark. It is similar to the sound of the glottal stop but the muscles at the back of the throat are gagged more forcefully (it has been described as the sound of someone being strangled!; or as the gagging sound made before vomiting). Not only is it a difficult sound to describe, but it is a difficult sound for non-Arabs to reproduce accurately. Therefore, to make this language guide easier for you to use, we have not distinguished between the glottal stop and the 'ayn', using the closing quote mark to represent both sounds. You'll find that Arab speakers will still understand you. Throughout the rest of this book the opening quote mark is used in Arabic words to represent the 'ayn'.

gh (the 'rayn'); tighten the muscles at the back of the throat and growl this sound; like a French 'r'.
dh as the 'th' in '**th**em' – pushes the preceding vowel to the back of the throat, as if when gargling. A sound rarely mastered by non-Arabs. There are several sounds ranging from 'd' as in 'dumb' through to 'z' as in 'zoo', but since even the locals confuse these sounds, it seems inappropriate to go into it here.
g soft, as the 'j' as in '**j**oin'.
H a strongly whispered 'h', almost like a sigh of relief.
q strong guttural 'k' sound. Often transcribed as 'k', although there is another letter in the Arabic alphabet which is the equivalent of 'k'. See Transliteration.
kh a slightly gurgling sound, like the 'ch' in Scottish 'lo**ch**'
r a rolled 'r', as in Spanish 'para'
s pronounced as in English '**s**it', never as in 'wisdom'
sh as in '**sh**elf'

Double Consonants In Arabic, double consonants are both pronounced. For example the word *istanna*, which means 'wait', is pronounced 'istan-na'.

Emphatic Consonants

There are four emphatic consonants - **ḍ, ṣ, ṭ** and **ẓ**. They are similar to their nonemphatic counterparts, except that they are pronounced with greater muscular tension in the mouth and throat and with a raising of the back of the tongue toward the roof of the mouth. This sensation can be approximated by prolonging the 'll' sound in 'pull'. The nearest example in English would be the first 't' in 'taught'. It's best to have a native speaker demonstrate these sounds.

Transliteration

It is worth noting here that transliteration from the Arabic script into English – or any other language for that matter – is at best an approximate science.

The presence of sounds unknown in European languages and the fact that the script is 'defective' (most vowels are not written) combine to make it nearly impossible to settle on one method of transliteration. A wide variety of spellings is therefore possible for words when they appear in Latin script – and that goes for place and people's names as well.

The whole thing is further complicated by the wide variety of dialects and the imaginative ideas Arabs themselves often have on appropriate spelling in, say, English (and words spelt one way in Jordan may look very different again in Syria, heavily influenced by French) – not even the most venerable of western Arabists have been able to come up with a satisfactory solution.

While striving to reflect the language as closely as possible and aiming at consistency, this book generally spells place, street and hotel names and the like as the locals have done. Don't be surprised if you come across several versions of the same thing!

When TE Lawrence was asked by his publishers to clarify 'inconsistencies in the spelling of proper names' in *Seven Pillars of Wisdom*, his account of the Arab Revolt in WWI, he wrote back:

> Arabic names won't go into English...There are some 'scientific systems' of transliteration, helpful to people who know enough Arabic not to need helping, but a washout for the world. I spell my names anyhow, to show what rot the systems are.

Pronouns

I	*ana*
you	*inta* (m)/*inti* (f)
he	*huwa*
she	*hiyya*
we	*naHnu/eHna*
they	*humma*

Greetings & Civilities

Arabs place great importance on civility and it's rare to see any interaction between people that doesn't begin with profuse greetings, enquiries into the other's health and other niceties.

Arabic greetings are more formal than in English and there is a reciprocal response to each. These sometimes vary slightly, depending on whether you're addressing a man or a woman. A simple encounter can become a drawn-out affair, with neither side wanting to be the one to put a halt to the stream of greetings and well-wishing. As an *ajnabi* (foreigner), you're not expected to know all the ins and outs, but if you come up with the right expression at the appropriate moment they'll love it.

The most common greeting is *salām alaykum* (peace be upon you), to which the correct reply is *wa alaykum as-salām* (and upon you be peace). If you get invited to a birthday celebration or are around for any of the big holidays, the common greeting is *kul sana wa intum bi-khīr* (I wish you well for the coming year).

After having a bath or shower, you will often hear people say to you *na'iman*, which roughly means 'heavenly' and boils down to an observation along the lines of 'nice and clean now, huh'.

Arrival in one piece is always something to be grateful for. Passengers will often be greeted with *al-Hamdu lillah 'al as-salāma* – 'thank God for your safe arrival'.

Hi.	*marHaba*
Hello.	*ahlan wa sahlan* (or just *ahlan*, 'Welcome')
Hello. (response)	*ahlan bēk*
Goodbye.	*ma'a salāma/ Allah ma'ak*
Good morning.	*sabaH al-khayr*
Good morning. (response)	*sabaH an-nūr*
Good evening.	*masa' al-khayr*
Good evening. (response)	*masa 'an-nūr*
Good night.	*tisbaH 'ala khayr*
Good night. (response)	*wa inta min ahalu*

Basics

Yes.	*aiwa/na'am*
Yeah.	*ay*
No	*la*
Please. (request)	*min faḍlak* (m) *min faḍlik* (f)
Please. (formal)	*law samaHt* (m) *law samaHti* (f)
Please. (come in)	*tafaḍḍal* (m) *tafaḍḍali* (f) *tafaḍḍalū* (pl)
Thank you.	*shukran*
Thank you very much.	*shukran jazīlan*
You're welcome.	*'afwan/ahlan*
Pardon/Excuse me.	*'afwan*
Sorry!	*āsif!*
No problem.	*mish mushkila/ mū mushkila*

Never mind.	*maalesh*
Just a moment.	*laHza*
Congratulations!	*mabrouk!*

Small Talk

Questions like 'Is the bus coming?' or 'Will the bank be open later?' generally elicit the inevitable response: *in sha' Allah* – God willing – an expression you'll hear over and over again. Another common one is *ma sha' Allah* – God's will be done – sometimes a useful answer to probing questions about why you're not married yet!

How are you?
kayf Hālak? (m)
kayf Hālik? (f)
How are you? (dialect)
shlonak? (m)
shlonik? (f)
Fine.
al-Hamdu lillah
(literally 'thanks be to God')
What is your name?
shu-ismak? (m)
shu-ismik? (f)
My name is ...
ismi ...
Pleased to meet you. (departing)
furṣa sa'ida
Nice to meet you.
tasharrafna
(literally 'you honour us')
Where are you from?
min wayn inta?

I am ...	*ana ...*
Australian	*ustrāli* (m)
	ustrāliyya (f)
American	*amrīki* (m)
	amrīkiyya (f)
Canadian	*kanadi* (m)
	kanadiyya (f)
English	*inglīzi* (m)
	inglīziyya (f)

Are you married?
inta mutajawwiz? (m)
inti mutajawwiza? (f)
How old are you?
Ay 'amrak? (m)
kam sana 'andak? (f)
I'm 20 years old.
'Andī 'ashrīn sana
I'm a student.
ana tālib (m)
ana tāliba (f)
I'm a tourist.
ana sa'iH (m)
ana sa'iHa (f)
Do you like ...?
inta batHib
I like ...
ana baHib ...
ana uHib...
I don't like ...
ana ma baHib ..
ana lā uHib ...

Language Problems

Do you speak English?
bitiHki inglīzi?
hal tatakallam(i) inglīzi?
I understand.
afham
I don't understand.
ma bifham
la afham

I speak ...	*ana baHki .../ana atakallam ...*
English	*inglīzi*
French	*faransi*
German	*almāni*

I want an interpreter.
urīd mutarjem
Please write it down.
mumkin tiktabhu, min fadlak?
What does this mean?
yānī ay?
How do you say ... in Arabic?
kayf taqul ... bil'arabi?

Getting Around

Where is ...?
wayn ... ?
Can you show me (on the map)?
wayn (fil kharīṭa)?

How many km?
kam kilometre?
What time does ... leave?
sa'a kam biyitla'...?
What time does ... arrive?
sa'a kam biyuṣal...?
How long does the trip take?
kam as-sa'a ar-raHla?

1st class	*daraja ūla*
2nd class	*daraja thāni*
ticket	*at-tazkarah*
ticket office	*maktab at-tazākar*
to/from	*ila/min*
airport	*al-maṭār*
bicycle	*al-'ajila*
boat/ferry	*al-markib/ as-safīna*
bus	*al-bāṣ*
bus station	*maHaṭṭat al-bāṣ/ karaj*
car	*as-sayyāra*
guide	*ad-dalīl*
railway station	*maHaṭṭat al-qiṭār*
train	*al-qiṭār*

Directions

on the left	*'ala yasār/shimāl*
on the right	*'ala yamīn*
opposite	*muqābil*
straight ahead	*'ala ṭūl/sawa/ dugri*
here/there	*hon/honāk*
in front of	*amām*
near	*qarīb*
far	*ba'īd*
east/west	*sharq/gharb*
north/south	*shimāl/junub*
this way	*min hon*

Around Town

I'm looking for ...	*ana abHath ...*
Where is the ...?	*wayn ...?*

bank	*al-maṣraf/al-bank*
beach	*ash-shāti'*
chemist/pharmacy	*as-ṣayidiliyya*
city/town	*al-medina*
city centre	*markaz al-medina*
customs	*al-jumruk*
entrance	*ad-dukhūl*
exit	*al-khuruj*
hotel	*al-funduq*
information	*isti'lāmāt*
market	*as-souq*
mosque	*al-jāma'/al-masjid*
museum	*al-matHaf*
passport & immigration office	*maktab al-jawazāt wa al-hijra*
police	*ash-shurṭa*
post office	*maktab al-barīd*
restaurant	*al-maṭa'am*
street/road	*ash-sharia*
telephone office	*maktab at-telefon*
temple	*al-ma'abad*
tourist office	*maktab as-siyaHa*
village	*al-qariyya*

Paperwork

date of birth	*tarīkha al-mūlid*
name	*ism*
nationality	*jensīya*
passport	*jawaz as-safar*
permit	*tasrīH*
place of birth	*makan al-mūlid*
visa	*sima*

Accommodation

Do you have a ...?	*fi ...?*
room	*ghurfa*
single room	*ghurfa mufrada*
double room	*ghurfa bi sarīrayn*

Can I see it?
mumkin atfarraj-ha?
How much is it for each person?
Qad aysh li kul waHid?
Where is the bathroom?
Wayn al-Hammam?
We are leaving today
eHna musafirīn al-yom

address	*al-'anwān*
air-conditioning	*kondishon*
blanket	*al-baṭāniyya*
camp site	*mukhaym*
electricity	*kahraba*
hotel	*funduq*
hot water	*mai Harra/sākhina*
key	*al-miftaH*

manager	*al-mudīr*
shower	*dūsh*
soap	*sabūn*
toilet	*twalet/mirhaḍ/*
	Hammām

Food

I'm hungry/thirsty.
ana ju'ān/aṭshān
What's this?
ma hādha?/shu hādha?
Another ... please!
... waHid kamān, min fadlak

breakfast	*al-fuṭūr*
dinner	*al-'ashā*
food	*al-akl*
grocery store	*al-mahal/ al-baqaliyya*
hot/cold	*harr/bārid*
lunch	*al-ghada*
restaurant	*al-maṭ'am*

Vegetarianism, by the way, is a non-concept in the Middle East. Even if you ask for meals without meat, you can be sure that any gravies, sauces etc will have been cooked with meat or animal fat. See Food in the Regional Facts for the Visitor chapter for more information.

Shopping

What is this?	*shu hadha?*
How much?	*qad aysh/bikam?*
How many?	*kam waHid?*
How much money?	*kam fulūs?*
Is there ...?	*fi ...?*
There isn't (any).	*ma fi*

big/bigger	*kabīr/akbar*
cheap	*rakhīs*
cheaper	*arkhas*
closed	*maghlūq/musakkar*
expensive	*ghāli*
money	*al-fulūs/al-maṣāari*
open	*maftūH*
small/smaller	*ṣaghīr/as-ghar*

Health & Emergencies

Go away!	*imshi!*
Help me!	*sā'idūnī!*
I'm sick.	*ana marīd* (m)
	ana marīda (f)
doctor	*duktūr/tabīb*
hospital	*al-mustash-fa*
police	*ash-shurta/al-bolis*

Time & Dates

What's the time?	*as-sā'a kam?*
When?	*matā/emta?*
yesterday	*imbārih/ams*
today	*al-youm*
tomorrow	*bukra/ghadan*
day after tomorrow	*ba'ad bukra*
minute	*daqīqa*
hour	*sā'a*
day	*youm*
week	*usbū'*
month	*shahr*
year	*sana*

Monday	*al-itnein*
Tuesday	*at-talata*
Wednesday	*al-arbi'a*
Thursday	*al-khamīs*
Friday	*al-jum'a*
Saturday	*as-sabt*
Sunday	*al-aHad*

Months

The Islamic year has 12 lunar months and is 11 days shorter than the western (Gregorian) calendar, so important Muslim dates will fall 11 days earlier each (western) year.

There are two Gregorian calendars in use in the Arab world. In Egypt and westwards, the months have virtually the same names as in English (January is *yanāyir*, October is *octobir* and so on), but in Jordan, Syria and eastwards, the names are quite different. Talking about, say, June as 'month six' is the easiest solution, but for the sake of completeness, the months from January are:

January	*kanūn ath-thani*
February	*shubāt*
March	*azār*
April	*nisān*
May	*ayyār*
June	*Huzayrān*

July	*tammūz*
August	*'āb*
September	*aylūl*
October	*tishrīn al-awal*
November	*tishrīn ath-thani*
December	*kānūn al-awal*

The Hijra months, too, have their own names:

1st	*MoHarram*
2nd	*Safar*
3rd	*Rabi' al-Awal*
4th	*Rabei ath-Thāni*
5th	*Jumāda al-Awal*
6th	*Jumāda al-Akhira*
7th	*Rajab*
8th	*Shaban*
9th	*Ramadan*
10th	*Shawwal*
11th	*Zuul-Qeda*
12th	*Zuul-Hijja*

Numbers

Arabic numerals are simple enough to learn and, unlike the written language, run from left to right.

¼	*ruba*
½	*nuṣṣ*
¾	*talāta ruba*

0	*ṣifr*
1	*waHid*
2	*itnein/tintein*
3	*talāta*
4	*arba'a*
5	*khamsa*
6	*sitta*
7	*saba'a*
8	*tamanya*
9	*tis'a*
10	*'ashara*
11	*Hid-'ashr*
12	*itn-'ashr*
13	*talat-'ashr*
14	*arba'at-'ashr*
15	*khamast-'ashr*
16	*sitt-'ashr*
17	*saba'at-'ashr*
18	*tamant-'ashr*
19	*tisa'at-'ashr*
20	*'ashrīn*
21	*waHid wa 'ashrīn*
22	*itnein wa ashrīn*
30	*talātīn*
40	*'arba'īn*
50	*khamsīn*
60	*sitteen*
70	*saba'īn*
80	*tamanīn*
90	*tis'īn*
100	*mia*
101	*mia wa waHid*
125	*mia wa khamsa wa 'ashrīn*
200	*miatein*
300	*talāta mia*
1000	*alf*
2000	*alfein*
3000	*talāt-alaf*

Regional Facts for the Visitor

The information provided in this chapter is of a general nature and applies to both Jordan and Syria. For more specific details on each country, turn to the appropriate Facts for the Visitor chapter in each country section.

PLANNING

Maps

There is not a huge range of maps on Jordan and Syria, but what is available can generally be found in quality specialist shops such as Stanford's bookshop in London (☎ 0171-836 2121), 12-14 Long Acre, London, WC2E 9LP. Those on Jordan are generally cheaper in Jordan itself.

Middle East Most of the main publishers produce maps of the Middle East, including Freytag & Berndt, Bartholomews and the Beirut-based GEOprojects. Because of the scale, they are of limited practical value to the traveller.

Jordan & Syria Lonely Planet's *Jordan, Syria & Lebanon travel atlas* is about the best map investment you could make for this part of the world. Hildebrandt publishes an average sort of map covering Jordan, Syria and Lebanon on a scale of 1:1,250,000.

Air Charts Probably the highest standard of maps available are the Operational Navigation Charts prepared by the UK Ministry of Defence and designed for pilots (scale of 1:1,000,000). They are further subdivided into Tactical Pilotage Charts (TPC) at 1:500,000. Their interest, however, is mainly topographical and not well suited to the needs of the average traveller. They cost UK£7.50 a sheet and are available at specialist shops, such as Stanford's in London. The TPC sheet numbers for Syria are G4A-D. These also cover substantial sectors of neighbouring countries, including Jordan. To complete the latter picture you'd need to get H5B as well.

What to Bring

For most travellers, the backpack remains the best option, and the only one if you end up having to do any walking. On the down side, they do not afford the greatest protection to valuable belongings and some airlines may refuse to take responsibility if they are damaged or broken into.

A travel pack is recommended, where the straps of the pack can be zipped away when not needed. This combines the carrying ease of a pack with the added strength of a bag. Another alternative is a large, soft zip bag with a wide shoulder strap so that it can be carried with relative ease if necessary. You can also get some tabs sewn on so you can partially protect it from theft with small padlocks.

A hat, sunglasses and water bottle are essential in summer. A few other handy items are: a Swiss army knife, a torch (flashlight), a few metres of nylon cord (for use as a clothesline), some pegs, a universal sink plug, earplugs, medical and sewing kits, padlocks, towel, a short-wave radio, a canteen, a sleeping sheet and/or sleeping bag.

If you're going to be in the region in winter, make sure you have plenty of warm clothes and a windproof & waterproof jacket. It gets surprisingly miserable at this time of year. Snow is not uncommon in Amman and Damascus and more likely still at higher altitudes. Bear in mind also that heating in most of the lower-end hotels, especially in Syria, is often inadequate or nonexistent. Otherwise, a pair of jeans, a pair of shorts, a few shirts and T-shirts, underwear and socks (at least one heavy pair), a pair of strong shoes and a pair of sandals or flip-flops (thongs) and perhaps an outfit for more formal occasions should just about complete your requirements.

Tampons are not always readily available. You should also bring your own contraceptives or any special medication you need. Other toiletries are generally easily found.

SUGGESTED ITINERARIES

The number of general route options through Jordan and Syria is pretty limited. The two countries combined are increasingly forming part of a longer travellers' trail linking Turkey to Egypt and the rest of Africa. You can take in the bulk of the more important sights in both countries by following a roughly north-south route from Aleppo all the way to Aqaba (and vice-versa of course). There are several variations on the theme, and a number of possible detours that largely depend on the time available. To do the two countries any justice, count on a two week minimum. For more details, see Suggested Itineraries and the boxed stories called 'The Best of Jordan' and 'Best & Worst' in Jordan and Syria's Facts for the Visitor chapters.

Major Archaeological Sites & Maps

Archaeological Site	*Page Numbers*
Apamea (Syr)	310-12
Bosra (Syr)	277-80
Crac des Chevaliers (Syr)	297-300
Dura Europos (Syr)	352
Jerash (Jor)	140-41
Palmyra (Syr)	333-42
Pella (Jor)	150-51
Petra (Jor)	173-85
Rasafeh (Syr)	348
Ugarit (Syr)	288-9

VISAS & DOCUMENTS

Passport

Everyone requires a full valid passport to travel to Jordan and Syria. If you've had it for a while, check that the expiry date is at least six months off, otherwise you may not be granted visas. If you travel a lot, keep an eye on the number of pages you have left in the passport. A Syrian visa, one extension and the usual stamps as you enter and leave the country will fill two pages. The same equation applies more or less for Jordan and Lebanon too. If you do run out of pages, options vary depending on where you are from. US consulates will generally insert extra pages into your passport, but others may require an application for a new one. If yours is nearly full and you are likely to have this trouble, do yourself a favour before leaving home and get a new one.

In both countries it is wise to have your passport handy at all times when travelling. In Jordan this is particularly so in sensitive areas near the Israeli frontier, which means most of the Jordan Valley, the Dead Sea and Wadi Araba, where ID checks still remain commonplace. It is less of an issue in Syria, but it still happens.

Visas

For specific information on acquiring visas for Jordan and Syria, refer to Visas & Documents in each country's Facts for the Visitor chapter.

Photocopies

It is a wise precaution to keep photocopies of all the data pages of your passport and any other identity cards, and even your birth certificate if you can manage it. Other worthwhile things to photocopy include airline tickets, travel insurance documents with emergency international medical aid numbers, credit cards (and international card loss phone numbers), driving licence, vehicle documentation and any employment or educational qualifications you may need if you are considering work or study. Keep all of this, and a list of the serial numbers of your travellers' cheques, somewhere separate from the originals of the documents.

Although theft is not a big problem in Jordan or Syria, some spare cash tucked away into a money belt, stuffed into a pair of socks or otherwise concealed could come in very handy if you lose your wallet, purse and/or money pouch. This is especially the case in Syria, where cash makes the world go around.

Travel Insurance

Don't, as they say, leave home without it. You may never need it, but you'll be glad you've got it if you get into trouble. These papers, and the international medical aid

HIGHLIGHTS

	Region	Comments
Archaeological		
Petra The great buildings of Petra, the rose-red city 'half as old as time', were hewn by the ancient Nabataeans into a towering rock wall on the edge of Wadi Araba.	South of Amman (Jordan)	One of the greatest attractions of the Middle East, Petra has unfortunately become an expensive tourist trap.
Kerak Dominated by the fortified citadel, Kerak is situated on the ancient caravan route that once linked Egypt and Syria.	South of Amman (Jordan)	It is possible to visit the Dead Sea from Kerak, but lack of facilities means that you'd be better off taking a dip at Suweimeh (see the North & West of Jordan chapter).
Crac des Chevaliers This extremely well-preserved Crusader castle dominates the gap in the mountain range between Turkey and Lebanon. This position assured control over the flow of people and merchandise from the ports to inland Syria.	Mediterranean Coast (Syria)	A torch (flashlight) is useful for exploring some of the castle's darker, more mysterious passage ways.
Palmyra One of the world's greatest historic sites, Palmyra is a spectacular archaeological oasis in the desert halfway between Damascus and the Euphrates.	The Desert (Syria)	If you only see one thing in Syria, see Palmyra.
Dura Europos This large, Hellenistic/Roman city is situated in a desert oasis which ends abruptly in a wall of cliffs dropping 90m into the Euphrates.	The Euphrates River (Syria)	French and Syrian archaeologists continue to work on the site.
Activities		
Diving & Snorkelling Some of the best coral reefs in the world are found off the Gulf of Aqaba.	South of Amman (Jordan)	It is a good place for beginners, with some of the most interesting things to see in the shallow depths.
Trekking & Climbing Wadi Rum and Petra are ideal places for long day walks, or in the case of Wadi Rum, treks that could take you off the beaten track for days.	South of Amman (Jordan)	Rock climbing is also a possibility in Wadi Rum, but only basic gear is available on site.
Camel Treks Fans of Lawrence of Arabia can be escorted by local Bedouin on camel treks from Wadi Rum to Petra.	South of Amman (Jordan)	Similar trips can be arranged in 4WD vehicles.

	Region	Comments
Activiities *cont*		
Ballooning		
Check out the exquisite scenery of Petra and Wadi Rum from a great height.	South of Amman (Jordan)	Ballooning season runs from March to November.
Language Courses		
If you want to gain more than a tourist's grasp of Arabic, enrol in one of the local language courses in Amman or Damascus.	Amman (Jordan) or Damascus (Syria)	Several schools operate in both cities.
Archaeological Digs		
Join archaeologists in the field, working (often unpaid) on an excavation.	All of Jordan and Syria	Plan ahead if you are interested in joining a dig – seasons are planned well in advance.
Shopping		
Aleppo		
Shop for kilims, gold, silver, silks, brocades, leather and food in the maze of bustling souqs in Aleppo, which arguably has the best market in the Middle East.	Aleppo (Syria)	A walk through the souqs can take you all day, especially if you accept the merchants' offers to drink tea with them.
Natural Beauty Spots		
Wadi al-Mujib		
The canyon of Wadi al-Mujib, one of the most spectacular natural sights in Jordan, is over a kilometre deep.	South of Amman (Jordan)	Approach Kerak on the King's Highway rather than the Desert Highway if you want to glimpse this natural wonder.
The Euphrates		
In contrast to stark desert landscape, the Euphrates offers a band of fertile land along its banks as well as a series of little-visited ancient sites.	North-Eastern Syria	Turkey's plans for new dam projects on the Euphrates are cause for considerable concern in Syria and Iraq.
Wadi Rum		
Bizarre sandstone and granite rockscapes rise out of the desert at majestic Wadi Rum.	South of Amman (Jordan)	You need to get well out of the village – by camel or 4WD – to fully appreciate the desert landscape.
Relaxation		
Turkish Baths		
Relax with a full wash, steam bath and massage package in one of the many public baths in Aleppo and Damascus.	Aleppo and Damascus (Syria)	The baths generally open for women and men separately.
Beach		
Bask in the sun on one of the public beaches at Aqaba.	South of Amman (Jordan)	There have been some reports of women being harassed on the beaches. This is not the place for bikinis.
Hot Springs		
A hot waterfall, natural spa baths and saunas, as well as a resort complex, tempt travellers to Hammamat Ma'in.	South of Amman (Jordan)	The therapeutic qualities of Hammamat Ma'in springs have been sought since ancient times.

numbers that generally accompany them, are valuable documents, so treat them like air tickets and passports. Keep copies of the details in a separate part of your luggage. For more on health & travel insurance, see the Health Appendix and the regional Getting There & Away chapter.

Driving Licence

An International Driving Permit is legally required if you intend to do any driving in Jordan or Syria, although in practice most car rental companies seem satisfied with national licences. For more information on driving in Jordan and Syria, see each country's Getting Around chapter.

Student Cards

Unhappily, ISIC cards and the like are next to useless in Jordan and Syria. They make no difference to museum entry prices and generally are not accepted for cut-price student fares on international flights. Of course, if you are travelling to neighbouring countries like Turkey, Israel and especially Egypt, you'll be glad you brought an ISIC card along.

If you are a student and can get a letter of introduction written for you on your institution's letter head, you may be able to arrange free entrance to Jordanian and Syrian monuments. See each country's Facts for the Visitor chapter for details.

MONEY

Carrying Money

Money is about the most precious stuff you'll have on your trip, so it is worth looking after it. Although theft is not a real problem in Jordan or Syria, it is always wise to take the basic precautions, especially in Syria, where you'll probably be carrying around a fair amount of cash. It is always better to carry your wallet (if you have one) in a front pocket, and not to have too much cash in it. The bulk of your money, travellers' cheques and documents are better off in a pouch worn close to the skin. There are many types of pouch and money belts that you can hang around the neck or wear around the waist – most travel equipment shops sell several versions of this sort of thing. The best material in hot places like these is cotton.

Hardened trans-Africa travellers (where theft often really is an issue) devise all sorts of strategies, sewing inner pockets into their trousers and other places not easily reached, but such measures can probably be discarded as overkill here. It is always sensible to leave some of your money hidden as a separate stash in your luggage (rolled up in a pair of thick socks for instance) in case you find yourself in deep trouble at some point.

For advice on what combinations of cash, travellers' cheques and credit cards you'll find useful in Jordan and Syria, see Money in each country's Facts for the Visitor chapter.

BOOKS

Most books are published in different editions by different publishers in different countries. As a result a book might be a hardcover rarity in one country but readily available in paperback in another. Fortunately, bookshops and libraries search by title or author, so your local bookshop or library is best placed to advise you on the availability of the following recommendations. For books specifically dealing with each of Syria and Jordan, see Books in each country's Facts for the Visitor chapter.

Lonely Planet

Travellers contemplating a longer swing through several countries of the Middle East should check out other Lonely Planet titles to the area, particularly *Middle East on a shoestring*.

Guidebooks

For a nostalgic look back, there are several wonderful old guidebooks to the region. *Cook's Traveller's Handbook: Palestine & Syria* had some good tips...in 1929. Going further back is MacMillan's 1908 *Palestine and Syria*. It deals largely with what today is Israel, but there is an enjoyable chapter on Damascus.

Islamic & Arab History

Among a couple of general histories of the Arabs to be recommended is Philip Hitti's *History of the Arabs*, which is something of a classic. A more recent and widely acclaimed work is *A History of the Arab Peoples*, by Albert Hourani. It is as much an attempt to convey a feel for evolving Muslim Arab societies as a straightforward history, with extensive treatment of various aspects of social, cultural and religious life.

For a more academic and somewhat drier historical approach, you could try *The Cambridge History of Islam* (edited by PM Holt et al), first published in hardback in 1970 but now available in four paperback volumes.

Those interested in early European interference in the Levant might care to look through Steven Runcimen's *A History of the Crusades*.

King Husain and the Kingdom of Hejaz, by Randall Baker, looks at the man who was in part responsible for fomenting pan-Arab nationalism prior to and during WWI. This controversial figure is an ancestor of the present king of Jordan. For a particular slant on the Arab world's relations with the west this century, it is instructive to read John Bagot Glubb's *Britain and the Arabs*, if you can find a copy. Otherwise known as Glubb Pasha, he virtually created the Jordanian army.

Contemporary Middle Eastern affairs are treated in *The Modern Middle East*, edited by Albert Hourani, Phillip Khoury and Mary Wilson.

Peter Mansfield has written several very readable works, including *The Arabs* and *A History of the Middle East*. A unique approach to the subject is *The Longman Companion to the Middle East Since 1914*, by Ritchie Ovendale. This presents a series of chronologies, biographies and dictionaries of key names and events – a handy reference work.

Undoubtedly the most comprehensive graphic distillation of recent Middle Eastern history is Martin Gilbert's *Dent Atlas of the Arab-Israeli Conflict*, a collection of maps detailing every conceivable angle of the region's troubled focal point.

Readers of French might find Joseph Burlot's *La Civilisation Islamique* a manageable introduction to the history not only of the Arab world, but of all those countries that have come under the sway of Islam. Dominique & Janine Sourdel's *La Civilisation de l'Islam Classique* is a more thorough work on the Islamic world in its glory days, from the 9th to the 12th centuries.

Arts & Architecture

A useful general reference work on artistic and architectural forms throughout the Muslim world is David Talbot Rice's *Islamic Art*. Another book carrying the same title has been written by Barbara Brend.

If you are serious about looking for quality rugs, kilims and the like in the markets of Syria (there is comparatively little in Jordan), it could pay to first consult *Oriental Rugs – A Buyer's Guide* by Essie Sakhai. The book includes colour photographs of different styles of carpets as well as information on the origins of the carpets. Also recommended (and with the same title) is *Oriental Rugs – A Buyer's Guide*, by Lee Allane.

More of a general display work is Johannes Kalter's *The Arts & Crafts of Syria*, a lavishly illustrated tome.

Several books deal with the intricate and complex artform of Arabic calligraphy. One such study is *Calligraphy and Islamic Culture*, by Annemarie Schimmel.

On a less exalted level, Heather Colyer Ross looks into popular art forms with her book, *The Art of Bedouin Jewellery*, a useful asset for those contemplating buying up the stuff in the souqs of Syria and Amman.

If you're interested in learning more about Muslim religious architecture and its permutations, *The Mosque*, edited by Martin Frishman and Hasan Uddin Khan, is a beautifully illustrated volume tracing the evolution of the mosque. ■

Religion

Getting a handle on Middle Eastern history and culture, and just to have an inkling of some of the reasoning behind much of what you see in day-to-day life in Jordan and Syria, requires at least some sketchwork knowledge of Islam. One of the better short accounts of Islamic belief and practices is *Mohammedanism – An Historical Survey*, by HAR Gibb. The Qur'an itself might seem daunting, but there are several translations around. AJ Arberry's *The Koran Interpreted* is considered among the better ones. Of course Muslims will tell you that the Qur'an cannot be translated, but must be read in Arabic to be truly appreciated. This may or may not be the case, but what is the non-Arabic reader to do?

Culture & Society

For a look at the life of women in Muslim countries, one introduction worth some time is Wiebke Walther's *Women in Islam – From Medieval to Modern Times*. Many tracts and often polemical texts have been brought out in recent years dealing with this, at times, delicate issue. *Women in Middle Eastern History*, edited by Nikki Keddie and Beth Baron also contains essays looking at the role of women down through the years.

The World of Islam, by Bernard Lewis, is a cross between a light introduction to the subject and a coffee-table size picture book. It is an unwieldy but highly attractive affair. For something a little more prosaic, there is Professor RM Savory's *Introduction to Islamic Civilisation*.

The secret world of the Druze is explored in Robert Brenton Betts' insightful *The Druze*.

Johann Ludwig Burckhardt spent the years from 1810-16 travelling extensively through Syria and the Holy Land, disguised as a pilgrim and compiling a unique and scholarly travelogue detailing every facet of the culture and society he encountered along the way. The result is *Travels in Syria and the Holy Land*.

Photography

For a rare look into a Syria and Jordan long gone, Malise Ruthuen's *Freya Stark in the Levant* provides a selection of this remarkable British writer's photographs from the region. Stark travelled all over the Middle East and left behind some 50,000 photos, many dating to the early decades of this century and as yet largely uncatalogued.

Bookshops Abroad

In London there are several good bookshops devoted to the business of travel literature. For guidebooks and maps, Stanford's bookshop (☎ 0171-836 2121), 12-14 Long Acre (WC2E 9LP), is acknowledged as one of the better first ports of call. A well-stocked source of travel literature with a strong leaning to collectors' items – 100 year old Cooks' guides and the like – is The Travellers' Bookshop (☎ 0171-836 9132), at 25 Cecil Court (W2N 4EZ). Another particularly good one is Daunts Books for Travellers (☎ 0171-224 2295), 83 Marylebone High Street (W1M 4AL).

In Australia, the Travel Bookshop (☎ 02-9241 3554), 20 Bridge Street, Sydney, is a travel book specialist. In the United States, try Book Passage (☎ 415-927 0960), 51 Tamal Vista Boulevarde, Corte Madera, California, and The Complete Traveler Bookstore (☎ 212-685 9007), 199 Madison Avenue, New York. In France, L'Astrolabe rive gauche (☎ 01-46 33 80 06), 14, rue Serpente, Paris, is recommended.

For books on all things Islamic and a fair spread of Arab history and books on contemporary Middle Eastern society, head for Al Hoda (☎ 0171-240 8381; fax 0171-497 0180), at 76-78 Charing Cross Rd. Eastern Books of London (0181-871 0880), at 125a Astonville St, are specialists in books on the Middle East, Eastern Europe and the Balkans.

PHOTOGRAPHY & VIDEO

Photography

Given the technology that goes into even the average pocket automatic camera, taking a halfway decent holiday snap is pretty much within everyone's reach. It is almost, but not quite, a matter of aiming and shooting. The single biggest factor to take into account is light. Try to work it so that you have your back to any sources of light (sunlight or artificial). The idea is to have light falling onto whatever it is you are taking a picture of. If the façade of a building you want to photograph is in shadow, come back at another time of day when it is lying in sunlight.

Think about what you want to capture on film. The best shots are usually the simplest ones, so focus in on the prime object of your lens' desires.

On the subject of light, the sun shines strong and hard in Jordan and Syria. Taking pictures in the middle of the day is virtually a guarantee of ending up with glary, washed out results. Where possible, try to exploit the softer light of the early morning and late afternoon, which enhances subtleties in colour and eliminates problems of glare. If you do need to take shots in bright light, think about using lens filters. As a rule, 100 ASA film is what you'll need most, although a couple of rolls of 200 ASA and/or 400 ASA can be handy for the odd occasion when light is not so strong.

Video

Properly used, a video camera can give a fascinating record of your holiday. As well as videoing the obvious things – sunsets, spectacular views – remember to record some of the ordinary everyday details of life in the country. Often the most interesting things occur when you're actually intent on filming something else. Remember too that, unlike still photography, video 'flows' – so, for example, you can shoot scenes of the countryside rolling past the train window, to give an overall impression that isn't possible with ordinary photos.

Video cameras these days have amazingly sensitive microphones, and you might be surprised how much sound will be picked up. This can also be a problem if there is a lot of ambient noise - filming by the side of a busy road might seem OK when you do it, but viewing it back home might simply give you a deafening cacophony of traffic noise. One good rule to follow for beginners is to try to film in long takes, and don't move the camera around too much. Otherwise, your video could well make your viewers seasick! If your camera has a stabiliser, you can use it to obtain good footage while travelling on various means of transport, even on bumpy roads. And remember, you're on holiday – don't let the video take over your life, and turn your trip into a Cecil B de Mille production.

Make sure you keep the batteries charged, and have the necessary charger, plugs and transformer for the country you are visiting. It is usually worth buying at least a few cartridges duty free to start off your trip.

Finally, remember to follow the same rules regarding people's sensitivities as for still photography – having a video camera shoved in their face is probably even more annoying and offensive for locals than a still camera. Always ask permission first.

Restrictions

Photography in military zones of both countries is forbidden. In Syria, they tend not to like you taking pictures of 'strategic areas' like bridges, public buildings (notably the ones with guards outside them) and the like.

Taking pictures of anything that suggests any degree of squalor, even the hectic activity of the marketplace, can offend some people's sense of pride. Sensitivity about the negative aspects of their countries leads some Jordanians and Syrians to become quite hostile about snappers.

Photographing People

A zoom lens is great for taking good people shots, usually without being noticed. A lot of people, women in particular, object to being photographed so you should ask first. Persisting if your snapping is unwelcome can lead to ugly scenes, so for the sake of your camera's health, exercise caution and common sense. Children will generally line up to be photographed.

Airport Security

Some but not all airports have X-ray machines for checking luggage. Despite assurances that they are safe for camera film, it's better to keep any unexposed film somewhere where it can be easily removed for examination.

TIME

Jordan and Syria are two hours ahead of GMT/UTC in winter (October to March) and three hours ahead in summer (April to September).

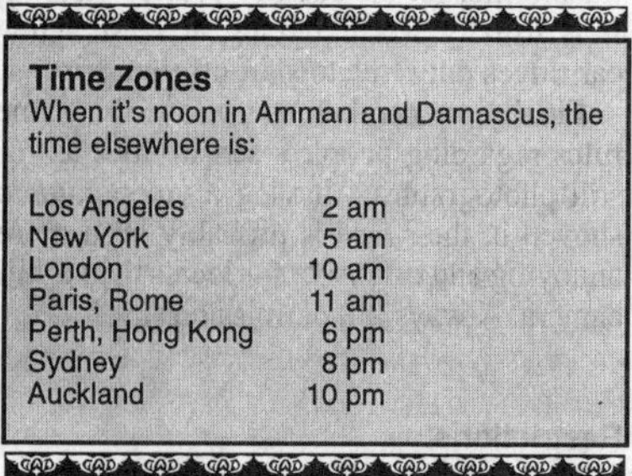

Time Zones

When it's noon in Amman and Damascus, the time elsewhere is:

Los Angeles	2 am
New York	5 am
London	10 am
Paris, Rome	11 am
Perth, Hong Kong	6 pm
Sydney	8 pm
Auckland	10 pm

Time is a commodity that Arabs always seem to have plenty of – something that should take five minutes will invariably take an hour. Trying to speed things up will only lead to frustration. It is better to take it philosophically than try to fight it. A bit of patience goes a long way here.

WEIGHTS & MEASURES

Jordan and Syria use the metric system. There is a standard conversion table at the back of this book.

HEALTH

Travel health depends on your pre-departure preparations, your day-to-day health care while travelling and how you handle any medical problem or emergency that develops. While the list of potential dangers can seem quite frightening, with a little luck, some basic precautions and adequate information few travellers experience more than upset stomachs. Please refer to the Health Appendix for details on pre-departure preparations, staying healthy and what to do in an emergency.

TOILETS

Toilets are generally the hole-in-the-floor variety and are in fact far more hygienic than sit-on toilets, as only your covered feet come into contact with anything.

It takes a little while to master the squatting technique without losing everything from your pockets. Carry your own toilet paper or adopt the local habit of using your left hand and water. There is always a tap at a convenient height for this purpose – whether any water comes out is something else again!

Toilet paper is widely available in Jordan, and although in Syria the familiar rolls may be a trifle harder to come by, most street vendors sell small packets of tissues that do just as well. Remember, for the sake of those who come after you, that the little basket usually provided is for your toilet paper. Trying to flush it will soon clog the system.

WOMEN TRAVELLERS

Attitudes to Women

Attitudes to foreign women in Jordan and Syria, as in indeed throughout much of the Middle East, can be trying to say the least. The reasons for this are complex, and of course it would be foolish to lump everyone together into the same category. These largely Muslim societies are, by contemporary western standards, quite conservative when it comes to sex and women, and most men have little or no contact with either before marriage – you'll soon notice your marital status (whether you are male or female) is a source of considerable interest to pretty much anyone you meet. 'Are you married?' usually figures among the first five standard questions Syrians or Jordanians put to foreigners. This in part reflects their own preoccupation with the issue. In general, a man has to gather a respectable sum of money or goods together to become an attractive prospect to eligible women – and their families.

Harassment of one sort or another does occur, and there is little point in pretending the contrary.

Western movies and TV give some men in these countries the impression that all western women are promiscuous and will jump into bed at the drop of a hat. An influx of prostitutes into Aleppo and Damascus from the former Soviet Union has created another problem – for some men all fair-skinned women are on the game, regardless of where they come from. The behaviour of some women travelling in these countries doesn't always help either. Flouting local sensitivities about dress not only gets the individuals concerned unwanted attention, it also colours the way locals perceive other travellers – however simplistic that may appear. Some women travelling in Syria and Jordan end up in short-term relationships with local men. Unfortunately this leads some locals to draw certain conclusions about all foreign women passing through.

Hassles & Avoiding Them

There will probably be times when you have male company that you could well live without. This may go no further than irritating banter or proposals of marriage and even declarations of undying love. Harassment can also take the form of leering, sometimes by being followed and occasionally being touched up.

You cannot make this problem go away and where possible, you should try to ignore this pubescent idiocy or you will end up allowing a few sad individuals spoil your whole trip. Plenty of women travel through Jordan and Syria, often alone, and never encounter serious problems.

The first rule of thumb is to respect standard Muslim sensibilities about dress – cover the shoulders, upper arms and legs at least, and not with skin-tight apparel. This is not a magic formula, but it certainly will help. Some women go to the extent of covering their head as well, although this makes little difference. Bear in mind that smaller towns and villages tend to be more conservative than big centres like Amman or Damascus, and that in general coastal towns are more relaxed than those of the interior.

Following a few other simple tips should also help reduce problems to a minimum. Avoid eye contact with a man you don't know; and try to ignore any rude remarks. Some women also find it's not worth summoning up the energy to acknowledge, say, being brushed up against. This is not to say that you should simply let everything go unremarked, and some behaviour may well warrant a good public scene. You'll be surprised how quickly bystanders will take matters into hand if they feel one of their own has overstepped the mark.

If you have to say anything to ward off an advance, *imshi* (clear off) should do the trick. A few women have found laughing at the importunate individual or staring at his shoes, as if to say, 'What kind of a cheap scumbag are you?', to be equally effective.

A wedding ring will add to your respectability in Arab eyes, but a photo of your children and even husband can clinch it – if you don't have any, borrow a picture of your nephew or niece.

Women travelling alone should think carefully before hitching to avoid unwelcome proposals.

Restaurants, Cafés & Hotels

Some activities, such as sitting in the tea shops, are usually seen as a male preserve and although it's quite OK for western women to enter, in some places the stares may make you feel uncomfortable. In Syria in particular, quite a few restaurants have a so-called family area. This is where the women generally go to eat. Women without male company will be more comfortable in these sections. As a rule, mixed foreign groups have no trouble wherever they sit, including in the tea shops and bars. In some of the local bars and cafés there is only one loo – since generally only men frequent these places. This doesn't mean women can't use them – but you should be aware of this unwitting unisex situation before settling in for a long tea or beer session.

Staying in budget hotels can sometimes be problematic if you're alone. You may have to take a room for yourself if there are no other travellers to share with, and it's not a bad idea to look around for cracks in interesting places. A wad of spare tissue paper or the like can come in handy for plugging up key and other holes if you're worried about peeping Toms.

GAY & LESBIAN TRAVELLERS

Homosexuality is prohibited in both Jordan and Syria and conviction can result in imprisonment. The public position on homosexuality in the Middle East is that it doesn't really exist. This is not to say that it doesn't, but Jordan and Syria are not ideal places to come out. Public displays of affection by heterosexuals are generally frowned upon, and the same rules apply to gays and lesbians.

For information on gay-friendly bars and hotels, see the *Sparticus International Gay Guide*.

DISABLED TRAVELLERS

Scant regard is paid to the needs of disabled travellers in Jordan and Syria. Every now and then in the big cities you might come across a wheelchair ramp when crossing the road, but that's about the extent of it.

Before setting off for Jordan and Syria, disabled travellers might wish to get in touch with the Royal Association for Disability & Rehabilitation (RADAR) (☎ 0171-250 3222), 250 City Rd, London, EC1V 8AS.

TRAVEL WITH CHILDREN

Taking the kids adds another dimension to a trip in Jordan and Syria, and of course it's not all fun and games. Firstly, it is a good idea to avoid travel in the summer and winter, as the extremes of heat and cold could really make your family journey quite unpleasant.

With very young children in particular, you will find yourself having to moderate the pace. Keeping the ankle-biters happy, well fed and clean is the challenge.

Always take along a bag of small gadgets and a favourite teddy bear or the like to keep junior amused, especially while on buses. Luckily, you will rarely have to embark on really long journeys in Syria or Jordan, so this should not pose too great a problem.

Powdered milk is available in both countries, and in Jordan pasteurised fresh milk is also around. Otherwise stick to bottled mineral water.

Kids already eating solids shouldn't have many problems. Cooked meat dishes, the various dips (such as hummus), rice and the occasional more or less western-style burger or pizza, along with fruit (washed and peeled) should all be OK as a nutritional basis. Nuts are also a good, safe source of protein and very cheap.

With infants, the next problem is cleanliness. It is impractical to carry more than about a half dozen washable nappies around with you, but disposable ones are not so easy to come by. As for accommodation, you are going to want a private bathroom and hot water. On occasion this will mean paying for something beyond the budget range.

Enough of the down side. The good news is that children are as loved in Jordan and Syria as anywhere else in the Middle East. Few people bring their young ones to this part of the world, so you'll find that your kids are quite a hit. In that way they can help break the ice and open the doors to closer contact with local people you might otherwise never have exchanged glances with.

For more comprehensive advice on the dos and don'ts of taking the kids away with you, check out Lonely Planet's *Travel with Children* by Maureen Wheeler.

ISLAMIC HOLIDAYS

As the Hijra calendar is 11 days shorter than the Gregorian calendar, each year Islamic holidays fall 11 days earlier than in the previous year. The precise dates are known only shortly before they fall, as they depend upon the sighting of the moon. The main Islamic holidays are the following. For the equivalent western calendar dates, see the Table of Holidays.

Major Islamic Holidays

Ras as-Sana
New Year's Day, celebrated on 1 Moharram.

Mulid an-Nabi
The Prophet Mohammed's birthday, celebrated on 12 Rabi' al-Awal.

Eid al-Fitr
Also known as the *Eid as-Sagheer* (small feast), it starts at the beginning of Shawwal to mark the end of fasting in the preceding month of Ramadan.

Eid al-Adhah
Known commonly as the *Eid al-Kabeer* (big feast), it is the time when Muslims fulfil the fifth pillar of Islam – the pilgrimage to Mecca. This period lasts from 10 to 13 Zuul-Hijja.

Ramadan

Ramadan is the ninth month of the Muslim calendar, when Muslims fast during daylight hours to fulfil the fourth pillar of Islam. There are no public holidays but it is difficult to deal with officialdom because of unusual opening hours.

During this month of fasting, pious Muslims will not allow *anything* to pass their lips in daylight hours. One is even supposed to avoid swallowing saliva.

Although many do not follow the injunctions to the letter, most conform to some extent. Foreigners are not expected to follow suit, but it is generally impolite to smoke, drink or eat in public during Ramadan. In the bigger cities it is less of a problem, but it remains sensible to avoid flaunting your kebabs.

Business hours tend to become more erratic and usually shorter, and in out-of-the-way places you may find it hard to find a restaurant that opens before sunset.

The evening meal during Ramadan, called *iftar* (breaking the fast), is always a bit of a celebration. Go to the bigger restaurants and wait with fasting crowds for sundown, the moment when food is served – it's quite a lively experience.

FOOD

Food in Syria and Jordan ranges from the exotic to the mundane. Unfortunately for the budget traveller, exotic food comes with exotic prices, so it's mostly the mundane you'll be relying on. The food is tasty as a rule but the lack of variety may have you dreaming about far away meals.

On the subject of *where* to eat, some places tend to cater almost exclusively to men. This is an issue mainly in Syria, but before women start worrying that they might starve, a couple of things need to be pointed out. Some of these restaurants also serve as drinking establishments (considered a male preserve) and others simply seem to attract mainly men. However, most restaurants where this may seem to be a problem have a 'family' section, basically set aside for women. Secondly, foreign women with male company will rarely, have any problem

Table of Holidays

Hejira Year	*New Year*	*Prophet's Birthday*	*Ramadan Begins*	*Eid Al-Fitr*	*Eid Al-Adha*
1417	20.05.96	28.07.96	10.01.97	09.02.97	18.04.97
1418	09.05.97	17.07.97	30.12.97	29.01.98	08.04.98
1419	28.04.98	06.07.98	19.12.98	18.01.99	28.03.99
1420	17.04.99	25.06.99	08.12.99	07.01.00	17.03.00
1421	06.04.00	14.06.00	27.11.00	27.12.00	06.03.01
1422	26.03.01	03.06.01	16.11.01	16.12.01	23.02.02
1423	15.03.02	23.05.02	05.11.02	05.12.02	12.02.03
1424	04.03.03	12.05.03	25.10.03	24.11.03	01.02.04

eating wherever they choose. It must be stressed that, in general, there is no real problem. But it is worth being aware of the issues.

Restaurant Meals

The most common way for a group to eat in any restaurant is to order *mezzeh* – a variety of small starters followed by several mains to be shared by all present. Otherwise, you can simply order one or two starters, bread, a main course (usually meat), salad and potato chips. Some smaller hole-in-the-wall places will specialise in one or two things only. Some just do chicken, while others have three or four stewed vegetables on show.

Starters *Hummus* is cooked chickpeas ground into a paste and mixed with tahini (a sesame-seed paste), garlic and lemon. It is available in virtually every restaurant and is usually excellent. It is generally eaten as a starter with bread, and goes very nicely with any of the meat dishes.

Baba ghanouj is another of the dips eaten

Bread & Snacks

The Arabic unleavened bread, *khobz*, is eaten with absolutely everything and is sometimes called *eish* (life), its common name in Egypt. It is round and flat and makes a good filler if you are preparing your own food. There is a variety of tastes and textures, depending on how it is baked, but the basic principle remains the same. On the streets of Amman, stalls sell *ka'ik*, which are round sesame rings and tastier than plain old khobz. A favourite breakfast staple is bread liberally sprinkled with *zata'* (thyme).

Felafel, shawarma and, to a lesser degree, *fuul* are the staple foods of the region and are eaten for breakfast, lunch or dinner. Fuul is a paste made from fava beans, garlic and lemon and is served swimming in oil – a bit hard to handle first thing in the morning. If you've arrived from Egypt, you will need no introduction.

Felafel is deep-fried balls of chickpea paste with spices and served in a piece of khobz with varying combinations of pickled vegetables ('*turshi*', not to everyone's taste), tomato, salad and yoghurt. This is one of the cheapest ways to eat and chances are you'll be thoroughly sick of felafels by the time you leave.

The meat equivalent of the felafel is the *shawarma*, and you'll probably have your fair share of these too as they are cheap and convenient. Slices of lamb are carefully arranged on a vertical spit and are topped with a few big chunks of fat, which drips down the meat as it cooks, and a tomato for decoration.

When you order a shawarma, more commonly known as a *sandweech*, the vendor will slice off the meat (usually with a great flourish and much knife sharpening and waving), dip a piece of flat bread in the fat that has dripped off the meat, hold it against the gas flame so it flares, then fill it with the meat and fillings similar to those for felafels. Chicken shawarmas are quite common too. Shops selling shawarma nearly always have the spit set up out by the footpath so you can just pick one up as you walk along.

In Syria, particularly in Aleppo, you'll come across bakeries selling what look like small pizzas, known as *safeeheh*. They are a type of bread topped with spices, cheese and sometimes meat. You can occasionally find these as far south as Amman in Jordan.

Other sandweech stalls specialise in offal of various kinds (liver, kidneys, brains, etc) and they are probably quite OK to eat if you can stomach that sort of thing. ■

Preparing *khobz* (unleavened bread)

with bread and is made from mashed eggplant and tahini. Fairly similar is another one called *mutabel*. A vaguely hot red dip is *daqqeh*.

Tabbouleh is largely a parsley and tomato based salad, with a sprinkling of sesame seeds, lemon and garlic. It goes perfectly with the hummus in bread.

A couple of more solid and tasty starters include *maqlubbeh*, steamed rice topped with grilled slices of eggplant or meat, grilled tomato and pinenuts, and *fareekeh*, a similar dish with cracked wheat. *Fattoush* is pretty much tabbouleh with little shreds of deep fried bread in it. Turkish-style stuffed vine leaves sometimes go by the name of *yalenjeh*.

A good dish that, ordered in sufficient quantity, could easily make a very satisfying main course itself is *mar-ya*, not unlike Turkish *lahmacun*. It is a kind of thin pastry with a tasty minced meat and spice topping, folded over and cut into sandwich-like squares. A similar Jordanian equivalent is called *arayis*.

The offal lover has the enticing options of brains, grilled or raw kidneys or even liver.

Main Courses For main dishes, you'll have the choice of eating either chicken, kebabs or meat and vegetable stews most of the time.

Chicken ('*farooj*') is usually roasted on spits in large ovens out the front of the restaurant. The usual serving is half a chicken ('*nuss farooj*') and it will come with bread and a side dish of raw onion, chillies and sometimes olives. Eaten with the optional extras of salad ('*salata*') and hummus, you have a good meal.

Kebabs are another favourite available everywhere. These are spicy minced lamb pieces pressed onto skewers and grilled over charcoal. They are usually sold by weight and are also served with bread and a side plate. *Shish Tawooq* is loosely the chicken version of the same thing.

Stews are usually meat or vegetable or both and, although not available everywhere, make a pleasant change from chicken and kebabs. *Fasooliya* is bean stew, *biseela* is made of peas, *batatas* of potato and *mulukiyyeh* is a kind of spinach stew with chicken or meat pieces. They are usually served on rice ('*ruz*') or more rarely macaroni ('*makarone*').

Starters

Spinach and Yoghurt Dip Dips are a ubiquitous part of the *mezzeh*. This version is less common in the west.

Ingredients

5 tbs olive oil
1 onion, very finely chopped
2 cloves garlic, crushed
1 bunch fresh spinach, washed and trimmed
500g plain yoghurt
1 tbs salt
freshly ground black pepper

Method

Heat oil in a frypan, toss in onion and saute until transparent. Turn down heat, stir through garlic and fry gently for one minute. Remove pan from heat and cool mixture in the pan.

Steam or boil the spinach for 3 minutes. Drain and squeeze out excess liquid. Cool then finely chop. Place yoghurt, onion mixture and spinach in a bowl. Whisk until smooth. Stir through salt and black pepper to taste.

Serve chilled.

Mains

Fasooliya Green bean stew in its many variations is a staple accompaniment in the Middle East.

Ingredients
5 tbs olive oil
3-4 cloves garlic, coarsely chopped
2 onions, finely chopped
1 tbs ground coriander
3 large tomatoes, skinned and coarsely chopped
1 kg green beans, washed and tailed
salt and freshly ground black pepper
juice of 1 lemon

Method
Heat oil in a large heavy-based saucepan, toss in garlic and fry gently for two minutes. Add onion and gently fry until transparent. Add coriander and stir through until the aroma is released. Add tomatoes and a little salt to help release their water and simmer for about 15 minutes, stirring occasionally.

Add beans, black pepper and lemon juice. Stir beans through the tomato sauce, cover saucepan and simmer until beans are cooked. Check seasoning.

Serve hot or cold.

Kibbeh Served both raw and cooked, in myriad variations, these meat and *burghul* (steamed, cracked wheat) 'balls' are pretty much the national dish of Syria (and Lebanon; versions known by other names exist elsewhere throughout the Middle East).

Traditionally, this dish is prepared entirely by hand, from the grinding of the wheat to the pounding of the lamb, and finally by thoroughly kneading the ingredients to ensure a fine consistency. In *A New Book of Middle Eastern Food*, Claudia Roden points to the mystique surrounding the preparation of this dish and says that women are 'said to be favoured by the gods if one is born with a long finger', which ensures the easy shaping of kibbeh.

The following recipe is a simple version which can be fried or char-grilled; a mincer or food processor will make your job a lot easier.

Ingredients
1 small onion, finely chopped
salt and freshly ground black pepper
400g minced lamb
1-2 tbs water
250g fine burghul, washed and drained
oil for frying

To Serve
cos lettuce
olive oil
lemon juice

Method
Mince the onion with salt and pepper.

Pound (or grind) the meat, adding sufficient water until smooth and well blended. Add onion mixture and burghul and knead (or blend) until combined into a smooth paste.

Mould into round flat discs (approximately 5 by 1 cm) and deep fry until golden. Alternatively char-grill until crisp.

Serve with lettuce drizzled with oil and lemon juice.

In Jordan, and less frequently in Syria, you can eat the Bedouin speciality *mensaf*. It is traditionally served on special occasions and consists of lamb on a bed of rice and pine nuts, topped with the gaping head of the lamb. The fat from the cooking is poured into the rice and is considered by some to be the best part. The Bedouin men sit on the floor around the big dishes and dig in (with the right hand only), while the women eat elsewhere in the town or camp. Traditionally, the delicacy is the eyes, which are presented to honoured guests! Don't worry if you miss out – there are other choice bits like the tongue. It's not always so easy to refuse if offered. Once all have had their fill, usually well before it has all been eaten, you move off to wash your hands while young boys take away the leftovers and tuck in. The meal is eventually followed by endless rounds of coffee and tea and plenty of lively talk. If you stay with the Bedouin you may be lucky enough to eat mensaf this way, but you can also buy a serve in restaurants in Amman. It is not cheap but should be tried at least once. A tangy sauce of cooked yoghurt mixed with the fat is served with it.

Fish ('*samak*') is not widely available and is usually so heavily salted and spiced that it tastes more like a large anchovy. Decent fish can be had in Aqaba, Jordan's Red Sea port, and occasionally in Syria's Mediterranean towns.

Desserts

Arabs love sugar and their desserts are assembled accordingly – they are very sweet. There are pastry shops in every town selling nothing but these (divinely) sickly sweets. Just wander in and have a look at the selection. The basic formula is pastry drenched in honey, syrup and/or rose water. Many of them, however different they look, fall into the general category of *baqlawa*. Buy only a small quantity as more than one of anything is too much.

In Syria, many of the pastry shops are sit-down places. You walk in, make a selection and take a seat. They serve you your order, some water to swig between each sweet and sometimes a coffee or tea as well. You pay on the way out. They are often good places for solo women travellers to relax. The most popular desserts are:

baqlawa – layered flaky pastry with nuts, drenched in honey
booza – ice cream
halawat al-jibna – a soft doughy pastry filled with cream cheese and topped with syrup & ice cream
isfinjiyya – coconut slice
kinaafa – shredded wheat over goat cheese baked in syrup
mahalabiyya – milk pudding
mahalabiyya wa festaq – milk pudding with pistachio nuts
mushabbak – lace-work shaped pastry drenched in syrup
zalabiyya – pastries dipped in rose-water

Desserts

Mahalabiyya This incredibly sweet dessert is common throughout the region.

Ingredients
6 tbs ground rice
1 litre milk
100g sugar
2 tbs rose water

Method
Make a smooth and runny paste with the ground rice and some of the cold milk.

Place the remaining milk and sugar in a heavy-based saucepan and bring to the boil. Gradually add the paste while stirring constantly with a wooden spoon. Reduce heat, simmer and continue to stir mixture until mixture begins to thicken. Add rose water, cook for one minute, then pour into a serving bowl.

Serve chilled.

Culinary Clues

Soup

soup	*shurba*
lentil soup	*shurbat al-'adas*

Vegetables

cabbage	*kharoum*

carrot	*jazar*
cauliflower	*arnabeet*
cucumber	*khiyaar*
eggplant	*bazinjan*
garlic	*tum*
green beans	*fasooliya*
lentils	*'adas*
lettuce	*khass*
okra	*baamiya*
onion	*basal*
peas	*biseela*
potatoes	*batatas*
salad	*salata*
tomato	*banadura*
turnip	*lift*
vegetables	*khadrawat*

Meats

camel	*lahm jamal*
chicken	*farooj*
kidney	*kelaawi*
lamb	*lahm danee*
liver	*kibda*
meat	*lahm*

Fruit

apple	*tufah*
apricot	*mish-mish*
banana	*moz*
date	*tamr*
fig	*teen*
fruit	*fawaka*
grape	*'inab*
lime	*limoon*
orange	*burtuqaal*
pomegranate	*rumman*
watermelon	*batteekh*

Miscellaneous

bread	*khobz* or *eish*
butter	*zibda*
cheese	*jibna*
eggs	*beid*
milk	*haleeb*
mineral water *maya*	*at-ta'abiyya*
pepper	*filfil*
salt	*milh*
sour milk drink	*ayran*
sugar	*sukar*
water	*mayy*
yoghurt	*laban*

DRINKS

Juice

All over the place, you will find juice stalls selling delicious freshly squeezed fruit juices ('*aseer*'). In Syria especially, these stalls are instantly recognisable by the string bags of fruit hanging out the front.

Popular juices include lemon, orange, banana, pomegranate and rockmelon, and you can have combinations of any or all of these. Some stalls put milk in their drinks which, in the case of Syria at least, you'd be well advised to stay away from if you have a dodgy stomach.

In Syria, you can be pretty sure you will get pure juice every time, but in Jordan, particularly in Amman, it pays to keep an eye on what's going on behind the counter – if indeed you can see. Diluting the juice with tap water or, worse, a sickly cordial, is a common enough and irritating practice. Often they seem to have plenty of the stuff ready, which they then top up with a couple of pieces of freshly squeezed fruit when you order.

Soft Drinks

Syrian soft drinks ('*gazoza*') are cheap (starting as low as 10 cents) and not too sweet. The orange drinks are called Crush and the coke seems to go by several names. A range of more expensive canned drinks, mostly produced under licence from Canada Dry or simply imported, is also widely available. They include 7-Up and other things called Oranta or Double Cola.

Jordan has Pepsi, 7-Up, Coca-Cola and a local product called Viva in bottles. They and others are also available in cans but are a little more expensive.

Alcohol

Despite the fact that Islam prohibits the use of alcohol, it is widely drunk and readily available.

Beer Both countries brew their own local

beers ('*birra*'). Syria has Al-Chark in Aleppo and Barada in Damascus, and both are quite palatable (Barada seems more reliable in quality) and cheap (about a dollar in most restaurants or almost half from liquor stores – including a S£5 deposit, so take your empties back!). Several imported beers, such as Bavaria and Carlsberg are also now freely available and go for anything from US$2 to US$4 a small bottle in restaurants.

Jordan brews Amstel and Henninger under licence from the parent European company. Amstel seems the more common, and you can buy 650 ml bottles of it for JD1.800 (US$2.50) from liquor stores – you get 800 fils back for returning the bottle. In Amman and Aqaba, you can also occasionally buy beer imported from all over the world – everything from Guinness to Fosters.

Liquor *Araq* is the indigenous firewater and should be treated with caution. It is similar to Greek *ouzo* or Turkish *raqi* and is availble in shops, bars and restaurants throughout Syria and Jordan. It is usually mixed with water and ice and drunk with food. The best araq is said to come from Lebanon. In Syria, the prized brands are Rayan, Al-Mimis and Nadim. Anything else may well bear a closer relationship to aircraft fuel than the aniseed-based drop it is supposed to be. In Jordan, Ghantous is a common brand that sells for US$4 in liquor stores.

Various other forms of hard liquor are available in liquor stores in both countries, including several whiskies and local concoctions. In Jordan it is possible to find all sorts of imported liquor in Amman and Aqaba, but you'll need a fat wallet if you are going to make a habit of it.

Wine This part of the world has an ideal climate for wine ('*khamr*') production, so in some senses it is a little surprising there isn't more about.

In Syria, the main wine-producing areas are to be found around the cities of Damascus and Homs. The output is hardly majestic, but it is drinkable. Bought in a liquor store, it is hard to beat for price, with lower quality bottles costing about US$1 and something slightly more acceptable closer to the US$2 mark. Among the latter is Doumani, a decent, slightly sweet red; Muscatel, a rosé, and Fayçal, a dry white.

Little wine is produced in Jordan. Brands such as Latroun, St Catherine and Cremisan, are instead imported from the West Bank and can be had for US$3.50 to US$5.50 a bottle in liquor stores. Again, they are nothing memorable, but at least they are there if you should feel like the grape. Cypriot wines are also available for about US$8.50, but they aren't much different.

THINGS TO BUY

The first and most important thing to know is that, for any kind of souvenir-hunting or serious stocking up on eastern goods, you are much better off making your purchases in Syria. There is, comparatively speaking, precious little around in Jordan, and what there is usually comes across from Syria at inflated prices. Apart from anything else, the experience of trawling through the great souqs of Damascus and Aleppo can in no way be matched in Jordan.

It could even be argued that Syria is a better choice for a good many items than the great markets of Cairo, which have been dealing with tourists all too keen to part with their money for just a little too long.

Carpets, Rugs & Kilims

The markets of Damascus and Aleppo are riddled with carpet dealers. The disappointing news is that the products, however decent they may be, do not represent the good value they once did. While it is still possible to stumble across a very good and aged handmade rug from Iran, the chances are that what you're looking at was sewn in an attic above you. This is not to say that the carpets are lousy, but it is worth taking a close look at quality. Inspect both sides of the carpet to get an idea of how close and strong the hand-sewing is. If you understand any Arabic, watch the locals haggle with salespeople and try to get an idea of what *they* think the merchandise is worth (bearing in mind that they are looking to use them as part of the household furnishing, not merely as a souvenir).

Designs generally tend to consist of geometric patterns, although increasingly the tourist market is being catered to with depictions of monuments, animals and the like – rather kitsch and a poor reflection of Middle Eastern artistic tradition.

Unlike in Morocco, where the distinction is instantly clear, the difference between what salespeople call carpets and kilims seems to be a little blurred here.

In Jordan, Bedouin rugs and tapestries made by Palestinian women are popular but you need to look carefully to make sure that they are actually handmade.

Gold, Silver & Jewellery

You can find gold shops scattered about the bigger cities of Syria and Jordan, but they are at their most concentrated in certain quarters of the Damascus and Aleppo souqs and Downtown Amman. As a rule, gold is sold by weight, and all pieces should have a hallmark guaranteeing quality. A hallmark normally indicates where a piece was assayed and a date. Verifying all this is difficult, and the best advice is to buy items you would be happy with even if you found on returning home that the gold content was not as high as you had been led to believe.

The same goes for silver, although of course its monetary value is in any case somewhat lower. For that reason, it is the most common material used by Bedouin women to make up their often striking jewellery. All sorts of things can be had, from crude earrings to complex necklaces and pendants laden with semiprecious stones. It is, by the way, wise to check on the nature of such stone, such as amber, with a lighted match. Black smoke, a mild stench and that melting feeling will reveal the plastic reality of some of the shysters' material. Depending on your tastes, a plethora of original and reasonably priced items can be purchased. Take most of the talk about antique jewellery with a shaker-full of salt. It is easy to make silver look very old.

Silver is not only used in women's jewellery, but to make carry-cases for miniature Qur'ans and other objects.

Metalwork

For centuries Damascus was, along with Toledo in Spain, one of the greatest centres for the production of quality swords. Tamerlaine forcefully transferred the Damascene sword-makers to Samarkand in the 15th century, but something of the tradition stuck. There is little use for such things these days, but several shops in Damascus still produce them for sale as souvenirs. Production seems rather half-hearted compared with the efforts of the city's Spanish counterparts.

Copper & Brassware

From Morocco to Baghdad you will find much the same sorts of brass and chased copper objects for sale. The good thing about this stuff is that it is fairly hard to cheat on quality. Most common are the very large decorative trays and tabletops, but other items typical of the Middle East include Arabic coffeepots and even complete coffee sets with small cups (the little traditional cups without handles should preferably be ceramic however). Incense-burners and teapots are among other possible buys.

Silk, Brocades & Textiles

Damascus in particular is known for its textiles, and has been since antiquity. This has to be one of the best places in the world to look for tablecloths and the like. They are generally made of fine cotton and handsomely adorned with silk. Brocade is another speciality, and the Bedouin-style vests on sale in some of the more reputable shops in the Damascus souqs are popular. Good ones will go for around US$10. Along the same line are *jalabiyyehs*, the long, loose robes that you'll see many men and women getting around in. The men's version tends to be fairly sober in colouring, while this kind of women's clothing can be almost blindingly gawdy.

Instruments

Quite a few souq stalls sell either *ouds* (Arabic lutes) or *darbukkas*, the standard Middle Eastern style drums. The latter can go quite cheaply, and even the lutes are hardly expensive at around US$40 for a typical model. Such an item's musical value must be considered unlikely to be high – it's the kind of thing you'd buy more for display than play.

Leatherware

Neither Syria nor Jordan is particularly good for leatherware. In Damascus you can find wallets, belts, pistol holsters and the like, but none of it is very exciting. There is nothing like what can be found in Cairo or Morocco.

Soap

Aleppo, in northern Syria, has a name for its soaps made with olive or even laurel oil (the latter is a costly product indeed). There are up to 40 small-scale manufacturers of such materials for soothing your skin.

Other Souvenirs

Another popular buy with foreigners are the woodwork items. They range from simple jewellery boxes to elaborate chess sets and backgammon boards. The better quality stuff tends to be of walnut and inlaid with mother of pearl. If the mother of pearl gives off a strong rainbow-colour effect, you can be almost sure it is the real McCoy. Otherwise it is more likely to be cheap plastic. The actual woodwork on many of these items tends to be a little shoddy, even on the better quality items, so inspect the joints and inlay carefully.

The ubiquitous waterpipes ('*nargilehs*') are about as vivid a reminder of a visit to the Middle East as one can imagine. Some of the smaller, simpler ones can start from as low as US$2 or US$3, but more ornate ones will cost considerably more. Remember to buy a supply of charcoal to get you going if you intend to use the thing when you return home – a couple of spare tubes would not go astray either. Of all the things you could buy, this has to be about the most awkward to cart around with you – and it's chances of surviving the post are not good.

Another simple idea, and much easier to carry around, is the traditional Arab headcloth, or *kafiyyeh*, and *'iqal* (the black cord used to keep it on your head) so characteristic of the region. Be aware that the quality of kafiyyehs varies considerably, with some being very bare strips of white cotton and others densely sewn in red or black patterns. Compare before you buy. Even the quality of the 'iqal can vary. A good set bought in Syria should not cost more than about US$4 to US$5 (S£200) at the most.

The small bottles of coloured sand from Petra are a speciality in Jordan. The sand is skilfully poured into bottles to form intricate patterns, and these are sold for anything from 500 fils upwards. Natural, coloured sand was originally used, but these days it is often artificially coloured (so what else is new?).

Dead Sea cosmetic products using the mud from the area are another possibility. The mud is supposed to be very good for the skin and you can buy such products in chic Amman boutiques or at the Dead Sea resorts.

Getting There & Away

However you're travelling, it's worth taking out travel insurance. Work out what you need. You may not want to insure that grotty old army surplus backpack – but everyone should be covered for the worst case: an accident, for example, that requires hospital treatment and a flight home. If you plan to travel for a long time, the insurance may seem expensive – but if you can't afford it, you certainly won't be able to afford to deal with a medical emergency abroad.

Check out policy fine print. In most cases you need to pay extra to cover yourself for 'dangerous sports' such as diving. Also, you often need to pay a surcharge for expensive camera equipment and the like. Standard insurance should in any case at least cover you for luggage theft and loss, cancellation of and delays to your travel arrangements.

Paying for your ticket with a credit card often provides limited travel accident insurance, and you may be able to reclaim payment if the operator doesn't deliver. Ask your credit card company what it will cover.

Once you have your ticket and policy, keep separate copies of the details in case the originals are lost or stolen.

Jordan and Syria are reasonably well connected by air with Europe, North Africa and the rest of the Middle East, but super cheap tickets hardly abound. Most independent travellers tend to enter the area by land or sea from neighbouring countries such as Turkey, Egypt and Israel. The political problems with the latter are complex, and one false move there could see you prohibited from entering Syria. Refer to Visas & Documents in each country's Facts for the Visitor chapter as well as the Jordan Getting There & Away chapter.

AIR

Always remember to reconfirm your onward flight or return bookings by the specified time – at least 72 hours before departure on international flights. Otherwise there's a risk that you'll turn up at the airport only to find you've missed your flight because it was rescheduled or that you've been classified as a 'no show'.

Buying Tickets

The plane ticket will probably be the single most expensive item in your budget, and buying it can be an intimidating business. It is worth putting aside a few hours to research the state of the market and check around the many travel agents hoping to separate you from your money. Start early: some of the cheapest tickets have to be bought months in advance, and some popular flights sell out early. Talk to other recent travellers – they may be able to stop you making some of the same old mistakes. Look at the ads in newspapers and magazines, consult reference books and watch for special offers. Then phone round travel agents for bargains. (Airlines can supply information on routes and timetables; however, except at times of inter-airline war they do not supply the cheapest tickets.) Find out the fare, the route, the duration of the journey and any restrictions on the ticket. (See the Air Travel Glossary.) Then sit back and decide which is best for you.

You may discover that those impossibly cheap flights are 'fully booked, but we have another one that costs a bit more...' or that the flight is on an airline notorious for its poor safety standards and leaves you in the world's least favourite airport in mid-journey for 14 hours. Alternatively they may claim to have the last two seats available for that country for the whole of July, which they will hold for you for a maximum of two hours. Don't panic – keep ringing around.

If you are travelling from the UK or the USA, you will probably find that the cheapest flights are being advertised by obscure bucket shops whose names haven't yet reached the telephone directory. They sell airline tickets at up to a 50% discount where places have not been filled, and although

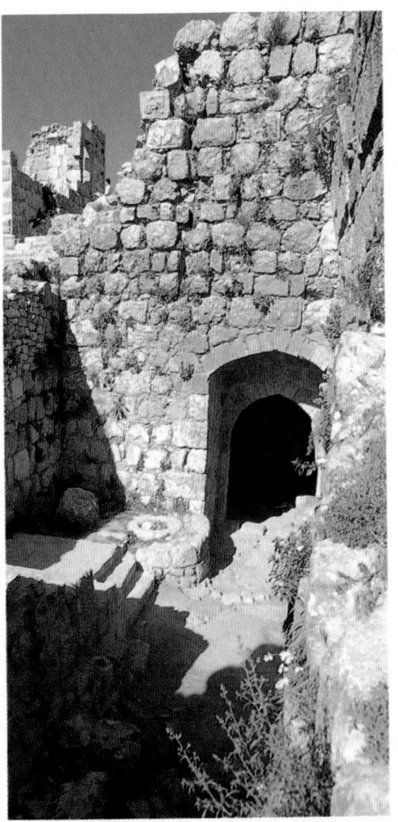

DAMIEN SIMONIS

OLIVIER CIRENDINI

HUGH FINLAY

OLIVIER CIRENDINI

A	B
A	C
D	D

Jordan

A: Qala'at ar-Rabad (Ajlun) – a fine example of Islamic military architecture.
B: Remarkable frescoes are housed in the desert castle Qusayr 'Amra.
C: Qasr al-Kharaneh, one of the first khans (caravanserais) for traders.
D: The majestic scenery of Wadi Rum.

DAMIEN SIMONIS

OLIVIER CIRENDINI

OLIVIER CIRENDINI

DAMIEN SIMONIS

Jordan

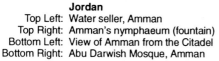

Top Left: Water seller, Amman
Top Right: Amman's nymphaeum (fountain)
Bottom Left: View of Amman from the Citadel
Bottom Right: Abu Darwish Mosque, Amman

airlines may protest to the contrary, many of them release tickets to selected bucket shops – it's better to sell tickets at a huge discount than not at all. Many such firms are honest and solvent, but there are a few rogues who will take your money and disappear, to reopen elsewhere a month or two later under a new name. If you feel suspicious about a firm, don't give them all the money at once – leave a deposit of 20% or so and pay the balance when you get the ticket. If they insist on cash in advance, go somewhere else. Once you have the ticket, ring the airline to confirm that you are actually booked onto the flight.

You may decide to pay more than the rock-bottom fare by opting for the safety of a better-known travel agent. Firms such as STA, which have offices worldwide, Council Travel in the USA or Travel CUTS in Canada are not going to disappear overnight, leaving you clutching a receipt for a nonexistent ticket, but they do offer good prices to most destinations.

Use the fares quoted in this book as a guide only. They are approximate and based on the rates advertised by travel agents at the time of going to press. Quoted airfares do not necessarily constitute a recommendation for the carrier.

Travellers with Special Needs

If you have special needs of any sort – you've broken a leg, you're vegetarian, travelling in a wheelchair, taking the baby, terrified of flying – you should let the airline know as soon as possible so that they can make arrangements accordingly. You should remind them when you reconfirm your booking (at least 72 hours before departure) and again when you check in at the airport. It may also be worth ringing round the airlines before you make your booking to find out how they can handle your particular needs.

Airports and airlines can be surprisingly helpful, but they do need advance warning. Most international airports will provide escorts from check-in desk to plane where needed, and there should be ramps, lifts, accessible toilets and reachable phones. Aircraft toilets, on the other hand, are likely to present a problem; travellers should discuss this with the airline at an early stage and, if necessary, with their doctor.

Guide dogs for the blind will often have to travel in a specially pressurised baggage compartment with other animals, away from their owner; though smaller guide dogs may be admitted to the cabin. All guide dogs will be subject to the same quarantine laws (six months in isolation etc) as any other animal when entering or returning to countries currently free of rabies, such as Britain or Australia.

Deaf travellers can ask for airport and in-flight announcements to be written down for them.

Children under two years of age travel for 10% of the standard fare (or free, on some airlines), as long as they don't occupy a seat. They don't get a baggage allowance either. 'Skycots' should be provided by the airline if requested in advance; these will take a child weighing up to about 10 kg. Children between two and 12 can usually occupy a seat for half to two-thirds of the full fare, and do get a baggage allowance. Push chairs can often be taken as hand luggage.

The USA

There's little direct traffic between the USA and Jordan and Syria. For specifics, see each country's Getting There & Away chapter. It may be worth your while getting a cheap flight to Europe (say London) first and trying from there.

The *New York Times*, the *LA Times*, the *Chicago Tribune* and the *San Francisco Examiner* produce weekly travel sections in which you'll find any number of travel agents' ads. Council Travel and STA have offices in major cities nationwide. *Travel Unlimited* (PO Box 1058, Allston, Mass 02134) publishes details of cheap air fares.

Standard fares on commercial airlines are expensive and probably best avoided. However, travelling on a normal, scheduled flight can be more secure and reliable, particularly for more elderly travellers and families who might prefer to avoid the potential inconveniences of the budget alternatives.

Discount and rock-bottom options from the USA include charter flights, stand-by and courier flights. Stand-by fares are often sold at 60% of the normal price for one-way tickets. Airhitch (☎ 212-864 2000), Suite 100, 2790 Broadway, New York, NY 10025, specialises in this sort of thing. You will need to give a general idea of where and when you need to go, and a few days before your departure you will be presented with a choice of two or three flights.

Courier flights are where you accompany freight or a parcel to its destination. There may not be much going to Jordan or Syria, but you never know your luck. Generally courier flights require that you return within a specified period (sometimes within one or two weeks, but often up to one month). You will need to travel light, as luggage is usually restricted to what you can carry onto the plane (the parcel or freight you accompany comes out of your luggage allowance), and you may have to be a US resident and apply for an interview before they take you on. Most flights depart from New York.

A good source of information on courier flights is Now Voyager (☎ (212) 431-1616), Suite 307, 74 Varrick St, New York, NY 10013. This company specialises in courier flights, but you must pay an annual membership fee (around US$50), which entitles you

Air Travel Glossary

Apex Apex, or 'advance purchase excursion' is a discounted ticket which must be paid for in advance. There are penalties if you wish to change it.

Baggage Allowance This will be written on your ticket: usually one 20 kg item to go in the hold, plus one item of hand luggage.

Bucket Shop An unbonded travel agency specialising in discounted airline tickets.

Bumped Just because you have a confirmed seat doesn't mean you're going to get on the plane – see Overbooking.

Cancellation Penalties If you have to cancel or change an Apex ticket there are often heavy penalties involved. Insurance can sometimes be taken out against these penalties. Some airlines impose penalties on regular tickets as well, particularly against 'no show' passengers.

Check In Airlines ask you to check in a certain time ahead of the flight departure (usually 1½ hours on international flights). If you fail to check in on time and the flight is overbooked the airline can cancel your booking and give your seat to somebody else.

Confirmation Having a ticket written out with the flight and date you want doesn't mean you have a seat until the agent has checked with the airline that your status is 'OK' or confirmed. Meanwhile you could just be 'on request'.

Discounted Tickets There are two types of discounted fares – officially discounted (see Promotional Fares) and unofficially discounted. The lowest prices often impose drawbacks like flying with unpopular airlines, inconvenient schedules, or unpleasant routes and connections. A discounted ticket can save you things other than money – you may be able to pay Apex prices without the associated Apex advance booking and other requirements. Discounted tickets only exist where there is fierce competition.

Full Fares Airlines traditionally offer first-class (coded F), business-class (coded J) and economy-class (coded Y) tickets. These days there are so many promotional and discounted fares available from the regular economy class that few passengers pay full economy fares.

Lost Tickets If you lose your airline ticket an airline will usually treat it like a travellers' cheque and, after inquiries, issue you with another one. Legally, however, an airline is entitled to treat it like cash and if you lose it then it's gone forever. Take good care of your tickets.

No Shows No shows are passengers who fail to show up for their flight, sometimes due to unexpected delays or disasters, sometimes due to simply forgetting, sometimes because they made more than one booking and didn't bother to cancel the one they didn't want. Full-fare passengers who fail to turn up are sometimes entitled to travel on a later flight. The rest of us are penalised (see Cancellation Penalties).

On Request An unconfirmed booking for a flight, see Confirmation.

Open Jaws A return ticket where you fly out to one place but return from another. If available this can save you backtracking to your arrival point.

to take as many courier flights as you like. Phone after 6 pm to listen to a recorded message detailing all available flights and prices. The Denver-based Air Courier Association (☎ (303) 278-8810) also does this kind of thing. You join the association, which is used by international air freight companies to provide the escorts.

Prices drop as the departure date approaches. It is also possible to organise the flights directly through the courier companies. Look in your Yellow Pages under Courier Services.

Charter flights tend to be significantly cheaper than scheduled flights. Reliable travel agents specialising in charter flights, as well as budget travel for students, include STA and Council Travel, both of which have offices in major cities. Agencies specialising in cheap fares include:

STA
- 48 East 11th Street, New York, NY 10003 (☎ (212) 477-7166)
- 914 Westwood Blvd, Los Angeles, CA 90024 (☎ (213) 824-1574)
- 166 Geary Street, Suite 702, San Francisco, CA 94108 (☎ (415) 391-8407)

Council Travel
- 148 West 4th Street, New York, NY 10011 (☎ (212) 254-2525)
- 205 East 42nd Street, New York, NY 10017 (☎ (212) 661-1450)
- 1093 Broxton Ave, Los Angeles, CA 90024 (☎ (213) 208-3551)
- 530 Bush Street, San Francisco, CA 94108 (☎ (415) 421 3473)

Overbooking Airlines hate to fly empty seats and since every flight has some passengers who fail to show up (see No Shows) airlines often book more passengers than they have seats for. Usually the excess passengers balance those who fail to show up but occasionally somebody gets bumped. If this happens guess who it is most likely to be? The passengers who check in late.

Promotional Fares Officially discounted fares like Apex fares which are available from travel agents or direct from the airline.

Reconfirmation At least 72 hours prior to departure time of an onward or return flight you must contact the airline and 'reconfirm' that you intend to be on the flight. If you don't do this the airline can delete your name from the passenger list and you could lose your seat. You don't have to reconfirm the first flight on your itinerary or if your stopover is less than 72 hours. It doesn't hurt to reconfirm more than once.

Restrictions Discounted tickets often have various restrictions on them – advance purchase is the most common (see Apex). Others are restrictions on the minimum and maximum period you must be away, such as a minimum of 14 days or a maximum of one year (see Cancellation Penalties).

Standby A discounted ticket where you only fly if there is a seat free at the last moment. Standby fares are usually only available on domestic routes.

Tickets Out An entry requirement for many countries is that you have an onward or return ticket, in other words, a ticket out of the country. If you're not sure what you intend to do next, the easiest solution is to buy the cheapest onward ticket to a neighbouring country or a ticket from a reliable airline which can later be refunded if you do not use it.

Transferred Tickets Airline tickets cannot be transferred from one person to another. Travellers sometimes try to sell the return half of their ticket, but officials can ask you to prove that you are the person named on the ticket. This is unlikely to happen on domestic flights, on an international flight tickets may be compared with passports.

Travel Agencies Travel agencies vary widely and you should ensure that you use one that suits your needs. Some simply handle tours while full-service agencies handle everything from tours and tickets to car rental and hotel bookings. A good one will do all these things and can save you a lot of money but if all you want is a ticket at the lowest possible price, then you really need an agency specialising in discounted tickets.

Travel Periods Some officially discounted fares, Apex fares in particular, vary with the time of year. There is often a low (off-peak) season and a high (peak) season. Sometimes there's an intermediate or shoulder season as well. At peak times, when everyone wants to fly, not only will the officially discounted fares be higher but so will unofficially discounted fares or there may simply be no discounted tickets available. Usually the fare depends on your outward flight – if you depart in the high season and return in the low season, you pay the high-season fare. ■

Another travel agent specialising in budget airfares is Discount Travel International in New York (☎ (212) 362-3636).

For the truly hi-tech traveller, another potential source of information and flights are the travel forums open to users of the Internet, and assorted computer information and communication services. They are a step further down the travellers' superhighway from television Teletext services – another source of flights and fares.

Canada

Travel CUTS, which specialises in discount fares for students, has offices in all major cities. Otherwise scan the budget travel agents' ads in the *Toronto Globe & Mail*, the *Toronto Star* and the *Vancouver Province*. The magazine *Great Expeditions* (PO Box 8000-411, Abbotsford BC V2S 6H1) is also sometimes useful.

For courier flights originating in Canada, contact FB on Board Courier Services (☎ (514) 633-0740 in Toronto/Montreal, or ☎ (604) 338-1366 in Vancouver). See The USA for more information on courier flights.

Australia

STA and Flight Centres International are major dealers in cheap airfares, although heavily discounted fares can often be found at the travel agency in your local shopping centre. The Saturday travel sections of the Melbourne *Age* and the *Sydney Morning Herald* have many advertisements offering cheap fares to Europe, but don't be surprised if they happen to be 'sold out' when you contact the agents – they are usually low-season fares on obscure airlines with conditions attached.

The following are some addresses for agencies offering good-value fares:

STA
- 224 Faraday Street, Carlton, Vic 3053 (☎ 03-9349 2411)
- 855 George Street, Sydney, NSW 2000 (☎ 02-9212 1255)
- 1st Floor, New Guild Building, Hackett Drive, University of Western Australia, Crawley, WA 6009 (☎ 09-380 2302)

Flight Centres International
- 19 Bourke Street, Melbourne, Vic 3000 (☎ 03-9650 2899)
- Shop 5, State Bank Centre Arcade, 52 Martin Place, Sydney, NSW 2000 (☎ 02-9235 0166)
- City Flight Centre, Shop 25, Cinema City Arcade, Perth, WA 6000 (☎ 09-325 9222)

NZ

As with Australia, STA and Flight Centres International are popular travel agents in New Zealand. Useful addresses include:

Flight Centre
- Auckland Flight Centre, Shop 3A, National Bank Towers, 205-225 Queen Street, Auckland 1001 (☎ 09-358 0074)

STA Travel & International Travellers Centre
- 10 High Street, Auckland 1001 (☎ 09-309 0458)

Campus Travel
- Gate 1, Knighton Rd, Waikato University, Hamilton 2001 (☎ 07-838 4242)

UK & Ireland

London is one of the best centres in the world for discounted air tickets. For the latest fares, check out the travel page ads of the Sunday newspapers, *Time Out*, *TNT* and *Exchange & Mart*. All are available from most London news-stands. Another good source of information on cheap fares is the magazine *Business Traveller*. Those with access to Teletext will find a host of travel agents advertising just as in the publications already listed. Computer buffs with access to the Internet may find useful information in the many travel forums floating around in cyberspace.

Most British travel agents are registered with the Association of British Travel Agents (ABTA). If you have paid for your flight with an ABTA-registered agent who then goes bust, ABTA will guarantee a refund or an alternative. Unregistered bucket shops are riskier but sometimes cheaper.

The Globetrotters Club (BCM Roving, London WC1N 3XX) publishes a newsletter called *Globe* that covers obscure destinations and can help in finding travelling companions.

STA (☎ 0171-9379962) is one of the more reliable agencies, but not necessarily cheap.

They have several offices in London, as well branches on many university campuses and in Bristol, Cambridge, Leeds, Manchester and Oxford, among other cities. The main London branches are:

86 Old Brompton Rd, London SW7 3LH
117 Euston Rd, London NW1 2SX
38 Store Street, London WC1E 7BZ
Priory House, 6 Wrights Lane, London W8 6TA

A similar place is Trailfinders (☎ 0171-938 3939), 42-50 Earls Court Rd, London W8 6EJ and 194 Kensington High Street, London W8 7RG. The latter branch offers an inoculation service and a research library for customers. They also have agencies in Bristol, Birmingham, Glasgow and Manchester.

Campus Travel is in much the same league and has the following branches in London:

52 Grosvenor Gardens, London SW1W 0AG (☎ 0171-730 3402)
University College of London, 25 Gordon Street, London WC1H 0AH (☎ 0171-383 5377)
YHA Adventure Shop, 174 Kensington High Street, London W8 7RG (☎ 0171-938 2188)
YHA Adventure Shop, 14 Southampton Street, London SO14 2DF (☎ 0171-836 3343)
South Bank University, Keyworth Street, London SE1 (☎ 0171-401 8666)

Council Travel (☎ 0171-437 7767), 28a Poland Street, London W1V 3DB specialises in student and under-26 fares.

Flying as a courier (see also The USA), might be a possibility. See the Yellow Pages to find companies that do this.

If you're coming from Ireland, you are almost guaranteed of getting a better deal by legging it across to London first.

Continental Europe

There are flights from most major centres to Jordan and Syria, although to get a good deal you may have to fly via one of the main hubs such as Frankfurt.

Germany In Munich, a great source of travel information and equipment is the Därr Travel Shop (☎ 089-28 20 32) at Theresienstr. 66. In addition to producing a very comprehensive travel equipment catalogue, they also run an 'Expedition Service' with current flight information available.

In Berlin, ARTU Reisen (☎ 030-31 04 66), at Hardenbergstr. 9, near Berlin Zoo (with five branches around the city) is a good travel agent. In Frankfurt a/M, you might try SRID Reisen (☎ 069-43 01 91), Bergerstr. 118.

Netherlands Amsterdam is a popular departure point. Some of the best fares are offered by the student travel agency NBBS Reiswinkels (☎ 020-620 50 71). They have seven branches throughout the city. Their fares are comparable to those of London bucket shops. NBBS Reiswinkels has branches in Brussels, Belgium, as well.

Italy The best place to look for cheaper flights is with CTS (Centro Turistico Studentesco). They have branches all over the country. In Rome (☎ 06-46 791) they are at Via Genova 16.

France In Paris, Voyages et Découvertes (☎ 01-42.61.00.01), 21 Rue Cambon, is a good place to start hunting down the best airfares.

Greece & Turkey Athens is something of a Mediterranean centre for bucket-shop flights and dodgy charters, although the pickings to Syria and Jordan are pretty slim. Likewise in Turkey, Istanbul's Sultanahmet area is the place to look around for cheap tickets.

North Africa & the Middle East

There's not much in the line of cheap flights to or from other Middle Eastern and North African countries.

Asia

Hong Kong is the discount air ticket capital of the region, although Singapore, Penang and Bangkok can also be good places to look for cheap fares. Jordan and Syria are a bit off the beaten track, however, and there is not much discounting on these routes. STA has branches in Hong Kong, Tokyo, Singapore, Bangkok and Kuala Lumpur.

You can often find reasonable, if unspectacular, deals between India or Pakistan and Syria or Jordan.

LAND

Bringing Your Own Vehicle

It's no problem bringing your own vehicle to Jordan or Syria, although you should get a *carnet de passage en douane* and your own insurance. The UK Automobile Association requires a financial guarantee for the carnet, which effectively acts as an import duty waiver, as it could be liable for customs and other taxes if the vehicle's exit is not registered within a year. The kind of deposit they are looking at can be well in excess of US$1000. It is essential to ensure that the carnet is filled out properly at each border crossing or you could be up for a lot of money. The carnet may also need to have listed any more expensive spares that you're planning to carry with you, such as a gearbox.

All this said, drivers have brought their vehicles into both Jordan and Syria without a carnet. In such a case, you have to buy what amounts to a temporary customs waiver on arrival. In Syria it appears this costs about US$50, plus possible bribes to grumpy customs officials.

In Jordan, you will be obliged to take out local insurance of JD17, plus a nominal customs fee of JD7 for most European registered vehicles.

In the case of Syria, third-party insurance has to be bought at the border at the rate of US$36 a month. This supposedly also covers you for Lebanon, but double check. The real value of these compulsory insurance deals is questionable, and it is worth making sure your own insurance company will cover you for Jordan and Syria.

Obviously, you will need the vehicle's registration and ownership papers, but you do not strictly speaking need an International Driving Permit – your national licence is generally sufficient.

Finally, you should bring a good set of spare parts and some mechanical knowledge, as you will not always be able to get the help you may need. This is especially the case for motorcycles. There are precious few decent bike mechanics in Jordan and virtually none in Syria who can deal with modern motorcycles.

Public Transport

Regular buses and service taxis connect Jordan and Syria with one another. Buses and in some cases service taxis connect Syria with Turkey and Lebanon, and buses link Jordan with Iraq and Saudi Arabia. There is also plenty of transport to both sides of the Jordan-Israeli frontier.

SEA

Jordan is connected by daily ferries to Nuweiba in Egypt and Syria by a weekly ferry to Beirut (Lebanon), Alexandria (Egypt) and sometimes Cyprus.

For information on passenger travel by cargo boat, readers should contact the Strand Cruise & Travel Centre (☎ 0171-836 6363; fax 497 0078), Charing Cross Shopping Concourse, Strand, London WC2N 4HZ.

Jordan

Facts about Jordan

HISTORY SINCE WWI

The Arabs joined the British drive to oust the Turks in June 1916, after British assurances that they would be helped in their fight to establish an independent Arab state. This was one month after the British and French had concluded the secret Sykes-Picot agreement, whereby 'Syria' (modern Syria and Lebanon) was to be placed under French control and 'Palestine' (a vaguely defined area including modern Israel, the Occupied Territories and Jordan) would go to the British.

This betrayal was heightened by the 1917 Balfour Declaration, a letter written by the British Foreign Secretary, Arthur Balfour, to a prominent British Jew, Lord Rothschild. It stated that:

> His Majesty's Government view with favour the establishment in Palestine of a National Home for the Jewish people, and will use their best endeavours to facilitate the achievement of this object, it being clearly understood that nothing shall be done which may prejudice the civil and religious rights of existing non-Jewish communities in Palestine, or the rights and political status enjoyed by Jews in any other country.

At the end of the war, Arab forces controlled, to a greater or lesser degree, all of modern Saudi Arabia, Jordan and parts of southern Syria. The principal Arab leader, Emir Faisal, set up an independent government in Damascus at the end of 1918, a move at first welcomed by the Allies, however, his demand at the 1919 Paris peace conference for independence throughout the Arab world was not so kindly greeted. He and his elder brother, Abdullah, were declared kings of Syria and Iraq in March 1920, but shortly afterwards the League of Nations awarded Britain a mandate over Palestine, separating it from Syria, where the French quickly forced Faisal to flee.

The British later came to an accommodation with Faisal, handing him Iraq and having Abdullah proclaimed ruler of the territory that came to be known as Transjordan (formerly part of the Ottoman province of Syria), lying between Iraq and the East Bank of the Jordan River. This angered the Zionists, as it effectively severed Transjordan from Palestine

JORDAN
Area: 91,860 sq km
Population: 4.95 million
Population Growth Rate: 3.4%
Capital: Amman
Head of State: King Hussein
Official Language: Arabic
Best Time to Go: Spring or Autumn
Currency: Jordanian Dinar
Exchange Rate: JD0.71 = US$1
Per Capita GNP: US$1373
Inflation: 4%
Time: GMT/UTC + 2

Umm al-Jimal (north of Amman, see page 148) flourished into Omayyad times, but never recovered after an earthquake in 747.

and so reduced the area of any future Jewish National Home.

Abdullah made Amman his capital, Britain recognised the territory as an independent state under its protection in 1923 and a small defence force, the Arab Legion, was set up under British officers, the best known of whom was Major JB Glubb (Glubb Pasha). A series of treaties between 1928 and 1946 led to almost full independence, and Abdullah was proclaimed king in 1946. A further treaty in 1948 reserved Britain privileges only in military affairs.

Palestinian Dilemma

Transjordan's neighbouring mandate of Palestine now became a thorn in Britain's side. The Balfour Declaration and subsequent attempts to make the Jewish National Home a reality were destined for trouble from the start. Arabs were outraged by the implication that they were the intruders and the minority group in Palestine, when in fact it is estimated that at the end of WWI they accounted for 90% of the population.

Jewish immigration in the 1920s caused little alarm, although there was some violence between the two groups. The situation deteriorated sharply with the rise of Hitler and the persecution of Jews in Germany and Europe in the 1930s. Jewish immigration accelerated, fuelling Arab fears of the creation of a Jewish state in which they would be the losers.

Fighting between the two groups and anti-British riots increased, prompting a series of proposals to partition Palestine that culminated in a White Paper in 1939. It called for the creation of a bi-national state within 10 years and joint Arab-Jewish participation in administration in the meantime. It also limited Jewish immigration to 75,000 over five years. Both sides rejected this, although the plan had found some favour with the Arabs. The conflict was muted by the onset of war, during which both sides cooperated with the British.

The crisis reached its high point in the years immediately following the war. After various plans had been rejected, the UN voted for the partition of Palestine in November 1947. More than half the territory, including much of the valuable coastal strip, was allotted to the Jews. The Arabs were shocked and conflict was inevitable. The State of Israel was proclaimed on 14 May 1948 and the next day the British Mandate finished. As British troops withdrew from the area, Arab armies marched into Palestine. However, highly trained and organised Israeli forces proved much too strong for the poorly led and ill-equipped volunteers from other Arab countries who had flocked to Palestine to support the Arab cause. Israel was soon well in control of its allotted area as well as entrenching itself in some strategic parts of territory that had been assigned to the Arabs. The massacre of an entire village of Arabs by Israeli forces was followed by a mass exodus of nearly one million Arabs, giving the Jews their much needed majority and at the same time placing strain on Jordan.

Fighting continued but by mid-1949 armistices had been signed between the new Israeli state and its Arab foes.

Jordan's Role

King Abdullah harboured dreams of a 'Greater Syria' to include all of the modern states of Syria, Lebanon, Transjordan and what was now Palestine and Israel in a single

King Abdullah ruled over Jordan for just five years until his assassination in 1951.

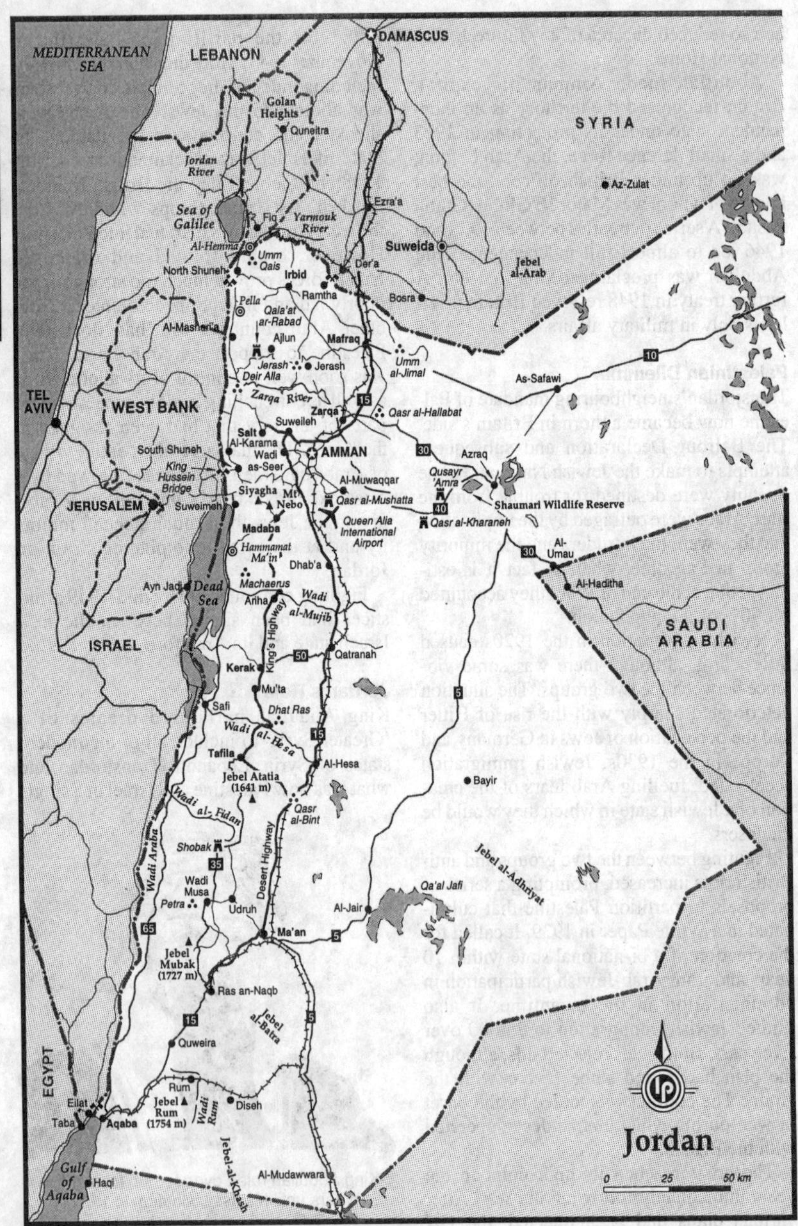
MEDITERRANEAN SEA
LEBANON
DAMASCUS
Golan Heights
Quneitra
SYRIA
Az-Zulat
Jordan River
Sea of Galilee
Fiq
Yarmouk River
Ezra'a
Al-Hemma
Umm Qais
Suweida
North Shuneh
Irbid
Der'a
Jebel al-Arab
Ramtha
Bosra
Pella
Qala'at ar-Rabad
Al-Mashari'a
Ajlun
Mafraq
Umm al-Jimal
Jerash
Deir Alla
10
As-Safawi
Zarqa River
TEL AVIV
WEST BANK
15
Qasr al-Hallabat
Zarqa
Suweileh
Salt
Al-Karama
Wadi as-Seer
AMMAN
30
South Shuneh
Azraq
King Hussein Bridge
Al-Muwaqqar
Qusayr 'Amra
Siyagha
Mt Nebo
Qasr al-Mushatta
40
Shaumari Wildlife Reserve
JERUSALEM
Suweimeh
Queen Alia International Airport
Qasr al-Kharaneh
Madaba
Hammamat Ma'in
Al-Umau
Dhab'a
Al-Haditha
Ayn Jadi
Dead Sea
Machaerus
Ariha
Wadi al-Mujib
SAUDI ARABIA
ISRAEL
King's Highway
Qatranah
50
Kerak
Mu'ta
5
Safi
Dhat Ras
Wadi al-Hesa
Tafila
Al-Hesa
Jebel Atatia (1641 m)
Bayir
Wadi al-Fidan
Qasr al-Bint
Shobak
Desert Highway
Jebel al-Adhriyat
35
Wadi Araba
Wadi Musa
Qa'al Jafi
Petra
Udruh
Al-Jafr
65
Ma'an
Jebel Mubak (1727 m)
Ras an-Naqb
Jebel al-Batra
EGYPT
Quweira
Rum
Jebel Rum (1754 m)
Wadi Rum
Diseh
Eilat
Taba
Aqaba
Jebel-al-Khash
Gulf of Aqaba
Haqi
Al-Mudawwara
Jordan
0
25
50 km

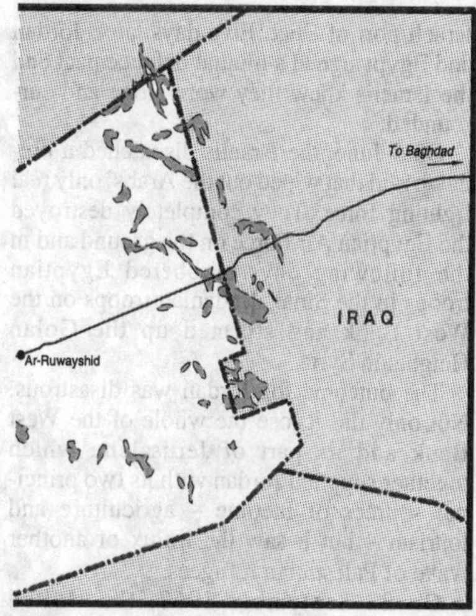

Arab state, later to include Iraq as well. For this, he was suspected by his Arab neighbours of pursuing quite different goals from them in their fight with the new state of Israel.

At the end of hostilities, Jordanian troops were in control of East Jerusalem and the West Bank. In response to the establishment of an Egyptian-backed Arab Government in Gaza in September 1948, King Abdullah had himself proclaimed King of All Palestine in Jericho in December. In April 1950, he formally annexed the territory, despite paying lip service to Arab declarations backing Palestinian independence and expressly ruling out territorial annexations. The new Hashemite Kingdom of Jordan won immediate recognition from the governments of Britain and the USA.

The mass migration of Palestinians virtually doubled Jordan's population as refugee camps sprang up in the Jordan Valley and near Amman.

King Abdullah was assassinated outside the Al-Aqsa Mosque in Jerusalem in July 1951, and after his son Talal ruled for a year, his grandson Hussein came to power at the age of 17. With great skill and a good deal of luck he has managed to stay there ever since. In 1956 he sacked Glubb Pasha (by now Chief of Staff of the Jordanian Army). After elections that year, the newly formed pro-Nasser (that is, supporters of President Nasser of Egypt) government broke ties with the UK and the last British troops left Jordanian soil by mid-1957. Hussein staged a coup against his own pro-Nasser government, partly because it had tried to open a dialogue with the Soviet Union.

With the union of Egypt and Syria in 1958, King Hussein feared for his own position and tried a federation with his Hashemite cousins in Iraq. This lasted less than a year as the Iraqi monarchy was overthrown and British troops were sent in to Jordan to protect Hussein.

The PLO

In February 1960, Jordan offered its citizenship to all Palestinian Arab refugees wanting it. In defiance of the wishes of the other Arab states for an independent Palestine, Jordan continued to insist that its annexation of Palestinian territory be recognised.

King of Jordan since 1952, Hussein is the great-grandson of King Hussein of Hejaz (the 37th in direct descent from Mohammed).

Despite Jordan's opposition, the Palestine Liberation Organisation (PLO), with its own army, was formed in 1964 with the blessing of the Arab League to represent the Palestinian people. The Palestine National Council (PNC) was established within the PLO as its executive body – the closest thing to a Palestinian government.

At about the same time, an organisation called the Palestine National Liberation Movement was set up. It was known as Al-Fatah (the reversal of its Arabic initials, making up the word 'conquest'). One of the stated aims of both the PLO and Al-Fatah was to train guerrillas for raids on Israel.

Al-Fatah emerged from a power struggle for control of the guerrilla organisations as the dominant force within the PLO and its leader, Yasser Arafat, became chair of the executive committee of the PLO in 1969.

After the disaster of the Black September hostilities in Jordan in 1970 (see The Six-Day War), the PLO concentrated its activities in Lebanon.

In 1974, the PLO made a major gain in its bid for international recognition. At the UN General Assembly it was invited to take part in a debate on the 'Palestine question' and the vote favoured the PLO as the legitimate representative of the Palestinians.

The Six-Day War

The early 1960s saw Jordan's position improve dramatically with aid from the USA and a boom in tourism, mainly in Jerusalem's old city, but it lost out badly in the Six-Day War of 1967.

The build-up to the war had seen severe Israeli warnings against increasingly provocative Palestinian guerrilla raids into Israel from Syria. With President Nasser of Egypt promising to support Syria in the event of an Israeli attack, the Syrians stepped up the raids and in May 1967 announced that Israel was massing troops in preparation for an assault. Egypt responded by asking the UN to withdraw its Emergency Force from the Egypt-Israel border, which it did. Nasser then closed the Straits of Tiran (the entrance to the Red Sea), effectively nullifying the Israeli port of Eilat. Five days later, Jordan and Egypt signed a mutual defence pact and the Israelis knew they were alone and surrounded.

On 5 June, the Israelis dispatched a pre-dawn raid that wiped out the Arabs' only real fighting force. They completely destroyed the Egyptian Air Force on the ground and in the following days clobbered Egyptian troops in the Sinai, Jordanian troops on the West Bank and stormed up the Golan Heights in Syria.

The outcome for Jordan was disastrous. Not only did it lose the whole of the West Bank and its part of Jerusalem, which together supplied Jordan with its two principal sources of income – agriculture and tourism – but it saw the influx of another wave of Palestinian refugees.

On 22 September 1967, the United Nations passed Resolution 242, which called on Israel to withdraw from the areas it had taken in the recent war, and for all countries in the Middle East to respect the rights of others 'to live in peace within secure and recognised boundaries'. Jordan was among the Arab countries to accept it but Syria and Iraq would not, as it implied recognition of Israel.

After the defeat of 1967, the Palestinians became more militant and although there was tacit agreement with the Jordanian government that they would operate freely out of their bases in the Jordan Valley, they also expected immunity from Jordan's laws. The country became increasingly unsettled and by 1970 the government had virtually become just one of many other factions vying for power.

Clearly this couldn't last and the showdown came in September of that year in an incident that came to be known as 'Black September'. The Palestinians, in their most daring deed to date, hijacked four commercial aircraft and flew three of them to the north of Jordan, holding passengers and crew hostage. This was part of a campaign in which thousands died as the guerillas took control of the northern strip of the country. Although the hostage crisis was resolved and a ceasefire put in place at the end of the month, fighting soon began again. Now the army went in with full force and in a brief civil war ending in July 1971 wiped out all resistance throughout the country. The guerillas were thus forced to recognise Hussein's authority and the Palestinians had to choose between exile or submission.

Camp David

Jordan was not directly involved in the October War of 1973 but did send a small number of troops to assist Syria.

In October 1974, King Hussein reluctantly agreed to an Arab summit declaration recognising the PLO as the sole representative of the Palestinians and its right to set up a government in any liberated territory, effectively nullifying Jordan's own claims to the West Bank.

When Egyptian President Anwar Sadat boldly decided to visit Israel and so begin the process leading to the 1978 Camp David accords and subsequently a full peace treaty with Israel, King Hussein joined the other Arab countries in rejecting the results. The Arabs complained that the Israeli-Egyptian peace neither required the Israelis to withdraw from occupied territories nor asserted Arab sovereignty over them.

Gulf Wars

Attention switched from the Arab-Israeli conflict to the Persian Gulf when Iraq invaded Iran in 1980. Jordan's backing for Iraq in the eight-year slogging match put a constant strain on its already poor relations with Syria, which backed Iran.

But Jordan's gulf woes did not really begin until Iraq decided to annex Kuwait in August 1990. Dependent on Iraq for a quarter of its trade and most of its oil imports, Jordan found itself caught between a rock and a hard place. Support among Palestinians in this country for Saddam Hussein, who promised to link the Kuwait issue to their own and force a showdown, was at fever pitch. King Hussein had little choice but to side with Saddam, against the majority of the Arab states and the multinational force sent to eject Saddam from Kuwait. The monarch played the game with typical dexterity. Although tending to side publicly with Baghdad, he maintained efforts to find a peaceful solution and complied with the UN embargo on trade with Iraq. This last step won him the sympathy of western financial bodies and, although US and Saudi aid was temporarily cut, along with Saudi oil, loans and help were forthcoming from other quarters, particularly Japan and Europe.

The West Bank

In August 1986, King Hussein unveiled a US$1300 million investment programme over five years for the West Bank, with Israeli approval. Palestinians reacted badly, saying this was a sign that Israel and Jordan were coming to some kind of arrangement at their expense. It also appeared to give the lie to Hussein's avowed support for the PLO and de facto renunciation of claims to the West Bank.

In July 1988, however, seven months after the beginning of the *intifada* – the not always so passive Palestinian revolt in the Occupied Territories – King Hussein announced that all administrative and legal ties with the West Bank were being cut, along with the development programme.

With the signing of the PLO-Israeli declaration of principles in September 1993, which set in motion the process of establishing an autonomous Palestinian authority in the Occupied Territories, Jordan appeared to have definitively abandoned all claims to the area.

Peace & Foreign Relations

Compared with its northern neighbour Syria, Jordan has long displayed greater flexibility in its attitude to Israel and the peace process. After the Madrid peace talks in 1991 set in train a rocky but slow progress towards a comprehensive peace between Israel and its Arab neighbours, movement along the Israel-Jordan track of these talks was much smoother than with the Syrians or many of the Gulf Arab states. Of course, since renouncing its claims to the West Bank in

1988, the territorial question was virtually removed as an obstacle. Nevertheless, the revelation of the Israeli-Palestinian declaration of principles in 1993 came as something of a surprise to King Hussein. The three-way relations between Israel, Jordan and Arafat's new Palestine National Authority (PNA) constitute a complicated game, and there is little doubt that Israel has aimed for separate peace arrangements between itself and the various Arab parties to keep the coordination of the latters' desires to a minimum.

In any event, on October 26 1994, Jordan and Israel signed a peace treaty in Wadi Araba. The treaty provides for the dropping of all economic barriers between the two countries and close cooperation on security, water and other issues. With economic relations expected to take off in a way that never happened between Israel and Egypt after they agreed to peace in 1979, the unknown element is how the Palestinians will fare, sandwiched as they are between the two sides. They have long feared cooperation between Jordan and Israel would ultimately undermine any nascent Palestinian state. The clause in the treaty recognising the 'special role of the Hashemite Kingdom of Jordan in Muslim holy shrines in Jerusalem' has sounded alarm bells in Palestinian circles. Does King Hussein still have designs on Jerusalem and the West Bank? Do the Israelis hope to get Jordanian recognition of Jerusalem as the Israeli capital in exchange for some form of territorial or other sop? For now, all this lies in the realm of speculation.

In the meantime, links between Jordan and the PNA are multiplying, with joint committees looking at possible confederation and other forms of cooperation. The complex Middle Eastern political poker match has, if anything, become still more Machiavelian with peace, throwing open at least as many questions as it has so far resolved.

The assassination of Israeli Prime Minister Yitzhak Rabin in November 1995 provided the occasion for a rare and emotionally charged symbolic expression of the new state of relations between Jordan and Israel. King Hussein's first official visit to Israel was not how he might have imagined it – he came to heap praise on his erstwhile enemy turned 'brother' in peace.

Perhaps seeking to capitalise on the momentum created by the peace deal with Israel, King Hussein managed to restore normal relations with Kuwait in February 1996 and also travelled to Saudi Arabia in a fence-mending exercise. Since Iraq's invasion of Kuwait, Jordan had found itself virtually cut off from the Gulf States. In the meantime, the king continues to play a delicate game vis-à-vis Iraq, but evidently distancing himself from Saddam Hussein.

Jordan Today

In November 1989, the first full elections since 1967 were held in Jordan in which women were allowed to vote for the first time. The exercise was repeated four years later, and this time some 20 political parties were allowed to participate. Although the Islamic Action Front (IAF) won 16 of the 80 lower house seats, royalist independents together constitute a large majority, thus assuring King Hussein a reasonable level of compliance.

Democratisation is fraught with dangers. The IAF has connections with the Muslim Brotherhood, and their opposition to the peace treaty with Israel and west-leaning politics of King Hussein are cause for some disquiet. The king has not hesitated to point out to the west that Algeria is not alone in having to deal with rising fundamentalism. King Hussein has also demonstrated on several occasions that he is quite happy to put democracy on hold when free debate and freedom of press expression have appeared to him more of a threat to than a guarantee of stability. Both leftists and IAF members still accuse the king of undermining democracy by curbing unions and muzzling the press. In local elections midway through 1995, the IAF actually registered losses, claiming government manipulation.

Whatever the truth of such claims, the king does genuinely seem desirous of seeing parliamentary democracy take root, and he has repeatedly called on politicians to reduce the number of parties and concentrate on legislation rather than petty rivalries.

GEOGRAPHY & CLIMATE

Jordan is a tiny country with a very curious shape. Its total area is 91,860 sq km, about the same size as Portugal. The strange kink in the Jordan-Saudi Arabia border is known as 'Winston's hiccup' because the story goes that the British Secretary of State, Winston Churchill, drew the boundary after having had a more than satisfactory lunch in Jerusalem one day back in 1920. Since King Hussein renounced claims to the West Bank in 1988, the country has the same boundaries as the former Transjordan.

Distances are short – it's only about 430 km from Ramtha in the north to Aqaba in the south. From Aqaba to the capital, Amman, it is 335 km. From Amman to the furthest point of interest in the east, Azraq, is just 103 km.

Jordan can easily be divided into three major regions: the Jordan Valley, the East Bank plateau, and the desert.

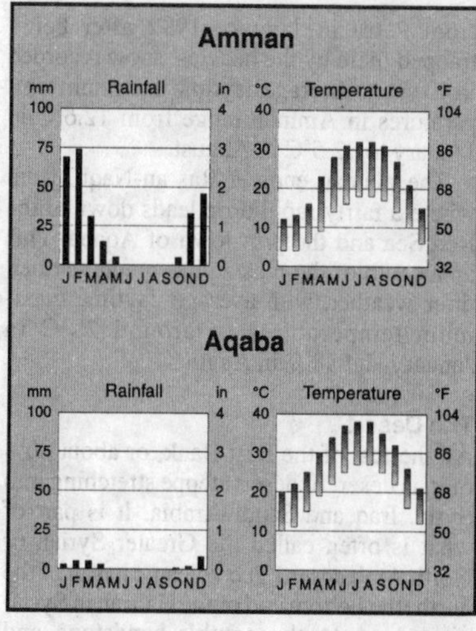

Jordan Valley

The dominant physical feature of the country is the fertile valley of the Jordan River. Forming part of the Great Rift Valley of Africa, it rises just inside Lebanon and runs the full length of the country from the Syrian border in the north to the salty depression of the Dead Sea, and south to Aqaba and the Red Sea. The river itself, 251 km long, is fed from the Sea of Galilee (Lake Tiberias), the Yarmouk River and the valley streams of the high plateaux to the east and west.

The Dead Sea, at 394m below sea level, is the lowest point on earth, and the highly saline soils of this central area of the Jordan Valley support little vegetation. The sea's water itself is loaded with salt and related chemicals, and in fact is chemically saturated at a depth of 110m.

South of the Dead Sea, the Wadi Araba is an extremely desolate region. Potash is mined at Safi and it is hoped the area contains other minerals as it is useless for anything else. On the western side of the Dead Sea, Israeli *kibbutzim*, some in occupied territory of the West Bank, provide fertile havens in the desert.

The only town of any size in the valley is Jericho, in Palestine National Authority territory on the western side.

The weather in the valley is oppressive in summer – it feels like you're trapped in an airless oven. Daily temperatures are well in excess of 36°C and have been recorded as high as 49°C. Rainfall is low, at under 200 mm annually.

East Bank Plateau

The East Bank plateau is broken up only by the gorges cut by the streams of the Wadi Zarqa, Wadi al-Mujib and Wadi al-Hesa, which flow into the Jordan River. ('Wadi' is the Arabic word for a valley formed by an often dry watercourse. Some begin to flow again when there has been substantial rainfall.)

This area contains the main centres of population: Amman, Irbid, Zarqa and Kerak. It's also the region with the sites of most interest: Jerash, Kerak, Madaba and Petra.

Snow in Amman is not unheard of and even Petra gets the occasional fall. A group of 300 European tourists had to be rescued from Petra in January 1992 after being trapped there by the heaviest snow recorded in 40 years. Average daytime maximum temperatures in Amman range from 12.6°C in January to 32.5°C in August.

The plateau ends at Ras an-Naqb, from where a fairly rapid drop leads down to the Red Sea and the port town of Aqaba. This area south of the plateau has much warmer, drier weather, with average daytime maximum temperatures of around 20°C in January and 38°C in August.

The Desert

All the rest of the East Bank, or about 80% of it, is desert or desert steppe stretching into Syria, Iraq and Saudi Arabia. It is part of what is often called the Greater Syrian or North Arab desert. The volcanic basalt of the north (the bottom end of the Hauran in Syria) gives way to the south's sandstone and granite, which sometimes produces amazing sights – the area of Wadi Rum is one of the most fantastic desert-scapes in the world.

The climate is extreme with summertime temperatures which can reach into the high 40s, and days in winter when cold winds howl down from central Asia. Rainfall is minimal – less than 50 mm annually.

ECOLOGY & ENVIRONMENT

The single biggest environmental problem faced by Jordan is water, or rather the lack of it. A rapidly growing population, rising living standards in the cities and heavy exploitation for agriculture are all contributing factors. Demand far exceeds supply and wastage on the land and in the cities exacerbates the situation (see also the boxed story called 'Water Works' later in this chapter). The thirst has put a huge strain on the country's subterranean aquifers – the most visible result being the virtual disappearance of the Azraq oasis in the east of the country, and all the wildlife that went with it. Attempts are being made to reverse some of that damage, but the main problem will not simply go away.

Water Works

As peace is achieved in what has been, since the end of WWII, one of the world's hottest trouble spots, thoughts are turning to what could prove to be the single greatest source of future friction. Neither oil nor embedded Israeli-Arab antagonism, but the very font of life – water. None know better than Jordan just how serious this issue is. In 1990, demand for water was almost double the available resources, and the situation will only get worse as the population grows and living standards rise. The country's only sources of water are the Jordan and Yarmouk rivers and subterranean aquifers already in many cases over-exploited.

Prior to the 1994 peace deal with Israel, Jordan had long accused the Israelis of extracting much more than their fair share of the River Jordan's water, pumping it into Lake Tiberias for their own uses. If this just meant that your average Amman resident had to make do with the odd shower less, it might not be so important, but chronic water shortages have already put a severe brake on agricultural and industrial growth.

The matter is complicated, and more efficient distribution of extant supplies would help. In addition, Jordan's farmers consume two-thirds of the total used, some of it in less than efficient style. One report has also suggested that half the water consumed in Amman is lost in leakage.

There is little doubt that the need for regional cooperation to maximise water efficiency helped spur Amman into reaching an accord with Israel. Similarly, the Israelis are as conscious as anyone of the potential for unrest in the region if water shortages are allowed to become a chronic problem. Both sides have allocated about US$9 billion each to water projects. Plans are afoot for a joint Israeli-Jordanian dam project on the Yarmouk. Meanwhile, a pipeline was laid in 1995 to carry 30 million cubic metres of water a year from Lake Tiberias to Jordan's King Abdullah Canal. Another more ambitious plan envisages the setting up of a water-conveyancing system from Turkey to Jordan via Israel.

In addition, ideas have been put on the table for the construction of a series of canals, desalination plants and hydroelectric power stations that would link up the Red Sea, the Mediterranean and the Dead Sea and serve Jordan, Israel and the Palestine National Authority's territory. ■

Industry itself causes problems. The Yamanieh coral reef off the coast at Aqaba is a treasure trove of marine life, but every year thousands of tonnes of phosphates are accidentally dumped at sea by loaders at the Aqaba sea terminal. How much damage this is doing can only be guesses at.

These and other pollution problems have not gone totally unnoticed. A handful of 'Greens' try to make their voices heard, but as yet environmental awareness is far from widespread. For that matter, the issue of water in particular is often seen less as an environmental issue that as a bone of regional political contention. Although they are cooperating now, Jordan and Israel were for a long time at loggerheads over the use of shared water sources – notably the River Jordan. And as long as Syria stays out of the peace process, a key player remains missing.

FLORA & FAUNA

The pine forests of the north give way to the cultivated slopes of the Jordan Valley where cedar, olives and eucalyptus are dominant. South towards the Dead Sea the vegetation gives way to mud and salt flats.

Animals found in the desert regions include the camel (of course), desert fox, sand rat, hare and jerboa (a small rodent). The hills to the north-east of the Dead Sea are home to boars, badgers and goats.

It is possible to see gazelle and oryx (a large antelope), once a common feature of the Jordanian desert, at the nearby Shaumari Wildlife Reserve, where they have now been reintroduced. Outside the reserve, and despite the apparent diversity of the wildlife, you'll be lucky to see anything more exotic than camels and goats.

For parts of the year, the Azraq Oasis is home to hundreds of species of birds migrating from Europe and the Middle East, although the number has dropped steeply as exploitation of the wetlands has destroyed much of the environment.

In the Gulf of Aqaba, there's a huge variety of tropical fish and coral that makes for some of the best scuba-diving in the world.

GOVERNMENT & POLITICS

The constitution of 1952 states that Jordan is a constitutional monarchy with representative government. The National Assembly (*'majlis al-umma'*) is bicameral, the Senate having half the number of members as the House of Representatives.

The king is vested with wide-ranging powers – he appoints and can dismiss judges, approves amendments to the constitution, declares war and is the commander of the armed forces. He approves and signs all laws, although his power of veto can be overridden by a two-thirds majority of both houses of the National Assembly.

The 80-member lower house is elected by all citizens over the age of 18 years, but the prime minister is appointed by the king, as are the president and 40 members of the Senate. The prime minister, or the king through the prime minister, appoints a Council of Ministers that is subject to the approval of parliament. The council is responsible for general policy and coordination of the work of various departments.

Although elections are supposed to take place every four years, polls in November 1989 were the first held since Jordan lost the West Bank in the 1967 war. During that period Jordan had in effect been under martial law.

In 1974 the king dissolved the House of Representatives; it was replaced four years later by a National Consultative Council, its 60 members appointed by the king. This in turn was dissolved and the House reassembled in 1984. There were no full direct elections – these were made impossible anyway by the continued Israeli occupation of the West Bank, which accounted for half the seats, and King Hussein's recognition of the PLO earlier as the sole representative of the Palestinians.

On 30 July 1988 the House was again dissolved. The following day the king announced that Jordan was cutting all administrative ties with the West Bank. New electoral laws paving the way for elections on the East Bank and increasing the number of deputies from 60 to 80 preceded the 1989 elections. In September 1992, parliament passed a law allowing political parties, which range from the Communists through to the Islamic Action Front (IAF). The latter managed to snap up 16 seats in the November 1993 elections, making it the single biggest party in parliament.

For administrative purposes the country is divided into eight *muhafazat* (governorates).

ECONOMY

One of the main economic victims of the Gulf War in 1990-91, Jordan has managed to weather the storm far better than many expected. One UN assessment put the total cost of the Gulf crisis to Jordan, in the 12 months from August 1990, at more than US$8 billion. In that period the country registered zero growth and observers were predicting the worst. It is estimated that the UN naval blockade of Aqaba (aimed at enforcing UN sanctions against Iraq) cost Jordan up to US$300 million a year in lost business after its implementation in 1991. Jordan breathed a sigh of relief when the blockade was dropped in mid-1994, as much of the shipping turned away had had nothing to do with Iraq. Merchandise is still inspected on the ground, however.

A quarter of Jordan's pre-war trade had been with Iraq. This was virtually wiped out. For a while too, Jordan was obliged to seek other sources of oil, 80% of which was being delivered by Baghdad prior to the war. Later, Amman was allowed to take Iraqi oil as direct debt repayment – so long as no cash changed hands.

Until the war an important source of income had been remittances from Jordanians and Palestinians working in the Gulf. By early 1992 most had left the Gulf States – 300,000 of them for Jordan. The loss of remittances was at first seen as a heavy blow, but the 'returnees' brought US$500 million home with them, and actually helped unleash an unprecedented boom – stimulating economic growth of a staggering 11% in 1992. Since then, growth has remained at a very healthy 5%.

Jordan's recent success is also partly due to close adherence to an International Monetary Fund reform plan that has greatly boosted confidence in Jordan. Big state monopolies such as Royal Jordanian Airlines and the telephone company are set for privatisation, further signs of growing dynamism in Jordan.

Nevertheless, with US$5.6 billion foreign debt, around 15% unemployment (down from 25% at the end of the 80s) and an estimated 20% to 25% living below the poverty line, Jordan still has considerable problems to deal with. Many price subsidies on basic goods (including water) remain in place. With average per capita income of JD150 a month, the pressure on average Jordanians would be too much if all subsidies were simply removed. Price-hike riots, such as those in 1989, live on in the memory of Jordan's rulers.

Agriculture makes up 8% of GDP and is concentrated in the Jordan Valley, where ambitious irrigation schemes like the King Abdullah Canal and several dam projects make cultivation possible on thousands of hectares. Modern methods ('plasticulture' and greenhouses) have greatly increased productivity, and Jordan exports much of the fruit, vegetables and cereals that are its most important crops. On the highlands that form the eastern edge of the Jordan Valley, crops such as tobacco, wheat, barley and beans are grown. Scarce water supplies, however, are a constant threat and farmers are sometimes ordered not to plant crops because there is not enough water to go around.

The various industries account for 26% of GDP. Phosphate mining is carried out from vast reserves at Wadi al-Hesa and Shidiya (near Ma'an) and is a major export. Potash is another important export. Although the world market for these products has declined since the late 80s, Jordan continues to widen the number of joint ventures with foreign companies to manufacture derivative products. Copper from Wadi Araba, south of the Dead Sea, is also exported. Manufacturing ranges from cement and batteries to toys, beer and matches.

Oil is yet to be found in commercially

viable quantities, and the government is placing greater hope in natural gas. Big reserves were found in the north-east of the country around Ar-Risha in 1987-88 and now meet 15% of Jordan's energy needs. It is hoped they will end up satisfying a quarter of national requirements. Imported oil is refined by the Jordanian Refining Company at Zarqa.

Tourism in Jordan took a long time to recover after the loss of Jerusalem but, aided by the 1974 decision to allow tourists to cross into the West Bank, it had begun to exceed pre-1967 levels when the Gulf crisis started. There were 446,032 tourist arrivals to Jordan in 1995 and 478,596 so far in 1996 at the time of going to press. These large numbers of tourists are offering a significant contribution to the Jordanian economy. The Israeli contingent means a huge boost to tourist numbers – enough indeed to have some people worried about Jordan's capacity to deal with them all.

The 1994 peace treaty with Israel fills Jordanians with optimism about the possible economic spin-offs. The long-term plans are ambitious. Moves to link up the two countries' power grids with those of neighbouring countries such as Egypt and Syria are symbolic of the hopes held by visionaries of a Middle Eastern common market. That is a long way off, but already Jordan and Israel are marketing themselves as a package – notably in tourism.

If one considers that Transjordan in 1948 was a country of some 400,000 inhabitants, mostly poor Bedouin, the transformation in the past 50 years has been remarkable, especially given the absence of petrol and the disasters wrought on the economy by war and internal dissent. It remains to be seen what dividends peace can deliver.

POPULATION & PEOPLE

The population of Jordan stood in December 1995 at about 4.95 million, of whom 900,000 were registered as refugees from the wars of 1948 and 1967 with the United Nations Relief & Works Agency (UNRWA) on the East Bank. At 3.4%, the rate of growth is perhaps faster than the authorities would like.

Some 1.57 million live in the capital, Amman, and a further 624,000 in neighbouring Zarqa and suburbs. The northern city of Irbid and its surrounding county are the next most densely populated area, with 746,000 inhabitants.

Ethnic & Religious Groups

The majority of Jordanians are Arabs descended from various tribes that have migrated to the area over the years from all directions. In addition, there are 25,000 Circassians, descendants of migrants from the Caucasus in the 19th century and a much smaller group of Chechens. Jordan also counts a small Armenian population.

More than 92% of Jordanians are Sunni Muslims and about 6% are Christians who live mainly in Amman, Madaba, Kerak and Salt. There are tiny Shiite and Druze populations, and a few hundred Bahais, another subsect of the Shiites.

The Circassians, who first settled in Jordan in Wadi Seer and Na'ur in about 1878 and can trace their heritage back to Indo-European Muslim tribes in the 12th century, form the most important non-Arab minority. Related to them is the small Shiite community of Chechens.

The majority of Christians belong to the Greek Orthodox Church, but there are Greek Catholics, a small Roman Catholic community, Syrian Orthodox, Coptic Orthodox and Armenian Orthodox.

Palestinians

About 60% of the population are Palestinians, many of them still registered as refugees. They fled fighting, mostly from the West Bank, during the wars of 1948 and 1967. All were granted the right to Jordanian citizenship and many have exercised that option, playing an important part in the political and economic life of Jordan. Since the Gulf War, some 300,000 Palestinians who have returned from Kuwait have joined their Jordan-based counterparts.

Occupying high positions in government

The Bedouin

These desert dwellers, the *bedu* (the name means nomadic), number several hundred thousand, but few can still be regarded as truly nomadic. Some have opted for city life, but most have, voluntarily or otherwise, settled down to cultivate crops rather than drive their animals across the desert in search of fodder.

Still, a few retain the old ways. They camp for a few months at a time in one spot and graze their herds of goats, sheep or camels. When the sparse fodder runs out, it is time to move on again. All over the east and south of the country you'll see the black goat-hair tents (*'bayt ash-sha'ar'*: house of hair) set up; sometimes just one, often three or four together. Such houses are generally divided into a *haram* for the women and another section for the menfolk. This latter part is the public part of the home. Here guests are treated to coffee and sit to discuss the day's events. Most of the family's belongings, stores and so on are kept in the haram, or forbidden area (strangers are not permitted inside).

The Bedouin family is a close-knit unit. The women do most of the domestic work. This includes fetching water, baking bread and weaving clothes. The men are traditionally the providers and warriors. There is precious little warring to do these days, and the traditional inter-tribal raids that for centuries were the staple of everyday Bedouin life are now a memory. With the kids often sent out to tend the flocks, the average Bedouin fellow can actually find himself distinctly under-employed.

Most of those still living in the desert continue to wear traditional dress, and this includes, for men, a dagger – a symbol of a man's dignity but rarely used in anger now. The women tend to dress in more colourful garb, but rarely do they veil the face. Instead, facial tattoos are displayed by Bedouin women.

Although camels, once the Bedouin's best friend, are still in evidence, they are now often replaced by the Land Rover or Toyota pick-up truck – Wilfred Thesiger would definitely not approve. Other concessions to modernity are radios (sometimes even TVs), plastic water containers and occasionally a kerosene stove.

The Jordanian government provides services such as education and housing to the 40,000 or so estimated truly nomadic Bedouin, but both are still often passed up in favour of the lifestyle that has served them so well over the centuries.

The Bedouin are renowned for their hospitality and it is part of their creed that no traveller is turned away. This is part of a desert code of survival. Once taken in, a guest will be offered the best of the available food and plenty of tea and coffee. The thinking is simple. Today you are passing through and they have something to offer; tomorrow they may be passing your camp and you may have food and drink – which you would offer before having any yourself. Such a code of conduct made it possible for travellers to cross the desert with some sense that the odds against survival in such a hostile natural environment were not stacked so high as to be impossible.

One has to wonder, if tourists continue to pass through in ever growing numbers (and 99 times out of 100 in no danger of expiring on a sand dune), how long outsiders can expect to be regaled with such hospitality. After all, the original sense of it has largely been lost. Perhaps the moral for travellers is to be open to such things, but not to deliberately search out the Arab 'hospitality experience', reducing it to a kind of prefab high to be ticked off from the list of tourist excitements automatically claimed as a virtual right. There is a world of difference between the harsh desert existence that engendered this most attractive trait in Arab culture and the rather artificial context in which most of us experience this part of the world today. ■

Bedu means nomadic, but increasing numbers of Bedouin are opting for a less traditional lifestyle.

and business, many Palestinians continue to dream of a return to an independent Palestine. It is partly because of this that so many continue to live in difficult conditions in the 30 or so camps that dot the East bank. UNRWA is responsible for the welfare of the refugees, and also provides health and education services. Nevertheless, it may cease operations if comprehensive peace accords are ever signed.

EDUCATION

Jordan is one of the better educated of the Arab countries, with 87% literacy and 97% of children attending primary school. There are three kinds of schools – government, private and missionary. School is compulsory to the age of 14 and 70% of pupils attend government schools. UNRWA runs schools for refugee children.

Of the six state-owned universities, the three big ones are: Jordan University in Amman, Yarmouk University in Irbid and the military Mu'ta University near Kerak. Fees tend to be in excess of US$1,000 a year – exorbitant for many. There are also 10 expensive private institutions. They all have difficult entrance requirements, forcing some students to look abroad for a place to study.

About 100,000 people, around half of them female, were in some form of higher education in 1992, according to a UNESCO survey. An oversupply of professionals, such as engineers, has been exacerbated by the return of many Jordanians and Palestinians from the Gulf States since the war in 1991.

Interestingly, Jordan became the only Arab country to scrap compulsory military service at the end of 1991.

SOCIETY & CONDUCT

For the predominantly Muslim population, religious values still greatly inform Jordanian social life. Although more westernised than most Arab countries, women still tend to take a back seat to men in the professions, with the emphasis on family. Contact between westerners and locals, including women, may be less fraught in some circles of Amman society than elsewhere in the Arab world, but the barriers remain high. Some of the better off and well educated use social events hosted by westerners as a chance to bend the norms a little – Jordanians can be seen to be partying in a more western sense on occasions like the Hash House Harriers' (see Activities in the Amman chapter) evening runs and barbecues.

Jordanians can become vociferous at the drop of the hat, but never more so than over football (soccer to some). It doesn't matter, for instance, that Jordan might not have a team competing in the World Cup – Jordanians will be glued to their television sets no matter who is playing.

The old tribal structure of the Bedouin remains more or less intact, but the number of true nomads is shrinking as most settle in towns.

Dress & Behaviour

Although fairly used to the odd ways of westerners, immodest dress is still a source of irritation and can lead to trouble for women.

Men can get around in shorts without eliciting much of a response, particularly in Aqaba. Women, too, can probably relax a bit in Aqaba but otherwise are advised to wear at least knee-length dresses or pants and cover the shoulders. Both sexes should be well covered when entering mosques.

Although getting your hands on a drink is not a problem in Jordan, moderation is the rule of thumb. Drunkenness in the streets is not a common sight, and trying to start a trend might have unpleasant consequences – use common sense. If you have crossed to Aqaba from Eilat, for instance, remember that there is a considerable cultural difference between the two places.

Facts for the Visitor

PLANNING

When to Go

The best time to visit Jordan is in spring or autumn, when the daytime temperatures aren't going to knock you flat and the winds aren't too cold. Spring is the optimal time to visit.

Should you come in summer, be well prepared with a hat, sunscreen and your other protective clothing. The entire country boils, and nowhere more than around Wadi Rum and the desert areas. Along the Jordan River the humidity can become quite suffocating.

Unlike in Syria, winter is not a complete washout in Jordan. It can be bitterly cold throughout most of the country and snow blizzards are not unheard of in Petra. Once you come off the high plateaux and head down to Aqaba and the Red Sea, however, it becomes very pleasant – as with Israel's playground in Eilat and Egypt's Sinai coast, Aqaba is quite a hit with deep-frozen northern Europeans.

Those heading north towards Turkey should try to do so in spring, aiming to be in Turkey, Greece or wherever they have planned in Europe for the summer. Conversely, those going south should do so for the winter. Reaching Aqaba and subsequently heading into Egypt by November is ideal.

What Kind of Trip?

Jordan lends itself to a fairly relaxing short-break from Europe. In two weeks you could take in all the main sights and finish off with some diving and beach time in Aqaba.

Many people opt to join a tour that combines Jordan with Syria or, more recently, Israel (see also Organised Tours in the Jordan Getting There & Away chapter), but this is much more expensive than simply doing it yourself. Jordan is easy to get around and perfectly suitable for independent travel. Language is rarely an insurmountable difficulty and frequent transport means you can get just about anywhere under your own steam.

The standard budget traveller approach to Jordan remains pretty much unchanged. Few come only to Jordan, but make it part of a tour encompassing Turkey, Syria, perhaps Lebanon and finally Israel. Many push on into Egypt's Sinai but often go no further. Those who cross the Suez canal enter the African continent, opening up a whole new travel vista.

Maps

Lonely Planet's *Jordan, Syria & Lebanon travel atlas* is about the best of the lot and saves on picking up a lot of unwieldy individual maps.

The Royal Jordanian Geographic Centre publishes a map of the country for JD1.500 (scale 1:750,000), but although it comes with extra details such as distances between major towns and sketch plans of Aqaba, Jerash and Amman, it is much the same as the free map you can get at the Ministry of Tourism. Beirut's GEOprojects produces a similar map for JD2, with small plans of Jerash and Petra, but it's little better.

The Royal Jordanian Geographic Centre also publishes city plans of Amman, Petra, Jerash, Kerak, Madaba and Aqaba (they sell for about UK£7 in London).

Although it's a bit of a toss-up, Freytag and Berndt's Jordan map (scale 1:800,000) is probably about the best available of the fold-out maps.

SUGGESTED ITINERARIES

The main route through Jordan is a fairly straightforward north-south undertaking. As the Desert Highway offers few attractions, the obvious choice for getting from Amman to Aqaba or vice versa is to follow the King's Highway. With a day or two spent on a diversion to Wadi Rum, you can pretty much cover all the main, and many secondary places of interest on or just off this highway.

Petra lies at its southern end, and on the way you can stop in at the castles of Kerak and Shobak, cross the great Wadi al-Mujib and admire the wonderful Christian mosaics of Madaba. Further diversions at the Dead Sea and the delightful hot springs of Hammamat Ma'in suggest themselves along the way, for those who have time.

Apart from this main route, you could take a day or two to do a circuit east of Amman through the Desert Castles, and then use Amman as a base to visit some of the country's greatest ancient sites, including Pella and, of course, Roman Jerash.

The Best of Jordan

For the traveller with little time to spend in Jordan, there is a handful of places that should not be missed, all of which could be seen in as little as five or six days. Heading from north to south, the Roman Decapolis city of Jerash is an easy day trip from the capital, Amman, and is one of the best preserved Roman provincial cities in the region. Excavations and restoration continue to reveal more of its impressive array of buildings. These include the Artemis Temple, two theatres, the strange Oval Forum and a number of churches.

Only 118 km south of Amman is the impressive Crusader fortress of Kerak. It can be visited on the way down to Jordan's main attraction, Petra, the city hewn into rock by the ancient Nabataeans. Although it really deserves at least a couple of days, you can still cover some of its more remarkable features in one (long) day. These would include the Treasury (remember *Indiana Jones & the Last Crusade*?), the theatre and Roman city centre, the tombs, and the monastery. If you only had a day in Jordan, this is where it should be spent.

To the south-east of Petra are the sandstone and granite rockscapes rising out of the desert at Wadi Rum, made famous by Lawrence of Arabia. Finally, you could do far worse than spend a day diving off the Red Sea port town of Aqaba.

Another natural wonder is the Dead Sea. While there is no doubt that a float here is a unique undertaking, travellers planning to head for Israel should probably save it for there, as the so-called resort facilities on the Jordanian side are rather a disappointment. ■

TOURIST OFFICES

Local Tourist Offices

Tourist information is sparse in Jordan, although the Ministry of Tourism & Antiquities does put out a few glossy brochures and posters and a reasonable map of Jordan and Amman. The most useful of these is the *Visitor's Guide* prepared by the Ministry. There are tourist offices in Amman, Petra, Jerash, Kerak and Aqaba which can occasionally be helpful.

Tourist Offices Abroad

Royal Jordanian Airlines' sales offices double as tourist offices all over the world, so don't try to extract information from Jordan's diplomatic missions. In London, you could also try the Jordanian Information Bureau (☎ 0171-630 9277), at the same address as the embassy (see Embassies later in this chapter).

If you buy a ticket at Trailfinders (☎ 0171-938 3366) in London, ask to see the library in the basement of their office at 194 Kensington High St, London W8 7RG. They have a collection of old brochures, travel articles and the like.

VISAS & DOCUMENTS

For general information on what kind of documents to carry, turn to Visas & Documents in the Regional Facts for the Visitor chapter.

Visas

Visas are required by all foreigners entering Jordan. These are issued at the border or airport on arrival, or can be obtained from Jordanian consulates outside the country. Unless you want a multiple-entry visa, or belong to one of the few nationalities that gets charged more on the frontier than in an embassy, wait until you get to Jordan for your visa.

Tourist visas are valid for stays of up to two weeks from the date of entry, but can be easily extended for up to three months (see also Visa Extensions later in this chapter). They are free to Australian citizens and range in cost up to US$60 for other nationalities.

Much depends on which nationalities apply for their visas where. Jordan's London embassy issues visas (single and multiple entry) free to Australians. It charges Canadians UK£39 for both kinds of visa, Britons UK£27/48, Germans UK£9/21, New Zealanders UK£12/21 and US citizens a whopping great UK£42 for a single entry. The Jordanian embassy in London prefers not to issue Americans multiple-entry visas.

In Damascus, Syria, one month tourist visas are issued on the same day, require two passport photos and cost anything from nothing (Australians) to S£1300 (Canadians). US citizens pay S£1100 and Britons S£900. At the time of writing, Britons were better off getting the visa in Damascus, as they were being charged JD23 on the border. Multiple-entry visas are also available. Australians again pay nothing (valid for six months); Canadians are charged S£1300 (three months); Americans S£1500 (one year) and Britons a staggering S£3400 (six months).

Multiple-entry visas can also be easily obtained in Cairo, Egypt, but elsewhere Jordanian embassies seem less willing to issue anything but single-entry visas. If you wait until you arrive in the country, you can only get single-entry visas. Charges for those obtaining visas on arrival are: JD15 for US citizens, JD8 for the French, JD7 for Germans, JD18 for Japanese and JD31 for Canadians. You'll notice that in some cases there is a saving to be made by waiting until you arrive (in the case of US citizens for instance).

Since peace has been achieved between Jordan and Israel, there are no longer any difficulties attached to crossing between the two countries. Take note, however, that Israeli stamps or other evidence of having been in Israel still bars you from travelling to several countries, including Syria, Yemen and most of the Gulf States (see also Visas for Neighbouring Countries). The Jordanian embassy in Tel Aviv issues Jordanian visas.

Visa Extensions Your visa entitles you to 15 days on arrival in Jordan – it will be stamped with a reminder to visit the police within that period. Failure to do so if you intend to stay longer will result in a JD1 per day fine being applied on departure for every day you have overstayed.

Registering with the police is tantamount to getting an automatic extension for two to three months. The process is quick enough, once you have found the *appropriate* police station. In Amman it is in Muhajireen (see the Amman chapter). They stamp your passport, ask a few routine questions and give you a yellow slip that you must present on departure. The appropriate office in the Muhajireen police station is open from 10 am to 1 pm daily except Friday.

For extensions beyond this time, you may be sent to the Directorate of Foreigners & Borders, in Suleiman an-Nabulsi St in Amman, which opens from 8 am to 2 pm Saturday to Thursday. It's right on the No 7 service-taxi route, up past the blue King Abdullah Mosque. It is the fourth big gateway after the side street by the mosque.

Student Permits

Given the price of entry into Petra, students with a valid, international student ID card should approach the office of the Director-General of the Department of Antiquities (☎ 644336; fax 615848), in Sultan al-Atrash St, near 3rd Circle in Amman, for a permit allowing free entry to all sights. To maximise the chances of success, the request should be made in writing, and preferably on your university's letter-head.

Visas for Neighbouring Countries

Egypt To find the Egyptian embassy, head towards 5th Circle from 4th Circle and take the fifth street off to the right. The embassy is next to the distinctively yellow Dove Hotel, and is open for visa applications from 9 am to noon Sunday to Thursday. Passports can be picked up on the same day at 3 pm. You need a passport photo and JD17. Visas are valid for presentation for three months and get you one month in Egypt. Unless you really need to get it here, the consulate in Aqaba is much quieter – and the fee is lower at JD12. In any case, most people can be issued with visas on arrival in Egypt.

Iran Those preparing a trip across the Middle East into western Asia may want to try their luck for an Iranian visa here. The embassy is around the corner from the Syrian embassy and open for business from 10 am to noon Monday and Wednesday only.

Iraq The Iraqi embassy is between 1st and 2nd Circles on Zahran St, but your chances of getting a visa – should you be foolhardy enough to want to go – are slim at best.

Israel Although Israel now has a consular office in Amman (in the Forte Grande Hotel building in Shmeisani), most nationalities do not need to drop in as they will not require visas to visit.

Lebanon The consular office of the Lebanese embassy, right on 2nd Circle, is open from 8.30 to 11 am Monday to Thursday and Saturday for visa applications. Take a photocopy of your passport details, a passport photo and JD14 (all nationalities). The visa is valid for a month. Unless you intend to fly in and leave by air or boat, the Lebanese visa is little use without a Syrian one (and Syrian visas are hard to come by in Jordan). Some travellers have reported difficulties obtaining Lebanese visas in Jordan in the past.

Syria The Syrian embassy is past 3rd Circle in a side street off to the right from the Spanish embassy. Take a No 3 service taxi and get out at the Ministry of Foreign Affairs.

If at all possible, get your Syrian visa before you end up in Jordan. At the time of writing, what had been about the easiest place to pick up a Syrian visa had become the most difficult. The official line is that processing applications will take at least 20 days without any guarantee that the visa will be granted. It appears only residents in Jordan can obtain visas with minimal trouble.

Under normal circumstances you need a letter of recommendation from your embassy, for which there may be a fee (the UK embassy charges JD7), one passport photo and the visa fee (which varies from nationality to nationality, from nothing for Australians through to JD38 for Britons).

Applications are accepted between 9 am and 11 am Sunday to Thursday, but if the present situation persists, you'd be wiser to try elsewhere.

Also bear in mind that if you wish to travel to Lebanon too, you really need a double-entry visa for Syria.

Citizens of those countries with no Syrian representation could try simply turning up at the border (see also the Syria Facts for the Visitor chapter) if obtaining the visa in Amman proves impossible.

Anyone who has crossed from Israel to Jordan via the Wadi Araba or Sheikh Hussein Bridge crossings will have stamps that automatically disqualify them from going to Syria (the Jordanian stamps are sufficient to disqualify you, regardless of whether the Israelis put one in or not). Travellers who 'sneak' across from Israel via the King Hussein Bridge (Jisr al-Malek al-Hussein), and have no stamps in their passports will still get no joy from the Syrians. Even if you obtained your Syrian visa before entering Israel, the absence of a Jordanian entry stamp will give you away and you will probably be turned back at the Syrian border.

Even if you do things in a more convoluted fashion, by visiting Israel from Egypt, returning to Egypt and coming to Jordan by the Nuweiba ferry, you run a good chance of acquiring unwanted evidence in your passport. Even if the Israelis do *not* stamp you in or out, the Egyptians may well do so (at Rafah at least). It is not unheard of for the Syrians to miss such Egyptian stamps, but you would be foolish to bank on it.

EMBASSIES

Jordanian Embassies Abroad

Visas can be obtained from Jordanian diplomatic missions in countries around the world.

Australia

20 Roebuck St, Redhill, Canberra, ACT 2603
(☎ 06-295 9951)

Belgium
104 Ave F D Roosevelt, 1050 Brussels (☎ 2-640 7755)
Canada
100 Bronson Ave, Suite 701, Ottawa, Ontario OT K1N 6R4 (☎ 613-238 8090)
Egypt
6 Al-Juhaini St, Doqqi, Cairo (☎ 2-348 7543)
France
80 Blvd Maurice Barres, 92200 Neuilly-Seine, Paris (☎ 01-46 24 23 78)
Germany
Beethovenallee 21, 5300 Bonn 2 (☎ 228-35 70 46)
(Consulates) Jordanian visas are also available at consulates in Berlin, Düsseldorf, Hanover, Munich and Stuttgart.
Iraq
House No 1, Street 12, District 609, Al-Mansour, Baghdad (☎ 1-541 2892)
Israel
14 Abba Hillel St, Ramat Gan suburb, Tel Aviv (☎ 3-7517722). Issues visas from 9 am to 1 pm Sunday to Thursday.
Italy
Via G d'Arezzo 5, 00198 Rome (☎ 6-862 05 303)
Japan
4a B Chiyoda House, 4th floor 17-8, Nagata-cho, 2-chome, Chiyoda-ku, Tokyo 100 (☎ 3-35 80 58 56)
Saudi Arabia
Diplomatic Area, Riyadh 11693 (☎ 1-4543192)
Spain
Paseo de General Martínez Campos 41, 28010 Madrid (☎ 1-419 1100)
Switzerland
Belpstr. 11, 3007 Berne (☎ 31-25 41 46)
Syria
Al-Jala'a Ave, Damascus (☎ 11-323 4642)
Turkey
Mesnevi, Dedekorkut Sokak No 18, Çankaya, Ankara (☎ 4-439 4230)
UK
6 Upper Phillimore Gardens, London W8 7HB (☎ 0171-937 3685)
USA
Washington DC: 3504 International Drive NW, 20008 (☎ 202-966 2664)
New York (consulate): 866 UN Plaza, New York (☎ 212-752 0135)

Jordan has no diplomatic representation in New Zealand or Ireland. New Zealand and Irish citizens can obtain visas on arrival (as indeed everybody can), although Irish citizens can obtain one through the London embassy if they wish.

Foreign Embassies in Jordan

Most of the foreign embassies and consulates are in Amman. Egypt also has a consulate in Aqaba.

Australia
Between 4th & 5th Circles, Zahran St, Jebel Amman (☎ 673246)
Austria
Mithqal al-Fayez St, Building 36, Jebel Amman (☎ 644635)
Belgium
Andalous St (near 5th Circle), Jebel Amman (☎ 675683)
Canada
Pearl of Shmeisani Building, Shmeisani (☎ 666124)
Denmark
24 Sharif Abdul Hamid Sharaf St, Shmeisani (☎ 603703)
Egypt
Qurtubah St, between 4th and 5th Circles (☎ 605202)
France
Mutanabi St, Jebel Amman (☎ 641273)
Germany
31 Benghazi St, 4th Circle, Jebel Amman (☎ 689351)
Holland
2nd Floor, Jordan InterContinental Hotel (☎ 619693/9)
Iraq
1st Circle, Jebel Amman (☎ 621375)
Israel
Forte Grand Hotel, Shmeisani (☎ 698541)
Italy
Hafiz Ibrahim St 5/7, Jebel al-Weibdeh (☎ 638185)
Japan
Between 4th & 5th Circles, Al-Aqsa St, Jebel Amman (☎ 672486)
Lebanon
2nd Circle, Jebel Amman (☎ 641751)
New Zealand
4th Floor, Khalas Building, 99 Al-Malek al-Hussein St, Downtown (☎ 636720)
Norway
33 Qais bin Saida St, 3rd Circle, Jebel Amman (☎ 644932)
Saudi Arabia
1st Circle, Jebel Amman (☎ 814154)
South Africa
Mohammed al-Madi St, North-West Abdoun (☎ 811194)
Spain
Zahran St, Jebel Amman (☎ 614166/7)

Sweden
 12 Embassy St, 4th Circle, Jebel Amman (☎ 669177)
Switzerland
 19 Embassy St, 4th Circle, Jebel Amman (☎ 686416)
Syria
 Afghani St, Jebel Amman (☎ 641935)
UK
 Abdoun (☎ 823100)
USA
 Between 2nd & 3rd Circles, Jebel Amman (☎ 820101)

CUSTOMS

You can import 200 cigarettes and up to one litre of wine or spirits into Jordan duty free. There are no restrictions on the import and export of Jordanian and foreign currency.

MONEY

Costs

Jordan is not the cheapest country in the area to travel in. The most basic accommodation will generally cost US$5 to US$7 for a single room, and if you've come from Egypt (or even Syria), you'll find the food and transport generally more expensive.

With careful budgeting, you can survive on about US$15 per day as long as you don't mind eating felafel and shawarma and staying in the cheapest of the cheapies. It wouldn't take too many 'extravagances' to push the daily budget closer to US$20.

A bed in a shared room or single in the cheapest hotels ranges from JD2.500 to JD5, and a hot shower sometimes costs another 500 fils. On rare occasions you can get a miserable bed for as little as JD1.500.

Snacks like felafels and shawarmas cost from 100 fils and 250 fils, respectively. All over the bigger cities you'll see perfectly good ice creams on sale for around 100 fils.

A cup of tea will normally cost up to 250 fils; Turkish coffee costs from 250 to 300 fils. Bottles of soft drink will be from 100 to 200 fils, and cans a little more. Large 1.5 litre bottles of mineral water come at 300 to 400 fils; fresh juices from juice stands from 350 fils for a small glass in Amman to JD1 or more for a pint in Aqaba (exotic fruits like mango can cost double). A 650 ml bottle of Amstel beer costs up to JD1.600 in local bars, but there is a returnable deposit of anything up to 800 fils for those buying in liquor stores. In Petra and resorts you'll be looking at closer to JD3 for a bottle.

Credit Cards

There are no local charges on credit card cash advances but the maximum daily withdrawal amount is JD500, whether over the counter or from Automatic Teller Machines (ATMs). Whether you can get this much or not will depend on the conditions pertaining to your particular card.

The British Bank of the Middle East, Jordan National Bank and the Bank of Jordan accept MasterCard for cash advances, but only at selected branches.

Visa is more widely accepted for cash advances, but again only at selected branches of the following banks: the Housing Bank, the Bank of Jordan, the Cairo-Amman Bank, the Arab Banking Corporation, the Jordan Arab Investment Bank and the Jordan Investment & Finance Bank. The first two each have a branch in Aqaba that will give cash advances on Visa, as will a branch of the Bank of Jordan in Irbid.

ATMs have made an appearance, but as yet the only ones that seem to accept some foreign cards (including Visa and MasterCard) are those of the British Bank of the Middle East – and there are still precious few about. If a machine swallows your card, call ☎ 06-669123 (Amman).

Credit cards can be used to pay hotel and restaurant bills in some cases as well as for a range of purchases. However, always be sure to ask if any commission is being added on top of your purchase price. This can sometimes be as much as 5%, making it better to get a cash advance and pay with the paper stuff.

If you have problems with Visa, its head office is the Jordan Payment Services Co, on the 3rd floor of the Housing Bank Centre in Amman (☎ 680554; fax 680570). They can help in the event of lost or stolen cards, even issuing you with an emergency replacement card if necessary. MasterCard holders with similar problems should head for the Jordan National Bank next to the Jordan InterContinental Hotel in Amman.

Currency

The currency in Jordan is the dinar (JD) – known as the *jaydee* among hip young locals – which is made up of 1000 fils. You will also often hear *piastre* or *qirsh* used, which are both 10 fils, so 10 qirsh equals 100 fils. Often when a price is quoted to you the ending will be omitted, so if you're told that something is 25, it's a matter of working out whether it's 25 fils, 25 qirsh or 25 dinar! Just to complicate things a little bit further, 50 fils is commonly referred to as a *shilling*, 100 fils (officially a *dirham)* as a *barisa* and a dinar as a *lira*. In fact, Jordanians rarely use the word fils at all, except for the benefit of foreigners.

The coins in circulation are 5, 10, 25, 50, 100, 250 and 500 fils. The values of the coins are written in English; the numerals are in Arabic only. Just to confuse things, 1, 2½, 5 and 10 piastre (that is, 10, 25, 50 and 100 fils) coins have been introduced. Be careful, as the 5s and 10s are virtually the same size.

Notes come in JD0.500, 1, 5, 10 and 20 denominations. For everyday travelling, the JD5 note is about as large as you want. Changing 20s especially can be a nuisance.

Changing Money

There is little trouble changing money in Jordan, and most hard currencies are accepted (you will get nowhere with the New Zealand dollar and the Irish punt, however). Most banks will change travellers' cheques, and the British Bank of the Middle East (there is a branch in Downtown Amman) will accept Eurocheques. American Express has representatives in Amman and Aqaba.

You can buy Jordanian currency before you leave home and take as much in with you as you like. It is possible to change dinars into foreign (including hard) currencies, but you will need to show receipts proving you changed your currency into dinars in Jordan.

Fees & Commissions All banks charge a standard JD5 fee for changing travellers' cheques. The charge is per *transaction*, irrespective of the amount, so it pays to change in bulk as few times as possible. Watch out for some banks, as they also apply a commission. Ask if this is the case.

One of the most irritating demands made by many banks is to see the sales receipts for the cheques before changing them – directly contradicting the standard instructions to keep them separate. Sometimes they will relent, sometimes they won't.

As a rule, the most widely recognised travellers' cheques are American Express.

In Amman, one of the best places to go is the 1st Circle branch of the Bank of Jordan, which is reasonably efficient and does not ask to see sales receipts. The Downtown branch on Al-Malek Faisal St is OK too.

Cash is no problem, but if you are asked for commission go elsewhere.

There are bank branches at Amman's Queen Alia airport where you can change cash or cheques or get a cash advance on Visa. They even charge commission on cash, so are not the best deal going, and late at night generally accept cash only. Beware when changing at the border, as some travellers have reported being charged US$6 and above as commission.

You can also change cash and cheques in the bigger hotels, but the rates vary greatly and are almost always lower than those offered by the banks.

In February 1989, privately-run exchange houses were shut down amid government

Currency Exchange

A$1	=	JD0.56
C$1	=	JD0.52
E£1	=	JD0.21
FF10	=	JD0.14
DM1	=	JD0.48
¥100	=	JD1.00
S£10	=	JD0.20
UK£1	=	JD1.11
US$1	=	JD0.71

accusations that speculation by the moneychangers was pushing the currency down. They have again sprung up all over Amman, Aqaba and Irbid. Many accept cash only and you should be careful about exchange rates (often quite acceptable) at these places, the main advantage of which is that they keep longer hours than the banks. In those few where you can change travellers' cheques, you may find they charge no commission or transaction fee, but the rate may be lower than in the banks. Before deciding, compare the bank rate (with fee) with the rate applied by the moneychangers.

Bank Holidays Banks close on Friday and holidays, so if you get stuck, you may have to settle for changing in one of the exchange houses or the big hotels. Many small hotel owners and shopkeepers will change cash, but not at a favourable rate.

There are two exceptions to the rule. You can change money at one of the airport bank branches seven days a week. If you are in Aqaba, try the Cairo-Amman Bank at the Arab Bridge Maritime Co. As Arab Bridge sells ferry tickets to Egypt in US dollars, the bank branch in the same building is open on holidays to change money.

Tipping & Bargaining

Tips of 10% are generally expected in the better restaurants. Bargaining, especially when souvenir-hunting, is essential but shopkeepers are less likely than their Syrian and Egyptian counterparts to shift a long way from their original asking prices.

POST & COMMUNICATIONS

Post

Letters to the USA and Australia cost 400 fils, postcards 300 fils. To Europe, letters are 300 fils and postcards 200 fils.

Letters posted from Jordan take up to two weeks to Australia and the USA; and more like three to four days to Europe. The postal service between Jordan and Israel has been re-established.

Parcel post is ridiculously expensive. If you want to send something by air to Australia, for instance, the first kg will cost you JD13.700 and each subsequent kilo JD9.400. To the UK the first kg is JD9.500 and each one after is JD3.400.

Express mail can also be sent from Jordan. A normal letter sent this way to Australia would cost JD2.200, or JD1.600 to Europe.

Couriers A wide range of major courier companies, and quite a few homegrown versions, are flourishing in Jordan. You can send packages or letters, or have them sent to you. Federal Express (☎ 618730), for example, have an office near 2nd Circle in Amman.

Note that packages can end up at Amman's Queen Alia airport, where you'll have to battle out whether or not customs duty is applicable.

Telephone

The local telephone system isn't too bad, and is being improved. Telecommunications are slated for privatisation, and Jordan has established its first mobile phone system. Those of us needing normal phones spend 100 fils for a local call. Most shopkeepers and hotel staff will let you use their phone, which is better than trying to use the few noisy public telephones.

Overseas calls can be made from offices in Amman and Aqaba but cost the earth, at up to JD2.750 per minute with a three minute minimum. It may take up to 30 minutes or so to get the connection.

Daytime calls cost JD1.650 a minute to Europe, JD2 to the USA and JD2.500 to Australia. Add 10% to all these charges. Night rates are in effect from 10 pm to 6 am. They are respectively JD1.160, JD1.400 and JD1.750 per minute, plus the 10%. Cheap rates apply all day Friday. It is not possible to make collect calls from Jordan.

In Amman a bunch of private phone/fax offices have sprung up in direct competition. They sometimes provide cheaper rates and do not impose a three minute minimum.

Private communications companies have set up too, offering on occasion slightly cheaper rates, no three minute minimum and the option of sending faxes.

Local Telephone Area Codes

Amman	06
Irbid	02
Jerash & Mafraq	04
Ma'an, Petra, Kerak & Aqaba	03
Madaba	08
Zarqa	09
Salt	05

You can make overseas calls from hotels, but they cost substantially more than from the offices. The smaller hotels will charge about JD3 to JD4 per minute for a call to Europe; the bigger ones, like the InterContinental in Amman, charge JD17 for the first three minutes to Australia and JD11.200 for the same to Europe.

It is now possible to make calls between Jordan, Israel and the West Bank.

For directory assistance for local calls, ring ☎ 121. Although a new telephone directory in English and Arabic was around in 1996, along with an English Yellow Pages, finding one or the other posed something of a problem. The cultural centres or bigger hotels *might* have a copy.

Fax, Telex & Telegram

The post offices in Amman and Aqaba will send telegrams, and the telephone offices will send telexes. Five star hotels will also send telexes and faxes for guests – for a fee. Even some smaller hotels will send faxes, as do most of the private phone offices.

Internet

For those of you lugging laptops around, Jordan *is* joining the communications revolution, but as yet hooking up is difficult for all but a lucky few. Few servers are yet operating, and there are only about 1500 local subscribers. You may also find your modem does not fit local phone sockets. In April 1996, the government licensed the US communications company Sprint to set up an Internet access network in Jordan in conjunction with a Jordanian company. ■

BOOKS

Lonely Planet

Annie Caulfield's *Kingdom of the Film Stars: Journey into Jordan* unravels some of the tightly-woven western myths about the Arab world, and does so in the intimate framework of a love story. With honesty and humour, the author tells of her relationship with a Bedouin man and offers a vividly personal account of Jordanian culture and society. This is one of the many exciting titles in Journeys, Lonely Planet's new travel literature series.

Guidebooks

The locally produced *Travellers' Guide to Jordan* (Josephine Zananiri) is not very useful, but the Franciscan friars' *Guide to Jordan*, compiled in 1953, has some interesting odds and ends in it.

Fodor's *Jordan & the Holy Land* (Kay Showker) is mainly for the group tourist, or those with a vehicle, and lists only up-market establishments. The Harvard *Let's Go* guide to Israel and Egypt includes a reasonable but slim section on Jordan. Boxer's *Jordan Revealed* and the Blue Guide's *Jordan* may be helpful, especially for historical information but they are not that strong on practical travel information.

Travel

In the late 19th century, the archaeologist Selah Merrill set off to the explore what is modern Jordan, the area he called *East of the Jordan*. His book is one of the very few to touch on this area before recent times.

History & Politics

On Jordan's recent history, there is the somewhat gushing *Hussein of Jordan* by James Lunt. A slightly more serious look at Jordanian history is Kamal Salibi's *The Modern History of Jordan*, which spans the short history of this 20th century creation from the 1920s to the Gulf wars. A more academic and dry work is Ma'an Abu Nowar's *The History of the Hashemite Kingdom of Jordan*. For a look at the country in the wider perspective of its position among shaky neighbours,

Archaeological Sites
For a detailed look at the main archaeological sites, there are a number of books available.

Petra and *Jerash & the Decapolis* by Iain Browning are well illustrated and detailed guides.

If you want something smaller, a couple of excellent guides by Rami Khouri, former editor of the *Jordan Times*, are titled *Petra – A Guide to the Capital of the Nabataeans* and *Jerash – A Frontier City of the Roman East*. They give full details of the two sites and have excellent maps and plans. You should be able to find them in the Jordan Distribution Agency in Amman.

The same author is largely responsible for a series of booklets, published by Al-Kutba, to most of the sites, great and small, in Jordan. They are available for JD3.

Written in 1959, *The Antiquities of Jordan* (G Lankester Harding) is a bit dated but is still the most comprehensive guide to archaeological sites in Jordan and includes those on the West Bank. The author was Director of the Department of Antiquities in Jordan for 20 years.

For a more academic approach to the whole subject, the Jordanian Department of Antiquities has published two substantial volumes entitled *Studies in the History and Archaeology of Jordan*.

Petra – A Travellers' Guide, by Rosalyn Maqsood, is a comparatively thorough and quite digestible description of Jordan's most famous sight. ■

Jordan in the Middle East – 1948-1985 is an insightful collection of essays edited by Joseph Nevo and Ilan Pappé.

Living in Jordan
If you want more practical information on everything from road rules to how to track down a plumber, *Welcome to Jordan* (American Women of Amman, Amman) might be for you. Produced mainly with expatriates in mind, it does have some information that could be of use to the short-term visitor. It is not easy to find, so try at the American Center or British Council libraries.

Trekking & Climbing
For rockclimbing and walking, *Treks & Climbs in Wadi Rum* by Tony Howard is an excellent handbook full of walks, climbs, and 4WD and camel treks. The new edition contains over 250 routes. *Walks & Scrambles in Wadi Rum*, also by Tony Howard, is a useful pocket guide. For further information see the boxed story called 'Trekking in Jordan' later in this chapter.

Photography
High Above Jordan, an officially sanctioned book of aerial photographs by Jane Taylor, is not a bad coffee-table book of the place, but a little pricey at JD20. Another classy glossy is *Journey Through Jordan* by Mohammed Amin, Duncan Willetts and Sam Wiley.

Bookshops
Most of the above books can be found in a handful of bookshops in Amman, and some in Aqaba as well (where prices tend to inflated). See the appropriate chapters for more information.

NEWSPAPERS & MAGAZINES
The press in Jordan is given a surprisingly free reign, but according to some journalists in the country, pressure is still exercised from time to time on those thought to be out of line. They also say that the bulk of newspapers all too often push an editorial line curiously similar to the government's position. By the region's standards, however, the controls are loose. At the time of writing, a controversial new, and in some respects restrictive, press and publications law was being debated in parliament.

The daily English-language newspaper, the *Jordan Times* (150 fils), has a reasonably impartial outlook and gives good coverage of events in Jordan, elsewhere in the Middle East and worldwide. It also has a limited 'What's On' listing that includes films, exhibitions, flight information, emergency telephone numbers and even the latest market prices of fruit and vegetables.

The *Star* (350 fils) is an English-language weekly tabloid with more feature articles, a section in French and with more extensive listings.

Foreign Press

The major European dailies and news magazines like *Time*, *Le Point* and *Der Spiegel* are available in several newsagents scattered about Amman, and to a lesser extent in Aqaba. The dailies are generally not more than two days old, but can cost as much as JD2 to JD3!

RADIO & TV

Radio Jordan transmits in Arabic and English. The English station is on 855 kHz AM and 96.3 kHz FM in Amman or 98.7 kHz FM in Aqaba. It's mostly a music station.

The best way to keep in touch with events inside and outside the country is through the BBC World Service, which can be picked up from about 4 am to midnight GMT/UTC on at least some of the following frequencies: 6195 kHz; 7325 kHz; 9410 kHz; 12,095 kHz; 15,070 kHz; 15,575 kHz; 17,640 kHz; and 17,705 kHz. As well, some broadcasts are transmitted on medium wave 1323 kHz. Anyone happening to have access to satellite services can pick up broadcasts on AsiaSat. The BBC alters its programming every six months or so, and the British Council in Amman usually has the latest information.

The Voice of America (VOA) broadcasts to the Middle East from 4 am to 10 pm GMT/UTC on a wide range of frequencies, including: 792 kHz; 1197 kHz; 1260 kHz; 1548 kHz; 3985 kHz; 5995 kHz; 6010 kHz; 6040 kHz; 7170 kHz; 11,965 kHz and 15,205 kHz.

Jordan TV broadcasts on two channels; the first in Arabic, and Channel 2 in a combination of English, French and Arabic. Jordanians are avid TV watchers and you can see them in the tea shops glued to the sets following the latest developments in American soaps (wrestling also draws big audiences). The foreign channel sometimes screens excellent movies and TV series. News is broadcast in English at 10 pm and in French at 7 pm.

In the north of the country you can pick up Syrian TV as far down as Azraq. Israeli TV can be seen in places like Aqaba and Kerak, not too far from the Israeli border. The locals have no qualms about tuning in to Israeli TV, especially if movies are being shown that would be cut to ribbons by Jordanian censors. In Aqaba, you can also watch Egyptian TV.

PHOTOGRAPHY & VIDEO

Film & Equipment

Kodak and other brands of film, including slides, are widely available at the tourist sites in Jordan and in Amman itself, but don't expect to pay less than you would at home (anything up to JD8 for a roll of 36 slides). Check the use-by dates before buying.

Getting your film developed in Amman and Aqaba is easy but fraught with danger. Even the best equipped shops seem to have a tendency to ruin a good batch of photos. Developing a roll of Kodak slide film can cost JD7.500. You've been warned!

For more general information on photography and video shooting, see Photography & Video in the Regional Facts for the Visitor chapter.

ELECTRICITY

Jordan's electricity supply is 220V, 50 AC. Sockets are generally of the European two pronged variety, although in Aqaba you're more likely to find the British three pronged ones. Those taking electrical appliances with different plugs should buy an appropriate adaptor. If you use a radio or walkman a lot in your room, it will work out cheaper than buying tons of batteries, which often turn out to have less life in them than expected.

Power is generated by the two large oil-fired generating plants in Zarqa and Aqaba. Supply is reliable and uninterrupted.

LAUNDRY

In the bigger cities, especially Amman, there are plenty of places (often displaying a sign saying 'Dry Cleaning') where you can have your laundry done. Ask your hotel. You can be charged around 600 fils to have a shirt cleaned and 750 fils for a pair of trousers. It can take as little as 24 hours, but sometimes longer.

DANGERS & ANNOYANCES

Jordan is a safe and friendly country to travel in. The military keep a low profile and you would be unlikely to experience anything but friendliness, honesty and hospitality here.

It is generally safe to walk around day or night in Amman and other towns.

Theft is usually no problem for people who take reasonable care with their gear. Leaving your bag in the office of a bus station or hotel for a few hours should be no cause for concern. Shared rooms in hotels are also quite OK as a rule, but don't take unnecessary risks.

LEGAL MATTERS

The Jordanian legal system is something of a cross-breed, reflecting the country's history. Civil and commercial law are governed by a series of courts working with a mix of inherited British-style common law and the French code. Religious and family matters are generally covered by Islamic *shari'a* courts, or ecclesiastic equivalents for non-Muslims.

The visitor will be unlucky to get caught up in the machinations of Jordanian justice. Note that penalties for drug use of any kind are stiff and apply to foreigners and locals alike. Traffic police generally treat foreign drivers with a degree of good-natured indulgence, so long as no major traffic infringements are made.

If you do get into trouble, there is little your embassy can do for you but contact your relatives and recommend local lawyers.

BUSINESS HOURS

Government departments are open from 8 am to 2 pm daily except Friday. Banks are open from 8.30 am to 12.30 pm and again from 4 to 6 pm daily except Friday (3.30 to 5.30 pm in winter). Businesses keep similar hours but are more flexible.

Small shops are open long hours, from about 9 am to 8 or 9 pm. Some close for a couple of hours in the middle of the afternoon. Friday is pretty dead, although a few shops are open, and you can still change money at the airport.

The souqs and street stalls are open every day and in fact Friday is often their busiest day.

During Ramadan, the Muslim month of fasting, business hours are shorter and because of the restriction on eating or drinking during the day, it can be difficult to find a place that's open in daylight hours, particularly in out-of-the-way places.

Museums are generally open daily except Tuesday, but opening hours sometimes vary.

PUBLIC HOLIDAYS

Holidays are either religious (Islamic or Christian) or celebrations of important events in Jordanian or Arab history. For a list of Islamic holidays, see the Regional Facts for the Visitor chapter.

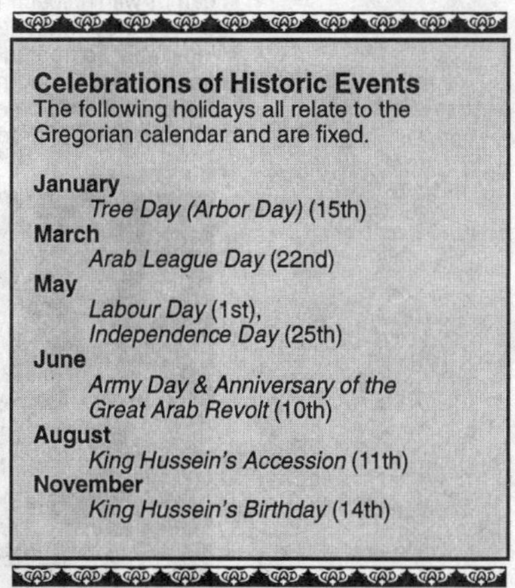

Celebrations of Historic Events

The following holidays all relate to the Gregorian calendar and are fixed.

January
Tree Day (Arbor Day) (15th)

March
Arab League Day (22nd)

May
Labour Day (1st),
Independence Day (25th)

June
Army Day & Anniversary of the Great Arab Revolt (10th)

August
King Hussein's Accession (11th)

November
King Hussein's Birthday (14th)

Christian Holidays

Most Christians in Jordan use the eastern (Julian) calendar to determine holidays; this can be as much as one month behind the Gregorian calendar, which is used by the Roman Catholics and Protestants. Easter is the main festival celebrated in the eastern Church.

Trekking in Jordan

Wadi Rum

Trekking in Jordan is in its infancy, though rock climbing took off in the mid 80s following our 'discovery' of the superb cliffs and canyons of Wadi Rum in 1984.

This uniquely beautiful desert area which is just one hour by bus from Aqaba has become acknowledged as 'one of the world's foremost desert climbing areas'. Alongside this the number of short walks, camel safaris and treks has gained increasing popularity and offers the visitor a remarkable variety of venues from a short stroll up to Lawrence's Well, through to canyon trails lasting half a day such as the impressive maze of Rakabat Canyon, or an ascent of Jordan's highest mountain, Jebel um Adaami, 1830m, in a remote part of the desert down on the border with Saudi Arabia. For those with a little rock climbing ability and a head for heights, there are wonderful scrambles such as those to the now famous Rock Bridge of Burdah or even to the summit of Jebel Rum, up traditional Bedouin hunting routes such as Sheikh Hamdan's Route. For routes like these, you should have a guide and a safety rope.

On the other hand, if you really want to get into the desert experience, you can walk for days among superb scenery as the rock domes and sandscapes change from the ghostly colour of a full moonlit night to the hot furnace hues of late afternoon. Such trips are also an opportunity to meet the local people. Despite a recent move (attracted by the tourism bonanza) to the newly built village in Wadi Rum, the Bedouin still retain most of their camps out in the desert, as well as a love of their traditional way of life which they are pleased to share with you. Approach their camps with respect. You should not go in if there are only women present, unless they make it obvious you are welcome. Once invited, you will inevitably be treated to tea, and you will be able to replenish your water for your onward journey. You may even be invited to stay the night, which will undoubtedly be a memorable experience. Ten years ago, this would all have been offered as a traditional gesture of hospitality. With increas-

Some of the extraordinary desert scenery of Wadi Rum. Note the bizarre rock formations which soar from the desert floor.

ing numbers of visitors, the welcome remains as genuine, but you may feel it reasonable to offer some payment in return (which may be refused). The choice is yours but clarify the position first, to save embarrassment later. As always, the further off the road you get the more sincere your welcome is likely to be.

There are over twenty routes described in the Al Kutba pocket guide *Walks and Scrambles in Wadi Rum* which, like the more technical and rock-oriented *Treks and Climbs in Wadi Rum* is available from Aqaba book shops (across the road from the post office) and many of the larger hotels, as well as from the rest house shop in Rum itself.

Petra

Outside Rum there is little available published information on walks and treks. Rami Khouri's excellent little book *Petra – a guide to the capital of the Nabataeans* published by Longman describes many of the walks in and around Petra and is invaluable if you want to do more than make a hectic one day visit to this legendary and inspiring ancient city. Unfortunately, stocks are dwindling so it could be hard to find though it may be updated and republished by Al Kutba in the next year or so. The current alternative is another guide by Rami Khouri in the Al Kutba series that is simply entitled *Petra*. Whilst this documents the city extremely well and

This stunning monastery is one of Petra's 'high places'. It can be reached by climbing up an ancient rock-cut path.

contains a good map of the immediate environs, it does not give many route descriptions. Nevertheless, if you can't find the Longman version, this is the next best bet.

Either book will get you up to the Monastery, or up the imposing cliffs to Iron Age remains on the top of Umm al-Biyara, its stone stairways, like those of Gormenghast, worn 'ankle-deep in time', or over the High Place of Sacrifice with its splendid panoramic view of Petra. The Longman book, however, describes how to enter Petra by paths such as those from Al-Beidha (or Little Petra) and will take you up to places like the tomb on the summit of Jebel Harun where tradition has it that Aaron, brother of Moses, died – a magical place to spend the night, high above Petra and the wilderness of Wadi Araba with the arid hills of Palestine and Israel beyond. From here, there are ancient trails down to Wadi Araba, and to the Roman theatre and springs of Wadi Sabra 'where only Allah and the Bedouin live', or so we were told by a Bedouin who offered us tea in one of the remote recesses of this beautiful and wild valley.

Many more trails penetrate the rugged hills around Petra, sometimes through narrow and tortuous canyons that dwarf the famous Siq. These will be included in Al Kutba's proposed book on trekking in Jordan to be published in the next couple of years. The surrounds of Petra are real wilderness country and should not be entered without a local guide. The only major canyon route published to date was in the first edition of the Wadi Rum Guide, now out of print, which included a small section on Petra. The route described is a one day canyon walk from Bir Madhkur in Wadi Araba up Wadi es-Siq (otherwise known as Wadi Siyyagh) to emerge in Petra, near the start of the way to the Monastery. This is a great trek with a little rock scrambling to bypass waterfalls and swimming pools, but again should not be entered into without a guide or route description, as the way is not always evident.

Dana – Shobak Area

Despite this being an outstandingly beautiful area with its own unique ambience there is no published trekking information, though details should be included in the proposed Al Kutba guide. Dana, the newly created Nature Reserve, is the feather in the cap of Jordan's Royal Society for the Conservation of Nature (RSCN). The ancient stone-built

The Bedouin are renowned for their hospitality and it is part of their culture that no traveller be turned away.

village with its vaulted houses perched on a cliff above the dramatic westward plunging valley of Wadi Dana was until recently falling into ruins. It has now been renovated in the traditional Dana style. Local people have re-learnt traditional crafts and the orchards have been replanted, offering work opportunities and incentives for local people to stay rather than join the drift to the towns and cities.

Round the rim of the escarpment to the north, a campsite is in an idyllic location amongst green 'alpine' meadows and white rock domes with magnificent views out across Wadi Araba to the west. The whole area is, primarily, a nature reserve and consequently the only trail officially approved at the moment runs between the campsite and village. There are plans to open others, down the valley of Dana to the 4000 year old copper mines of Feinan on the edge of Wadi Araba, and back up little known caravan routes to Shobak Castle, brooding in grim austerity on the ramparts of the bare hills to the south.

From Shobak there are ways on south through the hills, past ancient stands of oak, to Al-Beidha and Petra. Conversely, from Dana there are also trails going north to other historic sites such as the cliff top refuge of Selah occupied from the early Bronze Age through to Biblical times. You will find it just north of the village of Es Sil on an isolated rocky hill in a deep gorge and, if necessary, one of the locals will guide you down to and then up the stone steps between the cliffs to this mountain top hideaway.

The Dead Sea Hills

North of Dana, and all the way to Amman, the high hills of the desert plateau rise from the abyss of Wadi Araba and the Dead Sea, and are slashed by huge canyons such as Hasa and al-Mujib. Over these hills and down the steep sides of these dramatic gorges, the thin ribbon of the King's Highway winds its way and forms the starting point for some short walks and great treks, a few of which emerge on the newly constructed Dead Sea Highway.

For example, you can break your journey at Wadi Hasa where, just south of the river crossing, it is a short climb up a conical hill to the ruins of the once magnificent Nabataean temple of Jebel Tannur. Considerably more strenuous is the trek down Wadi al-Mujib, 'The Grand Canyon of Jordan'. This takes two or three days and needs ropes to descend the waterfalls of the last kilometre which passes through a narrow flooded ravine (which can be avoided by an old route out to its south). Al-Mujib is, however, currently being studied by the RSCN and may well become another Nature Reserve. In this case, the trek down this awe-inspiring valley may need special permission.

North of al-Mujib, the site of Machaerus, where John the Baptist reputedly lost his head, is connected by seldom trodden paths to the hot springs of Herod's Baths by the Dead Sea, and to those at Zerqa Main. Again, as with all the long treks in this area, local guides are recommended if one is to find the right way through these unforgiving hills.

North of Amman

The high hills of Jerash and Ajlun offer a different, almost unexpected terrain. In the spring, carpets of red crown anemones fill the meadows beneath the pine forested and sometimes snow-capped rolling hills. Here, numerous short walks are possible along trails through the woods and into quiet valleys where you may meet local farmers tending their crops. Flowers and bird life are plentiful and it can be a relaxing way to while away a few hours.

To the west, the hills drop into the Jordan Valley, now no longer the dust-bowl of Wadi Araba but a fertile agricultural valley cradling a tightly knit patchwork of fields dotted with plastic greenhouses. Down here are 4000 year old burial mounds and tucked in a side valley are the Graeco-Roman ruins of Pella which can be reached on foot from the hills above by small trails leading into the valley. Finally, to the north again, the area around the Graeco-Roman ruins of Gadara at Umm Qais offers short walks and views of the Golan Heights with the Sea of Galilee and the Yarmouk River below.

All this northern area is, in general, easy walking country usually on small roads or stony trails between villages that are rarely too far apart. If you have the time, it's an opportunity to get away from the crowds, breathe some fresh country air in beautiful surroundings and meet the local people. That, after all, is surely the essence of travel.

Some Tips

The Jordanian authorities don't look too kindly on wild-camping or sleeping out away from recognised camping areas. This is not because they want to squeeze you for your last penny. The situation arose when the borders with Israel opened and the Jordanians suddenly had the possibility of Israelis, not to mention a massive influx of other tourists, wandering around their country and camping off-site. Rightly or wrongly this was seen as a security risk, particularly for the Israelis and for their protection the authorities always insist on everyone camping in approved places.

While trekking, an approach of maximum safety and minimum impact is good practice. This is true of anywhere in the world, but some issues are especially important in this region. Employ a local guide for long treks or rock climbing. Leave no litter – even though you may be faced with an approach to litter by locals that seems less than responsible, you can still

Ancient inscriptions carved into the rock can be admired at Wadi Rum.

carry out what you carry in. Don't burn excessive amounts of wood or leave fire-marks on the ground – even better still, cook with a stove. Be sensitive to the local people – adopt a mode of dress considerate of the local standards and seek permission before entering a camp or taking photographs. How you treat the locals will affect how they treat others in the future.

The best time to go is undoubtedly spring – late March through to the end of April: it's not too hot, the rains should have finished, the flowers should be in bloom and the wells and springs should be full. The down-side of this is that in early spring canyon trips like the Mujib Gorge or some of the side entries to Petra such as Wadi es Siq may be either too fast-flowing or flooded in their lower reaches to be passable. Late September to mid October are usually dry months without the excessive heat of summer.

Speaking of floods and rain, either can happen throughout the winter months of November to March, and this is consequently not a good time to be considering walking or camping in narrow wadis and ravines when flash floods can sweep unheralded out of the hills. People have been killed in the Petra Siq by flash floods. Such instances are, fortunately, rare. The most usual problem with water is a lack of it! Drink more than you need before starting and carry plenty: two litres each is a minimum, take more if you can, unless you're absolutely certain of its availability ahead.

The journey can be longer and take more out of you than you think – walking in sand is not easy, nor is going uphill in the hot sun! There are almost always unexpected encounters with local people who pop up unannounced in the most remote places. Wildlife is also not uncommon and you may be lucky enough to see almost anything from tortoises through to ibex or desert fox. Hyenas prowl the gorges and hills above the Dead Sea and can be dangerous though fortunately they are very reclusive. However, their undoubted presence not only adds spice to your camping but also provides the Bedouin with opportunities for some outrageous tales! Also around the Dead Sea valley, there are wild boar, mongoose and, of course, as elsewhere in Jordan snakes and scorpions, so tread gently – or rather, noisily!

Up above, you're likely to see eagles and vultures and, in the Dana Reserve, lammergeiers are not too uncommon. Smaller birds abound and are far too numerous to mention as Jordan lies on one of the main migration routes between Africa, Europe and Asia, as well as having its own endemic species from colourful Palestinian sunbirds through to hubara bustards.

Allow yourself plenty of time for your journey – you may be an experienced walker, but you may never pass this way again. Give yourself time to linger and enjoy the view and time to chat with passers by, or simply time to sit in the shade at midday and relax. Let people know where you're going and roughly what time, or what day, you expect to arrive: don't leave your tent empty for days without telling anyone where you've gone – it causes others no end of worry!

Knowing precisely where you're going can often be a bit of a problem. Apart from Wadi Rum, where there is a 1:50,000 map on the rest house wall that gives you an excellent idea of the complexity of the area, maps other than road maps are hard to come by. Generally you will either have to use the maps in the existing guide books to Rum and Petra (which aren't too bad), or ask directions locally. This can have unexpected results and may not always lead to answers that you want to hear or choose to believe. For instance, you may be told that the path to Jebel Harun is 'forbidden' or the descent of the al-Mujib Gorge is 'impossible'. Whether either of these is true or not you must decide for yourself!

As for clothing, a lightweight wind-proof top is well worth having, as is a thin fleece jacket for the evening. Lightweight waterproofs are rarely needed except perhaps for some of the wetter mid-winter days unless you're spending more time from October through to April in the north which is undoubtedly colder and wetter than the south. Most people walk in lightweight cotton clothes or the modern equivalent and trainers are the most usual footwear, although some people prefer modern lightweight walking boots which give more ankle support. It's really not advisable to wear shorts or sleeveless tops. Don't forget your hat, sunscreen, medical kit, knife, torch (flashlight) and matches. Water purifiers and insect repellent may be useful.

For camping, the lightest of tents and sleeping bags should suffice. In southern Jordan, if you're only spending a few nights out you may prefer simply to sleep under the stars and not bother carrying a tent, though after a clear, cold night on the top of Jebel Rum, you may wake with your sleeping bag covered in frost. Indeed, we once woke up after a cold night near Dana in late March to find a couple of centimetres of snow on our tent!

Other than that, the only things you need to know are that you can buy just about any basic camping food you may need in any of the larger towns and villages, including fresh bread and dehydrated foods. The smaller ones are only likely to have pasta, rice, tinned foods and Jordan Valley produce (sometimes of dubious freshness). Small camping gas cylinders tend only to be available in large towns.

Enjoy your trekking and try not to put yourself in a situation where you will need to be rescued. There really isn't a search and rescue service in Jordan, though the helicopter pilots of the Royal Jordanian Air Force have been called out on two occasions to assist injured climbers in Wadi Rum and they did a first class job. However, don't rely on them – if you get yourself into trouble, be prepared to get yourself out!

Finally, if you find any interesting walks or meet some good local guides or have any interesting anecdotes about trekking in Jordan, please write to us, care of Lonely Planet: it all helps to make other people's journeys better.

Tony Howard & Di Taylor
NOMADS, July 96

Recommended Reading

- *Treks and Climbs in Wadi Rum* (Tony Howard, Cicerone Press)
- *Walks and Scrambles in Wadi Rum* (Tony Howard & Diana Taylor, Al Kutba)
- *Petra – a Guide to the Capital of the Nabataeans* (Rami G Khouri, Longman)
- *Petra* and other booklets (Rami G Khouri, Al Kutba)
- *Introduction to the Wildlife of Jordan* and other booklets (RSCN)
- *The Antiquities of Jordan* (G Lankester Harding, Jordan Distribution Agency)

SPECIAL EVENTS

Jordan's best known cultural event is the Jerash music festival, which generally takes place about July each year, although since the Gulf War in 1991, it has been under a cloud. At the time of writing it appeared it would go ahead. For information, call the Jerash Festival Office on ☎ 675199.

The foreign cultural centres have regular films, lectures and exhibitions, such as the French film festival. Enquire at the centres. Since 1989, an annual European Film festival has been held in Amman around May.

The Royal Cultural Centre quite regularly holds music recitals. Occasionally, concerts are held in Amman's Roman theatre as well.

ACTIVITIES

Diving & Snorkelling

The coast south of Aqaba port up to the Saudi border is home to one of the world's better diving spots, with plenty of coral and colourful fish life. There are four dive centres in Aqaba. A single dive will cost from about JD20, depending on the gear you have with you and the centre you dive with. All three run PADI and CMAS courses for beginners and beyond, for which you'll be looking at up to JD290.

There are fears that pollution from the port will damage the sea life at Aqaba – thousands of tons of phosphates are dropped into the water during loading every year. Nevertheless, the diving offers great variety and is relatively easy. Egypt's Ras Mohammed is thought by most to be better, but requires deeper dives in more dangerous circumstances.

Camel Treks

Enterprising Bedouin are prepared to take you on camel treks from Wadi Rum to Aqaba or even Petra. Similar trips can be done in 4WD but obviously lose a good deal of their charm.

Ballooning

For a bird's eye view of Petra and Wadi Rum, a hot air balloon could be for you. The season runs from March to November and inquiries should be made to Balloons Over Jordan in Amman (☎ 825224).

LANGUAGE COURSES

For those taken enough by the mystery of the Arab world to want to learn something of the language, there are several possibilities. University of Jordan, in University Street, Amman (☎ 843555; fax 832318) offers summer courses in Modern Standard Arabic (MSA) as well as more leisurely courses through the rest of the year. Enquiries should be made to the director of the Language Centre in the Arts Faculty. On occasion the Language Centre can help find accommodation with Jordanian families.

The British Council (☎ 636147) has recently revamped its Arabic courses and aims now to offer not only classes in colloquial Jordanian Arabic, but alternative classes in MSA as well. The French, German and Spanish cultural centres all offer some level of Arabic tuition.

WORK

Language Teaching

Work in Jordan is probably not an option for most foreigners passing through. Teaching English is the most obvious avenue, but the top two schools, the British Council and the American Language Center (☎ 659859) mainly recruit in the UK and the USA, respectively. This does not mean that someone passing through cannot get work. Vacancies can arise at short notice and it is

> **Archaeological Digs**
>
> You may be able to get work on archaeological digs, but it is usually unpaid. If the Department of Antiquities is no help, try the British Institute for Archaeology & History (☎ 841317) or the American Center of Oriental Research (ACOR; ☎ 846117). A more extensive list of organisations involved in the field appears in the *Visitor's Guide* available at the Ministry of Tourism in Amman. For more on archaeology in Jordan and Syria, see the boxed story called 'Digging up the Past'. ■

JORDAN

definitely possible to get part-time positions. For the British Council, minimum requirements are the RSA Preparatory Certificate (the Diploma is preferred) or equivalent and two years' experience. Pay generally starts at about JD13 to JD15 per hour.

Two other possibilities are the Yarmouk Cultural Centre in Shmeisani (☎ 671447) and the Modern Language Center, at 39 Murtadha al-Zubaida St in Jebel al-Weibdeh (☎ 638373).

Diving

If you are a diving instructor, you could always try your luck at one of the dive centres in Aqaba.

ACCOMMODATION

There are no youth hostels in Jordan. A bed in a shared room in a cheap hotel will not cost under JD1.500 and, generally, will be more like JD2.500 to JD5 without shower. It's sometimes possible to sleep on the roof, which in summer is a good place to be, but this will still cost at least JD1.

Especially in Amman, the cheap places can be incredibly noisy because of traffic and the hubbub of the cafés and shops, so try to get a room towards the back of the building.

The most surprising thing about accommodation in Jordan is that there are towns, some of them quite large like Jerash, that have no hotel at all. Other towns, like Madaba and Ajlun, offer little or nothing in the bottom end of the market, and you may find yourself obliged to shell out up to JD20 for a single room.

The cheap hotels may insist on hanging on to your passport to put in the 'safe', which is usually the drawer in the desk at the front. If you want to keep it with you (where else is there to have it?), a little friendly persuasion usually works.

There is a reasonable selection of middle-range hotels in Amman, Aqaba and Petra, where a single may cost from JD8 to JD20. Beyond that, there is no shortage of the top-end stuff, where rooms can easily break the JD100 barrier.

Women Travellers in Jordan

Jordan is one of the safest places to travel but don't flaunt your body on public beaches and make sure that you respect the culture of the country.

Now that the Israeli borders are open it's all getting pretty cosmopolitan and the hotels are getting used to the idea of 'travellers', single women or otherwise.

I have found the following places to stay pleasant and secure, although I must stress that I have rarely travelled solo:

Al-Monzer Hotel, Amman (☎ 639469)
Hisham Hotel, Amman (☎ 642720; fax 647540)
Jerusalem Hotel, Aqaba (☎ 314815)
Jordan Flower Hotel, Aqaba (☎ 314377)
Nairoukh 1 Hotel, Aqaba (☎ 319284)
Al-Anbat Hotel, Wadi Musa (☎ 336265; fax 336888)
Mussa Spring Hotel, Wadi Musa (☎ 336310; fax 336910)
Government Rest House, Wadi Rum

Staying in the Bedouin camps around Wadi Rum is also OK provided you behave and dress appropriately (no bare flesh). However, single women travelling alone are inevitably seen as being available, so don't be surprised if you get amorous advances out in the sands under the stars! If you can't handle it, don't go alone.

Di Taylor, NOMADS

ENTERTAINMENT

Jordan is not exactly thumping with night life. The big hotels offer the usual expensive and often dull discos and nightclubs and occasionally present Arab musicians and belly dancing. The smart set and generally better off of Amman hang around the restaurants and cafés in Shmeisani or Abdoun, which can be quite busy, but almost everything is shut by about 11pm.

The bars in the bigger hotels are one exception to the rule and sometimes stay open quite late. There are also one or two discos open for a late night.

Amman has a few reasonable cinemas where you can catch comparatively recent movies that haven't been too badly mauled by the censors.

Getting There & Away

For general information about travel to and from Jordan, as well as advice on where to look for cheap tickets and taking your own vehicle, see the regional Getting There & Away chapter.

Jordan can be reached by air, overland from Israel, Syria, Iraq or Saudi Arabia and by sea from Egypt. Royal Jordanian, the national carrier, flies to many destinations in the Middle East, Europe, the USA and Asia.

AIR

Airports & Airlines

The modern Queen Alia international airport, about 35 km south of Amman, is the country's main gateway. You will find banking facilities open 24 hours a day and seven days a week. Although you should be able to change travellers' cheques and even get cash advances on Visa cards during the day, cash only may be exchanged from about 10 pm to 8 am. Postal, telephone and telex facilities are also available. There is a hotel information counter in the transit lounge. If you are getting a visa on arrival, try to have the exact change (the fees are posted at passport control, and some of the bank branches are located *before* passport control).

If you arrive at a crazy hour, there are some good seats for sleeping around the transit desk.

A former military airfield east of central Amman in Marka is used for flights to Aqaba and also the newly established Tel Aviv link. There are plans to direct Cairo and Damascus flights to this airport too.

Some direct charter flights serve Aqaba, particularly in winter, when pasty Europeans are ferried in for some sun treatment. There is talk of establishing a joint Jordanian-Israeli international airport to serve Aqaba and Eilat, but the idea remains on the drawing board for now.

North America

The cheapest way from the USA or Canada to Jordan is generally a return flight to London and a bucket-shop deal from there. That said, it is worth checking around carefully first. It might also work out cost effective to take a flight to Israel and complete the trip overland (or include Israel in the trip – bearing in mind the complications this can cause with onward travel to Syria and some other Arab countries).

Royal Jordanian (☎ 212-949 0050), flies from New York via Amsterdam. The cheapest quoted return fare is an Apex deal valid for up to two months and costing US$1300. The cheapest one-way ticket is US$789. Other airlines fly from New York via Europe to Amman. At the time of writing, about the cheapest one going was with Balkan Airlines (overnight layover in Sofia, Bulgaria) for US$598 (plus US$32 in taxes).

Royal Jordanian also have flights from Toronto and Montreal. The lowest fares from Toronto to Amman are C$1968 (not great value) one way and a two-month Apex return is far cheaper. Local reductions and special fares are available, which could bring the return fare down to little over C$1000.

The UK

Royal Jordanian (☎ 0171-734 2557), 177 Regent St, London W1R 7FB, flies direct to Amman from London every day except Monday. The one way flight costs UK£552. A cheap return valid for up to two months costs UK£535. As you might have guessed, this is not the cheapest way to fly, so you should look around. With most other airlines you will have to make connecting flights. All fares quoted here are exclusive of the UK£10 Air Passenger Duty.

About the cheapest low season fare going from London is with Olympic Airways, which is reasonable value at UK£237 for an open ticket valid for 12 months. Turkish Airlines has a similar low season fare of UK£242. If you're a student or under 26, you [illegible] Airways' return youth fare [illegible]esting.

[illegible] competitive are the low [illegible] with Cyprus Airways and Alitalia. Their tickets cost UK£297 and UK£293 respectively and are valid for up to three months.

If you want to leave in high season, which by most calculations starts up some time in March, most airlines will charge considerably more. Air France has a ticket valid for 12 months for UK£401 (via Paris). A summer fare ticket valid for six months with KLM comes in at UK£535.

A small UK-based airline, British Mediterranean, flies twice a week from Heathrow to Amman (and Damascus) via Beirut.

Continental Europe

KLM and Lufthansa are among the more popular Continental European airlines operating into Jordan. Travellers from neighbouring countries such as France tend to opt for these two as well, even though the flights generally entail picking up connections in Amsterdam and Frankfurt respectively.

It is usually possible to dig up flights from Athens and Istanbul for around US$150 one way to Amman.

North Africa & Middle East

There are daily flights with Royal Jordanian and EgyptAir between Amman and Cairo. The one way fare is JD78, or JD160 round trip. Flights connect Amman and Tunis on Wednesday and Sunday and the trip costs JD170 one way or double return. Several daily flights with various airlines link Amman and Damascus. The one way fare is JD43 and double for a return ticket.

The Royal Wings subsidiary of Royal Jordanian runs five flights a week from the Marka airport to Tel Aviv for JD50 (one way) and JD85 return. El Al also has a service to Amman.

It is, of course, much cheaper to go overland to Israel and Syria. As far as Egypt is concerned, the overland routes via Israel and the Sinai or the Aqaba-Nuweiba ferry are cheaper and more interesting alternatives to flying.

Australia & New Zealand

There are no direct connections between Australia or New Zealand and Jordan but STA Travel offers a fare of A$1800 return and A$1200 one way from the east coast of Australia with Qantas and Royal Jordanian. They regularly have specials in the market, however, starting at about A$1100 one way and A$1550 return. The fare can change depending on the date of travel and where you fly via – travelling with Qantas to Jakarta and Royal Jordanian onwards is usually cheaper than travelling via Bangkok or Singapore.

The full economy low season fare quoted by Royal Jordanian is A$2318 return and A$1461 one way.

Asia

Royal Jordanian flies to Singapore, Karachi and New Delhi. The quoted economy fare from New Delhi to Amman is Rs 16,410 one way and Rs 24,615 return (three month excursion). The quoted fare from Singapore to Amman is S$2426 one way and S$4852 return. From Karachi in Pakistan there are flights for Rs 13,440 one way and Rs 20,215 return (four month excursion). If you look around local travel agents, you should turn up hefty discounts on these fares and those with competing airlines.

LAND

Syria

Bus The only border crossing between Syria and Jordan is at Ramtha/Der'a and, as the traffic is heavy, it gets extremely crowded during the day.

Twice a day air-conditioned JETT (Jordan Express Tourism Transport) and Karnak buses (the Syrian government bus company) run between Amman and Damascus. The trip takes about seven hours depending on the border formalities and is the easiest way to make the crossing. It costs JD4.500 from Amman but only JD4 or US$5 from Damascus. You can't pay in Syrian pounds either way and you need to book in advance as demand often exceeds supply.

For more details see Getting There & Away in the Amman, North & West of Amman and Damascus chapters.

Train The famous Hejaz railway line built early this century to transport pilgrims to Medina from Damascus has been resurrected between Damascus and Amman. A slow diesel train with ancient carriages now operates once a week – some travellers have had the good fortune to have a steam engine for the Syrian leg, but this appears to be an exception rather than the rule. It leaves Amman on Monday at 8 am and returns the following Sunday. Tickets cost JD2.500 and you should count on a journey time of about 11 hours.

Should the peace process one day include Syria, plans for a modern Amman-Damascus line with a branch to Haifa (Israel) may become a reality.

Service Taxi The *servees* are slightly faster than the buses and run at all hours, although it is harder to find one in the evening. They usually get a far more thorough search at the border, so you often save no time at all. They leave from around the Abdali bus station in Amman – you can't miss the distinctive American-made yellow taxis – and from next to the Karnak bus station in Damascus. The trip costs JD5.500 or S£385.

There are competing service taxi companies down in Shabsough St that go to Damascus and other destinations. They also operate between Damascus and Irbid in northern Jordan for the same price.

Hitching It is possible to cross the Jordan-Syria border with a combination of local bus, walking and hitching. See Irbid (Jordan) and Der'a (Syria) for details.

Iraq

Bus In the wake of the Gulf War, Iraq, even if you could get a visa, is probably not a sensible place to go at the moment. The crackdown on Shiites in the south and Kurdish infighting in the north-east add ... the danger.

If you can and need to go, there are two daily JETT buses between Amman and Baghdad. They cost JD12, depart at 8.30 am and 2 pm and take about 14 hours.

Hijazi buses, which are much the same as JETT's, leave each day from the Abdali bus station at 1 pm and cost JD10.

Service Taxi The service taxis are faster than the buses, but over a long distance the bus is probably more comfortable. You'll find taxis for Baghdad around Abdali bus station and in Shabsough St in Downtown Amman, although demand is not so high.

Hitching If you are determined to go, the steady stream of trucks heading to Baghdad used to make hitching fairly easy, although drivers may be reluctant to be seen with foreigners now. From Amman, ask for a town bus from Raghadan bus station that will drop you near the highway to Azraq.

Saudi Arabia

Bus There are regular JETT and Saptco buses from Amman to Jeddah (10 am), Dammam (11 am) and Riyadh (11.30 am), all costing JD31 and taking up to 24 hours, depending on your destination. Buses also depart from Aqaba. Transport can be arranged to destinations beyond, such as Abu Dhabi and Kuwait. For direct JETT services to Kuwait, ask at the company's Marka office (☎ 894872). Hijazi has buses to Saudi Arabia for similar prices, and several other private companies around Abdali station sell long distance tickets of this type. Regular buses run from the JETT office in Aqaba for the same prices.

Unless you are a Muslim or doing business in Saudi Arabia, the hard part is getting a visa. The only ones dished out to tourists are transit visas, which sometimes allow you to travel along the Tapline (Trans Arabia Pipeline) in three days, but sometimes only let you fly in and out and spend a day in Riyadh.

The main land route into Saudi Arabia is along the highway south of Azraq, 103 km

... There are two other crossing ... on the coast of the Gulf of ... ra, the other further east via ...

Hitching This may be possible on the route from Azraq, but from Aqaba can be difficult as the cars are often full to bursting with people and their goods and chattels.

Israel & the West Bank

Peace with Israel and the setting up of the partially autonomous Palestine National Authority has created a totally new situation. There are now three border crossings. Private cars can now be taken across the northern and southern crossings. Israeli vehicles are required to change number plates when they enter Jordan, but no such restriction applies to Jordanian vehicles going the other way. Vehicles with plates from other countries should have no problem.

Wadi Araba This handy crossing (Arava to the Israelis) in the south of the country links Aqaba to Eilat. The border is open from 6.30 am to 10 pm Sunday to Thursday; 8 am to 8 pm Friday to Saturday. To get there from Aqaba you need to take a taxi (JD3) the 10 km to the border. Only about two km from central Eilat, you can simply walk in from the Israeli side, or catch bus No 16 for NIS4. Bus No 16 runs between Arava crossing and the Taba crossing into Egypt, via Eilat's central bus station. If coming to Jordan this way, there are service taxis to central Aqaba – they cost JD4.

If you come down from Jerusalem on the No 392 and you want to skip Eilat, ask the driver to let you off at the turn-off for the border, a short walk away.

A bus service between the two towns was due to begin operation in April 1996, but there was still no sign of it by the end of that month.

There are money changing facilities, phones and cafés on both sides of the border, and if you are coming from Israel the Jordanians will issue visas on the spot. This route makes a viable alternative to the Nuweiba ferry for heading into Egypt. Leaving Israel, there is an exit tax of NIS48.70. Going the other way the Jordanian tax is JD4.

Jisr Sheikh Hussein The northernmost Jordan River crossing, and perhaps the least convenient for most travellers, the Jisr (bridge) Sheikh Hussein links Beit She'an in Galilee with northern Jordan. If coming from Israel, get a Tiberias bus and change at Beit She'an. From here another bus takes you to the Israeli side for NIS8.40. The Israeli official name for this crossing point is Jordan Border. After passport formalities, a compulsory bus takes you to the other side for NIS3.

From the Jordanian side you can wait for a minibus to Irbid (300 fils) or get a taxi about three km to the main road, where you can try your luck flagging down minibuses.

The Jordanian exit tax is JD4, while the Israelis charge NIS48.70. The crossing is open the same hours as the Wadi Araba crossing, and you can obtain a Jordanian visa here.

Jisr al-Malek al-Hussein/Allenby Bridge Long the only crossing between Jordan and the West Bank (and hence tacitly Israel), this crossing over the Jordan River remains somewhat of an anomaly. The procedure is more straightforward than used to be the case, and you no longer require permits.

The border is open from 8 am to 10.30 pm Sunday to Thursday; from 8 am to 1 pm Friday and Saturday. You can catch the JETT bus from Amman at 6.30 am (JD6). The fee includes the short ride over the bridge. Or you can get a minibus (JD1) or service taxi (JD1.500) to the Jordanian frontier (JD2 going the other way) from Abdali bus station. The odd service taxi also connects from this border crossing to Irbid.

The ride to the Israeli side costs another JD1.500, and although extremely short can seem to last an eternity with repeated stops for passport checks. The bridge itself is rather disappointing, an unimpressive 30m long structure over what seems little more than a dribble of the River Jordan. It's not possible to walk, hitch or take a private car.

The historic oddity of this crossing has remained enshrined in the fact that, on leaving Jordan, you are not really considered to be leaving Jordan (you with me?). Prior to 1988 Jordan still laid claim to the West Bank as its own territory, and somehow this idea has remained in the approach to visas. If you wish to return to Jordan from Israel within the validity of your present Jordanian visa, you need only keep the stamped exit slip and present it on returning by the same crossing (it won't work at the other crossings). For this reason there is no Jordanian exit tax either. Going the other way, the Israeli exit tax is a hefty NIS83.50 (US$31), supposedly because you are paying to leave Israel *and* the Palestine National Authority's territory.

The Israeli passport control process can be a little wearying, with plenty of waiting and bag checking. There is a change booth on your way to the exit. Note that, if you are entering Jordan this way and intend to return to Israel, you must conserve the entrance form given to you by the Jordanians – they could well insist on you prolonging your stay in Jordan if you cannot present it.

Once outside you have two choices if you wish to proceed to Jerusalem. First there is the easy way – a *sherut* (direct share taxi) for NIS26 per person. These taxis arrive at a garage opposite the Damascus Gate in Jerusalem.

Since the Palestine National Authority was set up, the cheap Arab bus to Jerusalem of yore is history. You can now catch a bus to Jericho (Areeha) for NIS5.50. There you can take a service taxi for NIS20 a person to Bethany, just outside central Jerusalem – taxis with PNA plates are not allowed to enter Jerusalem proper. From Bethany you need to get a local service taxi to the Damascus Gate for NIS1.50.

Coming from Amman, you can be in Jerusalem by 10 am – but not every day is a lucky one.

Although known as the Allenby Bridge to the Israelis, the bridge is the Jisr al-Malek al-Hussein (King Hussein Bridge) to the Jordanians and Palestinians. Asking for the Allenby Bridge is likely to meet with blank stares. Although it can get quiet, the traffic through this crossing is pretty constant, so you shouldn't have too much problem with the public transport either way.

Note Middle Eastern politics being what they are, all the above information should be considered highly perishable. Things can alter at short notice and it is as well to be prepared for changes – at least in the procedural minutiae.

SEA

Egypt

Bus & Ferry You can book a ferry and bus right through to Cairo at the JETT bus office. The ticket costs about US$45, but you can pick up Cairo-bound buses on arrival at Nuweiba anyway.

Ferry & Fast Boat There is at least one daily car ferry and a fast (foot passenger only) boat between Aqaba and Nuweiba in Sinai. Until the Jordan-Israeli border was thrown open, the ferry was the only way (except by air) to get between Egypt and Jordan.

There is an Egyptian consulate in Aqaba where visas are issued with relatively little fuss on the same day. It's a lot easier than doing battle at the crowded embassy in Amman. Most nationalities can also obtain tourist visas on arrival at Nuweiba.

Beware of buying ferry tickets in Amman, as you may be charged for nonexistent 1st class places.

The car-ferry trip is meant to take three hours but can often take much longer. Occasionally, a southerly wind blows up that can oblige ferries coming to Nuweiba to wait until it subsides, but the problem is more likely to be chaos at one port or the other. Although some travellers have reported the luxury of travelling on a near-empty boat, the more common experience is of ferries packed beyond capacity. Be prepared for a trip that could last as long as eight hours.

The fast turbo-catamaran is a new beast on this route, and on a good day takes just one hour to complete the trip.

The worst time for travelling is just after the *Hajj*, when Aqaba fills up with *Hajjis* (pilgrims) returning home from Mecca to

Egypt and all points west with their overloaded cars. At the peak, they sometimes put on two extra boats, and although foot passengers should have little problem getting a ticket, the delays and confusion are a rude introduction to the bureaucratic frustrations that await in Egypt.

For details on ticket prices see the Aqaba Getting There & Away section.

Saudi Arabia

Before the Gulf War it was possible to travel between Aqaba and Jeddah by boat, but this service had not been resumed at the time of writing.

LEAVING JORDAN

You will be stamped out and, if you have a single-entry visa and wish to return, will require a new visa, regardless of how long you have been in Jordan. This, however, does not apply to the West Bank.

Departure Tax

There are three departure taxes from Jordan: JD4 across land borders (except to the West Bank); JD6 from Aqaba by sea; and JD10 by air. Note that you are not supposed to pay the airport departure tax if you are in Jordan less than 72 hours. If this is the case, fill out a transit card and save yourself some money.

ORGANISED TOURS

If money is not an object and time is, a number of organisations offer guided tour possibilities to Jordan. For English speakers, there are quite a few based in the UK, although travel agents or Royal Jordanian offices in other countries should be able to put you on the trail of local operators.

To get an idea, Prospect Art Tours Ltd (☎ 0181-995 2151/2163), 454-458 Chiswick High Rd, London W4 5TT, organises nine-day guided tours from UK£1250.

The Imaginative Traveller, which has offices around the world including in the USA, the UK, Australia, Canada, New Zealand and South Africa, offers various programmes of differing duration in Jordan. Costs vary depending on season and country of departure.

Jasmin Tours (☎ 01628-531121), High St, Cookham, Maidenhead, Berks SL6 9SQ, has a wide programme of tour possibilities to Jordan. A couple of these cover Jordan only from six to eight days and cost anything from around UK£700 to UK£1200, depending on the season and accommodation option. A series of other tours ranging up to 13 days combine Jordan or some of its main sights (such as Petra and Jerash) with Syria, Israel, or the Sinai peninsula in Egypt.

British Museum Traveller (☎ 0171-323 8895), 46 Bloomsbury St, London WS1B 3QQ, offers a unique tour opportunity to the museum's site at Tell as-Sa'idiyyeh for a week (UK£825).

The programmes on such trips are usually fairly tight, leaving little room for roaming around on your own, but they take much of the hassle off your plate. As there are quite a few tour operators, it pays to shop around to see what suits you. Check itinerary details, accommodation, who does the ticketing, visa and other documentation footwork, insurance and tour conditions, carefully.

Warning

The information in this chapter is particularly vulnerable to change: prices for international travel are volatile, routes are introduced and cancelled, schedules change, special deals come and go, and rules and visa requirements are amended. Airlines and governments seem to take a perverse pleasure in making price structures and regulations as complicated as possible. You should check directly with the airline or a travel agent to make sure you understand how a fare (and ticket you may buy) works. In addition, the travel industry is highly competitive and there are many lurks and perks.

The upshot of this is that you should get opinions, quotes and advice from as many airlines and travel agents as possible before you part with your hard-earned cash. The details given in this chapter should be regarded as pointers and are not a substitute for your own careful, up-to-date research. ■

Getting Around

AIR

Domestic Air Services

Being such a small country there is hardly any need for an internal air network, but Royal Wings, a subsidiary of Royal Jordanian, runs 50 seater aircraft daily from Marka airport near Amman to Aqaba. Royal Jordanian international flights also occasionally connect the two. For details see Getting Around under Amman and Aqaba.

BUS

There are a few small bus companies, but as yet no serious competition for the state-run JETT company has emerged on the country's main routes, despite the decision to revoke JETT's monopoly in 1995.

JETT Bus

The 150 enormous blue and white buses belonging to the JETT bus company service limited routes within the country and run charter tours. Buses run from Amman to Aqaba, King Hussein Bridge (Jisr al-Malek al-Hussein), Petra and Hammamat Ma'in.

See Getting There & Away in the Amman chapter for details of destinations, transport routes and ticket prices.

Bus/Minibus

Large private buses, usually air-conditioned, run north from Amman to Irbid (850 fils) and south to Aqaba (JD2).

All smaller towns are connected by 20 seat minibuses. These leave when full and on some routes operate infrequently. The correct fare is nearly always posted in Arabic somewhere inside the front of the bus. If you can see a sign with (for most shorter trips) a three digit figure, you've probably found the price in fils, so it pays to learn the Arabic numerals. Ask the other passengers what to pay, although if you *are* being ripped off – it happens rarely – they may side with the bus operators.

You sometimes have to pay full fare even if you are not going to the end of the line, or you pick the ride up along its route. However, they usually work out a lower rate based on the distance you're travelling. As a rule, it's sensible anyway to establish the fare before taking the ride.

TRAIN

Goods trains use the Hejaz railway line south of Amman and the line built to take the phosphate from Al-Hesa to Aqaba. There are no internal passenger services.

SERVICE TAXI

By far the most popular mode of transport is the service taxi. These are usually Peugeot 504 or 505 station wagons with seven seats or Mercedes sedans with five seats.

They operate on most routes and because of the limited number of seats, it usually doesn't take long for one to fill up. They cost up to twice as much as the minibuses but are faster as they stop less along the way to pick up or set down passengers.

CAR & MOTORCYCLE

Road Rules

Vehicles drive on the right-hand side of the road in Jordan. Rules are not always given great attention by locals, and the police tend to be fairly indulgent towards foreigners so long as they do nothing serious. The prudent driver should have little trouble, but take particular care in built-up places, where people and cars tend to jostle for space. Note also that scant regard is paid to lane divisions, and use of the indicator seems to be an optional extra. Horn-honking, on the other hand, is a national past-time.

The general speed limit inside built-up areas is 50 km/h, increasing to 70 km/h on multi-lane highways in Amman. On the open road, the general speed limit is 90 km/h, or 110 km/h on the Desert Highway. Roads are generally not bad.

Most places you are likely to be heading

for are signposted in English as well as Arabic, although there are occasional exceptions to this rule.

Rental

Most things in Jordan are expensive and hire cars are no exception, but if there are several of you to split the cost it can be a good way of seeing a bit of the country, especially the desert castles, some of which are not serviced by public transport. Other areas where a car can come in handy are down the Wadi Araba and around the Dead Sea.

You'll find any number of rental agencies in Amman and a few in Aqaba. The smaller companies can be substantially cheaper than the international crowds like Budget, Hertz and Avis. See Amman and Aqaba for details.

You'll be lucky to find a small car with unlimited km for much under JD25 a day with a three day minimum. Limited-km deals work out to be much more expensive if you intend to do more than 100 km per day. They cost from about JD20 per day plus 50 to 80 fils for every extra km.

Note that although insurance is usually included, you will generally be liable for around JD200 excess in case of accident. You may also be asked for a deposit of up to JD300, sometimes not until you've all but signed on the dotted line. If you spoke on the phone before arranging anything and no mention was made of it, tell them you haven't got that kind of money and that you'll go elsewhere; sometimes they will relent. Also, watch out for the unwritten clause that says you also pay daily rental for the length of time the car is off the road due to an accident – in addition to the excess you pay.

Long-term rentals (a week or more) generally come in more cheaply per day. At the time of writing hire cars could not be taken into neighbouring countries.

Some hire-car places will drop the car at your hotel. You can also hire cars with drivers if you want but there is really no need as the driving is relatively easy.

You can pay with credit card, but most companies will slap a 5% fee on top of the rental costs. Cash rules in this case.

Petrol

There is no trouble getting petrol in the towns, but stations are scarce even along main roads. *Benzin 'adi* (regular) costs 220 fils (about US35c) a litre, and the less frequently available *mumtaz, khas* or *aka* (super) 300 fils a litre. Forget about unleaded petrol. Diesel is available at about 110 fils a litre.

BICYCLE

Cycling is an option in Jordan but not necessarily a fun one (and some travellers have reported difficulty getting their bikes into Jordan, particularly from Israel). The desert in summer is not a good place to indulge in any kind of movement. Cycling north or south (most travelling will be done in those directions) can be hard work too. There is a strong prevailing wind from the west that can wear you down. Bring plenty of spare parts.

Bicycles can travel by air. You *can* take them to pieces and put them in a bike bag or box, but it's much easier simply to wheel your bike to the check-in desk, where it should be treated as a piece of baggage. You may have to remove the pedals and turn the handlebars sideways so that it takes up less space in the aircraft's hold; check with the airline well in advance, preferably before you pay for your ticket.

HITCHING

Hitching is never entirely safe in any country in the world, and we don't recommend it. Travellers who decide to hitch should understand that they are taking a small but potentially serious risk. People who do choose to hitch will be safer if they travel in pairs and let someone know where they are planning to go.

Hitching is definitely feasible in Jordan. The traffic varies a lot from place to place but you generally don't have to wait long for a lift on main routes.

Some drivers will pick a passenger up as a way of subsidising their own trip. If you want to avoid a possibly unpleasant situation when you get out, ask beforehand if payment is expected and if so, establish how much they want. Otherwise, simply offer a small amount when you get out.

Make sure you have a hat and some water to fight the heat if you have to wait a while for a lift. Hassles when hitching are rare, but women travelling alone should definitely not hitch.

LOCAL TRANSPORT

The Airports

You can reach central Amman by local bus and taxi, or rent a car at the Budget or Avis desks at the airport. Service taxis connect Amman's minor Marka airfield with the centre.

Taxis connect central Aqaba with its local airport.

Bus

Amman has an efficient and cheap public bus network but none of the buses have the destination in English (although some have the number), so unless you can read Arabic or know which one to catch, their usefulness is limited.

Service Taxi

Amman is also well served by service taxis which, like buses, run along set routes through the city, and these are by far the best way of getting around. They too have nothing posted in English but are a lot easier to track down than the buses.

The city service taxis are generally white, but the important feature is the *white* panel on the driver's and front passenger's door with the number and route in Arabic. They wait until full at their terminus stop and will drop you wherever you want along their route and pick up other passengers along the way. You pay the full fare wherever you alight.

Irbid also has a couple of service taxi routes.

Taxi

Outside Amman and Irbid you'll have to walk, which poses no problems, or take one of the many regular taxis. These tend to be yellow but are distinguished from the service taxis by the *green* panel on the front doors. They are equipped with meters and the drivers usually speak a fair amount of English, especially in Amman. After 8 pm they charge up to 20% more.

ORGANISED TOURS

The only scheduled tours are operated by JETT from Amman to Petra and Hammamat Ma'in. They are really only for those who have limited time in Amman and want to see something of these two sites. The drive to Petra takes three hours' each way, which doesn't leave much time for sightseeing.

Only a few of the multitude of travel agents in Downtown Amman will try to help you put together your own tour; some of those are in or near the big hotels. Beware of the latter. Royal Tours (☎ 644267), a subsidiary of Royal Jordanian with offices in the InterContinental Hotel in Amman, will put you in a chauffeur-driven car for a few days and work out an itinerary (as hectic as you please) to cover sites from Jerash in the north to Petra and Wadi Rum in the south. They book you (and your driver) into hotels (three-star at least) and take into account a mile of 'extras'. A typical tour like this lasting three days would cost at least US$140 for car and driver alone, and you may find yourself being put in a car with other people without being told so in advance! If you have a large enough group you can hire a bus with them instead, and the cost comes down. Royal Tours also does a range of half and full-day excursions from Amman.

Another such tour operator is Grand Travel (☎ 690401), just behind the Housing Bank Centre in Shmeisani, Amman. A sample of their quoted prices per person for car hire from Amman with an English-speaking driver is: US$40 for a half-day in Jerash (including lunch); US$45 for a half-day at the Dead Sea, Madaba and Mt Nebo; US$85 for a full day in Petra.

A reasonable daily rate for car and driver seems to be about JD40. You might also try Jerusalem Express Travel (☎ 622151) on Al-Malek al-Hussein St, Amman, or Jordan

Regular Transport (☎ 622652), near Abdali bus station in Amman. If you just organise the car through the agent, you can then settle on hotels of your choice, and save yourself a lot of money along the way.

There is another option – bargain with regular taxi drivers. You can sometimes convince them to go just about anywhere for the day for about JD25 to JD30.

Amman

Amman will certainly never win any prizes for most interesting city in the world – the town centre, known as Downtown is a busy, chaotic jumble of traffic, and just crossing the street is an achievement. Nevertheless, Amman is really quite pleasant and is the hub of all roads in Jordan so it's highly unlikely that you will not pass through it.

A village of about 2000 people at the turn of the century, Amman has grown incredibly in recent years and now sprawls over a large area. Surveying the scene from atop one of the hills ('*jebels*') the city is built on, it's easy to get the impression that it is nothing more than an interminable spread of thousands of concrete blocks.

On closer inspection, however, the situation is not quite so dire. There are some leafy, agreeable areas in the city and, while there is no feeling of being in one of the ancient metropolises of the Orient (since Roman times Amman had never been much more than a village), Downtown has a good deal of atmosphere. It teems with locals hunting through the flea markets, food stalls and gold souqs; its old cafés hum with the activity of card and backgammon players hunched over teas and smoking nargilehs, and over it all, like clockwork, waft the mesmerising tones of the eternal call to prayer. And there are just enough leftovers from the city's distant Roman past, particularly the main theatre, to keep you occupied for a half day's sightseeing.

Amman is also one of the friendliest cities you're likely to visit. Many residents are Palestinians who fled from the area west of the Jordan River during the wars of 1948 and 1967. They are generally well educated, speak a fair amount of English and are happy to chat with a foreigner. In almost every encounter a Jordanian (or Palestinian – although most hold Jordanian passports, the Palestinians are proud of their separate identity) will greet you with 'Welcome in Jordan', and you get the feeling they really mean it.

History

Excavations in and around Amman have turned up finds from as early as 3500 BC. Occupation of the town, called Rabbath Ammon in the Old Testament, has been continuous and objects found in a tomb dating back to the Bronze Age show that the town was actively involved in trade with Greece, Syria, Cyprus and Mesopotamia.

Biblical references are many and reveal that by 1200 BC Rabbath Ammon was the capital of the Ammonites. During David's reign, he sent Joab at the head of Israelite armies to besiege Rabbath, after having been insulted by the Ammonite king Nahash.

It seems David was not the most benevolent of rulers. Before capturing Rabbath he sent Uriah the Hittite 'in the forefront of the hottest battle' (II Samuel 11) where he was bound to be killed, simply because David had taken a liking to Uriah's wife Bethsheba. And after taking the town David burnt the inhabitants alive in a brick kiln (II Samuel 12).

The town continued to flourish and supplied David with weapons in his ongoing wars. His successor, Solomon, erected a shrine in Jerusalem to the Ammonite god Molech. From here on, the only Biblical references to Rabbath are prophecies of its destruction at the hands of the Babylonians, who did in fact take over but did not destroy the town.

The history of Amman between then (circa 585 BC) and the time of the Ptolemies of Egypt is unclear. Ptolemy Philadelphus (283-246 BC) rebuilt the city during his reign and it was named Philadelphia after him. The Ptolemy dynasty was succeeded in turn by the Seleucids and, briefly, by the Nabataeans, before Amman was taken by Herod around 30 BC and so fell under the sway of Rome. The city, which even before Herod's arrival had felt Rome's influence as a member of the semi-autonomous Decapolis (a kind of loose commercial union that included Jerash and Gadara, the present-day

JORDAN

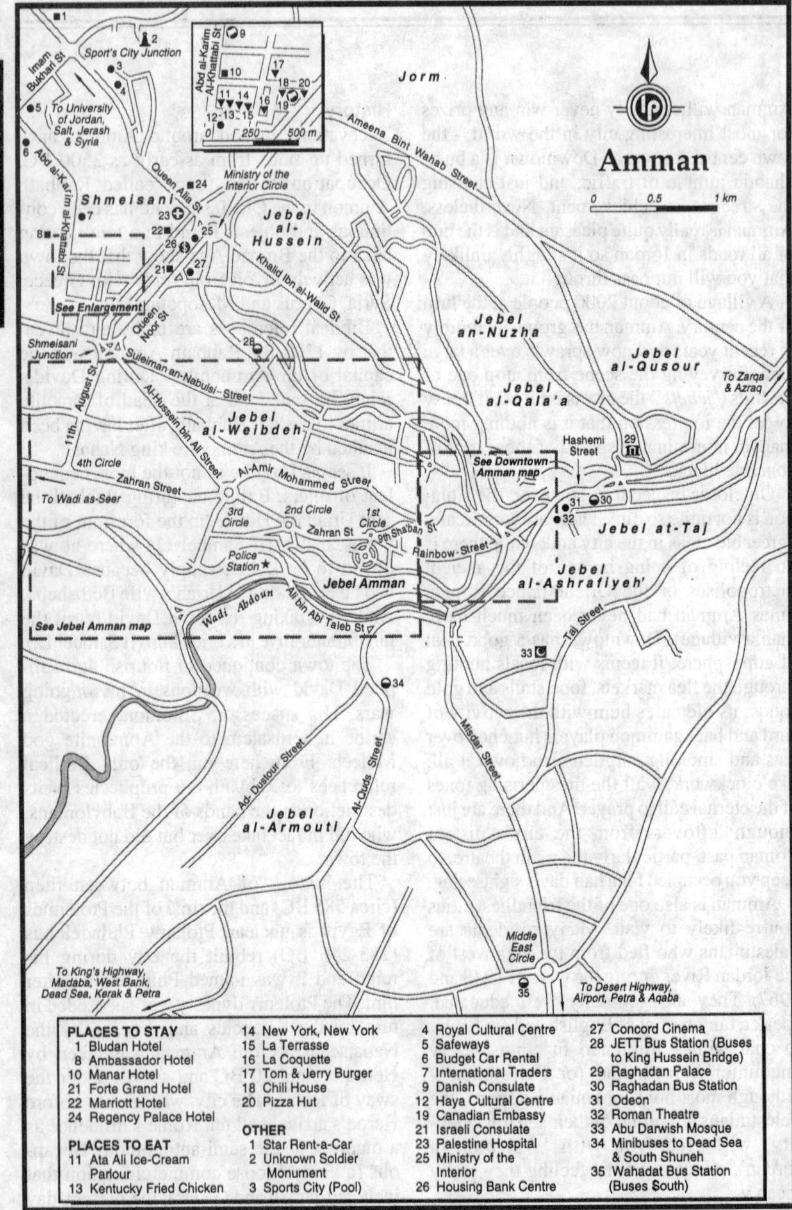
Amman
0 0.5 1 km
Jorm
Sport's City Junction
Imam Bukhari St
To University of Jordan, Salt, Jerash & Syria
Abd al-Karim al-Khattabi St
Ameena Bint Wahab Street
Ministry of the Interior Circle
Queen Alia St
Shmeisani
Jebel al-Hussein
Khalid Ibn al-Walid St
See Enlargement
Queen Noor St
Shmeisani Junction
Jebel an-Nuzha
Jebel al-Qusour
To Zarqa & Azraq
Jebel al-Qala'a
Suleiman an-Nabulsi Street
Al-Hussein bin Ali Street
11th August St
Jebel al-Weibdeh
4th Circle
Zahran Street
To Wadi as-Seer
Al-Amir Mohammed Street
3rd Circle
2nd Circle
1st Circle
Zahran St
9th Sha'ban St
Rainbow Street
Police Station
Jebel Amman
Hashemi Street
See Downtown Amman map
Jebel at-Taj
Jebel al-Ashrafiyeh'
Wadi Abdoun
Ali bin Abi Taleb St
See Jebel Amman map
Taj Street
Misdar Street
Ad-Dustour Street
Al-Quds Street
Jebel al-Armouti
Middle East Circle
To King's Highway, Madaba, West Bank, Dead Sea, Kerak & Petra
To Desert Highway, Airport, Petra & Aqaba
Abd al-Karim Al-Khattabi St
0 250 500 m
PLACES TO STAY
1 Bludan Hotel
8 Ambassador Hotel
10 Manar Hotel
21 Forte Grand Hotel
22 Marriott Hotel
24 Regency Palace Hotel
PLACES TO EAT
11 Ata Ali Ice-Cream Parlour
13 Kentucky Fried Chicken
14 New York, New York
15 La Terrasse
16 La Coquette
17 Tom & Jerry Burger
18 Chili House
20 Pizza Hut
OTHER
1 Star Rent-a-Car
2 Unknown Soldier Monument
3 Sports City (Pool)
4 Royal Cultural Centre
5 Safeways
6 Budget Car Rental
7 International Traders
9 Danish Consulate
12 Haya Cultural Centre
19 Canadian Embassy
21 Israeli Consulate
23 Palestine Hospital
25 Ministry of the Interior
26 Housing Bank Centre
27 Concord Cinema
28 JETT Bus Station (Buses to King Hussein Bridge)
29 Raghadan Palace
30 Raghadan Bus Station
31 Odeon
32 Roman Theatre
33 Abu Darwish Mosque
34 Minibuses to Dead Sea & South Shuneh
35 Wahadat Bus Station (Buses South)

The Decapolis

The Roman commercial cities of the Middle East first became known as the Decapolis sometime in the 1st century AD. By this time the network of trading centres had been in existence for nearly a century. Despite the etymology of the word, it seems that the Decapolis consisted of more than 10 cities. No one knows for certain the reason behind such a grouping – in all likelihood the association of the cities served a double function: to unite the Roman possessions and to enhance commerce. The cities were linked by paved roads that allowed wagons and other traffic to circulate rapidly. At Umm Qais and Jerash, the ruts carved by these wagons can still be seen in the stones of the city streets. The influence of the Decapolis cities stretched from the Gulf of Aqaba to Syria. The cities flourished during the period of Roman dominance in the east, but fell into decline with the dawn of the Omayyad era. Afterwards, the choice of Baghdad as the centre of the Muslim world dealt the Decapolis a final blow. ■

Umm Qais), was totally replanned in typically grand Roman style.

Philadelphia was the seat of Christian bishops in the early Byzantine period, but the city declined and fell to the Sassanian Persians (or Sassanids) about 614 AD. Their rule was short-lived, collapsing before the forces of Islam around 630 AD.

At the time of the Muslim invasion, the town was still alive and kicking, and living on the caravan trade. Its fortunes declined and some believe it was reduced to a prison town for exiled princes and notables. It was nothing more than a sad little village when a colony of Circassians was resettled here in 1878. It became the centre of Transjordan when Emir Abdullah made it his headquarters in the early 1920s.

In 1950 it was officially declared the capital of the Hashemite kingdom, and since then has gone ahead in leaps and bounds to become a modern bustling city, with a population of more than a million.

Orientation

Amman was born on seven major hills (like Rome) but today spreads across 19 jebels. It can be mighty confusing to begin with. Downtown is at the bottom of four of these hills, which means that wherever you want to go from there is up, and these hills are steep! The centre of Downtown is the area immediately around the King Hussein Mosque (built in 1924 and also known as the Al-Husseini Mosque). The cheap hotels are clustered in this area, about a half-hour walk downhill from the bus stations in Abdali where most travellers arrive.

The only way to make any sense of Amman in a short time is to pick out the major landmarks on the jebels. Most streets are signposted, but unfortunately the official name often means nothing to the locals. Just to note one example, Abu Bakr as-Sadiq St is so named on the street sign and official maps, but is actually known to everyone as Rainbow St. Under the circumstances, asking for directions to a street is generally useless.

From the citadel on top of Jebel al-Qala'a you have a view of the surrounds and can try to get your bearings. The main hill is Jebel Amman, where you'll find most of the embassies and some of the flash hotels. The traffic roundabouts on Jebel Amman are numbered as you leave Downtown, so you go from 1st Circle up to 7th Circle and beyond. Just to confuse matters, the circles from 4th on are not circles at all but regular junctions with traffic lights. The main landmark on Jebel Amman is the Jordan Tower Centre just below 3rd Circle – it's the high, circular white tower topped by a 'crown'.

Jebel al-Hussein is the next one to identify, as there are two major bus stations here. It's north-west of the citadel and the Housing Bank Centre sticks out a mile – it's the tall, terraced building with the creepers hanging down the sides. Closer to Downtown, also on Jebel al-Hussein, is the big, blue dome of the spanking new King Abdullah Mosque. It's also easy to identify as it's one of the few buildings that is not grey or white! Close to the mosque are the Abdali and JETT bus stations.

To the south of Jebel al-Qala'a is Jebel

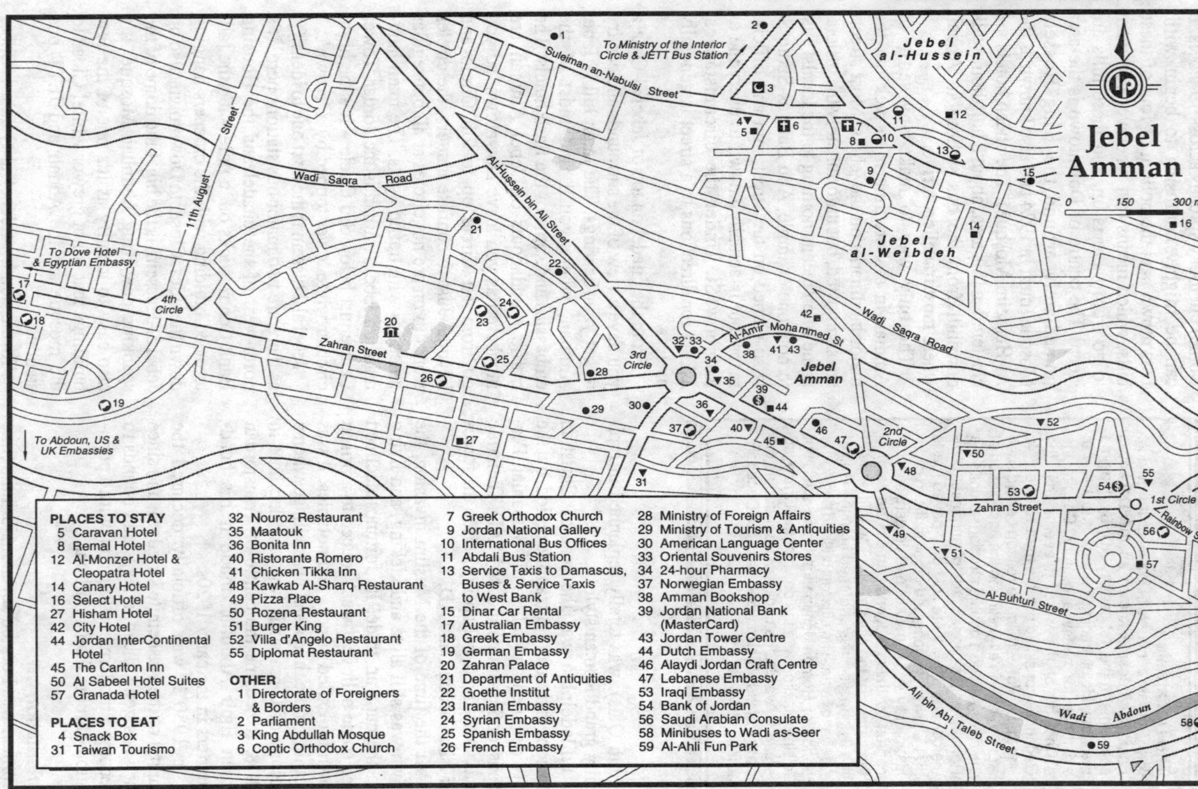
Jebel Amman
0 150 300 m
Jebel al-Hussein
Jebel al-Weibdeh
Jebel Amman
To Ministry of the Interior Circle & JETT Bus Station
Suleiman an-Nabulsi Street
Al-Hussein bin Ali Street
Wadi Saqra Road
Zahran Street
Al-Amir Mohammed St
1st Circle
2nd Circle
3rd Circle
4th Circle
Rainbow St
Al-Buhturi Street
Ali bin Abi Taleb Street
Wadi Abdoun
11th August Street
To Dove Hotel & Egyptian Embassy
To Abdoun, US & UK Embassies
PLACES TO STAY
5 Caravan Hotel
8 Remal Hotel
12 Al-Monzer Hotel & Cleopatra Hotel
14 Canary Hotel
16 Select Hotel
27 Hisham Hotel
42 City Hotel
44 Jordan InterContinental Hotel
45 The Carlton Inn
50 Al Sabeel Hotel Suites
57 Granada Hotel
PLACES TO EAT
4 Snack Box
31 Taiwan Tourismo
32 Nouroz Restaurant
35 Maatouk
36 Bonita Inn
40 Ristorante Romero
41 Chicken Tikka Inn
48 Kawkab Al-Sharq Restaurant
49 Pizza Place
50 Rozena Restaurant
51 Burger King
52 Villa d'Angelo Restaurant
55 Diplomat Restaurant
OTHER
1 Directorate of Foreigners & Borders
2 Parliament
3 King Abdullah Mosque
6 Coptic Orthodox Church
7 Greek Orthodox Church
9 Jordan National Gallery
10 International Bus Offices
11 Abdali Bus Station
13 Service Taxis to Damascus, Buses & Service Taxis to West Bank
15 Dinar Car Rental
17 Australian Embassy
18 Greek Embassy
19 German Embassy
20 Zahran Palace
21 Department of Antiquities
22 Goethe Institut
23 Iranian Embassy
24 Syrian Embassy
25 Spanish Embassy
26 French Embassy
28 Ministry of Foreign Affairs
29 Ministry of Tourism & Antiquities
30 American Language Center
33 Oriental Souvenirs Stores
34 24-hour Pharmacy
37 Norwegian Embassy
38 Amman Bookshop
39 Jordan National Bank (MasterCard)
43 Jordan Tower Centre
44 Dutch Embassy
46 Alaydi Jordan Craft Centre
47 Lebanese Embassy
53 Iraqi Embassy
54 Bank of Jordan
56 Saudi Arabian Consulate
58 Minibuses to Wadi as-Seer
59 Al-Ahli Fun Park

al-Ashrafiyyeh. It's the tallest and steepest of the jebels and has the curious Abu Darwish Mosque on the top, built in alternating layers of black and white stone. To get to the top for an excellent view, take a No 25 or 26 service taxi from behind the Church of the Saviour.

Some street name variations are worth bearing in mind in Downtown. Al-Malek al-Hussein St is sometimes known in English as King Hussein St. The same can be said of the following: Al-Malek Faisal St (King Faisal St) and Al-Amir Mohammed St (Prince Mohammed St).

Information

Tourist Office There's no tourist office in Amman but you can go to the Ministry of Tourism (☎ 642311) just up from 3rd Circle. It has a few glossy brochures (the most useful called *Visitor's Guide)* and sometimes has acceptable maps of Jordan and Amman. Unless you want a few free wall posters, it's not really worth the effort. To get there from Downtown, catch a No 3 service taxi from near the Rhum Continental Hotel and get out at the last stop, a block south of 3rd Circle. The ministry is about a block west across the main road.

Your Guide to Amman is a free monthly booklet that lists embassies, airlines, travel agencies and car rental companies and has other useful and not-so-useful information. Pick up a copy at any of the airline offices or travel agents.

Visa Extensions If you plan to stay in Jordan more than 15 days, you are supposed to register with the police. This effectively means applying for a visa extension of two to three months. In Amman you need to go to the Muhajireen police station (ask for the 'Markaz Amn Muhajireen'). You can get service taxi No 35 from near the Church of the Saviour – ask where to be let off, as you could easily find yourself disappearing well away from your intended destination. The relevant office at the station is open from 10 am to 1 pm Saturday to Thursday. If you want further extensions, you may be sent to the Directorate of Foreigners & Borders, in Suleiman an-Nabulsi St.

Foreign Embassies See the Jordan Facts for the Visitor chapter for addresses of foreign embassies in Amman, and for information on visas.

Money There are numerous banks all over Downtown as well as in Jebel Amman and Shmeisani. The rates don't vary but the commissions and other charges can. For travellers' cheques, the best place is probably the Bank of Jordan branch on 1st Circle. The one on Al-Malek Faisal St in Downtown is also fine.

There are several places where you can use a Visa card for cash advances, including the InterContinental and Mariott hotels and several banks in Shmeisani. You can use MasterCard and cash Eurocheques at the British Bank of the Middle East – there is a branch on Al-Malek al-Hussein St, Downtown. The same bank also has a reliable ATM for Visa and MasterCard. If your card is swallowed, call ☎ 669123. See the Jordan Facts for the Visitor chapter for more details.

The American Express agent is International Traders (☎ 607014) in Shmeisani, opposite the Ambassador Hotel in Abd al-Karim al-Khattabi St. The office is open from 8 am to noon and 3 to 6 pm daily except Friday. It is not on any public transport route, so you'll have to take a taxi or walk from the last stop on the No 7 service-taxi route.

Thomas Cook is represented by Space Tourism & Travel (☎ 668069) in Shmeisani, behind the Haya Cultural Centre. See Money in the Jordan Facts for the Visitor chapter as well.

Post The central post office is in Downtown, on Al-Amir Mohammed St. The poste restante mail is kept in a box on the counter directly in front of you as you walk in – you just look through the lot. If there are bulky items for you, a slip is usually placed in the box for you to pick out and hand in. Some of the employees don't seem to be aware of the significance of these slips, so you should insist that there must be a parcel stashed away there for you until someone who knows what's going on comes to your aid. The office is open from 7 am to 7 pm (5 pm in winter) daily except Friday, when it closes at 1.30 pm.

The post office will also send telegrams and faxes.

You can also have mail forwarded to the American Express representative in Amman. Technically you should be a customer, which means having cheques or a credit card, although generally they don't seem to mind one way or the other. See Money earlier in this chapter.

Parcels The parcel post office is in the same street as the telephone office, but closer to the corner of Al-Amir Mohammed St. It looks more like a shop-front than a post office and is opposite a rear entrance to the main post office. The parcel office is open from 8 am to 2 pm.

Posting a parcel is time-consuming but simple enough, although the asking prices are out of this world (see Post in the Jordan Facts for the Visitor chapter). Take the parcel *unwrapped* to the parcels office, from where you'll be directed to the customs office on the 1st floor of the main post office. After a perfunctory search it is cleared and you're sent back to the parcel office, where the parcel is weighed and you pack it. Cotton is provided for wrapping.

Telephone The main office for international telephone calls ('*centraal*') is in the street up behind the post office, opposite the Al-Khayyam Cinema. It's open from 7.30 am to 11 pm daily.

For details on the cost of international calls from Amman see the Jordan Facts for the Visitor chapter. From 10 pm, the rates are cheaper. Be prepared for a bit of a crush, though.

You need to fill out a yellow sheet (it's in Arabic) with your name, the destination city and country, and the number you want to call. You specify a theoretical amount of time for the call and attach an appropriate sum of money. If your call goes over you pay the difference; if it goes under they give you the change – and they do, so don't worry about handing over too much.

You can send telexes from the telephone office, but not faxes.

International calls and faxes can also be made from the collection of little communications offices that have sprung up in direct competition to the phone office – on the same street. Check around as their rates vary. They generally open longer hours (at least one claims to stay open around the clock).

International calls made from five star hotels are charged at more extortionate rates.

Travel Agencies There is a plethora of travel agencies dotted around the city, with a crowd of them along the Downtown end of Al-Malek al-Hussein St. Although some claim to organise tours within Jordan, the bulk of them appear to be little more than ticketing agents for international air travel.

It is inadvisable to book sea passage to Nuweiba (Egypt) with these agents, as some travellers have reported paying for 1st class cabins that don't exist. If you can, simply buy a ticket in Aqaba.

For land travel you are better off going to the JETT offices (see the Jordan Getting Around chapter and Getting There & Away later in this chapter) or using other buses and service taxis. For more information on tours see the Jordan Getting Around chapter.

Bookshops There are some bookshops in Amman worth mentioning, but don't hold your breath about any of them. The most irritating thing is that none seem to have the full range of available books on Jordan – if you want something specific, you may have to trudge around a few. Bear in mind that some of the souvenir shops in hotels and near the Amphitheatre sometimes have just as good a range of books.

Possibly the best bookshop is the one at the Jordan InterContinental Hotel, which has a range of books on Jordan and the Middle East, not a bad selection of fiction and foreign press. It is the best pick of the hotel bookshops, although the Marriott's has some different material on Jordan.

The Jordan Distribution Agency (☎ 630191) is the closest to Downtown, just where 9 Sha'ban and Al-Amir Mohammed Sts meet. It has a reasonable range of books on the Middle East, a small stock of fiction and some foreign press. The Amman Bookshop (☎ 644013), just below 3rd Circle, has just been refurbished and offers an excellent range of English language books. The Majdalawi Masterpieces Bookshop (☎ 658859) is an excellent bookshop which stocks mainly children's books. The Jordan Book Centre (☎ 606882), Al-Jubeiha, has a great stock of (mainly American) books: both hardcover and paperback. The University Bookshop (☎ 606271), Luweibeh Gardens St has an extensive range of books on all subjects, including Lonely Planet titles. It is a little out of town, but worth a visit.

Cultural Centres & Libraries The British Council (☎ 636147) on Rainbow St (or Abu Bakr as-Sadiq St), Jebel Amman, east of 1st Circle, has a good library, current newspapers, and regularly shows films. The library is open from 10 am to 6.30 pm Saturday to Monday; from 10 am to 8 pm Tuesday and Wednesday and from 10 am to 1.30 pm on Thursday.

The American Center (☎ 822471) also has a library (open from 8 am to 7 pm Sunday to Thursday), newspapers and a video library. It shows feature films twice a week, but is a little inaccessible as it's in the embassy block way out in Abdoun.

The Centre Culturel Français (☎ 637009) is by the roundabout at the top of Jebel al-Weibdeh, the hill directly behind the post office. It is open from 9 am to 1 pm and 4 to 7 pm Saturday to Thursday. It also has a library and organises films.

For German speakers, the Goethe Institut (☎ 641993) is the place to go. It is only open from 9 am to 12.30 pm Saturday to Wednesday and again for an hour from 5.45 pm on Saturday.

The Spanish Instituto Cervantes (☎ 624049) is behind the Jordan InterContinental Hotel near 3rd Circle. It opens from 9 am to 1 pm and 4 to 7 pm Sunday to Thursday.

Medical Services You could choose worse places to get ill, as Amman has more than 20 hospitals. Among the better are the Hussein Medical Centre in Wadi as-Seer (☎ 813 813/32) and the Palestine Hospital in University St, Shmeisani (☎ 607071). *Your Guide to Amman* contains a complete list of hospitals and doctors on night duty throughout the capital (a list of such doctors also appears daily in the *Jordan Times)*, as well as 24-hour pharmacies (there's one on 3rd Circle).

Emergency

In case of emergency, you can contact the police (☎ 192 or 621111). For an ambulance or first aid call ☎ 193. The fire department can be contacted on ☎ 199. The number for the traffic police is ☎ 656390. In the case of a car accident, call them on ☎ 896390. ■

Roman Theatre

Amman does not have a lot to offer in terms of sights, but a handful of buildings, museums and the ruins on the citadel testify to the city's long history. One can only imagine what Roman Philadelphia must have been like in its heyday.

The restored Roman theatre, five minutes' walk east of Downtown, is the most obvious and impressive remnant of Philadelphia. It is cut into the northern side of a hill that once served as a necropolis and has a seating capacity of 6000 people.

It is thought the theatre was built in the 2nd century AD during the reign of Antoninus Pius, who ruled from 138 to 161. These theatres often had religious significance, and the small structure built into the rock above the top row of seats is believed to have housed a statue of the goddess Athena, who was prominent in the religious life of the city.

Restoration began in 1957, but unfortunately different materials from the original were used and reconstruction was in part inaccurate. Just in front of the theatre are the remains of a colonnaded square that once formed part of the city's forum. In recent years it has once again become a place of entertainment, and productions are put on at irregular intervals.

Entrance to the theatre is free, although you will probably be accosted by 'guides' trying to rope you into a tour of the theatre and anything else you care to suggest, in and out of Amman.

Odeon

On the eastern end of what was the forum stands the Odeon, which is still being restored. Built about the same time as the Roman theatre, it served mainly as a venue for musical performances. You can't get in yet, but if you walk up the stairs behind you can peek inside to see the rows of seats facing west. It is thought that the building, much taller in its original state, was enclosed with a wooden or temporary tent roof to shield performers and audience from the elements.

Nymphaeum

Philadelphia's chief fountain stands with its

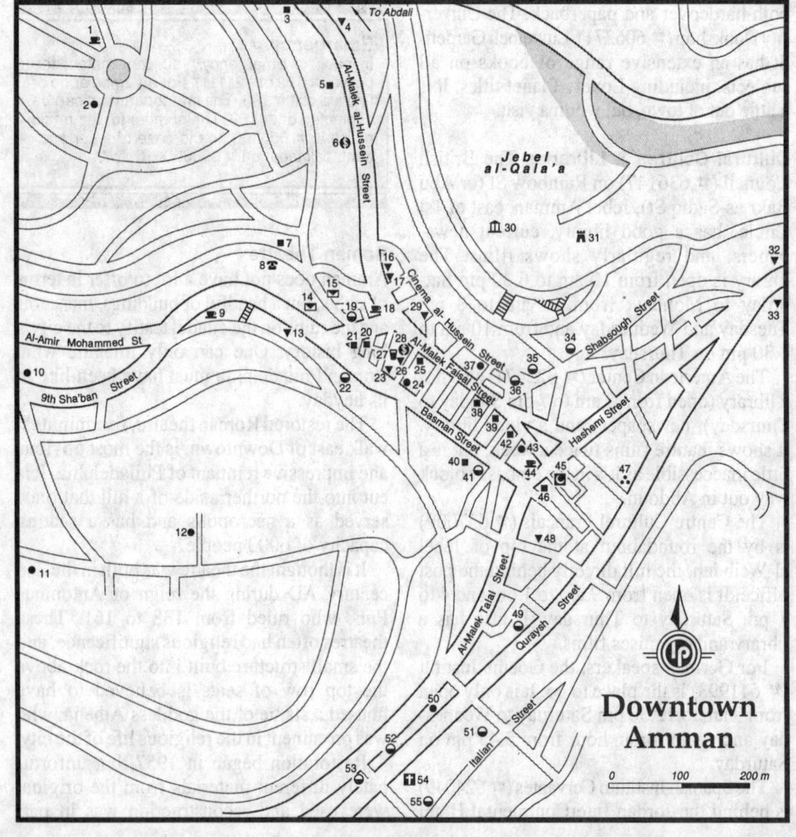

back to Quraysh St, west of the theatre and not far from the King Hussein Mosque. In the past few years all the housing that used to all but completely hide it from view has been cleared away. It is thought to have been built a little later than the theatre and Odeon.

Citadel

Although much of the citadel's buildings have disappeared or been reduced to rubble, you can see evidence of Roman, Byzantine and Islamic construction. Artefacts dating from the Bronze Age show that the hill served as a fortress and/or agora for thousands of years.

The most impressive building, which stands behind (north of) the National Archaeological Museum, is now simply known as the **qasr** (palace). Generally believed to be the work of the Omayyad Arabs, dating from the early 8th century, no-one seems certain about what its function was. To the north and north-east are ruins of Omayyad palace grounds. A Spanish team is working on excavations here.

Closer to the museum (it is signposted) is a small **Byzantine basilica**, of which little is left standing. Thought to date from the 6th or 7th century, it contained mosaics that have been covered by excavators for their own protection.

About 100m south is what is commonly identified as a **temple to Hercules**. A US restoration team has re-erected modest sections of the wall and three columns. The temple dates from the reign of the emperor Marcus Aurelius (161-180 AD). The Romans also fortified the hill with defensive walls, partly restored by the Omayyads and still visible in parts today. On the northern slope of the citadel is an enormous water cistern cut into the rock.

From the south-eastern side you have sweeping views of the theatre and the centre of town.

Folklore Museum

One of two small museums in the wings of the Roman theatre, the Folklore Museum (to the right) houses a modest collection of items displaying the traditional life of the local people – a Bedouin goat-hair tent complete with all the tools and utensils, musical instruments (note the single-string '*rababah*', a classic Bedouin instrument), woven rugs and a camel saddle. It's open from 9 am to 5 pm

PLACES TO STAY
- 3 Park Hotel
- 5 Lords Hotel
- 7 Bdeiwi Hotel
- 20 Cliff Hotel
- 21 Vinice Hotel & Salamon Bar
- 25 Baghdad Grand Hotel
- 38 Reyad Hotel
- 39 Yarmouk Hotel
- 40 Rhum Continental Hotel
- 42 Palace Hotel
- 46 Zahran Hotel

PLACES TO EAT
- 4 Abu Rasheed Fual Restaurant
- 13 Wimpy
- 16 Al-Quds Restaurant
- 17 Jabri (Café & Pâtisserie)
- 23 Abu Hatem Restaurant
- 26 Abu Khamis & Abu Saleh Restaurant
- 29 Beefy Café
- 32 Fast Meal
- 33 Al-Saha al-Hashemieh Restaurant
- 48 Cairo Restaurant

OTHER
- 1 Rooftop Café
- 2 Centre Culturel Français & University Bookshop
- 6 British Bank of the Middle East
- 8 Telephone Office
- 9 Jordan Café
- 10 Natour Car Rental
- 11 British Council
- 12 Bani Hamida House
- 14 Central Post Office
- 15 Parcel Post Office
- 18 Central Café & Hilton Bar
- 19 Service Taxi No 4
- 22 Service Taxi No 2
- 24 Raghadan Cinema & Kit Kat Bar
- 27 Jordan Bar
- 28 Bank of Jordan
- 30 National Archaeological Museum
- 31 Citadel
- 34 Service Taxis to Damascus, Beirut & Baghdad
- 35 Service Taxi No 6
- 36 Service Taxi No 7
- 37 Gold Souq
- 41 Service Taxi No 3
- 43 Liquor Store
- 44 Arab League Café
- 45 King Hussein Mosque
- 47 Nymphaeum
- 49 Local Bus to Wahadat Bus Station
- 50 Fruit & Vegetable Souq
- 51 Service Taxi No 27
- 52 Service Taxi No 29
- 53 Service Taxi No 35
- 54 Church of the Saviour
- 55 Service Taxi Nos 25 & 26

Saturday to Thursday (except Tuesday), and from 10 am to 4 pm Friday and holidays. Entry is JD1.

Traditional Jewels & Costumes Museum
This is in the left wing of the Roman theatre and has well-presented displays of traditional costumes, jewellery and utensils. The best, however, is the mosaic collection, most of it from churches in Madaba and dating back to the 6th century. It keeps the same hours as the Folklore Museum and also costs JD1, marginally better value in this case.

National Archaeological Museum
Just north-west of the Hercules Temple in the grounds of the citadel is the Archaeological Museum. Although small, it has quite a good collection of ancient bric-a-brac ranging from 6000 year old skulls from Jericho to artwork from the Omayyad period. There are some examples of the Dead Sea Scrolls, a copy of the Mesha Stele (see Kerak in the South of Amman chapter for details) and some odd-looking Iron Age anthropomorphic cocoon-like coffins. Entry costs JD2 and opening times are the same as for the previous museums.

Jordan University Archaeology Museum
If you have a special interest in archaeology, or happen to be out at Jordan University, check out the small museum containing artefacts found at various sites in Jordan – mostly ceramics and some statuary – from the Bronze and Iron ages, as well as the Roman, Hellenistic and Islamic periods. Entrance is free and it's supposedly open from 8 am to 5 pm Saturday to Wednesday.

Jordan National Gallery
If you're interested in what contemporary Jordanian painters and sculptors are up to, pop by this small gallery in Jebel al-Weibdeh, at 6 Hosni Fareez St. It's open from 10 am to 1.30 pm and 3.30 to 6 pm daily except Tuesday.

Monument to the Unknown Soldier
The simple and solemn memorial to Jordan's fallen is out by the Sports City complex and houses a small and not uninteresting museum on Jordan's military history. It starts with the Arab Revolt in WWI, scrupulously avoiding all mention of Lawrence of Arabia and the British involvement, and continues through to the Arab-Israeli wars. It opens from 9 am to 4 pm daily except Friday. Entrance is free.

King Hussein Mosque
Restored in 1987, this mosque was built by King Abdullah in 1924. It stands on the site of a mosque built in 640 AD by 'Umar, the second caliph of Islam.

King Abdullah Mosque
Completed in 1990 as a memorial to the present king's grandfather, the unmistakable blue-domed mosque is worth a quick look inside. Women will be required to wear an *'abaaya* (full-length black robe) that covers their hair. Baksheesh of anything up to JD1 will be expected too.

Activities

Hash House Harriers If you want to meet a few of the local expatriates, the Hash House Harriers is a social jogging club where the emphasis is on the social side of things rather than the jogging. They meet every Monday night at about 6 pm and after a run of up to 10 km (you can bail out before) there's a barbecue and drinks at one of the members' homes. You bring your own meat, although first-timers are not really expected to.

Men pay JD3.500 and women JD2.500, which pays for the barbecue and copious quantities of Amstel beer. To find out where it's on, ask someone at the British embassy or British Council. First-timers be warned that they will be identified as 'virgins' and obliged to do a bit of high-speed drinking at some point in the evening. At the time of writing the Hash Master was Richard Martin, who could be contacted on ☎ 666320.

Friends of Archaeology If you are interested in archaeology, get in touch with this group (☎ 695682), which regularly organises trips to places of interest all over Jordan with an expert guide. If you have no joy with this number, try the British Council for tips on their whereabouts.

Swimming If you want to cool off there are not many cheap options. You can try the big hotels, where you'll pay more than JD5. For an Olympic-size pool, there is Sports City (Al-Medina ar-Riyadiyya), but here too you'll be up for JD5 for a swim and locker. The cheapest alternative in pools appears to be the Manar Hotel, which charges non-guests JD3.

Bowling There is a bowling alley – virtually next door to the British Council – on Rainbow St.

Language Courses

It is possible to enrol for courses in Arabic in Amman. There are several choices; the best bet is probably Jordan University. See Language Courses in the Jordan Facts for the Visitor chapter for more details.

Places to Stay – bottom end

Downtown is thick with cheap hotels. Along Al-Malek Faisal St practically every building is a hotel. A lot of these places have shops on the ground floor, a tea shop on the 2nd and then rooms on the 3rd and 4th floors. They are nearly all noisy as hell; the din from the street and neighbouring buildings is penetrating and seems no better on the upper floors. For what it's worth, try to get a room at the back.

The *Zahran Hotel* (☎ 625473) is about as basic as they come at JD1.500 per person (JD3 for a double to yourself if you want) and is virtually welded onto the King Hussein Mosque – just right for early risers.

If that doesn't grab you, there's any number of cheapies to choose from where you'll be looking at around JD3 for a bed. The *Yarmouk Hotel* (☎ 624241), on Al-Malek Faisal St, has beds for JD2.500 and doubles for JD5 (whether double or single occupancy). It's basic enough. A lane further away from the King Hussein Mosque is the *Reyad Hotel* (☎ 624260), where a bed in a share room costs JD3 and a double JD8. The *Baghdad Grand Hotel* (☎ 625433), on the same street, is much of a muchness and charges JD2.500 for a bed or JD6 for a double (it might knock a JD1 off for single occupancy). You'll find many other hotels in the same category.

The long-time backpacker favourite is the *Cliff Hotel* (☎ 624273), a slight jump for the better in quality but not the cheapest around. It is up a side alley just off Al-Malek Faisal St. A bed in a double costs JD5, or JD8 for the whole room. You can sleep on the roof (a good idea in the heat of summer, especially as some rooms don't have fans) for JD2. A hot shower costs 500 fils extra, and soft drinks are sold on the premises. You can do your own cooking and store luggage for free. The staff also organises day trips to the Dead Sea and elsewhere, but some travellers have warned of problems with at least one of the drivers contracted. In any event, the owner, Abu Suleiman, is a mine of information on what to do and how to do it.

One lane up towards the post office is the *Vinice* (☎ 638895), whose signs each present a variation on the spelling. Beds in a shared room cost JD3, and doubles JD6 (JD5 for single occupancy). It is quite OK, and becoming increasingly popular as a rival to the Cliff.

Up by the telephone office is a tidy new place called the *Bdeiwi Hotel* (☎ 643394) on Omar al-Khayyam St. Rooms are clean and comfortable and you pay JD4 per person (in doubles and triples). Single occupancy of a room costs JD8. Hot showers are free, and the guy here also runs a busy phone and fax business.

The *Lords Hotel* (☎ 622167) on Al-Malek al-Hussein St is big and cavernous and a bit gloomy but this does help to keep it cool in summer. It's a bit pricey at JD7/12 for singles/doubles with fan and hot water. It is centrally heated in winter and even has room service. Worn around the edges, it's OK without being exceptional.

In much the same league is the *Palace Hotel* (☎ 624326), Al-Malek Faisal St.

Rooms with good ensuite bath and phone, but rather saggy beds, come in at JD8/13.

Edging a little further up the scale, the *Park Hotel* (☎ 648145), further up Al-Malek al-Hussein St from the Lords, is better value at JD10/14 for rooms with phone, TV, balcony and bathroom – bargaining is possible.

Heading into the middle bracket and a nice deal is the *Select Hotel* (☎ 637101), Baoniya St, on Jebel al-Weibdeh. The rooms, which cost JD11/16, are about the same quality as those of the Park Hotel, but many have very shady balconies and the attached Negresco bar is an added attraction.

Places to Stay – middle

The *Al-Monzer Hotel* (☎ 639469) by the Abdali bus station has acceptable singles/doubles with fan, phone and piping hot showers for JD14/18 plus 10% taxes – a little steep for what you get. Try to avoid the top-floor rooms, which are stuffy in summer. The *Cleopatra Hotel* next door wants similar money without any of the quality – although it is quicker to drop the price by a couple of dinars.

On the other side of the road, tucked away in a side street opposite the police department, is the *Remal Hotel* (☎ 630670; fax 655751), which has much more comfortable rooms – some with huge double beds – for JD14/18 plus taxes. Most rooms have ensuite bathroom and they are very clean. You can have breakfast and taxes included if you stay for a few days.

Not too far away (a steep walk or taxi ride from Abdali bus station) is the *Canary Hotel* (☎ 638353; fax 654353) on Jebel al-Weibdeh, opposite the Terra Sancta college. Rooms come for JD16/24. They are clean and quiet, and the leafy location is quite accessible – the No 4 service taxi passes fairly close by. The rooms have phone, TV and bathroom and the price includes taxes and breakfast.

A trifle more expensive but also of a high standard is the *Caravan Hotel* (☎ 661195; fax 661196), close to the King Abdullah Mosque on Police College St. Singles/doubles with spotless bathroom, TV and phone cost JD20/26 plus taxes. The price includes breakfast.

Also pretty good is the *Rhum Continental Hotel* (☎ 623162) – also spelt 'Rum', as in the wadi. It's on Basman St in Downtown and has spotless if rather small rooms with air-con, heating in winter, hot ensuite shower, TV and mini-bar for JD16/25 plus 10% tax. There's a restaurant, bar and fax service open to customers.

The *Granada Hotel* (☎ 622617), which has a cosy bar that is quite popular with expats, has singles/doubles/triples for JD24/32/40 plus 20% taxes. It's opposite the Sri Lankan consulate near 1st Circle. For a bit of three star comfort, try the *City Hotel* (☎ 642251; fax 652634) on the road up to 3rd Circle from Downtown. It has a small pool and gym facilities and the rooms cost JD25/30 for singles/doubles, plus 10% tax.

A particularly good choice is the *Dove Hotel* (☎ 697601; fax 674676), Qurtubah St, next to the Egyptian embassy between 4th and 5th Circles in Jebel Amman. Rooms cost JD20/26 plus 20% taxes, and there's a restaurant and bar.

A new place that is pleasant enough is *Al Sabeel Hotel Suites* (☎ 630571), with rooms at JD24/30 plus 20% taxes. To find it, head a block east of 2nd Circle and take the first right (look out for the Rozena Restaurant, in the same building).

Up on Abd al-Karim al-Khattabi St in Shmeisani is the *Manar Hotel* (☎ 662186; fax 684329) with singles/doubles for JD29/39, including breakfast, taxes and swimming pool.

Further up the same road is the *Ambassador Hotel* (☎ 665161; fax 681101) with good rooms from JD40/55 plus 20% taxes.

If the top-range hotels are a bit beyond the wallet's reach, you can get a pretty luxurious deal at *The Carlton Hotel* (☎ 654200; fax 655833), opposite the InterContinental between 2nd and 3rd Circles. It has perfectly good rooms for JD45/55 plus 20% taxes.

Very popular with journalists and other visitors is the quiet, leafy *Hisham Hotel* (☎ 642720; fax 647540), a couple of blocks south of the French embassy on Zahran St, between 3rd and 4th Circles. Singles/doubles with satellite TV, bath, air-con and direct phone cost JD40/55 plus 10% tax.

Places to Stay – top end

Amman also has its share of four and five star international hotels. Among the biggies, the closest to Downtown is the *Jordan Inter-Continental Hotel* (☎ 641361; fax 645217), midway between 2nd and 3rd circles. Singles/doubles go for JD130/140 plus 10% tax. Along with the *Marriott* (☎ 607607; fax 670100), which charges JD145 plus 20% in taxes for doubles, it is the most expensive. The Marriott, a block behind the Ministry of the Interior, has all you would expect of such a hotel; 24-hour international telephone and fax, swimming pools, restaurants and bars. Virtually across the main road heading out to the university is the slightly gloomy *Regency Palace Hotel* (☎ 607000; fax 660013), with rooms at JD70/85 plus 20% in taxes.

The *Forte Grand Hotel* (☎ 696511; fax 667137) to the south of the Housing Bank Centre in Shmeisani has bright new rooms for JD115/125 plus 20% taxes.

Places to Eat

Amman offers quite a range of food options, with several non-Middle Eastern cuisines represented. If you're on a tight budget though, you won't be seeing much of this kind of food. Don't leave it too late to head out for your evening meal – many places start shutting up their kitchens as early as 9 pm.

Cheap Eats If money's scarce, your mainstay in Amman will be felafel and shawarma and, in summer at any rate, plenty of ice cream.

Breakfast is easy. Right by the Cliff Hotel are a couple of alleys with small shops that sell yoghurt, milk, fruit, butter, bread and all sorts of cheeses. Stock up with goodies and put your own breakfast together. There is a great bakery in the same lane as the entrance to the Cliff – try the local breakfast staple – bread covered with za'atar (thyme).

In the alley across Al-Amir Mohammed St from the Vinice Hotel is *Hashem*, a good cheap restaurant for felafel, hummus and fuul or combinations of some or all of the above. A filling meal with bread and tea is only about 500 fils and the place opens 24 hours. Or you can buy a bag full of felafel – eight balls for 100 fils.

You'll find several shawarma stalls dotted around Downtown. The price of a shawarma is around 250 fils, but you'll need a couple to make a decent lunch.

In the same lane as the Baghdad Grand Hotel is a place called the *Abu Khamis & Abu Saleh Restaurant* (you can also enter it from the back lane). It's a big place with a chicken-roasting oven out the front. It has a good range including chicken, stuffed green peppers, potato chips, a variety of meat and vegetable stews, rice, and soup as well as salads, hummus and bread. A filling meal will cost between JD1 and JD2.

The *Al-Quds Restaurant*, on Al-Malek al-Hussein St, is a good place. The front window is full of sweets and pastries. The best dish here is the traditional mensaf with a delicious cooked yoghurt sauce. It's not cheap at JD2.200 but it is excellent. Other standard meat dishes cost about JD1.500. For dessert try the mahalabiya wa festaq for 280 fils.

Cheaper, and with a similar range to the Abu Khamis, is the *Cairo Restaurant* a block south-west of the King Hussein Mosque. A meal of chicken, mulukiyyeh, rice salad and a soft drink – more than one can eat – will set you back about JD1.500. There are several little restaurants of its ilk on the same street.

There is another good place in the first lane south of the one with the Cliff Hotel (they are connected). It's the last door on the left before you emerge on Basman St. The restaurant (the *Abu Hatem* in Arabic) has a tiny upstairs section. The speciality here is 'arees, a kind of grilled sandwich made of the standard khobz (minced meat, tomato, garlic and spices). One of these makes a pretty filling meal, and will cost 400 fils.

The main attraction of the *Abu Rasheed Fual Restaurant* (no sign in English) on Al-Malek al-Hussein St is the little one-table balcony shaded by a tall eucalypt. An omelette for breakfast here is a pleasant option. It's above the Pan Pacific travel agency.

Just off Cinema al-Hussein St is the *Beefy* café, a fast-food type place with good hamburgers, pizzas and chips. Best of all, it must do one of the best milkshakes in the region. You can sit at one of the couple of tables or by the window, or just take away. A basic hamburger is 450 fils. The pizzas (which are quite good, but lacking in tomato) are a bit expensive at JD1.650. The milkshakes are tasty and cost 500 fils.

If that's not enough burger choice, head for the *Wimpy* on Basman St, accompanied by *Southern Fried Chicken*. If you're up around 2nd Circle, there is a series of quick takeaway style places just south-east off the roundabout along Al-Buhturi St, including a pizza place and home-grown *Burger King*.

By far and away superior to all of them is *Snack Box*, up on Suleiman an-Nabulsi St behind the King Abdullah Mosque. Run by a charming Cardiff exile, the fine stir fries and meat-and-pasta meals (eat in or take away) cost JD2 or under and are a very tasty alternative to the standard fare.

Mid-Range A few doors down from the Amman Bookshop, before you get to the Jordan Towers building, is the *Chicken Tikka Inn* with good curries for around JD2.500. It's open from noon to 4 pm and 6.30 pm to midnight.

Right on 1st Circle, the *Diplomat Restaurant* has a good range of dishes for JD1 to JD3, including reasonable pizza. It's open until quite late and has tables on the footpath where you can sip on an Amstel (JD1.800). Up on 2nd Circle is a similar place called the *Kawkab al-Sharq*. The lady in green on the sign is Umm Kolthoum, the Arab world's most revered singer.

The *Nouroz* ('Nairuz' in Arabic) restaurant up on 3rd Circle does an edible version of pizza, but don't waste time asking for the ham version. A bottle of Latroun wine will cost you JD8. Another place for pretty much standard stuff is *Maatouk*, also on 3rd Circle.

Just behind the nearby hospital and down a side street two blocks south of 3rd Circle is the *Taiwan Tourismo*, where a filling and good Chinese meal for two can be had for around JD10.

Back Downtown is the *Al-Saha al-Hashemieh*, opposite the Roman theatre. Outside you can dine under a 'Bedouin' tent roof in the company of a stuffed hyena. This place has become a bit too posh for its own good. The traditional Middle Eastern fare is of a high standard, but you'll be lucky to get away for less than JD8 per person. Ever wondered just what the delicacy known as 'sheep's eggs' are? One guess.

Across the road is a string of bright cheerful places, including *Fast Meal*, where locals munch on burgers and slurp huge fruit cocktails.

In Shmeisani there is a whole string of places where you won't come away with much change from JD10, except at the western takeaways: *Pizza Hut* and *Kentucky Fried Chicken*. Actually, imitation western fast food seems to be all the rage. You could get an approximation of an American chilli dog at *Chili House* or hamburgers and chicken nuggets at *Tom & Jerry Burger*.

Popular and somewhat more swish places include *La Terrasse*, which often has Arab musicians in the evening, *La Coquette*, for French dining, and *New York, New York*. These are all clustered around Queen Noor St, but the easiest thing to do is jump into a cab and ask for the *Jabri* pâtisserie in Shmeisani.

In the same area, the *Ata Ali* ice-cream parlour, on Abd al-Karim al-Khattabi St before the Manar Hotel, has 36 mouth-watering flavours of ice cream to take away. The sit-down section is expensive and disappointing.

Also out this way, a bit of a hike north of the previous cluster of restaurants, is Safeway – open 24 hours a day for all your shopping requirements!

Expensive For a meal with a view, try the restaurant on the 23rd floor of the *Jordan Towers* building (known simply as the *burj*, or tower), just below 3rd Circle. It's worth the trip just for the view. Mezzeh is JD4, most main dishes JD5 to JD8 and a modest glass of draught beer in the bar a cool JD2.700. A cup of coffee is JD1.

Ristorante Romero is a fairly pricey Italian restaurant at Mohammed Hussein Haikal St 32, a side street across the main road from the InterContinental Hotel. The next side street up towards the 3rd Circle, Qiss bin Sa'edeh St, has the Spanish version, the *Bonita Inn*. Although it does a version of paella and the odd tapa, much of the menu is given over to an odd international assortment of dishes. A full meal with wine in either of these places will easily cost at least JD20. The *Rozena Restaurant* is in much the same league, as is another nearby Italian place, the *Villa d'Angelo*.

The big hotel restaurants are generally expensive and not as good as some of those outside. None have very good breakfast deals either, most charging JD4 or more for non-guests.

Entertainment

Cinemas The two best cinemas in town, which often get comparatively recent releases in a not too censored form, are the Philadelphia in the basement of the Jordan Towers complex and the Concord up near the Housing Bank Centre in Shmeisani. Tickets are JD3. See the *Jordan Times* for what's on.

Then there are the typical Middle Eastern cinemas, where heavily censored Chuck Norris style movies are the staple. Seats for these movies, which can occasionally be entertaining, cost JD1. One or two Downtown cinemas specialise in fairly sweaty old erotic numbers.

The cultural centres often have films on free. A European film festival is staged in May and a French film festival is also held annually.

Nightclubs Some of the big hotels run modest nightclubs. *Jugglers* at the Forte Grand Hotel in Shmeisani is OK. Another disco is *Scandals* in the San Rock Hotel (☎ 813800) in Um Utheina, well away from the centre around 6th Circle.

Exhibitions & Music The various cultural centres regularly organise lectures, exhibitions and musical recitals. The jaded Royal Cultural Centre also occasionally puts on concerts and drama.

Bars Apart from the *Hilton*, which is off to the right of the stairs just up Al-Malek al-Hussein St (and seems to be the most expensive), there are numerous tiny little bars tucked away in the rabbit warren of alleys around the Cliff Hotel. In the first lane east of the lane where the Cliff is, you'll find one called the *Jordan Bar*. Another, the *Kit Kat*, is up in Basman St, just next to the Raghadan Cinema. Another of this kind is the *Salamon Bar*, next to the Vinice Hotel. It closes at about 11.30 pm, and a beer costs around JD1.300. Women should take into account that they are likely to attract a fair amount of unwanted attention, especially if unaccompanied. Slightly 'classier' is the bar attached to the Rhum Continental Hotel on Basman St.

A little further away is a quieter more mixed bar, the *Negresco*, which is attached to the Select Hotel in Jebel Al-Weibdeh. It closes at 11 pm.

Up on Jebel Amman, the *Hisham Hotel* has a nice beer garden where a pint of draught lager will cost you JD2.500. The Granada Hotel has a bar popular with expats (the British Council is nearby) called *After Eight* and the Dove Hotel, near 5th Circle, has an *Irish pub* that has become very popular with expats and stays open until about 1.30 am.

There are several liquor stores around the traps if you want to drink 'at home' – you'll find one on Al-Malek Faisal St.

Cafés Some of the Downtown cafés make good places to sit and write letters, meet the locals and maybe play a hand of cards or backgammon with them. These are generally men-only places, but western women have no trouble soaking this atmosphere up, especially if accompanied by a male. One of the best is the *Arab League Café*, whose entrance is shared with that of the hotel of the same name. It's a big old place looking out over the King Hussein Mosque.

The *Central Café* is right on the corner of Al-Malek al-Hussein St and Al-Malek Faisal St, but has lost some its charm since the outdoor terrace was ripped away. It shares an entrance with the Hilton bar. The café is on the left. Others to look for are crammed into the lanes around the Cliff Hotel – the *Auberge* is one floor below the Cliff. Further up Al-Amir Mohammed St is another fairly pleasant little spot, the *Jordan Café* (sign in Arabic only), which has quite a large open-air terrace.

For mixed company and wonderful pastries, try the upstairs café at *Jabri*, on Al-Malek al-Hussein St.

If you happen to be up around Jebel al-Weibdeh with kids in the summer, the *rooftop café* above the small shopping arcade at 5 Ibn Tufail St could be the go. Up on the 4th floor (take the lift off to the left inside the arcade) is a terrace café with great views, slot machines inside and a children's play area.

Things to Buy

The Alaydi Jordan Craft Centre (☎ 644555) is right by 2nd Circle. It looks like a normal house but inside are some excellent hand-made articles for sale. Prices are high but this is quality stuff, a lot of it made by Palestinian refugees. It is open from 9 am to 6 pm daily except Friday.

Down by 1st Circle at the Bani Hamida House (☎ 658696) you can get your hands on Bedouin rugs made by the tribe of the same name. It's about four blocks east of the British Council. The quality is high, but then prices aren't exactly low either.

There's another good shop, Oriental Souvenirs Stores, around the corner from the Nouroz restaurant on 3rd Circle. Some of the souvenir shops in Downtown are worth hunting around in too.

If you need to replenish your tape collection, Black & White Music Centre, beneath the Concord Cinema in Shmeisani, is not a bad place to look.

Getting There & Away

Air Amman is the main arrival and departure point for international flights, although a few touch down in Aqaba too. For details of airlines that service Jordan see the Jordan Getting There & Away chapter.

The following airlines have offices in Amman:

Aeroflot
Jordan InterContinental Hotel, Jebel Amman (☎ 641510)
Air France
Shmeisani (☎ 666055)
British Airways
Hashweh Corporation Building, Kalha St (☎ 828801)
EgyptAir
Zaatarah & Co, Al-Malek al-Hussein St (☎ 630011)
KLM
Al-Malek al-Hussein St (☎ 655267)
Lufthansa
Shmeisani (☎ 601744)
Middle East Airlines
Al-Malek al-Hussein St (☎ 636104)
Royal Jordanian
Abdali (☎ 678321)
Saudia
Al-Malek al-Hussein St (☎ 639333)
Syrianair
Al-Amir Mohammed St (☎ 622147)

Domestic The only internal air route is between Amman and Aqaba. Royal Wings has a daily flight from Marka airfield at 7.30 am for JD20 each way. Some Royal Jordanian flights also land in Aqaba, as a stop on international routes.

JETT Bus The JETT bus office/station (☎ 664146) is on Al-Malek al-Hussein St, about 500m past the Abdali bus station. A separate office (☎ 696151) about 20m farther up deals exclusively with international runs. If you arrive from Syria on a Karnak bus, this is where you'll end up. To get to the centre try to pick up a No 6 service taxi (70 fils) heading downhill and ride it to the end. It drops you in Cinema al-Hussein St right in the centre. A normal yellow taxi costs about 400 fils. If you want to walk it takes about 20 minutes. Tickets for JETT buses should be booked two days in advance.

There's one bus daily to the King Hussein Bridge (Jisr al-Malek al-Hussein) for the West Bank and Israel at 6.30 am (JD6). See the Jordan Getting There & Away chapter for more details on crossing to the West Bank and Israel.

JETT buses for Damascus leave at 7 am and 3 pm (JD4.500), for Baghdad at 8.30 am and 2 pm (JD12) and there's a daily bus to Petra at 6 am for JD5.500.

There are at least four daily services to Aqaba (JD4.300).

To get to the JETT bus station, the No 6 service taxis start running at about 5.30 am so you can catch one from Downtown for any of the early-morning departures.

Bus/Minibus The main bus stations in Amman are: Abdali for transport north and west, Wahadat for buses south, and Raghadan for local buses, Madaba and Zarqa (from where you can get buses heading east and north-east). There are also a few less well-defined bus stops for certain destinations.

Abdali bus station is on Al-Malek al-Hussein St, about 20 minutes' walk (uphill) from Downtown. A No 6 or 7 service taxi from Cinema al-Hussein St goes right by it. Minibuses run to Jerash (270 to 350 fils, about one hour), Ajlun (450 fils, 1½ hours), Irbid (530 fils, up to two hours), Salt (175 fils, 45 minutes), Suweileh (85 fils, 20 minutes) and Deir Alla in the Jordan Valley (400 fils, one hour). They simply leave when full, but tend to stop running at about 5 pm. Minibuses also run between Abdali and Zarqa.

There are also air-con Hijazi buses every 15 to 20 minutes to Irbid (850 fils). Buy tickets from its office at the Abdali station. Other big old buses charge 500 fils.

From the southern end of the station you can get minibuses (more frequent in the morning) to Jisr al-Malek al-Hussein; the ride costs JD1 and takes 45 minutes.

All buses and service taxis heading south leave from Wahadat station, way out to the south of town by the traffic roundabout called Middle East Circle (Duwaar Sharq al-Awsat). It is connected to Abdali bus station by service taxi (120 fils, no number), or you can get a No 27 service taxi from Downtown near the fruit and vegie souq or even a local bus from along Quraysh St to Middle East Circle. This is where you'll arrive if you come from anywhere south by minibus.

There are minibus departures for Kerak (750 fils), Ma'an (JD1.050) and Wadi Musa/Petra (JD2). There are also large air-con buses for Aqaba for JD2 and minibuses for JD3, as well as occasional minibuses to Tafila and Shobak. Very irregularly minibuses run direct to Hammamat Ma'in for JD1.500. Buses (200 fils) and minibuses (220 fils) run to Madaba, although it's more convenient to get one from Raghadan. The fares are generally posted at the front inside the buses in Arabic only, but you may have to bargain to pay the correct amount. Nothing runs to a schedule so it's just a matter of getting a seat and waiting.

From Raghadan bus station, a few minutes' walk east of the Roman theatre, there are minibuses to Madaba (220 fils). The ride takes about an hour. Minibuses and local buses run to Zarqa for anything up to 150 fils.

Minibuses for Wadi as-Seer (100 fils, 30 minutes) depart from Ali bin Abi Taleb St, a 10 to 15 minute walk from the King Hussein Mosque. Minibuses for South Shuneh (400 fils, about one hour) and occasionally direct to the Dead Sea resort of Suweimeh (600 fils) leave from Al-Quds St (the area commonly known as Ras al-'Ain). Take a No 29 service taxi from Quraysh St, a little past the Church of the Saviour, and get off as it veers right off Al-Quds St.

Train The Hejaz railway train to Damascus leaves on Monday at 8 am and costs JD2.500. The trip takes about 11 hours and you can expect to get a diesel engine attached to your ancient carriages (although you might get truly lucky with a steam engine on the Syrian leg – some travellers have).

Service Taxi The service taxis are faster and more convenient than the buses but are more expensive. Because they only carry five or seven people, they fill up a lot faster than the buses and don't stop along the way. They use the same stations as the buses (Abdali, Wahadat and Raghadan). As with the buses, service-taxi departures are considerably more frequent in the morning.

From Abdali bus station they run to Irbid (850 fils, about 1½ hours), Jerash (650 fils, 45 minutes), Ajlun, Salt, the King Hussein Bridge (JD1.500, 45 minutes) and even occasionally to Ramtha, the Jordanian border crossing with Syria (JD1).

They also run to Damascus for S£385 or JD5.500.

From Wahadat there are departures for Kerak (JD1, two hours), Madaba (300 fils, 30 minutes), Wadi Musa/Petra (JD2.500, three hours), Ma'an (JD2, 2½ hours), Shobak and Tafila (JD2) and Aqaba (JD3.250, five hours).

From Raghadan, the only service taxi that might be of interest is the one to Marka (100 fils), which can drop you by the Hejaz railway station to the east of central Amman, as well as Marka airfield. Tell the driver your destination: *mahattat sikkat hadid al-Hejaz* (the Hejaz railway station) or *al-matar* (the airport).

Car Rental One of the cheapest car rental agencies is Star Rent-a-Car (☎ /fax 604904) out by Sports City Junction. The guy there is helpful and willing to do a deal. He charges JD25 per day for unlimited km with a three day minimum. This includes insurance above the first JD200 and he'll deliver the car to you Downtown. You can also arrange to leave the car at the airport, in Aqaba or at the King Hussein Bridge.

If you're going to be doing less than 100 km per day, Dinar (☎ 654238), near the Merryland Hotel just south of Abdali bus station, can offer you a Toyota Starlet for JD18 a day with 100 free km per day and a three day minimum. Each 100 km above this costs JD8. You're required to leave a JD300 deposit in cash or with a credit card.

Natour (☎ 627455) in 9 Sha'ban St, Jebel Amman, is not bad. It offers a reasonably new model Toyota Corolla or Mitsubishi Lancer for JD25 a day with unlimited km. A deposit isn't required and you're charged an excess of JD200 in the event of an accident. The hitch is that you must pay daily rental for the number of days the vehicle is in the garage.

Budget (☎ 698131) has an office in Shmeisani near Safeway, at the airport and the InterContinental Hotel. Rates start at JD33 a day for a Daihatsu Charade with unlimited km. Avis (☎ 699420), out at the airport, is more expensive still. Europcar has reps at the Marriot, Regency Palace and Forte Grand hotels. See the Jordan Getting Around chapter for more information.

Motorcycle The increasing number of motorcyclists coming through Jordan and Syria may have noted that there are distressingly few qualified mechanics around. One you can try in Amman is the Atlas Centre, Bayder Wadi as-Seer, in the industrial sector of town. Ask for Yassir.

Hitching To hitch you need to start out of town. For the King's Highway it's easiest to catch a town bus to Madaba and hitch from there. For the Desert Highway take an airport bus (750 fils) and get off where it turns off the highway.

If you're heading north take a minibus from Abdali bus station to Suweileh, which will put you right on the highway.

Getting Around

The Airport The Queen Alia international airport is about 35 km south of the city. Buses make the 50 minute run irregularly from 6.30 am to 8.30 pm from the Abdali bus station for 750 fils. There is a small stand marked for the airport bus at the top end of the bus station, but it's not easy to find. From the airport, buses start at 7.15 am and stop running at 9.45 pm.

You can also get special airport taxis for the trip into town. They cost about JD8 (JD10 from about 10 pm to 8 am).

If you need to get to the small airfield at Marka, take a Marka service taxi from the Raghadan bus station.

Service Taxi The local bus system is hard to figure out as nothing is in English so service taxis are the way to go. For details on how to identify service taxis see the Jordan Getting Around chapter.

There's a standard charge of 70 to 80 fils for most, depending on the route, and you pay the full amount regardless of where you get off. An exception is the Abdali-Wahadat service taxi, which costs 120 fils. After 8 pm the price goes up by 25%.

The cars queue up and so do you. Often the queue starts at the bottom of a hill – you get into the last car and then the whole line rolls back a car space and so on.

Service Taxi Routes

No 2 – leaves from Basman St, near the post office, for the 1st and 2nd circles (70 fils)

No 3 – leaves from Basman St for the 3rd and 4th circles (80 fils)

No 4 – leaves from the side street near the post office for Jebel al-Weibdeh (70 fils)

No 6 – leaves from Cinema al-Hussein St for the Ministry of the Interior Circle, going past the Abdali and JETT bus stations (70 fils)

No 7 – leaves from Cinema al-Hussein St, continues up Al-Malek al-Hussein St past Abdali bus station and King Abdullah Mosque, and along Suleiman an-Nabulsi St (80 fils)

Nos 25, 26 – leave from behind the Church of the Saviour, Downtown and continue to the top of Jebel al-Ashrafiyyeh at the Abu Darwish Mosque for a good view (70 fils)

No 27 – leaves from near the fruit and vegie souq and continues to the Middle East Circle for Wahadat bus station (75 fils)

No 29 – leaves from near the front of the Church of the Saviour (past Dead Sea buses) for Jebel al-Armouti (70 fils)

No 35 – leaves from near the front of the Church of the Saviour for Muhajireen, passing close by to the Muhajireen police station en route (70 fils)

Taxi The guys who drive the regular taxis are keen and if you do any walking in Amman you'll get sick and tired of getting honked at as they prowl for fares. Although generally they do use the meter, keep your eyes open. The flagfall is 150 fils, and any cross-town journey you want to make should never cost more than 800 fils. Don't stand for any non-sense about having to pay more for baggage or other extras they may feel inclined to tack on to the price.

Late at night they will often only take you for a negotiated price and nothing will change their minds. When this is the case you just have to bargain – you know at least what the upper limit should be. (See Local Transport in the Jordan Getting Around chapter for further details.)

Around Amman

SALT

The village of Salt, 30 km north-west of Amman, was the area's administrative centre under Ottoman rule. It was passed over as the new capital of Transjordan in favour of the small village of Amman. The result is that Amman has been transformed out of all recognition into a sprawling modern city, while Salt has retained much of its charm – if you have a day to kill, it's worth a bit of exploration. Although little merits particular attention, you will see some fine examples of Ottoman architecture as you meander through the town centre. Salt is about the only town in Jordan where you don't get the feeling that it has been thrown together in the past 20 or so years.

Take a walk downhill from the bus station into Wadi She'ib, a refreshing valley with some interesting caves.

While in the town centre, you might want to track down the Salt Handicraft Centre (☎ 05-551781), where you can buy textiles and ceramics made in the vocational school here.

Getting There & Away

A minibus from Abdali bus station costs 175 fils for the 45 minute trip. A service taxi will cost you 300 fils. From Salt there are also minibuses heading down into the Jordan Valley to South Shuneh.

WADI AS-SEER & 'ARAQ AL-AMIR

The narrow fertile valley of Wadi as-Seer is a real contrast to the bare, treeless plateau around Amman to the east. The ruins of the **Qasr al-Abd** (Castle of the Slave) and the caves known as 'Araq (or 'Iraq) al-Amir (Cave of the Prince), are 10 km down the valley from the largely Circassian village of Wadi as-Seer.

As you cross a small waterway just beyond Wadi as-Seer an ancient **aqueduct** appears on the right, followed shortly after, on the left, by the façade cut into the rock known as **ad-deir** (the monastery), although in fact it was probably a medieval dovecot.

The 'Araq al-Amir caves are up to the right of the road a few km farther on, and arranged in two tiers – the upper one forms a long gallery along the cliff face. The caves were apparently used as cavalry stables, but local villagers now use them to house their goats and store chaff. One of the caves, easily recognised by its carved doorway, has historians guessing, for to the right of the entrance the name Tobias is engraved in Aramaic. Some say it is the Jewish version of Hyrcanus.

Half a km farther down the valley and visible from the caves stands the **castle**. A degree of mystery surrounds the reason for its construction, and even its precise age, but it is believed Hyrcanus, of the powerful Jewish Tobiad family, had it built in the 2nd century BC. The 1st century historian, Josephus, in his *Antiquities of the Jews*, talks of a castle of white stone decorated with carvings of 'animals of a prodigious magnitude'.

Today, reconstruction of the palace is complete. A French archaeologist spent three years making detailed drawings of the fallen stones, creating cardboard cutouts of each stone and trying to piece it all together. Another seven years were spent on the actual reconstruction. The result is a fine monument which, until now, has been completely ignored by tourists.

The best part is the north entrance with one of the original carved beasts, an enormous lion, in place over the north-west corner. The building was once covered in such figures. Note the lion on ground level on the east façade, which was used as a fountain. The place is unique in that it was built out of some of the biggest blocks of any ancient structure in the Middle East – the largest measures seven by three metres. The blocks were, however, only 20 cm or so thick, making the whole edifice quite flimsy, and a perfect victim for the earthquake that flattened it in 362 AD.

Getting There & Away

A minibus from Ali bin Abi Taleb St takes half an hour and costs 100 fils. There are also minibuses from Suweileh and local town buses.

From Wadi as-Seer you catch a minibus for 100 fils that will take you right to the end of the road at 'Araq al-Amir. You might have to wait a while for this bus to fill up, although on Friday it's a little quicker as a lot of people head down to various parts of the wadi for picnics.

KAN ZAMAN

How seriously can you take a place called Once Upon A Time? You know there is something wrong when a lanky Bedouin wearing full dress sword and other paraphernalia emerges to take the keys of your car and park it for you. This so-called restored turn-of-the-century walled Ottoman village is little more than a series of semi-stylish souvenir shops together with a very pleasant restaurant set beneath the vaulted ceiling of what could look for all the world like a venerable old souq. The bigger Amman hotels ferry visitors in here by the busload to sample the set buffet dinner (JD10.200) accompanied by some Arabic music after a heavy shopping session. A coffee in the neighbouring café costs double the usual price, but then you *are* paying for ambience.

It is a curio of sorts, but without private means of transport it is hardly worth attempting to reach. It lies about 15 km out of Amman along the airport highway. When you see the Madaba exit, leave the airport highway and head east (not west for Madaba). The 'village' is off to the left after a couple of km – look out for the Coca Cola billboard along the road.

North & West of Amman

The area to the north of Amman is the most densely populated in Jordan, with the major centres of Irbid and Jerash as well as dozens of small towns dotted in amongst the rugged and relatively fertile hills. In this area lie the ruins of the ancient Decapolis cities of Jerash and Umm Qais (Gadara), and the 12th-century castle of Ar-Rabad (Ajlun).

North-east of Irbid, the country flattens out to the plains of the Hauran (and the strange black basalt town of Umm al-Jimal) that stretch away into Syria. To the west lies the Jordan Valley, one of the most fertile patches of land in the Middle East.

JERASH

Situated 51 km north of Amman, Jerash is one of Jordan's major attractions, second only to Petra. Lying in the Gilead Hills right on the road that leads to Ramtha and on to

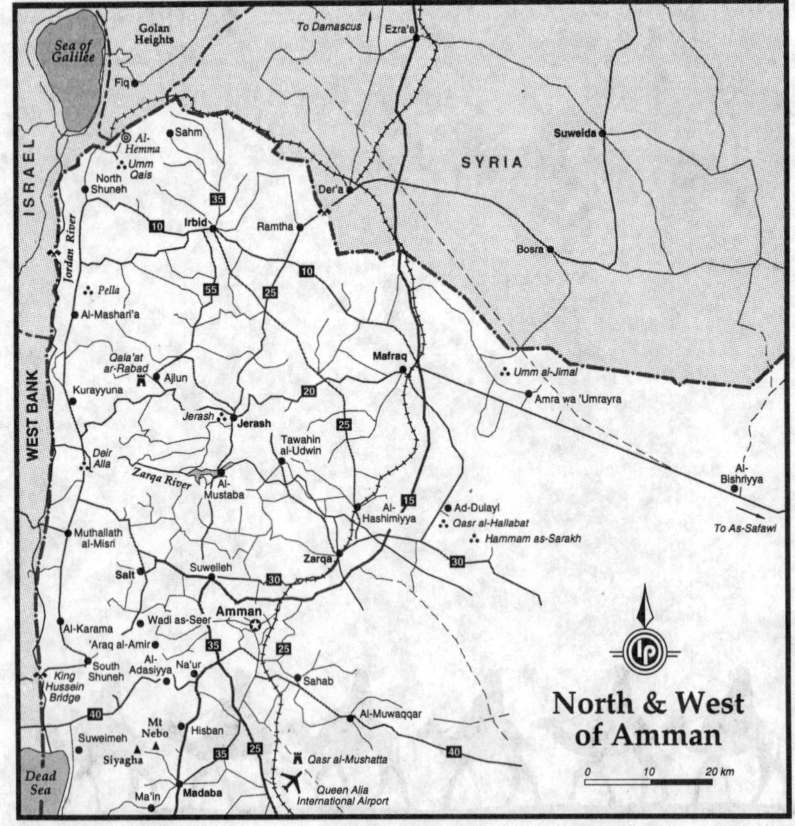

Syria, it is the best example in the Middle East of a Roman provincial city and is remarkably well preserved.

The modern town of Jerash, which lies on the east bank of a small tributary of the Zarqa River, has a sizable population of Circassians settled here by the Turkish authorities late last century.

The main ruins of Jerash are on the west of the same stream and were rediscovered in 1806 by a German traveller, Ulrich Seetzen. Restoration began in 1925 under the British Mandate, and three years later the first excavations were carried out. Prior to that most of the city had been buried under sand, which accounts for the good condition of many of the buildings.

In its heyday it is estimated Jerash had a population of around 15,000 and, although it wasn't on any of the main trade routes, its citizens prospered from the good corn-growing land that surrounds it. The ancient city preserved today was the administrative, civic and commercial centre of Jerash. The bulk of the inhabitants lived on the east side of Wadi Jerash.

Excavations have revealed two theatres, an unusual oval-shaped forum, temples, churches, a marketplace and baths. Restoration work continues on various parts of the site.

The rising tide of tourists coming to Jordan has been felt here, and you will usually be accompanied by several busloads of the package crowd – as well as a few locals flogging 'antiquities' – exercise the usual sceptical caution.

History

Although there have been finds to indicate that the site was inhabited in Neolithic times, it was from the time of Alexander the Great (332 BC) that the city really rose to prominence.

In the wake of the Roman general Pompey's conquest of the region in 63 BC, Jerash became part of the Roman province of Syria and, soon after, a city of the Decapolis. Over the next two centuries trade with the Nabataeans flourished and the city grew extremely wealthy. Local agriculture and iron-ore mining in the Ajlun area contributed to the city's wellbeing. A completely new plan was drawn up in the 1st century AD, centred on the typical feature of a colonnaded main street intersected by two side streets.

With Emperor Trajan's exploits around 106 AD, which saw the annexation of the Nabataean kingdom and even more wealth finding its way to Jerash, many of these buildings were torn down to be replaced by even more imposing structures.

In 129 AD, when the Emperor Hadrian visited and stayed for some time, the town administration went into top gear again. To mark a visit of such importance, the Triumphal Arch at the southern end of the city was constructed.

Jerash reached its peak in the beginning of the 3rd century, when it was bestowed with the rank of Colony, but from then on it went into a slow eclipse. With the overland caravans now defunct because of the sea trade and disturbances such as the destruction of Palmyra in 273 AD, the decline continued steadily. The only respite came during the reign of Diocletian (circa 300 AD), which saw a minor building boom.

By the middle of the 5th century, Christianity had become the major religion of the region and the construction of churches proceeded apace. Under Justinian (527-565 AD) no less than seven churches were built, mostly out of stones filched from the earlier pagan temples and shrines. No more churches were built after 611.

With the Persian invasion of 614 and the Muslim conquest of 636, followed by a series of earthquakes in 747, Jerash was really on the skids and its population shrank to about 25% of its former size.

Apart from a brief occupation by a Crusader garrison in the 12th century, the city was completely deserted up until the arrival of the Circassians in 1878. Conservation and restoration began in 1925 and continues today.

Information

There's a visitors' centre with a souvenir

Jerash: the Ruins

Approaching from Amman, the **Triumphal Arch** is first to come into view. Although its present height is daunting, it was twice as high when first built. One unusual feature of the construction is the wreaths of carved acanthus leaves above the bases of the pillars, which look like they'd be more at home on the top.

Behind the arch is the **hippodrome**, the old sports field once surrounded by seating that held up to 15,000 spectators. Some of the seating has been restored in ongoing conservation work. The 244 by 50m pitch hosted mainly athletics competitions and, as its name suggests, horse races.

The entrance to the main site is from behind the Government Rest House which is about 50m outside the **South Gate**. The gate, originally one of four in the 3500m long city wall (little of which remains), also bears the acanthus leaf decoration of the Triumphal Arch. It is thought that a new city quarter was planned between the two gates.

Once inside the gate, the **Temple of Zeus** is the ruined building on the left. It is being restored to its former glory, when a flight of stairs led up to it from a lower sacred enclosure, itself supported by a vaulted corridor built to compensate for the unhelpful local geography. The corridor (part of which is now open) was probably used as stables, barracks or as a warehouse. The temple was built in the latter part of the 2nd century on a holy site from earlier times. The lower level ('*temenos*') had an altar and served as a holy place of sacrifice. Of the main temple building, little remains but the outer walls.

The **forum** (marketplace) is unusual because of its oval shape, and some attribute this to the desire to link gracefully the main north-south axis ('*cardo*' – the standard Roman main street) with the existing Hellenistic sacred site of the Zeus temple or its predecessor. In fact, some historians dispute that it was a forum in the strict sense, suggesting it too may have been a place of sacrifice connected to the temple. The reconstructed Ionic columns surrounding it are an impressive sight. The centre is paved with limestone and other softer blocks. It is believed the podium in the centre was the base for a statue.

The **south theatre**, behind the Temple of Zeus, was built in the 1st century and could once hold 5000 spectators. The back of the stage was originally two storeys high and has now been rebuilt to the first level. From the top of the seats you have an excellent view of the ruins, with the modern town of Jerash in the background.

On the far side of the forum the cardo, or **colonnaded street**, stretches for more than 600m to the North Gate. The street is still paved with the original stones and the ruts worn by thousands of chariots over the years can be clearly seen. The columns on the west side are of uneven height and were built that way to complement the façades of the buildings that once stood behind them.

At the two main intersections ornamental *tetrapyla* were built. The **southern tetrapylon** consisted of four bases, each supporting four pillars topped by a statue. Only the bases have been rebuilt, of which the south-eastern one is the most complete. The intersection was made into a circular plaza at the end of the 3rd century.

The cross street ('*decumanus*') runs east, downhill to a bridge spanning the small river and on to the **eastern baths**, just behind the present bus station, and west to a gate in the city wall. On the left, before this cross street, is the city's restored **agora**. There was a fountain in the middle.

The steps of the 4th century **cathedral** (so called, although there is little proof it was more than another church) are on the left, about 100m after the intersection. The gate and steps actually cover the remains of an earlier temple to the Nabataean god Dhushara.

Behind the cathedral lies the **Church of St Theodore**, built in 496 AD, and between the two a large courtyard with fountain. Just south of the church lies an **Omayyad building**, the existence of which supports the theory that the newly arrived Muslims lived in reasonable harmony with the city's earlier, largely Christian inhabitants.

Next along the cardo is the **nymphaeum**, the main ornamental fountain of the city and a temple to the nymphs. Built in 191 AD, the two storey construction was elaborately decorated and faced with marble slabs on the lower level and plastered and painted on the upper level. Water used to cascade over the façade into a large pool at the front and the overflow from this went out through carved lions' heads to drains in the street below.

The daunting Triumphal Arch, Jerash

Next on the left is the most imposing building on the site, the **Temple of Artemis**, dedicated to the patron goddess of the city. After the Great Gate ('*propylaem*') of the temple come two flights of stairs leading up to the courtyard where the temple stands. Large vaults had to be built to the north and south of the temple to make the courtyard level. Originally, the temple was surrounded by pillars but only the double rows at the front remain, as they and much of the material of which the temple was built were taken and reused in later buildings, such as the churches. The temple was fortified by the Arabs in the 12th century, but this work was destroyed by the Crusaders.

Back on the main street, opposite the Great Gate, is the **Viaduct Church** built over what was once the road leading up to the Temple of Artemis. Further up the main street is the second major intersection and the **northern tetrapylon**, dedicated to the Syrian wife of the Emperor Septimus Severus. This was different from the southern one in that it consisted of four arches surmounted by a dome.

The **western baths** are just downhill from the northern tetrapylon. Dating from the 2nd century, they represent one of the earliest examples of a dome atop a square room. It's all a bit of a jumble today.

The **north theatre**, just to the west of the tetrapylon, is smaller than the south theatre and is only beginning to look itself after much restoration that is still to be completed. Virtually next door are the remains of the 6th century **Church of Bishop Isaiah**. From the Northern Tetrapylon it is about 200m to the **North Gate.**

Just to the south of the Temple of Artemis lie the ruins of a number of **churches**. In all, 13 have been uncovered and it is widely believed that there are more to be found. To the west of the church of St Theodore are the churches of St Cosmos & St Damianus, St John and St George. They were all built around 530 AD and opened on to one another. The floors of all three were finely decorated with mosaics, some of which you can still see in St Cosmos and St Damianus and also in the Traditional Jewels & Costumes Museum in Amman. Little remains of the other churches.

In the tiny **museum** just to the east of the forum is a good selection of artefacts from the site, ranging from pottery theatre tickets to jewellery, glass and Mameluke coins. The main attraction is the gold jewellery and coins found in a family tomb near the Triumphal Arch. The staff are friendly and will show you around if you want. It supposedly opens from 8 am to 5 pm (3 pm on Friday and from 9 am to 3 pm on holidays), and entry is covered by the main entrance ticket.

The whole site takes a good few hours to wander around and absorb and one can only imagine what it would be like if the other 90% were excavated! ■

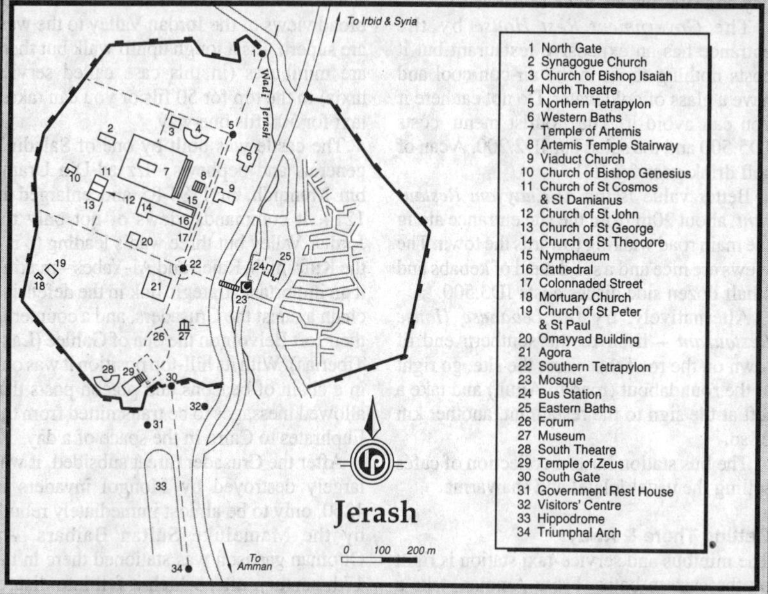

shop and post office, and this is the place to hire a guide for JD4 if you really want one – they have quite a few languages covered, but the commentary can be uneven.

The Government Rest House sells unashamedly expensive refreshments and meals. There used to be a nightly sound & light performance at 8.30 pm, but it has not been staged for years. The crowd of souvenir stands just outside the South Gate is growing visibly fat on the passing trade, and prices for maps and books are a few JD up on the Amman average.

The site is open daily from 7.30 am until dark and entry is JD2 (250 fils for Jordanians).

Places to Stay & Eat

Surprisingly, there is no hotel in Jerash, but its proximity to Amman makes it an easy day trip. Otherwise, you could go on to stay at Ajlun, but be warned that the cheapest single on offer there is around JD20 (with an early start, you can cover Jerash and Ajlun in one day and still make it back to Amman).

The *Government Rest House* by the entrance has an expensive restaurant but it costs nothing to sit in the air-con cool and have a glass of cold water. Do not eat here if you can avoid it. The 'tourist menu' costs JD5.500 and the salad bar JD2.200. A can of soft drink goes for JD1.

Better value is the *Al-Khayyam Restaurant*, about 20m from the site entrance along the main road walking towards the town. The views are nice and a solid meal of kebabs and a half dozen side dishes costs JD3.500.

Alternatively, try the *Lebanese House Restaurant* – head to the southern end of town on the road that skirts the site, go right at the roundabout (road to Ajlun) and take a left at the sign to the restaurant, another km or so.

The bus station hosts a collection of cafés selling the usual felafel and shawarma.

Getting There & Away

The minibus and service-taxi station is right by the eastern baths. From Amman, take a service taxi (650 fils, 45 minutes) or minibus (270 to 350 fils, one hour) from Abdali bus station, or hitch from the Suweileh roundabout.

From Jerash, there are minibuses to Irbid (290 fils), Mafraq (270 fils) and Ajlun (170 fils), 25 km to the west.

If you stay in Jerash after about 5 pm, be prepared to hitch back to Amman as all transport stops running soon after that. The Tourist Police, who for the most part hide in the air-con visitors' centre, may help by flagging down a car for you.

AJLUN

The trip to Ajlun, 22 km to the west of Jerash, goes through some beautiful small pine forests and olive groves.

The attraction of the town is the **Qala'at ar-Rabad**, built by the Arabs as protection against the Crusaders. The castle is a fine example of Islamic military architecture. It stands on a hill two km to the west of the town and when you reach the top you understand why the location was chosen – the broad views of the Jordan Valley to the west are superb. It's a tough uphill walk but there are minibuses (in this case called service taxis) to the top for 50 fils or you can take a taxi for 500 fils one way.

The castle was built by one of Saladin's generals and nephews, 'Izz ad-Din Urama bin Munqidh, in 1184-85 and enlarged in 1214. It commands views of not only the Jordan Valley but three wadis leading to it – the Kufranjah, Rajeb and Al-Yabes – making it an important strategic link in the defensive chain against the Crusaders, and a counter to their fort Belvoir on the Sea of Galilee (Lake Tiberias). With its hill-top position it was one in a chain of beacons and pigeon posts that allowed messages to be transmitted from the Euphrates to Cairo in the space of a day.

After the Crusader threat subsided, it was largely destroyed by Mongol invaders in 1260, only to be almost immediately rebuilt by the Mameluke Sultan Baibars. An Ottoman garrison was stationed there in the 17th century, after which it fell into disuse. Earthquakes in 1837 and 1927 damaged it badly, but it has since been partly restored.

It is open from 8 am to 7 pm (5 pm in winter) daily. The entry fee is JD1.

In the town of Ajlun itself, the only thing of interest is the mosque in the centre. Its minaret is said to date back some 600 years.

Places to Stay & Eat

There are two hotels along the way up from the town to the castle. The first and more expensive is the *Al-Rabad Castle Hotel* (☎ 462202), about 500m before the castle. It has very comfortable rooms (no fans though) and commanding views of the valley and town but the prices are just as stunning – JD24/32 plus 10% tax for singles/doubles with bath and balcony. The manager is willing to come down a few dinars, and there's a pleasant restaurant and pergola at the front.

About 100m further up is the more austere *Ajlun Hotel & Restaurant* (☎ /fax 462524). Rooms go for JD24/32 plus 10% tax with bath, heating and balcony. Breakfast is thrown in and the management will also bargain in price. It's not surprising that both places seem empty most of the time.

If you have your own tent, it is possible to camp in the small patch of forest just to the west of the castle. Take the track to the right 50m before the castle, pass the Al-Rabadh restaurant and after the second concrete shed, there's a small track off to the right. Watch out for old gaping cisterns and the occasional ant nest.

It's good advice to pass by the *Al-Rabadh* restaurant. It has the nerve to ask 500 fils for a coke and the only food on offer is a tomato and egg salad! If you bring your own food, join the locals for a picnic around the base of the castle. There is a drinks stand by the entrance.

The *Green Mountain Restaurant*, by the traffic roundabout in the centre, has – surprise, surprise – roast chicken, hummus, salad and bread. Next door is the *Abu al-'Az* café, which will feed you well if the Green Mountain is shut – but it will serve you more items than you can possibly consume and charge you accordingly if you are not paying close attention. There are a couple of felafel and shawarma joints around the bus station.

The *Ajlun Tourist Park*, where you can sit down for a meal of kebabs and a beer, is on the left-hand side of the road about one km from Ajlun towards Jerash. It has a beautiful view of the castle across the valley.

Getting There & Away

There are regular minibuses from Jerash for 170 fils (22 km and about half an hour) or direct from Amman for 450 fils (1½ hours).

At a push it would be possible to go from Amman to Jerash and Ajlun and on to Irbid in one day.

To get to Irbid, minibuses cost 270 fils for the 45 minute trip. On working days there are also large air-con buses, for which competition is keen in the mornings with all the students heading off to Yarmouk University.

IRBID

Although artefacts and graves in the area show Irbid has been inhabited since the Bronze Age, it has little to offer the visitor. Still, it is a handy base for trips to Umm Qais and Al-Hemma on the Syrian border (where there are views of the Golan Heights and the Sea of Galilee) and to Pella.

The university campus, more than a km south of the town centre, is a world of its own, busy with fast-food restaurants and cafés. In early 1986 the university was a focal point of unrest, when students demonstrated for greater participation in the running of the university. In the ensuing clash with police, three protesters were trampled to death. The riot was seen as part of a growing resentment in the country at the lack of participation in government, which culminated in the price-hike riots of April 1989.

Information

Money There is no problem changing money as most of the big banks are represented in the centre of town. You can get Visa cash advances at the Bank of Jordan, on the 1st floor of the same building containing the Abu Baker Hotel. The Arab Bank, across the road from the Hotel al-Wahadat al-Arabiyya,

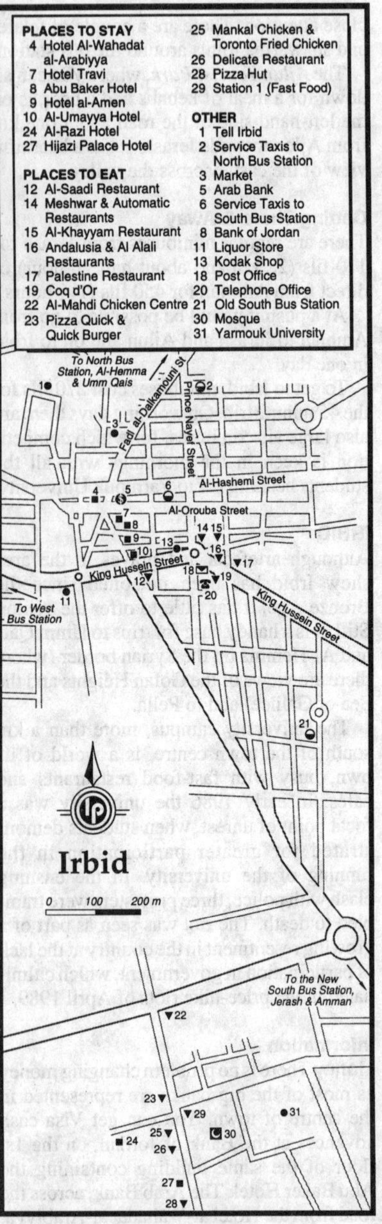

also accepts Visa card and changes cash and travellers' cheques. The banks generally open from 8.30 am to 12.30 pm and 4 to 6 pm, Saturday to Thursday.

The moneychangers clustered around the same hotel offer decent rates but accept cash only.

Post & Communications The post office is on King Hussein St and opens from 7 am to 7 pm (5 pm in winter) daily except Friday, when it closes at 1.30 pm. The centraal is around the corner on Prince Nayef St.

Film There's a modern Kodak store in a side alley west of the Meshwar restaurant.

Things to See

Not much is the short answer, but there are two museums at the university. From the main entrance walk straight up the main thoroughfare about 200m. Off to the right is the **Museum of Jordanian Heritage**, open from 10 am to 3 pm (5 pm in winter), daily except Tuesday. It is considered the best archaeological museum in the country, with modern displays far superior to those found in the museum in Amman and explanations in English. Be warned that, in spite of the official opening times, the museum quite often seems to be out of action.

If you go back to the main thoroughfare and proceed straight towards the stadium, you'll come to the **Natural History Museum**, open from 8 am to 3 pm (5 pm in winter), daily except Tuesday and Friday. Admission, if it's open, is free.

Places to Stay – bottom end

There are a few basic hotels in the busy downtown area. The best is probably the *Hotel al-Wahadat al-Arabiyya* (☎ 242083), although it's a bit of a toss-up. It's friendly and clean and you pay JD5/8/10.500 for singles/doubles/triples. A shower is 500 fils, and the guy who runs it has set up a tiny indoor tent for sipping tea – a bit silly really but the idea is nice. Almost directly opposite is the *Hotel Travel* (☎ 242633). It offers much the same deal and has undergone a whitewash job recently. No-one seems to speak any English here.

The *Hotel al-Amen* (pronounced 'ameen'; ☎ 242384) has good clean doubles for JD8, or JD6 for single occupancy. There are hot showers (500 fils), some rooms have fans and you can use the fridge and stove. The staff are also quite friendly.

The entrance to the *Abu Baker Hotel* (☎ 242695) is upstairs from the Bank of Jordan. It charges JD5/8 for basic singles/doubles, but the former can mean having a room with three beds to yourself – some of the rooms on the upper floors have sweeping views of central Irbid – for what they are worth.

Places to Stay – middle

For something a bit more up-market, try the *Al-Umayya Hotel* (☎ 245955) on King Hussein St. It's on the 2nd floor above the Jordan Arab Investment Bank and has good, clean rooms with ensuite bath, TV and fan at JD14/18. You may be able to bargain down a little.

Out by the university, about 100m down a side street opposite the mosque, is the *Al-Razi Hotel* (☎ 275515). It has singles/doubles for JD22/27.500, but this may come down with some bargaining. The rooms are clean and airy, with TV and fan. It's in a nice spot, although a little out of the way (if the centre of Irbid is what you want to see), and mostly houses more affluent students.

Irbid's premier establishment, the *Hijazi Palace Hotel* (☎ 279500; fax 279520) is further south along the main road. It has three to four star service with rooms for JD48/60 a single/double, including breakfast.

Places to Eat

There is a huddle of felafel and shawarma stands around the Hotel Travel. For something different, the *Meshwar Restaurant* near the roundabout by the post office does all sorts of filled sandwiches. Some look a little off-putting, but for a tasty change from felafel and shawarma, try the 'fish sandwich'. This bright and cheery place also sells fresh juices for 300 fils, and there is a standard coffee shop upstairs.

Next door, the *Automatic Restaurant* will serve you up the usual kebabs, chicken and so on, or the local version of a hamburger cooked before your hungry eyes. You can also get a beer.

The *Palestine* does fairly standard fare and doubles as a tearoom, and the *Al-Saadi* across the road from the Al-Umayya Hotel is similar. The hotel itself has a restaurant too.

The *Al-Khayyam Restaurant*, around the corner from the Meshwar (look for the Bell's Scotch sign) is more of a bar than anything else, but you can get a decent meal here too. A generous plate of kebabs costs JD1.500, and the beer is JD1.400. It also sells takeaway liquor, discreetly placed in a paper bag. On that note, there are several liquor stores dotted about the centre of town too.

The *Coq d'Or* has the usual half chicken for JD1, and across the road you'll find a couple of high-rise restaurants. Head inside the arcade and take the lift to the 6th floor for the *Andalusia Restaurant* or the *Al Alali*, two floors higher. Both serve up fairly standard fare for slightly above-average prices.

Out by the university there is a plethora of eateries, and the area seems to be the liveliest part of Irbid. Turn left when leaving the university's main entrance and you hit a main road. On the corner turning south is *Station 1*, a fast-food joint just by the mosque where an acceptable burger costs 350 fils. Virtually across the road, *Pizza Quick* and *Quick Burger* offer pizzas of a sort for JD1.750 and hamburgers for 450 fils. Heading north you can grab half a chicken at *Al-Mahdi Chicken Centre* for 900 fils. Further sources of this flightless bird are *Mankal Chicken* and *Toronto Fried Chicken*. Just south of these is the *Delicate*, a pizza joint! If this sounds dubious but it's a pizza you desire, you could also walk on down past the Hijazi Palace and find a western favourite – *Pizza Hut*.

Getting There & Away

Bus/Minibus Irbid has four bus stations. The northern one is about a 20 minute walk from the centre; alternatively, service taxis and minibuses run past it from near the souq for 80 and 60 fils respectively. There are minibuses from this bus station to Umm Qais (220 fils, 45 minutes) and Al-Hemma (280 fils, one hour).

The old south bus station is no longer of much interest to travellers, servicing only a few local destinations, and should not be confused with the main bus station to the south-east of town.

From the new south bus station (ask for the '*mujama' Amman al-jadeed*')there are air-con Hijazi buses to Amman's Abdali bus station. They leave every 15 to 20 minutes until about 6.30 pm for 850 fils. You buy seated tickets at the office and the trip takes about 1½ hours, depending on the traffic. Alternatively, there are other buses (500 fils) and minibuses (530 fils) until about 8.30 pm and service taxis (up to two hours, 850 fils). There are also minibuses to Ajlun (270 fils, 45 minutes), Jerash (300 fils), Ramtha (see the following section), Zarqa and Mafraq.

From the west bus station, off Palestine St and near the town centre, there are minibuses to Al-Mashari'a (300 fils, 1½ hours), within walking distance of the Roman city of Pella in the northern Jordan Valley. From Al-Mashari'a you can also get to any other Jordan Valley destination. This is also the place to get a minibus for Israel (see the following section).

Syria If you want to go direct to Damascus there are Syrian service taxis operating out of the new south bus station. The trip takes three to four hours depending on border formalities and costs JD4 or S£300.

To cross on your own, take a minibus from the same bus station to Ramtha (or Ar-Ramtha), the last town before the Jordanian border post, for 150 fils. You can then hitch the last few km to the border post, and after the formalities the soldiers will flag down a vehicle to take you to the Syrian side. Once you're through, it's a three or four km walk or hitch to Der'a, the first town, from where there are buses to Damascus and Bosra.

Alternatively, you can get a service taxi from Ramtha to Der'a for JD2 or S£150.

If you're coming from Syria, you can follow the same options in reverse. Once in Ramtha, you can take the minibus to Irbid and another to Amman, or a minibus to Zarqa via Mafraq for 500 fils. From Zarqa there are town buses and minibuses (up to 150 fils) that take you the 20 km to Downtown Amman. If the one you catch doesn't stop at Raghadan bus station, jump out at the King Hussein Mosque.

Israel Minibuses leave from the west bus station for the Jisr Sheikh Hussein (Sheikh Hussein Bridge) crossing (aka Jordan Border) into Israel. The trip takes about an hour and costs 300 fils. From the Jordanian side a bus takes you across to the Israeli border post for NIS3. From there you catch another bus to Beit She'an for NIS8.40. For more details on crossing formalities, see the Jordan Getting There & Away chapter.

Getting Around

Irbid can be used as a staging post for heading elsewhere (it is quite possible to get to Umm Qais and Al-Hemma via Irbid from Amman in one long day), and you can get from one bus station to the other without getting caught up in the town at all. Service taxis (often in the form of minibuses) run between all the stations and the middle of town. Service taxis leave from near the souq to the north bus station. The minibuses charge 60 fils, the service taxis 80 fils.

From the main drag, Al-Hashemi St, service taxis leave for the new south bus station (running past the old one, too). There are also service taxis and minibuses to Yarmouk University from near the same spot for 50 fils. The north, west and new south bus stations are all linked by the same kind of service taxi (the ride costs 100 fils), so you need never stop in the town itself.

UMM QAIS

Right in the corner of Jordan, 30 km north-west of Irbid, is Umm Qais, with views over the Golan Heights and the Sea of Galilee

(Lake Tiberias) to the north and the Jordan Valley to the south. The area is reputed to have the oldest olive trees in the region and the olives are said to be so good that even Israelis have started flocking here to get a hold of some.

This is the site of the ancient Graeco-Roman town of Gadara, one of the cities of the Decapolis and, according to the Bible, the place where Jesus cast out the devil from two men and cast it into a herd of pigs (Matthew 8:28-34).

The city was captured from the Ptolemies by the Seleucids in 198 BC, and the Jews under Hyrcanus captured it from them in 100 BC. When the Romans (led by Pompey) conquered the east and the Decapolis was formed, the fortunes of Gadara, taken from the Jews in 63 BC, increased rapidly and building was undertaken on a typically large scale.

The Nabataeans controlled the trade routes as far north as Damascus. This interference with Rome's interests led Mark Antony to send Herod the Great to conquer them. This he failed to do completely, but he did wrest a sizable chunk of territory from them in 31 BC. Herod was given Gadara following a naval victory and he ruled over it until his death in 4 BC, much to the disgust of the locals, who had tried everything, in vain, to put him out of favour with Rome. On his death, the city reverted to semi-autonomy as part of the Roman province of Syria.

Gadara continued to flourish with the downfall of the Nabataean kingdom at the hands of Trajan in 106 AD, and was the seat of a bishopric until the 7th century. By the time of the Muslim conquest, however, it was little more than a small village. Since 1974, German and Danish teams have been excavating and restoring the site.

Only a few years ago this place saw hardly any visitors, but it is becoming increasingly popular, especially with the waves of Israeli tourists.

Things to See

Just after the town, on the way down to Al-Hemma, turn off on a dirt track signposted to the Government Rest House. On a rise to the left (once the acropolis?) stands an old Ottoman building, Bayt Rusan, now a small **museum**. Open from 8 am to 5 pm (4 pm in winter) daily except Tuesday, it contains artefacts and mosaics from the area. One of the mosaics, a 4th century example found in one of the town's mausoleums, is one of the most interesting exhibits, overshadowed perhaps by the headless, white marble statue of a goddess that was found sitting in the front row of the **Western Theatre**.

The theatre, in a sorry state of repair, can be found on the other side of the Government Rest House, further past the museum down the track that shows signs of better days as a Roman road. It provides incredible views out over the Sea of Galilee.

Next to it is a **colonnaded street** that was once probably the town's commercial centre. The theatre and some of the columns are made of black basalt, as indeed are many of the modern homes in the area, built by vandalising the ancient ruins. Further west along what's left of the main Roman street, are a **mausoleum** and then **baths** on the right and, further along still, another mausoleum on the left. A few hundred metres more take you to the barely visible contours of what was once a hippodrome.

Admission to the site, open daily from 8 am to 7 pm (5 pm in winter) costs JD1.

Places to Stay & Eat

The *Umm Qais Hotel* (☎ 02-217081; fax 242313) is a very comfortable place that opened in 1995. Room prices seem to vary, but JD6 a person seems the approximate figure. The place, which also incorporates a small restaurant, is well worth it and even accepts Visa and MasterCard. You can part with more money at the overpriced *Government Resthouse* if you are looking for some nosh during your visit to the ruins. It's a pleasant place to sit and a grilled fish will set you back JD5.500. A coffee is 500 fils.

Getting There & Away

There are regular minibuses to Umm Qais from Irbid for 220 fils (45 minutes). Keep

JORDAN

your passport handy for possible military checkpoints.

AL-HEMMA

The baths of Al-Hemma are a further 10 km from Umm Qais, down the hill towards the Yarmouk River and Golan. The area near the river and springs is a lush green, in stark contrast to the bare, steeply rising plateau of the Israeli-occupied Golan to the north, where you can see the occasional jeep patrol on the other side.

The baths were famous in Roman times for their health-giving properties and are still used today, but you have to be keen to want to jump into the smelly water. If you do, there are separate timetables for men and women.

Places to Stay & Eat

The hotel (☎ 02-249829, ext 5) by the baths has rooms for JD8, and a terrace café. Or you could try the *Sah al-Noum Hotel* (☎ 02-273158), heading left into the town from the baths. Simple but acceptable doubles with washbasin cost JD8. The *Al-Ahmeh Restaurant* by the baths is pleasant enough but a bit of a rip-off – a tea costs 500 fils. You'll find a few simple restaurants in the village.

Getting There & Away

There are regular minibuses from Irbid to Al-Hemma for 280 fils (one hour). From Umm Qais, just wait by the side of the road for a passing minibus or hitch a ride with another vehicle. You need your passport for the trip down as there's a military control point on the edge of Umm Qais and at least one other closer to Al-Hemma.

UMM AL-JIMAL

Comparatively little is known about this strange, black city in the south of the Hauran (also called Jebel Druze), only about 10 km from the Syrian border and about 20 km east of Mafraq.

It is thought to have been founded in about the 2nd century AD and formed part of the defensive line of Rome's Arab possessions. Roads lead north to Bosra (in present-day Syria) and south-west to Philadelphia (modern Amman) and it served as an important trading station for Bedouins and passing caravans. The town, which may have had as many as 10,000 inhabitants in its heyday, continued to flourish into Omayyad times, but was destroyed by an earthquake in 747 and never recovered.

Things to See

Much of what remains, some of it more interesting for archaeologists than tourists, is simple urban architecture – ordinary peoples' houses and shops. When you enter the site, the first big building with a square tower has been identified as a **barracks** and **church** combined. The most easily identifiable building, with its four arches, is the **western church**. Between the two is a **cathedral** on the right (looking towards the western church) and what has been called the **Praetorium** on the left.

Getting There & Away

It is possible to do the trip in a day from Amman, from where you would take a local bus or minibus to Zarqa (up to 150 fils), a minibus from there to Mafraq (350 fils) and from there another minibus to Umm al-Jimal for 200 fils. By car, you head away from Mafraq on Highway 5 towards As-Safawi where the other main road east from Amman via Azraq joins up on its desolate way to Baghdad. There is little reason for heading out this way, but should you want to, a minibus from Mafraq to As-Safawi costs 800 fils.

The Jordan Valley

Forming part of the Great Rift Valley of Africa, the fertile valley of the Jordan River was of considerable significance in Biblical times and is now the food bowl of Jordan.

The river rises from several sources, mainly the Anti-Lebanon Mountains in Syria, and flows down into the Sea of Galilee (Lake Tiberias), 212m below sea level, before draining into the Dead Sea which, at

392m below sea level, is the lowest point on earth. The actual length of the river is 360 km, but as the crow flies the distance between its source and the Dead Sea is only 200 km.

It was in this valley some 10,000 years ago that people first started to plant crops and abandon the nomadic lifestyle for permanent settlements. Villages were built, primitive water-harnessing schemes were undertaken and by 3000 BC, produce from the valley was being exported to neighbouring regions. The river itself is highly revered by Christians because Christ was baptised by St John the Baptist in its waters.

Since 1948, the Jordan River has marked the boundary between Israel and Jordan from the Sea of Galilee to the Yarbis River. From there to the Dead Sea the river marked the 1967 cease-fire line between the two countries, but since the two sides signed a peace agreement in 1994 instead marks the continuation of the official frontier.

In the 1967 war with Israel, Jordan lost the land it had annexed in 1950, the area known as the West Bank, now partly under Israeli control and partial Palestine National Authority administration. The population on the east bank of the valley dwindled from 60,000 before the war to 5000 by 1971. During the 70s new roads and fully serviced villages were built and the population has now soared to over 100,000. There are no cities along the river course, although the Roman city of Pella (Tabaqat Fahl) used to occupy a commanding position on the eastern bank.

Ambitious irrigation projects such as the East Ghor (now King Abdullah) Canal, extended in the late 80s and early 90s, have brought substantial areas under irrigation. A new dam at Al-Karama, 50 km from Amman, will irrigate another large area of new agricultural land when it is finally completed. The giant Al-Wahda dam project with Syria on the Yarmouk River has been stalled because international investors won't chip in without Israeli approval of the project.

The hot dry summers and short mild winters make for ideal growing conditions and two or even three crops a year are grown. Thousands of tonnes of fruit and vegetables are produced annually, with the main crops being tomatoes, cucumbers, melons and citrus fruits. The introduction of portable plastic greenhouses saw a sevenfold increase in productivity and this has meant that Jordan can now afford to export large amounts of its produce to the surrounding countries.

Apart from the Dead Sea and Pella, there is little to attract the visitor to the valley today, although Deir Alla might also be of interest to budding archaeologists.

Note

Keep your passport handy anywhere along the Jordan Valley and the Dead Sea area, as military checkpoints are frequent and ID is required. People without their passports have been known to be sent back to Amman. This also, by the way, goes for Wadi Araba.

The Jordanian people first cultivated the Jordan Valley 10,000 years ago when they abandoned a nomadic lifestyle.

PELLA

Another 30 km north of Deir Alla, near the village of Al-Mashari'a, are the ruins of the ancient city of Pella (Tabaqat Fahl), two km east of the road (it's not signposted, so ask). It is a steep walk up to the site, and the heat can be punishing in summer, so get some water at one of the shops in Al-Mashari'a before heading up.

Although the site was inhabited from as early as 5000 BC, and Egyptian texts make several references to it in the 2nd millennium BC, it was during the Graeco-Roman period that Pella flourished. The city's original name, Pehel, appears to have been altered to that of the birthplace of Alexander the Great. Pella followed the fate of many other cities in the region, coming successively under the rule of the Ptolemies, the Seleucids and the Jews, who largely destroyed Pella in 83 BC because its inhabitants were not inclined to adopt the customs of their conquerors.

Pella was one of the cities of the Decapolis, the commercial league of 10 cities formed by Pompey after his conquest of Syria and Palestine in 64 BC. It was to Pella that Christians fled persecution from the Roman army in Jerusalem in the 2nd century AD.

The city reached its peak during the Byzantine era and by 451 AD Pella had its own bishop. The population at this time is estimated to have been about 25,000. It was a popular bathing place, and the locals still enjoy a splash around in the cool springs of Wadi Al-Jirm. The defeat of the Byzantines by the invading Arab armies near the city in 635 was quickly followed by the knockout blow at the Battle of Yarmouk the next year.

There is strong evidence that, until the massive earthquake that shook the whole region in 747, the city of Fahl (its Arabic name) continued to prosper under Omayyad Arab rule. Archaeological finds show that even after the earthquake the city remained inhabited on a modest scale. The Mamelukes occupied it in the 13th and 14th centuries, but afterwards the town was all but abandoned until the 19th century.

In 1967 American excavations began. They were joined by an Australian team in 1978, which has since taken over the bulk of the work. Although it will never throw up classical monuments to the extent of, say, Jerash, it is a far more important site as it has revealed evidence of life from the Stone Age through to medieval Islamic times.

Things to See

The first building on the site you'll see emerges on the left of the track. Dubbed the **West Church**, it was built in the 6th century – you'll know it by its three standing columns. After passing through an area still under excavation, you pass the archaeologists' dig house on the left before coming to a

Part of a marble screen which separated the chancel from the nave and the trancepts in a church at Pella.

graveyard and the remains of a 14th century Mameluke mosque. Further off to the left is a Byzantine cistern that held 300,000 litres of water.

You then approach an area known dryly as the **main mound**. Here is a maze of houses, shops, store houses and the like. If you look across the valley, you can see a new building with three arches – the Government Rest House (what else?). Down below to the right lies a concentration of Byzantine and Roman structures, the most important of the city's public buildings.

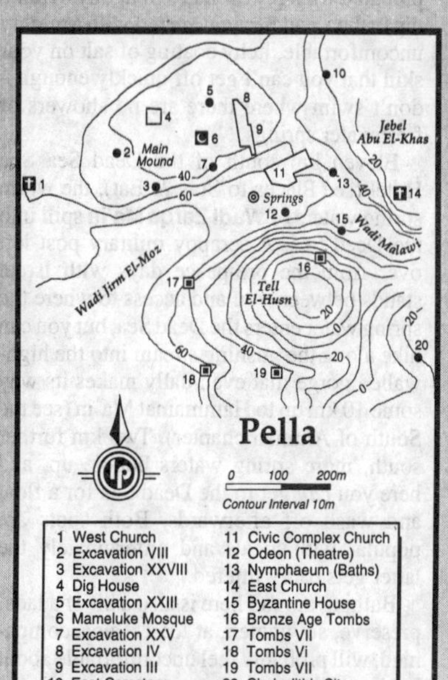

Right next to the imposing **Civic Complex Church**, built in the 6th and 7th centuries, is a small 1st century *odeon* or **theatre**, which sits on the Wadi Al-Jirm. Just east of the church are the remains of a Roman **nymphaeum** (baths), and further east again, perched up on a rise, is the **East Church**. To the south is **Tell Hosn**, on top of which was a Byzantine fort. To the west of the Civic Complex Church rise up imposing remnants of Bronze Age city walls.

Places to Stay & Eat

The *Government Rest House* has the predictable expensive eating option, and in the immediate vicinity it is the only option if you can't save your hunger for when you get back down to the main road or Al-Mashari'a. They can point you to a nearby guesthouse (no phone) where a room for two costs JD15. The rest house itself is separated from the site by a fence, although you can crawl under it in parts. Otherwise it's one helluva long walk uphill along the road that curls up around and behind the site.

Getting There & Away

From Irbid you can catch an Al-Mashari'a minibus from the west bus station. From Amman, take a minibus for Suwalha and change for Al-Mashari'a. You can also catch a series of minibuses up the valley from South Shuneh or down from North Shuneh.

Hitching is also a possibility. ■

DEIR ALLA

The site of Deir Alla, 35 km north of South Shuneh, is to the left of the main road heading north. Although there is little to see today, it is of historical importance. According to the Old Testament book of Joshua, Jacob is said to have rested here after wrestling with an angel and named the place Succoth. Some archaeologists have cast doubt on this claim.

An impressive sanctuary was built on the small tell (artificial hill) around 1500 BC. It was in use up until 1200 BC, when it was abandoned after being destroyed, some say by earthquake, others by Egyptian troops. Dutch archaeologists have found figurines and incense burners on the site, suggesting it may have been a temple.

Deir Alla was a Persian settlement in the 3rd century BC, but it was later abandoned until the arrival of the Muslim Arabs, from which time it served as a cemetery for nearby villages. There is a sign up at the base of the tell indicating what there once was to see.

Getting There & Away

The direct minibus from Abdali bus station

in Amman (400 fils) doesn't leave very often, so you could catch another minibus heading for Suwalha (370 fils – not to be confused with Suweileh), an important minibus interchange a few km south of Deir Alla. From here you can get buses to any destination (you may have to change once or twice along the way) north or south along the valley.

If you're coming from South Shuneh, take the Al-Karama minibus (70 fils) and change there for Deir Alla (200 fils). You can also make the trip down from Al-Mashari'a.

THE DEAD SEA

The Dead Sea (Al-Bahr al-Mayit or Bahr Lut – the Sea of Lot) is 75 km long, from six to 16 km wide and has no outlet. The name becomes obvious when you realise that the high salt content (33%) makes any plant or animal life impossible. The concentration of salt has nothing to do with the sea being below sea level. Rather, it comes about because of the high evaporation rate which has, over the years, led to the build-up of salts. The Jordan River flows into it, but the level of the sea is falling as more water is diverted from the river each year for irrigation.

At the southern end of the sea the Jordanians are exploiting the high potash content of the mineral-rich water. Each day more than one million tons of water are pumped into vast evaporation ponds covering some 10,000 hectares. The concentrated potash salts are then refined at the processing plant south of Safi. The project is now producing more than 1.9 million tons of potash annually, making Jordan one of the world's largest producers. However, with world prices failing to reach the levels predicted in feasibility studies, the project has not been the money-spinner that had been hoped for.

Whatever the reason for the Dead Sea's salt build-up, it certainly makes for an unusual swimming experience. The higher density of the water makes your body more buoyant, so drowning or sinking is a tricky feat. Swimming is also just about impossible as you're too high in the water to stroke properly, but of course you can always float on your back while reading the newspaper and have your picture taken. While paddling about you will probably discover cuts you never knew you had as the water gets into them, and if any gets into your eyes, be prepared for a few minutes of agony. After a dip in the Dead Sea you are left with a mighty uncomfortable, itchy coating of salt on your skin that you can't get off quickly enough – don't swim where there are no showers or freshwater springs.

Eleven km south of the Dead Sea Spa Hotel (see Places to Stay & Eat), the warm spring waters of **Wadi Zarqa Ma'in** spill into the Dead Sea. A scrappy military post left over from the pre-peace days with Israel stands between you and access to where the spring water enters the Dead Sea, but you can hike along the gushing stream into the high-walled gorge that eventually makes its way some 10 km up to Hammamat Ma'in (see the South of Amman chapter). Two km further south, more spring waters bubble up, and here you *can* get to the Dead Sea for a float and wash off afterwards. Both spots are popular with locals and unfortunately the latter gets badly littered.

Bathing around here is also a bit of a lads' preserve, so women, at least if unaccompanied, will probably feel uncomfortable about having a dip.

Places to Stay & Eat

In the wake of the peace treaty with Israel, a string of proposals for hotel and resort construction along the east (Jordanian) bank of the Dead Sea has emerged, and in mid-1996 investment of US$7 billion for new resorts was approved by the government. Watch this space.

For the moment, the 'resort' at Suweimeh is where most people go for a float. The government-owned *Dead Sea Rest House* (☎ 05-572901) provides day-trippers with showers, change rooms and an air-con restaurant. The prices in the restaurant are high so bring something to eat if you are staying for the day.

Entry costs JD1, which includes use of change rooms and a shower (bring your own soap). The place gets crowded on Friday and Sunday, and there are no showers after sunset.

An all-body Dead Sea mud pack, supposed to do wonders for your skin, will cost you JD2. Women are advised to insist on applying their own mud.

You can doss down in much overrated rooms here for JD33/42, including breakfast, but there is little incentive to do either this or eat in the pricey restaurant. As for the camels awaiting tourists at the entrance, make up your own mind.

A rather more up-market option is the *Dead Sea Spa Hotel* (☎ 09-802028), 5½ km further south. It costs JD7.500 to walk in and use their bit of beach, pool and spa, and lunch comes in at about JD10. Rooms, which you must book through their Amman office (☎ 06-602554), cost US$106/120.

Getting There & Away

You can get to the Dead Sea direct from Amman by the minibus (600 fils) that leaves from Al-Quds St. There are not many of these, and the last one back to Amman leaves about 4 pm. They go right to the resort.

There are more frequent buses from Amman to South Shuneh (ash-Shuneh al-Junubiyyeh) for 400 fils. From there another minibus leaves about every half hour for Suweimeh. The trip costs 200 fils, which for some odd reason you have to pay in 100 fils instalments, the second of them about halfway. This drops you about one km away – follow the sign to the rest house. You can also get to South Shuneh from Salt.

Friday and Sunday are the best days for hitching as families head down to the sea on their day off, although many cars are full.

If you plan to visit Israel, the resorts on the western side at 'Ain Feshka (West Bank) and Ein Gedi (Israel) are far more accessible.

East of Amman

To the east of Amman, the stony desert plain rolls on to Iraq and Saudia Arabia. It is cut by the Trans Arabia Pipeline and the highway to Iraq, and if not for these, east Jordan would be left alone to the Bedouin. Apart from Azraq and As-Safawi, there are no towns to speak of and no points of interest except for the desert castles and a small wildlife reserve.

The Desert Castle Loop

A string of what have become known as 'castles' lies in the desert east of Amman. Most of them were built or taken over and adapted by the Damascus-based Omayyad rulers in the late 7th and early 8th centuries. Two of the castles, Azraq and Hallabat, date from Roman times and there is even evidence of Nabataean occupation.

There are various theories about their use. The early Arab rulers were still Bedouin at heart and it is thought their love of the desert led them to build or take over these pleasure palaces, which appear to have been surrounded by artificial oases teeming with wild game and orchards.

Here they pursued their habitual pastimes of hawking, hunting and horse-racing for a few weeks each year. The evenings were apparently spent in excessive festivities with plenty of wine, women, poetry and song. Some historians believe that only here did the caliphs feel comfortable about so flouting the Qur'an. Others say they came to avoid epidemics in the big cities or even to maintain links with, and power over, their fellow Bedouin, the bedrock of their support in the conquered lands.

The castles can be visited in a loop from Amman out to Azraq and back and are never more than a couple of km off the road. With the exception of Qasr al-Mushatta, it is quite feasible to see all the main castles in one day using a combination of public transport and hitching. There are several so far off the

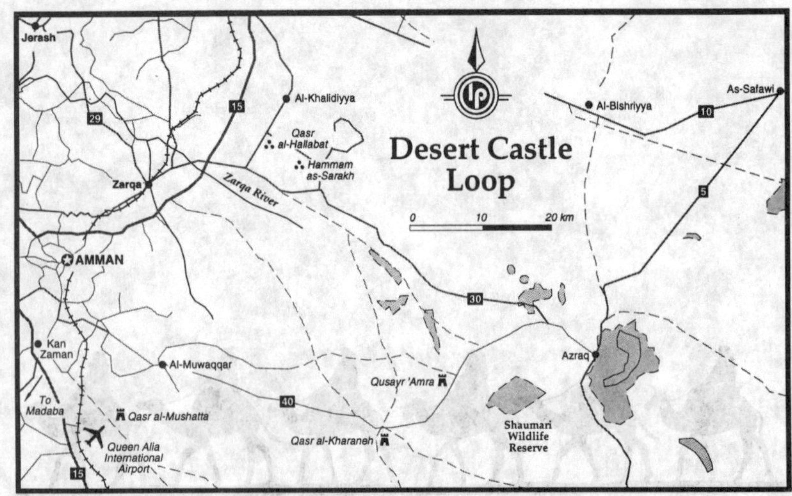

beaten track that only 4WDs and experienced guides will do. A private car would simplify matters, or you could arrange a taxi for the day from Amman. The Cliff Hotel can help with this, or you could negotiate directly with a taxi driver.

From Amman take the road for Zarqa and then turn off to Azraq. Hallabat is signposted off to the left after about 20 km. It is about another 10 km to the Qasr al-Hallabat (following a sometimes confusing route – you may need to ask a couple of times), and then a further three km to the Hammam as-Sarakh. Follow the same road eastwards back onto the main highway to Azraq, a further 70 km. An excellent road then heads back to Amman going right past the castles of Qusayr 'Amra and Qasr al-Kharaneh, before joining the Desert Highway on the southern outskirts of Amman.

At one stage this road widens out and has runway markings on it! Don't panic. You haven't strayed into the airport, it's just an emergency strip should the Queen Alia international airport be put out of action at any time. Traffic along this once very busy highway has slowed greatly due to the UN embargo on Iraq in place since 1990 over its invasion of Kuwait. Some illicit cargo still trundles along here, but it appears largely to have been choked off – effectively meaning the shutdown of one of Iraq's main lifelines.

QASR AL-HALLABAT

This was originally a Roman fort built during the reign of Caracalla (198-217 AD) as a defence against raiding desert tribes, although there is evidence that Trajan before him had established a post on the site of a Nabataean emplacement. During the 7th century it became a monastery and then the Omayyads further fortified it and converted it into a pleasure palace.

Today it is a jumble of crumbling walls and fallen stone, and many of them bear Greek inscriptions. The site is sometimes locked but the custodian will wander over and let you in if you wait by the gate. He may also feel inclined to point out the sites of interest among the ruins, or simply invite you to tea.

HAMMAM AS-SARAKH

A few km down the road heading east is this bathhouse and hunting lodge built by the Omayyads. It has been almost completely reconstructed over the years and you can see the channels that were used for the hot water and steam. These baths often had a hot ('*caldarium*'), lukewarm ('*tepidarium*') and cold bath ('*frigidarium*'). Here, the latter is absent. You can wander around the site pretty much at will.

Getting There & Away

From Amman take a minibus to Zarqa (up to 150 fils). Take a local service minibus to the other bus station in Zarqa (a matter of a few minutes), from where you can get a minibus to Hallabat (230 fils). The same bus drives right by the two sites. For reference, the Qasr is in west Hallabat (Hallabat al-Gharbi) and the Hammam in east Hallabat (Hallabat ash-Sharqi). From the Hammam it's probably easiest to hitch to the Azraq highway and on to Azraq.

A minibus runs between Zarqa and Azraq for 450 fils (1½ hours). You can either catch the Hallabat minibus back to Zarqa and start again from there, or simply wait to pick up an Azraq minibus on its way past.

AZRAQ

The oasis town of Azraq lies 103 km east of Amman and forms a junction of roads heading north-east to As-Safawi and on to Iraq, and south-east into Saudi Arabia.

To the south the wide, shallow valley of Wadi Sirhan stretches away to Saudi Arabia. Once a major caravan route, TE Lawrence used it on his journeys between Aqaba and the headquarters he established for a time in the castle here.

Azraq is one of the few places with water in the entire eastern desert and used to be one of the most important oases in the Middle East for birds migrating between Africa and Europe. It was also home to water buffalo and other wildlife. Until the mid-1990s, the water level in the swamps had fallen drastically because of the large-scale pumping from wells to supply Amman with drinking water. In the 1960s the swamp in and around Azraq covered some 10 sq km; 30 years later it was little more than a pool. In the past couple of years, attempts have been made to revive the oasis, reversing the pumping *to* the wells and making tentative moves to protect the area. The water buffalo and most other wildlife is gone forever, and few of the many species of migratory birds that once stopped here does so any longer – most settle on the shores of the Sea of Galilee in Israel instead. Still, there are hopes that aquatic life can be re-established and perhaps other improvements will follow. A visitors' centre was due to open at the end of 1996, and plans are afoot to use the oasis as a selling point in promoting Azraq more in the context of desert castle tourist jaunts from Amman.

The water that initially gave the oasis life originates in Syria, filters slowly through underground streams and surfaces at Azraq. It is estimated that this process takes 10,000 years. Until recently it was not being replenished at anything like the rate at which it is consumed.

The area was once home to various species of deer, bear, cheetah, ibex, oryx and gazelle. In the Shaumari Wildlife Reserve to the south-west of Azraq, an attempt is being made to reintroduce some of these animals to the area. Another reserve is planned for the north-east.

Information

There's a post office in the northern part of Azraq and a few exchange booths in the southern part – most do cash only.

Azraq is divided into two parts – north and south. From the intersection with the road to Amman, it is about five km to north Azraq, where the Qasr al-Azraq is located. South Azraq stretches for a few km to the south on the road to Saudi Arabia and is basically a truckies' paradise of restaurants, cafés and mechanics. Semitrailers, buses, long-distance service taxis and private cars from Saudi Arabia, Kuwait, Iraq, Syria and even Turkey all stop in at this frontier interchange. There are no service taxis or the like between the two halves of Azraq.

Qasr al-Azraq

The large castle here is built out of black basalt and in its present form dates from the beginning of the 13th century. It was originally three storeys high, but much of it crumbled in an earthquake in 1927. Greek and Latin inscriptions date earlier constructions on the site to around 300 AD – about the time of the reign of Diocletian. The Omayyads followed and maintained it as a military base, as did the 13th century Ayyubids. In the 16th century the Ottoman Turks stationed a garrison there.

After the 16th century, the only other recorded use of the castle was during WWI. For here in the winter of 1917 TE Lawrence made his desert headquarters during the Arab Revolt against the Turks. He set up his quarters in the room immediately above the southern entrance. His men used other areas of the fort and covered the gaping holes in the roof with palm branches and clay. They were holed up here for months in crowded conditions with little shelter from the cold, of which more than one man died.

The southern door is a single massive slab of basalt and Lawrence describes how it 'went shut with a clang and crash that made tremble the west wall of the castle'. Some of the paving stones inside the door have small indentations. These were carved by former gatekeepers who played an old board game using pebbles to pass the time.

In the middle of the courtyard is a small mosque that is possibly Omayyad. Opposite the entrance are storerooms and stables, and in the north-west corner what is thought to have been a prison. The old caretaker will tell you that the remaining three level structure in the west wall housed a Roman general.

The site is open daily and entrance is free.

Shaumari Wildlife Reserve

Established in 1975, the reserve was set up to reintroduce wildlife that had long since disappeared from the region. In 1978, for

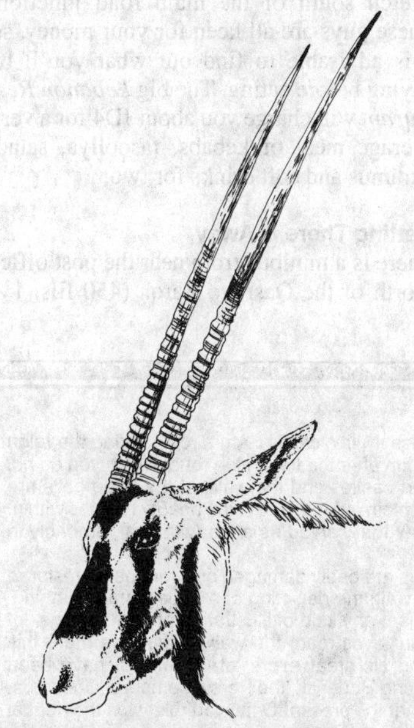

Oryx (large antelope) were once common in the Jordanian desert. Today they can be admired in the Shaumari Wildlife Reserve.

example, eight oryx were imported from the USA – in 1996 there were 222. Also roaming the reserve are several hundred gazelle (others are still found wild in the Jebel Druze area bordering Syria and south of Petra, but are in danger of extinction due to hunting). In 1981, two blue-necked ostriches were reintroduced – there were 14 of them at the time of writing.

There are plans to move half the oryx to a new reserve in Wadi Rum and so expand the project. In the meantime, the UN Development Programme allocated US$4 million in 1993 to sponsor conservation projects in the reserve. Other plans include establishing a new reserve to the north-east, around the Qasr Burqu north of the Iraq highway.

Unfortunately, you may not see much in this reserve apart from the ostriches, which tend to stick close to an enclosure not far from the entrance to the park. The gazelle and oryx largely roam free, so although you can borrow binoculars from the park attendants and climb up a viewing tower, don't expect to see hundreds of animals – the odd gazelle and oryx may be the limit. There are also some enclosures where sick animals are kept under observation.

Entrance costs 300 fils, or 100 fils for students. There are some brochures and a tiny natural history museum in the office.

The only way to this quite small reserve, about 10 km south of the old junction in Azraq, is by car or hitching. You can also arrange a taxi with one of the hotels in Azraq. Travel five km down the road to Saudi Arabia and turn right. After about five km what appears to be a eucalyptus copse in the stony desert rises up on the left. This is the reserve.

Places to Stay

Just south of the Qasr on the main road is the *Hotel Al-Sayad*. You may see signs for the *Hunter Hotel* too – they are one and the same, as *sayad* is Arabic for hunter. Although it looks quite flash with a pool and well manicured gardens, the rooms are fairly disappointing and overpriced at JD24/32 for singles/doubles that can't even boast a private bathroom. Bargaining is possible.

A few km further south and signposted on a side road to the west is the *Azraq Rest House*, also known as the Azraq Tourist Resort. If you're coming from Amman, turn left at the intersection and left again at the signpost down an oddly out of place tree-lined avenue. At JD26/32, the dowdy but adequate rooms come with breakfast, a bathroom and old TV. Like the Al-Sayad, the rest house has a restaurant (for about an extra JD5 per person, you can add dinner to the room price) and pool. It's a little sterile, and without a car a huge pain to get to.

A much better deal is the *Al-Zoubi Hotel*, about one km south of the intersection and just back from the road to Saudi Arabia. As everywhere else here, prices are negotiable, but you may be able to get a room with up to four beds for JD12. There are no singles. The penniless may choose the *Funduq Al-Waha* (no sign in English), a few hundred metres north of the Al-Zoubi along the same highway. A bed costs JD3 in a share double. Water is hot when the sun is. All these places can be reached through the Azraq telephone exchange – dial ☎ 647610 or 647611 and tell the operator who you want.

Places to Eat

A bunch of small restaurants lines the one km stretch south of the main road junction. These guys are all keen for your money, so it is advisable to find out what you'll be paying before eating. The big *Lebanon Restaurant* will charge you about JD4 for a very average meal of kebabs, fasooliya, salad, hummus and soft drinks for two.

Getting There & Away

There is a minibus from near the post office (north of the Qasr) to Zarqa (450 fils, 1½

Qusayr 'Amra

Heading back towards Amman on Highway 40, the Qusayr (little castle) 'Amra, built during the reign of caliph Walid I (705-715 AD), appears on the right 25 km after the fork in the road (which you do *not* take) to Zarqa. This is the best preserved of the desert castles and the walls of the three halls are covered with frescoes – some 350 sq metres all up. The plain exterior belies the beauty that lies within. It is believed the building was part of a greater complex that served as a caravanserai, probably in existence before the arrival of the Omayyads.

You first enter the audience hall. Many of the frescoes are badly damaged but were partly restored by a Spanish team in the 70s. Note on the right (west wall) the depiction of a nude woman bathing. What makes such a fresco remarkable is that under Islam any kind of illustration of living beings, let alone nudes, was all but prohibited (and the more your eyes roam the walls within, the more this particular theme becomes apparent). To her left stand six great rulers, of whom four have been identified – Caesar, a Byzantine emperor, the Visigoth king Roderick, the Persian emperor Chosroes, and the Negus of Abyssinia. The fresco either implies that the present Omayyad ruler was their equal or better, or is simply a pictorial list of Islam's enemies.

The small room with the dome was the steam room and had benches at either end. The dome is of special interest because it has a map of the heavens on it.

The floors of the two rooms at the back of the main hall bear a modest layer of mosaics.

A UNESCO world heritage site, it is now the subject of work by a French team to protect the frescoes from the occasional flash floods that can strike in this otherwise blisteringly dry desert.

From Azraq you can get a Zarqa minibus to where the highway forks to Zarqa and Amman. Get off there and you have 25 km left to hitch. Alternatively, you could organise a taxi in Azraq – the bigger hotels can help there. You're looking at about JD5 to Qusayr 'Amra, or about double to include Qasr al-Kharaneh. ■

The well-preserved desert castle of Qusayr 'Amra – now a world heritage site.

hours). It runs up and down the length of north and south Azraq in search of passengers before hitting the highway.

QASR AL-KHARANEH

This castle is a further 16 km along the road to Amman, stuck in the middle of a treeless plain to the left (south) of the highway. It seems it was the only one of the castles built solely for defensive purposes, although no-one is really sure what its use was. One popular explanation is that it was one of the first Islamic khans, or caravanserais, for travelling traders. The date of construction is uncertain but a painted inscription above one of the doors on the upper floor puts it at 710 AD. The presence of stones with Greek inscriptions in the main entrance frame suggests it was built on the site of a Roman or Byzantine building.

The long rooms either side of the entrance were used as stables. The castle is built around a central courtyard, in which are pillars that used to support a balcony. Right in the centre of the courtyard was a basin for collecting rainwater.

The castle is remarkably well preserved and most of the rooms, particularly those of the upper level, are decorated with carved plaster medallions set around the top of the walls. There are also Kufic inscriptions scattered around the upper level. Stairs in the south-east and south-west corners lead to the 2nd floor and the roof.

From Qasr al-Kharaneh it is also possible to visit Qasr al-Mushatta. There are tracks from the main road that cut across the desert to the airport, but these should not be attempted without a guide. The other alternative is to take the highway to the outskirts of Amman and then take the road to the airport.

JORDAN

The Omayyads

Princes of conquest rather than princes of religion, lords of the desert not disciples of prayer, the Omayyad caliphs have never ceased to intrigue historians and archaeologists alike. And for a good reason: the Omayyads occupy an important place in history as the first dynasty of Islamic rulers.

The main aspects of Omayyad history are well known: their headquarters was in Damascus, their authority lasted from 661 to 750, and history records the names of four famous rulers: Mu'awiya, 'Abd al-Malik, Walid I and Walid II. However, their culture and the details of their political and religious lives are clouded in mystery. One thing is certain, they left behind an unexpected image of a flourishing Islam and precious few clues for today's scholars. The most extensive remains of their culture are to be found in the Jordanian desert castles. It would perhaps be more accurate to speak not of castles but of organised residences comprising baths, hydraulic irrigation systems, and hunting and agricultural shelters. These palaces were places, away from the religious demands of the holy cities, where the caliphs could indulge in the fruits of their victories. The unexpected presence – notably inside Qusayr 'Amra – of numerous representations of naked women seems to agree with the identification of these palaces as centres of pleasure and indulgence. One can easily imagine the 'nouveaux riche' caliphs and their entourage celebrating at a sumptuous feast. However, this thesis is contested by certain historians who believe that the women are depicted in domestic rather than erotic scenes.

Others see in the choice of a semi-desert zone the sign of obvious nostalgia. Although the success of their conquests led to a more sedentary lifestyle, the Omayyad caliphs found in their desert castles a return to the ambience of their earlier nomadic existence.

Places of relaxation or of pleasure; nostalgic havens of a nomadic lifestyle now gone or palaces dedicated to debauchery; edifices erected to proclaim their glory and triumph or isolated retreats in the desert – no one knows for sure which of these depictions is most accurate. The opinion presented by Oleg Grabar – an eminent specialist – seems to be the most convincing. She favours a middle approach, placing the Omayyad lifestyle at a point between the serious and the sensuous. Whatever the balance, the success of the Omayyad regime was short-lived. The Omayyad form of government was quickly proven to be 'insufficiently Muslim' in the eyes of the fervent. They were pursued, massacred and replaced by the Abbasids.

Deposed, the Omayyads only surfaced again after some years in Spain. Their residences in the Jordanian desert survived them – they remain shrouded in myth. ■

JORDAN

QASR AL-MUSHATTA

Qasr al-Mushatta is 35 km south of Amman near the airport. It was the biggest and most lavish of all the Omayyad castles (its name means winter camp or residence) but for some unknown reason it was never finished. It is believed to have been begun under the caliph Al-Walid II, and that he also intended to establish a city in the area. Arab historians recount that he was assassinated by angry forced labourers, many of whom had died during the building because of a lack of water in the area.

Today it looks far from grand, especially as the elaborate carving on the façade was stripped and shipped off to a museum in Berlin after the palace was given to Kaiser Wilhelm, just before WWI, by Sultan Abd al-Hamid of Turkey. Some pieces of this are still lying around the site and they give some idea of how it must have once looked.

One unusual feature of the building is that the vaults are made from burnt bricks – an uncommon material in buildings of this style.

This site is kept locked at night but is opened each day by the soldiers who are part of the airport security.

Getting There & Away

The Qasr al-Mushatta is not more than two km from the airport but cannot be reached on foot, as security guards will not allow you to walk past the control tower to get to it. The only option is to drive the 10 km around the airport perimeter: turn right at the roundabout by the Alia Gateway Hotel as you approach the airport and the road will take you past at least two checkpoints and on to the castle. You will be asked to leave passports, and possibly car documents, with the checkpoints – to be picked up on the return trip.

If you take the airport bus (see Getting Around in the Amman chapter) as far as the turn-off, you might be able to hitch around, although little traffic heads out that way. You might also bargain with a taxi at the airport to take you.

Diving

Many people come to Aqaba just for the diving. The best diving is just off the beach on the Yamanieh Reef, north of the Saudi Arabian border, and although the general consensus is that Ras Mohammed in the Sinai is more spectacular, the diving here is still some of the best in the world.

Dive Centres Aqaba's dive centres accept the usual dive cards, but it is recommended that you go down with an instructor if you haven't dived for more than six months. The Gulf is a good place for beginners, as there is plenty to see at fairly shallow depths (visibility is close to 20m). According to Jordanian law, diving deeper than 30m is prohibited. March and April are the worst times to dive because of algae bloom.

The Royal Diving Centre (☎ 317035; fax 317097), which has been operating since 1987, is on the beach, about 12 km out of town. It charges JD15 a dive or JD27 for two dives in a day, including all equipment hire. A one-off trial dive costs JD25. A day's snorkelling costs JD3.500, or you can just hang around the pool for JD2. There is a cafeteria but no accommodation. A private bus does a round of the big hotels in town at about 9 am and returns at 4.30 pm.

The longest established dive centre is at the Aquamarina I Hotel (☎ 316250; fax 314089). It is the most expensive, too. It does boat dives only. These dives cost a whopping JD48, including equipment – a strong incentive to pay for the second dive too (JD16.800). A half-day trial dive from the boat with basic instruction costs JD45.

The dive centre at the Al-Cazar Hotel (☎ 314131; fax 314133) charges from JD18 to JD28 per dive, depending on the amount of equipment you need. It also offers trial dives, courses for most levels and night dives.

The recently opened Red Sea Diving Centre (☎ 322323; fax 318969), run by Mohammed al-Momany, charges JD24 for one dive with full equipment and JD40 for two dives in the same day. You can also hire out snorkelling gear for JD8.

Courses PADI (Professional Association of Diving Instructors – sometimes known as Pay And Dive Immediately) open-water courses and the CMAS certificate, both of which take from four to seven days to complete, cost anything from about JD200 at the Royal Diving Centre to JD290 at the Aquamarina. All centres offer more advanced courses.

OLIVIER CIRENDINI

The Gulf of Aqaba is home to a selection of exotic marine life and spectacular coral reef.

OLIVIER CIRENDINI

DAMIEN SIMONIS

Jordan

Top: The road to the three peaks of Mt Nebo; the Siyagha peak is thought by some to be the site of Moses' tomb.

Bottom: Amman's 6000-seat Roman theatre viewed from the Citadel.

South of Amman

With the notable exception of Jerash, the bulk of Jordan's top attractions lie well south of the capital. There is little doubt that the growing influx of tourists swarming all over Petra, Aqaba and, as yet to a lesser extent, Wadi Rum, is beginning to have a telling effect on the relationship between locals and foreign visitors. With so many videocam-toting outsiders tramping around, it is understandably hard to resist the temptation to extract a little extra. This is a nice way of saying that the rip-off is becoming a more widely practised sport in the south. So it is worth being a little more vigilant with people trying to separate you from your money. In all, the atmosphere remains relaxed and low key – certainly the Jordanians have a long way to go before reaching the virtuoso levels of hustle and rip-off known in other parts of the world, and the warmth and hospitality for which they are justly known survives largely intact in even the most heavily touristed areas.

There are three routes south of Amman to Aqaba: the Desert Highway, the King's Highway and the Wadi Araba road via the Dead Sea. If you only have limited time, the Desert Highway is the road to use – but it is the least interesting. Fast and flat, there is little to stop for until you reach the turn-off for Wadi Rum, beyond which lies Aqaba.

Ideally, travel the King's Highway, which is by far the most interesting route taking you past ancient towns, castles and through some spectacular country. If returning to Amman from Aqaba, the Wadi Araba road, which hugs the Israeli border and then the Dead Sea, makes a decent alternative to the Desert Highway. From the Dead Sea you can turn north-eastwards for Madaba or Amman.

Note

You must always have your passport ready for military checkpoints along the Wadi Araba and Dead Sea (and the Jordan Valley if you intend to pursue the route directly north). There are also very few petrol stations between Aqaba and the northern end of the Dead Sea – make sure your tank is full.

The King's Highway

The picturesque King's Highway (known in Arabic as 'At-Tariq as-Sultani', the Sultan's Rd) twists and winds its way south, connecting the historic centres of Madaba, Kerak, Tafila, Shobak and Petra. Transport along the route is reliable but not always frequent.

Hitching is often the quickest way to go as you don't have to wait for minibuses (which you can often pick up on the road anyway) to fill up at bus stations, but be prepared for waits of an hour or two on deserted stretches. Towns along the way are connected by a series of minibuses and/or occasional service taxis.

MADABA

This easy-going little town 30 km south of Amman is perhaps best known for its Byzantine-era mosaics, including the famous 6th century map of Palestine. In recent years a lot of work has been done to reveal still more of these priceless treasures, and this greater attention focussed on the city's past is raising its profile as a stop on the tourist trail. One sure sign that it is having the desired effect is the mushrooming of souvenir shops in the past couple of years.

The most important Christian centre in all Jordan, Madaba has long been a good example of religious tolerance. Increased activity by the Muslim Brotherhood in the late 70s and early 80s did little to endear the two communities to one another, but since the mid-80s, tension between them has again dropped away.

History

Madaba, the Biblical Moabite town of

Medeba (Isaiah 15:2, Joshua 13:9,16), was one of the towns divided among the 12 tribes of Israel. It is also mentioned on the famous Mesha Stele (Moabite Stone) raised in about 850 BC by the Moab king Mesha and detailing in its inscriptions his battles with the kings of Israel.

The Ammonites were in control of Madaba by 165 BC, but it was taken by Hyrcanus I of Israel about 45 years later and later promised to the Nabataeans by Hyrcanus II in return for helping him recover Jerusalem. Under the Romans from 106 AD, it became a prosperous provincial town with the usual colonnaded streets and impressive public buildings. That prosperity continued during the Byzantine period up until the Persian invasion in 614 AD, and most of the mosaics that can now be seen date from this period.

Further damage was inflicted after the Persians by a devastating earthquake which occurred in the middle of the 8th century, leading to the town's abandonment. It wasn't until the late 19th century that the mosaics were uncovered when 2000 Christians from Kerak migrated here and started digging foundations for houses.

Information

The tourist office (☎ 543376) is at the site of the Burnt Palace, about 100m away from St George's Church in a side street off to the left. It opens from 8 am to 2 pm daily. The guy running the small shop of the National Society for the Preservation of the Heritage of Madaba and its Suburbs (quite a mouthful!) in the same spot is more than willing to help with information if the office is closed.

You can change cash and travellers' cheques in several banks, including the Bank of Jordan and the Jordan National Bank. The post office is near St George's.

St George's Church

The most interesting mosaic, in the Greek Orthodox St George's Church, is a clear map of Palestine and lower Egypt. Although now far from complete, many features can still be made out, including the Nile River, the Dead Sea and the map of Jerusalem showing the

Church of the Holy Sepulchre. More than two million pieces made up the original mosaic, laid out around 560 AD over an area of 25 by five metres. News that the mosaic map had been found reached Europe in 1897, leading to a flurry of exploratory activity in the region. The church is open from 8.30 am to 6 pm (from 10.30 am on Friday and Sunday). Entry costs JD1.

Archaeological Park

Careful excavation and restoration from 1991 to 1995 has led to the creation of this 'park'. Its core takes in the sites of the 7th century churches of the Virgin and of the Prophet Elias, along with parts of an earlier structure now known as the Hippolytus Hall. Between the two churches lies the well-preserved remains of a Roman road, which ran east to west between the then Roman city's gates. Several mosaics have been uncovered and ramps built to allow visitors to examine them.

By far the most impressive is that in the **Hippolytus Hall**, depicting scenes from the classic Oedipal tragedy of Phaedre and Hippolytus. The main mosaic in the **Church of the Virgin**, a masterpiece of geometrical design, appears to have been executed in Omayyad times, but by Christians, not Muslims. The surviving mosaics in the **Church of the Prophet Elias** are not as eye-catching. At the eastern end of the Roman road, a projected Mosaic School, partly funded by the Italian government, aims to teach locals how to restore mosaics. It is housed in what remains of yet another Byzantine church, known now as the **Church of the Sunna Family**, after the property's former owners.

Across the road from this compound, more work remains to be done at the Burnt Palace and Church of Al-Khadir. Excavations have been carried out and the mosaics found – it remains to set up a similar system of ramps and viewing positions to fully incorporate them into the Archaeological Park. Work was due to begin in mid-1996.

There seems to be some confusion about when the site is open. From 8.30 am to 5.30 pm seems to be the winning answer, but only until 3 pm or closed altogether on alternate Fridays. Entrance is free.

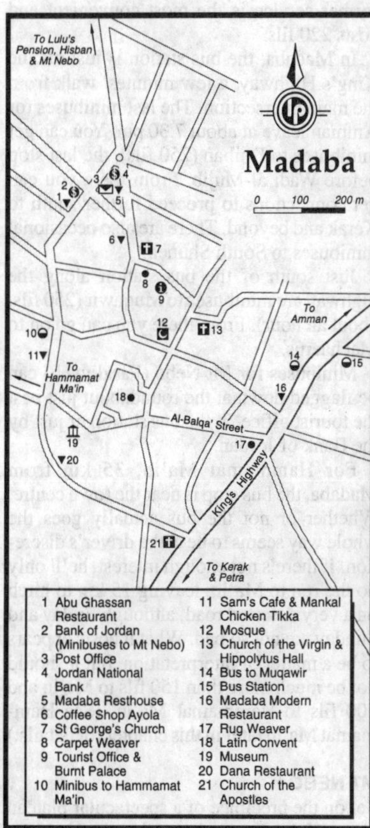

Church of the Apostles

As part of the overall programme to rehabilitate the town's heritage, yet another extraordinary mosaic, dedicated to the 12 Apostles, is on view in a tastefully designed building to replace what little was left of the Church of the Apostles, down by the King's Highway about one km from St George's Church. Opening times are supposed to be the same as for the Archaeological Park, but you can take this with a grain of salt.

Museum

The museum, taking in several old Madaba homes containing some fine mosaics, is tucked away at the end of a small alley. Apart from mosaics, the museum houses jewellery, traditional costumes, a small archaeological display – mostly pottery, seals and the like – and a copy of the Mesha Stele. The most interesting mosaics are the 6th century *Banche & Satyrs* in a room marked **Traditional House of Madaba** (50 years old), and one depicting paradise and its fruits in an unmarked room. The museum is open from 9 am to 5 pm (10 am to 4 pm on Friday and holidays) and closed Tuesday. Entry is JD1.

Carpet Weaving

Madaba is also famous for its colourful rugs; in a couple of small shops in town you can see them being woven on large hand looms. Unfortunately they are catching on to the tourist lure, and new carpet-weaving shops seem to be popping up all over the joint.

Places to Stay & Eat

There's one fine place to stay, but it is often full. *Lulu's Pension* (☎ 08-543678) is about a 10 minute walk from St George's. Head out along the road for Mt Nebo, but at the second roundabout go straight on (rather than left for Mt Nebo). Open since mid-1995, it has 13 beds in very clean, comfortable rooms. The price of JD10 per person includes breakfast and use of a communal kitchen. There's a big TV and music area, where you can roll out your sleeping bag for JD6. You can camp in the yard if you have a tent.

Along the King's Highway there are a few cheap restaurants. The *Madaba Modern Restaurant* serves a half chicken, hummus and salad for JD1.700. The *Abu Ghassan Restaurant* is a similar sort of place. The ubiquitous *Mankal Chicken Tikka* chain has a place near the minibus stop for Hammamat Ma'in. Next door, you can have a beer at *Sam's Café*.

Opposite St George's is the *Coffee Shop Ayola*, a swish new place that offers good but expensive felafels (500 fils), filter coffee for JD1 and great ice cream in a pseudo Bedouin atmosphere. The tour bus people usually get dragged around to the equally new *Dana Restaurant*, not far from the Church of the Apostles. The food is OK and the place very clean, but again you are paying more than really necessary for pretty standard stuff. The other option at this end is the *Madaba Resthouse*, which puts on quite an attractive all-you-can-eat buffet for JD6.

Getting There & Away

Madaba is served by minibuses from Amman's Raghadan and Wahadat bus stations. The former service is the most convenient and costs 220 fils.

In Madaba, the bus station is just off the King's Highway, a few minutes' walk from the main intersection. The last minibuses for Amman leave at about 7.30 pm. You can get minibuses to Dhiban (250 fils), the last stop before Wadi al-Mujib. From there you can get connections to proceed further south to Kerak and beyond. There are also occasional minibuses to South Shuneh.

Just south of the bus station along the highway are minibuses to Muqawir (250 fils, about an hour). From there you can go on to Machaerus.

Minibuses for Mt Nebo (Fasaliyyeh) can be flagged down at the roundabout just past the tourist office, at the bus station or just by the Bank of Jordan.

For Hammamat Ma'in, 35 km from Madaba, the bus stop is near the town centre. Whether or not the bus actually goes the whole way seems to be at the driver's discretion. If there's not enough interest, he'll only do the run to Ma'in, leaving 15 km to hitch on a very deserted road, although Friday and Sunday are not so bad. What it costs appears to be a matter of interpretation, but it should not be much more than 150 fils to Ma'in and 500 fils to Hammamat Ma'in. (See Hammamat Ma'in later in this chapter for details.)

MT NEBO

Set on the precipice of a spectacular plateau about 10 km west of Madaba, the Mt Nebo area is celebrated as a memorial to Moses. There are actually three peaks, the first called Nebo and the last Siyagha ('monastery' in Aramaic), which commands sweeping views from right on the edge of the plateau and is one of the supposed sites of Moses' tomb. On a clear day you can see the Dead Sea and even the spires of the churches in Jerusalem.

Inside the church you will find souvenirs for sale, and with luck an interesting guide to Jordan written by the Franciscan Fathers. The Franciscan monastery is out of bounds for tourists.

There is a strange 500 fils collective ticket 'for services' that seems to be issued to people entering in groups of one or more.

The Siyagha Mosaics

The Franciscan brothers bought the site at Mt Nebo in the 30s and have excavated the ruins of a church and monastery. The existence of the church was reported by a Roman nun, Etheria, in 393 or 394 AD, and by the 6th century it had expanded to a large Byzantine church and baptistry. Although little remains of the buildings that housed them, the mosaics from this period can be seen today, protected by a modern structure erected by the Franciscans.

The main mosaic is yet another remarkable work of patient artistry in the school of what you have already seen in Madaba. Measuring some three by nine metres, it is well preserved and depicts scenes of wine-making as well as hunters and an assortment of animals, such as a panther, bear, fox, lion, sheep and hens. ■

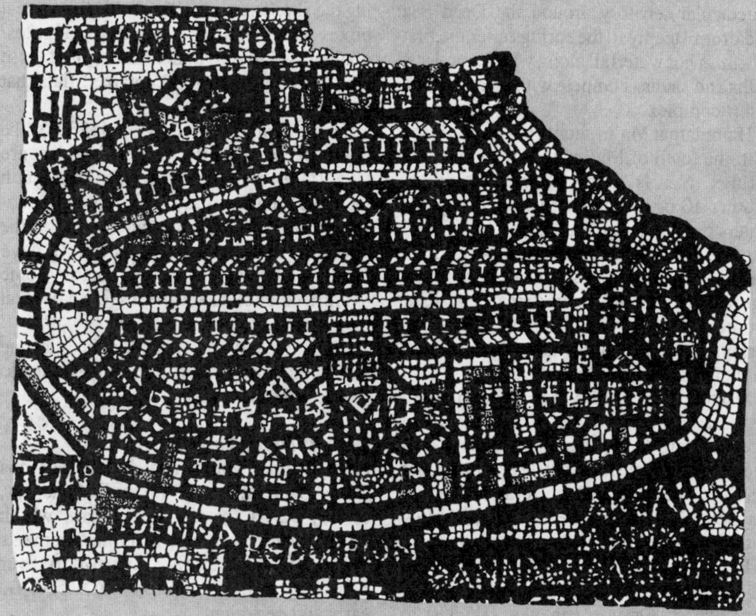

This mosaic map of Jerusalem can be found in Madaba.

The site is open from 7 am to 7 pm (5 pm in winter) daily. The rest house was closed at the time of writing, but you can eat and drink at the roadside *Siyagha Restaurant* a couple of km short of the site on the Madaba road.

Getting There & Away

From Madaba take a minibus from the traffic roundabout (near the tourist office) or by the Bank of Jordan heading for Mt Nebo (Fasaliyyeh) for 100 fils. From there it's about a four km walk. There are a few vehicles along this section so it may be possible to hitch. A taxi will take you from Madaba and back (giving you half an hour to wander around) for JD5.

HAMMAMAT MA'IN

The hot springs and resort of Hammamat Ma'in lie 35 km south-west of Madaba. The serpentine road crosses some of the most spectacular territory around the Dead Sea and drops steeply to the springs after the first 30 km. A hot waterfall along with natural spa baths and saunas compete with an expensive resort complex.

Hammamat Ma'in should not be confused with the town of Ma'in, 15 km short of the springs. Nor is it the Biblical Callirhoe, another 10 or so km west where the spring waters carried along Wadi Zarqa Ma'in spill into the Dead Sea. The therapeutic value of Callirhoe's waters was made famous by figures such as Herod the Great, and their source also feeds the Hammamat Ma'in springs, whose qualities have equally been known since ancient times.

A road connection has been mooted between Hammamat Ma'in and the Dead Sea, but until then the spring waters at that end of the wadi are most easily reached along the Dead Sea road north of Kerak or south of the Dead Sea resorts (see The Jordan Valley in the North & West of Amman chapter).

Before you even get into this place, you're hit for money. It's a minimum JD2 just to approach it. Or you can pay JD3.850 to access the pool (which you could actually pay for separately if you so choose once inside). As you walk down to the Ashtar Hotel, you'll see a 25m waterfall fed by warm spring water. You can go across the stream and, if you can find a vaguely dry spot, drop your stuff and splash around.

For a free sauna and spa, walk along the road passing under part of the hotel and after a few hundred metres you'll reach a mosque. Continue past this another 50m and you'll come to a natural sulphur spa bath. The cave to the right is as good a sauna as you'll ever have. Women should be aware that this is, unfortunately, generally a male-dominated activity – the usual warnings apply and going alone is not a good idea.

Places to Stay & Eat

There is no cheap accommodation here, unless you search for a spot to camp around the stream. The cheapest is the *Safari Caravans* park just behind the Drop & Shop 'supermarket' on your left shortly after entering the site. These claustrophobic little sweat boxes are JD15/20 a night for singles/doubles – plus 10% tax! To the right of these are 'chalets', small self-contained flats that go for JD27/37 plus tax.

In the *Ashtar Hotel* (☎ 08-545500), the heart of the resort, singles/doubles are US$70/90. The hotel has spa and health facilities for guests only. It also has an expensive restaurant. The only alternative is the poolside restaurant which doesn't have much to offer anyway. Or you can buy some overpriced biscuits and drinks (even beer) at the so-called supermarket.

There is a drink stand by the mosque which, like everywhere else, feels entitled to charge over the odds.

Getting There & Away

From Amman you can catch the JETT bus from Abdali station at 8 am for JD4 one way, or pay JD10 for the round trip, which includes entry and lunch. From Amman's Wahadat station there are up to four minibuses in the morning for JD1.500. Be early and be patient.

From Madaba the odd minibus runs to Hammamat Ma'in (about 500 fils), although more often than not it only goes as far as

Ma'in (150 fils). It is not uncommon for the minibus driver to try on a nasty rip-off at this point. In that case you have a long hitch in front of you – sometimes easier said than done. Returning, there is the JETT bus to Amman (JD4), which leaves from the pool at around 5 pm. There may also be a minibus or service taxi back to Madaba (JD1). The Drop & Shop supermarket seems to be the best place to pick something up, but be there at about 4.30 pm and keep your eyes peeled.

MACHAERUS

Perched on a 700m high hill about 50 km south-west of Madaba are the ruins of Herod the Great's fortress Machaerus. His successor, Herod Antipas, had John the Baptist beheaded here. The hill, which commands splendid views over the Dead Sea to the west and surrounding valleys, was first fortified about 100 BC and expanded by Herod the Great in 30 BC. From here, Jewish troops were supposed to keep the Nabataeans in check.

Herod Antipas feared John the Baptist's popularity and did not take kindly to criticism of his second marriage to Herodias, but whether or not he really wanted him killed is not entirely clear. One night he promised Salome, Herodias' daughter, anything she wanted for her dancing and she, on her mother's prompting, asked for the head of John the Baptist.

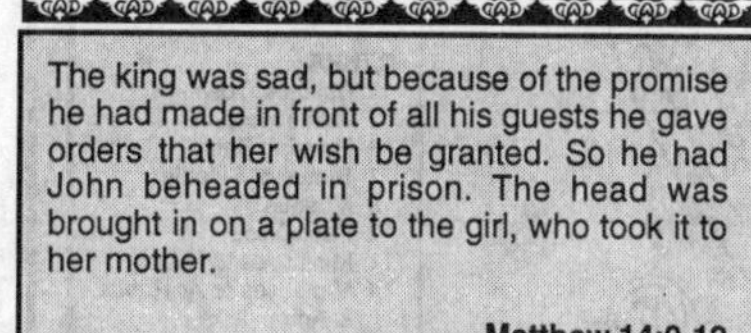

The king was sad, but because of the promise he had made in front of all his guests he gave orders that her wish be granted. So he had John beheaded in prison. The head was brought in on a plate to the girl, who took it to her mother.

Matthew 14:9-12

Things to See

The fort, known to the locals as **Qala'at al-Meshneq**, is approached up a set of stairs. Excavations are still going on. There's not an awful lot to see, but as you pass the workers' hut you come upon **baths** and around them to the east and north are vestiges of Herod Antipas' **palace**. On the west side are parts of the fortress **wall** and defensive **towers**. From here you can see clearly across the Dead Sea into the West Bank. Bring your own food and water as there is nowhere to buy anything here.

Getting There & Away

From Madaba take a Muqawir minibus (250 fils, about one hour), which follows the King's Highway to Libb and turns right. This is not exactly a heavily touristed spot, so tell the driver what you want and he'll let you out at an appropriate place. You can see the hill and fort to the west.

It is about half an hour's walk directly across a goat path and down to an unfinished road that will take you to the stairs. On the way along the road you'll see some artificial caves (tombs?). The minibuses back to Madaba are infrequent and finish at about 5 pm, so keep a watch out.

KERAK

The town of Kerak (often spelled Karak) can be reached from the Desert Highway, but if you go this way you'll miss one of the most spectacular natural sights in Jordan, the canyon of **Wadi al-Mujib**, about 50 km north of Kerak on the King's Highway. The canyon is over a km deep and the road winds precariously down one side and up the other. At the bottom, there is only a bridge over the wadi and a rather forlorn-looking post office. This canyon is the Arnon of the Bible and formed a natural boundary between the Moabites in the south and the Amorites in the north.

The greater part of Kerak, 900m above sea level, lies within the walls of the old Crusader town and is dominated by the fortified citadel (or *'qasr'*) – one in a long line built by the Crusaders stretching from Aqaba in the south right up into Turkey in the north.

History

Kerak lies on the routes of the ancient caravans that used to travel from Egypt to Syria in the time of the Biblical kings, and were also used by the Greeks and Romans. It is mentioned several times in the Bible as Kir, Kir Moab and Kir Heres and later emerges as a provincial Roman town, Characmoba.

The arrival of the Crusaders launched the town back into prominence and the Crusader king, Baldwin I of Jerusalem, had the castle built in 1132 AD. This site was chosen because it was strategically placed midway between Shobak and Jerusalem and had a commanding position. It became the capital of the Crusader district of Oultrejourdain and, with the taxes levied on passing caravans and food grown in the district, helped Jerusalem prosper.

After holding out for years against attacking Arab armies, it finally fell to the forces of Saladin in 1188 AD. The governor of the fort at the time, Renauld de Chatillon, who was killed by Saladin shortly after the Crusaders' defeat at the Battle of Hittin, had the charming habit of throwing his enemies over the battlements of the castle into the valley 450m below. He even went to the trouble of having a wooden box fastened over their heads so they wouldn't lose consciousness before hitting the bottom!

The Mameluke Sultan Baibars strengthened the fortress in the late 13th century, but three towers later collapsed in an earthquake. In the 1880s, local infighting compelled the Christians of Kerak to flee north to Madaba and Ma'in, and peace was only restored after thousands of Turkish troops were stationed in the town.

Information

The tourist office in the same building as the Castle Hotel seems to exist primarily for decorative purposes. You can try your luck from 8 am to 2 pm daily except Friday. You can change cash and travellers' cheques at several banks, and get a cash advance on Visa at the Housing Bank – the process is wearying, but you'll get there in the end. It opens

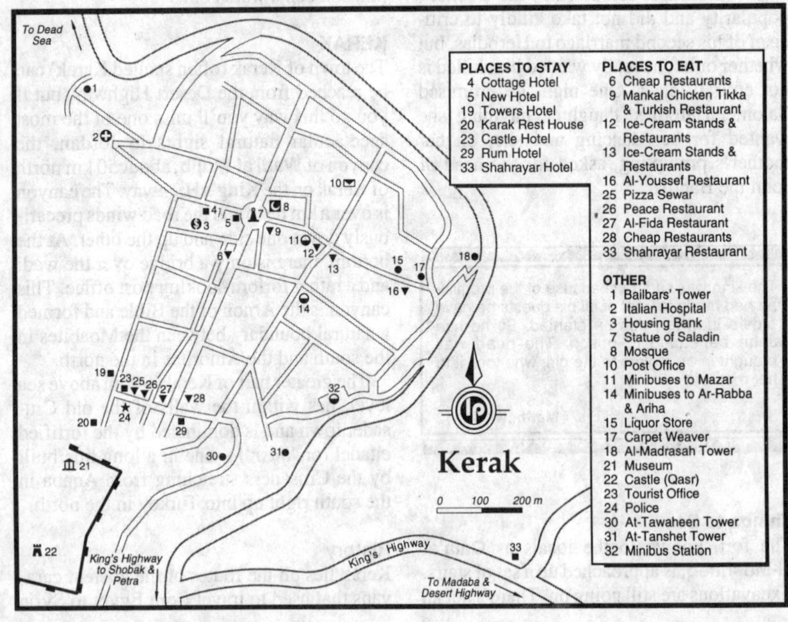

from 8.30 am to 1 pm and again from 4 to 5.30 pm (3.30 to 5 pm in winter). There is also a small post office.

Qasr

The citadel ('*qasr*') itself has been partially restored and is a jumble of rooms and vaulted passages. It is still possible to see the cisterns where water was stored, but not much else. A torch (flashlight) would be useful for poking around some of the darker places, but watch your step as there are gaping light shafts and collapsed ceilings all over the place.

Shortly after entering, stairs lead down to the museum, or you can veer up to the right and double back to find yourself in the lower of two long vaulted rooms, probably used as stables or dining halls. The multistoreyed building at the southern end was the *donjon* (dungeon).

Ask the museum caretaker to show you the underground vaulted rooms entered by a locked door about 30m opposite the museum. This is the best preserved and deepest part of the castle. The hall is 150m long and divided by a larger room with four *iwans* (vaulted halls). On the west side of the iwan room is the original entrance to the castle. Stacked at the southern end are piles of ancient and medieval pottery and artefacts.

The castle is open daily during daylight hours and admission is JD1.

Museum

The museum is down a flight of stairs on the right as you enter the castle. Apart from a selection of Neolithic tools and Bronze and Iron Age pottery, it also has one of the many copies of the Mesha Stele and a translation of its text.

The museum is open from 8 am to 5 pm daily except Tuesdays, and the castle admission covers entry.

Places to Stay

The number of hotels operating in Kerak doubled in the first half of the 90s, which might be a little overdone given that for many tourists Kerak is just a stopover between Amman and Petra. Practically all the hotel owners will bargain down – don't simply accept the first room rate offered.

The cheapest, and worst, place in town is the *New Hotel* (☎ 351942) in the centre, away from the castle. A bed in pretty basic rooms costs JD2.500 and the amenities are grotty. You can cook in the kitchen if that tempts you.

Next up is the *Castle Hotel* (☎ 352489), near the old fortress. Singles/doubles/triples go for about JD5/7/10. The rooms are cleaner than those at the New Hotel and showers are communal. The loos are a bit smelly.

Just around the corner, the same people operate the *Towers Hotel* (☎ 354293), which has clean rooms, some with private shower and loo. You get two sheets, a decent mattress, a small towel and even toilet paper is provided. As ever, room prices are flexible, but it appears JD10/15 are the basic rates. In bigger rooms, prices are negotiated on the basis of JD7 per person, regardless of whether the room has its own bathroom or not.

A Stele at Twice the Price

The original Mesha Stele was found by a missionary at Dhiban, just north of Wadi al-Mujib, in 1868. It was a major discovery because it not only provided historical detail of the battles between the Moabites and the kings of Israel, but was also the earliest example of Hebrew script to be unearthed. After surviving intact from about 850 BC (when it was raised by King Mesha of Moab to let everyone know of his successes against Israel) to 1868 AD, it came to a rather unfortunate end.

After finding the stele, the missionary reported it to Charles Clermont-Ganneau at the French Consulate in Jerusalem who then saw it, made a mould of it and went back to Jerusalem to raise the money which he had offered the locals for it. While he was away the local families argued over who was going to get the money and some of the discontented lit a fire under the stone and then poured water on it, causing it to shatter. Although most pieces were recovered, inevitably some were lost. The remnants were gathered together and shipped off to France and the reconstructed stone is now on display in the Louvre in Paris. ■

JORDAN

Just as good and in the centre of town is the *Cottage Hotel* (☎ 354359). The sign only makes it as far as *Cot* in Cottage. It is very clean and has some large rooms. Doubles without private bathroom go for JD7; those with bath cost JD10. The loos here are absolutely spotless.

The lads at the *Rum Hotel* (☎ 351351) have possibly overdone the self-promotion bit, with billboards as far back as Wadi al-Mujib and plenty of hard sell if they can collar you. The place is a bit boxy and seems to have been built a little too hastily, but the rooms are quite OK at JD6 to JD10 per person, depending on their size.

Outside of town on the road to Madaba lies the rather odd *Shahrayar Hotel* (☎ 353549), where rooms start at JD10/15. A room for four with private bathroom up the spiral staircase costs JD20. Like everywhere else, they'll bargain down. The huge restaurant downstairs has an outdoor section boasting views across the valley to the castle.

Next to the castle is the *Karak Rest House* (☎ 351148), which charges JD27.500/40 for comfortable rooms, including taxes and breakfast. The views are excellent, as it is right on the edge of the escarpment.

Places to Eat

From the restaurant of the *Karak Rest House* you have splendid views over the Dead Sea on a clear day, but the prices are high and the food average. A small can of Amstel beer costs about JD2.

Apart from the rest house there are a few cheap eateries around, but after 9 pm it can be difficult to find one open. The *Peace Restaurant*, a couple of doors down from the Castle Hotel, serves up a filling mixed grill of meat with several dips and salad for about JD3.500, including a soft drink. A block further on is *Al-Fida* restaurant, which serves up fare of much the same quality for similar prices. The difference is you can get a beer. Next to the Peace Restaurant stands the rather unfortunately named *Pizza Sewar*, a kind of fast-food place.

There are a couple of other cheapies a block east of the Al-Fida, and a small group of cheap-food places and ice-cream stands a block east of the central roundabout, where a statue of Saladin now stands instead of a Roman column. Virtually on the roundabout is the *Turkish Restaurant*, typical of the genre. Next door is the vaguely Indian-style *Mankal Chicken Tikka* joint. Further east again down the same road you'll find another restaurant in the same range as the Al-Fida, the *Al-Youssef Restaurant*, which is also quite decent. There's at least one liquor store, across the road from the Al-Youssef.

Getting There & Away

From the bus station there are minibuses and service taxis for Amman along the Desert Highway. Minibuses depart until 6 pm and cost 750 fils. They also run south to Tafila (500 fils, 1½ hours). Public transport along the King's Highway is infrequent and, from Tafila at least, you're probably better off hitching. That way you can jump on a minibus if one comes and also have the chance of getting a lift with a truck or private car.

Minibuses along the King's Highway for Ar-Rabba and up as far as Ariha (300 fils; just before Wadi al-Mujib) depart from a side street in the centre of town, although some people wait for them on the main road by the bus station. From Ariha you can connect with minibuses to Dhiban and then on to Madaba.

Minibuses to Aqaba run down Wadi Araba (JD1.750, three hours) every hour or so. They stop in Safi for the Dead Sea, should you really want to get to this part of it.

AROUND KERAK

The Dead Sea

It is possible to visit the Dead Sea from Kerak, but it's a bit pointless as there's nothing to see and nowhere to wash the salt off after a swim. Find a minibus heading for the phosphate-mining town of Safi. This will drop you at a road junction in the Wadi Araba. From here it's about a five km walk to the water. The trip is more hassle than it's worth. If you're driving, it can be another story, with the Wadi Araba road making an

In Search of Sodom

There is nothing new in the assumption that the world's naughtiest town lay somewhere around the southern end of the Dead Sea. But a team of British geologists think they have found the key to its precise location. An area of the Dead Sea north of the Lisan Peninsula (and south of Kerak) produced bitumen, a saleable item in those days and probably the 'slimepits' referred to in the Old Testament. The geologists think Sodom, and neighbouring Gomorrah, could not have been far away, since their inhabitants would have made their money from the bitumen. If they are right, the site has been underwater off the east bank of the sea since Biblical times.

The Book of Genesis suggests God was rather unhappy with the locals' behaviour, and so 'the Lord rained upon Sodom and upon Gomorrah brimstone and fire...and he overthrew those cities, and all the plain, and all the inhabitants of the cities, and that which grew upon the ground...' Fanciful legends of a fevered Biblical imagination? Not necessarily. The whole area is located on a fault line, and it would not have been the first time that such a zone has been simply swallowed up when the ground collapsed in a kind of massive implosion. Also known as 'liquefaction', or collapse of the soil, the observer reporting for the Book of Genesis may well have been describing a terrible natural disaster instead of the wrath of God.

Archaeologists who have long puzzled over the whereabouts of this Biblical Soho now have a clue they alone might never have stumbled upon. ■

alternative route to the King's Highway to Amman or the combination of King's and Desert highways to Aqaba.

Ar-Rabba

About 20 km north of Kerak, this small town boasts a Roman temple and other Roman and Byzantine remains just west of the highway. The two niches in the temple contained statues of the Roman emperors Diocletian and Maximian. The local authorities thought it would be a good idea to place chunks of Roman columns at regular intervals along the median strip down the length of the town.

You can reach Ar-Rabba by any northbound minibus from Kerak.

Mazar

A dishevelled, straggly place about 15 km south of Kerak, Mazar is home to a small Islamic Museum, open from 9 am to 3 pm daily except Tuesday. Admission is free. It's of minor interest, but if you want to go, minibuses depart regularly from central Kerak for 150 fils.

Dhat Ras

The crumbling ruins of a Nabataean and Roman settlement can be seen in this small village about 25 km south of Kerak. The remains of a wall and column belonging to a 2nd century temple lean at a crazy angle and look set to tumble down.

The village is five km east of the King's Highway and minibuses run from Kerak (250 fils, 30 minutes).

Tafila

Second only to Wadi al-Mujib, the deep gorge of Wadi al-Hesa bisects the King's Highway about 45 km south of Kerak. Some 32 km further on lies Tafila, a busy market centre where surrounding fruit and olive growers sell their produce.

Tafila was part of the Crusaders' line of bases; a large, squat building a couple of hundred metres west of the highway, about halfway into the town, probably dates from then. It's locked and the keeper seems to keep out of sight. You can see in through the gate anyway, which will satisfy most visitors. Tucked in among sprawling houses, it overlooks valleys that fall away steeply from the town's edge.

If you get stuck, you can stay in the rather basic *Afra Hotel* in the centre of town. Minibuses from Kerak cost 500 fils and take about 1½ hours, taking a back route off the King's Highway and into Wadi al-Hesa.

Hammamat Burbita & Hammamat 'Afra

If thermal springs are your thing, you can track down a couple of local 'hot' spots in Wadi al-Hesa. Heading south from Kerak, you need to keep a watch for white-on-brown signs indicating these two places south of Mazar. The road is an alternative route to Tafila and a spectacular drive into the heart of Wadi al-Hesa.

About 23 km short of Tafila, the two springs are signposted off to the right (west). From the signpost it is six km to the turn-off (right again, unsignposted) to Hammamat Burbita. It's a green patch in the base of the wadi, where you'll find a small rock pool with a makeshift galvanised iron roof. Hot, slightly sulphurous water bubbles up here. Another six km on, the road ends in a stream rising from another spring, Hammamat 'Afra. It is a more beautiful spot and a favourite with Jordanians on excursion. As with Hammamat Ma'in, women are likely to feel uncomfortable stripping down to bathe here if local men are around in any numbers. That said, the drive itself is worth it. Hitching is difficult in these parts.

Dana Nature Reserve

Stretching west away from the King's Highway town of Al-Qaddisiyyeh, the newly developed Dana Nature Reserve is something of a novel experiment in Jordan – an attempt to promote eco-tourism, protect wildlife and improve the lives of local villages all at once.

Run by the Royal Society for the Conservation of Nature (RSCN), the reserve aims to protect endangered species, including a few ibex, mountain gazelle, badgers, red fox and even the odd wolf. At the eastern end of the reserve lies the old stone village of Dana – a rare change from the modern concrete monstrosities characteristic of modern Middle Eastern towns. The project aims to preserve the village and improve its inhabitants' prospects. They are being helped to market local products, such as dried fruit, pottery and jewellery. In the recently opened Dana Guest House are RSCN labs for the study of wildlife in the area, workshops for the locals and even a small adult literacy school.

Only limited parts of the reserve may be visited. When approaching from Tafila, you will see a turn-off to the Dana Camp a few km before reaching Al-Qaddisiyyeh. This takes you to the reserve's visitors' centre, known as Al-Burj (the Tower Centre). From there you can take a shuttle bus to the camping ground and walk along three marked trails (a solid half-day's walking for the fit). You are not allowed to hike beyond the trails without pre-arranged authorisation, which should be sought at the RSCN in Amman. Camping beyond the camping ground is also forbidden. Entry to the area around the Tower Centre and a viewpoint is 250 fils per person or JD1 per car. If you want to walk and/or stay overnight, you pay JD5, which lets you in, covers the shuttle bus from the Tower Centre to the camping ground and trails, as well as access to Dana village.

You can also reach Dana directly by turning right off the King's Highway at the southern end of Al-Qaddisyyeh – Dana is 2.5 km away and signposted off to the right. Not yet enforced, a JD2 charge is envisaged for entry to the village, half of this to go into projects to aid Dana residents.

A shuttle bus between Dana and the RSCN camping ground is also planned.

If you want to stay, you can try the camping ground, where it costs JD7 per person, plus JD5 for tent hire and JD2 for sheets and pillow. Mattresses and blankets are free – which they'd want to be after you've added all this up. In Dana itself, the *Dana Guest House* (☎ 03-368497; fax 368499) has comfortable enough rooms for JD25/40. The views from the terrace are breathtaking, but let's face it, so are the prices for everything, including the local handicrafts. Bookings can be made through the RSCN in Amman (☎ 837931). Minibuses connect Al-Qaddisiyyeh with Tafila.

SHOBAK

Shobak, another Crusader castle/fort in the chain, has a commanding position over some incredibly desolate land. The fortress, called Mons Realis (Montreal), stands 60 km south of Tafila and was built by Baldwin I in 1115. It suffered numerous attacks from Saladin before finally succumbing to him in 1189. Much of its present form is owed to the restoration carried out by the Mamelukes in the 14th century.

Built on a small knoll right on the edge of the plateau, the castle is at its most imposing when seen from a distance. The inside is in a decrepit state, although restoration work is under way. There are two churches in the castle, the first of them on the left of the entrance and up the stairs, and evidence of baths, cisterns and rainwater pipes. The caretaker will happily point out a well reached by 365 steps (about an hour's dangerous walk) cut into the rock. The Arabic inscriptions on the walls of the castle were left by Saladin.

At the foot of the hill you can see abandoned Bedouin houses.

Getting There & Away

A side road leads to the castle from the King's Highway, about two km north of the small village. It is marked by two signs and is hard to miss. From there it is four km to the castle, although it comes into view on the right after about 2½ km. If you are on foot head straight for it as soon as you see it and you'll cut off a km or so.

There's not much transport to Shobak village and, again, hitching is probably the best option. Minibuses linking Wadi Musa and Ma'an, up the Desert Highway to the north-east, pass through Shobak. There are irregular connections to Tafila and even Aqaba.

PETRA

Hewn from a towering rock wall, the imposing façades of the great buildings and tombs of Petra are a testament to the one-time wealth of the ancient capital of the Nabataeans – Arabs who dominated the Transjordan area in pre-Roman times.

A remarkable reminder of the commercially-minded Nabataean's genius, they stand today witness to an almost equally impressive, if less edifying, talent for making a fast buck. Certainly the single greatest attraction in Jordan and indeed one of the top drawcards of the entire Middle East, Petra must also stand alone as about the most expensive tourist trap in the world. For all that, and the locals are well aware of this, few people will refuse to shell out what is required to explore the wonders of Petra having gone to the trouble of reaching Jordan in the first place.

So many words have been written about Petra (which means 'rock' in Greek), including the much overworked 'rose-red city half as old as time' (from Dean Burgen's poem, *Petra)*, but these can hardly do the place justice. You have to spend at least a couple of days walking around and getting the feel of the place.

Much of Petra's fascination comes from its setting on the edge of the Wadi Araba. The sheer and rugged sandstone hills form a deep canyon easily protected from all directions, to which the easiest access is through the Siq, a narrow winding cleft in the rock anything from five to 200 metres deep. Although the sandstone could hardly be called rose-red, it takes on deep rusty hues interlaced with bands of grey, yellow and every shade in-between. The soft rock has plied itself to erosion by wind and water, but at the same time is being quite simply eaten away by the salt carried on ill winds from the Dead Sea: a source of considerable concern to scientists here.

Few buildings in Petra stand free, for the bulk are cut into the rock – hundreds of them. Until the mid-1980s many of these caves were home to the local Bedouin. They have since been moved to a 'new village' to the north – an arrangement they are less than happy with. You can see the village north of the colonnaded street from a vantage point up by the Pharaon Column. A handful of families still pitch their black goat-hair tents in the area and live in the caves. They make their money from Pepsi stands, handicrafts and other artefacts – usually scraps of the distinctive pottery and 'old' coins – which they sell to the tourists.

Not so long ago it was an arduous journey from Amman to Petra, only affordable by the lucky few. Now good bitumen roads link it with the outside world and from Amman it can be reached in three hours via the Desert Highway and Shobak, or five hours down the historic King's Highway. Awaiting you are all types of accommodation, ranging from the five star Forum Hotel to simple backpackers' digs.

Since Jordan and Israel ended their state of war, Petra has turned from a popular tourist destination into bedlam. The adjoining village of Wadi Musa is expanding apace as the rush continues to erect ever more hotels – whole hillsides look set to disappear at any moment under a thick layer of concrete.

Luckily, Petra itself is shielded from all the visual horrors, although with up to 3000 people entering every day, fears are growing that the tourist onslaught may not be sustainable. For some time now the authorities have been toying with the idea of imposing a daily ceiling of 1500 visitors.

For the moment, the bulk of visitors rush the place, spending a couple of hours taking happy snaps and then zooming off to the next place on their itinerary. This is great, for it means that in the best parts of the day, early morning and late afternoon, the place is comparatively clear. Spend a couple of days exploring to do it any justice.

History

Excavations carried out in the 1950s in the region unearthed a Neolithic village at Al-Beidha, just to the north of Petra, which dates from about 7000 BC. This puts it in the same league as Jericho on the West Bank as one of the earliest known farming communities in the Middle East.

Between that period and the Iron Age (circa 1200 BC), when it was the home of the Edomites, nothing is known. The Edomite capital Sela in the Bible (II Kings 14:7, Isaiah 16:1) was, probably mistakenly, once thought to have been the massif Umm al-Biyara (the Mother of Cisterns) which is part of the western wall of the canyon. The actual site of Sela appears in fact to lie to the north, about 10 km south of Tafila. Sela (which also means 'rock'), was where the Judaean king Amaziah, who ruled from 796 to 781 BC, threw 10,000 prisoners to their deaths over the precipice.

The Nabataeans were a nomadic tribe from western Arabia who settled in the area somewhere around the 6th century BC and became rich, first by plundering and then by levying tolls on the trade caravans for safe passage through the area under their control. The Seleucid ruler Antigonus, who had come to power in Babylonia when Alexander the Great's empire was parcelled up, rode against the Nabataeans in 312 BC and attacked one day when all the men were absent. His men killed many of the women and children and made off with valuable silver and spices. The Arabs retaliated immediately, killing all but 50 of the 4000 raiders. Antigonus tried once more to storm Petra but his forces, led by his son Demetrius, were driven off.

Petra then became the sophisticated capital of a flourishing empire that extended well into Syria. The term empire is used loosely, for it was more a zone of influence. As the Nabataeans expanded their territory, more caravan routes came under their control and their wealth increased accordingly. It was principally this, rather than territorial acquisition, that motivated them.

The Roman general Pompey, having conquered Syria and Palestine in 63 BC, tried to exert control over the Nabataean territory but the Nabataean king Aretas III was able to buy off the Roman forces and remain independent. Nonetheless, Rome exerted a cultural influence and the buildings and coinage of the period reflect the Graeco-Roman style.

The Nabataeans weren't so lucky when they chose to side with the Parthians in the latter's war with the Romans, finding themselves obliged to pay Rome heavy tribute after their defeat of the Parthians. When the Nabataeans fell behind in paying this tribute, they were invaded twice by Herod the Great. The second attack, in 31 BC, saw him gain control of a large slice of territory. Finally in 106 AD, the Romans took the city and set about transforming it with the usual plan of a colonnaded street, baths and the rest of the trappings of modern Roman life.

With the rise of Palmyra in the north and the opening up of the sea-trade routes,

Petra's importance started to decline. During the Christian era a Bishopric was created in Petra and a number of Nabataean buildings were altered for Christian use. By the time of the Muslim invasion in the 7th century, Petra had passed into obscurity and the only activity in the next 500 years was when the Crusaders moved in briefly in the 12th century and built a fort.

From then until the early 19th century, Petra was a forgotten city known only to the local Bedouin inhabitants. These descendants of the Nabataeans were not inclined to reveal its existence because they feared the influx of foreigners might interfere with their livelihood.

Finally in 1812, a young Swiss explorer and convert to Islam, Johann Ludwig Burckhardt, while en route from Damascus to Cairo, heard the locals tell of some fantastic ruins hidden in the mountains of Wadi Musa. In order to make the detour to Wadi Musa without arousing local suspicions, he had to think of a ploy.

> I, therefore, pretended to have made a vow to have slaughtered a goat in honour of Haroun (Aaron), whose tomb I knew was situated at the extremity of the valley, and by this stratagem I thought that I should have the means of seeing the valley on the way to the tomb.
>
> **Johann Ludwig Burckhardt**

This is exactly what happened and he was able to examine very briefly only a couple of sites, including the Khazneh (Treasury) and the Urn Tomb, which aroused the suspicions of his guide. He managed to bluff his way through and report to the outside world that 'it seems very probable that the ruins at Wadi Musa are those of the ancient Petra'.

Information

Tourist Office There is a visitors' centre near the entrance, but the Tourist Police staffing the desk don't seem to have much knowledge to impart. It is open from 7 am to 5 pm daily.

Money You can change cash and travellers' cheques, or get a Visa cash advance, at a branch of the Arab Bank in the same building as the visitors' centre. It is supposed to be open from 8.30 am to 12.30 pm only, but appears to open for a couple of hours from about 3 pm too. The bank's head office is in Wadi Musa, and you can also change money at the nearby Housing Bank. Failing that, most hotels will change money at unfavourable rates.

Post & Communications There is a small post office at the site, supposedly open from 8 am to 7 pm daily except Friday. The main post office is in central Wadi Musa (near the Wadi Petra restaurant), and there is another small office up by the Mussa Springs Hotel. It too opens from 8 am to 7 pm and for a couple of hours on Friday morning.

Books Several souvenir stands sell various guidebooks to Petra, but everything is at least a few JD more expensive than in Amman.

Medical Services There is a medical centre in Wadi Musa. With the steady influx of tourists into the area, the Governorate of Ma'an has called for the construction of a full hospital in Wadi Musa.

Entry Fees & Conditions Are they going to kill the goose that laid the golden egg? Admission for one day costs a staggering JD20. Since most people will want more than one day, the two/three day passes (JD25/30) are manifestly better deals. The multi-day tickets are not transferable as you have to sign them and present them each subsequent day with proof of identity. Children under 12 pay half price and Jordanian citizens JD1. The site is open daily from 6.30 am.

The fun does not necessarily stop there. People unfortunate enough to be travelling in organised tours often get to shell out JD7 for a compulsory horse ride from the main entrance to the beginning of the Siq – a grand

JORDAN

Petra: the Ruins

From the point where you buy tickets a track leads down to the Siq – the narrow winding wadi leading in to Petra. Off to the left is the **Brooke Hospital for Animals**, a haven for local wildlife and where some of the horses end up after being given too hard a time. This is where you can hire one if you really feel an uncontrollable urge to sit in the saddle and go nowhere much.

In any event, it's more interesting to walk through the ruins, and this gives you time to look at the first of the monuments – three square freestanding tombs on the right. No evidence of bones has been found and it may be that, rather than tombs, they are a kind of outsize tombstone.

Further on to the left is the **Obelisk Tomb**, which originally reached seven metres high. Five graves were found inside the monument, four represented by the pyramid-shaped pillars and the last by a statue between the middle pillars.

Just past the Obelisk Tomb a path leads up to the left to what was a place of religious worship called **Al-Madras** (signposted). This is not the most spectacular of Petra's offerings, but is full of small memorials, inscriptions, and niches for making offerings. A similar area people rarely bother to poke around in is just opposite the Obelisk Tomb – scramble up and you can't help stumbling on to tombs and memorials cut from the stone.

After a party of 23 tourists was drowned in a flash flood in the Siq in 1963, the entrance was blocked by a dam that diverts the intermittent flow of water into an ancient tunnel on the right and into Petra the long way. During construction, engineers working on the project found the foundations of a Nabataean dam and used them as the base for the new one. In spite of all the work, a rain burst can still cause a mighty uncomfortable torrent of mud down the Siq.

Once inside the Siq, the path narrows to about five metres and the walls tower up to 200m overhead. At some points it is no more than two metres wide. The original channels cut in the walls to bring water into Petra are visible and in some places the 2000 year old terracotta pipes are still in place. In Roman times the path was paved and one section is still intact. The niches in the walls used to hold figures of the Nabataean god Dushara.

The Siq is not a canyon, a gorge carved out by water, but rather is one block that has been rent apart by tectonic forces. You can see at various points that the grain of the rock on one side continues on the other. The entrance to the Siq was once topped by an arch built by the Nabataeans. It survived until the late 19th century, and you can still see remains of it as you enter the gorge.

The walls close in still further and at times almost meet overhead, shutting out the light and seemingly the sound as well. Just as you start to think that there's no end to the Siq, you catch glimpses ahead of the most impressive of all Petra's monuments – the Khazneh.

Khazneh (Treasury) Tucked away in such a confined space, the Khazneh is well protected from the ravages of the elements, and it must be from here that Petra gained its 'rose-red' reputation. Although carved out of the solid iron-laden sandstone to serve as a tomb, the Treasury gets its name from the story that pirates hid their treasure here, in the urn in the middle of the second level. Some locals have obviously believed this story for the 3.5m high urn is pockmarked by rifle shot, the result of vain attempts to break open the solid-rock urn.

Like all the rock-hewn monuments in Petra, it is the façade that captivates (the final scenes of *Indiana Jones & the Last Crusade* were shot here); the interior is just an unadorned square hall with a smaller room at the back. The Khazneh, which is 40m high, is at its best between about 9 and 11 am (depending on the season) when it is in full sunlight, or late in the afternoon when the rock itself seems to glow.

Barely distinguishable reliefs on the exterior of the monument have aroused much speculation, little of it conclusive, about their identification, although it is felt they represent various gods. The Khazneh's age has also been a subject of debate, and estimates range from 100 BC to 200 AD.

From the Khazneh, the Siq turns off to the right, and diagonally opposite is a sacred hall, which may have had ritual connections with the Treasury. It features the most characteristic expression of this Nabataean architecture, the 'crow-step' decoration, which is like a staircase on top of the façade.

As you head down towards the city, the number of niches and tombs increases, becoming a virtual graveyard in rock arching around the back of the amphitheatre, so that it has in fact become known as the Theatre Necropolis.

Amphitheatre The 8000 seat amphitheatre, thought to hold only 3000 until it was fully excavated, comes into view ahead and to the left. Originally thought to have been built by the Romans after they defeated the Nabataeans in 106 AD, it is now felt the Nabataeans themselves cut it out of the rock around the time of Christ, slicing through many caves and tombs in the process. Under the stage floor were storerooms and a slot through which a curtain could be lowered at the start of a performance. Through this slot an almost-complete statue of Hercules was recovered.

Not all the caves around the theatre served as tombs; some of them were houses. Just before the theatre on the left is a staircase leading up to the High Place of Sacrifice.

Royal Tombs The wadi widens right out after the theatre and after passing a few Pepsi-and-souvenir stalls you come to the main city area covering about three sq km. Up to the right, carved into the face of Jebel Khubtha, are the three most impressive burial places, known as the Royal Tombs. The whole rock façade sometimes goes by the name of the Kings' Wall, although who the 'kings' were, no-one knows.

The first is the **Urn Tomb** with its open terrace built over a double layer of vaults. The room inside is enormous, measuring 20 by 18m, and the patterns in the rock are striking. It's hard to imagine how the smooth walls and sharp corners were carved out with such precision. A Greek inscription on the back wall details how it was used as a church in Byzantine times.

Next in line is the **Corinthian Tomb**, a badly weathered monument similar in design to the Khazneh. Beside it stands the **Palace Tomb**, a three storey imitation of a Roman palace and one of the largest monuments in Petra. The top left-hand corner is built out of cut stone as the rock face didn't extend far enough to complete the façade. The four doors lead into small uninteresting rooms.

Further north and little visited is the **Mausoleum of Sextius Florentinus**, a Roman administrator under emperor Hadrian, which his son had made in 130 AD. There is plenty of room here for wider exploration of still more graves and religious sites.

North of Jebel Khubtha is one of Petra's important artificial water channels, which carried water from Moses' Spring into city aqueducts.

The Colonnaded Street A few of the columns have been re-erected in the colonnaded street that runs alongside the wadi. The slopes of the hills either side are littered with the debris of the ancient city.

The street follows the standard Roman pattern of the east-west *decumanus.* What is puzzling is that there is no evidence of a *cardo*, or north-south axis, which traditionally was always the main street. In Petra it would probably have had to be as much staircase as street, but to date no trace of it has been found.

Coming from the amphitheatre, a **marketplace** lay to the left and on the other side of the street a **nymphaeum**, or public fountain. Little remains to be seen today. Further along on the left is a **Nabataean bath**, possibly used for ritual cleansing of believers. The street finishes at the **Temenos Gateway**, which was originally fitted with wooden doors and marked the entrance to the *temenos*, or courtyard, of the Qasr al-Bint. Immediately to the south-east of the Temenos Gateway lie the remains of what has been named the **Southern Temple**. Probably destroyed by an earthquake, excavations still underway suggest it was a major Roman temple raised in the 1st Century AD and used into early Byzantine times.

Qasr al-Bint Firaun This is Nabataean and dates from around 30 BC. The Qasr al-Bint Firaun (Castle of the Pharaoh's Daughter, the picturesque Bedouin title for it) is also known as the Temple of Dushara, after the god who was worshipped there, and was probably the main place of worship in the Nabataean city. It is the only freestanding structure in Petra and has been partially restored, which the building was in need of as it seemed close to toppling over.

Temple of the Winged Lions Up on the rise to the north of the Temenos Gateway is the recently excavated Temple of al-'Uzza-Atargatis or Temple of the Winged Lions, named after the carved lions that topped the capitals of the columns. The temple was dedicated to the fertility goddess, Atargatis, who was the partner to the main male god, Dushara.

The excavation of the temple, started in 1975 by an American group and still continuing, soon revealed that this was a building of great importance and had a colonnaded entry with arches and porticoes that extended right down to and across the wadi at the bottom. Fragments of decorative stone and plaster found on the site and now on display in the small museum suggest that both the temple and entry were handsomely decorated.

Byzantine Church To the east of the Temple of the Winged Lions, an American team is excavating a Byzantine church and preparing to carry out restoration on what the Americans believe may be the oldest Byzantine mosaic ever discovered. It is planned to have it open to public viewing, protected by a roofing structure to be erected when the restoration work is complete.

Al-Habis Just beyond the Qasr al-Bint Firaun is the small massif of Al-Habis (The Prison). In the old cave dwellings at the base are a couple more of the small souvenir-and-Pepsi shops found dotted around the whole city. Steps to the left of these shops lead up the face of Al-Habis to the small, free **museum**, which has a collection of artefacts found here over the years.

Next to the nearby fancy Forum Restaurant is another museum containing pottery, jewellery, statues and coins found across the site.

From here a track to the right leads across the wadi and up to the monastery (or '*deir*' in Arabic), another 'High Place' that takes an hour to reach but which shouldn't be missed on any account. ■

total of 500m. Such groups are also obliged to pay for local guides they generally do not need or want – and the guides' horses too! There appears no way around any of this.

Independent travellers are not affected by this blatant daylight robbery, but of course cannot avoid the main admission fee.

As for the horses, there is precious little point in hiring one, if you are given any choice in the matter, as you can't take them through the Siq. Horse-drawn carriages are another story, and may be worthwhile for the elderly or ill. The carriages are allowed through the Siq into Petra proper and they cost JD8 (one passenger) or JD14 (two passengers).

Note that all the official prices for horse and carriages are posted in the visitors' centre.

'Ain Musa

The first thing you come across as you enter Wadi Musa from Amman or Aqaba is a small building on the right with three white domes. This is not a mosque but 'Ain Musa (Moses' Spring), where Moses supposedly struck the rock and water gushed forth. The road then winds down the two km to the village of Wadi Musa (formerly Elji), and a further three km to the site entrance at the Petra Hotel & Rest House.

High Places

A number of other objectives well worth seeing require a bit of hard sweat to reach, but the effort is repaid by the spectacular views. As well as the following climbs, if you're really keen you can make the six hour climb to the top of **Mt Hor** and **Aaron's Tomb**, passing the **Snake Monument** (a stone reptile on a rock pedestal overlooking the dead buried in the area) on the way. You are now supposed to do this hike only in the company of an official guide – for information, enquire at the visitors' centre.

Crusader Fort The easiest of these climbs is up to the Crusader fort on top of Al-Habis. With so many other fine monuments around, the ruins of the castle itself are of little interest. The steps leading to the top start from the base of the hill on the rise behind the Qasr al-Bint Firaun. A track goes all the way around Al-Habis, revealing still more caves on its western side.

Monastery The climb to the monastery will take you from half to one hour, but the ancient rock-cut path is easy to follow and not steep. The walk is itself a spectacle of weird and wonderfully tortured stone, and the monastery itself every bit as breathtaking as the Khazneh.

If you really don't wish to walk, there is no shortage of people hiring out donkeys to take you up – the poor animals' owners want silly money like JD5 and will invent all sorts of stories about the difficulties ahead in order

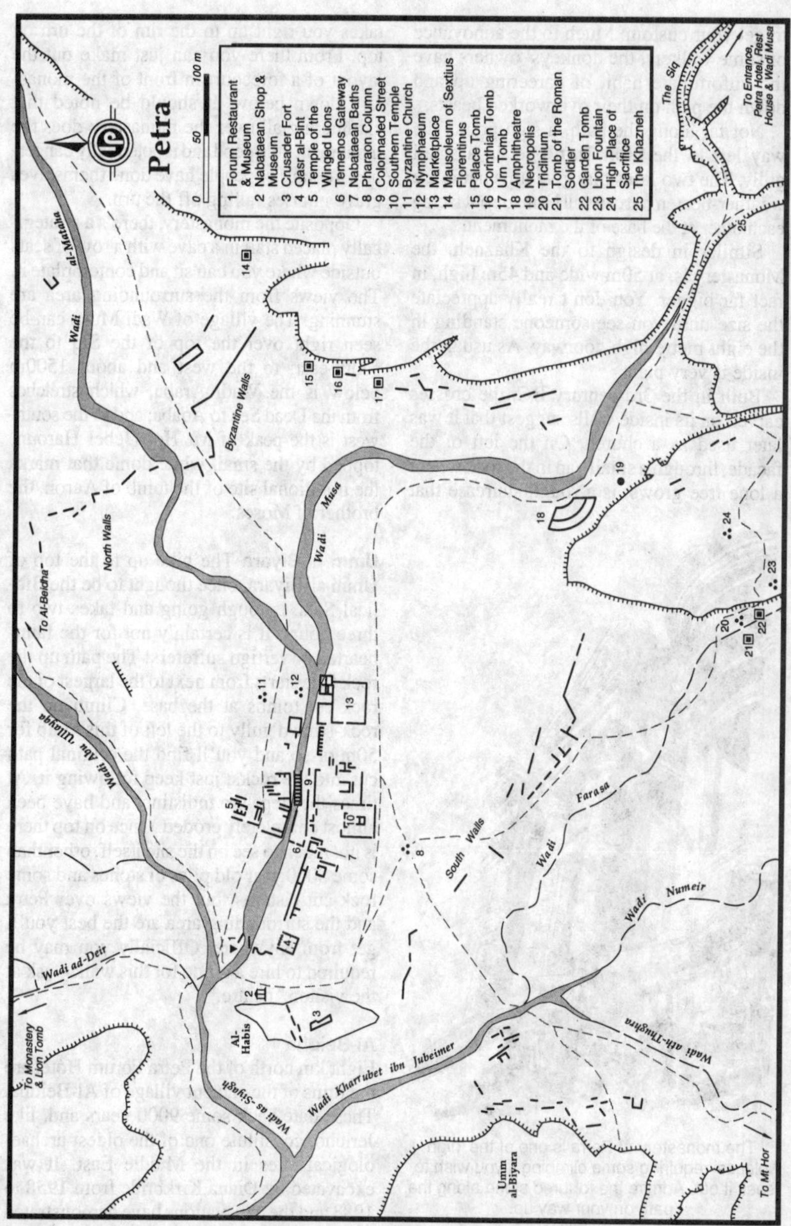
Petra
0
50
100 m
1 Forum Restaurant & Museum
2 Nabataean Shop & Museum
3 Crusader Fort
4 Qasr al-Bint
5 Temple of the Winged Lions
6 Temenos Gateway
7 Nabataean Baths
8 Pharaon Column
9 Colonnaded Street
10 Southern Temple
11 Byzantine Church
12 Nymphaeum
13 Marketplace
14 Mausoleum of Sextius Florentinus
15 Palace Tomb
16 Corinthian Tomb
17 Urn Tomb
18 Amphitheatre
19 Necropolis
20 Triclinium
21 Tomb of the Roman Soldier
22 Garden Tomb
23 Lion Fountain
24 High Place of Sacrifice
25 The Khazneh
To Entrance, Petra Hotel, Rest House & Wadi Musa
The Siq
Wadi al-Mataha
Byzantine Walls
North Walls
To Al-Beidha
Wadi Abu Ulllayqa
Wadi Musa
Wadi ad-Deir
To Monastery & Lion Tomb
Al-Habis
Wadi as-Siyagh
Wadi Kharrubet ibn Jubeimer
South Walls
Wadi Farasa
Wadi Numeir
Wadi ath-Thughra
Umm al-Biyara
To Mt Hor

to get your custom. Much to the annoyance of some walkers, the donkeys' owners have the unfortunate habit of careering up and down the path on their overworked beasts.

Not far along the path, a sign points the way left to the **Lion Tomb** set in a small gully. The two lions that give it its name are weather-beaten but can still be made out facing each other at the base of the monument.

Similar in design to the Khazneh, the Monastery is, at 50m wide and 45m high, in fact far bigger. You don't really appreciate the size until you see someone standing in the eight metre high doorway. As usual, the inside is very plain.

Built in the 3rd century BC, the crosses carved on its inside walls suggest that it was later used as a church. On the left of the façade, through a small gap in the rock where a lone tree grows, is a rough staircase that takes you right up to the rim of the urn on top. From there you can just make out the layout of a forecourt in front of the monastery down below. It should be noted that clambering all over the monastery does the monument little good and is potentially dangerous: a couple of people have done themselves grave injuries falling off the urn.

Opposite the monastery, there's a strategically placed stall in a cave with a row of seats outside where you can sit and contemplate it. The views from the surrounding area are stunning. The village of Wadi Musa can be seen right over the top of the Siq to the south-east; to the west and about 1500m below is the Wadi Araba, which stretches from the Dead Sea to Aqaba; and to the south-west is the peak of Mt Hor (Jebel Haroun) topped by the small white dome that marks the traditional site of the tomb of Aaron, the brother of Moses.

The monastery at Petra is one of the 'high places' requiring some climbing if you wish to seek it out. Admire the tortured stone along the path on your way up.

Umm al-Biyara The hike up to the top of Umm al-Biyara, once thought to be the Biblical Sela, is tough going and takes two to three hours. It is certainly not for the faint-hearted or vertigo sufferers! The path up the rock face starts from next to the largest of the rock-cut tombs at the base. Climb up the rock-strewn gully to the left of this tomb for 50m or so and you'll find the original path cut into the rocks; just keep following it. At times the steps are indistinct and have been almost completely eroded. Once on top there is not much to see on the site itself, other than some 8000 year old piles of stones and some rock-cut cisterns, but the views over Petra and the surrounding area are the best you'll get from anywhere. Officially you may be required to hire a guide for this walk – ask at the visitors' centre.

Al-Beidha

Eight km north of the Petra Forum Hotel are the ruins of the ancient village of Al-Beidha. These date back some 9000 years and, like Jericho, constitute one of the oldest archaeological sites in the Middle East. It was excavated by Diana Kirkbride from 1958 to 1983 and the excavations have demonstrated

High Place of Sacrifice

The third climb is up to the High Place of Sacrifice near the Siq and beyond to a series of other sights. This 1½ hour climb and descent is best done in the early morning so you have the sun behind you. Coming from the Khazneh, the steps head up to the left just as the theatre comes into view. After a half-hour climb, the track cuts sharply back to the right as you reach the High Place.

The top of the ridge has been quarried flat to make a platform, and large depressions with drains show where the blood of sacrificial animals flowed out. Altars were cut into the rock and just to the south are obelisks and the remains of buildings, probably used to house the priests. Once again the views over the ruined city to the west and Wadi Musa to the east are excellent.

From here you could simply turn back the way you came. However, the path also continues down the other side from the High Place between the obelisk and the ramshackle souvenir-and-Pepsi shop to the **Lion Fountain**, where the water used to run down the rock from above and out of the lion's mouth. The lion is about 4.5m long and 2.5m high. A stone altar diagonally opposite suggests the fountain had some religious function. The steps wind further down the side of the cliff to the **Garden Tomb**, although archaeologists believe it was more probably a temple. To its right are the remains of a high wall, part of what was once a water reservoir.

A little further on is the **Tomb of the Roman Soldier**, so named because of the statue over the door. Opposite this is the **Triclinium** (hall for religious feasts held for the dead of the Tomb of the Roman Soldier), unique in Petra for its decorations on the interior walls. A bit past this on the right are two less interesting classic façades, one with the appearance of two columns either side of the entrance. The path then flattens out and follows the Wadi Farasa, the site of the ancient rubbish dumps, and ends up at the **Pharaon Column**, the only surviving column of another temple. A few drums of other columns that once stood next to it lie abandoned on the desert floor. ■

One of the obelisks at the High Place of Sacrifice

to archaeologists that it was occupied during the 7th century BC.

On the various levels are the ruins of houses of different design, fireplaces and workshops. The ruins can be reached by road from outside Petra itself. On the way you can see the vestiges of a Crusader fort to the left, **Al-Wueira**, of which only some of the outer walls remain intact. You can also take a two hour walk from the centre of Petra – just keep heading north.

A taxi (from near the entrance to Petra) will take you out to Al-Beidha, wait an hour or so while you look around and bring you back for JD7.

Organised Tours Petra Moon Tourist Services (☎ 336665) organises 4WD trips to Wadi Rum (JD35 per person per day) and along Wadi Araba, the Dana Nature Reserve and Shobak (JD50 per person per day).

Places to Stay

Things have changed a little over the years in Petra. Back in 1908, MacMillan's guide to *Palestine and Syria* had the following advice:

At Petra there is no sleeping accommodation to be found, and travellers therefore have to bring with them camp equipment, unless they prefer to put up with the inconvenience of sleeping in the Bedawin huts at Elji, half an hour distant from Petra, or spend the night in some of the numerous temples. Such a course cannot be recommended to European travellers, especially if ladies are of the party.

Until fairly recently, travellers could still elect to sleep in the temples or even camp, but that's all history now, and with the opening of the border to Israel, Petra has come to know a tourist flood and consequently a hotel building boom that have already irrevocably changed the nature of the place for the worse. Virtually all the hotels line a five km stretch of road that passes through Wadi Musa and leads down to Petra. For simplicity's sake, the hotels are listed in that order.

In the overwhelming majority of cases it can be said that these places, especially in the lower and middle range, are uniformly bland and hastily built. There is no transport along this stretch apart from the swarms of taxis.

Prices can fluctuate at the whim of hotel owners depending on the season and how business is going. Most places have a restaurant of some description and the cheaper ones advertise 'student rates' – an invitation to bargain on rates for beds in a dorm. Although practically all the hotels will offer you half-board – and consequently higher rates, you should in no way feel obliged to pay for anything but the room. If you want breakfast or dinner in the hotel, you can always pay for them separately as you go.

Note that in winter heating will come in very handy. Most places seem equipped with some form of it, but make sure before choosing your quarters for the night.

Wadi Musa The *Mussa Spring Hotel* (☎ 336310; fax 336910) was one of the first of the budget hotels to see dollar signs written on the walls of Petra. It has the advantage of being the first hotel you come across, right after 'Ain Musa. A bed on the enclosed roof costs JD2, one in a room of three people or more JD4 and doubles JD10 (without private bath) and JD16 (with). Although still popular with backpackers, it is not necessarily the best choice. An all-you-can-eat buffet costs JD3 (it's OK but hardly spectacular), accompanied by reruns of a scratchy *Indiana Jones & the Last Crusade* video, starring Petra's Treasury in the final scenes. It's been playing nightly for four years. The hotel can also give you a lift down to Petra early in the morning, returning at about 5 pm – saving you an hour's walk. You may also find yourself being picked up by a taxi for free – the hotel has a deal with some taxis under which they pay to get their guests back from Petra. If not, never pay more than JD1.

Across the road is the new and luxurious *King's Way Inn* (☎ 336799; fax 336796). Spacious and spotless rooms with ensuite bathroom, TV, phone and so on cost a hefty JD70/85 plus 20% taxes.

A few hundred metres down the road is the *Al-Anbat Hotel* (☎ 336265; fax 336888). The name is Arabic for 'the Nabataeans'. It has an impressive reception area, but the rooms are hardly any better than those at the Mussa Spring. The basic charge seems to be JD6 per person, with the buffet dinner costing JD4.

Almost a km further downhill you come across the *Acropolis Hotel* (☎ 336355). There are no singles, and doubles/triples cost JD10/15 without bath and JD20/25 with. It is comfortable and clean enough, but the rooms are small and the place utterly charmless. Virtually across the road is the *Araba Hotel* (☎ 336107; fax 336107), a much better prospect. The owner charges JD10/15 for good little rooms with bath, but will bargain. Room Nos 310 and 309 have views across Wadi Musa and the latter a gigantic double bed.

The *Petra Stars Hotel* (☎ 336915) is not a bad choice, but rather pricey for the small rooms you get. Doubles/triples range from JD10/15 to JD20/25 (with bathroom), but as everywhere else, a bit of bargaining is worthwhile.

Past the roundabout and the road to Tayyibeh is the *Cleopetra Hotel* (☎ 337099). Aside from the awful pun, this is one of the better deals at this end of the scale. You pay JD10/14/16 for singles/doubles/triples with private bathrooms. The rooms are a little small, but the bathrooms are very clean.

Down a side lane to the left, the *Amra Palace Hotel* (☎ 337070; fax 337071) is an excellent mid-range place that is frequently full. The smallish but comfortably appointed rooms have satellite TV and ensuite bathroom, and cost JD30/42. The price includes breakfast, dinner and all taxes.

In much the same category as the Cleopetra, if a little more ramshackle, is the *Petra Gate Hotel* (☎ 336908), with small, clean rooms at JD8/14/18. All rooms have their own shower and some have grand views of the Wadi Musa sprawl. Across the road and downhill a little, the *Peace Way Hotel* (☎ 336963) is a comfortable place with a good reputation – so good it can often be booked out for months in advance. Singles/doubles with heating, private bathroom and telephone come in at JD21/25.

At this point you find yourself in the heart of Wadi Musa. If you turn left at the roundabout (you'll see the Wadi Petra Restaurant on your right) you'll come across the *Midtown Hotel* (☎ /fax 337054). At JD10/15 for singles/doubles, the rooms with private bath have the distinction of being a deal more ample than the average – a decent choice. Also in this part of town is the *Orient Hotel* (☎ /fax 337020) – turn right around the block when you pass the Midtown and you'll see it down a street to the left. If you can deal with the mauve décor, you can get a comfy bed in rooms with private bath for JD8/15.

Back at the roundabout, you'll notice the *Al-Rashid Hotel* (☎ 336800; fax 336801). It's not quite finished, but reasonable singles/doubles with private bathroom cost JD15/20.

Keep heading down the road to Petra and you strike the *Elgee Hotel* (☎ /fax 336701). This rather oddly laid out establishment charges JD25/35 for pokey rooms with TV, and breakfast thrown in – not the best deal in town. Across the road, the *Rose City Hotel* (☎ 336440; fax 336448) charges JD20/30 for its rooms – also well overpriced.

Further up the same side street is the *Treaury Hotel* (☎ 336221). Despite its half-finished look, the rooms aren't too bad. Singles/doubles without TV but good beds, and in some cases reasonable views, come in at JD25/35 – try to talk the price down.

As the road sweeps down towards Petra, the *Moon Valley Hotel* (☎ 336824; fax 337131) emerges on the right. It is in much the same league as the previous three, with singles/doubles/triples going for JD15/25/35 plus 10% in tax.

Petra From the Moon Valley the road describes a couple of broad curves as it drops down to the final strip leading in to Petra.

A few hundred metres before you reach the ancient site is the *Petra Palace Hotel* (☎ 336723; fax 336724). The rooms in the so-called old wing are attractively furnished but have no air-con or any of the other extras like TV, and so are too expensive at JD22.500/30. The brand new rooms in the new wing cost JD29/42, also a little too much for what you get. All prices are with breakfast.

Virtually next door is what was once the best deal in Petra. The *Sunset Hotel* (☎ 336579; fax 336950) is sadly now just one of many ordinary lower mid-range hotels, although the cheapest this close to Petra. Singles/doubles without private bath cost JD10/15, or JD15/20 with. The roof has been converted into a restaurant.

Up a side lane still bordered by the debris of recent construction, the *Candles Hotel* (☎ 336779; fax 336954) is like most of the remaining hotels down here, mainly interested in the passing stream of tour groups. Reasonable rooms cost JD24/30/50 including breakfast (10% tax on top).

A little further on, the *Edom Hotel* (☎ 336995; fax 336994) is in much the same category and charges an inflated JD33/45.

Just short of the visitors' centre, the Swiss hotel group *Mövenpick* is erecting a huge place.

If you turn up the road towards Al-Beidha, you'll find a couple more mid-range places that are frequently full and popular if only for their position right by Petra. They are much of a muchness and quite OK. The

JORDAN

Petra Moon Hotel (☎ /fax 336220) charges JD25/35 including breakfast, and seems prepared to bargain down. The *Flowers Hotel* (☎ 336771; fax 336770) is a little higher up and charges JD24/30/50.

The *Petra Hotel & Rest House* (☎ 336014; fax 3366868), about as close to the entrance as you can get, has good rooms that, given what all the neighbours are asking, are not unreasonably priced at JD30.800/60 in the older part and JD40.800/72 in the new wing. Part of the hotel is built around an old Nabataean tomb.

The *Petra Forum Hotel* (☎ 336266; fax 336977) is the premier hotel with singles/doubles for JD80/90 plus 20% tax. From the poolside bar there is a nice view over the rocky terrain north of the Siq, but bring a well-stuffed wallet with you. Several people have written in to say they were less than satisfied with the place. You can camp near the car park for JD4 per person plus taxes. Not surprisingly, it's rare to see any campers there.

Road to Tayyibeh The hotel plague is spreading its tentacles far and wide. Two luxury hotels have appeared on the road south to Tayyibeh about four km from Petra. Their selling point is the extraordinary view afforded over Petra's rockscape. The *Grand View Hotel* (☎ 336871; fax 336984) boasts swimming pool, snooker tables and bars, and its well-appointed rooms cost a whopping JD75/100 plus taxes. Next door, the *Petra Plaza Hotel* (☎ /fax 336407) reaches for the sky, with rooms at an even more painful JD100/120 plus taxes. More hotels are going up on this road, which should go a long way towards destroying what remains of the area's wild beauty.

Places to Eat

Rule number one: equip yourself with supplies before entering the ruins of Petra, otherwise you will be clobbered for everything from bottles of water (JD1) to the omnipresent 'lunch box' offered by numerous tent cafés spread out across the centre of the site. This generally consists of a couple of slices of dry bread, some yoghurt, cheese, tomato, cucumber and an orange for JD2.500.

For the cheapest eats, investigate the little restaurants clustered in the centre of town – which incidentally is where you can buy your own foodstuffs in shops frequented mainly by locals. The place marked *Fresh Food* is a good little eatery. With luck you can get yourself some decent kebabs or some such meal for JD2 to JD3 at the most.

The *Wadi Petra Restaurant*, right on the roundabout in town, is a curious little place where you can find a few dishes beyond the usual stuff. The chicken and mixed vegetable stew is good value at JD1.800 and makes a nice change. A big bottle of Amstel costs JD2.750 here, but it's as cheap as you'll find in Petra.

The *Sunrise Restaurant*, below the Sunset Hotel (very drole), is a complete rip-off, with a plate of kebabs going for JD5.

Nearby, you can have pseudo American-style pizza at *Papazzi*. A small pizza costs a big JD3 to JD4. Or you could do the hamburger equivalent at *Petra Burger*, near the Petra Palace Hotel.

The *Petra Hotel & Rest House* and *Petra Forum Hotel* both have expensive restaurants, and all the other hotels have restaurants attached. About the cheapest is at the Mussa Spring and Al-Anbat hotels, which charge respectively JD3 and JD4 for their all-you-can-eat buffets – now a popular dining method in mass-tourism Petra.

Getting There & Away

JETT Bus There is one JETT bus daily from Amman, leaving at 6 am. It is mainly for day-trippers who don't have the time to spare for a longer stay and the JD32 price reflects this. The fare includes entry to the site. As the drive from Amman is three hours each way, it doesn't leave much time for exploring the ruins. To take the bus one way without entry fees or extras is still JD5.500. It leaves Wadi Musa at about 3 pm. Tickets for the return trip can be bought from about 10.30 am on the day of travel at Jeff's Bookshop, a souvenir stand near the Petra Hotel & Rest House.

Minibus/Service Taxi Public transport connections to Petra are irregular. There are supposed to be three daily departures for Amman (Wahadat bus station) from the visitors' centre that also pass through the town, the first at 6 am, the last at around 7 am (JD2). Minibuses also supposedly leave for Aqaba at similar times (JD2.500).

Occasional service taxis run to and from Wahadat bus station in Amman for JD2.500, and charge up to JD1 for luggage. Don't expect to find anything in the afternoon going either way.

The most frequent connection is the minibus to Ma'an (750 fils), which is supposed to leave about once an hour. From Ma'an you can get another minibus or service taxi to Amman or Aqaba, or just get off on the highway and hitch.

At about 6.30 am a minibus leaves for Wadi Rum (JD2.500).

If you're staying at the Mussa Spring or Al-Anbat hotels, ask the managers to arrange for one of the minibuses to keep you a place and stop by on their way out. If you're not up when they arrive, they won't wait.

Taxi Yellow taxis will also do just about any trip you want – for a price. They will go to Wadi Rum for JD20, Aqaba for JD25 or even to Amman via the King's Highway for JD150!

Hitching Hitching is easy enough if you get yourself up to the junction by Moses' Spring ('Ain Musa). Allow five hours to get to Kerak and three to Aqaba – if you get lucky it could be a lot less.

A lot of the traffic coming out of Wadi Musa is only going as far as Ma'an, 50 km to the south-east on the Desert Highway, but from here there's plenty of traffic in both directions.

AROUND PETRA

Tayyibeh

About 15 km south of Wadi Musa along the continuation of the King's Highway, this quiet little village is being dragged out of its splendid isolation by the tourist dollar. That said, what has been done here is an interesting experiment. In the lower part of town, a typical stone village has been recreated to house the *Taybet Zaman* hotel complex (☎ 339111; fax 339101). Each room is a modest little stone, flat-roof house with brightly painted door, for which guests pay JD85/106 plus taxes.

It is really quite a tasteful way to set up a hotel. In addition, the complex has a terrace restaurant with magnificent views (it is not hard to see why Tayyibeh was selected for this experiment) and handicraft shops.

Local minibuses from Wadi Musa cost 300 fils. A taxi will run there for about JD1. The King's Highway continues from here to Ras an-Naqb, where it meets the Desert Highway for the final run into Aqaba via Wadi Rum. With your own vehicle, this is the route of preference.

The Desert Highway

The Desert Highway is exactly that – a strip of bitumen running through the monotonous desert for the 300 km from Amman to Ras an-Naqb, where it then winds down off the plateau to Aqaba. It used to be a bit of a nightmare stretch in parts, but its development into a (mostly) dual carriageway and the UN embargo on Iraq have combined to reduce the hazards. However, it can still be pretty hairy around Amman and Aqaba, and eventually truck traffic will probably again reach the crazy pre-1990 levels. These guys have scant regard for the niceties of road etiquette – they drive hard to scrape together a living and don't worry too much about regulation rest breaks.

Minibuses and service taxis operating between Amman and Aqaba, Petra and Kerak use this route, so if you want to take the King's Highway you'll need to take short hops (with your first stop in Madaba if coming from Amman).

MA'AN

There's nothing of interest in Ma'an, the biggest town in southern Jordan and the administrative centre of the region, but you may find yourself coming through en route from Amman to Aqaba and Petra (or vice versa).

The Desert Highway skirts the west side of the town, so if you are hitching through there's no need to go into Ma'an itself.

Places to Stay & Eat

Petra and Aqaba offer far better accommodation alternatives, but there is a trio of hotels here if you get stuck. The best is in the centre of town on the same roundabout as the main mosque. The *Hotel el-Jezira* (☎ 332043), has a nice old 1st floor verandah and comfortable beds in share rooms for JD2 to JD3, or triples for JD10.

If this fails, head west for the feeder road onto the Desert Highway (it branches east off the Desert Highway at points north and south of Ma'an, meeting at a roundabout in the middle that has a third road heading into the centre of town). North of the roundabout is the not overly inviting *Hotel Shaweekh* (☎ 331880), where a double with ensuite bath costs JD6 – try to bargain down for single occupancy. The front rooms have plants all over the balconies and inside. It is marginally better than the *Hotel Tabok* (no telephone), just up the road, which charges similar prices. Both have restaurants, and you'll find the usual felafel, chicken and kebab places in the centre of town.

If there is an attraction in Ma'an, it's the *Khoury Rest House*, about 500m along the feeder road when you come off the Desert Highway from the north. If you're driving down, it's worth stopping there for a drink. The owner looks and talks like someone still well entrenched in the Sixties, and his bar (he no longer runs the hotel or restaurant) is a truly psychedelic experience – stuffed with what seems like hundreds of clocks, assorted weapons, coloured lights and crazy sounds. You can hardly see the bar for 'the collection', and if he were in New York, London or Sydney, he'd make a mint. A taxi from the centre will cost you about 500 fils.

Getting There & Away

The minibus and service-taxi station in Ma'an is awkwardly placed on the south-eastern side of town, about a 20 minute walk into the centre. However, it can be a useful place to pick up transport north or south if you're coming from Petra.

Minibuses to Amman cost JD1.050 and service taxis JD2. Minibuses to Aqaba cost JD1. Minibuses to Wadi Musa (Petra) are meant to leave more or less hourly (750 fils).

QUWEIRA

From Ma'an the Desert Highway continues to Ras an-Naqb and then descends tortuously down through the hills. It's one of the most dangerous sections of road and tankers sometimes lose control and explode. The antics of the trucks as they jockey for a position makes for some hair-raising entertainment.

Quweira is the only town between Ma'an and Aqaba and the nearest to Wadi Rum, about 30 km to the south-east. The turn-off for Wadi Rum is five km south of town; the sign just says 'Rum' and there's a couple of little restaurants at the intersection.

WADI RUM

Wadi Rum offers some of the most extraordinary desert scenery you'll ever see and, along with Petra, is a 'must' in Jordan. Although more and more people flock here, the area has as yet lost none of its forbidding majesty. Luckily there is still no hotel, so those who decide to stay overnight are a blessed minority. How long will this remain the case? It is to be hoped that the powers that be resist the temptation to move into full tourism gear in Wadi Rum. Nightmare visions of phalanxes of jerry-built luxury hotels and restaurants selling overpriced 'genuine' Bedouin cuisine accompanied by 'traditional' Bedouin dancing and music are enough to keep the most serene spirited awake at night. It has happened elsewhere, so there is no reason why it might not happen here.

Wadi Rum is not of the sand-dune variety. What makes this place unique are the often bizarre rock formations soaring out of the desert floor.

During the Arab Revolt in 1917-18, it was one of the stamping grounds of the enigmatic TE Lawrence, and the desert shots in the film *Lawrence of Arabia* were taken around here. In his book, *Seven Pillars of Wisdom*, he describes his approach by camel from the south.

> (The hills) drew together until only two miles divided them: and then, towering gradually till their parallel parapets must have been a thousand feet above us, ran forward in an avenue for miles...The Arab armies would have been lost in the length and breadth of it, and within the walls a squadron of aeroplanes could have wheeled in formation. Our little caravan grew self-conscious, and fell dead quiet, afraid and ashamed to flaunt its smallness in the presence of the stupendous hills.
>
> **TE Lawrence, *Seven Pillars of Wisdom***

At 6000 feet (5788 feet or 1754m to be exact) above sea level Jebel Rum is even higher than Lawrence describes.

The rusty jebels of Wadi Rum rise sheer from the two-km-wide valley floor and are capped with smooth, pale sandstone. They completely dominate the settlement of Rum, which is a collection of about 20 Bedouin families in their black goat-hair tents, a few concrete houses, a school, a shop and the 'Beau Geste' fort, headquarters of the much-photographed Desert Patrol Corps. All up, villagers and desert nomads throughout the Wadi Rum area number a total of 4000 people.

A German-led consortium is now planning to build an experimental 30 megawatt solar tower in Wadi Rum, chosen for the obvious abundance of this particular raw material.

The only telephone here connects the police post with Amman.

Things to See

The JD1 you pay to enter Wadi Rum entitles you to a cup of coffee or tea. If you bring in a 4WD you pay an extra JD4 or JD5, depending on whether you've hired it or it's private.

There are a few things of interest in the immediate vicinity of the village. **Lawrence's Well** is a spring about two km south-west of Rum, about halfway up the slope. If you scramble up, the disappointment in finding little more than a stagnant pool will be compensated by the startling views south-east to Jebel Khazali and beyond. There are many Nabataean inscriptions by Lawrence's Well, as well as some written by the camel drivers of the Thamud tribe in Saudia Arabia.

A more beautiful spring is tucked away at the base of Jebel Rum, only 500m from the rest house. Just follow the white paint to a clump of small trees. This spring is the largest of many in the area and supplied the settlement with water before the government laid a water pipeline from Diseh.

Between the Government Rest House and the face of Jebel Rum are the ruins of a 1st century **Nabataean temple** which was a square courtyard surrounded by rooms on three sides. On the north side of Jebel Khazali there is a narrow *siq* (gorge) with Bedouin rock carvings. The whole area is dotted with examples of Thamudic and Kufic inscriptions and rock art.

The main attraction of a visit to Wadi Rum, however, is the desert, and to fully appreciate it you need to get well out of the village. There are a few alternatives here: 4WD, camel and your own two feet. The local Bedouin population have the monopoly on the first two and know it.

Exploring the Desert

To hire a 4WD will cost you anything from JD15 (just to get down to Lawrence's Well and back) to JD39 for a full day (although officially a full day means no more than 50 km). If you want a guide, they hope to get

Desert Patrol

The camel-mounted Desert Patrol was originally set up to keep dissident tribes in order and patrol the border. Today, they have exchanged their camels for blue armoured patrol wagons, with heavy machine guns mounted at the back and specially adapted for the desert. They can achieve speeds of over 100 km/h through the desert as they pursue their prey (drug smugglers on the Saudi border, or so they say), and occasionally rescue tourists who have lost their way.

The men of the patrol can be quite a sight in their traditional full-length khaki robes, bandoleer, dagger at the waist, pistol and rifle slung over the shoulder, but mostly they wear khaki uniforms like anywhere else. Even their value as a tourist attraction seems unable to halt the tide of modernisation. Inside the compound, the officer and men on duty (often from as far away as Irbid) sit under the shady eucalyptus trees and while away the time entertaining visitors with traditional Arabic coffee, heavily spiced with cardamom, followed by sickly-sweet tea. ■

Camel-mounted desert patrol officer

JD5 an hour out of you. The locals have cooked up a few itineraries that include a couple of naturally eroded 'bridges' and spots where views of the sunset are particularly enchanting.

The prices are posted in the rest house. Remember they are prices per vehicle, so the more people you can round up to share the expense the better (up to six people can fit into the back of these 4WDs with no problem). Use the prices as the upper limit in bargaining, for as you walk away towards the desert from the rest house, you'll be surprised how many locals will be prepared to do some kind of deal that undercuts the officially posted rates.

It is worth suggesting at this point that hiring your own 4WD in Aqaba (see also Aqaba later in this chapter) might well be a better alternative. Having your own 4WD allows you considerable freedom of movement, although any trips planned well away from Rum village might be better conceived in the company of a local guide.

Whichever way you organise the vehicle, you can obviously cover a lot of ground this way, but you don't escape the noise.

Camels are a better choice from this point of view. You can hire them to certain destinations or for several days, say to Aqaba by the desert track, at JD15 a day, staying with Bedouin families camped in the desert on the way. For the Aqaba trip you must also pay to get the camels back from Aqaba – the whole trip may cost as much as JD75. You can even organise such trips to Petra (reckon on about a week in the desert).

Otherwise you can do it on your own, although care must be taken as this is inhospitable country and it is easy to get lost. For any treks longer than a day that take you far from Rum itself, you should consider hiring a guide or at least getting Tony Howard's book on trekking and climbing in the area (see the boxed story called 'Trekking in Jordan'). It should not be attempted in summer as the temperatures are extreme and dehydration and exhaustion are real dangers.

The only gear you need is a sleeping bag,

hat, good shoes and adequate food and water. Five-litre water containers can be bought at the shop in Rum and this should be enough water for one person for two days. Water is the key issue – pay careful attention no matter how you are organising your exploration.

Once you're prepared, just head off south down the wadi and camp the night somewhere. There is enough small dead wood around for a fire and the experience of a sunset in the desert is unbeatable. At night the silence is so strong it rings in your ears, unless you hear the strange sounds of Bedouin singing wafting down the valleys.

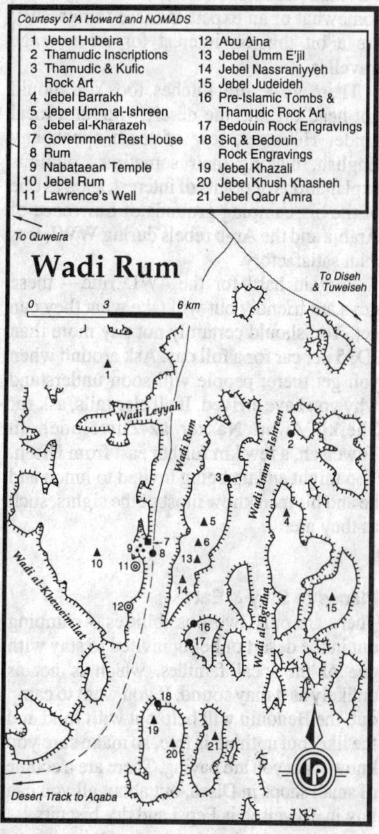

JORDAN

There are the occasional Bedouin camps dotted around and you'll generally be welcomed, but don't just waltz in – wait for an invitation. The Bedouin are incredibly hospitable people and will rarely turn away a stranger, but presumptuous behaviour is not likely to win you friends among them.

Rock Climbing

If rock climbing is your thing, Wadi Rum offers some challenging routes, equal to just about anything in Europe. Little has been done towards catering to the climber so you need to have your own gear.

In the 1980s the Ministry of Tourism commissioned a British climber, Tony Howard, to explore the area and map the climbs he did. The result is the excellent and detailed book *Treks & Climbs in the Mountains of Wadi Rum & Petra*, available from the Ministry of Tourism and in some bookshops. The 2nd edition (1993) has over 250 walks, 4WD routes, camel treks and rock climbs of all standards. He has also written a book called *Walks & Scrambles in Rum* (Al-Kutba Publishers).

You might also want to ask for a guy called Sabah Atiq when you get to Rum. He knows climbing routes and has some basic gear. A few rock faces have had bolts hammered in, but if you intend to go your own way, note that there have been several bad accidents. The rock is soft and can be treacherous. (See also the boxed story called 'Trekking in Jordan'.)

Places to Stay & Eat

The *Government Rest House* has quite reasonable two-person tents out the back for JD3 per person. Or you can sleep on the roof (mattresses and blankets are provided) for JD2. Take note that even in summer it gets pretty cool in the evenings. The rest house has showers, kitchen and luggage storage.

If this doesn't appeal, head out into the desert and sleep under the stars. You may be asked in by Bedouins to sleep under their tents instead – but don't turn up uninvited.

The rest house has an overpriced restaurant. A plate of mediocre kebabs will set you back JD3 plus taxes, while a 1.5-litre bottle of mineral water costs 750 fils.

The best advice is to bring your own food or hang on until you find the general store, just past the Desert Patrol's 'fort'. Here prices are slightly more down to earth. It also sells canned foods and some vegetables. Bread you can probably get for nothing at the rest house.

Getting There & Away

There is at least one daily minibus between Wadi Rum and Petra and another to Aqaba. The Petra bus leaves at 8.30 am and costs JD2.500 (it leaves Petra for Wadi Rum at about 6.30 am). The bus for Aqaba leaves Wadi Rum at 6.30 am and costs JD1.500. All these times are subject to the usual vagaries of this kind of transport – if they fill up earlier, they leave earlier.

Otherwise, you'll have to stick out your thumb. The turn-off for Wadi Rum is five km south of Quweira and the 26 km road from there is surfaced. From Aqaba take a Quweira minibus (500 fils) or a Ma'an minibus (JD1) to the turn-off.

After about 14 km, the road to Rum forks to the right for another 12 km. The left fork goes to the Bedouin towns of Diseh and Tuweiseh. Traffic along the Rum road is infrequent and you may well have to wait a couple of hours. You may be asked absurd sums for lifts this way, but really 500 fils should be enough to get you between Rum and the Desert Highway.

The only other possibility is to ask the drivers of tour buses that sometimes arrive in the afternoon and stay for an hour or so – just long enough for the tourists to ride a camel and take a few snaps – and then head back to Amman or Aqaba.

Hiring a taxi for the trip or even a 4WD to drive around inside Wadi Rum are options for those with a little more financial flexibility. See Aqaba later in this chapter for more details on the possibilities. Also refer to Exploring the Desert earlier in this chapter.

DISEH & TUWEISEH

If you find the number of tourists at Wadi Rum is too much, you could do worse than follow up with an excursion out to the towns of Diseh and Tuweiseh, about 12 km north-east of Rum. The terrain is not quite as breathtaking as Wadi Rum, but still more deserted.

There is no formal accommodation here at all, nor are there any places to eat, although there are a few basic shops in Diseh. The local Bedouin are keen to get some of the tourist biscuit and will happily drive you out into the desert area north of the Aqaba railway line. The place is dotted with old Nabataean and Roman dams, at least three artificial rock bridges, and assorted rock carvings and inscriptions, but unless you are somewhat of an expert in these things, they are a bit thin on interest for the average traveller.

There are several hitches, too. You should not head off into the desert without a local guide. However, few of them speak any English, making their sometimes dubious explanations of points of interest, such as one of the big camping grounds of Lawrence of Arabia and the Arab rebels during WWI, less than satisfactory.

Bargain hard for the 4WD ride – these guys are friendly but will take what they can get. You should certainly not pay more than JD35 per car for a full day. Ask around when you get there; people will soon understand why you have arrived. If all else fails, ask for Sheikh Awad Nasser az-Zuweibdeh in Tuweiseh, a few km further east from Diseh. You might end up being invited to lunch and he and his men know most of the sights, such as they are.

Places to Stay & Eat

There are only two possibilities – camping out in the desert or being invited to stay with one of the local families, which is not as unlikely as it may sound. If you want to camp out, the Bedouin will help out with food and the like, but nothing is free, so make sure you know what you are paying. There are a couple of small shops in Diseh, but about all you can buy in Tuweiseh is Pepsi and dry biscuits.

Getting There & Away

A minibus heads from Tuweiseh to the Desert Highway via Diseh at about 7 am (300 fils). Or you can hitch, as there is a much steadier stream of traffic from these towns than from Rum.

Aqaba

The balmy winter climate and idyllic setting on the Gulf of Aqaba make this Jordan's aquatic playground. While Amman shivers with temperatures around 5°C and the occasional snowfall, the mercury hovers steadily around 25°C in Aqaba. The water is clear and warm and as an added bonus offers some excellent diving for the underwater enthusiast. In summer, the weather is uncomfortably hot with daytime temperatures around 35°C and higher.

The town itself, Jordan's only access to the sea, is of little interest but with the beaches, cheapish hotels and a couple of restaurants offering something a bit different, it's not a bad place to stay for a few days.

The bulk of Jordan's exports and imports go through the port to the south of town, and in spite of the UN embargo against Iraq, it remains a busy economic hub. Now that Israel and Jordan are at peace, all sorts of ideas are being bandied about for developing the area. There is talk of building an international airport to serve Aqaba and Eilat, sharing port facilities and coordinating tourist development. The most perturbing news is that the strip of coast between Aqaba and the Saudi border may play host to a huge US-made theme park, complete with luxury hotel and all the usual gismos. No, Goofy won't be the star. The American promoters are promising a theme park based on Middle Eastern history and legends...one assumes not recent history.

Day and night there's a steady stream of road tankers into and out of Aqaba, but the activity is not as great as it was prior to August 1990, and fortunately the trucks are kept out of the town centre and directed to the enormous truck park three km north of town.

History

And King Solomon made a navy of ships in Ezion Geber, which is beside Eloth, on the shore of the Red Sea, in the land of Edom.

This verse from the Old Testament (I Kings 9:26) probably refers to present-day Aqaba. The name Eloth is a reference to the Israeli town of Eilat. Excavations at Tell al-Khalifa to the west of Aqaba right on the Jordan-Israel border have revealed copper smelters, held to be the site of Solomon's Ezion Geber. Smelting was carried out here from the 10th to the 5th century BC with ore coming from mines in Wadi Araba.

As trade with southern Arabia and Sheba (present-day Yemen) developed, it became a thriving settlement. In Roman times, the great road from Damascus came through here via Amman and Petra and then headed off west to Egypt and Palestine.

At the time of the Muslim invasion in the 7th century, there was a church and even a Bishop of Aqaba, or Ayla. The Crusaders occupied the area in the 12th century and fortified the small island called Ile de Graye, now known as Pharaoh's Island, about 10 km offshore. By 1170 both the port and the island were in Saladin's hands. In 1250 the Mamelukes took over and by the beginning of the 16th century had been swallowed up by the Ottoman Empire. The small fort in the town was built some time around the 14th century.

For the 500 years or so until the Arab Revolt during WWI, Aqaba remained an insignificant fishing village. Ottoman forces occupied the town but were forced to withdraw after a raid by TE Lawrence and the Arabs. From then on the British used it as a supply centre from Egypt for the push up through Transjordan and Palestine.

After the war the Transjordan-Saudi Arabian border had still not been defined, so Britain arbitrarily drew a line a few km south of Aqaba. The Saudis disputed the claim but took no action. As the port of Aqaba grew the

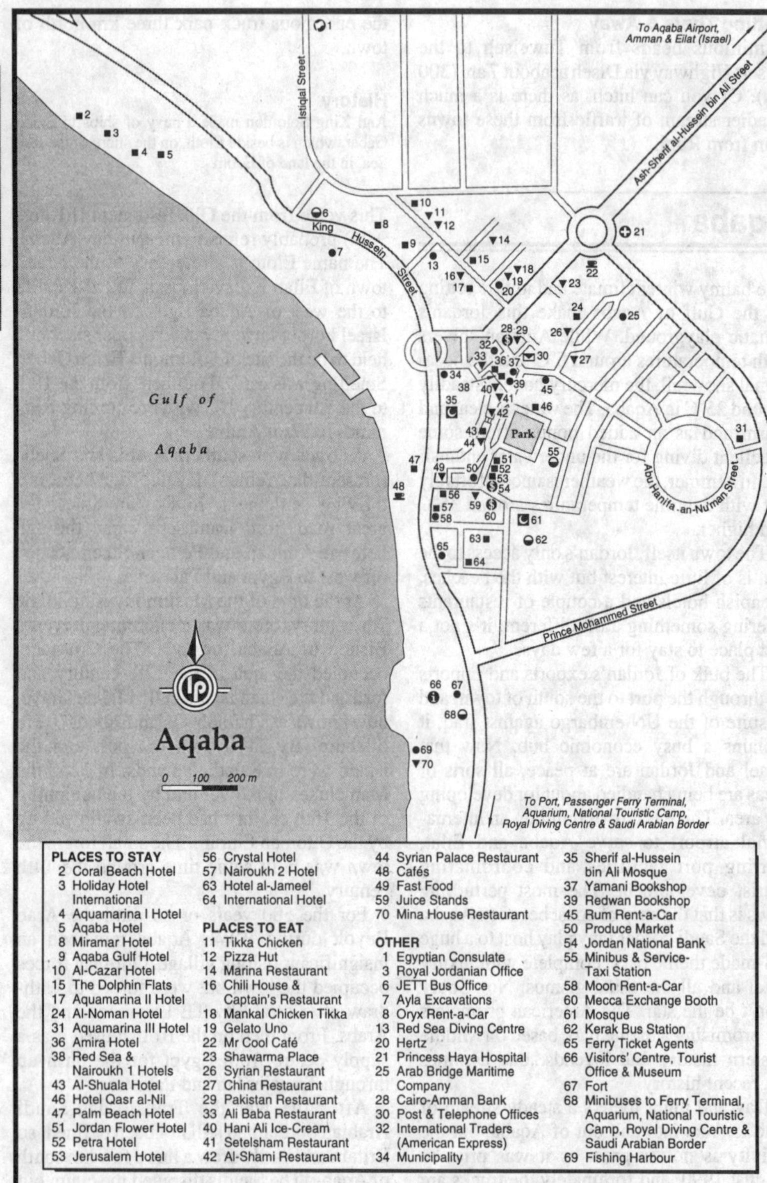
To Aqaba Airport, Amman & Eilat (Israel)
Ash-Sherif al-Hussein bin Ali Street
Istiqlal Street
King Hussein Street
Gulf of Aqaba
Park
Abu Hanifa an-Nu'man Street
Prince Mohammed Street
Aqaba
0 100 200 m
To Port, Passenger Ferry Terminal, Aquarium, National Touristic Camp, Royal Diving Centre & Saudi Arabian Border
PLACES TO STAY
2 Coral Beach Hotel
3 Holiday Hotel International
4 Aquamarina I Hotel
5 Aqaba Hotel
8 Miramar Hotel
9 Aqaba Gulf Hotel
10 Al-Cazar Hotel
15 The Dolphin Flats
17 Aquamarina II Hotel
24 Al-Noman Hotel
31 Aquamarina III Hotel
36 Amira Hotel
38 Red Sea & Nairoukh 1 Hotels
43 Al-Shuala Hotel
46 Hotel Qasr al-Nil
47 Palm Beach Hotel
51 Jordan Flower Hotel
52 Petra Hotel
53 Jerusalem Hotel
56 Crystal Hotel
57 Nairoukh 2 Hotel
63 Hotel al-Jameel
64 International Hotel
PLACES TO EAT
11 Tikka Chicken
12 Pizza Hut
14 Marina Restaurant
16 Chili House & Captain's Restaurant
18 Mankal Chicken Tikka
19 Gelato Uno
22 Mr Cool Café
23 Shawarma Place
26 Syrian Restaurant
27 China Restaurant
29 Pakistan Restaurant
33 Ali Baba Restaurant
40 Hani Ali Ice-Cream
41 Setelsham Restaurant
42 Al-Shami Restaurant
44 Syrian Palace Restaurant
48 Cafés
49 Fast Food
59 Juice Stands
70 Mina House Restaurant
OTHER
1 Egyptian Consulate
3 Royal Jordanian Office
6 JETT Bus Office
7 Ayla Excavations
8 Oryx Rent-a-Car
13 Red Sea Diving Centre
20 Hertz
21 Princess Haya Hospital
25 Arab Bridge Maritime Company
28 Cairo-Amman Bank
30 Post & Telephone Offices
32 International Traders (American Express)
34 Municipality
35 Sherif al-Hussein bin Ali Mosque
37 Yamani Bookshop
39 Redwan Bookshop
45 Rum Rent-a-Car
50 Produce Market
54 Jordan National Bank
55 Minibus & Service-Taxi Station
58 Moon Rent-a-Car
60 Mecca Exchange Booth
61 Mosque
62 Kerak Bus Station
65 Ferry Ticket Agents
66 Visitors' Centre, Tourist Office & Museum
67 Fort
68 Minibuses to Ferry Terminal, Aquarium, National Touristic Camp, Royal Diving Centre & Saudi Arabian Border
69 Fishing Harbour

DAMIEN SIMONIS

DAMIEN SIMONIS

TONY WHEELER

Top Left: Originally a Muslim stronghold, the Crusader fort of Qala'at al-Marqab (Syria) commands spectacular views of the Mediterranean.

Top Right: Roman-era mausoleum, Cyrrhus (Nabi Houri), Syria.

Bottom: Jerash's oval-shaped forum; Jerash (Jordan) rose to prominence in the time of Alexander the Great.

Tea & Coffee

Tea ('*shay*') and coffee ('*qahwa*') are the national obsessions in Jordan and Syria. These beverages are enjoyed in copious quantities by locals and are extremely strong.

Relaxing in a café sipping tea or coffee, sucking a water pipe ('*narjileh*') and chatting or playing cards or backgammon is a common pastime for Jordanian and Syrian men. Every town has at least one café, and they are good places to meet the locals. Arab women don't frequent cafés but it is generally no problem for western women to enter, although in the smaller towns you may get a few strange looks.

Tea is served in small glasses and is incredibly sweet unless you ask for only a little sugar ('*shwayya sukar*') or medium ('*wassat*'). If you want no sugar at all, ask for it *bidoon sukar*, but beware – this version is bitter and has a strong tannin after-taste. In Syria, the local version of a light chamomile tea is called *zuhurat* (known to some waiters as '*zuzu*'); it makes a pleasant alternative to shay. In Jordan, a refreshing option is *yensoon*, an aniseed-based hot drink that is great for colds, sore throats and indigestion. Another one is thyme-flavoured tea, or *zata'*.

Coffee, usually Turkish, is served in small cups and is also sweet. It is thick and muddy so let it settle a bit before drinking. Don't try to drink the last mouthful (which in the small cups is about the second mouthful) – it's like drinking silt.

The traditional Arabic or Bedouin coffee is heavily laced with cardamom and served in cups without handles that hold only a mouthful. It is poured from a silver pot, and your cup will be refilled until you make the proper gesture that you have had enough – do this by holding your cup out and rolling your wrist from side to side a couple of times. It is good etiquette at private occasions to have at least three cups, although you are unlikely to offend the host if you have less. Coffee is followed by tea *ad infinitum*. In some restaurants, a coffee-bearer wanders around at meal times offering Arabic coffee. The man is doing it for a tip, and better heeled patrons tend to take two or three cups as a matter of course, as part of the ritual of the meal.

OLIVIER CIRENDINI

Tea and coffee are enjoyed throughout cafés in Jordan and Syria.

limited coastline proved insufficient and in 1965 King Hussein traded 6000 sq km of Jordanian desert for another 12 km of the coastline. This gave the port room to expand and saw the fine Yamanieh coral reef become Jordanian territory.

Orientation

The main axis of Aqaba runs north-south along the coast through the centre of town and follows the gulf around to the west, ending at King Hussein's winter residence.

On the western side of the gulf, just across the border fence from Aqaba, is the Israeli resort of Eilat, now easily accessible since the outbreak of peace between the two countries. Still, depending on which side of the fence you're on, the gulf is known as either the Gulf of Aqaba or the Gulf of Eilat.

The airports serving the two towns lie close to each other either side of the border, which has led to the occasional stuff-up.

In 1986 a plane carrying Israeli tourists to Eilat landed. The pilot confirmed with the traffic controller that he had landed but was somewhat startled when the reply came back: 'Where? You're not on my strip.' He had in fact managed to land at the Aqaba airfield. A Jordanian official came on board, wished the passengers a happy flight and the plane took off for the two minute hop to Eilat. Plans for a joint airport are still on the drawing board.

Beyond Eilat, the coast of Egypt extends down the western side of the gulf, and Saudi Arabia on the east.

The city counted 3000 inhabitants in the 1950s, but by the year 2000 could have as many as 160,000. Most of the charmless expansion is taking place in the north and west of the town, while the port facilities lie about seven km south of the centre along the road to Saudi Arabia, which is 20 km from the centre. Most of the cheap hotels, restaurants, banks and the post office are clustered in the centre, with the more expensive ones at the north-western end of the beach.

Maps You're not likely to need a map of Aqaba, but the Royal Jordanian Geographic Centre's sporadically available version is the best you'll find.

Information

Tourist Office Housed in the visitors' centre behind the old fort on the waterfront, the office is open from 8 am to 2 pm daily and the staff are quite helpful with local information. They also have a free hand-out with some useful (and useless) telephone numbers. The museum is also housed here.

Egyptian Consulate The Egyptian consulate is in the new part of town, about 20 minutes' walk north of the centre. Tourist visas are issued on the spot for JD12 (cheaper than in Amman) with a minimum of fuss and the place is deserted – a great contrast to the shambles at the embassy in Amman. The visa office is open from 9 am to noon daily, except Friday.

A taxi from the Municipality will cost 500 fils with bargaining.

Money There are numerous banks around. If you are stuck without cash on a Friday or holiday, try the branch of the Cairo-Amman Bank at the Arab Bridge Maritime Company, which is open seven days so that people can change money to pay for ferry tickets in US dollars.

If you have a Visa card, you can process cash advances quickly at the Cairo-Amman Bank in the centre of town. MasterCard holders should head for the Jordan National Bank.

Outside normal banking hours (roughly 8.30 am to 12.30 pm and 3.45 to 5.45 pm), you can change cash and, in some cases, travellers' cheques also at the various moneychangers near the Jordan National Bank. Check their rates. Mecca Exchange seems reliable and changes cash and cheques.

The agent for American Express is International Traders (☎ 313757) near the Municipality, just along from the Ali Baba Restaurant. It's open from 8 am to 1 pm and 4 to 7 pm daily except Friday.

Post & Communications The post and telephone offices are next to one another right in the centre of town. The post office is open from 7.30 am to 7 pm daily except Friday, when it closes at 1.30 pm. The telephone office is open from 8 am to 10.30 pm daily.

American Express (see Money) can hold mail in Aqaba or even send it on to Amman, and the post office has a poste restante service.

Bookshops The Yamani bookshop opposite the post office has a good range of books on Jordan and the Middle East as well as current local and international newspapers. A few doors up, the Redwan bookshop (☎ 313704) has an equally wide range of newspapers, magazines and novels in English and German as well as a good range of books on Jordan. Book prices are higher than in Amman.

Radio If you have an FM radio there's a good music station broadcasting from Eilat on 102 kHz, and Radio Jordan is at 98.70 kHz.

Electricity In a touching reminder of Britain's better days, the sockets in Aqaba are generally of the three-prong UK type.

Medical Services The Princess Haya hospital is well equipped, even to the extent of having decompression chambers, and the staff are trained to deal with any diving accidents which occur.

Ayla

A few minutes' walk north along the main waterfront road beyond the Municipality is the site of old Aqaba, the early medieval port city that bore the name of Ayla (or Ailana). Signs in English and Arabic clearly pinpoint items of interest in the 120 by 160m city centre, including vestiges of the 80m long north-western wall and towers.

The history of the Egypt Gate reflects that of the whole city. From an impressive arch on columns in about 650 AD it was reduced to a small, roughly hewn doorway by 950 (now restored to this state) as the city declined, to end up filled in with just a sewage pipe poking through. The US-funded excavations have made considerable progress, but are still a long way from being complete.

Fort

The small fort down on the waterfront is worth a quick look. The Hashemite Coat of Arms above the main entrance to this 14th century Arab construction went up during WWI after the Turks were thrown out by combined British-Arab forces in 1917. Built under one of the last Mameluke sultans, Qansah al-Ghouri, the fort has been substantially altered several times since, and was partly destroyed by Royal Navy shelling. Entrance is free and the fort is usually open seven days a week, although Fridays may be dodgy.

Museum

Since excavations of medieval Ayla got seriously under way in 1987, the little museum in the back of the visitors' centre has acquired greater interest, with artefacts, plans and plenty of information on the old city. Ceramics showing Iraqi, Egyptian and Chinese influence is evidence that Ayla was a busy trading port in the Middle Ages.

Entrance is JD1 and the museum opens from 8 am to 1 pm and 3 to 5 pm daily except Tuesday.

Aquarium

Inaugurated in 1980, this aquarium has a small but varied collection of the many-coloured and sometimes bizarre local sea life. It's in the Marine Sciences Centre, 100m south of the passenger ferry terminal. If you can't go diving, this will at least give you a glimpse of what's down there. The staff are more than willing to explain which fish are what. It is open every day from 8 am to 5 pm and costs JD1 to get in.

Pharaoh's Island

The Aquamarina Hotel chain is the place to go for this one day excursion to what was once called the Ile de Graye, an island about eight km south of Taba in Egyptian waters. There is evidence that the island was inhabited as far back as the Bronze Age.

The JD20 fee includes transport from the hotel, visas, lunch and a visit to Saladin's castle (actually built by the Crusaders in 1115). The trip only goes if enough people have expressed interest. Several other hotels organise similar trips. The Aqaba Gulf Hotel's version (which departs from and returns to the Aqaba Gulf) costs JD24 and leaves an hour earlier (9.30 am) than the Aquamarina trip. Both return at about 4 pm.

Beaches

The public beaches in town aren't bad, and stretch from south of the big hotels to the marina and again from the marina down to the visitors' centre. There are small drink and snack stands dotted around the place. Glass-bottom boats cruise around trying to net tourists. The going rate seems to be about JD5 per boat for half an hour, although they'll try to hassle you into going out for an hour. There are plenty around so take no prisoners when bargaining. There are also pedal boats for hire.

Unfortunately, in spite of all the rubbish bins, the locals seem to care little about how much litter they leave around, and the beaches can become quite mucky. Furthermore, few women will feel comfortable on these beaches.

South of the port there is a cleaner beach with clearer water. You can pay 500 fils to use the beach at the National Touristic Camp, or JD2 at the Royal Diving Centre.

Finally, the hotel beaches are generally kept quite clean, but cost from JD2 at the Aqaba Hotel to JD6 at the Coral Sea. The guy at the Aqaba will drop his price in the afternoon, but the whole thing is ridiculous, as the Aquamarina I Hotel next door will usually let you onto its beach – which it shares with the Aqaba Hotel – for nothing! You can hire snorkelling gear at the Aqaba and Aquamarina hotels and deck chairs cost JD1.

It appears no private sailing is allowed in the Gulf for security reasons.

Warning

A few women travellers have reported varying degrees of harassment from the local lads on the beaches, even on some of those belonging to the hotels. Single western women are advised not to wear bikinis on the beaches. ■

Water Sports

The Aquamarina I Hotel will allow you to zip around a small course three times on its water-skis for JD4, or give you an hour's windsurfing for JD5. The Aqaba Hotel also has windsurfing gear and pedal boats for JD1.500.

Horse-Riding

Ask at the Aqaba Gulf Hotel about horse-riding with the Royal Horse Riding Club. At JD4 a half hour it's not particularly cheap, and possibly a little frustrating as galloping is prohibited. For information ask at the hotel or call ☎ 318100.

Hash House Harriers

Believe it or not, there is another of the worldwide running and drinking clubs here too. They take a small run and a drink or two on Monday night. Ask at the Al-Cazar dive centre for details.

Organised Tours

A bunch of taxi agents around the centre of town will gladly organise half and full-day trips to Petra and Wadi Rum. A full day to Petra should not cost more than JD35 for the car and JD25 for an afternoon to Rum. Given the entry charges to Petra, this kind of thing really is only an option for the independently wealthy with little time.

If you just want quick transport to these places, pay no more than JD15 one way for a taxi to Wadi Rum and JD25 to Petra.

On a completely different note, it is possible to organise horseback expeditions to places like Wadi Rum. If interested, ask after Wilfried Colonna at the Al-Cazar Hotel. When he's in town, he's most likely to be around from 10 am to 2 pm. He has had years of experience in the area.

Places to Stay – bottom end

Camping It is possible to camp in the garden of the *Aqaba Hotel* for JD5.500, which isn't too bad and gives you free access to the beach (not that you need it, since you can get onto the beach next door for free anyway).

If you want to get away from things, south of the port is the *National Touristic Camp*, where you can pitch a tent for JD1. There are sun shelters, showers and a cafeteria on the beach.

Hotels Standing alone next to a car park, the *Hotel Qasr al-Nil* (☎ 315177) is one of the cheapest and more squalid places. Doubles cost JD5, but most come with balconies and reasonable views. The showers are cool and the loos none too enticing. It's a desperation stop if all else fails.

There are three cheapies next to each other on the main street in the centre of town, and none is noticeably better than the others. The *Petra Hotel* (☎ 313746) has rooms at the front on the 3rd and 4th floors with balconies and a great view of the town, the gulf and Sinai. Singles/doubles with fans and hot water cost JD5/7. A bed in a shared room costs JD1.500.

The *Jerusalem Hotel* (☎ 314815), or 'Al-Quds' in Arabic, has much the same deal, while the *Jordan Flower Hotel*, or 'Zahrat al-Urdun' in Arabic, (☎ 314377) does not offer beds in shared rooms and is pricier. Rooms go for JD6/9, but bargaining down a dinar or two is not too hard when business is slow.

The *Red Sea Hotel* (☎ 312156) is one block back from the main street, near the post office. It's quite decent at JD6/10/18 for small rooms with fan and TV, and you get your own (usually) hot shower. Try not to get a room on the top floor in summer. Some of the rooms have great views and the owner is a friendly fellow.

The *Hotel al-Jameel* (☎ 314118), fronting a dirt car park, has air-con rooms for JD6/8. It's a little depressing really, but not too bad if you have no luck elsewhere. The rattly old air-con would keep all but the soundest of sleepers well awake.

The cheaper rooms at the *Al-Noman Hotel* (☎ 315142), at JD7/10, are OK but unspectacular. The cleaner ones at JD10/15 can, for a couple of JD more, be substantially bettered by a number of mid-range hotels.

Places to Stay – middle

Next door to the Red Sea Hotel is the slightly more up-market *Nairoukh 1 Hotel* (☎ 319284). Or rather there are two hotels of the same name. It appears there was a bit of a family feud, so both establishments use exactly the same name. The one closest to the Red Sea Hotel has rooms of a slightly higher quality than in the Red Sea, featuring TV, mini-bar, air-con and private bath. Rooms start at JD12/18/22 for singles/doubles/triples, but some determined bargaining can bring them down a little. Prices at the family competitor next door (☎ 312984) are virtually the same, as indeed are the rooms.

Better than either, unless you are determined to have a TV in your room, is the *Amira Hotel* (☎ 318840), just around the corner. Comfortable rooms (some double beds are huge) with private bath come in at JD12/18.

If you can scrape together a few more dinars, you make quite a qualitative leap with the *International Hotel* (☎ /fax 313403). The place is attractively decorated and the rooms extremely good value at JD18/28 with private bathroom, TV and phone.

Moving up the price scale but down the quality ladder, the *Palm Beach Hotel* (☎ 313551) is a strange beast. Somewhat dilapidated and scrappy, the rooms are quite OK nevertheless. What it lacks in crisp, new appearance, it makes up for in its tumble-down location in among palm groves and on the beach – it owns its own stretch. It also has a restaurant and bar. Although the asking price is JD22/26/28.500, a little bargaining should see breakfast thrown in.

The brand new *Crystal Hotel* (☎ 322001; fax 322006) is probably about the best value in its range. Spotless and relatively spacious singles/doubles cost JD24/36, equipped with what you'd expect of a more expensive place.

If you don't get in here, there are a couple of solid alternatives in a similar price bracket: the *Nairoukh Hotel 2* (☎ /fax 312980/1) on the waterfront and the *Al-Shuala Hotel* (☎ 315153; fax 315160), just across the lane from the Al-Shami Restaurant. Of the two, the Al-Shuala is a little cheaper and marginally better at JD24/28 plus 10% taxes. The modern rooms all have double beds, air-con, TV, mini-bar, ensuite bathroom and some have good views out over the gulf. The price includes breakfast. The Nairoukh 2 charges JD24/35.

A group might like to take a self-contained, furnished flat for JD50 at *The Dolphin* (☎ 314296), just up from the Al-Cazar Hotel. Sleeping four, the flats are spacious with TV, kitchen, lounge and bathroom.

The *Aquamarina Hotel* now has three branches. Aquamarina I (☎ 316250; fax 314271) is right on the beach next door to the Holiday Hotel International, while No II (☎ 315165; fax 315169) is closer to the centre. The latest addition to the stable is a little further out and is also known as the *Aqaba Inn* (☎ 319425; fax 313569). Standard prices in all three are JD48/66 for singles/doubles, including taxes. You can bargain for variations depending on the aspect of the rooms.

The *Aqaba Hotel* (☎ 314090; fax 314089), to the left of the beachside Aquamarina, has well-equipped bungalow-style rooms for JD44/58, which includes breakfast. It has all the mod cons and there's a seafood restaurant at the end of the pier.

Away from the beach, the *Al-Cazar Hotel* (☎ 314131; fax 314133) has reasonable rooms for JD40/55, including breakfast and taxes. The *Miramar Hotel* (☎ 314340/1; fax 314339) is a little dowdier but quite OK, with singles/doubles for JD30/36 including taxes.

Places to Stay – top end

At the top end of the scale, only the *Aqaba Gulf Hotel* (☎ 316636; fax 318246) is not on the waterfront. It asks a steep US$70/90 plus 20% taxes. Bargaining in the off season should see the price tumble.

To the right (north) of the Aquamarina I is the *Holiday Hotel International* (☎ 312426; fax 313426), the most expensive place in Aqaba. Starting prices are JD96/120 for singles/doubles, plus 20% taxes, but again a bit of persuasive bargaining in the off season will see the tariff collapse. It charges non-residents JD6 to use its strip of beach.

Next door, the *Coral Beach Hotel* is a little more reasonable, charging US$80/100, including taxes.

Places to Eat

Aqaba has quite a few choices when it comes to food. The *Ali Baba Restaurant* is the most up-market in town and has tables set up outside. Although a little expensive, it does a wide range of meals, including reasonable versions of Indian biryanis for JD5, a selection of fish meals for about JD7 and even ham and cheese submarines. A large can of imported Heineken costs a rather dear JD3.

As Aqaba climbs aboard the tourism bandwagon, it is becoming a little harder to find value for money. But there are exceptions. The *Setelsham Restaurant*, opposite the park in the centre of town, is simple but serves up good food for reasonable prices. The tasty shish tawooq (lightly spiced chicken pieces on a skewer) costs JD1.700.

The *Syrian Palace Restaurant*, next door to the Al-Shuala Hotel, also offers good food at moderate prices. Service is a little lethargic. Close by, the *Al-Shami Restaurant* is another decent place in the same vein, charging about JD2 for mains and dispensing free tea or coffee after your meal. Both places have upstairs sections with views across the Gulf.

The *China Restaurant* does some pretty good meat and rice dishes for around JD2 to JD4 and great soups for 500 fils. The cook is Chinese and the place has long maintained a high standard. The *Pakistani Restaurant* does some imitation subcontinental food.

By the Aquamarina II there are a few

places. The *Captain's Restaurant* does filet mignon (JD2.500), pasta, fresh fish (from JD5 to JD7) and the usual kebabs. Next door is the American-style fast food *Chili House*. The double hamburgers are OK but the tiny Chilli hot dogs are a washout. If it's fast chicken you want, try *Tikka Chicken* across the road – two pieces with fries and bread for JD2.500. Or there is the ubiquitous *Mankal Chicken Tikka* nearby. At the *Pizza Hut*, in the same area, you can pay with credit cards. Small pizzas start at JD1.650. Finally, the *Marina Restaurant* has similar prices to those of the Captain's Restaurant, but little or no atmosphere.

Down by the fishing harbour, it is hard to beat the location of the *Mina House Restaurant*, a small boat moored offshore. It specialises in fish dishes at around JD7 and even claims to do lobster Thermidor for JD35. Meat dishes come can cost from about JD3 to JD4.

Then of course there are the old favourites, roadside stands and cheapies with the usual stuff – you'll find a few of them in the centre of town. The *Syrian Restaurant* is a good example of the species for standard cheap snacks. There is also a very popular shawarma place on the road up to the Princess Haya Hospital. If you have late-night munchies, try *Fast Food* (aka *Quick Meel*), opposite the Crystal Hotel. It claims to stay open 24 hours a day.

For dessert, go to *Hani Ali*, just up from the Ali Baba. It's a sugar-addict's paradise of traditional sweets and delicious ice cream. An alternative for ice cream is *Gelato Uno*, near the Aquamarina II Hotel. The *Mr Cool* café, on the same roundabout as the Princess Haya Hospital, also has some decent ice creams.

There are a couple of reasonable juice places diagonally across the road from the Jerusalem Hotel. A pint of orange juice costs JD1.500. If you look around you'll turn up several of the standard coffee and tea shops. Or for something that panders a little more to the imagination, try the couple of local beachside cafés virtually in front of the Nairoukh 2 Hotel. Here you can sip a Coke or coffee in the shade of palm trees and contemplate the Gulf before you.

The shops along the main street are well provisioned with all sorts of food, so if you are heading for Wadi Rum stock up with goodies like dates, cheese and bread. The souq also has plenty of fresh fruit and vegetables.

Getting There & Away

Air Royal Wings, the Royal Jordanian subsidiary, generally has two daily flights to Amman, and occasional international Royal Jordanian flights also connect the two cities. The fare each way with either airline is JD20, and the trip takes 45 minutes. The main office (☎ 314477, 312403) is at the Holiday Hotel International.

Egypt Once or twice a week, Royal Jordanian puts on an unscheduled flight to Cairo from Aqaba for JD84 one way.

JETT Bus The JETT office (☎ 313222/3) is on the waterfront road opposite the Ayla site. The smooth and fast air-con buses run four times daily to Amman, the last at 4 pm. The five hour trip costs JD4.300. You should book at least a day in advance.

Saudi Arabia Saudi Saptco buses depart daily from the JETT terminal for most destinations in Saudi Arabia. The trip to Riyadh costs JD31. You can forget it around the period of the *Hajj* (pilgrimage to Mecca) and Eid al-Adhah.

Minibus/Service Taxi The main bus station is a couple of minutes' walk from the main street in the centre of town. A few buses and minibuses (JD2 to JD3) and service taxis (JD3.250) head for Amman in the morning. If there's nothing around, take a bus to Ma'an (JD1, departures until 5 pm) and try again from there. One or two minibuses leave in the morning for Wadi Musa (Petra) for JD2.500 per person. A minibus a day is supposed to go to Wadi Rum (JD1.500), usually fairly early in the morning – it depends entirely on when it fills up. If you miss it, get one for Ma'an or Quweira (500 fils). Tell the driver where you are going and he'll let you off at the turn-off, about five km before Quweira. Occasional minibuses also leave from this station for Tayyibeh and Shobak.

On Fridays and holidays minibuses to Petra and Rum are doubtful.

Buses leave for Kerak irregularly when full from a small bus station behind a mosque, not far from the Al-Jameel Hotel. The last one goes at about 2 pm (JD1.750, three hours).

Saudi Arabia Minibuses for the Saudi border (Ad-Durra) leave from the main road near the fort for 250 fils.

Israel You may get lucky and find a service taxi running to the Israeli border crossing for JD4 (JD1 per person if you can fill it), otherwise the going price for a standard taxi is JD3. For more details of the crossing, see the Jordan Getting There & Away chapter.

Car Rental There are several car-rental agencies dotted around town but, as in Amman, they are far from cheap. It is, however, worth thinking about hiring a 4WD to tour Wadi Rum (see also Wadi Rum earlier in this chapter).

Rum Rent-a-Car (☎ 313581) will rent you a small Suzuki 4WD for JD29.500 a day (100 km free; 65 fils each extra km). For three days you pay JD72.500, including insurance.

Moon Rent-a-Car (☎ 313316), near the Nairoukh 2 Hotel, offers late-model Toyota Corollas for JD40 per day with unlimited km. Ask at the Red Sea Hotel and you may get a discount.

Oryx Rent-a-Car (☎ 313133) concentrates on 4WDs alone. These are sturdy beasts manufactured in South Korea, but don't come cheap at JD55 a day for three days, including insurance and unlimited km (which you may well not use). Oryx is at the Miramar Hotel.

Hertz (☎ 316206) has an office opposite the Aquamarina II Hotel.

If you're hiring a car for any length of time and want to cover the whole country that way, it would be cheaper to do so in Amman.

Hitching If you arrive in Aqaba by truck, you may be dropped off at the truck park about three km north of town. A taxi into the centre shouldn't cost more than 500 fils, as you can usually find other people going into town.

For hitching north from Aqaba, the truck park is also a good place to start.

Ferry Although several ticket agents along the waterfront road sell ferry tickets to Nuweiba (Egypt), you are probably best off going direct to the offices of the Arab Bridge Maritime Company. The ferry terminal is south of the port, seven km from the centre (see Getting Around).

There is at least one daily car ferry between Aqaba and Nuweiba. On Sunday it leaves at noon and 6.30 pm; the rest of the week at 4 pm. There is also a fast turbo-catamaran for foot passengers only. It leaves daily at noon. From Nuweiba the ferry adopts a more or less identical timetable (11 am and 6 pm; 4 pm), while the fast boat leaves at 3 pm. The ferry trip under ideal conditions takes about three hours, while the fast boat can whisk you to the other side in an hour.

You will often find boats leave much later than scheduled, and peak times, such as around the Hajj, can be complete chaos.

The one-way trip from Jordan on the car ferry costs US$19 (plus a 200 fils charge). Don't worry if you don't have dollars – a bank branch within the premises will change your JD for the appropriate amount. Return tickets are valid for a year and cost US$32. A car costs US$100 one way.

The one-way fare on the fast boat is US$27 (plus the 200 fils charge), or US$42 for a return (also valid for one year).

Usually tickets can be bought on the day of departure and you only need to be at the dock about one hour before sailing.

You can buy a ferry and bus ticket to Cairo at the JETT bus office for US$45, although it's easy enough to pick up a local bus for Cairo in Nuweiba anyway.

From Nuweiba the one-way fare is US$32 on the ferry and US$42 on the fast boat.

Don't forget you must pay a departure tax of JD6 at the port. For most nationalities, Egyptian visas can be obtained on arrival (paperwork generally beginning on board).

For more details see the Jordan Getting There & Away chapter.

Getting Around

The Airport The Aqaba airport is about 10 km north of town and a taxi costs JD3.

The Ferry Terminal A local minibus leaves from the main road near the fort for the Saudi border. It passes the ferry terminal and costs 250 fils. A taxi between the port and central Aqaba should not cost more than JD1.500. A lot of the drivers are real sharks who don't use their meters.

Minibus Taxi Apart from the above cases, you may want a taxi to get down to the Aquarium, National Touristic Camp or the Royal Diving Centre. This should never cost more than JD3 under any circumstances. And of course the same minibus running to the Saudi border passes all these spots on the way down.

Syria

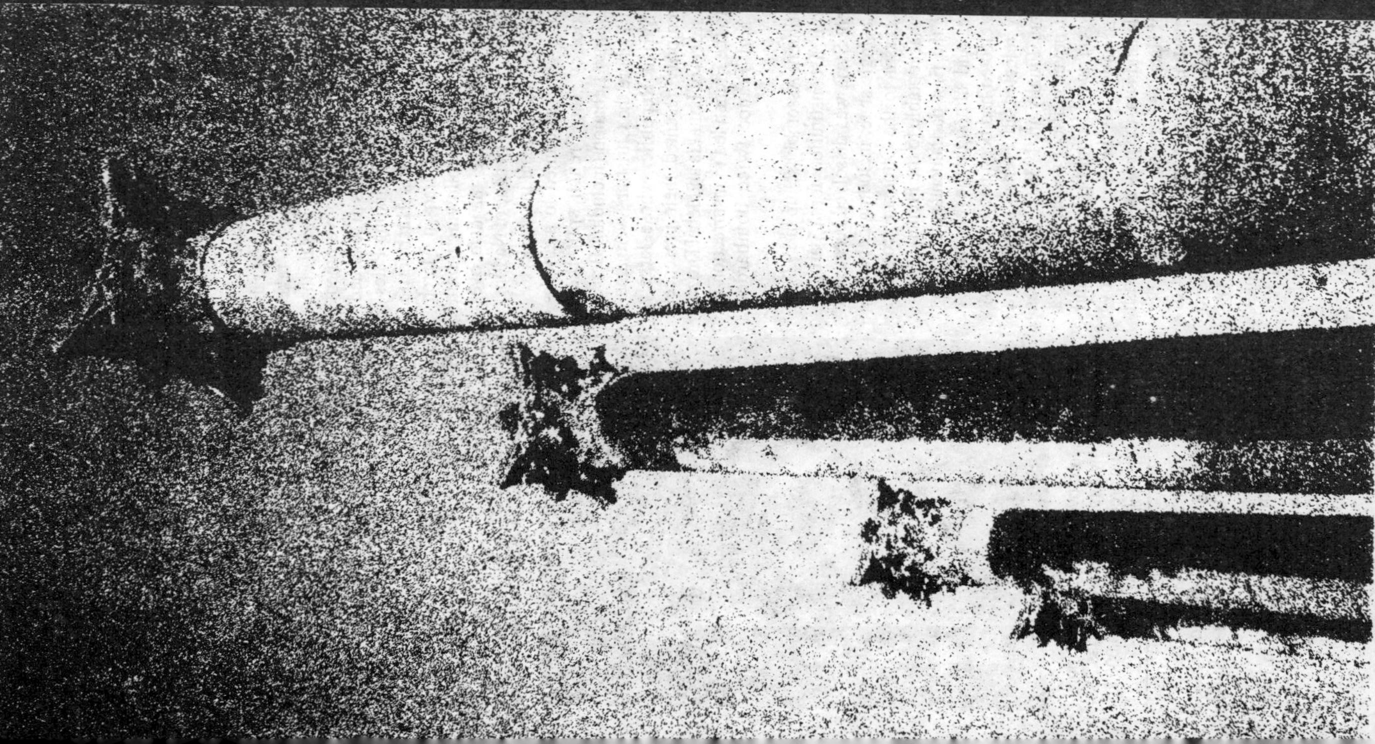

Facts about Syria

HISTORY SINCE 1920

In the dying days of WWI, TE Lawrence and other British officers involved with the Arab Revolt encouraged Arab forces to take control of Damascus and Emir Faisal, the leader of the revolt, to set up a government in 1918. When Arab nationalists proclaimed him king of Greater Syria (including Palestine and Lebanon) and his Hashemite brother, Abdullah, king of Iraq in March 1920, the French, who the following month were formally awarded the mandate over Syria and Lebanon by the League of Nations, moved swiftly to force Faisal into exile.

Employing what amounted to a divide-and-rule policy, the French split their mandate up into Lebanon (including Beirut and Tripoli) where the Christians were amenable; a Syrian Republic, whose largely Muslim majority resented their presence; and two districts of Lattakia and Jebel Druze. Hostility to the French led to insurrection in 1925-26 and France twice bombarded Damascus.

A Constituent Assembly set up in 1928 to hammer out a constitution for a partially independent Syria was dissolved because it proposed a single state, including Lebanon, as the successor to the Ottoman province. This was unacceptable to the French.

In 1932 the first parliamentary elections took place, and although the majority of moderates elected had been hand-picked by Paris, they rejected all French terms for a constitution. Finally in 1936, a treaty was signed but never ratified; under the deal, a state of Syria would control Lattakia and Jebel Druze as well as the *sanjak* (sub-province) of Alexandretta, the present-day Turkish province of Hatay. After riots by Turks in the sanjak protesting against becoming part of Syria, the French encouraged Turkey to send in troops to help supervise elections. The outcome favoured the Turks and the sanjak became part of Turkey in 1939. Syria has never recognised the outcome, which further sharpened feeling against France. Maps printed in Syria still show the area as Syrian territory.

When France fell to the Germans in 1940, Syria and Lebanon came under the control

SYRIA

Area: 185,180 sq km
Population: 17 million
Population Growth Rate: 3.6%
Capital: Damascus
Head of State: President Hafez al-Assad
Official Language: Arabic
Best Time to Go: Spring or Autumn
Currency: Syrian pound (*lira*)
Exchange Rate: S£42 = US$1
Per Capita GNP: US$991
Inflation: 12%
Time: GMT/UTC + 2

Part of the tetrapylon, four groups of four pillars, at Palmyra (see feature on pages 333-42). Each of the groups supports 150,000 kg of solid cornice.

of the puppet Vichy government until July 1941, when British and Free French forces took over. The Free French promised independence, but this did not come for another five years, after violent clashes in 1945 had compelled Britain to intervene. Syria took control of its own affairs when the last of the British troops pulled out in April 1946.

Meanwhile, what had been originally the mainly Christian Turkish province of Mt Lebanon became, with the annexation of some non-Christian (mainly Sunni, Druze and Shiite) territories, the state of Greater Lebanon. The French governor was forced to bow to Lebanese demands for self-rule and, when the new constitution was adopted, Greater Lebanon became the Lebanese Republic. Full independence came in 1946, when France withdrew the last of its troops.

United Arab Republic

Civilian rule in Syria was short-lived. The Kouwatli government was overthrown by the army in March 1949, and successive military coups brought to power officers with nationalist and socialist leanings. By 1954, the Ba'athists in the army, who had won support among the Alawite and Druze minorities, had no serious rival.

Founded in 1940 by a Christian teacher, Michel Aflaq, the Ba'ath Party was committed to a form of pan-Arabism that led to Syria forfeiting its sovereignty. In a merger with Egypt under President Nasser in 1958, Syria became what amounted to the Northern Province of the United Arab Republic. In 1960, a united National Assembly came together, with 400 Egyptian and 200 Syrian deputies. Although at first a popular move with many Syrians, the Egyptians treated them as subordinates, and after yet another military coup in September 1961, Damascus resumed full sovereignty. Although outwardly civilian, the new regime was under military control and it made few concessions to Ba'ath and pro-Nasser pan-Arabists, resulting in yet another change of government in March 1963.

A month before the Ba'ath takeover in 1963, which first propelled an air force lieutenant-general, Hafez al-Assad, into a government headed by General Amin al-Hafez, the Iraqi branch of the party seized power in Baghdad. Attempts were made to unite Iraq, Egypt and Syria but the parties failed to agree on the tripartite federation. Syria and Iraq then tried to establish bilateral unity but these efforts also came to nothing when the Ba'ath Party in Iraq was overthrown in November 1963.

Syria was now on its own. The Ba'ath Party's economic policy of nationalisation was meeting with much dissatisfaction, expressed in a bloodily repressed revolt in the city of Hama in 1964. Worse, the Ba'athists' pan-Arabism now posed an awkward dilemma. The existence of Ba'ath Party branches in other Arab countries implicitly gave non-Syrians a significant say in Syrian affairs, an issue that led to a party split. In February 1966, the ninth coup saw Amin al-Hafez ousted and the self-proclaimed socialist radical wing of the party in control of the government. Hafez al-Assad, commander of the air force and the rising strongman, was instrumental in bringing about the fall of the party old guard and facilitating the arrival of the extreme left of the party to power. Amin al-Hafez was later imprisoned as a 'traitor'.

The Six-Day War

The socialist government was severely weakened by defeat in two conflicts. The first disaster came at the hands of the Israelis in the June 1967 war. Later known as the Six-Day War, it was launched by Israel partly in retaliation for raids by Syrian guerillas on Israeli settlements. Israel attacked after President Nasser, having pledged support for Syria, closed the straits of Tiran (at the entrance to the Red Sea) to Israeli shipping. The end result was a severe political and psychological reversal for the Arab states and saw vast areas of land fall into Israeli hands. Syria was the target for a furious assault; the Golan Heights were taken and Damascus itself was threatened.

Next came the Black September hostilities in Jordan in 1970. In this clash, the Jordanian

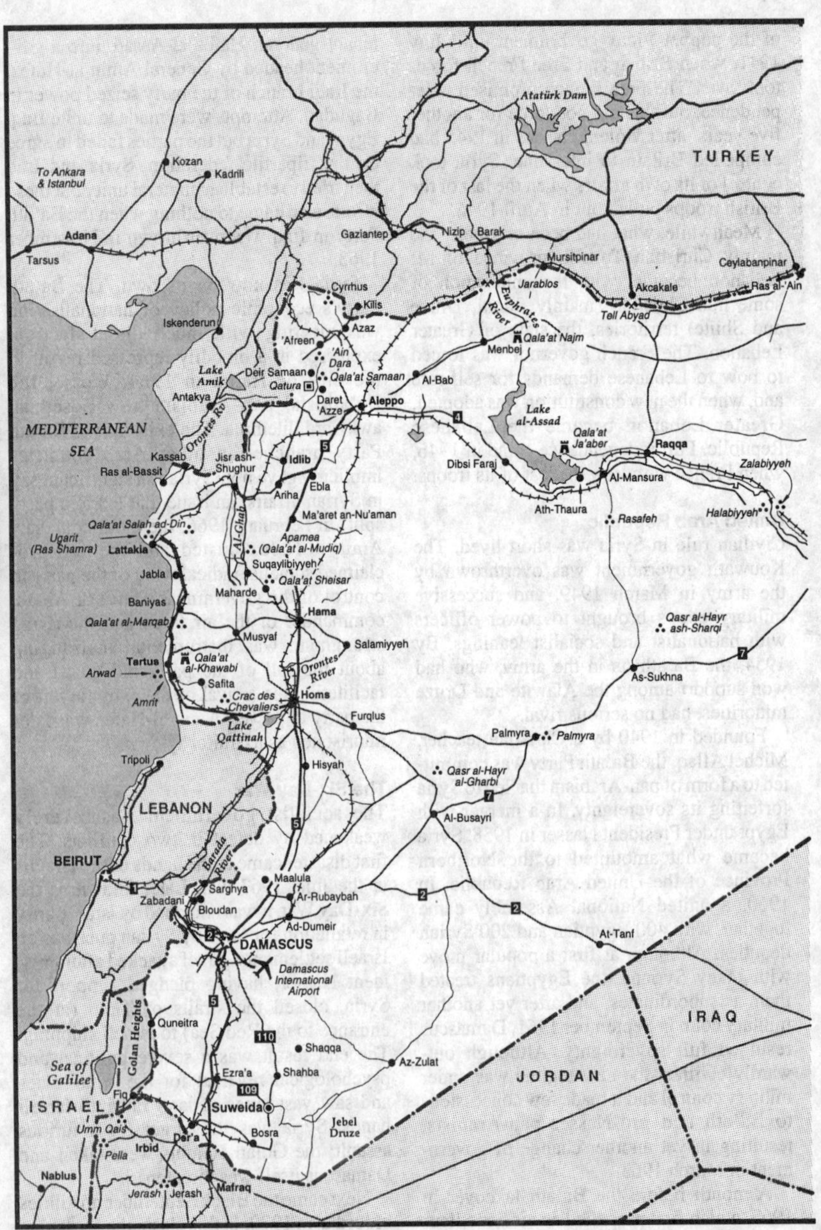
Atatürk Dam
TURKEY
To Ankara & Istanbul
Kozan
Kadrili
Adana
Tarsus
Gaziantep
Nizip
Barak
Mursitpinar
Ceylabanpinar
Ras al-'Ain
Akcakale
Tell Abyad
Jarablos
Euphrates River
Cyrrhus
Kilis
Azaz
Iskenderun
'Afreen
'Ain Dara
Qala'at Najm
Menbej
Lake Amik
Deir Samaan
Qala'at Samaan
Al-Bab
Qatura
Antakya
Daret 'Azze
Aleppo
Lake al-Assad
Qala'at Ja'aber
MEDITERRANEAN SEA
Orontes River
Kassab
Jisr ash-Shughur
Idlib
Ras al-Bassit
Ariha
Ebla
Dibsi Faraj
Raqqa
Al-Mansura
Zalabiyyeh
Ath-Thaura
Halabiyyeh
Rasafeh
Qala'at Salah ad-Din
Ma'aret an-Nu'aman
Al-Ghab
Ugarit (Ras Shamra)
Lattakia
Apamea (Qala'at al-Mudiq)
Suqaylibiyyeh
Jabla
Qala'at Sheisar
Maharde
Baniyas
Hama
Qala'at al-Marqab
Musyaf
Qasr al-Hayr ash-Sharqi
Salamiyyeh
Tartus
Qala'at al-Khawabi
Arwad
Orontes River
As-Sukhna
Safita
Amrit
Crac des Chevaliers
Homs
Lake Qattinah
Furqlus
Palmyra
Palmyra
Tripoli
Hisyah
Qasr al-Hayr al-Gharbi
LEBANON
Al-Busayri
BEIRUT
Baradā River
Maalula
Sarghya
Ar-Rubaybah
Zabadani
Bloudan
Ad-Dumeir
At-Tanf
DAMASCUS
Damascus International Airport
IRAQ
Golan Heights
Quneitra
Shaqqa
Sea of Galilee
Az-Zulat
Ezra'a
Shahba
JORDAN
Fiq
ISRAEL
Suweida
Umm Qais
Der'a
Bosra
Jebel Druze
Irbid
Pella
Nablus
Jerash
Jerash
Mafraq

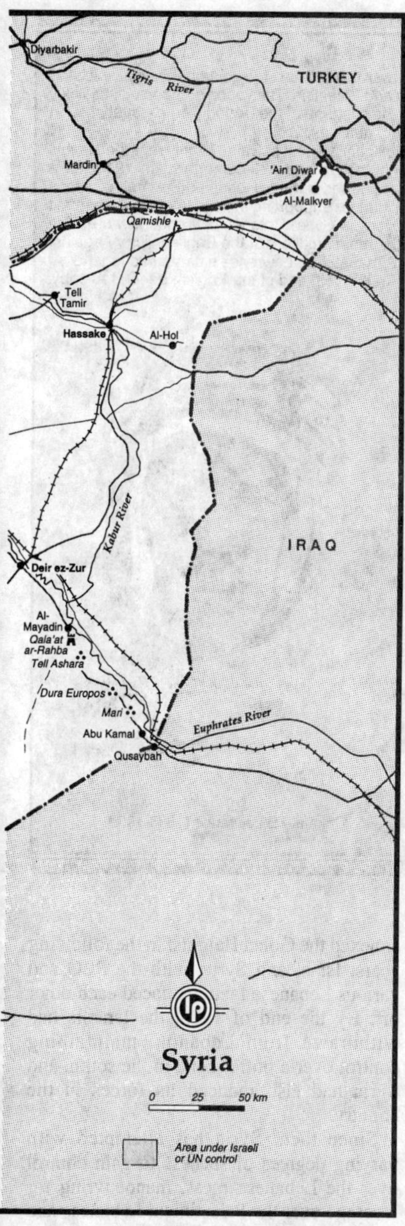

army moved against and defeated Syrian-supported Palestinian guerilla groups who were vying for power in Jordan. At this point Assad, who had opposed backing the Palestinians against the Jordanian army, seized power in November 1970 and ousted the civilian party leadership. He was sworn in as president for seven years on 14 March 1971.

On 6 October 1973, Egypt and Syria launched a surprise attack on Israel in an attempt to recover lost territories. After initial Arab gains, the Israelis managed to hold their ground and indeed in Syria came to within 35 km of Damascus. Although Assad grudgingly accepted a UN cease-fire on October 22 (as Egypt had done), his troops kept up low-level harrying actions in the Golan area, enough to keep the front on the boil without pushing Israel into another full-scale fight. Egypt signed an armistice in January 1974, but it was not until the end of May that Syria did the same.

Assad's Success

Since 1971, Assad has managed to hold power longer than any other post-independence Syrian government with a mixture of ruthless suppression and guile. His success can be attributed to a number of factors: giving disadvantaged and minority groups a better deal; stacking the bureaucracy and internal security organisations with members of his own Alawite faith (which has led to widespread repression and silencing of opposition both at home and abroad); and an overall desire, no doubt shared by many Syrians, for political stability. In 1992, he was elected to a fourth seven-year term with a predictable 99.9% of the vote. Assad rules through the so-called National Progressive Front, a Ba'ath-dominated body of allied parties. The 25th anniversary of the founding of his so-called Correctionist Movement in November 1995, a prelude to his definitive rise to power, was celebrated with much organised fanfare throughout Syria.

Lebanon

Since civil war erupted in Lebanon in 1975, Syria's involvement in its neighbour's affairs

Lawrence of Arabia

Born in 1888 into a wealthy English family, Thomas Edward Lawrence studied archaeology, which led him in 1909 and 1910 to undertake excavations in Syria and Palestine. The young archaeologist quickly familiarised himself with the region and even adopted the costume of the Bedouin on excavations, on which he also showed his organisational and leadership qualities.

With the outbreak of WWI, Lawrence became an intelligence agent in Cairo. Highly regarded in this capacity, he adopted an attitude which was both unobtrusive and anti-conformist. In 1915, as a specialist on Middle Eastern military and political issues, he recorded his ideas on the Arab question and these were taken into consideration by British intelligence. Supporting the cause of the Arab revolt and manifesting his own hostility towards French politics in Syria, Colonel Lawrence favoured the creation of a Sunni and Arab state. He also became the main architect of the English victory against the Turks. But it was the desert revolt of October 1918 that etched Lawrence's name into legend. At the side of Emir Faisal, who he made the hero of the Arab revolt, and of the English general Allenby, Lawrence conquered Aqaba. He then entered Damascus in triumph, marking the final defeat of the Ottoman forces. Syria then became a joint Arab-English state.

Returning to England, Lawrence defended his ideas at the peace conference and served as the special interpreter of the Hashemites. It was at this time that he started his principal work, *The Seven Pillars of Wisdom*, in which he recounted his adventures. In 1921, following the conference in Cairo at which both Lawrence and Churchill participated, he was sent to Transjordan to help the emir Abdullah – the grandfather of the current king Hussein of Jordan – to formulate the foundations of the new state. Nevertheless, he later left this position and enrolled in 1922 with the RAF, under the assumed name of Ross, first as a pilot, then as a simple mechanic. In 1927, he left on a mission to India, he returned home because of rumours that he had encouraged an uprising of Afghan tribes. He left the RAF in February 1935 and died on 19 May after a motorbike accident. He left behind him a myth – the myth of the man of the desert and the builder of empires, a myth magnified, and in part created by, David Lean's celebrated film, *Lawrence of Arabia* (1962). ■

Colonel TE Lawrence (1888-1935)

has waxed and waned. After several Arab summits, a 30,000-strong peace-keeping force, mostly Syrians, was sent in to quell fighting in Lebanon. At the same time, Soviet military support for Syria grew – by 1983 there were about 6000 Soviet military advisers in Syria.

Israel's invasion of Lebanon in 1982 and quick advance on Beirut heightened tensions, and for a while it seemed conflict between the two was inevitable. The invasion came shortly after Israel had formally annexed the Golan Heights. In the following years, Israel and Syria, with the PLO and various Lebanese factions, faced each other off. By the end of 1985, the Israelis had withdrawn from Lebanon, maintaining control over a buffer zone in the south, and Syria had also reduced its forces in the country.

Since then, Syria has attempted with varying degrees of success to gain control over the Lebanese mess, manoeuvring for leverage over the Palestinian, Lebanese and other factions at large in the country. Now that peace has returned to most of Lebanon, Syria seems to have won greater control over the country's affairs than ever. The cooperation pact signed between the two in 1991 has done nothing to diminish Damascus' role, and its troops remain stationed in eastern Lebanon. The fact that neither country has diplomatic representation in the other's capital is seen as confirmation of a Syrian policy of 'two countries, one nation', and even a prelude to eventual moves for a 'Greater Syria'.

Opposition

In the 80s, economic difficulties helped fuel growing discontent with Assad's regime. The main opposition came from the militant Muslim Brotherhood, who particularly object to Alawite-dominated rule,given that the Alawites account for only 11.5% of the population. Membership of the Brotherhood became a capital offence in 1981, but in 1985 the official attitude softened and some 500 members were freed from jail. By the end of 1992, a further 2000 political prisoners had gone free. In 1995 another 1200 political prisoners were released and exiled leaders of the Brotherhood were allowed to return to Syria.

The Brotherhood's opposition has sometimes taken a violent course. In 1979, 32 Alawite cadets were killed in a raid in Aleppo and anti-Ba'ath demonstrations were held in Aleppo in 1980. In February 1982 as many as 25,000 people were killed in the town of Hama when the army, under Assad's brother Rifa'at, moved in to brutally quash a revolt led by Sunnis who ambushed Syrian security forces and staged a general insurrection. Since then, little has been heard of the opposition.

Gulf War, Peace Talks & Water

Syria joined the Allied anti-Iraq coalition in 1990, no doubt spurred on by the collapse of the Soviet Union, its main superpower backer. Although no friend of Baghdad, having supported its enemy Iran throughout the first Gulf war, Assad saw in 1990 a chance to get into the good books with the west. In return for its modest contribution to the Allied effort, Syria hoped to be dropped from Washington's list of states supporting international terrorism, something it is still waiting for. In another gesture of goodwill in 1992, Assad opened the emigration door to Syria's few thousand remaining Jews – most packed their bags and left for the USA, leaving only a few hundred behind.

Assad has, by his moves, brought Syria out of the cold, and his decision to join in the peace process begun in Madrid in 1991 was another step in the same direction. Syria's main preoccupation in its relations with Israel remains the return of the Golan Heights, and while Jordan and Yasser Arafat's PLO have come to an accommodation with Israel, Syria remains cagey about committing itself to a peace deal. Damascus has always maintained that no deal should have been signed with Israel in the absence of a comprehensive peace agreement, arguing not without foundation that separate deals weaken the Arabs' bargaining position. Since the assassination in November 1995 of Israel's foremost peace crusader, Labour Prime Minister Yitzhak Rabin, international pressures for a peace deal have mounted, but Syria plays a mean game of poker and to date no obvious fruit has been born of the five years' tentative talks held by the both sides since Madrid.

Syria wants Israel to withdraw completely from the Golan, and it appears Israel may be prepared to do so, although it will have problems with the 13,000 Jewish settlers there. Mutual security arrangements and the establishment of demilitarised zones constitute the nuts and bolts of the public areas of disagreement, although ultimately Israel will want Syria to strangle the Hezbollah and other groups in Lebanon that still regularly provoke Israeli air and land assaults by their attacks on northern Israel.

In the longer term, Syria's foreign policy problems may come from a quite different direction. Turkey's plans to push ahead with new dam projects on the Euphrates River are cause for considerable alarm not only in

Syria, but in Iraq too. Water is set to become the most vital issue in the Middle East, and there is little doubt that Turkey is in a position to use its dams as a political weapon. Damascus has already accused Turkey of cutting the flow of the Euphrates on several occasions in retaliation for alleged Syrian backing of Kurdish guerillas operating in south-east Turkey.

After Assad?

The biggest question mark hanging over the country is what happens after Assad finally goes? Back in 1984, when Assad was recovering from a heart attack, a vigorous internal power struggle ensued when his brother Rifa'at apparently attempted to seize power and was effectively exiled to France. In 1986 he was allowed back but has since been forced to take a back seat.

For a time Assad's son, Basil, was being groomed for the top slot, but his death in a car accident (he liked fast cars) in January 1994 has reopened succession worries. Officially, the entire country remains in a state of deep bereavement over the dashing playboy son's death, but in late 1995 a new portrait began to appear in public places next to those of Hafez and Basil, that of Bashar, the president's younger son. Basil, who was respected in the army and had gone a long way to squashing the drug-production business in Lebanon, will be a hard act for his quiet, eye-doctor brother to follow.

Part of the problem is the question mark hanging over Hafez al-Assad's health, but his cautious style of rule has at least created a sense of relative stability. Whether any successor will be able to take the baton cleanly is open to speculation.

GEOGRAPHY & CLIMATE

Syria is not a large country – with an area of 185,180 sq km, it is a bit over half the size of Italy. It is very roughly a 500 km square with Lebanon intruding in the south-west, Jordan and Iraq in the south and east, and Turkey to the north.

There are four broad geographical regions in Syria: the coastal strip, the mountains, the cultivated steppe and the desert.

The Coastal Strip

The coastline of Syria stretches for about 180 km between Turkey and Lebanon. The Jebel an-Nusariyah (Ansariyah Mountains) almost front the coast in the north but give way to the Sahl Akkar (Akkar Plain) in the south. The fertile alluvial plains are intensively farmed year-round. The two major ports are Lattakia and Tartus and there's a large oil-refining complex at Baniyas.

Average daily maximum temperatures range from 10°C in winter to 29°C in summer and the annual rainfall is about 760 mm.

The Mountains

The Jebel an-Nusariyah peaks form a continuous jagged ridge running north-south just inland from the coast. With an average height of 1000m, they form a formidable and impenetrable barrier dominating the whole coast. Snowfalls on the higher peaks are not uncommon in winter. The western side is marked by deep ravines, while to the east the mountains fall almost sheer to the Orontes,

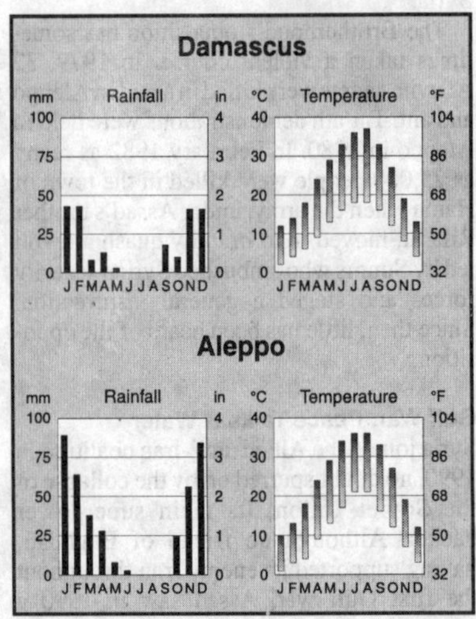

the fertile valley of the Nahr al-Assi (the Rebel River) that flows north into Turkey.

The Jebel Lubnan ash-Sharqiyah (Anti-Lebanon Mountains) mark the border between Syria and Lebanon and average 2000m in height. Syria's highest mountain, Jebel ash-Sheikh (Mt Hermon of the Bible), rises to 2814m. The main river flowing from this range is the Barada, which has enabled Damascus to survive in an otherwise arid region for over 2000 years.

Other smaller ranges include the Jebel Druze, which rise in the south near the Jordanian border, and the Jebel Abu Rujmayn in the centre of the country, north of Palmyra.

The Cultivated Steppe

The Fertile Crescent is, as the name suggests, Syria's main agricultural region and forms an arc in which are cradled the major centres of Damascus, Homs, Hama, Aleppo and Qamishle. The Euphrates and Orontes rivers provide water for intensive farming, while away from the water sources, dry-land wheat and cereal crops are grown. Irrigation is in fact stretching the area under cultivation, and another historically rich zone, the Jezira, is re-emerging. The name literally means 'island' and the area is bounded by the Euphrates and Tigris rivers in Syria and Iraq.

Daily highs average around 35°C in summer and 12°C in winter. Rainfall varies from about 215 to 500 mm.

The Desert

The Syrian desert, a land of endless and largely stony plains, occupies the whole south-east of the country. The oasis of Palmyra is on the northern edge of this arid zone and along with other oases used to be an important centre for the trade caravans plying the routes between the Mediterranean and Mesopotamia.

The Bedouin are at home in this country. During the winter months they graze sheep until water and fodder becomes scarce, and then move west or into the hills.

Temperatures are high and rainfall low. In summer the days average 40°C and highs of 46°C are not uncommon.

ECOLOGY & ENVIRONMENT

One of the worst things that could have happened to Syria is plastic, and certainly a 'sight' that leaps out at the eyes are grand sweeps of country whose sparse vegetation, scrappy fencing and any other obstacles are liberally draped with cheap plastic bags.

It is true there was a time when the nomadic Bedouin, as they moved on from one zone to another, would simply abandon whatever they could no longer use. This was OK when what little they could leave behind was generally biodegradable and easily absorbed into the environment. The habit has remained among their sedentary descendants, but what they discard, from plastic to scrap metal, has a more lasting and unpleasant effect.

Unfortunately, while Syrians have relatively recently embraced the technology of well-off western nations that has made plastic bags available to them, they have yet to develop waste management strategies, and appear not to have addressed the seriousness of this kind of pollution.

And while there is little doubt that the kind of ugly mass littering you will at times witness is depressing, remember that the majority of Syrians have considerably more pressing economic problems to deal with. This is not to say you can't make a contribution. The most obvious is to resist the local tendency to indifference on the subject and to do with your own rubbish what you would expect people in your own homes to do – bin it. If there's no bin, hang on to it until you find one.

FLORA & FAUNA

Heavy clearing has all but destroyed the once abundant forests of the mountain belt along the coast of Syria, although some small areas are still protected. Yew, lime and fir trees predominate in areas where vegetation has not been reduced to scrub. Elsewhere, agriculture dominates, with little or no plant life

SYRIA

in the unforgiving stretches of the Syrian Desert.

Your chances of coming across anything more interesting than donkeys, goats or the odd camel are next to nil. Officially, wolves, hyenas, foxes, badgers, wild boar, jackals, deer, bears, squirrels, and even polecats supposedly still roam around in some corners of the country, but don't hold your breath.

The yew tree (*T. baccata*) with its needle-like leaves and red cones can still be found throughout Syria.

GOVERNMENT & POLITICS

Actual power resides in the president as leader of the Arab Ba'ath Socialist Party. He can appoint ministers, declare war, issue laws and appoint civil servants and military personnel. Under the 1973 constitution, approved overwhelmingly by the Syrian electorate and defining the country as a 'Socialist popular democracy', legislative power supposedly lies with the people and freedom of expression is guaranteed. Enforcement of these principles has been less than thorough to say the least.

At the time of the promulgation of the constitution, which guarantees freedom of religious thought and expression, there was outrage that Islam was not declared the state religion. Bowing, but not all the way, to the pressure, Assad and his government amended it to say that the head of state must be Muslim.

All political parties are officially affiliated through the National Progressive Front, of which Assad is also the leader. Dominated by the Ba'ath Party, the Front is to all intents and purposes ineffective, serving as a tool by which Assad's regime can influence the non-Ba'ath parties. The 250 member People's Council has limited legislative powers, but just as the Ba'ath Party is the dominant force in the Front, so the Front dominates the council.

The president has three vice-presidents, possibly including his disgraced brother, Rifa'at, although some reports suggest he resigned as long ago as 1988. That there is no clarity on that score is a measure of the lack in transparency of the Syrian political apparatus. Until his death in January 1994, however, it was Assad's son Basil who was being prepared for the succession. That role now appears to have fallen to Bashar, Assad's second son.

The country is divided into 14 governorates, or *muhafazat,* which in turn are subdivided into smaller units of local government.

ECONOMY

After a particularly bad decade in the 80s, the outlook for Syria's economy has continued to improve slowly over the first half of the 1990s. The cautious process of reform has seen a loosening up in trade and finance laws, breathing some life into an economy otherwise stifled by regulations.

A more concrete ray of hope came from the development of petrol and gas finds in the Deir ez-Zur area along the Euphrates in the country's east. Production of the reasonably high quality light crude began in 1986 and reached nearly 400,000 barrels a day by the end of 1992. Most is produced by the Al-Furat Petroleum Company, a consortium of several foreign companies with a Syrian government component. Until then, only a small amount of poor, heavy crude was being extracted in the north-east of the country. Oil production appears to have peaked, but natural gas is also coming on line, with production standing at some 600 million cubic feet a day in 1995.

Agriculture accounts for about 25% of GDP and employs a quarter of the workforce, although a rural flight to the cities is slowly reducing this. Cereals and cotton are the main products of the Fertile Crescent and the Jezira, and improved irrigation in the first half of the 90s led to a rapid increase in production. In the mountains and on the coast tobacco, various fruits, especially citrus, and olives are all intensively grown. Plans are afoot to grow tea on the Mediterranean coast too.

Industry accounts for 23% of GDP, including the production of phosphates and fertilizers at Palmyra and Homs, iron and steel in Hama, and cement in Tartus. Syrians are proud of their drive towards some degree of self-sufficiency, and other products include rubber, glass, paper, food processing, along with the assembly of TVs, fridges, tractors and some other vehicles.

Power generation remains a burning issue in Syria, although the blackouts that were a feature of daily life in Syria in the 1980s and early 90s appear to be a thing of the past. The dam built on the Euphrates River at Lake Assad was designed to solve the difficulties but has failed to meet expectations, partly because of Turkey's exploitation of Euphrates' water upstream for its own dams in southeast Anatolia. According to observers in Damascus, however, the biggest problem is the vintage and make of most of the industrial equipment and power network. It's old, badly maintained and simply inadequate.

In the early 90s Syria embarked on a programme to construct gas-powered plants across the country to make up for the disappointing results of hydroelectric power.

Severe strain is placed on the economy by defence, which still accounts for over 50% of total expenditure, more than five times what is spent on education.

Syria's participation in the anti-Iraq coalition was partly calculated to win it lucrative new aid deals, not only with Gulf States, but in the west. Some of the aid received went into weapons procurement, but much was also used to invest in a new telephone system, power stations and a sewage system. Syria needs all the help it can get – national debt still stands at more than US$16 billion. Three quarters of it is owed to the former Soviet Union and much may never be paid back. Syrian business people are also hoping to cash in on the peace dividend expected if agreement is ever reached with Israel.

Although business is benefiting from the slow process of reform, the reduction in control and subsidies has had its down side. Prices are rising – many items have doubled in price since 1992, including basic foodstuffs. True, wages have gone up too. The average government employee takes home from S£6000 to S£8000 a month, virtually double the pay in 1992. Most private companies tend to follow the trend.

For the average Syrian, housing remains a tough problem. A decent apartment or house in a better area of Damascus can cost anywhere from US$500,000 to US$1,000,000. Laws designed to protect tenants from eviction have resulted in a rental accommodation shortage – 150,000 houses in Damascus are said to be boarded up because their owners prefer not to rent them out. Car ownership is equally out of reach, with import taxes at an astonishing 700%.

Syria has long been the perfect candidate for a thriving black market. Everything from narcotics to steel used to find its way into the country from Lebanon, but in July 1993 a serious clampdown began to have an effect. One visible result is that people now buy their western cigarettes in tobacconists at government regulated prices instead of from street vendors.

POPULATION & PEOPLE

Syria has a population of 17 million, and its annual growth rate of 3.6% (one of the highest in the world) is way out of proportion with its economic growth. The two biggest cities are Damascus and Aleppo, and rumoured figures from a census carried out in late 1995

Approximately 90% of the Syrian population are Arabic, with the remainder made up of Kurds, Armenians, Circassians and Turks.

put their respective populations at about six million and three million inhabitants.

Ethnic Groups

Ethnic Syrians are of Semitic descent. About 90% of the population are Arabs, which includes some minorities such as Bedouin people (about 100,000).

The remainder is made up of smaller groupings of Kurds, Armenians, Circassians and Turks.

Of the estimated 20 million Kurds in the region, about one million are found in Syria and, along with their counterparts in Turkey, Iran and Iraq, would like to have an independent Kurdish state – a wish unlikely to be fulfilled in Syria. They have been blamed for some acts of terrorism in Syria, which were seen as part of their push for self-government, although the Kurds' main efforts have in past years been concentrated on Turkey and Iraq. Since the late 80s, Turkey has repeatedly accused Syria of sheltering Kurdish rebels making incursions into southern Turkey, an allegation Damascus flatly denies. Syria's Kurds will often say things are just fine, but many are quick to tell outsiders, discreetly, of their desires for greater autonomy.

The Armenians, much in evidence in Aleppo, where they inhabit whole quarters and signs in their language abound next to signs in Arabic, are mostly descendants of those who fled the Armenian genocide in Turkey during WWI.

Linguistic Groups

Arabic is the mother tongue of the majority. Kurdish is spoken in the north, especially towards the east, Armenian in Aleppo and other major cities, and Turkish in some villages east of the Euphrates.

Aramaic, the language of the Bible, is still spoken in two or three villages.

English is widely understood and increasingly popular as a second language, while French, although waning, is still quite common among the older generations.

Religious Groups

Islam is practised by about 86% of the population – one-fifth of these are minorities such as the Shiite, Druze and Alawite, while the remainder are Sunni Muslims.

Christians account for most of the rest of the population and belong to various churches including the Greek Orthodox, Greek Catholic, Syrian Orthodox, Armenian Orthodox, Maronite, Roman Catholic and Protestant.

Until 1993, a few thousand Jews remained in Syria, mainly concentrated in Damascus. They used to be regularly wheeled out in the usual spontaneous demonstrations of undying loyalty to the president, but that has all changed since late 1992. Then, in yet another move to ingratiate itself with the west, Damascus granted most of the Jews passports and exit visas. Most took advantage of the offer and got one-way tickets to the USA, leaving only a few hundred behind.

EDUCATION

In the 1970s, the literacy rate in Syria was estimated by some at about 50%. This has been increased, perhaps to around 70%, but it is difficult to be sure of the figure. Officially at least, primary education from the age of six is free and compulsory. Secondary education is only free at state schools and there is fierce competition for places.

Although there are private schools, they follow a common syllabus.

Jostling for places in the universities is also tough. Damascus and Aleppo have the two main universities, with two smaller universities in Lattakia and Homs, and another small higher education institute in Deir ez-Zur.

The United Nations Relief & Works Agency for Palestine Refugees (UNRWA) runs schools for Palestinian refugees living in Syria, who also have the right to free places in Syrian schools.

About 170,000 students attend higher education institutions. Something that most young Syrians have to contend with is 2½ years military service.

For a long time, French was the foreign language of choice. But that has all changed, and English is now the favourite of most young people. Compulsory instruction in English or French now takes place in school from the age of eight. The effects of the change have been dramatic over the past five years, with noticeably more people able to converse to some extent in English.

Facts for the Visitor

PLANNING

When to Go

Spring is the best time to visit as temperatures are mild and the winter rains have cleared the haze that obscures views for much of the year. Autumn is the next choice.

If you go in summer, don't be caught without a hat and water bottle, especially if visiting Palmyra or the north-east. A siesta in the heat of the afternoon is a popular habit, and in summer you may well find you have little energy to do anything more.

Winter can be downright unpleasant on the coast and in the mountains, when the rains begin and temperatures drop. In fact, from November to February be prepared for some nasty weather all over the country. The change from mild or even hot days right up to the end of October can be quite dramatic when it comes, and bear in mind that most of the cheaper hotels (and quite a few of the more expensive ones) are not well equipped to deal with this kind of weather.

What Kind of Trip?

Syria is a comparatively easy place to get about in and lends itself to independent travel. Public transport is cheap, generally fairly fast and plentiful. As Syria becomes a more popular destination, the number of solo travellers passing through continues to rise. Some may not see that as positive, but it is confirmation of the country's 'do-ability'. Women travelling alone generally have few problems, but inevitably must be prepared for problems men won't encounter. See Women Travellers in the Regional Facts for the Visitor chapter.

Quite a few people opt to join an organised tour. Obviously if time is limited and your primary interest lies in visiting the main sights with a minimum of fuss, this can be an appropriate, but inevitably more expensive choice. See Tours in the Syria Getting There & Away chapter.

Even more so than in Jordan, Syria is an archaeologist's paradise, and the true aficionado of ruins and excavations could spend an eternity here. See also the boxed story called 'Digging up the Past' in the Facts about the Region chapter.

Maps

Apart from the free maps available at Syrian tourist offices, GEOprojects, based in Beirut, publishes a slightly better map of Syria on a scale of 1:1,000,000. Marginally better still is one published by Avicenne in Syria, available in Damascus and Aleppo. Lonely Planet's own travel atlas to Jordan, Syria & Lebanon is the ideal solution.

SUGGESTED ITINERARIES

Increasingly, travellers are using Syria and Jordan as a kind of overland link between Turkey and Egypt, often not spending more than a week in Syria. You could easily dally longer, but the busy mover can take in the main sights in this time. Coming from the north, you could start in Aleppo for a day or two, and then move down to Hama. This makes a good base for several day and half-day trips – including one to the Crusader castle known as the Crac des Chevaliers. From there you could proceed to Homs, change buses to head east to Palmyra for a day or two, and finally slew south-west to Damascus and on to Jordan. The same route works just as well in reverse.

If you have more time, an other less well-beaten trail takes in the coast. The main towns (Lattakia and Tartus) are nothing too remarkable, but several ancient sites and Crusader castles in the mountains just inland are best visited from the coast. You could do this as part of a loop via Aleppo and Hama. The Euphrates River offers a series of little visited ancient sites, including the better known ones of Dura Europos and Mari. An alternative departure route to Turkey via the border town of Qamishle would take you up

The Best & The Worst

Everyone in Syria is looking for something different, but there is little doubt about the main attractions. The Roman-era ruins of **Palmyra**, lying proud in a spectacular desert oasis setting halfway between Damascus and the Euphrates, constitute arguably the country's most astonishing sight. In a quite a different vein, but no less imposing for that, is the mammoth **Crac des Chevaliers**. Perched on a high point and dominating the main gap through the mountains that stretch from Turkey into Lebanon, it is a 'must'. Syria's two main cities, Damascus and Aleppo, each offer the chance to lose yourself in the chaos of their historic medieval quarters. For some, the maze of vaulted markets ('*souqs*') in **Aleppo** are themselves the high-point of a trip to Syria, but the ancient city of **Damascus**, with its great **Omayyad Mosque**, bustling markets and noble buildings, is the perfect place for days of wandering around and discovering.

Of course there is much more, and the independent traveller could spend weeks tracking down castles, the ruins of 5th century Byzantine towns, Roman settlements and **archaeological sites** of still greater antiquity – according to one claim, there are some 20,000 sprinkled about the country!

Syria has beaches, but we're not on the Red Sea or in the Greek islands here! If you want a sun and fun holiday, don't come to Syria.

It is perhaps a matter of taste, but some towns have a distinctly unattractive feel about them. Homs, for one, is a place that can and probably should be skipped. You will probably have to pass through this transport hub, but with some good timing you need only see the bus station. One of the bigger disappointments is Syria's only island, Arwad. Lying just off Tartus, it requires little effort to visit, so you may well want to have a wee look. Pity it's so mucky! ■

into the rich farming country of the Jezira, in Syria's north-east.

TOURIST OFFICES

Syria has begun to wake up to the potential bonanza in tourism, and is slowly moving to encourage more visitors to the country. There is no doubt that, whatever the reason, interest in the country is growing. Officially, 2.3 million people visited Syria in 1993, but the bulk of these were from other Arab countries and motivated largely by business, work or family reasons. Still, the numbers are rising. The tour bus is a more common sight at the main monuments, and a steadily growing stream of backpackers is on the march between Jordan and Turkey. For those who find this bad news, take heart. There is still plenty of scope for winding up in many fascinating places and having them entirely to yourself.

Local Tourist Offices

There is a tourist office in every major town, but don't expect too much in the way of information. All they generally have is a free hand-out map of often indifferent quality, although the Damascus one isn't bad.

Many of the museums and some of the archaeological sites have small booklets on sale, usually hidden away somewhere in a cupboard. Occasionally there'll only be one or two booklets – about somewhere else!

Tourist Offices Abroad

For information about Syria before your arrival, contact any of the Syrian diplomatic missions overseas. It is worth being insistent as these offices often have a complete set of the free hand-out maps available for each town in Syria. Syrianair agents also occasionally have some information. There are no tourist bureaus as such outside Syria.

The library at Trailfinders (☎ 0171-938 3366), in the basement of its office at 194 Kensington High St, London, W8 7RG, has some handy scraps of information, maps and so on.

VISAS & DOCUMENTS

For general information on what kind of documentation to carry, see Visas & Documents in the Regional Facts for the Visitor chapter.

Visas

All foreigners entering Syria must obtain a visa. These are available at Syrian consulates outside the country, or in some cases on arrival at the border, port or airport. To be on

SYRIA

the safe side, however, it is wise to get a visa before showing up at the border.

A warning: most travellers in the region tend to pick up their visas as they go. If you plan to do so in Jordan before proceeding north to Syria (and/or Lebanon and Turkey), think again. There was a time when it was the easiest place of all to get Syrian visas, but the embassy now delays decisions up to 20 days simply on whether or not to even process visa requests. As a rule, visas are *not* issued to non-residents of Jordan. This could change, but under the circumstances it would be prudent to obtain a Syrian visa elsewhere before reaching Jordan.

If there's any evidence of a visit to Israel in your passport, you generally won't be allowed into Syria. That said, mistakes on the Syrians' part are not unknown. Exit or entry stamps from the Egyptian crossings to Israel may well go unnoticed, although of course you cannot bank on it. A passport with a lot of stamps in it could slow you down at times. It can take two Syrian officials half an hour to decide that a trekking permit from Nepal has nothing to do with Israel! Should you plan on going to Israel after Syria, don't say so. Don't be fooled by any references to Occupied Palestine. A new section has appeared on visa forms along the lines of: 'Have you ever visited Occupied Palestine?' Trick question for which a yes response has the same effect as walking into a Syrian consulate waving the Israeli flag.

There have been varying reports on the validity of visas, but the standard set-up is the following. A tourist visa is valid for 15 days inside Syria and must be used within three months of the date of issue. Don't be misled by the line on the visa stating validity of three months – this simply means the visa is valid *for presentation* for three months.

On entry, you will fill out a yellow or white entry card (in English). Keep this, as you'll need it to get visa extensions and on leaving Syria.

Visa Costs The cost of visas varies according to nationality and on where you get them, and it is *not* always cheaper the closer you get to Syria. There seems to be little rhyme or reason in deciding which nationalities pay what, except in the case of UK passport-holders, who *always* pay a lot.

In the UK, Britons, Australians and New Zealanders pay a whopping UK£34 for a single-entry visa or double that for a multiple-entry visa. US passport-holders cough up UK£22 and UK£30.50 respectively. Germans on the other hand, come in at UK£7/18, while Canadians only pay UK£3.50/7. Cash only is accepted.

In Turkey, you can get Syrian visas in Ankara and Istanbul, and for most nationalities they are cheaper. Australians pay nothing, while Canadians and New Zealanders pay TL300,000 (about US$6). The Germans and French come in at TL600,000 while US citizens pay a hefty TL1,950,000. Britons take all the prizes though, with a whopping TL2,950,000 (about US$60). In addition, the Syrians here don't like issuing anything but single-entry visas, highly inconvenient if you intend to go to Lebanon, as this could mean you'll have to pick up another Syrian visa in Jordan (this time double entry), to allow you in and out of Lebanon. If this is indeed your intention, you may be advised to try for a multiple-entry visa before you get to Turkey. You cannot get a Syrian visa in Lebanon, and so might be forced to get a boat or fly out without a multiple-entry visa to allow you back into Syria.

Non-residents in Turkey need a letter of recommendation from their embassy, for which you may be charged. Australians, for instance, pay A$15 (in Turkish currency) and Germans DM20. New Zealanders note that they must pay for their letter in US currency. And you lucky Brits again take all the prizes, with a letter of recommendation apparently costing as much as UK£20!

You also need one passport photo. Visas in Turkey take one working day to issue. Note that the Syrian consulate in Istanbul is only open for applications from 9.30 to 11 am, and for pick-up from 2 to 2.30 pm the next working day.

Visas at the Border The number of stories floating about of successful and not so successful attempts to enter Syria without a visa is astounding. The official line is that if there is no Syrian representation in your country, you are entitled to be issued a visa on arrival at the border, airport or port. Australians, New Zealanders and Dutch travellers, for instance, *should* fall into this category.

The rules seem to be applied somewhat arbitrarily, however. There may be more chance of it working if you enter by less frequented border posts, such as at Kassab. If you manage to enter in this manner, and you are not obliged to pay for the visa, you will probably be issued with a slip stating that you still owe for it. This sum will be charged when you leave or apply for a visa extension. On the other hand, one Australian who reportedly got in this way ended up being arrested inside Syria and spending three nights in the cooler for his trouble!

It is also possible to apply for a pass in Damascus that allows you to leave the country for up to a month and then return without a visa. On your return you are reissued with a visa at the border. At the main immigration office in Damascus head for the second room on the left on the 1st floor. As it is not such a straightforward request, it seems to require a good many signatures (and a S£10 revenue stamp).

Visa Extensions If your stay in Syria is going to be more than 15 days you have to get a visa extension. This can be done at an immigration office, which you'll find in all main cities. You can get more than one extension and their length appears to depend on a combination of what you're willing to ask for and the mood of the official you deal with.

Extensions are usually only granted on the 14th or 15th day of your stay, so if you apply earlier expect to be knocked back. If, as sometimes happens, you are allowed to extend it earlier, check that the extension is from the last day of your visa or previous extension, and not from the day of the application.

The cost, number of passport photos and the time taken to issue the extension all vary from place to place. The cost is never more than US$1; you'll need anything from three (Damascus) to five (Aleppo) photos; and processing time varies from on-the-spot (most places) to 1 pm the following day (Damascus). There are also several forms to fill in, in French and/or English, usually containing questions repeated several times in slightly different ways – it is a challenge to think of sensible things to put down.

Residence for a year or so is an option, but you have to enrol in an approved Arabic language school or get an approved teaching job; for details see Language Courses and Work later in this chapter.

SYRIA

Travel Permits

It is possible to visit Quneitra, once the main town in the disputed Golan Heights area and destroyed by Israel during the 1973 war. It is maintained as a kind of propaganda showpiece, but to get in you need a permit from the Ministry of the Interior in Damascus. See Golan Heights in the South of Damascus chapter for more details.

Student Permits

Given the way entry prices to all sights in Syria have skyrocketed, anyone with a valid international student ID card should attempt to apply for a permit for free entry to the sights at the Department of Antiquities, next door to the National Museum in Damascus. The request needs to be made in writing, preferably on university letterhead. Success is not guaranteed, but if you get the permit, you'll have free entry to all sights as often as you please for one month.

Visas for Neighbouring Countries

Jordan Jordanian visas are available at the border, but if you want to get one in Damascus the embassy is on Al-Jala'a Ave, about five minutes walk over the bridge from the National Museum. Two-week tourist visas are issued the same day, require two passport photos and cost anything from nothing for

Australians to S£1300 for Canadians. US citizens pay S£1100 and Britons S£900.

At the time of writing, Britons were better off getting the visa in Damascus, as they were being charged JD23 on the border.

Multiple-entry visas are also available. Australians again pay nothing (valid for six months, Canadians are charged S£1300 (three months), Americans S£1500 (one year) and Britons a staggering S£3400 (six months).

The embassy is open for applications from 8.30 am to 12.30 pm daily except Friday.

Visa extensions are easily obtained in Jordan. See the Jordan Facts for the Visitor chapter for more details.

Iraq & Lebanon The Iraqi embassy has been closed for years. There is no Lebanese diplomatic representation in Damascus, presumably a testament to the Syrian policy of 'one nation, two countries'.

EMBASSIES

Syrian Embassies Abroad

Syria maintains embassies in the following countries:

Belgium
Avenue Franklin Roosevelt 3, Brussels 1050 (☎ 02-6480135)
Egypt
Sharia Abd ar-Rahim Sabri 18, Doqqi, Cairo (☎ 02-718320)
France
20 rue Vaneau, 75007 Paris (☎ 1-45 51 82 35)
Germany
Berlin: Otto Grotewohl Str 3 (☎ 030-220 20 46)
Bonn 2: Andreas Hermes Str 5, 5300 (☎ 228-81 99 20)
Italy
Piazza Coeli 1, Rome (☎ 06-679 7791)
Japan
Homat-Jade No19-45, Akasaka Minato-ku, Tokyo 107 (☎ 03-35 86 89 78)
Jordan
Afghani St, Jebel Amman (☎ 06-641392)
Saudi Arabia
Jeddah: Cnr Sharia al-Andalus and Sharia Mahmoud Rasif (☎ 02-6605801)
Riyadh: Cnr Sharia ath-Thamaneen and Sharia ar-Riyadh (☎ 1-4633198)
Spain
Plaza de Plateria de Martinez 1 (☎ 91-420 1602)
Switzerland
72 Rue de Lausanne, 1202 Geneva (☎ 022-32 65 22)
Turkey
Ankara: Abdullah Cevdet Sokak No 7, Çankaya (☎ 312-440 9657)
Istanbul (consulate): 3 Silahhane Caddesi (aka Maçka Caddesi), Ralli Apt 59, Teşvikiye (☎ 212-248 2735)
UK
8 Belgrave Square, London, SW1 (☎ 0171-245 9012)
USA
New York (consulate): 820 Second Ave, NY 10017 (☎ 212-661 1313)
Washington: 2215 Wyoming Ave NW, Washington DC 20008 (☎ 202-232 6313)

Foreign Embassies in Syria

Some of the foreign embassies and consulates to be found in Damascus are:

Australia
128/A Farabi St, Al-Mezzeh (☎ 666 4317)
Austria
Chafik Mouayad St, Sabri Malki Building, Rawda (☎ 333 6617)
Belgium
Ata Ayoubi St, Hashem Building (☎ 333 8098)
Canada
Block 12, Al-Mezzeh (☎ 223 6851)
Denmark
Chakib Arslan St, Abu Roumaneh (☎ 333 1008, 333 7853)
Egypt
Al-Jala'a Ave (☎ 661 3490)
Finland
West Malki Hawakir, Yaçoubian Building (☎ 333 8809; fax 373 4740)
France
Ata Ayoubi St (☎ 224 7992)
Germany
53 Ibrahim Hanano St (☎ 332 3800/1)
Ireland
No diplomatic representation in Syria, see UK embassy.
Italy
82 Al-Mansour St (☎ 333 8338)
Japan
18 Al-Mahdi bin Baraka Ave (☎ 333 8273)
Jordan
Al-Jala'a Ave (☎ 223 4642).
Lebanon
No diplomatic representation in Syria.
Netherlands
Al-Jala'a Ave (☎ 333 6871 or 333 3702 for emergency after hours). The embassy is open from 9 am to noon Sunday to Thursday.

SYRIA

New Zealand
No diplomatic representation in Syria, see UK embassy.

Norway
1st floor, Shaheen Building, Ahmed Shawki St, Malki (☎ 333 7114)

Saudi Arabia
Al-Jala'a Ave, Abu Roumaneh (☎ 333 4914)

South Africa
No diplomatic representation in Syria.

Spain
Al-Jala'a Ave, Abu Roumaneh (☎ 333 2126)

Sweden
Catholic Patriarchate Building, Chakib Arslan St, Abu Roumaneh (☎ 332 7261)

Switzerland
26 Al-Mahdi bin Baraka Ave, Chora Building (☎ 331 1870)

UK
11 Mohammed Kurd Ali St, Kotob Building, Malki (☎ 371 2561/2/3)

USA
2 Al-Mansour St, Abu Roumaneh (☎ 333 2814). The embassy opens from 8 am to 3.15 pm Sunday to Wednesday (2 pm on Thursday), while the consular service (round the back) is open from 7.30 am to 2 pm Sunday to Thursday.

CUSTOMS

You can bring in up to US$5000 without declaring it. Officially, you can only export US$2000 without declaring it, or S£5000 to Jordan or Lebanon. If you are travelling with considerably greater sums, you should play it safe and insist on declaring it all when you enter the country in order to be quite sure of avoiding any problems upon leaving.

MONEY

The banking system in Syria is entirely state-owned. Although there has been talk of creating openings for private and even foreign institutions, that still looks some way off, and initially would concern investment banks alone. The Commercial Bank of Syria is the public face of the state system and there's at least one branch in every major town. The system seems to have loosened up a little, and a majority of branches of the bank seem willing to change cash *and* travellers' cheques in most major currencies.

Costs

Syria remains a comparatively cheap country to travel in, but there is no doubt that it is slowly becoming more expensive. Continued inflation and easing of subsidies on staples has maintained upward pressure on prices since Syria's big inflationary heave in November 1991. In fact, the cheaper hotels and food cost much the same as in neighbouring Jordan. Public transport remains very cheap.

It is possible, although increasingly difficult, to stay within the US$10 to US$15 a day mark, but only if you are prepared to sleep in the cheapest hotels and stick to a diet of felafels, shawarma and juice.

With some exceptions, the cheapest beds in Syrian hotels come for around S£150, although if you want a single room you are looking at more like S£200. For more details on hotel costs, see Accommodation later in this chapter.

You can expect to pay in the vicinity of S£200 a head for an average meal in a mid-range restaurant. As in Jordan, waiters in the better restaurants expect tips, and occasionally deduct them themselves when giving you change.

A felafel on the street will cost S£15 to S£25 depending on its size, while a shawarma will usually cost S£25 to S£35. A small bottle of local soft drink bought from a street vendor is S£6 (S£10 if taken inside a café), while the various 330 ml canned soft drinks, some made under licence in Syria and others imported, cost S£20 to S£30. Bottles of local beer cost from S£30 in liquor stores to S£50 in most restaurants. A bottle of locally produced wine can go for as little as S£50, a bottle of araq around S£90 and a can of imported foreign beer S£100.

The standard cup of tea and coffee costs S£5 and S£10 respectively, but this can vary a lot, and you can easily find yourself paying S£20 for a big glass of tea in Damascus.

A kg of apples costs S£30, while bananas sell for about S£50 a kg. Fruit juices can cost anything from S£20 to S£50, depending on the size of the glass (the latter is generally a pint glass of pure juice).

Super ('*mumtaz*') petrol costs S£20.40 a litre, while diesel ('*mazout*') is very cheap at about S£2.66 a litre.

Entry Fees Since early 1995 the big expense has been entry to museums, castles and other sights. Many now cost S£200, which at the official exchange rate is about US$5. While such a fee can be justified in the case of the Crac des Chevaliers and a couple of the bigger museums, there will be plenty of times when you have to ask yourself whether any one sight is worth paying such money. It is irksome to note that locals pay S£25 at the most to enter these places.

The icing on the cake is a still more recent development. In some places, such as the Citadel in Aleppo and Qala'at Samaan, greed has frankly overwhelmed common sense. Where do they get off demanding S£500 for the right to take photos and S£1000 to shoot video tape? It can only be hoped that whoever dreamed up this revenue-raiser has some sort of mystical experience and realises the absurdity of these charges.

SYRIA

Currency

The currency is the Syrian pound (S£), known locally as the *lira*. There are 100 piastres ('*qirsh*') to a pound, but it's unlikely you'll ever need to know this, as few transactions nowadays involve the use of coins at all. Indeed only the one pound coin is still around, and the main purpose for keeping it alive seems to be for use in public telephones. Notes are S£5, S£10, S£25, S£50, S£100 and S£500.

Changing Money

Cash & Travellers' Cheques Cash is definitely king in Syria, although travellers' cheques are obviously the safer alternative.

Most major brands of travellers' cheque are accepted by the Commercial Bank of Syria, but a minimum one-off commission of S£25 is paid per transaction, whether you change one or several cheques.

Occasionally you'll be asked to present sales receipts when changing travellers' cheques, which of course you are not supposed to have together with the cheques. Not all branches do this, but you may find you have no choice, since in some towns there is only the one bank. You could try presenting them with photocopies of the sales slips.

There is no commission for changing cash and, as with cheques, most major currencies are accepted.

More often than not, you'll find yourself being diddled for a pound or two, as bank employees (and others) tend to round everything off to the nearest five pounds.

When shopping, some store-owners will accept not only foreign hard currency, but travellers' cheques and even some personal cheques – they will ask you to keep it quiet though. Travellers cheques are also often accepted by bigger hard-currency hotels as direct payment.

Currency Exchange

The Commercial Bank of Syria has not altered its exchange rates much in some five years. The US dollar has not moved at all and fetches S£42, which is not bad, but as much as S£8 short of the black market rate. Aside from this, there is another rate travellers should be aware of, the so-called 'official rate' used to calculate room prices in hotels charging hard currency. That rate is S£11.20 to the US dollar, so when taking extras like breakfast, try to pay on the spot in Syrian pounds – which you will have changed in the bank at S£42 to the US dollar. Anything that goes on the room bill may well be worked out at the official hotel rate.

A$1	=	S£32.83
C$1	=	S£30.55
FF10	=	S£82.20
DM1	=	S£28.11
¥100	=	S£39.00
JD1	=	S£59.13
TL10,000	=	S£5.10
UK£1	=	S£64.94
US$1	=	S£42

You may find it difficult to change Turkish lira in the banks, although in Aleppo at least it should not be a problem. The Turkish currency was on something of a devaluation roller-coaster at the time of writing and the best way to calculate comparative rates is to work out dollar equivalents. ■

Credit Cards Although still no good for cash advances, major credit cards such as American Express, Visa, MasterCard and Diners Club are increasingly accepted by bigger hotels and stores for purchases. They are also handy for buying air tickets (as the only alternative is hard currency cash) and with some car rental companies (it will save you having to leave a large cash deposit). And remember that you *can* use credit cards for cash advances in neighbouring Jordan, Lebanon and Turkey.

If you are in real trouble, some shopkeepers in the Damascus souqs will give a cash advance on credit cards, disguising the transaction as a sale. The rate, however, comes to about S£40 per US dollar – needless to say this is an illegal activity (see also Black Market).

Changing Money Outside Syria You can buy Syrian pounds in Jordan and in Turkish border areas. In the latter case, the bus station at Antakya is swarming with moneychangers and you can generally get a better deal there than on the black market inside Syria. It is a good idea to buy at least a small stash here to avoid being caught short when you first get inside Syria. You can also exchange money officially on the border, but at the inferior official rate.

If you leave Syria by land, you can trade your leftover pounds for dinars in Jordan or for lira in Turkey with little trouble. In Turkey, it is best to change at the border, but in Jordan most banks should accept Syrian pounds. That said, it is obviously better to be left with as little Syrian cash as possible when you leave the country.

Black Market

The black market in currency is alive and well, in spite of a 1986 law providing for up to three years in prison for the unwarranted possession of hard currency or its illegal exchange. The thirst for hard currency is easily enough explained. It can be used to make many purchases, mainly of foreign goods, that otherwise remain inaccessible to Syrians. As it happens, the release in December 1995 of some 5300 prisoners, many for so-called economic crimes, was interpreted by some as a prelude to the lifting of the 1986 law.

Although it is increasingly common practice, and at its most alive in Damascus, do exercise caution if you decide to change money this way.

Cash is obviously the most welcome object of illicit exchange, and the US dollar the preferred currency. At the time of writing, the best rate you could hope for was S£50 to the dollar. Outside Damascus you are looking at more like S£48. Treat the black market like any other transaction and bargain – often enough the initial offer will be for S£45. In some cases you will find people willing to change travellers' cheques in this way, although for a rate usually a couple of S£ lower than you would get with cash.

You may well be approached in the street, in your hotel (by staff) or in the souqs to change money. If you want to change and have not been approached, jewellery stalls in the souqs are a logical place to start. Be discreet, as there is a degree of risk involved for all sides.

Tipping

Baksheesh, the tip, is part of the oil that makes the Middle East run. Syrians are not particularly shrill about tips, which makes a nice change from some other countries in the area. Waiters in better restaurants generally expect a tip, and some will even help themselves by short-changing you a little. Other services are also carried out with a view to being tipped – everything from having your luggage taken to your room to having doors opened for you comes into this category. Judge each situation on its merits. The difficulty of getting your hands on small change (ie one pound coins) means that often you may find yourself skipping the tip.

Bargaining

Whatever you buy in the way of souvenirs, remember that bargaining is an integral part of the process and listed prices are always inflated to allow for it. When shopping in the souqs, bargain – even a minimum effort will see outrageous asking prices halved. Unlike in other countries, such as Egypt and Morocco, where the stream of tourists has been long and steady for many years, Syria is a pretty relaxed place to trawl the markets and have a dabble at the ancient game of haggling.

If you are interested in picking up souvenirs (and Syria is a much better place to do it than Jordan), take your time as you wander around the souqs. The main ones of interest to the souvenir hunter are the great vaulted markets of Aleppo and those of Old Damascus. The more time you can take to meander and compare asking prices the better.

Many items have prices written up in Arabic numerals. The fact that these prices often have nothing to do with reality is as good an indication as any that the bargaining game is not just something reserved for foreigners. Observe how locals quibble over prices of rugs and jewellery and you'll begin to get an idea.

When something catches your eye, show no more than a casual interest and inquire about a starting price. Calculators will be pulled out and, after a lot of digital gymnastics, a price reached. Depending on the object, shopkeepers and the degree of gullibility they assign to you, the price might be inflated by as much as 10 times. At any rate, the first sign of resistance on your part will probably see this first ambit claim tumble with astonishing speed. Even then you should take your time. Indulge in the chit-chat, take a cup of tea when offered and keep working away. When the going gets tough it is time to decide whether you are really willing to pay the price to which you have reduced the shopkeeper (or rather to which he has allowed himself to fall). If you can get him down no more, expressing regret at your mutual failure to agree on a price and walking off can sometimes have an electrifying effect. In any event, you will probably find what you want around the corner. Always remember that you are under no obligation to buy. Badgering by shopkeepers is pretty mild in Syria, but it does occur – there is absolutely no reason why you should allow yourself to be railroaded into any purchase you don't feel comfortable with.

See also Things to Buy in the Regional Facts for the Visitor chapter.

Begging

Although you are unlikely to encounter a lot of begging in Syria, it is something to take into account. Perhaps most obvious are the young 'baksheesh brats' with their demands for money or pens. While many clearly live in straitened circumstances, it is difficult to promote ceding to these demands. On the other hand, the decision over whether or not to give money or other objects away to such children must ultimately be a personal one.

POST & COMMUNICATIONS

Postal Rates

Letters to any destination seem to be up to S£18; postcards to Australia and the USA cost S£11, and to Europe S£10. In addition to post offices, you can also buy *tawaabi'* (stamps) from most tobacconists.

Sending Mail

The Syrian postal service is slow but effective enough. Letters mailed from the main cities take about a week to Europe and anything up to a month to Australia or the USA.

To send a parcel from Damascus or Aleppo, take it (unwrapped) to the parcel post office for inspection. After it's been cleared it has to be wrapped and covered with cotton material. You have to buy the material from one guy, pay another to give you some cardboard tags for the address, and yet another to wrap it! It's basically the enforced baksheesh gravy train for unemployed Syrians, which will cost you about S£30.

For all that, the process doesn't usually take more than about half an hour. A 10 kg parcel to Australia costs S£3500, S£2850 to the USA and S£1670 to the UK.

Receiving Mail

The poste restante counter at the main post office in Damascus is more or less reliable.

Take your passport as identification and be prepared to pay an S£8 pick-up fee.

Telephone

International calls can be made from the telephone offices in major cities, the occasional entrepreneurial store-owner or through any of the five star hotels. Syria is investing in satellite and optic fibre cable projects to modernise its long disastrous phone system, and the phone card has arrived in Syria. There are precious few card phones away from the phone offices, but there are considerable advantages to them. The system is satellite-based and good for national and international calls. Local calls have to be made with normal coin-operated telephones (see later in this section).

Normal rate phone calls with card phones or through the operator cost S£115 per minute to Australia, S£125 to the USA and S£100 to most destinations in Europe. There is a cheap rate, but the hours differ wildly from one country to the next. For Australia, cheap rate calls cost S£58 per minute from 2 to 7 pm. The rate to the USA is S£63 and calls can be made from 3 to 8 am. Cheap calls to Europe cost S£50 and can be made from 1 to 7 am.

You can book an international call through the operator at the phone office. In this case there is a three minute minimum and you can wait up to two hours for a connection to be made. Bring your passport along, as the operator will want to see it. Much easier if you can afford it is to buy a phone card (S£900) at the same counter and join a queue to a card phone in the same office. You dial direct and there is no minimum call period. The international access code is 00. Then dial the country code, city code and number.

The other option is to place a call through a big hotel or one of the several private international phone offices that are beginning to spring up. This is the most expensive way of doing things, with calls to Australia being charged at S£290 a minute and to the UK at S£250.

Reverse-charges calls cannot be made from Syria. If you need to call through an operator, the number is ☎ 944.

For local calls you need S£1 coins to operate the telephone booths – if you can find one in working order. It's much easier to make such calls from your hotel. The best bet with national calls is the phone card. Dial 0, the town code (see the Telephone Area Codes table) and the number.

Telephone Area Codes

Some of the important area codes in Syria are:

Aleppo	21
Damascus	11
Deir ez-Zur	51
Der'a	15
Hama	33
Hassake	52
Homs	31
Lattakia	41
Maalula	12
Palmyra	31
Raqqa	22
Safita	32
Tartus	44
Qamishle	53

Fax, Telex & Telegram

It is possible to send telexes and telegrams from telephone offices, but they are also expensive. It is also possible to send faxes from the main post offices. Normal phone call rates are charged, and what you pay depends on how long it takes for the fax to go through.

BOOKS

For a guide to more general works on Middle Eastern history, arts and the like, see Books in the Regional Facts for the Visitor chapter.

Lonely Planet

For unique insights into everyday life, read *The Gates of Damascus* by Lieve Joris. Through her friendship with a local woman and her family, the author paints a compellingly intimate portrait of contemporary Syria. This is one of the many exciting titles in Journeys, Lonely Planet's new travel literature series.

Guidebooks
A few books have appeared on the market in the past three years, but the line-up is still pretty thin. Michael Haag's *Syria & Lebanon* is one of the few general English-language travel guides covering Syria. It is good on sights but weak on practical advice.

You could try the officially sanctioned *Guide to Syria* by Afif Bahnassi (published locally by Avicenne), complete with maps copied from earlier editions of this guide. It's a saccharine but in places informative book that covers most of the sites. Another Avicenne publication is E Claire Grimes' *A Guide to Damascus*. Slightly better are Bahnassi's *Damascus* and *The Mosques of Damascus* – he may be an official mouthpiece, but he does seem to know his stuff.

Travel
Lady Gertrude Lowthian Bell was one of that rare breed of adventurous women to launch herself into the Middle East at a time when few people, men or women, travelled anywhere. *Syria – The Desert & the Sown* is her sympathetic if quirky account of the area known as Syria prior to WWI, an ill-defined province of the crumbling Ottoman Empire.

History & Politics
The Struggle for Syria by Patrick Seale is a highly readable account by an *Observer* correspondent of the political intrigues in Syria from independence in 1945 until the ultimately aborted attempts at pan-Arab union in 1958. For a more general summary, look for Derek Hopwood's *Syria – 1945-1986*.

For a look at the period immediately prior to this, you might want to leaf through *Syria and the French Mandate*, by Philip S Khoury. Another rather academic approach to the subject can be found in Stephen Hemsley Longrigg's *Syria and Lebanon Under French Mandate*.

A little studied subject is that of Syrian nationalist desires. *Greater Syria – The History of an Ambition* by Daniel Pipes looks at the great Syrian dream – control over an area that would not only include modern Syria and Lebanon, but Hatay in Turkey, and even Jordan and Israel.

Syria's human rights record has improved somewhat in recent years, but has not stopped US-based Middle East Watch from publishing a damning report in *Syria Unmasked*.

As Syria and Israel edge closer to peace, Moshe Ma'oz analyses the importance of an end to hostilities between these neighbours in his *Syria & Israel – From War to Peacemaking*.

Photography
If it's coffee-table tomes you're after, you

Archaeology & Monuments
English readers have been blessed in the past few years with a couple of thorough new titles covering most angles of Syria's ancient past. One is *Monuments of Syria*, by Ross Burns. It covers in considerable detail 115 sites across the country, but can be a bit weighty to drag around in your backpack. Another worth investigating is Warwick Ball's *Syria – A Historical and Architectural Guide*.

For more general background information, try *From Ebla to Damas: Treasures of Ancient Syria*, by Harvey Weiss et al. The archaeologist who made a name for himself with the discovery of the cuneiform tablets of Ebla, Paolo Matthiae, also wrote a fairly decent book covering the history of excavation of the main sites. It's called *Ebla and Empire Rediscovered*.

Something along more quirky lines is a reprint of TE Lawrence's *Crusader Castles*, a study originally published as a limited edition in the 1930s.

A multilingual and not awfully detailed little volume called *Dura Europos*, by Mohammed Ali Al-Souki, has recently joined the thin ranks of books produced in Syria on local sites. A ragbag of other slim booklets to specific sites such as Bosra and Ebla can occasionally be turned up on the dusty shelves of museums throughout Syria. These are generally pretty old, but contain interesting (if clumsily translated) information nonetheless.

For those who read German, there is an extremely solid guide to the historical sites called *Syrien*, by Johannes Odenthal. It is heavy going in parts, but thorough. ■

DAMIEN SIMONIS

DAMIEN SIMONIS

DAMIEN SIMONIS

DAMIEN SIMONIS

Syria

Top Left: Azem Palace, Damascus, is a peaceful haven boasting beautiful gardens.
Top Right: Omayyad Mosque (Damascus) – one of the jewels of Islamic architecture.
Bottom Left: Damascus' Saida Zeinab Mosque – burial place of Mohammed's grand-daughter.
Bottom Right: The old treasury (Omayyad Mosque), decorated with 14th century mosaics.

HUGH FINLAY

HUGH FINLAY

DAMIEN SIMONIS

DAMIEN SIMONIS

Syria

Top Left: One of Hama's *norias* (wooden water wheels).
Top Right: Aleppo's citadel dominates the city.
Bottom Left: Maalula's Convent of St Thecla is tucked snugly against a cliff.
Bottom Right: Homs' Khalid Ibn al-Walid Mosque is topped by nine cupolas.

could do worse than Michael Jenner's *Syria in View*, which contains some stunning photography and is available in Damascus. Bahnassi has also done a weighty illustrated volume called *Damascus*.

Bookshops in Syria

For information on bookshops outside Syria, see Books in the Regional Facts for the Visitor chapter. In Syria itself, the choices are pretty limited. For books on Syria, you are generally best off trying bookshops in the top hotels of Damascus and Aleppo. A fair selection of the above works and some of the general studies on Arab and modern Middle Eastern society are available in Syria. A couple of decent bookshops are also listed under individual city entries. Oddly, the ticket office in the Temple of Bel, in Palmyra, sells one of the best ranges of books on Syria.

CD ROM

At the time of writing, there appeared to be only one CD ROM in circulation about Syria. It is called *Syria – History & Culture* and is billed as an 'interactive encyclopedia about Syria covering geography, tourism, economy, education, culture, music and heritage'.

NEWSPAPERS & MAGAZINES

Although censorship is undeniably a feature of Syrian life, the locals do have a broad range of Arabic-language papers and magazines to choose from, not only Syrian, but from Jordan, Egypt, Lebanon and some of the Gulf States.

For everyone else, the situation is a bit more dire. The English-language daily newspaper, the *Syria Times*, is published under direct government control and is predictably big on anti-Zionist, pro-Arab rhetoric and short on news. It does have a 'What's on Today' section listing exhibitions, lectures and films as well as important telephone numbers and radio programmes.

Foreign newspapers and magazines such as the *The Middle East*, the *International Herald Tribune*, *Le Monde*, *Der Spiegel* and *Newsweek* are intermittently available in Damascus, Aleppo and Homs. Any articles on Syria or Lebanon are so lovingly torn out you'd hardly notice there was something missing.

RADIO & TV

The Syrian Broadcasting Service used to have a foreign-language service with programmes in French, English, Turkish, German and Russian. This seems to have bitten the dust (at least a determined dial-twiddling stint by the author turned up nothing), and the broadcast times of this service no longer appear in the *Syria Times*.

In any case, the best way to keep in touch with events both inside and outside the country is through the BBC World Service, which can be picked up from about 4 am to midnight GMT/UTC on at least some of the following frequencies: 6195 kHz; 7325 kHz; 9410 kHz; 12,095 kHz; 15,070 kHz; 15,575 kHz; 17,640 kHz; and 17,705 kHz. As well, some broadcasts are transmitted on medium wave 1323 kHz. It is also possible to pick up medium wave broadcasts on 9.41 MHz, 9.51 MHz, 21.7 MHz and 15.31 MHz.

Anyone happening to have access to satellite services can pick up broadcasts on AsiaSat. The BBC alters its programming every six months or so, and the British Council in Damascus usually has the latest information.

The Voice of America (VOA) broadcasts to the Middle East from 4 am to 10 pm GMT/UTC on a wide range of frequencies, including: 792 kHz; 1197 kHz; 1260 kHz; 1548 kHz; 3985 kHz; 5995 kHz; 6010 kHz; 6040 kHz; 7170 kHz; 11,965 kHz and 15,205 kHz. Some of these broadcasts can also be picked up on medium wave frequency 11.84 MHz.

The Syrian TV service reaches a large audience and programmes range from news and sport to American soaps. There is news in English on Syria 2 at around 10 pm and in French at about 8 pm.

You can see Turkish TV as far south as Aleppo, Iraqi TV in the east of the country and, since jamming was stopped in 1994, Jordanian TV in the south. Better still, some hotels, even at the budget end, provide satellite TV.

PHOTOGRAPHY & VIDEO

Kodak, Fuji and Konica print film is readily available. Slide film is usually only available in Damascus and Aleppo, and then with difficulty. There are places around to have your film developed, but quality is often poor.

Both VHS and Betamax video systems work in Syria – and movies for both are available for hire.

For more general information on photography and video shooting, see Photography & Video in the Regional Facts for the Visitor chapter.

ELECTRICITY

The current in Syria is 220 volts, 50 AC. Sockets are the two-pronged variety.

A lot of Syria's electricity is generated using thermal power, but the single biggest source of electricity is the hydroelectric generating station at the Lake Al-Assad dam on the Euphrates River. Daily power cuts seem largely a thing of the past, although they do occur occasionally.

LAUNDRY

Syria's laundries are not always that easy to find, so if you want to use one ask your hotel where the nearest is. It may organise things for you. The going price is S£25 to S£35 an item, but we are not talking about one hour laundromats. Expect anything up to a three or four day turnaround time, so try to establish when you'll get your clothes back if you are in any kind of a hurry. Don't be surprised to find things scribbled in wash-resistant black felt pen inside your garments – that's just to remind them who they belong to!

DANGERS & ANNOYANCES

Despite being depicted in the western media as a land full of terrorists and similar nasties (many Syrians are aware of and hurt by this reputation), Syria is a safe country to travel in. You can walk around at any time of the day or night without any problem, although the area around the bars in central Aleppo and the quasi red-light zone in Damascus should be treated with a little caution.

Most Syrians are very friendly and hospitable. Don't hesitate to take up an offer if someone invites you to their village or home.

Tourists are becoming more common currency in Syria, and in some cases this means *your* currency. Independent travellers who have found their feet and at least look as though they know what they are doing will usually pay the standard price for transport, food and the like. But in the end, few avoid the odd petty rip-off here and there. Attempts at ridiculous overcharging do seem to be a growing phenomenon – a sad and perhaps inevitable by-product of increasing tourist traffic. In all, the problem is a minor one, and the courtesy, generosity and sometimes simple curiosity that are a hallmark of the Syrians remain unaltered.

Theft

As in Jordan, the general absence of theft has got to be one of the most refreshing things about travelling in Syria. Your bags will be quite safe left unattended virtually anywhere. This is no excuse for inviting trouble through carelessness, but at least you don't have to keep a hawk-like watch over your stuff as you do in other parts of the world.

LEGAL MATTERS

The modern Syrian legal system has inherited elements from the Ottoman system and its French successor. The heirachy of courts culminates in the Court of Cassation – the ultimate appeal court for cases not connected with the constitution.

The law is not necessarily a paragon of equal treatment. The country is full of political prisoners and the law can be an arbitrary arm in the hands of the government. That said, tourists should have few opportunities to get to know the system personally. Drug-smuggling, long a problem in Lebanon, has been heavily clamped and carrying any kind of narcotics or even marijuana/hash is a foolish undertaking. If you are caught in possession, you could well wind up doing a heavy jail sentence or even being sentenced to death. If you do cross the law in any way, remember that your embassy can do little to help but contact your relatives and recommend local lawyers.

BUSINESS HOURS

Government offices, such as immigration and tourism, are generally open from 8 am to 2 pm daily except Friday and holidays, but the hours can swing either way by an hour or so. Other offices and shops keep similar hours in the morning and often open again from 4 to 6 or 7 pm. Most restaurants and a few small traders stay open on Friday.

Banks generally follow the government office hours, but there are quite a few exceptions to the rule. Some branches keep their doors open for three hours from 9 am, while some booths are open as late as 7 pm.

In smaller places, the post office closes at 2 pm. In bigger cities it stays open longer; until 8 pm in Damascus and Aleppo, where it is open on Friday too. As a rule, telephone offices are open much longer hours; in Damascus, for example, around the clock.

Principal museums and monuments open from 9 am until 6 pm in summer (4 pm from October to the end of March), while others generally open from 8 am to 2 pm. Most are closed on Tuesday.

Police

Syria has outwardly become a much more relaxed place since the late 80s. Nevertheless, you'll probably notice more people armed and in uniform than you are accustomed to at home (depending of course on where home is!). Military service is 2½ years and compulsory. Not only that, but there is an impressive array of semi-military police units and divisions as well, and some of them end up doing guard duty outside sensitive buildings and in strategic points like bridges. Out around the embassies and swish parts of Damascus, many of the armed men you'll see belong to virtually private armies attached to one or other bigwig or retired general – don't aggravate them, and they'll leave you alone.

The regular passport checks and baggage inspections that travellers have had to put up with on buses and trains have all but disappeared. That said, it is always a good idea to have your passport handy, on the off chance your bus or car is subject to a check.

Secret Police Syria has several internal intelligence organisations and it's no exaggeration to say that there are secret police all over the place. If a Syrian starts talking politics to you or tries to drag you into a conversation about Assad, don't reciprocate unless it's someone you know well. The official line is that Assad is the best thing since sliced bread and to say anything to the contrary would be inadvisable. Common sense is all that's required and you shouldn't worry too much. One guy even announced to me that he was with the *mukhabarat* (intelligence service) and proceeded to expound the virtues of Assad, then asking for an opinion. 'I think he's a clever man' is a safe, fairly accurate and non-committal response to this type of question.

Just to give an idea of the array of security forces, the following is a list of the main ones known to Amnesty International, the international human rights organisation.

Siraya ad-Difa' 'an ath-Thawra – the Brigades for the Defence of the Revolution are estimated to number between 15,000 and 25,000. Their main function is to protect the president and the administration.

Al-Wahdat al-Khassa – the Special Units comprise about 5000 to 8000 paratroopers and commandos.

Al-Mukhabarat al-'Ama – the General Intelligence responsible to the Minister of Interior.

Al-Mukhabarat al-'Askariyya – the Military Intelligence collects and acts upon intelligence affecting the armed forces. It is responsible to the Ministry of Defence.

Mukhabarat al-Quwwa al-Jawiyya – the Air Force Intelligence is the same as Military Intelligence, but with respect to the air force.

Al-Amn as-Siyassi – the Political Security monitors political activity and acts upon information gathered. It is responsible to the Ministry of Interior.

Al-Amn ad-Dakhili – the Internal Security is responsible to the Ministry of Interior.

Maktab al-Amn al-Qawmi – the National Security Bureau is responsible to the Presidential Security Council. ■

PUBLIC HOLIDAYS

Most holidays are either religious (Islamic and Christian) or celebrations of important dates in the formation of the modern Syrian state. Most Christian holidays fall according to the Julian calendar, as in Jordan, which can be as much as a month behind the Gregorian (western) calendar.

Although they are all supposedly official holidays, only some of them appear to be celebrated, when you may well find it's business as usual (see also Islamic Holidays in the Regional Facts for the Visitor chapter).

SYRIA

Official Holidays

January
New Year's Day (1st)
February
Union Day (22nd)
March
Revolution Day/Women's Day (8th)
Arab League Day (22nd)
April
Evacuation Day (17th)
May
Martyrs' Day (6th)
Security Force Day (29th)
August
Army Day (1st)
Marine's Day (29th)
October
Veteran's Day (6th)
Flight Day (16th)
November
Correctionist Movement Day (16th)
December
Peasants' Day (14th)
Christmas Day (25th)

SPECIAL EVENTS

The Roman Theatre at Bosra, south of Damascus, occasionally plays host to theatre and music performances, but its main annual festival takes place in September.

Since 1993, a folk festival mainly aimed at tourists has been staged annually in Palmyra around the end of April. It lasts three or four days and appears to be a successful idea. Bedouin music performances are the main drawcard, and indeed it was the Bedouin themselves who formed most of the audience first time around.

Every year, in September, Damascus holds a two week trade fair, of virtually no interest to the traveller, but usually accompanied by various cultural events. Check the *Syria Times* for details.

Every couple of years in November, Damascus hosts a so-called film festival. This is a chance for locals to see all sorts of foreign cinema, and not overly censored either. It is not quite a film festival in the commonly accepted meaning of the words, however. Rather than a celebration of current cinema and recent prizewinners, it seems more of an historical lucky dip. In the 1995 festival, one of the hits was *Murder on the Orient Express* – not exactly a celluloid spring chicken!

The foreign cultural centres occasionally show films and organise lectures. Notices of what's on sometimes appear in the *Syria Times* on Wednesday and Thursday, otherwise check with the centres themselves.

ACTIVITIES

Hiking

There are nó organised facilities for hikers in Syria, but one or two possibilities suggest themselves. The desert is not really wonderful hiking territory, but the mountainous strip between Lebanon and Turkey (around the Kassab border crossing) might well appeal to some. You could for instance set out to walk between some of the Crusader castles and similar sites. The Crac des Chevaliers, Safita and Hosn Sulayman are all linked by road. Pushing on, you could strike out north-east from Hosn Sulayman towards Musyaf (castle) and swing more or less westwards towards Qala'at Marqab. The problem with all this is that you are virtually obliged to follow roads as there are simply no maps available to guide you off the asphalt track. That detracts from the experience, but at least it means the odd microbus might come your way if you do get sick of the walk. Also worth bearing in mind is that in many small villages there are no hotels or banks. Weather is another important consideration. In summer it is really too hot for this sort of caper, and winter can be miserably wet and bitterly cold.

Turkish Baths

If you've never had a full Turkish bath, Syria is not a bad place to start. There are several good public baths in Aleppo and Damascus, and the full wash, steam bath and massage package does wonders for the body. As a rule, the baths are open for men only or women only. Those having more to do with foreigners are prepared to close their doors to the general public and take in mixed groups for a special price to be fixed by negotiation.

LANGUAGE COURSES

If you develop a more than passing interest in the Arabic language, there are several options in Damascus. The Arabic Teaching Institute for Foreigners (☎ 011-222 1538), PO Box 9340, Jadet ash-Shafei No 3, Mezzeh-Villat Sharqiyyah, Damascus, has two courses a year: from June to September and October to May. Tuition is in classical Arabic only and costs US$450 a term. Classes are held from 9 am to noon daily, and the institute makes no distinction in fees between the two terms, even though the winter term is patently longer! The quality of tuition appears to be quite variable. AIDS tests are compulsory for students.

Those wishing to stay long-term in Syria should note that this is one of the few ways of acquiring residence, saving you the hassles of continually applying for small visa extensions, which tend not to be granted beyond the second or third time anyway. A few people enrol in the course to gain residence and then go off and do something else.

The Goethe Institut and the Centre Culturel Français run courses in colloquial Arabic, and there is an expensive school used mostly by embassies and foreign companies working in Syria, MATC (☎ 011-224 3997). Enrolment in these or any 'cowboy' school will not allow you to get residence.

WORK

Language Teaching

Just as Syria is not top of the pops as a tourist destination, so it is few people's dream location for work, which means teachers *do* have limited possibilities. The American Language Center (ALC; ☎ 011-332 7236) is probably the best place to try your luck, followed by the British Council (☎ 011-333 8436). These are the only institutions that can secure residence for their employees.

Because the British Council is smaller and tends to recruit direct from the UK rather than locally, the ALC should be your first port of call. The school, if it needs anyone, prefers people with a Bachelor's degree and some form of teaching experience. Pay is calculated on a points system, so the better your qualifications, the better your chances of getting a job and the higher the dosh. A TEFL certificate or second language qualification, knowledge of Arabic, postgraduate studies and length of experience in teaching all improve your chances.

The ALC no longer pays in US currency. The bottom rate is S£420 per teaching hour, but bear in mind that new employees rarely get more than about 10 hours of work a week initially. The ALC also likes a commitment to at least six months. The best time to try is shortly before the beginning of a new term. This roughly means: late February, late May, early September and early December. The only people ALC hires direct from the US are highly qualified MAs.

The local schools, including the language faculty of the university, all tend to pay around S£100 an hour (around US$2). Tutoring is another possibility, but that requires time to build up a clientele – tutors generally charge S£400 to S£600 an hour. For tutoring, the best thing to do first up is contact the ALC for tips and possible contacts.

German and French travellers could try their luck at the Goethe Institut and the Centre Culturel Français (see Cultural Centres in the Damascus chapter).

Archaeological Digs

Work (often unpaid) occasionally crops up

on archaeological sites. It's obviously better to check this out through universities before leaving home, but your embassy might be able to help in Damascus. Or go to the Deutsches Archäologisches Institut (see the boxed story called 'Digging up the Past' in the Facts about the Region chapter for information on how to get on a dig).

ACCOMMODATION

There is only one so-called youth hostel in Syria, at Bosra. Otherwise, it's hotels or camping, although, as in Jordan, the formal possibilities for the latter are limited. You'll find every level of hotel accommodation in Syria, from the five star, characterless, could-be-anywhere hotels down to the noisy, filthy hellholes that you can also find in virtually any city in the world, all with prices to match.

Rooms in many of the cheap hotels are let on a share basis and will have two to four beds. If you want the room to yourself you may have to pay for all the beds, or just as likely an intermediate sum. For solo male travellers these shared rooms are quite OK and your gear is generally safe when left unattended (lock it up though). Where there are no other travellers about and no single rooms available, solo females will generally have to take a room with more than one bed to themselves. In practice, this generally doesn't work out to be too much of problem.

The biggest drawback with cheap hotels is that more often than not they are noisy affairs. Rooms often open on to common TV salons, or look over busy, chaotic streets. A pair of earplugs can mean the difference between a good night's sleep and being kept awake by loud chatter, music and the TV. Rooms at the back, away from the street, are usually quieter and sometimes cheaper.

Most hotels will want to keep your passport overnight, usually in a drawer at the reception desk. Initially this is so that they can fill in a standard police registration slip (sounds more sinister than it is), but the principal motivation is to have a security for payment of your bill. Tell the receptionist you need the passport to change money and you should be fine. Most hotels now have hot water at least in the evening or early morning. This is not always the case, so you should always ask.

With about a half dozen truly notable exceptions throughout the country, the

Women Travellers in Syria

Syria is not at all difficult for lone women travellers to get around in. Public transport between cities is easy to use, and as a woman alone I usually got one of the front seats to myself. The people I encountered were courteous and friendly; on several occasions the women I sat next to on the microsbuses invited me to their homes for tea, and one even paid my fare!

I do make a point of locking my valuables away when I leave the hotel room during the day, but I have often left baggage at hotel receptions and collected it later, so I really don't believe that theft is too much of a problem.

I've never felt myself to be in physical danger, but I think it's best to go with one's instincts, and not to stay in places that make one uncomfortable, no matter what the guide book says! With a bit of common sense I don't think a woman travelling alone through Syria will get into much trouble.

When I was last in Syria, I found the following hotels to be comfortable and secure places to stay for women travelling alone:

Sultan Hotel, Damascus (☎ 222 5768)
Citadel Hotel, Palmyra (☎ 910537)
Hotel Raghdan, Deir ez-Zur (☎222053)
Hotel Tourism, Raqqa (phone unavailable - see the Euphrates River chapter for details)
The Daniel Hotel, Tartus (☎ 220582)

Vicky Clayton
Melbourne, Australia

bottom level hotels are fairly simple affairs. Beds come with one sheet (two if you're lucky) and a blanket or two, and most rooms have a ceiling fan. Many rooms have a washbasin, but showers and toilets are generally outside. It is always worth looking around a bit, as the difference between basic and bloody awful is sometimes decisive.

You won't often get a bed for less than S£150, and for a single room the bottom rate is about S£200. A couple of the better cheapies charge up to about S£300/500 for singles/doubles, but in a few particular cases the difference is well worth it.

Hotels officially rated two star and up generally require payment in US currency or the equivalent in another hard currency and often actually want *cash*. Increasingly, the use of credit cards is filtering through to Syria for settling this kind of bill, but it is far from general practice. In some it is also possible to change travellers' cheques for the appropriate amounts.

The hard-currency hotels use a separate official exchange rate (S£11.20 to the dollar) to calculate their rates, so that what might be quite reasonable in Syrian pounds (at S£42 to the dollar) becomes absurd in hard currency. It is important to realise that just because you are being charged a lot of hard currency does not automatically mean you get a good hotel. It is in fact difficult to recommend many of the mid-range hotels because, frankly, they often offer little that the better cheapies don't. In essence, you can find yourself paying hefty sums for rooms you wouldn't touch at such prices in your own country.

All this may be about to change. Apparently aware of the insanity of this situation, the Ministry of Tourism announced plans at the time of writing to oblige five and four star hotels to charge hard currency at the normal bank rate. This would mean prices charged to foreigners tumbling to almost a quarter. Such a result is unlikely, but there were signs that rooms prices could fall by as much as half in the top hard-currency hotels.

Winter is cold in Syria and the cheap hotels are rarely adequately heated. Even many of the more expensive hotels have poor heating. Another good reason for staying away from the place between November and about March.

ENTERTAINMENT

There is not a huge range of night-time entertainment to choose from. Most of the cinemas run heavily censored martial arts movies or Turkish titillation, and are only interesting for the (largely all-male) crowds that have no alternative. Of course, the names change, and Arnold Schwarzenegger and Jean-Claude van Damme seem to be among the present favourites. The cultural centres in Damascus, along with one or two cinemas in the big cities, occasionally show more serious films.

Other than the belly dances and cabaret-style performances the big hotels often stage, the only other real possibility is the sleazy nightclubs, of which there is no shortage in Aleppo and Damascus.

Getting There & Away

For introductory and general information about travel to and from Syria, as well as advice on where to look for cheap tickets, taking your own vehicle and the like, see the regional Getting There & Away chapter.

There are three ways of getting to Syria: by air, overland or sometimes by sea. Most travellers will be arriving by the overland routes from either Turkey or Jordan.

AIR

Syria has two international airports: Damascus and Aleppo. Both have regular connections to Europe, other cities in the Middle East, Africa and Asia. Most air travellers, however, will arrive in Damascus, and indeed it is not always easy to find an agent who can get you on an international flight to Aleppo. Oh yes, and Lattakia has also been promoted to an 'international' airport – it has one flight a week to Cairo!

On destinations to Africa and the Middle East, there is generally only a choice between Syrianair and the respective national carrier of the country concerned. Most agents seem to quote the Syrianair fares as the cheapest, although the difference is not always breathtaking.

You must pay for tickets purchased in Syria in hard currency or with a credit card. The problem with the latter is that not all airlines or agents accept the main international cards. Syrianair, at the time of writing, took only American Express. However, other agents selling Syrianair tickets often did accept Visa and MasterCard. With these three cards you should be able to pay for a ticket – you just have to find an agent accepting yours. Only residents in Syria can pay for tickets with Syrian pounds. Now that the so-called aviation rate of exchange is virtually the same as the standard 'neighbouring countries' rate of S£42 to the US dollar, this does not represent the rip-off it once was.

There is a branch of the Commercial Bank of Syria and a next-to-useless tourist office at Damascus airport. For information on how to get to and from the airports, see the appropriate city chapters.

North America

You are probably better off grabbing a cheap flight to London and searching around for the best bucket shop deals there. Syrianair has no direct flights from North America. If you do want to fly with other airlines, you're looking at about C$1150 return from Montréal in high season and around US$1000 (with Gulf Air) from New York. Another possibility is to fly to Jordan or Turkey and travel overland from there.

The UK

As it's not a popular destination you won't find much discounting on fares to Syria. The national airline, Syrianair (☎ 0171-493 2851), is at 27 Albemarle St, London W1X 3HF. It flies to Damascus on Tuesday, Thursday and Sunday. Return fares for stays of two months or less are UK£290. Tickets valid for a year cost UK£330. These and all other fares quoted here are exclusive of the UK£10 UK Air Passenger Duty.

It is worth shopping around for competition flights. At the time of writing, Lufthansa was offering a return fare of UK£270, but the ticket was valid for a month only and was fixed dated. Another attractive deal for those with some time is with Czech Airlines. It offers a 12 month ticket with a free stopover in Prague for UK£299. Turkish Airlines flies via Istanbul for UK£242 (validity two months) and Air France for UK£294 via Paris (also two months). KLM offers a low-season fare valid for six months for UK£420.

If you're planning to tour both Jordan and Syria, you should consider flying to Amman, as a greater range of airlines serve that city with a variety of fare options (see also Jordan Getting There & Away).

Another option worth looking into is

taking a charter plane to Adana, in southern Turkey, and a local bus from there (see Land).

A small UK-based airline, British Mediterranean, flies twice a week from Heathrow to Damascus (and Amman) via Beirut.

Continental Europe

Amsterdam and Frankfurt are the two main hubs through which the bulk of flights for Syria are directed. At the time of writing, KLM and Lufthansa were offering some of the better deals available. Even French travellers were getting tickets routed through Frankfurt with Lufthansa.

From Athens and Istanbul, some agents offer one-way flights with Syrianair to Damascus for US$165 one way and US$316 return. From Turkey, for instance, there are two flights a week each with Syrianair and Turkish Airlines to Damascus. The student fares were US$148 one way and double for a return. Going the other way tends to be more expensive. Syrianair's one-way flight to Athens was US$223, and US$179 to Istanbul from Damascus.

It is actually more expensive to fly from Istanbul to Aleppo than to Damascus, so there seems little point in doing it.

Australia & New Zealand

With the increase in Middle Eastern carriers flying into Australia, fares to Damascus are now pretty cheap, with fares starting at about A$950 one way/A$1600 return on carriers like Emirates, Gulf Air or Middle East Airlines. Other carriers such as Alitalia and Olympic are not much more expensive (A$1050/A$1700), and allow stopovers in Rome and Athens respectively.

It's not the same story in New Zealand however – the cheapest fare around is a New Zealand/Emirates combination to Damascus (via Dubai) starting at a low season return of about NZ$2250.

It may also be worth looking around for better deals on more popular destinations, like Turkey, Egypt or even Greece and then going overland.

Asia

Syrianair has flights to Delhi
India. The quoted fare is US
The standard one-way fare to
stan is US$365.

North Africa

Syrianair has regular connections to Cairo and Tunis, but unless you have to fly it is certainly cheaper and more interesting to go overland. The cheapest available flight to Tunis, for example, is US$394. The deal to Cairo, at US$170 one way, is more reasonable.

LAND

Turkey

Bus There are at least four commonly used border posts between Syria and Turkey. The most popular one links Antakya and Aleppo via the Bab al-Hawa border station. Traffic can get fairly congested here and crossing usually entails a wait of a couple of hours. Other posts may be less crowded.

You can buy tickets direct from Istanbul to Aleppo (approximately 22 hours), Damascus (30 hours) and even beyond to Amman and Medina if you wish. The ticket costs in the vicinity of TL1,200,000 to TL1,500,000 (US$24 to US$30), depending on which company you travel with, regardless of whether you are going to Aleppo (ask for Halep) or Damascus (ask for Şam). Buses leave daily, usually with five or six departures between about 11 am and the early evening.

You will almost certainly have to change buses in Antakya for the trip to Aleppo (where you'll have to change again for the onward leg to Damascus). Thus, you could simply get a ticket for Antakya (TL850,000) and another on the spot for Aleppo, but with the latter costing TL500,000 to TL600,000, there's no real saving. By the way, if you're looking for a ticket to Aleppo at Antakya, go for the cheapest offer, as everyone ends up on the *same* bus.

On the subject of money, the best black market rates you'll ever get for buying Syrian pounds are right here in Antakya.

There are a few things to note in Istanbul too. If the bus company or agent is any good, the ticket price should include a free service bus between the city centre and the new Topkapı bus station to the west. You need to be at the pick-up point about 1½ hours before the bus departure time. The Istanbul metro also serves the bus station. In the Sultanahmet area of Istanbul, some agents advertise bus tickets for inflated prices (usually quoted in dollars): US$40 to Aleppo or Damascus (when at the time of writing the maximum should not have been more than US$30, TL1,500,000) represents a healthy cut for the agent, don't you think?

You could also catch a *dolmuş* from Reyhanli to the border, cross it on foot (a long and sweaty couple of km in summer) and try to pick up a lift on the Syrian side. This can greatly lengthen an already tiresomely slow procedure.

Going the other way, it was marginally cheaper to buy a ticket through to Istanbul from Aleppo (S£1000) than buying separate tickets to Antakya and on to Istanbul from there. With the Turkish currency all over the place, that situation could easily change.

At least one bus a day connects Aleppo with Gaziantep, while crossings such as Qamishle (in the north-east) and Kassab (north of Lattakia) require you to use a combination of local transport and your two pins.

For direct buses to Istanbul and several other Turkish destinations, book through the Karnak bus offices in Damascus or Aleppo, or at the Turkish bus stations in those cities. You can also find Turkish buses running from Lattakia and Homs. It's much cheaper to get local transport to Aleppo and catch a bus from there. For other destinations and details of fares see Getting There & Away in the Damascus chapter.

Train Every Thursday a train leaves Haydarpaşa railway station on the Asian side of Istanbul at 8.55 am for the 40 hour trip to Aleppo. No advance booking is necessary. There are no sleepers, and in Istanbul you will only be sold 1st class tickets at TL2,205,000 (about US$45). Don't believe travel agents who tell you the train only goes as far as the border, although you may have to change trains there. For details of the journey from Aleppo to Istanbul see Getting There & Away in the Aleppo chapter.

Jordan

There's only one border crossing between Syria and Jordan and that's at Der'a/Ramtha. Consequently, it's extremely congested at times. That said, it's easy to tackle on your own. You can cross by direct bus, service taxi or by using a combination of local transport and walking. For details see Der'a in the South of Damascus chapter and Irbid in the North & West of Amman chapter.

Bus There is one air-con Karnak bus and one JETT bus daily in each direction between Amman and Damascus.

Tickets cost US$5 or JD4 from Damascus and JD4.500 from Amman. Book in advance as demand for seats is high. The trip takes about seven hours, depending on the wait at the border. For details of departure times see Getting There & Away in the Damascus and Amman chapters.

Train The Hejaz railway, a narrow-gauge line that once linked Damascus to Medina for the annual pilgrimage, is alive and kicking feebly between Damascus and Amman. Trainwatchers and nostalgics should be warned that the locomotive is generally a diesel-run machine, not a romantic, sooty steam job (but some travellers have had the luck to get the sooty version on the Syria leg).

Given the length of the trip, it may as well be a steam train though! The 10 hour plus excursion starts in Damascus at 7.30 am on Sunday and returns the following day at 8 am. Tickets in 1st/2nd class cost S£160/120.

Desultory talks on the possibility of resurrecting the Hejaz railway in its full glory to Medina, in Saudi Arabia, have concluded that such a project would only be viable if the line were connected to the European rail network – a long-term goal of more visionary thinkers in the Middle East, but some way from becoming reality.

Service Taxi The service taxis are faster than the buses and depart frequently. They tend to be more thoroughly searched because of smuggling, but given the routineness of this activity, it is hard to escape the conclusion that a lot of nodding and winking goes on while these searches are carried out. Damascus to Amman costs JD5.500 or S£385 either way. Service taxis run between Damascus and Irbid for JD4 or S£300.

Lebanon

The stream of independent travellers heading for what was once known as the Switzerland of the Middle East may not yet be a flood, but it is gathering force.

Bus Daily buses run regularly to Beirut and Tripoli. For details see Getting There & Away in the Damascus and Aleppo chapters.

Service Taxi Service taxis operating out of Damascus run to Tripoli for S£416 or to Beirut for anything from S£191 to S£291, depending on which part of the city you want to reach.

Saudi Arabia & Kuwait

Bus It is possible to go direct from Syria to Saudi Arabia, simply passing through Jordan in transit. There are also irregular services all the way across to Kuwait.

For details see Getting There & Away in the Damascus chapter.

Service Taxi For S£3000 a head, you can take a service taxi from near the Karnak bus station in Damascus to Riyadh.

SEA

Every Wednesday a ferry leaves Lattakia for Alexandria (Egypt) via Beirut (Lebanon). The trip is a bit of an epic, and can last up to three days. In summer the same vessel may well call in at Cyprus too. The cheapest fare is US$140 for an airline-type seat, with no meals included. That could be rather rough going over the best part of three days. For more details, turn to Lattakia in the Mediterranean Coast chapter.

LEAVING SYRIA

On leaving Syria, have your yellow entry card, or the equivalent you received on getting a visa extension, ready to hand in. There may be a small fine to pay if you don't have it – which could be awkward if you have carefully made sure to spend your last Syrian pounds before crossing the frontier.

Departure Tax

People flying out of Syria must pay S£200 airport departure tax, but there is no tax for those leaving by land.

Warning

The information in this chapter is particularly vulnerable to change: prices for international travel are volatile, routes are introduced and cancelled, schedules change, special deals come and go, and rules and visa requirements are amended. Airlines and governments seem to take a perverse pleasure in making price structures and regulations as complicated as possible. You should check directly with the airline or a travel agent to make sure you understand how a fare (and ticket you may buy) works. In addition, the travel industry is highly competitive and there are many lurks and perks.

The upshot of this is that you should get opinions, quotes and advice from as many airlines and travel agents as possible before you part with your hard-earned cash. The details given in this chapter should be regarded as pointers and are not a substitute for your own careful, up-to-date research. ■

ORGANISED TOURS

Many tourists to Syria opt to join organised tours and, as with Jordan, there are quite a few organisations to choose from. British Museum Traveller (☎ 0171-323 8895), 46 Bloomsbury St, London WS1B 3QQ, offers several trips accompanied by museum lecturers. A combined tour taking in parts of Syria, Jordan and Israel costs UK£1990.

Jasmin Tours (☎ 01628-531121), High St, Cookham, Maidenhead, Berks SL6 9SQ, has 14 day tours with half-board for up to around

UK£2000. It also runs a nine day trip to Syria, and combined tours to Syria and Jordan.

Prospect Art Tours Ltd (☎ 0181-995 2151/2163), 454-458 Chiswick High Rd, London W4 5TT, organises 14 day guided tours from UK£1795. They cover most of the major sights and include a quick excursion to Baalbek in Lebanon.

You should hunt around for the deal that suits you best, looking especially at the content and the speed of the programme, amount of free time, the level of accommodation, the extent to which visas, tickets and other documentation is handled by you or the operator, insurance, tour conditions as well as obligations.

SYRIA

Getting Around

AIR

Domestic Air Services

Syrianair operates a limited internal air service that has been cut back to essential routes since big price hikes in November 1991. By western standards, flights are cheap, but they are out of reach for most Syrians.

There are internal connections from Damascus to Aleppo (S£600), Qamishle (S£900), Lattakia (S£500) and Deir ez-Zur (S£600).

Bear in mind that, given the time taken to get to and from airports, check in and so on, you're unlikely to save much time over the bus. The Damascus-Qamishle run is the only exception to this.

BUS

Syria has a well-developed road network and, partly because private car ownership is comparatively rare, public transport is frequent and, by western standards, very cheap. Distances are short so journeys are rarely more than four hours. About the longest single bus ride you can take is around nine hours from Damascus to Qamishle in the north-east.

Whatever type of transport you use, carry your passport with you, as the occasional ID check en route is still a remote possibility.

In the past few years, a plethora of private bus companies has sprung up in Syria, in many cases offering very comfortable and modern services much like those of the better bus companies in neighbouring Turkey. There are several general categories worth identifying, although in some cases the distinctions are not always totally clear cut.

Bus/Minibus

At the bottom rung of the road transport ladder are buses and minibuses of a hard-to-determine vintage that formed the bulk of Syria's public bus system until the end of the 1980s. While it would appear that they are destined for extinction, for now they represent the most colourful, crowded, slowest and cheapest way to get around.

As a rule, locals refer to the minibuses as *meecros* (for microbus). For the sake of clarity, however, we have chosen to distinguish between this clattery old dinosaur version and the modern vans that are increasingly taking over Syrian roads (see Microbus).

On the outside, these buses look fairly plain, but on the inside they are decorated with an extraordinary array of gaudy ornaments – plastic fruit and plants, lights and mirrors. The driver usually has just enough uncluttered window to see some of the road ahead! Then there's the cassette player – no bus would be complete without one. The sound is invariably tinny, the tapes worn out and the volume loud. These buses are far less comfortable than the more modern alternatives, but as the distances are short it's no real hardship, and it is one of the best ways to meet the local people.

Buses connect all major towns, while the minibus variety work on short hops and serve more out-of-the-way places. They have no schedule and leave when full, so on the less popular routes you may have to wait for an hour or so until they fill up. For Arabic readers, virtually all these buses have their destinations written somewhere on the front of the bus; everyone else will just have to ask and allow themselves to be swept along to the right bus.

Sometimes you are obliged to buy tickets for pre-allocated seats – those right up the front behind the driver are not numbered but titled *khususi* (special), a spot sometimes assigned to foreigners.

If you find yourself being shunted around by passengers or the conductor, as they point to your ticket, it'll be because this time you've actually bought a seated ticket and chosen the wrong seat. On popular routes one reason for all this kafuffle is that people holding tickets *get* a seat, while those who just pay when they jump on must stand.

SYRIA

Journey times are generally longer than with the other buses, as they set people down and pick them up at any point along the route. This has earned them the nickname of 'stop-stops' among some locals. Conversations on buses will often lead to an invitation to someone's house or village, so try to keep your schedule flexible enough to make the most of Syrian hospitality.

Fares are cheap. For instance, the trip from Damascus to Aleppo costs S£60 – less than US$1.50! Often you will be charged marginally more on minibuses where they cover the same route as their bigger brothers.

SYRIA

Microbus

The term microbus (*'meecrobaas', 'meecro'*) is a little blurred, but in general refers to modern (mostly Japanese) vans that have been adapted to squeeze in a few more people. These are used principally on short hops between cities (such as Homs to Hama) and many routes to small towns and villages. They are increasingly replacing the clattering old minibuses with which they compete, and are generally more expensive. They too leave when full but because they are smaller and there is no standing room, departures are considerably more frequent. Again, destinations are usually posted somewhere at the front of the microbus, and in some cases the fares are also posted inside, but all of this is in Arabic only.

In most (but not all) cases you pay for the trip on the microbus. The etiquette is admirable. On a request by the driver, the passengers start passing money towards the front of the bus, with one of them becoming the de facto conductor. One advantage of this is that you can wait to see what other people are paying (don't forget, however, that some may pay less for getting out before the final stop) before putting in your bit. This trust system means you generally need not fear being ripped off.

Karnak & Pullman Buses

The orange-and-white buses of the state-run Karnak company were once the deluxe carriers of the Syrian highways. The company and its buses have barely changed and that is their principal problem, for with so many rival companies now employing faster, sleeker vehicles, Karnak looks a pretty poor cousin by comparison. Its buses are perfectly acceptable and connect most major centres, but its network is shrinking. To give a comparative idea of price, the Damascus-Aleppo run costs S£100.

Towards the end of the 80s, a series of private companies began to emerge with buses of much the same vintage as Karnak, and in some cases superior in quality. As a rule, they were (and remain) cheaper than Karnak by a few pounds and went by the general name of Pullman. The denomination seems to have fallen into disuse, but for the purposes of this guide is as good as any to distinguish them from the most recent crop of modern buses now roaming Syria's roads. For instance, the trip from Damascus to Aleppo costs S£86. The quality of these buses can vary greatly, and the real distinction is between these and the antique buses in circulation mentioned above. You must always buy a ticket, with seat assigned, prior to boarding. Unlike the old buses, there is no standing in these, and they leave according to a set timetable. They generally do not set down and pick passengers along the way, but this is not an absolute law.

Luxury Buses

For want of a better word, we are calling the latest crop of buses 'luxury'. These new companies arrived on the scene in the course of the early 90s, and in general their buses distinguish themselves by being considerably more expensive than any others (eg S£150 between Damascus and Aleppo) and more comfortable. A rigid no-smoking rule is imposed on most, and in the course of the journey a steward will distribute sweets and the occasional cup of water. If you're unlucky, you'll get to see a video as well.

Tickets must be bought before boarding and these buses leave according to a timetable – on the dot. It is worth booking in advance, as demand can be high. In some towns all these companies share a bus station, but in others it is a matter of tracking down each company's office. While mostly in handy central locations, the latter are occasionally hidden away. Some, but not all, of these companies have been located on city maps throughout this book.

Among the better companies are Qadmous, Al-Ahliah and Al-Ryan. The clapped-out old buses mentioned at the beginning of this section are by far the most interesting way to get around, but if you are not counting every single penny, time is limited or you simply want to move painlessly from A to B, the luxury buses are definitely the way to go.

Holidays

You pay up to 25% extra on virtually all buses and microbuses on official holidays (this does not apply to normal Fridays).

> **Caution**
> It can be considered offensive for men to sit themselves next to women on the buses – at least more elderly and conservative women. If, when boarding, a male traveller only finds free seats next to local women, it would be prudent to remain standing. Often passengers will rearrange themselves so that women sit together, or with family members, and free the spare seats. If a male traveller does sit down next to a local woman and people get animated, the best advice is not to argue with them about it. ■

TRAIN

Syria has a fleet of slowly ageing trains supplied by Russia back in the 1970s. Money is now being put into overhauling the locomotives. Although more than 2000 km of track connect most main centres, the train is not the transport form of choice. The main line snakes its way from Damascus north to Aleppo via Homs and Hama before then swinging south-east for Deir ez-Zur via Raqqa. At that point it turns on itself again, proceeding north-east to Hassake and finally to Qamishle. Trains also operate on a couple of secondary lines, one of which runs from Aleppo to Lattakia, and then along the coast to Tartus and on to Homs and Damascus.

The trains are cheap and sometimes even punctual, but there are never more than three services a day between any given destinations, and often fewer. Worse, the stations are usually awkwardly located a few km from the centre of town, so that unless you are particularly enamoured of trains, you are better off with the more practical, if admittedly more prosaic, buses and service taxis.

First class is air-con with aircraft-type seats; 2nd class is the same without air-con. Sleepers ('*manaama*') are also available.

In 1908, the French-built Hejaz Railway was opened to take pilgrims from Damascus to Medina (Saudi Arabia). The station is a bit of a propaganda show piece – only the Sunday and Friday service to Der'a (and on to Amman on Sunday) and the summertime steam trains to Zabadani in the Barada Valley run along the Hejaz line. For this last trip, see Around Damascus in the Damascus chapter.

SERVICE TAXI

The share taxis, which also go by the name of service taxis ('*servees*'), in Syria are usually old American Desotos and Dodges from the 50s and 60s – and some from before. One driver called his an ancient monument. There's a chronic shortage of spare parts but ingenuity and improvisation keep them running. Although more modern vehicles have begun to appear, most drivers persist with their old favourites – largely for their robustness and size (good for squeezing people in).

They only operate on some major routes and in some cases seem to have succumbed to competition from the modern microbuses. They can cost a lot more than the buses. For instance, the trip from Aleppo to Hama costs S£150 per person, while on the old minibus you're looking at S£25. Unless you're in a tearing hurry, or you find yourself stuck on a highway and it's getting late, there's really no need to use them.

CAR & MOTORCYCLE

Road Rules

Traffic runs on the right-hand side of the road in Syria and, as in Jordan, a good dose of common sense is the best advice. The speed limit in built-up areas is generally 60 km/h, 70 km/h on the open road and 110 km/h on major highways.

The roads are generally quite reasonable in Syria, but when heading off into the back-blocks you will find that most signposting is in Arabic only. Always take care when driving into villages and other built-up areas, as cars, people and animals all jostle for the same space.

Long distance night driving can be a little hairy, as not all drivers believe in using headlights all the time. Beware also of the mad overtaker. Some people appear to consider it something of a test of their courage to overtake in the most impossible situations.

Rental

For a long time there was only one car hire firm to choose from in Syria, Europcar, but this has changed. Several major companies, including Budget and Avis, are now represented in Syria, if only in Damascus. Budget's cheapest standard rate is US$45 a day for a Ford Fiesta or something similar, including all insurance and unlimited km. Rental for a week comes out at US$259. The main advantage with such companies is that you generally know where you stand and staff usually speak English. The rates are comparable with anywhere else in the world (although somewhat lower than in neighbouring Jordan).

A plethora of local companies has also appeared since the beginning of the 90s. You want to be careful with these, as many charge ridiculous rates and seem to have dodgy rules on insurance – or none at all. The best advice is to look around or go straight to Marmou on Maysaloun St in Damascus, one of the oldest establishments and a fairly reliable place. Small car rental companies can be found in other towns too, but they are not as plentiful. If possible, get advice from locals or your hotel. When your luck is in, you can get something along the lines of a Renault 19 for as low as US$26 a day with unlimited km.

You need to be at least 21 years old to rent a car in Syria. Most companies will require a deposit in cash of up to US$1000 – not a comfortable or easy arrangement – unless you are paying by credit card.

Fuel

If you are driving a car in Syria you'll be better off if it runs on diesel ('*mazout*'), which is widely available and dirt cheap at S£2.66 per litre. Regular petrol ('*benzin*') costs S£6.85 a litre and S£20.40 for super (sometimes referred to as '*mumtaz*'). The latter is fairly widely available, but you can forget about lead-free petrol.

Customs

On the off chance that you bring a vehicle into Syria without a carnet, and for whatever reason need to leave Syria briefly and return, it is possible to do so without taking your vehicle out of the country. Those travelling without a carnet will want to avoid crossing borders as much as possible because of the costs and red tape involved. The single most likely reason for doing this is heading to Amman to get a Lebanese visa and returning.

You need to go to the customs ('*jumruk*') building on Palestine Ave (Sharia Filastin) in Damascus to get a paper (S£10 revenue stamp) allowing you to leave Syria and return without getting into trouble for not having your vehicle (details of which are scribbled into your passport when you first arrive). You may be obliged to have the vehicle impounded during your absence.

The Customs building is also the place to go if you stay more than a month and need to renew your Syrian third-party insurance or customs waiver (see also the regional Getting There & Away chapter).

BICYCLE

A growing number of independent travellers are choosing to cycle through Syria as part of a wider bike tour around the Mediterranean or indeed overland from Europe to

Asia. This can be hard work for several reasons. Syrians are not used to seeing long-distance cyclists, which means you need to pay extra attention on the roads. The extreme temperatures, especially in summer, need to be taken into account. You should also have a very complete tools and spares kit, as you cannot rely on being able to find what you need on the way.

HITCHING

Hitching is never entirely safe in any country in the world, and we don't recommend it. Travellers who decide to hitch should understand that they are taking a small but potentially serious risk. However, many people do choose to hitch, and the advice that follows should help to make their journeys as fast and safe as possible.

Hitching is even easier in Syria than in Jordan, as still fewer people have private cars, and it is an accepted means of getting around. Similar rules apply in Syria as in Jordan; some payment is at times expected, as the driver will take passengers to subsidise his own trip. Unless you are skint, the best policy is to offer a small amount (try not to be insulting, though) and often you'll find it being knocked back. The same warnings about hitching apply in Syria as anywhere and women, especially when travelling alone, should not attempt it.

LOCAL TRANSPORT

The Airport

Damascus international airport is about 25 km south-east of the city. A local bus leaves from outside the terminal every half hour for S£10, and takes roughly 45 minutes to the centre. From the city, it leaves from Choukri Kouwatli Ave. The service begins at 5.30 am and ends at 11 pm.

Taxis are a rip-off from the airport, but if you must take one don't offer more than S£300. They will start at S£700 or more but stand your ground – or just catch a bus.

Aleppo airport is about 25 km east of the city. Buses run from the Karnak bus station for S£10 and take about half an hour.

The two km from Qamishle to the airport can be reached by service taxi or any bus heading to Hassake. Lattakia airport is 25 km south of town. A service taxi costs S£300.

Bus

All the major cities have a local bus and/or microbus system but, as the city centres are compact, you can usually get around on foot. This is just as well because neither the buses nor the microbuses have signs in English (and often nothing in Arabic either).

That said, they can be useful (and cheap) for getting out to distant microbus or railway stations, especially in the capital.

Service Taxis & Taxis

Taxis in most cities are plentiful and cheap. In Damascus they have meters, although not all drivers use them – a cross-town trip should never cost more than S£25, although from the centre to Mezzeh you'd be looking at more like S£40. In Aleppo a cross-town ride should not cost more than S£15. There is a flagfall of S£3. Where they don't use a meter, it's a matter of negotiating the fare when you get in.

It's a real surprise to find taxi drivers who aren't all sharks. In Syria, if you get into a taxi and ask how much it is to the bus station (or wherever) you will often be told the correct fare and bargaining will get you nowhere. This is not, however, an invitation to drop your guard.

Although they are not in evidence in the capital, some other cities, notably Aleppo, are served by local service taxis that run a set route, like a bus or microbus, picking up and dropping passengers along the way for a set price. For the outsider, there is no obvious way to distinguish between them and normal taxis – both are yellow, although you can generally bet the big old lumbering American relics are service taxis.

If you read Arabic, it's easy. Regular taxis have a sign on the doors reading 'Ujra medinat Halab, raqm...' (City of Aleppo Taxi, Number...), while the others have a similar-looking sign reading 'Khidma Medinat

Halab' (City of Aleppo Service) followed by the route name.

Should you end up sharing with other people and the taxi doesn't take you exactly where you want to go, you're probably in a service taxi!

ORGANISED TOURS

If time is important or you're just in Damascus for a couple of days, several travel agents in the area around the Cham Palace Hotel offer half-day and one day excursions as far afield as Palmyra and Bosra. They operate mainly in spring and summer, and you're looking at around US$35 per person for the transport – if there is sufficient demand to fill a microbus. You're better off getting around under your own steam to such places, but if you really want to do this, one reader has recommended Dawn ('Al-Fajar') Travel (☎ 331 6006), Al-Brazil Street (see Central Damascus map).

SYRIA

Damascus

Until the turn of the century, Damascus could still boast itself to be the 'Pearl set in Emeralds'. However, the emeralds, or green fields watered by the Barada River, have long since been submerged in the urban sprawl that is home to some six million people. It is nevertheless still the bright light in Ash-Sham, which loosely translates as southern Syria. Words change their meaning, and 'Dimashq ash-Sham' (the modern Arabic for Damascus) is often simply referred to as Ash-Sham by locals.

Syria's capital and by far its largest metropolis, Damascus is a city of fascinating contrasts. Veiled women in traditional garb mix with country Bedouin ladies and other city folk sporting trendy western-style fashion. Old men in *jalabiyyehs* and *kafiyyehs* shuffle past go-ahead young public servants in natty suits and pushy young hawkers in the crowded souqs of the old city.

Beyond the timeless oriental bazaars and blind alleys of the old city stretches the largely modern administrative and commercial district, with its seemingly lawless traffic and the hustle and bustle you'd expect of a busy capital. Above it all, like a permanent leitmotiv, Arabic pop music wafts from music stands and cassette shops at every turn, sweeping you along with its unmistakable rhythms.

By midnight an eerie quiet descends upon the city, and occasionally you may see lorries moving around with a huge spray pipe, heaving out a misty grey fog that hangs in the air. It is in fact an insecticide, and apparently the posher parts of town get a double serving. Whatever it does to the bugs, it sure can't do much for people being sprayed in the streets!

The city owes its existence to the Barada River, which rises high in the Jebel Lubnan ash-Sharqiyyeh (Anti-Lebanon Mountains). The waters give life to the Ghouta Oasis, making settlement possible in an otherwise uninhabitable area.

History

Damascus claims to be the oldest continuously inhabited city in the world, although its northern rival, Aleppo, hotly disputes this. Hieroglyphic tablets of Egypt make reference to 'Dimashqa' as being one of the cities conquered by the Egyptians in the 15th century BC, but excavations from the courtyard of the Omayyad Mosque have yielded finds dating back to the 3rd millennium BC. The name Dimashqa appears in the Ebla archives and also on tablets found at Mari (2500 BC).

It has been fought over many times and some of the earliest conquerors include King David of Israel, the Assyrians in 732 BC, Nebuchadnezzar (circa 600 BC) and then the Persians in 530 BC. In 333 BC it fell to Alexander the Great. Greek influence declined when the Nabataeans occupied Damascus in 85 BC. The Romans soon sent the Nabataeans packing in 64 BC and Syria became a Roman province. It was here that Saul of Tarsus was converted to Christianity and became St Paul the Apostle.

Damascus was an important city under the Romans and it became a military base for the armies fighting the Persians. Hadrian declared it a metropolis in the 2nd century AD and during the reign of Alexander Severus it became a Roman colony.

By the end of the 4th century AD most of the population had adopted Christianity. The Temple of Jupiter became a cathedral dedicated to St John the Baptist, whose head supposedly lies in a tomb inside the Omayyad Mosque.

With the coming of Islam, Damascus became an important centre as the seat of the Omayyad caliphate from 661 to 750. The city expanded rapidly and the Christian cathedral was turned into a mosque. When the Abbasids took over and moved the caliphate to Baghdad, Damascus was plundered once again.

After the occupation of Damascus by the

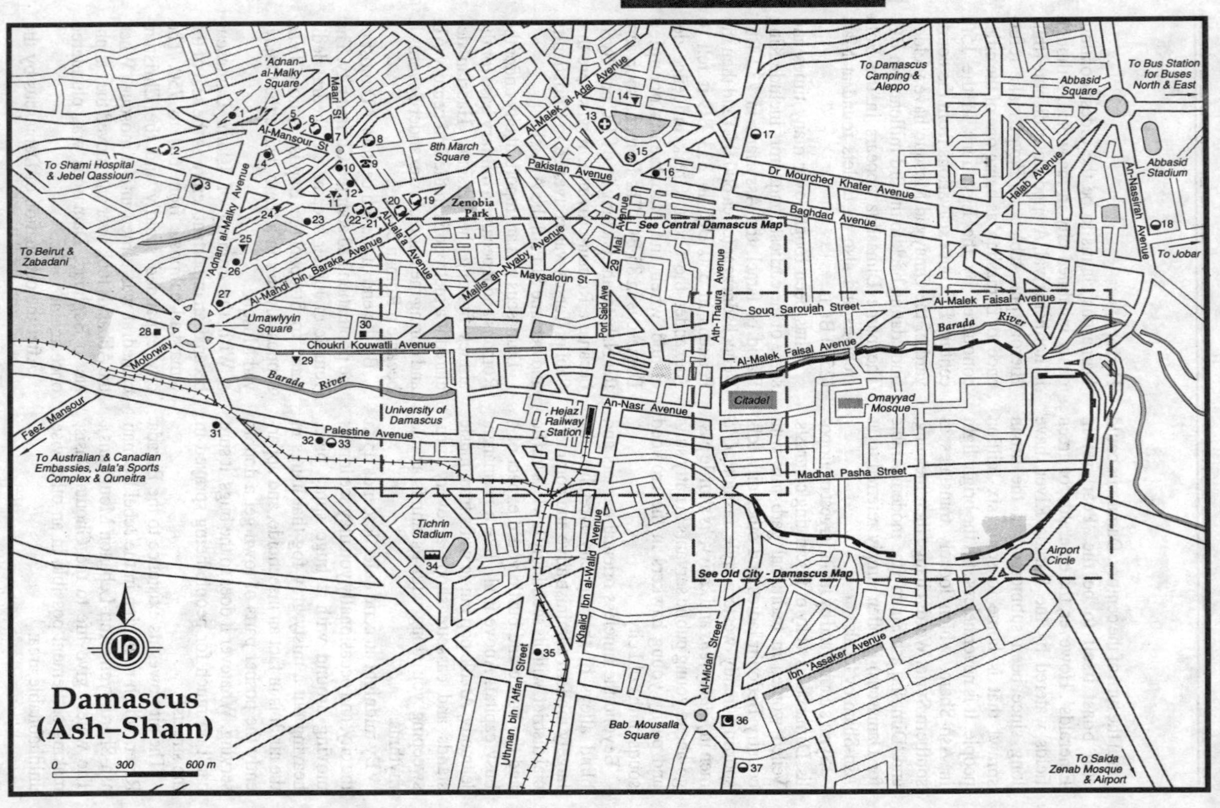
Damascus
(Ash–Sham)
0
300
600 m
'Adnan al-Malky Square
Maari St
Al-Mansour St
To Shami Hospital & Jebel Qassioun
'Adnan al-Malky Avenue
8th March Square
Al-Malek al-Adal Avenue
Pakistan Avenue
Zenobia Park
To Damascus Camping & Aleppo
Abbasid Square
To Bus Station for Buses North & East
Abbasid Stadium
Halab Avenue
An-Nassirah Avenue
Dr Mourched Khater Avenue
Baghdad Avenue
To Jobar
See Central Damascus Map
To Beirut & Zabadani
Al-Mahdi bin Baraka Avenue
Al-Jala'a Avenue
Majlis an-Nyaby Avenue
29 Mai Avenue
Maysaloun St
Port Said Ave
Ath-Thaura Avenue
Souq Saroujah Street
Al-Malek Faisal Avenue
Barada River
Umawiyyin Square
Motorway
Choukri Kouwatli Avenue
Citadel
Omayyad Mosque
University of Damascus
Hejaz Railway Station
An-Nasr Avenue
Faez Mansour
Palestine Avenue
To Australian & Canadian Embassies, Jala'a Sports Complex & Quneitra
Madhat Pasha Street
Tichrin Stadium
Khalid Ibn al-Walid Avenue
Airport Circle
See Old City - Damascus Map
Uthman bin 'Affan Street
Al-Midan Street
Ibn 'Assaker Avenue
Bab Mousalla Square
To Saida Zenab Mosque & Airport

PLACES TO STAY
28 Sheraton Hotel
30 Meridien Hotel

PLACES TO EAT
11 'Restaurant Circle'
14 Sakura Restaurant
24 Toledo Restaurant
25 Aldar Restaurant
29 Palais des Nobles

OTHER
1 Ministry of the Interior (Quneitra Passes)
2 German Embassy
3 British Embassy
4 American Cultural Center
5 Italian Embassy
6 US Embassy & Consular Section
7 American Language Center
8 Turkish Embassy
9 Telephone Office
10 British Council (Cultural Centre & Language School)
12 Newsstand
13 Italian Hospital
15 Central Bank Building
16 Syrianair
17 Microbus to Harasta Camping Ground
18 Maalula & Saydnaya Microbus Station
19 Japanese Embassy
20 Swiss Embassy
21 Dutch Embassy
22 Saudi Consulate
23 Newsstand
26 Deutsches Archäologisches Institut
27 Al-Assad National Library
31 Customs Building
32 Budget Car Rental
33 Al-Ahliah Bus Company
34 Swimming Pool
35 Avis
36 Mosque
37 Bus Station (Southern Areas)

Seljuq Turks in 1076, the Crusaders tried unsuccessfully to take it in 1148 before it finally fell to Nureddin, a general of Turkish origin, in 1154. Many of the monuments in the city date from the time of his successor Saladin, when Damascus became the capital of a united Egypt and Syria.

The next to move in were the Mongols who, after only a brief occupation, were ousted by the Mamelukes of Egypt in 1260. During the Mameluke period, Damascene goods became famous worldwide and attracted merchants from Europe. This led to the second Mongol invasion under Tamerlaine, when the city was flattened and the artisans and scholars were deported to the Mongol capital of Samarkand. The Mamelukes returned soon after and proceeded to rebuild the city.

From the time of the Ottoman Turk occupation in 1516, the fortunes of Damascus started to decline and it was reduced to the status of small provincial capital in a large empire. The only interruption in 400 years of Ottoman rule was from 1831 to 1840, when it once again became the capital of Syria under the Egyptians, following the rise to power there of Mohammed Ali Pasha. Fearing the consequences of an Ottoman collapse, the west intervened to force Ibrahim Pasha, Ali's lieutenant, to withdraw from Syria.

By 1878 the city's population had grown to 150,000, great improvements had been made in sanitary conditions and a transport system built. By 1908 Damascus had a network of tramlines and was connected by rail to Beirut and Medina.

The Turkish and German forces used Damascus as their base during WWI. When they were defeated by the Arab Legion and the Allies, the first, short-lived Syrian government was set up in 1919.

The French, having received a mandate from the League of Nations, occupied the city from 1920 to 1945. They met with a lot of resistance and at one stage in 1925 bombarded the city to suppress rioting. French shells again rained on the city in the unrest of 1945, which led to full independence a year later when French and British forces were pulled out and Damascus became the capital of an independent Syria.

Orientation

The city centre of Damascus is fairly compact and finding your way around on foot is no problem, although the official street signs do not always correlate with their commonly known names.

The real heart of the city is the Martyrs' Square (Saahat ash-Shuhada) which the locals all know as 'Al-Merjeh' (a name dating from Ottoman times and meaning something along the lines of 'pasture' or 'park'). The martyrs were victims of the French bombardments in

1945. The rather curious bronze colonnade in the centre commemorates the opening of the first telegraph link in the Middle East – the line from Damascus to Medina. Most of the cheap hotels and restaurants are around here, and many decades ago the heart of the city's now extinct tram system beat here.

The main street, Said al-Jabri Ave, begins at the Hejaz railway station and runs north-east, changing its name to Port Said Ave at the Choukri Kouwatli Ave flyover, and then again to 29 Mai Ave at the Peasant's Monument (Youssef al-Azmeh Square), finishing at the Central Bank building. The whole street is only about one km long and along here you'll find the post office, tourist office, various airline offices and many mid-range restaurants and hotels. Al-Jala'a Ave heads out to the Jordanian embassy. The area around it is known to everyone as Abu Roumaneh.

The Barada River is unfortunately not much more than a smelly drain flowing from north-west to south-east through the city, although it tumbles quite strongly past the old city after some rain. Right in the centre it has been covered over. On its banks to the west of the Martyrs' Square is the Takiyyeh as-Sulaymaniyyeh Mosque and the National Museum, and close by are the university, Karnak bus station and the immigration office.

The old city lies to the south of the river, just east of Martyrs' Square. Apart from the old Roman road, the Street Called Straight (no need to explain why) or 'Via Recta', it's a tangle of narrow and twisting lanes and alleys with the old houses often almost touching overhead.

To get a good view of the city, take a local microbus to Muhajireen from opposite the Hotel Venezia. Ride the bus to the end and then climb the stairs to higher up on Jebel Qassioun. It's best to go in the late afternoon when the sun is behind you.

Information

The American Women of Damascus have compiled a useful booklet with practical information about the city. It is called *Living in Damascus* and is available at the small library opposite the US consulate. It is aimed mainly at residents.

Tourist Office This is on 29 Mai Ave, just up from Youssef al-Azmeh Square. It's open from 9 am to 7 pm daily except Friday, and the friendly, English-speaking staff can be very helpful. There's a good free map of Syria with plans of Damascus, Aleppo and Palmyra on the back. The Damascus map is quite reasonable, and maps of other parts of the country are also available.

An Unhappy Chapter

Travel guidebook writers often take upon themselves, for better or for worse, the delicate task of political and social commentary. Back in 1908, MacMillan's guide to *Palestine & Syria* was no different. Among much lavish praise for the wonders of Damascus, came this less than flattering and no doubt somewhat jaundiced account:

> The one foul blot on the fair fame of Damascus is the cold-blooded massacre of 6000 Christian inhabitants of the city by their Moslem fellow-citizens in the month of July 1860. About that time a deadly feud between the Druses and Maronites of the Lebanon district had culminated in an open conflict, in which many thousands on both sides perished; and the Moslems of Damascus, who have always been notorious for their fanatical hatred of Christianity, seized the opportunity of the disturbed condition of the region to wreak their malice upon the unoffending native Christians of the city.
>
> Some acute observers, acquainted with the internal condition of Damascus, are of the opinion that the bad blood is as strong as ever between the partisans of the two religions in the city, and that it would need but a very tiny spark to set the angry sentiment into a flame once more. Let us hope that the introduction of European civilisation with the advent of the railways, electric light, and tramways, will tend to modify the oriental stubbornness of religious hatred, and that no such hatred or disaster will ever again defile the 'Pearl set in Emeralds'. ■

SYRIA

If you go to the Ministry of Tourism by the Takiyyeh as-Sulaymaniyyeh Mosque, you can get the same maps and sometimes colour posters as well. That office is open Saturday to Thursday from 9 am to 2 pm.

The information booth at the airport is staffed irregularly, not overly informative and sometimes plain misleading – don't believe them when they claim you should pay taxis into the city S£500 in hard currency.

Visa Extensions For visa extensions, the central immigration office is on Palestine Ave (Sharia Filastin), one block west of the Karnak bus station. As with all government departments, it's open from 8 am to 2 pm every day but Friday. You'll need three passport photos (a couple of photographers with ancient cameras across the road can do some awful photos for you), and a revenue stamp (S£3) from the stall outside the building. Go to the 2nd floor to begin filling in the four forms; you can get extensions of up to one month. They cost S£25 and take a working day to process – pick them up at 1 pm the next day.

There is another immigration office at Furat Ave, closer to Martyrs' Square, but you'll probably be moved along to the main building anyway.

Foreign Embassies See the Syria Facts for the Visitor chapter for addresses of foreign embassies in Damascus.

Money There are several branches of the Commercial Bank of Syria as well as more straightforward exchange booths where you can change money fairly easily. The booth on Martyrs' Square is open from 9 am to 6 pm Saturday to Thursday and 10 am to 2 pm on Friday and will change cash and travellers' cheques. So will the booth opposite the Hejaz railway station, which is open from 10 am until 5 pm seven days a week.

Several bank branches take cash and cheques, but are not open as long (usually 8.30 am to 12.30 pm). Branches in the Meridien and Sheraton hotels also accept cash and cheques. The branch on Youssef al-Azmeh Square has a booth open from 8.30 am to 8 pm. The Commercial Bank of Syria branch at the airport is supposedly open seven days a week. There is also an exchange booth in the old city, just inside Bab ash-Sharqi.

The American Express agent (☎ 221 7813; fax 222 3707) is in the Sudan Airways office in an alley off Fardous St. The postal address is PO Box 1373, Damascus. The financial services on offer are extremely limited.

Thomas Cook is represented by Nahas Travel on Fardous St. It reportedly can arrange to have money wired to them (and hence to you) in a matter of hours. It even claims to be able to forward the money on to other branches of Nahas throughout the country. Nahas also represents MasterCard and Visa in Syria, but about all it can do is report theft or loss of these cards to the respective companies.

You might be able to have money or cheques simply stashed into a DHL bag, *if* DHL agrees to it. It has an office just off Choukri Kouwatli Ave, near the Chachati bookshop. The next problem is convincing the Commercial Bank of Syria to cash the cheque(s) in hard currency rather than turning them all into Syrian pounds.

Post The central post office is on Said al-Jabri Ave. You can't miss it – it's an imposing building, open from 8 am to 7 pm every day, except Friday and holidays, when it closes at 1 pm. When the power goes out, the interior is very dark and gloomy. The poste restante counter is to the left when you enter and is fairly efficient. You'll need to have your passport as proof of identity and there is a S£8 charge per letter for any mail you pick up. The poste restante window closes down at 5 pm.

The parcel post office is outside and around the corner.

You can also have mail sent to you c/o American Express (see Money earlier in this chapter). The office is open for client mail Saturday to Thursday from 8.30 am to 1.30 pm and 5 to 8 pm.

Telephone The telephone office is a block east of the Hejaz railway station on An-Nasr Ave, and is open around the clock. The best bet for international or regional calls within Syria is to buy a phone card at the crowded counter on the right and join a card-phone queue. Otherwise, in addition to money and your passport, you will need to come equipped with oodles of patience. Go to the counter already mentioned, fight your way to the front and tell them the country, city and number you want. They'll call for you an hour or two later when they have a line. For details of call costs, discount rates and so on, see Post & Communications in the Syria Facts for the Visitor chapter.

Telegrams can be sent from this office during vaguely set daytime hours. They are even more expensive than phone calls.

Note that Damascus phone numbers have been undergoing changes as the system is improved. They are now generally seven-digit numbers. If you have a six digit number that does not work, doubling the first digit will usually do the trick.

Bookshops Possibly the best bookshop in Damascus is the Librairie Avicenne (☎ 221 2911), a block south of the Cham Palace Hotel. It has a fair range of books on Syria, some novels in English and French, and a selection of days-old press, including *The Financial Times*, *The Times* and *Le Monde*. Not quite as good is the Librairie Universelle (☎ 231 0744), which is at the corner of Port Said and Basha Sts.

The Meridien and Sheraton hotels both have fairly decent bookshops, with some foreign press and a selection of books on Syria and, in the case of the Meridien, even the odd book on surrounding countries. These two shops are owned and operated by Librairie Avicenne.

The Cham Palace Hotel Bookshop (☎ 223 2300) has a good selection of paperbacks, art and design books and books on Syria.

There are newsstands which sell a better than average range of magazines and foreign press, often stocking more than the bookshops. To get to them, make your way to Al-Jala'a Avenue. Follow this boulevard north and you'll find one newsstand not far short of the British Council. For the other, turn left off Al-Jala'a Avenue at the Saudi embassy and where the road forks, take the left branch. When you reach the park, take a right and the newsstand is there.

Predominantly French material is on sale at the Librairie Chachati, virtually across the flyover from the Turkish bus station.

Cultural Centres The American Cultural Center (☎ 333 8443) is off Mansour St near the US embassy. Its library is stocked with books, newspapers, videos and also shows CNN news. It is open Sunday to Thursday from 10 am to 1 pm and 2 to 5 pm. Don't be daunted by the massive security screen.

The British Council (☎ 333 8436; fax 332 1467), at the northern end of Al-Jala'a Ave, serves as a language school and also has a small library. Occasionally it puts on films.

The Centre Culturel Français (☎ 224 6181) is in a lane just off Midan Youssef al-Azmeh St. Its primary vocation is the teaching of French, but films are often organised too.

Other cultural centres include the German Goethe Institut (☎ 333 6673), in the Dar as-Salam building, just off Maysaloun St, the Spanish Cultural Centre (☎ 714003) in Nazem Pasha St and its Russian equivalent (☎ 427155) on 29 Mai Ave.

Photography For camera repairs the Haig shop on Youssef al-Azmeh Square has been recommended by travellers.

Medical Services If you can, it is always a good idea to consult your embassy for referrals to recommended doctors. Damascus has several hospitals. Among the better ones is the Shami Hospital (☎ 371 8970). Another possibility to try is the Italian Hospital (☎ 222 9316).

The booklet *Living in Damascus* has lists of doctors and dentists.

Emergency If you need the police in a hurry, call ☎ 112. An ambulance can be reached on ☎ 110. In case of fire, call ☎ 91.

Walking Tour
Most visitors to Damascus will want to begin their explorations with the old city. The most enjoyable 'method' for coming to know it is simply to wander slowly and absorb, but you might like to plan some sort of route through the labyrinth. What follows is merely a suggestion for getting acquainted with the main points of interest. The nooks and crannies are over to you.

The most obvious starting point is by the massive and brooding walls of the **citadel**, to the right of which yawns the cavern of the city's main market street, **Souq al-Hamadiyyeh**. Meander into this and you get a full-frontal blast of the oriental market, although perhaps not as evocative as those of Aleppo. This covered street leads directly to what remains of the Western Gate of the Roman **Temple of Jupiter** and, immediately beyond it, the splendour of one of Islam's greatest architectural triumphs, the **Omayyad Mosque**. To gain access, follow the walls to the left and then right – tourists enter by the gate in this, the northern wall. In this same area is clustered a couple of important buildings, including **Saladin's Mausoleum** and the former 15th century madrassa which has been turned into the Arab Epigraphy Museum. A detour a block west of the mosque and off to the right will bring you to a pair of majestic 13th century **madrassas**.

Proceed a little further and veer off to the left to behold the spectacle of modern Iranian religious architecture – the **Saida Ruqqaya Mosque**, built over an important Shiite shrine. If you turn heel and follow the main lane as it twists and turns in a vaguely southerly direction, you'll emerge on a pretty arboured street that leads back to the (closed) eastern gate of the Omayyad Mosque. The cafés make an ideal rest stop. From here you could head back eastwards along this road past an intriguing madrassa and into the little-visited north-eastern quarter, but this is perhaps better saved for later missions.

An alternative is to circle around the Omayyad Mosque's south wall and take a left just as you reach the west façade. About 100m south along this busy souq street you arrive at an uneven intersection, presided over by a mosque you might hardly notice, such is the confusion around here. Heading south (left) gets you to the **Azem Palace**, one of the old city's principal monuments, while off to the right lies the **Azem Ecole**, a fine 18th century madrassa turned classy souvenir shop. A little further on, and with its entrance just in off the first side lane to the left, is the unassuming **Madrassa an-Nuri**, where the great Nureddin is buried. If you continue west along Mu'awiyyeh St and take a right (north) towards Souq al-Hamadiyyeh, you'll reach one of Nureddin's legacies, the 12th century **Maristan Nur ad-Din**.

Back at the intersection, you can then bowl straight ahead, but keep your eyes open on the left for the **Hammam Nureddin** and the fine entrance to the **Khan As'ad Pasha**. When you reach the next intersection you have another khan virtually in front of you. Turn left here and you can head east into what eventually becomes the **Street Called Straight**, which leads all the way down to Bab ash-Sharqi, or the **East Gate**. Several possible diversions along the way involve navigating backstreets to find a handful of old Ottoman-era **noble houses** and the odd pretty mosque, before you eventually pass the modest **Roman arch** and finally hit the East Gate. In the lane just inside the city wall, and heading north from the Street Called Straight, is the **Chapel of Ananias**. If you want to have a quick look at St Paul's Chapel, you're best off exiting by the East Gate and following the wall around to your right.

Plunging back inside the old city or following the south wall almost back around to the Souq al-Hamadiyyeh entrance, take a stroll down Al-Midan St for a series of **Ottoman mosques** and the **cemetery**.

The Old City
City Walls & Citadel The old city wall, first erected in grand style by the Romans, has been flattened and rebuilt several times over the past 2000 years. What stands today dates largely from the 13th century. It is pierced by a number of gates ('*bab*' – the Arabic plural is '*abwab*'), only one of which (the restored

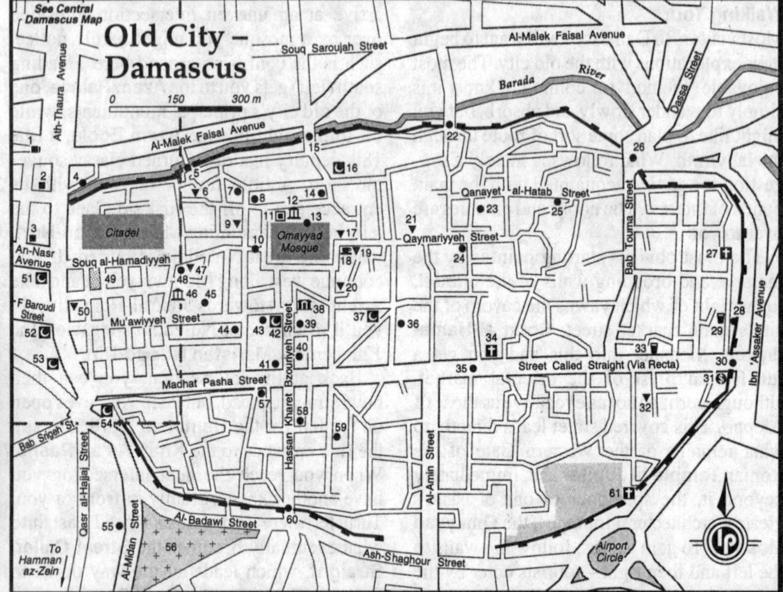

SYRIA

PLACES TO STAY
1 Alaa Tower Hotel (No 2)
2 Hotel Qasr al-Chark
3 Syrian Grand Hotel

PLACES TO EAT
6 Old Damascus Restaurant
9 Abu al-'Azz Restaurant
17 Ash-Sham Restaurant/Café
19 Felafel Place
20 Omayyad Palace Restaurant
21 Alf Layla Wa Layla Restaurant
32 Restaurant La Guitare
47 Bakdach Ice-Cream Parlour
50 Cheap Restaurant

OTHER
4 Leather Souq
5 Bab al-Faraj
7 Madrassa al-Adiliyya
8 Madrassa az-Zahiriyya
10 Western Gate of Temple of Jupiter
11 Saladin's Mausoleum
12 Arab Epigraphy Museum
13 Tourists' Entrance to Omayyad Mosque
14 Hammam as-Silsila
15 Bab al-Faradis
16 Saida Ruqqaya Mosque
18 Café Naufara
22 Bab as-Salama (Gate of Safety)
23 Hammam al-Qaymariyyeh
24 Madrassa al-Fatihiyyeh
25 Hammam Bakri
26 Bab Touma (Thomas Gate)
27 Chapel of Ananias
28 Bayt Nassan
29 Piano Bar & Café La Terrasse
30 Bab ash-Sharqi (East Gate)
31 CBS Exchange Booth
33 Liquor Store/Bar
34 St Mary's Church
35 Roman Arch
36 Dar Anbar
37 Amr al-Jabli as-Safar Jalani Mosque
38 Azem Palace
39 Hammam Nureddin
40 Khan As'ad Pasha
41 Spices Souq
42 Mosque & Herbs & Potions Market
43 Azem Ecole
44 Madrassa An-Nuri
45 Gold Souq
46 Science & Medical Museum
48 Tony Stephan's Store
49 Rug Souq
51 Mosque
52 Ad-Darwishiyyeh Mosque
53 As-Siba'iyyeh Mosque & Madrassa
54 As-Sinaniyyeh Mosque
55 Madrassa as-Sabuniyyeh
56 Bab as-Saghir Cemetery
57 Khan Suleiman Pasha
58 Bayt as-Siba'i
59 Bayt Nizam
60 Bab as-Saghir & Cemetery
61 Bab Kisan (St Paul's Chapel)

Bab ash-Sharqi or East Gate) dates from Roman times. The best preserved section is between **Bab as-Salama** (Gate of Safety) and **Bab Touma** (Thomas Gate – named after a son-in-law of the emperor Heraclius) in the north-east corner. For most of its length, the wall is obscured by new buildings constructed over and around it. Bab as-Salama is a beautiful example of Ayyubid military architecture, but unfortunately it is now draped with electric cables and telegraph wires.

Bab Kisan houses St Paul's Chapel. This is where tradition has it that the Christians lowered St Paul out of a window in a basket to escape the wrath of the Jews (Acts 9:25).

The whole area is a labyrinth of winding alleys and chaotic markets, stretching from the mainly Muslim and touristed souqs around the Omayyad Mosque to the mostly Christian sector around Bab ash-Sharqi.

The citadel itself forms part of the western wall at the end of An-Nasr Ave. It used to be home to the National Guard but is now closed for restoration. Originally the site of a Roman fort, it was expanded in the 13th century to resist Crusader attacks. Destroyed by the Mongols in 1400, it was later partially restored by the Turks. It affords good views over the city if you manage to slip in through the occasionally open gates without raising the worker's hackles.

Souq al-Hamadiyyeh Just right of the citadel is the entrance to one of the main covered markets, the Souq al-Hamadiyyeh. The vaulted cobbled souq with its bustling crowds, hawkers and tenacious merchants is worlds away from the traffic jams of the streets outside. It's also the closest thing to a mild tourist trap in Syria.

Among the souvenir stalls in the initial stretch of the souq is the old city's main rug and carpet market. It is in this area that foreigners are accosted by merchants the most and a lot of moneychanging goes on too. For more information on souvenir hunting, see Things to Buy later in this chapter.

Temple of Jupiter Only parts of the western gate of this once imposing Roman temple, at the eastern end of Souq al-Hamadiyyeh, remain in a decent state of repair. The outer walls of the Omayyad Mosque mark the position of the 3rd century temple itself, but the entire complex was considerably grander, covering an area of 315 by 270m. The street leading east from the mosque once ended in Roman Damascus' agora (marketplace). South of the mosque are outlines of what may have been a governor's palace and theatre on Madhat Pasha St.

As you emerge from Souq al-Hamadiyyeh today, you are confronted with two enormous Corinthian columns supporting a decorated lintel. The gateway is draped with electric cables, telegraph wires and lights. At the foot of the columns lies a hive of bookshops and stalls selling all manner of religious memorabilia – Qur'ans, pictures of Mecca and wall hangings with calligraphic messages of the 'god is great' variety.

Omayyad Mosque Just behind the columns rise the walls of one of the jewels of Islamic architecture, the Omayyad Mosque – daunting in size and impressive in its construction. Take your time on a visit. It's a peaceful place and a respite from the heat and bustle outside.

The history of the site goes back almost 3000 years to the 9th century BC, when the Aramaens built a temple to their god, Hadad (mentioned in the Book of Kings in the Old Testament). Then followed the Temple of Jupiter, subsequently replaced by a basilica named after St John the Baptist. When the Muslims entered Damascus in 636 they converted the eastern part of the temple into a mosque and allowed the Christians to continue their worship in the western part.

This arrangement continued until 705, when the sixth Omayyad caliph, Al-Walid, decided to 'build a mosque the equal of which was never designed by anyone before me or anyone after me'. Consequently, all the old Roman and Byzantine constructions within the enclosure were flattened and for the next 10 years over 1000 stonemasons and artisans were employed in the construction of the grand new mosque. Most of the interior had to be reconstructed at the end of the last century after a fire gutted the original building in 1893.

The three minarets all date from the original construction but were renovated and restored at later dates by the Ayyubids, the Mamelukes and Ottomans. The one on the northern side is the **Minaret of the Bride** (Minaret al-'Arous), while the one on the south-eastern corner is the **Minaret of Jesus**, so named because local tradition has it that this is where Jesus will appear on Judgement Day.

The northern part of the rectangular mosque is an open courtyard with a beautiful, marble floor that remains cool even in summer. The courtyard is flanked on three sides by a double-storeyed portico that used to be covered with veined marble. The two pillars either side of the ablution fountain ('*kubbet an-naufara*') in the centre used to hold lamps to light the courtyard. Many of the columns could well have been simply pilfered from the earlier temple. Some of them have been raised again in higgledy-piggledy fashion outside the north wall.

The small octagonal structure on the western side, decorated with intricate 14th century mosaics, is the old treasury ('*bayt al-hal*') once used to keep public funds safe from thieves. It is counterbalanced by another domed structure built in the 18th century.

On the southern side of the courtyard is the rectangular prayer hall, its three aisles divided by a transept. High above the transept is the Dome of the Eagle, so called because it represents the eagle's head while the transept represents the body and the aisles are the wings. If you stand under the dome facing the mihrab (prayer niche) to the south and look up, you'll see eight names in Arabic. From the bottom right clockwise they are Allah, Mohammed and then the first four caliphs (who had been Companions of the Prophet), Abu Bakr, Omar, Othman and Ali. The last two names are Hassan and Hussein, Ali's two sons.

Looking somewhat out of place in the sanctuary is the structure surrounding the shrine of John the Baptist (the Prophet Yahia to the Muslims). It is believed his head (and according to some accounts the rest of his body too) was buried on this spot. The

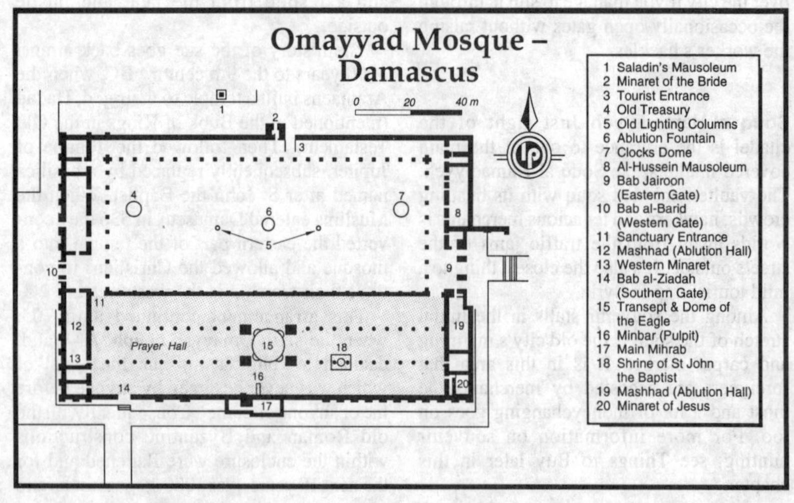

wooden tomb was replaced by the present marble one after the fire of 1893.

The eastern side of the mosque contains a shrine of primary significance to Shiite visitors to Damascus. The head of Hussein, son of Ali, is supposedly buried in an inner sanctuary here. He was killed by the Omayyads at Kerbala in Iraq, but whether or not his head ended up here is more a matter of legend than fact.

The tourist entrance is through the northern Bab al-'Amarah. Here you pay the S£10 entry fee. All women, and men in shorts, have to use the black robes supplied. Some travellers report not being allowed in with shorts, whether wearing a robe or not. As in all mosques, you must remove your shoes, and it's best to keep them with you. Non-Muslims are admitted on Friday too, but not during the main midday prayer time, when the mosque is closed to tourists for a couple of hours. The mosque's doors close in the evening after the final prayers. It's quite OK to take photos anywhere inside.

Mausoleum of Saladin Saladin's mausoleum was originally built in 1193 and restored with funds made available by Kaiser Wilhelm II of Germany during his visit to Damascus in 1898. The walnut-wood cenotaph is richly decorated with motifs of the Ayyubid period and still contains Saladin's body. Next to it is a modern tomb in marble donated by Kaiser Wilhelm. All but an arch of the original madrassa that contained the mausoleum has disappeared.

The mausoleum itself is topped by a red 16-part 'melon' dome and is in a pleasant garden setting outside the northern wall of the Omayyad Mosque. The caretaker almost seems reluctant to let you in, but will do his best to answer questions in broken English. You supposedly need your ticket to the mosque to get in here, but he seems oblivious to this. Doubtless a tip would be appreciated. As a rule, the mausoleum is open daily from 10 am to 5 pm.

Arab Epigraphy Museum This is a case of a museum building being more engaging than its contents for most visitors. The small calligraphic exhibit will attract those with a particular interest, but it is limited. It is in the 15th century Madrassa al-Jaqmaqiyya (about 20m down from Saladin's Mausoleum) a fine example of the characteristic

SYRIA

The Pigeon Breeders

In Damascus, as in most cities in Syria, there is a ritual performed among the clouds. If you climb mount Qassium, or stand on the terrace of a house, it is possible to watch the strange dance of pigeons as they soar in the air.

They fly in clusters, coming together then separating and going their own way. The loud cries from the roofs mingle with the soft coos emanating from the terraces. A faded red flag flutters at the end of a pole; another a little further away raised on the top of a building also begins to wave. The *kashash* are there. They devote themselves to their passion: the breeding and trapping of pigeons (a practice that the law condemns). The kashash are often branded as thieves, bandits as well as people of ill-repute.

The domain of the kashash is an island suspended above the frantic activity of the city, a mysterious world with strict codes where they take refuge, at the end of a working day. No women are allowed to climb on to the roof where the pigeons are bred. Strangers are also not welcome. There are days of fortune and days without, days when the breeding is enriched by a trapped pigeon and days when they lose one of their own.

The kashash know all the species of pigeon and can identify their origins and the distances that they have travelled. The *Rjerni*, with its black and chestnut plumage, is the most valuable and is worth about S£25,000. The *Rihani*, with its tender, delicate yellow neck is worth roughly S£4000. The *Mazouzin*, with its feathers of grey, white and black has a value of S£8000. The black-and-white *Abla* is worth about S£22,500. Who would have believed it? The roofs of Damascus, like the ones of most Syrian villages, are worth a veritable fortune. ■

Mameluke-era penchant for layering differently coloured stone in the façade. It's open from 8 am to 2 pm daily except Tuesday, and entry is S£100.

Al-Adiliyya & Az-Zahiriyya Madrassas Not more than 100m down the market lane to the left (west) of the Western Gate of the Temple of Jupiter, you will find two old Qur'anic teaching schools, erected in the 13th century during the ascendancy of the Ayyubids. The first, on the left, is the Madrassa al-Adiliyya, begun under Nureddin and continued under a brother of Saladin, Al-'Adil Saif ad-Din, whose grave it contains. Its façade is considered a classic example of Ayyubid architecture. It is now a library.

The Madrassa az-Zahiriyya opposite, begun in 1277, houses the body of Sultan Baibars, who went a long way to expelling the last of the Crusaders from the Levant. Look for someone to open up the room where the great Sultan lies, as there are some interesting mosaics to inspect there.

Apart from his burial chamber, the focal point of interest is again the entrance façade, with its alternate levels of black and cream stonework and complex decoration.

Saida Ruqqaya Mosque For centuries the mausoleum of Ruqqaya Bint al-Hussein ash-Shaheed bi-Kerbala (Ruqqaya, the Daughter of the Martyr Hussein of Kerbala) was hidden among the clutter of tumbledown Damascene housing just to the north of the Omayyad Mosque. In 1985, construction of a new Shiite mosque began, largely funded by the Iranians and consequently very much in the Iranian style. Like its sister Saida Zeinab Mosque on the outskirts of Damascus, the predominantly blue hues of the tiles and the onion-shaped dome strike an uncanny and some might even say discordant note in a country where this style of Islamic architecture is otherwise quite unknown. To get to it, proceed east from the Arab Epigraphy Museum and take the first left past the Hammam as-Silsila. Head straight on and you cannot miss it.

Azem Palace The peaceful haven of the Azem Palace, just to the south of the Omayyad Mosque, was built in 1749 by the governor of Damascus, As'ad Pasha al-Azem. The black basalt and limestone used to create alternating layers of white and black are a characteristic theme throughout Levantine and Egyptian architecture, and were particularly popular under the Mamelukes, from whom this aspect of the palace undoubtedly takes its inspiration. The cool, flourishing gardens and intricate interior decoration of some of the rooms lend the palace a restrained beauty and charm.

The rooms of the palace also house exhibits of the **Museum of the Arts & Popular Traditions of Syria**. The displays are rather disappointing but do manage to give some idea of Syria as it was. It is not well labelled, so try to latch on to one of the attendants to show you around.

This kind of display, featuring mannequins dressed in the traditional costumes of people from all walks of life, seems to be a well-worn museum genre throughout the Middle East, and you'll find no shortage of them in Syria.

The palace is open from 9 am to 6 pm daily (4 pm in winter) except Tuesday. On Friday it closes for about two hours from 12.30 pm. Entry is S£200.

Azem Ecole Built in 1770, the Madrassa Abdullah al-Azem is a little gem of Ottoman urban architecture. Today known as the Azem Ecole, it houses a quality souvenir store, where you can also get a chance to see the production of hand-woven silk garments, tablecloths and the like.

Madrassa an-Nuri Nureddin, Saladin's uncle who united Syria and paved the way for the latter's successes against the Crusaders in the latter 12th century, lies buried in a modest chamber in this madrassa around the corner from the Azem Ecole. Apart from the great man's memory, the other outstanding feature is the crimson *muqarnas* (cupola). The style is an Iraqi-Persian import and quite

Heroes of Islam

The oft divided Islamic states' long struggle against invading Crusaders produced three knights in shining armour who lie resting in Damascus today: Nureddin (Nur ad-Din or 'Light of the Faith'), Saladin (Salah ad-Din or 'Rectitude of the Faith') and Baibars as they are known to the west.

Nureddin, son of Imad ad-Din, the founder of the Zangi dynasty, was the first to gain any momentum in the struggle against the 'Franks', gradually laying the foundations for a united front to face them off. In 1154, he removed Damascus from potentially pro-Christian hands and cleared the Syrian hinterland of the vestiges of Crusader presence. He also made inroads into the principality of Antioch, capturing its ruler and also that of Tripoli, Raymond III.

Meanwhile, Nureddin had a Kurdish general gradually take control of the decrepit Fatimid state in Egypt, which lay dangerously open to Crusader assault. The general soon died, but his son, Saladin, soon proved a more than capable successor. By the time Nureddin died in 1174, Saladin had already taken over de facto control of Egypt and blocked any threat from Christian Palestine. His brother then took over Yemen, and the Holy Cities of Arabia fell under Saladin's sway. He quickly took control of Syria and in the next 10 years extended his control into parts of Mesopotamia, careful not to infringe too closely on the territory of the by now largely powerless Abbasid caliphate in Baghdad.

The year 1187 was one for Saladin. He took Tiberias in July, crushed the Crusaders in the Battle of Hittin and stormed Jerusalem in October. By the end of 1189, he had swept the Franks out of Lattakia and Jabla to the north and castles such as Kerak and Shobak inland. Only Antioch (Antakya in present-day Turkey), Tyre and Tripoli (both in Lebanon) remained in European hands. The blitzkrieg provoked western Europe into action, sending the Third Crusade under the command of Richard the Lionheart, Frederick Barbarossa and Philippe Auguste of France. In a desperate bid to reverse the Latins' fortunes in the Holy Lands, the European forces laid siege to Akka (in modern Israel) and Saladin attempted for two years to break it. Once taken, Akka became the Crusaders' capital. After a bloody massacre of some 30,000 captives in Akka, Richard the Lionheart called for peace. This was finally signed in November 1192, giving the Crusaders the coast and the interior to the Muslims. Saladin died three months later in Damascus.

Both Nureddin and Saladin had not only fought ceaseless military campaigns, the latter creating a single Islamic state stretching from North Africa to the Tigris. Both built hospitals and other public works. It was Saladin who began the Citadel of Cairo, one of that city's most extraordinary lasting monuments, and he in particular associated with philosophers and poets. Finally, he proved a true knight in the romanticised European tradition of chivalry. Standing in stark contrast to the barbarous antics of most of the Crusaders, Saladin was a stickler for treaties and fair play. His treatment of captives after taking Jerusalem was lenient compared with Richard the Lionheart's massacre at Akka, and it was not his habit to plunder, at least not for his own enrichment.

The fourth of the Mameluke sultans of Egypt, Sultan Baibars, who also controlled much of Syria, was the next great champion to take to the field against the Crusaders. He began operating in 1263. Within five years he had taken Jaffa, Kerak and most importantly Antioch. Not as nice a fellow as Saladin, he torched the place, a blow from which the city never recovered. As a side event, he cleared western Syria of the Ismaelis, taking all their castles. He also took the magnificent Crac des Chevaliers, leaving only a small, if determined, group of Crusaders holed up in Tartus and Qala'at al-Marqab. He died in 1277. Within 15 years of his passing, the last of the Crusaders was finally ejected from the Levant, never to return. ■

Saladin's Castle – built by the Crusaders in 1115

striking, creating the impression of multiple layers of ice-cream-like shells.

Maristan Nur ad-Din Nureddin was not just a fighting man and politician, he had something of a social conscience, the memory of which lives on in this hospital, which he built in the 12th century. It was for centuries renowned in the Arab world as an enlightened centre of medical treatment. Of particular note is the crimson muqarnas dome and the remarkable decoration of the entrance. If approaching from the Souq al-Hamadiyyeh, turn right (south) just before the Tony Stephan shop. You'll see the Maristan on your left about a block south towards Mou'awiyah Street.

Around the cool, peaceful courtyard inside are displayed the hodge-podge exhibits of the so-called **Science & Medical Museum**. The old medical and surgical odds and ends from Roman to Ottoman times look more like implements of torture – there's even an old electric-shock machine. It's easy to see why many patients carried good-luck charms. There's also a display of 100 or so medicinal herbs and spices used in ancient times. What the room full of stuffed animals and birds is doing here is anybody's guess.

The Maristan and museum are open from 8 am to 2 pm daily except Friday. The entry fee is S£100. Descriptions are in French and Arabic.

Around the Azem Palace Along the vaulted souq running south from near the Azem Palace (Hassan Kharet Bzouriyeh St) stand virtually side by side the Hammam Nureddin (see Hammams later in this chapter), the most elegant of Syria's old bathhouses, and the grand entrance to the Khan As'ad Pasha, built in 1752 by the Damascus Governor responsible for the Azem Palace. Inside, you can still appreciate the grand scale of this caravanserai. The market stands here are particularly pungent, specialising in herbs and spices, with several stalls given over to sweets and chocolate.

A walk through some of the back lanes in this area throws up the odd find. Close to each other about a block and a half south of Madhat Pasha St (also known as Souq Madhat Pasha and virtually part of the original Roman Via Recta, or Street Called Straight) are a couple of old Ottoman noble houses. The 18th century **Bayt Nizem** was once the residence of the British consul, and as is always the case, the expansive interior is belied by a blank façade. You can visit this one from 8 am to 2 pm (bang on the door), but the nearby **Bayt as-Siba'i** is now the German ambassador's residence and getting a peek inside virtually out of the question.

North of Madhat Pasha St, the **Dar Anbar** was erected in 1867 for a wealthy Ottoman merchant. As you pass inside, the first courtyard was a reception area, the second reserved for men of the household and guests (the '*salamlik*') and the third the domain of the women ('*haramlik*'). A fourth patio out the back was used as servants' quarters. In 1920, the elegantly sprawling building became Syria's first secondary school. It now houses offices for experts working to preserve the best of old Damascus. You can wander in here from about 8 am to 1 pm on working days.

Virtually across the road, the 17th century **Amr al-Jabli as-Safar Jalani Mosque** boasts a particularly engaging minaret.

The Street Called Straight About two-thirds of the way along the Street Called Straight (Via Recta) are the remains of a **Roman arch**, roughly marking the boundary of what might be called the Christian quarter.

There are a few churches in this area but the only one of any historical interest is the **Chapel of Ananias** (Kaneesat Hananya), the old cellar of which is reputedly (but quite probably not) the house of Ananias, an early Christian disciple. He was charged to 'go into the street which is called Straight, and enquire in the house of Judas for one called Saul of Tarsus (St Paul) (Acts 9:11) so that he might be able to touch him and restore Saul's sight'.

The entrance to the chapel is just inside the wall between Bab ash-Sharqi and Bab Touma. Take the last left before exiting the

CHRISTINE COSTE

CHRISTINE COSTE

Syria

Top: Tartus, Syria's second port. The old city has been little touched by modernity, and one can get a feel for the city's Crusader past.

Bottom: Sweet shop, Lattakia. A busy port city, Lattakia was once a crossroads of ancient trade routes.

HUGH FINLAY

DAMIEN SIMONIS

DAMIEN SIMONIS

DAMIEN SIMONIS

HUGH FINLAY

Syria

Clockwise from top left: Ruins of the 2nd century AD city of Palmyra; 17th century Arab castle, Palmyra; Euphrates River viewed from Dura Europos; Roman rock tombs, Qatura; Basilica, Rasafeh.

old city through Bab ash-Sharqi and follow it to the end. The chapel is in a crypt below the house where you (sometimes) pay to enter. It is open daily except Tuesday from 9 am to 1 pm and 3 to 6 pm. In the chapel, the story of Paul is told in a series of panels in Arabic and French.

About halfway between the chapel and Bab ash-Sharqi is another old noble family's house, **Bayt Nassan**. It is a luxurious old house with some sublime Islamic ornamentation in the courtyard, particularly the doors.

St Paul's Chapel in Bab Kisan purportedly marks the spot where the disciples lowered St Paul out of a window in a basket one night so that he could flee from the Jews, having angered them after preaching in the synagogues. You can't enter the Bab from the outside. Follow the driveway up to the new convent on the left and push open heavy wooden doors into the back of the Bab, now containing the small chapel.

Al-Midan Quarter

No more manifest than where Al-Midan St heads away from the old city is the desire of successive Ottoman governors of this ancient seat of Islam to leave a mark. A trail of grand if dishevelled mosques clutters up this choking roadway through markets and bustling workshops as it winds its way south. It seems odd that such a string of holy places should be laid out here until you realise that, prior to the advent of the Hejaz railway, this street led through the Gates of God (Bawabat Allah) on the long road south to Mecca. Once a year, great caravans of pilgrims would set off from this very spot on the Hajj. It must once have been, judging by the report in the 1908 edition of MacMillan's guide to *Palestine & Syria*, quite a spectacle:

> The starting of the Hajj is a sight that should be witnessed by every traveller in Palestine who can arrange to be at Damascus on the day when the great event occurs, even though it has lost much of its former grandeur now that the railway runs into the Hauran, and is likely to be shorn gradually of all its glory when the new Hejaz railway is completed. The ceremony which takes place is the despatch of the *Mahmal*, containing the covering for the Ka'aba, or sacred stone at Mecca. The actual pilgrimage does not leave until some weeks later, as a large section of the tedious journey is now performed by rail.

Across the road from the Mu'awiyyeh St entrance into the old city stands the **Ad-Darwishiyyeh Mosque** built by Darwish Pasha, governor of Damascus, in 1574. Darwish lies buried in a tomb next door. A few metres further south of this is the **As-Siba'iyyeh Mosque** and madrassa, built in the early 16th century, and again named after the governor responsible for it, Siba'i. It is about the last Mameluke-era contribution to the Damascus cityscape. Next along the other side of the street as you head south is the **As-Sinaniyyeh Mosque** built in 1590 by Sinan Pasha, another governor of Damascus. What most stands out is the green enamel colouring of the brickwork.

Further south again, past the junction with Al-Badawi St, the **Madrassa as-Sabuniyyeh** was built in the 15th century and is fronted by an elaborately decorated façade, especially the entrance. As you continue south, you pass several imposing mausoleums and the Bab as-Saghir cemetery. In a sign of Al-Midan St's one-time importance as the official pilgrims' road out of Damascus, approximately the following three km are punctuated by still more mausoleums , mosques and madrassas.

New City

Takiyyeh as-Sulaymaniyyeh Mosque

Lying on the banks of the Barada River just to the west of the post office, this mosque was built in 1554 by one of Ottoman Turkey's foremost classic architects, Sinan. His work adorns Istanbul and various other cities of Turkey, Syria and the Balkans. The Takiyyeh is particularly graceful, built in alternating layers of black and white stone with a central dome and pencil-shaped minarets so typical of the Turkish taste. It's peaceful to sit by the fountain and watch the world go by, away from the traffic outside. The grounds also house the Army Museum.

Next to the mosque is the **Artisanat** – a

handicraft market in a caravanserai built under the Ottoman Sultan Selim in 1516 to accommodate poor pilgrims. The former quarters, kitchens and offices are now workshops where you can see all sorts of crafts practised, from weaving to glass-blowing.

Across Choukri Kouwatli Ave are the remains (closed to the public) of the 12th century **Madrassa al-'Aziyyeh**, next to An-Nadwa Restaurant.

National Museum This, the most important of the city's four museums, is next to the Takiyyeh as-Sulaymaniyyeh Mosque. It could well be argued that you would profit from a visit before and after seeing the main sites around the country.

The shady garden in the front has bits and pieces of statuary from sites all around the country and the small café sells tea and soft drinks. To sit under the large eucalyptus trees and sip a *shay* on a hot afternoon is a good way to recharge your system.

The façade of the museum is imposing – it is the entrance to the old Qasr al-Hayr al-Gharbi (a desert palace/military camp west of Palmyra dating from the time of the Omayyad caliph Hisham in 688). It was transported to Damascus stone by stone and reconstructed, but looks somewhat cramped by the wings of the museum.

Inside is a fantastic array of exhibits: written cylinders from Ugarit using the first known alphabet, dating from the 14th century BC; statuary from Mari, dating from the 3rd to 2nd millennium BC; two halls full of marble and terracotta statues from Palmyra; a reconstruction of an underground burial chamber ('*hypogaeum*') from the Valley of the Tombs, Palmyra; frescoes from Dura Europos; sculptures of black basalt from the Hauran around Bosra; Damascene weapons; old surgical instruments from doctors' graves; Islamic glassware from the 13th century; a collection of Qur'ans dating from the 13th century; a room decorated in the style of the Azem Palace of the 18th century; and an extensive collection of coins and gold jewellery.

To get to the latter exhibit, known as the **Homs collection** because much of it was found in and around that city, you'll need to ask the curator's permission, but it's worth the effort. They say the room (upstairs above the Byzantine and Palmyra displays) is generally kept locked due to a lack of staff.

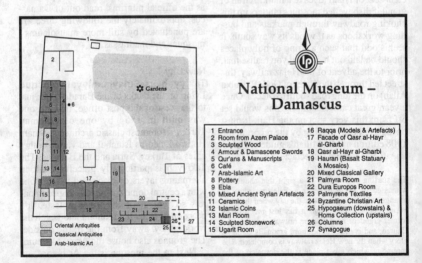

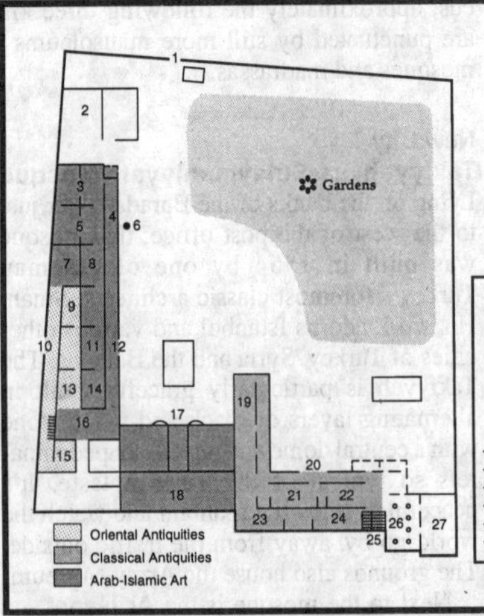

National Museum – Damascus

1 Entrance
2 Room from Azem Palace
3 Sculpted Wood
4 Armour & Damascene Swords
5 Qur'ans & Manuscripts
6 Café
7 Arab-Islamic Art
8 Pottery
9 Ebla
10 Mixed Ancient Syrian Artefacts
11 Ceramics
12 Islamic Coins
13 Mari Room
14 Sculpted Stonework
15 Ugarit Room
16 Raqqa (Models & Artefacts)
17 Facade of Qasr al-Hayr al-Gharbi
18 Qasr al-Hayr al-Gharbi
19 Hauran (Basalt Statuary & Mosaics)
20 Mixed Classical Gallery
21 Palmyra Room
22 Dura Europos Room
23 Palmyrene Textiles
24 Byzantine Christian Art
25 Hypogaeum (dowstairs) & Homs Collection (upstairs)
26 Columns
27 Synagogue

Alongside some exquisite gold jewellery, there are coins depicting Venetian Doges, the Roman emperor Phillip the Arab as well as Alexander the Great, among other leaders through history.

The **synagogue**, removed from Dura Europos and reconstructed here, is out the back past a small colonnaded courtyard. Inside, the synagogue you can see benches around the sides and niches where the five books of the Torah were kept. The frescoes around the walls of the synagogue depict episodes from the Old Testament, from the crowning of King Solomon through the reign of David, the story of Moses and the flight from Egypt.

The museum is open from 9 am to 6 pm (4 pm in winter) every day except Friday, when it opens from 9 am to 11.15 pm and 1 to 6 pm. One traveller has reported that the museum was closed on a Tuesday. This should not be the case, but bear it in mind when planning your sightseeing. The entry fee is S£200. All bags and cameras have to be left in the office at the entrance. Unfortunately, most of the exhibits are labelled only in French or Arabic and some have no label at all.

Army Museum This museum, in the grounds next to the Takiyyeh as-Sulaymaniyyeh Mosque, has a mixed collection of weapons and armour. Outside are various cannons and planes, mostly relics of attacks by the French on Damascus during rebellions under the mandate, notably in 1925 and 1945, or leftovers from WWII and the Arab-Israeli war of 1967. There's also a pile of the twisted remains of planes shot down in the war in 1973.

On the same theme, a whole room is dedicated to captured Israeli war material from the 1973 war, and one of the soldiers who act as curators of the museum is bound to want to explain to you the ins and outs of the war. It is a sobering propaganda showroom covering what was a ferocious but largely failed attempt by the Syrians to recover territory in the Golan Heights which was lost to Israel in 1967.

An interesting anachronism is a display on the theme of Soviet-Syrian space cooperation. Hammers and sickles and smiling portraits of Gorbachev seem to indicate the Syrians' desire to keep alive memories of the good old days.

The museum is open daily from 8 am to 2 pm, except Tuesday, and the fee for admission is S£5.

Salihiyyeh Quarter Strung out along the lower slopes of Jebel Qassioun, the Salihiyyeh quarter first really got off the ground when Nureddin settled Arab refugees from Jerusalem there in the 12th century. What grew up in the subsequent four centuries was a lively if straggly zone of mosques, mausoleums and other religious institutions. Many of them can still be seen from the outside, although only a few can generally be visited. Exceptions to this rule are the early 13th century **Hanbila Mosque** and the 16th century **Mohi ad-Din Mosque**, in which are housed the important tomb of the great 12th century Sufi mystic, Sheikh Mohi ad-Din Ibn al-Arabi.

Saida Zeinab Mosque

About 10 km south of the city centre stands an extraordinary Iranian-built mosque on the site of the burial place of Saida Zeinab, grand-daughter of Mohammed. The glistering gold of the onion-shaped dome topping the mausoleum and the brilliant shades of blue tile work that covers the edifice and its twin, freestanding minarets comes as something of a shock – in much the same way as do the great Shiite monuments of Kerbala in southern Iraq.

The main entrances to the sanctuary are on the northern and southern sides, and non-Muslims may enter the courtyard that surrounds the central mausoleum. This itself they may not penetrate, but you can have a look inside to the riot of colour and chandeliers that bedazzles the faithful. The latter kiss and stroke the silver grate surrounding Zeinab's tomb, seemingly in the hope of thus attracting to themselves some of the holiness of the much venerated descendant of the Prophet.

To get here, take a microbus for *karaj as-Sitt* (S£5) from the microbus station on F Baroudi St. This takes you to a minibus station, from where you can reach the mosque itself by yet another microbus (S£3).

Hammams

Turkish baths are a great way to spend a couple of hours but unfortunately it is usually a men-only activity. A few are close to the Omayyad Mosque, but the more you look the more you will find. Most of them have no signs in English.

The one with the most appeal is the Hammam Nureddin, in the covered street that runs between the Omayyad Mosque and the Street Called Straight. It was founded in the mid-12th century and although often altered in the succeeding centuries, remains one of the grandest as well as oldest functioning hammams in the country. The full massage, bath and sauna with towel, soap and tea will cost you S£240. Men can even have their hair-cut. Open from 9 am to 11 pm daily.

Next door to the Madrassa az-Zahiriyya is a hammam of the same name, most of it in use since the 12th century. The works cost you S£220, and it is open from 8 am to midnight seven days a week.

More or less opposite the Minaret of the Bride is the comparatively bland Hammam as-Silsila, also open seven days a week – from 9 am to 11 pm. It has cottoned on to tourists and charges S£300. Women generally can't get in, but mixed groups can arrange to take the place over – for a hefty consideration in dollars.

Out near Bab Touma is a much less touristed bathhouse, the Hammam Bakri. It opens daily from 8 am to midnight and charges about S£160 for the full scrub and massage. Women can get in by special reservation only.

A couple of blocks west, the Hammam al-Qaymariyyeh on Zuqqaq Hammam (Baths Lane) is a local establishment with no sign in English and a daily women's session from midday to 5 pm.

The 15th century Hammam az-Zein on Qasr al-Hajjaj St is not designed for tourists and charges about S£100. You are probably better off bringing your own soap, towel and the like. Its opening hours are much the same as at the Hammam al-Qaymariyyeh.

Out in the suburb of Jobar are a couple of local hammams near one another. Women's sessions are held at both Hammam al-Atiq (Old Hamman) and Hammam al-Jadid (New Hammam) from midday to 5 pm. Take a taxi and ask for Mawqif al-Hammamat in Jobar.

Don't take any valuables with you to the baths, only the money you need.

Swimming

The Olympic pool at the Tichrin sports complex is open all year round from 6 am to 8 pm, although in the afternoons it is generally open to women only. A single entry ticket costs S£40 (if anyone's taking any notice) or you can get a monthly pass for S£500.

Otherwise, most of the big hotels open their pools in summer. They don't come cheap – the Cham Palace charges S£500 a day to non-guests.

Language Courses

It is possible to enrol in Arabic language courses in Damascus. Most people who desire to secure residence start off at the government Arabic Teaching Institute for Foreigners. For details see the Syria Facts for the Visitor chapter.

Special Events

The Damascus International Fair is a trade exhibition that takes place annually in the first two weeks of September. Although it is of little interest to the traveller, parallel cultural events are occasionally staged by some of the participating countries. Check the *Syria Times* for what's happening.

Places to Stay

With a couple of notable exceptions, the bulk of the cheap accommodation is to be found grouped around Martyrs' Square. A good number of the more expensive hotels are also within quick walking distance of the square. Remember that virtually all hotels above the two star mark (not, by the way, a guarantee of any minimum of quality) charge in US dollars. The prices they ask are quite absurd, largely because they are calculated at the rate of S£11.25 to the dollar. However, there are enough cheap places, and a few of higher quality, that will accept Syrian pounds to make it generally unnecessary for the traveller on a tight budget to worry about parting with lots of dollars for little comfort.

In addition, it appeared at the time of researching that dollar hotels would soon be calculating prices at the standard bank rate of S£42 to the dollar.

Accommodation can get short at peak periods of the year, and especially around the time of the Hajj, when many locals and Turks stop in on their way to or from Mecca. Try to arrive in the morning before places fill up.

If you are looking to stay long term and want to rent a room or an apartment, you could start your search at the noticeboards at the American Language Centre (ALC), British Council, Goethe Institut and the Centre Culturel Français.

Places to Stay – bottom end

Camping If you really want to pitch a tent in an approved ground, *Damascus Camping*, also known as *Harasta Camping* (☎ 445 5870), four km out of town on the road to Homs, charges S£250 per person a day. It has a toilet, shower and cooking facilities, but is hardly worth it, particularly when you consider the inconvenience of having to make your way into the centre and out again. A local microbus runs out there from along Ath-Thaura St. It is popular with some of the overland truck tours that make their way through here.

Hotels Some of the cheapies around Martyrs' Square double as brothels, and either turn away foreigners who genuinely want just a bed or invite them in for a bed with extras. Some will give you a bed and hit you for more than it's worth the next day, since you've taken up valuable space.

In any case, the true travellers' ghetto lies in the Sarouja district. Or more precisely in Bahsa St, a pretty little lane north off Choukri Kouwatli Ave. The *Al-Haramein Hotel* (☎ 222 9487) is an enchanting old Damascene house converted into a hotel. The rooms on three floors are gathered around a pleasant, open courtyard. Beds in share rooms cost S£150, while singles/doubles go for S£200/325. There are two hot showers in the cellar, but you need to time when you go to avoid disappointment. You can even watch satellite TV in the lounge while sipping a tea.

A couple of doors up the road is the equally good *Al-Rabie Hotel* (☎ 221 8373), with rooms and beds for the same prices and, if anything, a still more pleasant courtyard.

If both these places are full but you want to stay in the area, the *Hotel Saadeh*, a couple of lanes west of Bahsa St, has beds for S£150 a throw. This place is fairly basic and not a patch on the other two.

In the Martyrs' Square area you could do worse than the *Syrian Grand Hotel* (☎ 221 5233), a block west of the citadel. It has beds for S£150 in sometimes quite large rooms with fan. Some of the doubles, with private toilet and cold shower, are not bad value at S£300. There is a hot communal shower.

A block west is another quite decent place, the *Radwan Hotel* (☎ 222 1654) which charges a flat S£200 per person in a single, double or bigger shared room. The beds are comfortable and some rooms have private shower and balcony.

Virtually opposite, the *Ghassan Hotel* (☎ 221 4606) is OK if you can get a double with balcony on the lower floors. Some of the singles at the top of the building are frankly quite awful. The communal hot shower is on the 1st floor. Singles/doubles go for S£200/350.

A good, clean place is the *Grand Ghazi Hotel* (☎ 221 4581) on Furat Ave. Decent sized rooms with basin and fan cost S£250/350.

Although far from spectacular, the *Hotel*

Qasr al-Chark (☎ 221 2864) has some acceptable doubles for S£300. Quite a few of the neighbouring hotels are brothels, and there have been reports that this place doubles as one too.

The *Zahraa Hotel* (☎ 222 5375) has pretty respectable rooms and a pleasant reception area. There is hot water in the communal showers, but in the morning only. Rooms cost S£250/400.

More of a last resort is the *Hotel Said* (☎ 221 1604). It's OK if you take a shared room with balcony (S£150 per person), but the singles are pretty awful and cost S£300. It costs S£50 for a hot shower too.

In the street next to the Hejaz railway station, *L'Oasis Hotel*, or 'Al-Waha' in Arabic (☎ 222 7724), is quiet and secure and the guys running it are helpful. Singles/doubles with fan and bath cost S£250/400.

Places to Stay – middle

Going up-market a bit generally means a fairly hefty leap in prices, and not always a commensurate increase in quality. You'll be lucky, even with bargaining, to find anything much under about US$15 for a single. Many of these places are two star on some technicality, but offer little more than the cheapies.

One of the best ones is the *Sultan Hotel* (☎ 222 5768) just west of the Hejaz railway station on Moussallam Baroudi Rd. Good, clean rooms with hot water and breakfast included are US$22/30, and the staff are helpful.

For a little more you will do even better with the *Alaa Tower Hotel* (☎ 223 1692). This is actually a chain, but if you try the one tucked away opposite the Centre Culturel Français you'll get quality singles/doubles with satellite TV for S£1300/2200. If it is full, it will send you to one of its other six branches.

Nearby is the *Hotel Venezia* (☎ 222 1224) on Midan Youssef al-Azmeh St. A favourite with Dutch tour groups and Russians, it is a

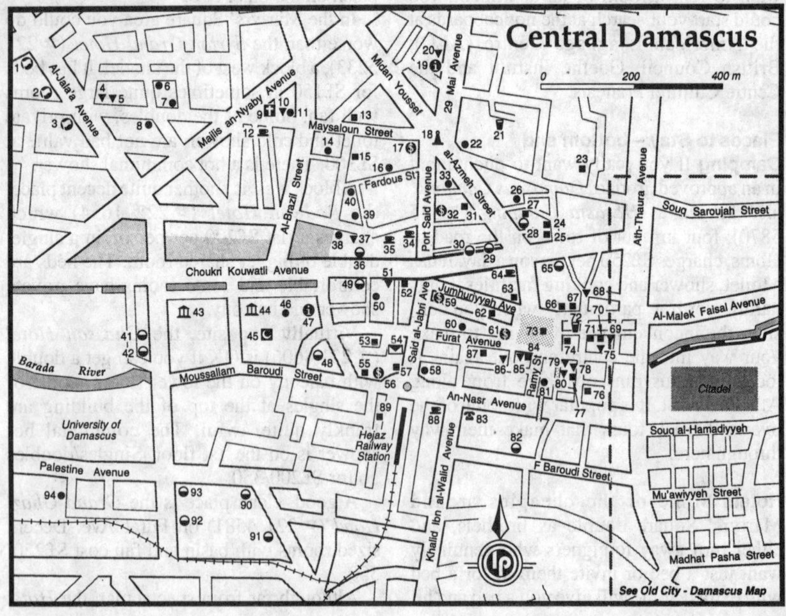

curious sort of place and reasonable (if hardly outstanding) value at US$36/40 plus taxes.

Right behind the post office is the *Afamia Hotel* (☎ 222 0182), which has adequate rooms with ensuite bath and noisy air-con. It is sometimes necessary to book rooms, which cost US$21/24, a day or two in advance.

Slightly grander is the *Orient Palace Hotel*, across the road from the Hejaz railway station. Rooms are a little expensive at US$32/39 (or US$34/41 with a TV and fridge). It has retained something of its old-world, French Mandate charm.

On Martyrs' Square itself is the *Omar al-Khayyam Hotel* (☎ 221 1666) which is overrated and overpriced at US$45/56. The price includes TV, noisy air-con and breakfast. More reasonable, and also on the square, is the *Ramsis Hotel* which has singles/doubles/triples for US$17/23/27. Other similar hotels include the *Hotel Siyaha* on Martyrs' Square and the *Samir Palace Hotel* (☎ 221 9502). The latter offers rooms for US$28/35. A couple of newer looking but fairly shoddily built establishments in Jumhuriyyeh Ave are the *Hotel Al-Imad* (☎ 222 5704), with rooms for US$25/33 including breakfast, and the *Hotel Altal* (☎ 221 9010).

PLACES TO STAY

13 Cham Palace Hotel
15 Fardoss Tower Hotel (& The Pub)
23 Hotel Saadeh
24 Al-Rabie Hotel
25 Al-Haramein Hotel
27 Alaa Tower Hotel
31 Hotel Venezia
52 Hotel Semiramis
53 Al-Afamia Hotel
55 Sultan Hotel
57 Orient Palace Hotel
62 Al-Fardous Tower Hotel
63 Omar al-Khayyam Hotel
66 Hotel Altal
67 Hotel Al-Imad
70 Zahraa Hotel
71 Hotel Said
73 Hotel Siyaha
74 Samir Palace Hotel
76 Radwan Hotel
77 Ghassan Hotel
84 Ramsis Hotel
87 Grand Ghazi Hotel
89 L'Oasis Hotel

PLACES TO EAT

4 Morocco Restaurant
5 Station One Restaurant
10 Pizza Roma
12 Shimi Café
20 Al-Kamal Restaurant
27 Alaa Tower Restaurant
35 Café
37 An-Nadwa Restaurant
51 Radwan Restaurant
68 Vegetable Market & Kebab Stalls
69 Al-Awami Restaurant
75 Sahloul Restaurant
78 Ghassan Restaurant
79 Al-Arabi Restaurant
80 Al-Arabi Restaurant (No 2)
85 Shawarma Stands
86 Al-Aricha Restaurant

OTHER

1 Belgian Embassy
2 Egyptian Embassy
3 Jordanian Embassy
6 Goethe Institut
7 Marmou Car Rental
8 Lido Music Store
9 Church
11 Dawn Travel
14 Librairie Avicenne
16 Syrianair
17 Commercial Bank of Syria
18 Midan Youssef al-Azmeh (Peasant's Monument)
19 Tourist Office
21 Damascus Workers Club
22 Haig Camera Repairs
26 Centre Culturel Français
28 Microbuses to Muhajireen
29 Zeitouni Bus Company
30 Airport Bus Station
32 Commercial Bank of Syria (Cash Only)
33 Librairie Universelle
34 Café Havana
36 Turkish Bus Station
38 Madrassa al-'Aziyya
39 Sudan Airways & American Express
40 Nahas Travel & Thomas Cook
41 City Microbus Station
42 Damas Tour & Qadmous Bus Companies
43 National Museum
44 Army Museum
45 Takiyyeh as-Sulaymaniyyeh Mosque
46 Artisanat (Handicraft Market)
47 Ministry of Tourism
48 Bus Station
49 Luxury Bus Station
50 DHL
54 Central Post Office
56 Commercial Bank of Syria
58 Syrianair
59 Commercial Bank of Syria
60 2nd Immigration & Passports Office
61 Exchange Booth
64 Rooftop Café
65 Microbuses to North/East Bus Stations & Jobar
72 Bar Karnak
73 Martyrs' Square (Al-Merjeh)
81 Liquor Store
82 Microbuses to South Bus Station &SaidaZeinab Stop
83 Telephone Office
88 Open Air Café
90 Microbuses (Mostly West)
91 Pullman Buses & Taxis to Saudi Arabia
92 Karnak Bus Station
93 Service Taxis to Amman & Beirut
94 Central Immigration Office

Heading up to the top end is the *Al-Faradis Hotel* (☎ 224 6546; fax 224 7009), tucked away in a side street a block west of Martyrs' Square. Good but fairly sterile rooms with TV and international phone go for US$76/92 plus 10% taxes, which includes breakfast. If you murmur the word 'discount' the price should drop by 25% at least. There is a collection of hotels in a similar price category (and some more expensive still) between the Choukri Kouwatli Ave flyover and Youssef al-Azmeh Square.

SYRIA

Places to Stay – top end

For those who want the best available, there's the Sheraton, Meridien and four hotels of the Cham chain, where the amount spent on a bed for the night is enough to keep most travellers going for a week or two.

The *Meridien Hotel* (☎ 371 8730; fax 371 8661) is on the north bank of the Barada River, about 10 minutes' walk north-west of the centre. Rooms start at US$205/240 and head upwards. The *Sheraton Hotel* (☎ 373 4630) is pleasantly located by the river, a km further west along Choukri Kouwatli Ave. You can read the latest news on agency teletype printouts in the foyer. It is a little more expensive again, at US$220/260 plus taxes.

The *Cham Palace* (☎ 223 2300; fax 221 2398), complete with revolving restaurant, is one of the more conveniently located of the biggies. It's just one block west of Youssef al-Azmeh Square and is one of a chain. Singles/doubles start at US$150/160, plus 10% taxes. Two smaller versions, the *Jala'a* and *Techrine* hotels, further away from the centre, have singles/doubles for US$90/110. The Techrine is near the Damascus International Fair and the Jala'a is out west in Mezzeh.

Out on the airport road, the *Ebla Cham* (☎ 224 1900; fax 541 0070) has singles starting from US$225 and peaking at US$4400 for a presidential room!

Not far from Martyrs' Square is the totally refurbished *Semiramis Hotel* (☎ 221 3813), with singles/doubles coming in at US$200/220 plus 10% tax.

Places to Eat

Old City Since most people like to spend the bulk of their time in Damascus in the old city, it's a logical place to look for a bite to eat too. There are a few possibilities ranging from the very cheap through to rather pricey. About 30m east of the Omayyad Mosque is probably the best value *felafel place* in all of the town. A truly fat felafel will cost you S£25. Just outside the city walls on the west side, opposite the Ad-Darwishiyyeh Mosque, is a good little restaurant with a 'family' section upstairs.

Along one of the covered market lanes a block west of the Omayyad Mosque is a clutch of hole-in-the-wall eateries. Among them is something of a surprise packet, the *Abu al-'Azz Restaurant*. Head upstairs and you'll find a bright, spacious place spread out over several floors. A wide choice of well-prepared dishes is on offer and you can eat well for under S£200. There's no alcohol – but sometimes there's a live band.

Considerably more expensive and tending to cater to tourists is the nearby *Old Damascus Restaurant* (☎ 221 8810), situated behind the citadel. It is sumptuously decked out in the manner of a well-to-do oriental mansion. The food is reasonable but you'll get little change from S£500. Along similar lines and pricier still is the *Omayyad Palace Restaurant* (☎ 222 0826) where a full dinner will cost S£750 with a somewhat dubious, if good-humoured, performance by a couple of whirling dervishes who don't so much as whirl as fall about the place. Another in the same genre is the *1001 Nights* ('Alf Layla Wa Layla' in Arabic) east of the Omayyad Mosque.

Restaurant La Guitare, just (south) off the Street Called Straight, has a pleasant rooftop eating area in summer.

Around Martyrs' Square This area is crowded with eateries, and several cheap juice and shawarma stands right on the square. Juices cost anything up to S£50, depending on how huge your glass is. For the do-it-yourself crowd, there is a good fruit and vegetable market wedged in-between

Martyrs' Square and Choukri Kouwatli Ave. An-Nasr Ave is also packed with places to pick up a quick shawarma.

Those on a skimpy budget in need of a change from felafel can head for the *Radwan Restaurant*, on Choukri Kouwatli Ave. You can feast on rice, potato and bean stews or even broiled chicken. With a soft drink thrown in you can eat a filling meal for under S£100.

A good sign is a full restaurant, and one of the best eateries in the cheapish bracket is the *Al-Arabi*, now a chain of two restaurants a little way off the square towards the citadel. It offers an unusually wide range of meat and vegetable dishes (including that old favourite, lamb's testicles). A hearty meal won't cost much more than S£250, and the filling vegetable dishes are cheaper still. There are menus in English and you can take away.

The *Ghassan Restaurant* has excellent chicken, and a filling meal with typical side orders like hummus, salad, bread and a Coke will cost you about S£160. Similar in terms of price and what you get is the *Al-Aricha Restaurant*, which has had some favourable reports from travellers.

The glitzy 'three star' *Sahloul Restaurant*, just off Martyrs' Square, has all the standard fare as well as a variety of meat and vegetable stews, rice and macaroni, but is rather overpriced. A big meal of chicken shish tawooq (marinated and barbecued pieces of chicken) and side orders costs S£250. Similar is *Al-Amawi*, with its main entrance around the block.

Elsewhere in Damascus There is any number of restaurants in Damascus, and throughout Syria for that matter, where a good meal will cost around S£200. There is a string of them along 29 Mai Ave, and the *Al-Kamal Restaurant*, next to the tourist office, is typical. Most of the more expensive places also serve beer, something that cannot always be taken for granted.

Better value is *An-Nadwa Restaurant* in the street behind the Turkish bus station. It's a pleasant location and S£200 will get you a decent meal of kebabs with the usual side dishes. If it's just a beer you want, a half litre of Barada costs S£40.

You can dine al fresco at the *Al-Khater Restaurant*, on the 3rd floor in the Hotel Venezia, but the food is overpriced and overdone. Better value are the restaurants in the Alaa Tower hotels. Several travellers have given them good reports. The *Toledo Restaurant*, up in the embassy district, has nothing to do with Spain but serves up decent Syrian cuisine in somewhat swisher than usual surroundings.

Morocco Restaurant, on Maysaloun St near Al-Jala'a Ave, is a reasonable version of a fast-food joint, doing hamburgers and other food more Middle Eastern in appearance. Next door, *Station One Restaurant* offers a mix of Syrian and European dishes. The menu of the day can be very good and makes a welcome change from the standard fare. It'll set you back about S£500 per person. This place serves no alcohol.

For a real splurge, head for the revolving restaurant in the *Cham Palace Hotel*. The food is unexceptional and pricey, but the atmosphere is great.

If you have access to private transport and you're in Damascus in the summer months, head out of town along the Beirut road. There is a string of riverside restaurants along a particularly pleasant and shady stretch of the Barada.

Foreign Cuisine *Pizza Roma*, just off Maysaloun St, is run by a guy who used to work for Pizza Hut in Abu Dhabi. He has adapted the idea and this eat-in or takeaway joint does a good American-style deep-pan pizza for less than S£100. *Aldar Restaurant*, overlooking the small park in off 'Adnan al-Malky Ave, also does an OK pizza, but the best of the lot is *Milano*, where the pizzas are good and cost up to S£90. It lies in a huddle of about a half dozen restaurants on a small square collectively known to the Damascus expat community as 'Restaurant Circle'. The offerings here include the vaguely French *Joy*, *La Chaumiére* and *Le Chevalier*.

For pricey Italian food with a good reputation among expats, try *Luigi's* at the

Sheraton. If you feel like Chinese, the restaurant in the Cham Palace Hotel is reasonably authentic. You will almost definitely spend more than S£500 in these places.

Syria's only Japanese eating house, the *Sakura Restaurant* has had the thumbs up from Japanese tourists, but you'll need S£500 or more per person.

Still in the process of creation is a kind of international restaurant bazaar known as the *Palais deș Nobles* off Choukri Kouwatli Ave, not far in from Umawiyyin Square. So far it has a mediocre and pricey Mexican place and similarly uninspiring French restaurant – but maybe it'll improve. For TexMex, you could pop into *La Hacienda* at the Meridien Hotel.

Dessert For one of the best ice creams you are likely to taste, head for *Bakdach* in the Souq al-Hamadiyyeh. There is at least one 'imitation' place before you get to it (they are both on the right heading towards the Omayyad Mosque), but wait for the best.

A bowl of ice cream, covered with pistachio nuts, or sahlab (a kind of smooth, sweet milk pudding) covered with same, costs S£10 and is worth every piastre. That's all they serve, but they do it well.

If you're inclined to enjoy sipping cappuccino and nibbling cakes, you could do worse than the *Shimi Café* in Maysaloun St near the Cham Palace hotel. Its patisserie is one of several along this rather swish drag, where you will also find imported American ice creams.

Entertainment

Cinema Most of the cinemas around show pretty appalling fare. This is not consistently the case however, and occasionally you will get a good, not overly censored flick at the Cham Palace cinema (in the hotel complex) and one or two other cinemas around the centre. Cheaper seats in the standard cinema cost S£25 to S£35. For better quality movies, the Cham Palace charges up to S£75 – but it has two very wide-screen cinemas.

Bars & Nightclubs Quite a few restaurants serve alcohol, but finding a straightforward bar can be a quite a challenge in Damascus. Inside the old city there is a pokey little men-only liquor store-cum-bar on the Street Called Straight. A classier act where a beer will cost you about S£100 is the *Piano Bar*, in the same building as Café La Terrasse.

A popular haunt with locals and backpackers alike is the *Bar Karnak*. You can eat here, but most people come to drink beer or araq until one or two in the morning. It's above the Hotel Siyaha – just head up the stairs in the street entrance off the square.

The *Damascus Workers Club*, off 29 Mai Ave, has a pleasant beer garden arrangement. It also serves food.

Otherwise, the only real choice seems to be between hotel bars and sleazy nightclubs. The latter you will find scattered about the new town. Of the former, *The Pub* in the Sheraton is popular with expats and one of the better places for meeting long-termers in Damascus. Another bar of the same name in the *Al-Fardous Tower Hotel* features a little light jazz piano in the evenings to accompany your S£175 can of Carlsberg.

The *Meridien Hotel* has quite a pleasant disco playing a mix of Middle Eastern and western pop. The entry price of S£500 includes one drink. Subsequent tipples cost S£250 a throw. It's a similar story at the *Jet Set* disco in the Cham Palace hotel.

Cafés There are several cafés of the traditional, men-only type scattered around the Martyrs' Square part of town, including a nice one on An-Nasr Ave, near the Hejaz railway station, and the rooftop place on the corner of the Choukri Kouwatli Ave flyover. But the two prize-winners are the *Café Naufara* and its more expensive opposite number just tucked away in the shadow of the Omayyad Mosque's eastern wall. Either of them make a fine spot for sipping tea or indulging in a nargileh. At the former, a local story-teller pops in for an hour or so in the early evening to entertain the locals.

A recent and very pleasant arrival is the *Café La Terrasse*, housed in a refurbished Damascene mansion between Ananias' house and Bab ash-Sharqi. It also has a bar and sells a little tourist kitsch as a sideline.

Café Havana, on Port Said Ave in the new town, has something of a history as a haunt for coup planners and other plotters in the days before Hafez al-Assad got a firm grip on the country.

Things to Buy

Many of the typical products foreigners look out for in the markets of Damascus can be found all over the old city. Nevertheless there are some general areas where certain wares predominate. Barely after entering Souq al-Hamadiyyeh from the west you find yourself surrounded by **rug and carpet stores**. They can be found elsewhere, but this is where you'll strike the greatest concentration of them – and the greatest pressure to buy. Plenty of other stuff can be found here too. Further in and covering a goodly sized patch between Souq al-Hamadiyyeh and Mu'a-wiyyeh St is the **gold souq**.

A little way south of the Omayyad Mosque you run into the **herbs & potions market**, which soon gives way along Hassan Kharet Bzouriyeh St to sweets stalls and then the **spice market**.

SYRIA

Pipe Dreams

When you arrive in New York for the first time, it is easy to feel you have just landed on a movie set – the cars really are that big and steam actually does puff up from grills in the streets. In much the same way, to walk into an old-style café in Damascus is to feel like you have just stepped into one of the great all-time cinema clichés. People really *do* smoke those complicated looking waterpipes – just like every self-respecting pasha in the movies!

Smoked pretty much wherever the Ottoman Empire held sway at one time or another, they have acquired a plethora of names. To Syrians such a contraption is known as the *nargileh (or 'narjileh'*, but the Egyptian pronunciation seems to have established itself). Just what the pipe has to do with the coconut, the other meaning of the word, is anyone's guess. To westerners it is known as the hookah or, more expressively, the hubble bubble (or even as hubbly bubbly). You'll understand why when you hear the gurgling sounds emanating from the glass water container as smoke is sucked down from the tobacco atop a long metal tube and passes on to another flexible tube on its way to your lungs. In Egypt they call it *shisha* and ask if you *tishrab shisha*? (Do wish to drink some shisha?)

Local men (it is almost exclusively a male activity) get hours of soothing pleasure from these pipes, but contrary to popular western wishful thinking, there is rarely any hash or dope burning under the lumps of red-hot charcoal. Apart from a standard rough shag tobacco, you can also get *'asl* (tobacco drenched in honey) or *tufah* (the apple version) both of which give off a much more pleasant odour. ■

A *nargileh* (or '*narjileh*') – more commonly known as the hookah

Other areas to look for souvenir shops include those around the west face of the Omayyad Mosque and the eastern end of the Street Called Straight.

There is no substitute for walking around and comparing quality yourself, but a reliable store worth inspecting early on is that of Tony Stephan (☎ 221 2198) at No 156 in Souq al-Hamadiyyeh. This place carries a good range of quality merchandise from textiles through inlaid woodwork and jewellery to copper and brassware. Pressure is at a minimum and a browse here will provide you with a good point of reference for further shopping.

Another pleasure to the eye is the Azem Ecole, housed in a former madrassa (see Azem Ecole earlier in this chapter) on Mu'awiyyeh St. Here you will also find a wide range of goods and have the chance to see silk products being hand-woven.

For a rundown on the kinds of souvenirs you might like to pick up, see Things to Buy in the Regional Facts for the Visitor chapter.

Getting There & Away

Air You'll find almost all the airline offices and travel agencies for international travel in or around Fardous St, a small side lane west of Port Said Ave, just before Youssef al-Azmeh Square.

For details on international flights to Damascus, see the Syria Getting There & Away chapter.

Some travellers have reported being subjected to repeated searches by unpleasant plain-clothes officials prior to boarding planes at Damascus airport.

There are several Syrianair offices scattered about the city centre (for example, in Fardous Street, Baghdad Avenue and Said al-Jabri Avenue), some of them marked on the Damascus maps in this section. Syrianair flies once or twice daily to Aleppo for S£600. Three times a week (Sunday, Tuesday and Thursday) a flight departs for Qamishle (S£900), and once a week to Deir ez-Zur (Wednesday, S£600) and Lattakia (Friday, S£500).

Bus/Minibus There are two main bus stations (known as 'garages') in Damascus for regular buses and minibuses. There are also a couple of minor bus stations. These buses run to no set schedule and just leave when full.

For buses north, east and to the coast, the station is about three km east of the centre past the traffic circle known as Abbasid Square (or Abbasayeen). To get there catch a local microbus for karajat (garages) from Choukri Kouwatli Ave, just short of the Ath-Thaura Ave flyover.

This is the cheapest category of buses. Estimated journey times should be taken with a grain of salt.

Bus/Minibus Fares

destination	fare	time (hours)
Aleppo	S£60	five-six
Deir ez-Zur	S£106	seven
Hama	S£32 (S£45 minibus)	three
Homs	S£27 (S£35 minibus)	2½
Qamishle	S£150	nine
Tartus	S£53	four

The station for buses south is just south of the huge Bab Moussala Square roundabout, about two km from the centre. Take a local microbus from the microbus station of F Baroudi St and get off at the first stop after the roundabout. Minibuses leave for Der'a (S£25, two hours), Suweida (S£22, 1¾ hours) and Shahba (S£18, 1¼ hours). More modern microbuses also serve Der'a (S£45) and Suweida (S£39).

In addition, there are two smaller bus stations for buses doing short runs north (such as Maalula and Saydnaya) and west (like Bloudan and Zabadani). See the appropriate Getting There & Away sections for these destinations.

Karnak Bus The Karnak bus station is about a 15 minute walk to the west of Martyrs'

Square. It's a big, bustling place that even has a reasonable restaurant. Although the country's flag bus line, it now competes with many other companies and is no longer anything particularly special. One sure sign that Syrians are not impressed has been the elimination of some routes and reduction in services.

Still, Karnak's buses go from Damascus to most major towns in Syria. Buses (not all of them Karnak) also leave here for destinations in Turkey, Lebanon, Jordan and the Gulf. It is a good idea to book at least one day in advance.

There is a daily departure at 10 pm for Istanbul (S£1200, 30 hours) that also stops at Iskenderun (S£500), Adana (S£600) and Ankara (S£1000). It is cheaper to get local transport to Aleppo or the Turkish border and get Turkish buses from there.

Twice daily, buses leave for Amman in Jordan and cost US$5 or JD4. You can't pay in Syrian pounds. The first departure is at 7 am; the second (actually the Jordanian JETT bus making the return trip) at 3 pm. The journey takes six or seven hours, depending on delays at the border.

Karnak buses leave at the same times for Beirut in Lebanon. The trip takes about three hours and costs S£125.

A Saudi bus company, Aman, has a daily service to Riyadh (S£2000, 24 hours), which also goes to Jeddah. There are occasionally departures for Kuwait, too. You will be asked to present your Saudi visa, and it may pay to get a transit visa for Jordan in advance.

Karnak Bus Fares

destination	fare	time (hours)
Aleppo	S£100	five
Der'a	S£30	1½
Hama	S£60	2½
Homs	S£50	two
Lattakia	S£90	five
Palmyra	S£90	four (via Homs)
Safita	S£75	three
Tartus	S£75	3½

There are departures at le[...] many destinations within Sy[...]

Pullman Bus The pullman bus station is next door to the Karnak bus station and competing companies run most of the main routes inside Syria at slightly lower rates than Karnak. Sample Pullman bus fares from Damascus are: Homs, S£39; Aleppo, S£86; Lattakia, S£80; Deir ez-Zur, S£110; Raqqa, S£130. See the Syria Getting Around chapter for more details.

Luxury Bus A new station for some of the more expensive bus companies is about 150m west of the Hejaz railway station. Al-Ryan is one of the firms that operates from here.

Luxury Bus Fares

destination	fare	time (hours)
Aleppo	S£150	five
Beirut (Lebanon)	S£200	three
Deir ez-Zur	S£150	six
Hama	S£100	2½
Hassake	S£250	seven
Homs	S£75	two
Lattakia	S£140	five
Palmyra	S£125	three (direct)
Qamishle	S£340	nine
Suweida	S£40 (microbus)	two
Tartus	S£110	3½

Be warned that some of the offices in fact act as agents for buses with different departure points. This is the case with the direct microbuses to Bosra with Damas Tour. These leave seven times a day from beneath the big flyover (Jisr ar-Rais or President Bridge) west of the National Museum and cost S£45. Another quality company, Qadmous, is based here. These big modern buses serve most destinations, particularly along the coast. The fare to Lattakia is S£150. Al-Ahliah, another good company, is based somewhat out of the centre along Palestine Ave. Zeitouni, with an office on

Choukri Kouwatli Ave, is also very good, but is probably about the most expensive company of the lot.

Turkish Bus There is a bus station for Turkish buses just where the Choukri Kouwatli flyover begins. Buses leave for Istanbul and other destinations from here at 10 pm and tickets can be bought at the bus station or from travel agencies dotted around the city. They cost more than the bus leaving from the Karnak station (S£1500 to Istanbul), but in any case the same advice applies on making your way first to Aleppo by internal transport before picking up a Turkish bus. It may be necessary to book in advance.

Train The Hejaz railway station is right in the centre of town. It's a majestic building, a fitting departure point for the Hajj with a classic, intricately decorated ceiling inside. Outside stands one of the old steam engines designed to take pilgrims on their way to Mecca. Before you get too excited, most trains nowadays actually leave from the Khaddam railway station, about five km away. Trains are infrequent and slower than the buses and run daily to Homs, Hama, Aleppo, Raqqa, Deir ez-Zur, Hassake, Qamishle, Tartus and Lattakia. The train trip to Qamishle can take 16 hours or more. A shuttle bus runs between the Hejaz station and Khaddam station to meet trains. It leaves the Hejaz station at 4 pm and 11 pm.

The only trains leaving from the Hejaz railway station are the Friday and Sunday run south to Der'a (S£26, three hours) and the summertime day-trippers' steam train to the mountain 'beauty spot', Zabadani (the train is known to some expat wits as the *Zabadani Flyer*). The Sunday Der'a train goes on to Amman (leaving at 7.30 am) and costs S£160/120 in 1st/2nd class.

The big disadvantage with the trains is that the railway station is usually right on the outskirts of town and it can be a hassle to get to the centre.

Train Fares

destination	sleeper	1st class	2nd class
Aleppo	S£325	S£85	S£57
Deir ez-Zur	S£500	S£153	S£103
Hama		S£57	S£40
Homs		S£47	S£34
Lattakia		S£90	S£60
Qamishle	S£740	S£198	S£132
Tartus		S£67	S£46

Service Taxi There is a service-taxi station next to the Karnak bus station. Taxis leave throughout the day and night for Amman (S£385 or JD5.500, five hours), Irbid (S£226, 3½ hours) and Zarqa (S£297, 4½ hours) in Jordan. Likewise the trains also run to various destinations in Lebanon and Aleppo.

There is another service-taxi station behind the Pullman bus station. Service taxis to Riyadh cost S£3000 a head.

Service Taxi Fares

destination	fare	time (hours)
Aleppo	S£150	five
Baalbek	S£173	two
Beirut Armoun	S£291	3½
Beirut Kahala	S£191	2½
Sidon	S£268	3½
Tripoli	S£416	4½

Car Rental Europcar has agents in most of the big hotels. Other companies include Avis (☎ 223 9664), 'Uthman bin Affan St and Budget (☎ 224 6725), Palestine Ave. The latter are also situated at Al-Baramkeh St (☎ 222 6964).

Of the many local companies that have appeared in recent years, Marmou (☎ 335959), has an office on Maysaloun St. For more information on what to expect in terms of prices and conditions, see the Syria Getting Around chapter.

Getting Around

The Airport Damascus international airport is 25 km south-east of Damascus. Local buses leave every half hour from next to the Choukri Kouwatli Ave flyover from 5.30 am to 11 pm. The trip costs S£10 and takes about 45 minutes.

Taxis should not cost more than S£300, and even that is fairly generous. Another option is to call the government-run Transtour (☎ 222 4414) and hire one of its cars. It has a taxi-style arrangement between the airport and central Damascus for US$10.

Bus Bigger town buses still operate, but the microbuses are handier. Tickets cost S£5 or you can get a book of five at the ticket booths for S£20.

Microbus Damascus old city buses are ceding ground quickly to a mass onslaught by nimble little microbuses (also known as '*servees*'). The city is compact and you shouldn't need to use either except in a couple of cases. The microbuses run set routes, and generally pick up and set down at marked stops, although the drivers are pretty flexible about this. The fare ranges from S£3 (if anyone has coins) to S£5.

The main central terminal is at Jisr ar-Rais, the flyover west of the National Museum. From here you can get microbuses to Bab Touma, Muhajireen, Mezzeh, Abbasid Square (or Abbasayeen; for Saydnaya and Maalula) and karajat (the north-east bus station). The latter two can also be picked up along Choukri Kouwatli Ave.

Microbuses for the south bus station ('*karaj*') near Bab Moussala leave from another station on F Baroudi St, as do others that take you to the minibus for Saida Zeinab Mosque.

Route names are posted in Arabic on the front of the bus.

Taxi All the taxis are yellow, and there are hundreds of them. They are cheap, but make sure the driver uses the meter. A cross-town ride should cost between S£15 and S£25. From Martyrs' Square (Al-Merjeh) to Mezzeh costs about S£40, while the ride from Bab ash-Sharqi to Mezzeh will come in at S£50.

Around Damascus

AD-DUMEIR

The so-called Roman temple of Ad-Dumeir (or Ad-Dmeir), a dusty, nondescript little village some 40 km north-east of Damascus on the Palmyra road, is something of a conundrum. The conventional wisdom has it as a temple dating from the 3rd century and dedicated to Zeus, but there is also some suggestion it had a double function, starting life as a public fountain. Other evidence points to an earlier Nabataean religious building on the same site.

The squat rectangular structure sits deep in a pit that resulted from intense excavations and subsequent reconstruction work. A local caretaker has the keys and will let you in (a small tip for his trouble is recommended). You can see Greek inscriptions on the wall as you enter and again in several spots inside. The temple is off the main drag about 100m east of the microbus stop. Transport from the main north-east bus station in Damascus is fairly regular and costs S£15. A few km further east and just off the road to Palmyra are the scant remains of a 2nd century Roman camp.

SAYDNAYA

At first glance you could just about mistake the modern Greek Orthodox convent lording it over the Christian town of Saydnaya for another Crusader castle. In fact the convent stands on the site of one of the most ancient and important places of Christian pilgrimage in the Middle East. In one of its chapels is housed an image of the Virgin Mary attributed by lore to St Luke and to which for centuries have been attributed all manner of miracles. The chapel – off to the left from the main entrance – is crammed with modern icons and other testimonies of faith by the convent's visitors.

The town itself, although set in a quite spectacular position in the heart of the Anti-Lebanon range, has little else of obvious interest, and so makes an easy half-day excursion from Damascus.

Getting There & Away

Microbuses run regularly from a small bus station south of the Abbasid Stadium, in the east of Damascus. The trip costs S£12 and takes about 40 minutes. To get to the microbus station, catch one of the local microbuses for Abbasayeen and get off at the stadium. From there walk a long block south and the station is on your left.

MAALULA

Set in a narrow valley in the foothills of the Anti-Lebanon range, Maalula is an interesting little village where many of the houses, plastered in pastel yellow, blue and mauve colours, cling precariously to the cliff face. The multicoloured paint job lends the place a splash of brightness missing in most of Syria's concrete-grey villages.

Although some Muslims live here, most of Maalula's residents are Greek Catholics. The village's real claim to fame, however, is that a dialect of Aramaic is still spoken here. Dating from the 1st millennium BC, Aramaic was the language that Jesus spoke, and in which were first written the Lord's Prayer and the Old Testament book of Daniel. Two nearby settlements, Jaba'deen and Bakh'a, are also Aramaic-speaking.

At the main intersection in the village, the road forks. The right fork leads to the Convent of St Thecla, tucked snugly against the cliff. The convent itself is of no particular interest, but carry on past it along a narrow cleft cut through the rock by the waters draining the plateau above the village. Turn back to the left where the cleft opens out and walk along the cliff edge for some spectacular **views** of the town and valley. The atmosphere is unfortunately spoiled by the presence of the sprawling Safir Hotel.

Past the hotel is another **convent**, dedicated to St Sergius (Mar Sarkis). The low doorway leads into the monastery where there is a small Byzantine church. Take the road leading down from the monastery and it brings you out at the road fork in the village.

Places to Stay & Eat

Maalula is an easy day trip from Damascus, and it is hard to believe that many people would want to spend the money availing themselves of the services of an expensive hotel there. However, the *Safir Hotel* (☎ 012-770250) offers four star accommodation at US$105/120 for singles/doubles, along with a bar, pool and restaurant. It also does a Sunday buffet for S£500.

In the centre of town and by the Convent of St Thecla there are a few small snack places and shops. You may be able to stay overnight at the convent.

Getting There & Away

Microbuses run to Maalula every hour or so from the same spot you get Saydnaya microbuses. The trip costs S£22 and takes about an hour.

ZABADANI, BLOUDAN & 'AIN AL-FIJEH

These three small towns are in the valley of the Barada River as it makes its way down from the Anti-Lebanon range to the Ghouta Oasis and Damascus.

The countryside is very pleasant but the main attraction is the narrow-gauge train trip up the valley, which you can take any day of the week in summer. Damascenes flock there on Friday to escape the city and picnic by the river. The train is loaded with a real variety of people – from elderly veiled women with children and grandchildren in tow, to teenage boys sporting their latest western clothes and ghetto-blasters.

The train crawls as far as Zabadani (1200m), taking about three hours to cover the 50 km from Damascus. It then stops for about three hours before making the return trip. If that's too long for you, catch a microbus down to 'Ain al-Fijeh to have a look around before picking up the train (or another microbus) on the downward journey, or simply ride all the way back to Damascus. Not far from Zabadani lies a small Druze monument marking the spot (according to the local tall tale) where Biblical Cain buried Abel after slaughtering him.

Bloudan (1400m) is seven km further on again from Zabadani and cannot be reached by train. Bloudan is another in place in a line of favourite weekend getaway spots for stressed out Damascenes. Although pleasant enough, it really doesn't have much to offer the traveller.

Getting There & Away

Trains (the *Zabadani Flyer*) only run during the summer, leaving from the Hejaz railway station at 8 am. The fare is S£12.

Microbuses leave from the station next to the Karnak bus station. They take about an hour and cost S£20 to Zabadani and S£22 to Bloudan.

South of Damascus

The area from Damascus south to the Jordanian border, about 100 km away, is fertile agricultural land and intensively farmed, particularly with watermelons. In the late summer you'll probably see more melons for sale by the side of the road than you've ever seen in your life. Often, however, it looks as though the farmers are trying to grow polythene bags – the fields are littered with them.

The Golan Heights in the south-west were originally Syrian territory but have been largely in Israeli hands since the Arab-Israeli war of 1967. For the Syrians, Golan remains the most pressing issue in the peace process, even ahead of resolution of the Palestinian dilemma. Until now, Damascus has maintained that any peace deal with Israel must involve the total withdrawal of Israeli forces and settlers from Golan.

The area known as the Hauran is a black

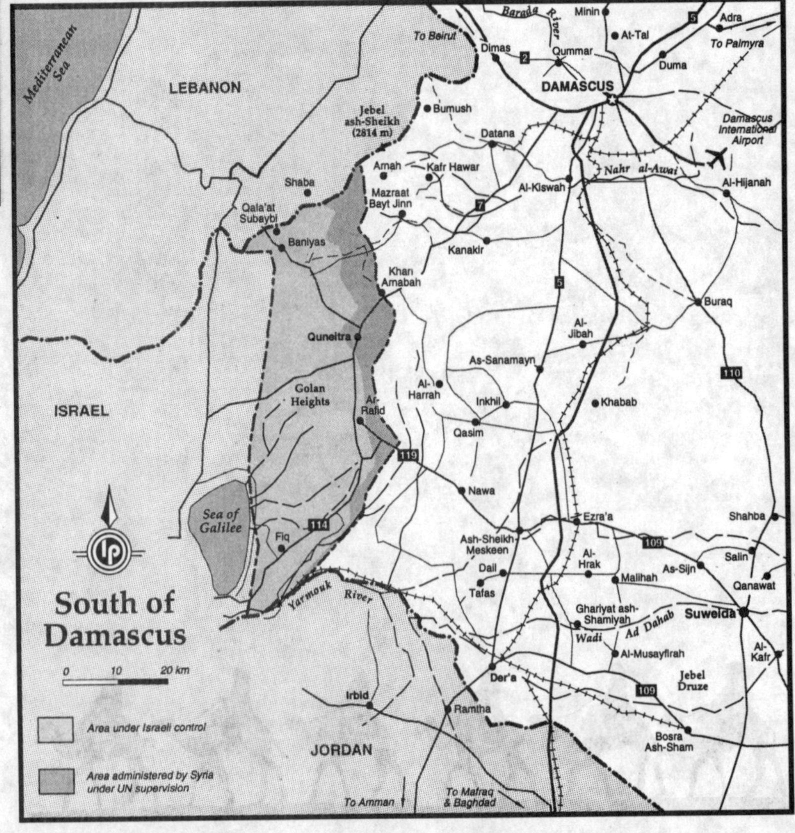

basalt plain that straddles the Jordan-Syria border and also goes by the names of Jebel Druze and Jebel al-Arab. The black rock used for construction gives the villages and towns of the area a strange brooding quality.

GOLAN HEIGHTS

Few people have not heard mention of the Golan (or Jawlan) in news reports on the Middle East, but most have only a vague notion of the area's whereabouts or significance.

Marking the only border between Israel and Syria, it has for decades been a bitter bone of contention. During the 1967 war, Israeli forces cleared the Golan of Syrian troops and even threatened Damascus. After the war of 1973, a delicate truce was negotiated between Israel and Syria by the US Secretary of State, Henry Kissinger, who spent almost a month shuttling back and forth between Damascus and Israel. The truce saw Syria regain some 450 sq km of territory lost to the Israelis during the war as well as some small, symbolically important pieces lost in the 1967 war. A complicated demilitarised buffer zone supervised by UN forces was also established, varying in width from a few hundred metres to a couple of km.

In 1981 the Israeli government upped the stakes by formally annexing part of the Golan and moving in settlers. In Israeli eyes the heights serve as an indispensable shield against potential Syrian attack. The Syrians, quite naturally, see things differently.

Since the Middle East peace process was kicked into gear with the 1991 Madrid conference, Israel and Syria have danced a reluctant tango without any tangible results so far. With peace signed between Israel and Jordan, and the Palestinians slowly regaining some autonomy, Syria remains in some senses the odd one out. Damascus' position, on the surface at least, is straightforward enough – Israel must execute a complete withdrawal from the whole area before Syria will contemplate peace. Though concessions have been forthcoming from Tel Aviv, such an unconditional withdrawal poses an enormous security gamble in the eyes of the Israeli military.

It is more than 20 years since a shot has been fired in anger here, but the ruins of Quneitra, once the area's administrative capital, serve as a bitter reminder of conflict. Before the Israelis withdrew from Quneitra after the 1973 cease-fire, they evacuated the 37,000 Arab population and systematically destroyed the town, removing anything that could be unscrewed, unbolted or wrenched from its position. Everything from windows to light fittings were sold to Israeli contractors, and the buildings of Quneitra thus stripped were then pulled apart with tractors and bulldozers. It is even reported that some graves were even broken open and then ransacked.

Quneitra today is a strange ghost town. Houses lie crumpled where they were pulled down, the empty shells of mosques and churches rise among the strangely peaceful scenes of devastation. The high street banks and shops are lifeless, and the pockmarked local clinic has become the centrepiece for what is in all something of a propaganda exhibit demonstrating the hard-nosed approach of the Israelis.

For some years, Quneitra has been under Syrian control within the UN patrolled demilitarised zone. There is in fact a UN checkpoint right in the town, and barbed wire on its outskirts marks where Syrian territory ends and Israeli occupied land begins. From the town you can easily make out Israeli communications and observation posts on the heights to the east. Much of this area is also mined.

To visit the town, you need a pass from the Ministry of the Interior. The appropriate building is three doors along from the Kuwaiti embassy, near 'Adnan al-Malky Square in Damascus. You'll know it by the young, T-shirted, armed guards. It's open from 8 am to 2 pm Sunday to Thursday, and you must bring your passport. You should have the pass within about half an hour, but remember that it is valid for use on the *following* day only. The pass will be taken from you by an intelligence official who will board the minibus to Quneitra and act as a kind of official 'tour guide'.

Getting There & Away

Microbuses from next to the Karnak bus station cost S£20 and take one hour. They don't quite take you all the way, dropping you in a town called Khan Arnahah about 10 km short of Quneitra. From there regular minibuses and microbuses (S£5) make the final run past Syrian and UN checkpoints into Quneitra itself.

SHAHBA

Lying about 90 km south of Damascus, Shahba entered into its own when refounded by its most famous son, Emperor Phillip, in 244 AD, the year of his accession to the ultimate position of authority in the Roman Empire. The only Arab to rule the empire, his reign lasted only five years, but Phillipopolis continued to thrive long after he had gone, as the magnificent 4th century mosaics now held in the museum of nearby Suweida testify.

The main street of modern Shahba follows the line laid down by the ancient town's *cardo*, intersected by the *decumanus* at the town centre. Head right along the partly intact paved **Roman road**, past four columns on the right, and you'll see a number of buildings of interest on the left.

The best preserved of them appears to have been a family **shrine**, dedicated to a god Martinus, probably Phillip's father. Just behind it lies a fairly modest **theatre**. Fish sculpted on the walls of the vaulted passages show the way to your seats. Back on the main road, head a little way south and on the left you can see the jumbled remains of the town **nymphaeum**, or public fountain. Further down the street is part of the original southern **gate** of the city.

In a street which runs parallel with the nymphaeum is a small museum. The principal exhibits are some fine 4th century mosaics dug up in Shahba. The scenes depicted include the *Wedding of Ariadne and Bacchus* and *Orpheus Surrounded by Animals*. The museum is open from 8 am to 2 pm daily except Tuesday, and entry costs S£200.

Getting There & Away

Minibuses run from the south bus station (or 'garage') in Damascus. The trip takes about 1¼ hours and costs S£18. Or you can get a regular Damas Tour bus for S£50. You can also pick up minibuses or microbuses coming up from Suweida.

SUWEIDA

Anything that might once have been of interest in this provincial capital, a largely Druze redoubt 15 km south of Shahba, has long been swept away by modern expansion. However, the **museum**, built and organised with the aid of the French and opened in November 1991, holds an impressive collection covering periods in Hauran history from the Stone Age to Rome. You can see prehistoric pottery, an extensive array of mostly basalt statuary, as well as a popular tradition section (the usual wax dummies in traditional garb and various other bits and bobs).

The main attraction, however, are more mosaics from Shahba, which alone make a visit worthwhile. The best preserved and most remarkable (you can't miss it) is entitled *Artemis Surprised While Bathing*. Unfortunately, all the labelling is in Arabic and French only.

The museum is open from 9 am to 6 pm (4 pm in winter) daily except Tuesday, and admission costs S£200. To get to the museum, walk one km directly east of the microbus station at the northern entry into the town. The outsized, modern and gleaming building is rather hard to miss.

Places to Stay & Eat

The *Rawdat al-Jabal Hotel* is a grubby dive with beds in share rooms for S£75. The nearby *Touristic Hotel* (☎ 016-221012) overcharges at US$20/25 for its singles/doubles with unappetising ensuite bathrooms. There are a few local eateries around the town centre.

Getting There & Away

A minibus from Damascus (from the south bus station) takes 1¾ hours and costs S£22. Or you can take a slightly faster microbus for

S£40, which leaves at set times. For the trip back book ahead for the microbuses or be prepared for a long wait if you leave it later than about 3.30 pm, as the number running after then is minimal.

QANAWAT

A 15 minute bus ride east of Suweida lies the town of Qanawat, once a member of the Roman-inspired Decapolis that included such cities as Jerash, Philadelphia (Amman) and Gadara (Umm Qais) in Jordan. The bus drops you at the most interesting monument, known as the **Seraglio**. Historians believe it was a combination of temples, the most intact building dating from the second half of the 2nd century AD. It was later converted into a basilica and the whole area given over to Christian worship. Admission costs S£100.

If you continue north from here (head left from the main façade), you will come towards a riverbed where you can see remains of a **theatre**, a **nymphaeum** and a few other scattered relics.

Getting There & Away

To use public transport, you need to head about one km towards the centre of Suweida from the northern microbus station. The Qanawat shuttle leaves fairly regularly from a side street off the main road, and about the only way you'll find it is by asking at regular intervals along the way for the Qanawat bus. The quick trip costs S£5.

BOSRA

The town of Bosra (or more properly Bosra ash-Sham) lies between two wadis, both of which run into the Yarmouk River, about 40 km east of Der'a and 140 km south of Damascus across fertile plains littered with black basalt rocks. Once important for its location at the crossroads of major trade and, under the Muslims, pilgrimage routes, it is now little more than a backwater.

It is a weird and wonderful place. Apart from having possibly the best preserved Roman theatre in existence, the rest of the town is built in, around and over old sections of Roman buildings, almost entirely out of black basalt blocks. Those in the new houses have mostly been filched from ancient structures.

Altogether it's a strange mixture of architectural styles and, as the *Cook's Travellers'*

SYRIA

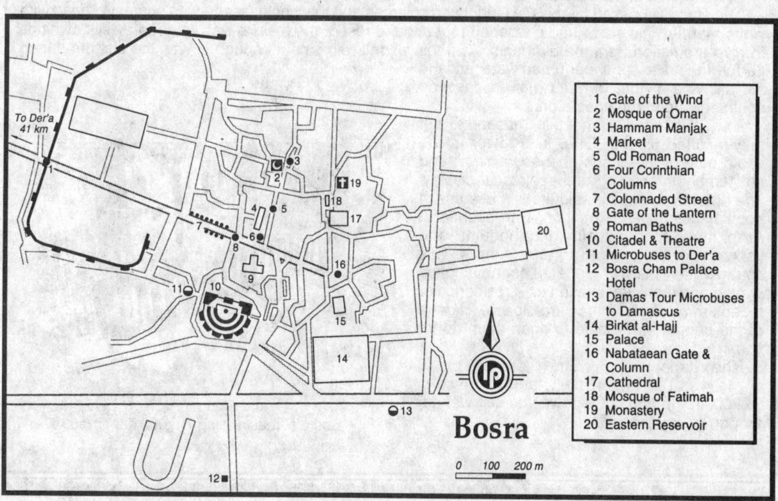

Handbook of 1934 says, 'a zealous antiquary might find weeks of profitable enjoyment among the ruins'. That probably remains quite true to this day, but for most people one day is enough to see everything at a leisurely pace. It is quite possible to visit Bosra ash-Sham in a day-trip from Damascus using public transport, so long as you make sure of your place in the bus for the return trip. You could also use Der'a as a base, which is closer and makes for a less hectic day.

History

Bosra is mentioned in Egyptian records as early as 1300 BC and during the 1st century AD it became the short-lived capital of the Nabataean kingdom as Petra was eclipsed in the south.

In 106 AD the Romans annexed the area and Bosra, then named Nova Trajana Bostra, became capital of the Province of Arabia and seat of a praetorian legate. He administered the region and was in command of the Third Legion, garrisoned mainly at Bosra. The town, which could trace its routes back to Bronze Age times, owed its considerable wealth in part to its new political functions, but the surrounding country in those days was also something of an agricultural bread basket, providing a sound economic foundation for the Bosrans' wellbeing. When Phillip became emperor of Rome, he raised

Bosra: Citadel & Theatre

The citadel is a curious construction as it is largely a fortified Roman theatre. The two structures are in fact one – the fort was built around the theatre to make it an impregnable stronghold. The first walls were built during the Omayyad and Abbasid periods, with further additions being made in the 11th century by the Fatimids.

After the Crusader attacks of 1140 and 1183, the Ayyubids found there was not enough room to house all their troops stationed here, so from 1202 to 1251 nine towers were constructed. They were encircled by a deep moat and a five span bridge was erected.

The big surprise on entering the citadel is to find the magnificent 15,000 seat theatre. Long obscured by the addition of later buildings, the theatre's full glory was only laid bare this century. It is a rarity among theatres of the time in that it is completely freestanding rather than built into the side of a hill.

The stage is backed by rows of Corinthian columns and the whole façade was originally faced with white marble. The stage had a wooden roof and the rest of the theatre was covered by silk awnings to give protection from the elements. As if this wasn't refinement enough, it was the custom during performances to spray perfumed water into the air, allowing a fine, fragrant mist to descend soothingly upon the spectators.

Two of the towers contain museums, but they're often closed. One, in a tower in the south-east of the citadel, houses a small and not terribly interesting archaeological display. The other is one of the ubiquitous museums of popular culture and tradition, with scenes of Arab life depicted using mannequins and various exhibits of clothing and utensils. This south-western tower appears to have once served some official function as a residence or reception quarters. If they are closed, ask one of the people in the café to open them up for you.

The citadel is open from 10 am to 6 pm (9 am to 4 pm in winter) daily, and entrance is S£200; in the rest of the town you can wander around at any time. ■

Bosra's freestanding, 15,000 seat theatre

the town to the status of metropolis and coins were minted here.

During the Christian era Bosra retained importance as the seat of a primate with 33 priests subject to him. Prior to its fall to the Muslims in 634, tradition has it that Mohammed encountered the Nestorian monk Boheira here. Although some say the monk did little more than introduce Mohammed to the basic tenets of Christianity, others claim he told him of his future vocation as a Prophet.

The Crusaders twice tried unsuccessfully to take the fortress in the 12th century and the Mongols seriously damaged it during their invasion in 1261.

Bosra's position on the pilgrimage route to Mecca long assured continued prosperity, and because of the tradition of Mohammed and the monk, pilgrims would often stop here for up to a week. When this route became unsafe about the end of the 17th century, the pilgrims started using a route further to the west – Bosra was on the way down.

Things to See

North of the citadel, the old city's **main street** runs roughly east to west. At its western end rises the Gate of the Wind (Bab al-Hawa), while along the cobbled main street are the remains of columns found on the site during excavations.

The Gate of the Lantern (Bab al-Qandil), on the main street near the citadel, dates from the 3rd century. An inscription on the right-hand pillar states that it was erected in memory of the Third Legion, which was garrisoned here.

Next up are the four enormous Corinthian **columns**, looking somewhat out of place. This is what is left of the **nymphaeum**, which supplied water to the people and gardens.

Just past these is another column and lintel that has been incorporated into a modern house. The thought of a few tons of basalt plummeting through the ceiling one night would surely be cause for insomnia. It is believed that this is what remains of a pagan sanctuary built by one of the kings of Bosra to protect his daughter from death. A dismal failure it seems, as the daughter was brought a bunch of grapes in which a scorpion was hiding. It promptly stung and killed her.

Right opposite this are the **Roman baths**. It was a complicated series of rooms where the bather moved from one pool room to the next, finally arriving at the steam bath.

The **Mosque of Omar** lies about 200m north of the main street. Although claimed by some to be one of the three oldest mosques in the world (the others are in Medina and Cairo) and built in 720, the more likely hypothesis has it being erected in 1112 by a Seljuq administrator.

Virtually opposite, the **Hammam Manjak** was fully revealed in the early 1990s. Built in 1372 under the Mamelukes, this rather odd little institution features a set of vaguely human-shaped cells for what look like individual showers. There's a small museum next door dealing with excavations past and present (closed on Friday; entry is free).

The **monastery** is the oldest church in Bosra and is thought to have been built in the 4th century. This is supposedly where Mohammed met the monk Boheira. The façade has been totally rebuilt but the side walls and apse are original.

Between the monastery and the main street lies the **cathedral** in a sorry state of decay. It represents one of the earliest attempts to surmount a square base with a circular dome, but it was poorly built in the first place (circa 512 AD) and had to be rebuilt a number of times before its final demise. The emperor Justinian used the church as the model for cathedrals he built at Constantinople and Ravenna. His architects managed to do a better job of it and those two cathedrals still stand.

At the eastern end of the main street is the **Nabataean gate & column**. The gate is the main entrance to the palace in which the Nabataean king Rabbel II lived. The column is the only one of its kind in Syria and bears the typical simple Nabataean capital.

Further out of town are two **cisterns** or reservoirs that used to supply the town with water. The one to the east of the Nabataean ar swimming location with the ough not overly inviting.

Places to Stay & Eat

There is only one hotel in Bosra ash-Sham, the expensive *Bosra Cham Palace* (☎ 015-790488), where singles/doubles will cost you US$100/120. It's a few hundred metres south of the theatre.

Otherwise, you can stay in a room in the so-called hostel inside the citadel itself for S£200 a night. You'll need a sleeping bag, as there is not much in the way of bedding. It is quite a unique experience, and some travellers have reported that you can even stay during the September festival. See Special Events in the Syria Facts for the Visitor chapter for details.

Around the entrance to the citadel are a couple of shops selling felafels and drinks, but they like to charge over the odds.

Getting There & Away

Damas Tour has a direct microbus between Bosra ash-Sham and Damascus (see also Getting There & Away in the Damascus chapter). The last one leaves Bosra ash-Sham about 8.30 pm. If you want to be sure of having a seat on one of these, book it as soon as you can (make it your first task if you plan to get back to Damascus on the same day).

Otherwise, there are minibuses and microbuses to Der'a. The trip takes about an hour and costs S£9/15 respectively. Be warned though, that the last ones leave town about 4.30 pm. There is no direct service from Suweida, but you may be able to make it with a combination of microbuses or minibuses and hitching. Don't leave this too late, as transport in this part of the country slows to a trickle from around 4 pm.

DER'A

There's not a lot of interest in this southern town, 100 km from Damascus, although it can make a good base for visiting the ruins at Bosra ash-Sham, and you'll end up here if you want to tackle the Jordanian border by local transport. There are a couple of sights worth a quick look if you are stuck here with time to kill. More importantly, the village of Ezra'a, to the north and accessible by local transport, is home to two of the oldest churches in Syria.

You'll find a tourist office on the Damascus road, just north of the railway line, and further up the same road is a post office.

Things to See

About two km south of the centre of town is the **Omari Mosque**, loosely based on the Omayyad Mosque in Damascus, although far less grand. It was built in the 13th century under the Ayyubids.

To get to it, head out along the Jordan road, then veer off it to the left before crossing the stinking dribble that passes for a river. Follow the road up around the left side of the knoll and beyond; the mosque will appear on the left.

As you leave the mosque, take the side street almost directly opposite and on your right you'll see the remains of a **Roman theatre** that are still being investigated.

Places to Stay & Eat

There's a couple of nondescript hotels in the centre of town. The *Hotel as-Salam* (☎ 221 157), in a side street south off the main road (which itself runs parallel to the railway line), is about as cheap as it gets. S£150 will get you a bed in a grungy share room, and S£250 an equally unexciting double. On the main road itself and marginally better is the *Hotel al-Ahram* (☎ 221791) where S£150 will get you a bed in a very basic share room. Overpriced but more comfortable doubles with bath cost S£600. The best place is predictably enough a dollar hotel. The *Orient Hotel* (☎ 222430), aka the Al-Chark, charges US$15/20 for good clean rooms with bath.

There are a few small felafel, chicken and shawarma places in the main street.

Getting There & Away

Bus The bus station lies about three km east of the centre of town – a real pain. Buses and minibuses to and from Damascus (south bus station) cost S£25 and take about two hours. Faster microbuses cost S£45. Minibuses to

Bosra ash-Sham take up to an hour and cost S£9, while microbuses cost S£15. Competition for the Damascus buses can be pretty tough in the afternoons.

There is a daily Karnak service between Der'a and Damascus. Tickets cost S£30 and the trip takes about 1½ hours. You can't pick up the Damascus-Amman (Jordan) bus here.

Train The diesel train for Amman passes through from Damascus at about noon on Sunday and costs S£115. The same train goes back to Damascus on Monday. There is an additional service between Der'a and Damascus on Friday.

Jordan This border is straightforward enough, although it can involve a bit of hiking. Service taxis shuttle between the bus stations in Der'a and Ramtha (on the Jordanian side), and cost S£150 or JD2 per person.

Otherwise you will need to hitch or walk. To save yourself some of the effort, try to get a local bus from the bus station into the centre; that will save you the first three km. From there head south out on the Jordan road (it's signposted) and hitch or walk the four km to the Syrian checkpoint. Once through formalities here, it's another three or four km to the Jordanian checkpoint. The soldiers here may not allow you to walk the last km or so to the immigration post, but are friendly and will flag down a car or bus for you. From Ramtha, minibuses go on to Mafraq, Irbid and Zarqa, from where you can proceed to Amman.

The number of trucks lining the road on this border is staggering – at times they are queued up for km waiting to cross. The drivers are well prepared. Each truck has a well-stocked food box on the side complete with teapot and gas stove, and you'll see the drivers sitting next to their trucks making a brew and having a chat while they sit it out.

Getting Around

There's little need for an extensive local transport system in Der'a. However, it is worth noting that if you arrive at the bus station and want to get back into the town centre, there are fairly regular local buses between the two for S£2.

EZRA'A

The Greek Orthodox **basilica of St George** (Mar Jirjis) has been in business since the 6th century and is worth the 30 km detour from Der'a. It is basically an octagon within a square base, its interior graced with a series of attractively simple arches. Virtually next door is the Greek Catholic **Church of St Elias**. It also dates from the 6th century but has been much altered over the years and consequently does not make the same impression as its Orthodox cousin.

From the main Der'a bus station you have to get a local bus to Ash-Sheikh Meskeen, where a local microbus conneets to Ezra'a.

Mediterranean Coast

The 183 km long Syrian coastline is dominated by the rugged mountain range that runs along its entire length. The coastal strip, narrow in the north, widens towards the south and is extremely fertile and heavily cultivated.

The port city of Lattakia ('Al-Lathqiyya') with its beach resorts, and the ruined ancient city of Ugarit, lie in the north. From here roads head on to Turkey, east across the mountains to Aleppo, and south to Tartus, a secondary port that still preserves remnants of its medieval Crusader past.

The mountains behind Lattakia contain Syria's only forests and these are easy on the eyes after the often monotonous country in the interior. Excessive clearing of the forests for timber have led to large areas being reduced to scrub, although the government has laid aside some areas for preservation.

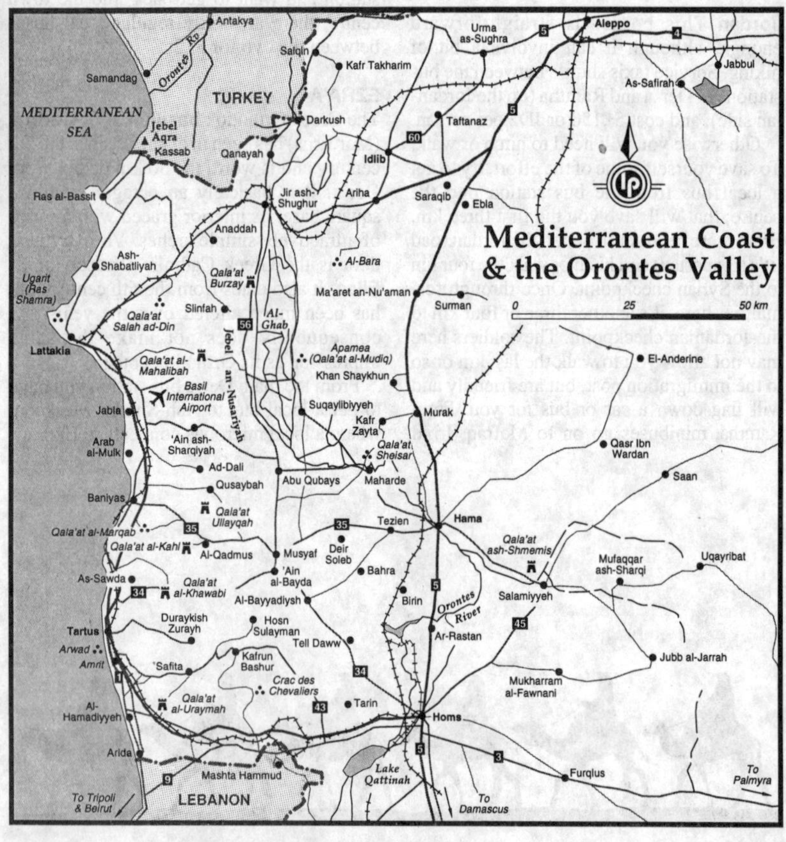

Perhaps more interesting still for the traveller, much of this area fell for centuries into Crusader hands. They left behind them a chain of hilltop eyries and precipitous castles, the undisputed king of which is undoubtedly the stalwart Crac des Chevaliers.

The beaches along the coast are unfortunately nothing to rave about as the water is murky and the sand littered with garbage. Popular though they may be with Syrians on holiday, the foreign tourist passing through would do better to save the sand, sea and sun experience for other Mediterranean neighbours, such as Turkey or Israel.

LATTAKIA

This busy port city is dominated by the harbour facilities and freighters anchored just offshore. Most of Syria's imports and exports come through here and a weekly ferry connects it with several other Mediterranean countries. The odd sign in Greek not only points to the town's openness to the sea and traffic with outsiders, but seems to survive as a dim reminder of the area's history on the crossroads of ancient trade routes. A contemporary note is struck by the recent addition of the odd shop sign in Russian. The visitors are a novelty on Lattakia's streets, but the commercial theme remains the same.

It's certainly not a typical Syrian town. With its wide, tree-lined boulevards and occasional sidewalk café, Lattakia has almost a European air about it. Not surprisingly then, Lattakia is also one of the least conservative cities in Syria. The people are snappy dressers and, apart from the odd *hijab* (woman's head scarf), you'll see little of the traditional dress prevalent in the towns of the interior.

The city itself has no real attractions but it makes a good base for visits to the ruins of the ancient city of Ugarit (now known as Ras Shamra), Jabla, Qala'at Salah ad-Din (Saladin) and, at a pinch, the northernmost beach of Ras al-Bassit.

History

Lattakia became a city of importance under the Seleucids in the 2nd century BC and was named Laodicea by Seleucus I. It came under Roman control in the 1st century AD and Mark Antony made it a free town.

A string of serious earthquakes during the Middle Ages took their toll and, with the rebellions of the Alawites against the ruling Ottoman administration in the 1800s, Lattakia had little chance of regaining its former prosperity. Only since Hafez al-Assad, whose family is from Lattakia, came to power in the 70s has it boomed with the development of the port facilities.

Orientation

The lower end of 14 Ramadan St, the main road running from the north-east into town and culminating at the central mosque, is where most of the cheap hotels, cafés and the like are gathered, spilling into the streets immediately around it. Most buses (except Karnak) and service taxis leave from somewhere along this road.

Baghdad Ave, the north-south boulevard that eventually becomes 8 Azar St, is the chic axis of Lattakia, with several charming (and pricier than normal) European-style cafés along the footpaths.

Information

Tourist Office The Tourist Centre is at the fork in the main road to Aleppo and Ras Shamra. It is open from 8 am to 7 pm daily except Friday, and the friendly staff will bend over backwards to help, even if they really don't have that much to offer in terms of literature or firm advice.

Visa Extensions For visa extensions, the immigration office is on the 2nd floor of the police building. The office is open from 8 am to 2 pm daily except Friday. Extensions are issued on the spot.

Money The Commercial Bank of Syria is on Baghdad Ave and is open from 8.30 am to 1.30 pm daily except Friday. There are three entrances. Take the middle one, which leads into a kind of exchange booth that is very

SYRIA

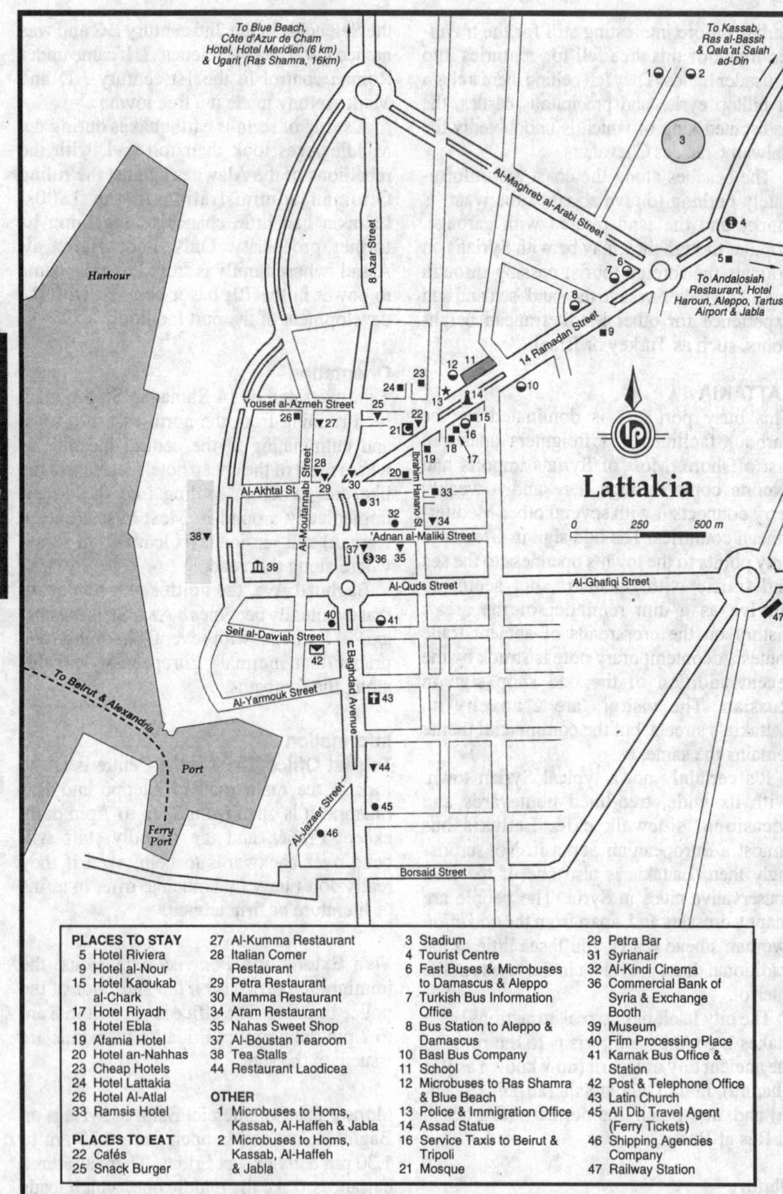
Lattakia
To Blue Beach, Côte d'Azur de Cham Hotel, Hotel Meridien (6 km) & Ugarit (Ras Shamra, 16km)
To Kassab, Ras al-Bassit & Qala'at Salah ad-Din
To Andalosiah Restaurant, Hotel Haroun, Aleppo, Tartus, Airport & Jabla
To Beirut & Alexandria
Harbour
Port
Ferry Port
Al-Maghreb al-Arabi Street
14 Ramadan Street
8 Azar Street
Yousef al-Azmeh Street
Al-Akhtal St
Al-Moutannabi Street
Ibrahim Hanano St
'Adnan al-Maliki Street
Al-Quds Street
Al-Ghafiqi Street
Seif al-Dawiah Street
Baghdad Avenue
Al-Yarmouk Street
Al-Jazaer Street
Borsaid Street
0 250 500 m
PLACES TO STAY
5 Hotel Riviera
9 Hotel al-Nour
15 Hotel Kaoukab al-Chark
17 Hotel Riyadh
18 Hotel Ebla
19 Afamia Hotel
20 Hotel an-Nahhas
23 Cheap Hotels
24 Hotel Lattakia
26 Hotel Al-Atlal
33 Ramsis Hotel
PLACES TO EAT
22 Cafés
25 Snack Burger
27 Al-Kumma Restaurant
28 Italian Corner Restaurant
29 Petra Restaurant
30 Mamma Restaurant
34 Aram Restaurant
35 Nahas Sweet Shop
37 Al-Boustan Tearoom
38 Tea Stalls
44 Restaurant Laodicea
OTHER
1 Microbuses to Homs, Kassab, Al-Haffeh & Jabla
2 Microbuses to Homs, Kassab, Al-Haffeh & Jabla
3 Stadium
4 Tourist Centre
6 Fast Buses & Microbuses to Damascus & Aleppo
7 Turkish Bus Information Office
8 Bus Station to Aleppo & Damascus
10 Basl Bus Company
11 School
12 Microbuses to Ras Shamra & Blue Beach
13 Police & Immigration Office
14 Assad Statue
16 Service Taxis to Beirut & Tripoli
21 Mosque
29 Petra Bar
31 Syrianair
32 Al-Kindi Cinema
36 Commercial Bank of Syria & Exchange Booth
39 Museum
40 Film Processing Place
41 Karnak Bus Office & Station
42 Post & Telephone Office
43 Latin Church
45 Ali Dib Travel Agent (Ferry Tickets)
46 Shipping Agencies Company
47 Railway Station

efficient. You can change cash and travellers' cheques.

Post & Communications The post office is south of the centre towards the harbour entrance. There are card phones and fax facilities here, and it's open from 8 am to 11 pm daily.

Photography There are several new shops on Baghdad Ave near Al-Quds St where you can have film processed with up-to-date equipment.

Museum

There's a small museum down near the waterfront housed in what was once an old khan, or caravanserai. The 2nd floor was built during the French Mandate. Most descriptions are in Arabic, but the caretaker is quite helpful if you don't speak the lingo. There's some pottery and written tablets from Ugarit, chain-mail suits and a section devoted to contemporary art. It's open from 8 am to 2 pm daily except Tuesday. Entry is S£200 and at that price a visit is of questionable value.

Places to Stay – bottom end

Lattakia offers a reasonable range of cheap hotels, most of them concentrated in a small area around the mosque.

The *Hotel Kaoukab al-Chark* (☎ 238 452), just by the Assad statue, has basic singles/doubles for S£150/300. Rooms with private bath cost S£200/325.

A marginally better deal is the *Ramsis Hotel* (☎ 238058), where prices are the same. There is a good common hot shower.

Closer to the mosque is the *Afamia Hotel*, where beds come in at S£130/250 for singles/doubles. A hot shower costs extra. Turn down the street to the left and you'll come across the *Hotel an-Nahhas* (☎ 238 030), where the friendly Algerian manager has rooms for S£150/250, many of them with a balcony. A hot shower costs S£25. The manager sells coffee, tea and juices on the premises and he speaks English and French also.

Tucked right away in a tiny lane is the *Hotel Ebla*, where rather simple, airless rooms look on to a central courtyard. Your man here wants S£200/250, but it's not a great deal. If you're curious, follow the signs off 14 Ramadan St (near the Hotel Riyadh) and turn first left into a side alley. It's on the left.

Right by the mosque are a few more cheapies, but they're so close by that you may as well have a loudspeaker hooked up in each room for the early morning call to prayer. That said, the *Hotel Lattakia* has been recommended by some sound-sleeping travellers. Singles/doubles cost S£150/200. There's a good shower and the rooms are clean.

Away from the town centre and closer to the port is Lattakia's best budget place, the *Hotel Al-Atlal* (☎ 236121). This quiet, family-run establishment charges S£250 per person for good beds in homey rooms. The sign on Youssef al-Azmeh St says 'Hotel' only.

Places to Stay – middle

A couple of doors down from the Kaoukab al-Chark is the *Hotel Riyadh* (☎ 239778), a comfortable place boasting fairly modern rooms high enough up to neutralise much of the street noise and with hot water and balconies. The snag is they cost too much at US$18/22.

Singles/doubles/triples set you back US$18/22/ 25 at the Hotel al-Nour (423980), opposite the first of the bus stations in Lattakia.

Further up the same road, just opposite the Tourist Centre, is the *Hotel Riviera* (☎ 421 803; fax 418287) where the reception is friendlier and rooms (with hot water, TV and fridge) are more expensive. Singles/ doubles cost US$54/59.

Another roundabout further on is the *Hotel Haroun* (☎ 427140). It's a bit sombre and has had scathing reports from some guests.

Places to Stay – top end

About six km north of town on Blue Beach

is the four star *Hotel Meridien* (☎ 229000). Rooms here cost US$90/115 plus 10% taxes, but in the off season it's pretty easy to get a 25% discount. You are only charged to use the reasonably clean beach in high season.

To get to the Meridien you actually pass Lattakia's premier establishment, the *Côte d'Azur de Cham* (☎ 228691), where room prices vary quite considerably depending on whether you want one facing the sea or not. The cheapest rooms are in the Residence part of the complex, starting at US$100. The hotel charges non-guests S£300 to use the beach.

Places to Eat

As with hotels, the cheap restaurants and street stalls are around the mosque area. A quick hunt will turn up the old faithfuls – felafel, chicken, kebabs and shawarma. Lattakia has a surprising concentration of restaurants and even a few spots that pass as bars.

For the same old food in better surroundings, the *Aram Restaurant* upstairs on the second corner south of the mosque is not a bad choice. A decent meal will cost you about S£200.

There's a whole string of restaurants along Al-Moutannabi Street. Among them, *Al-Kumma* is a pleasant place up on the 2nd floor. Try to get a window seat. Prices are fairly average for this kind of restaurant, and a standard meal of half a chicken, side dishes and a beer will cost about S£200.

Italian Corner Restaurant is a popular place offering a few not terribly well-prepared Italian dishes and pizza of sorts for about S£80. It also does a wide range of Arabic dishes. Better still, there's a bar serving bottles of imported beer for S£85 and cocktails for S£100 plus. Just around the corner, the *Petra* bar/restaurant is good for Middle Eastern cuisine and drinking. The dishes marked on the menu as cooked in clay pots are particularly recommended.

Another possibility for a halfway decent pizza is *Mamma*. Its pizzas cost about the same as those at Italian Corner and are quite good. There's also spaghetti bolognaise, escalope and hamburgers!

A block further north, you can get a reasonable imitation takeaway burger and chips from *Snack Burger*, a bright little spot in a side street. Another reasonable western-style fast-food place is the *Andalosiah*, across the roundabout from the Haroun Hotel.

A bright new choice is *Restaurant Laodicea*, south down Baghdad Ave on the site of what was once a Franciscan convent.

In summer, shops all over Lattakia sell a luridly coloured but quite edible locally produced ice cream.

On the subject of things sweet, the *Nahas* sweet shop, not far up a side street from the Commercial Bank of Syria, has an amazing range of local and imported chocolates and sweets. If you've been on the road for a while and have forgotten what, say, Maltesers taste like, this is about the only place in Syria you're likely to be able to remind yourself.

Among the more stylish of the handful of sidewalk cafés along Baghdad Ave is the *Al-Boustan* tearoom, a great place to start the day and not a bad choice for whiling away the early evening.

Getting There & Away

Air Lattakia's airport lies about 25 km south of town, close to Jabla. This is Assad territory, and the airport is among the rapidly expanding list of items across the country to be named after the president's son Basil, who died in a car accident in January 1994. A grand total of two flights leave this 'international' airport each Friday, one for Damascus (S£500) and the other for Cairo (hence the grandiloquence), which costs US$170 one way. Syrianair has an office on Baghdad Avenue.

Bus Myriad bus companies have departures from up and down 14 Ramadan St.

Clapped-out buses to Aleppo and Damascus leave from a station opposite the Hotel al-Nour. The buses cost S£30 to Aleppo and S£55 to Damascus. Old-style minibuses also serve Aleppo, and the ride costs S£40.

About 100m further up the road away

from the centre is an assortment of private companies with modern buses, and in some cases microbuses, to several destinations. The trip to Damascus with such companies costs about S£140 and it's S£100 to Aleppo.

The Karnak bus station and office is at the southern end of the town centre, just off Baghdad Ave. Book one day in advance for buses running daily to Aleppo (S£50), Damascus (S£90, stops in Tartus and Homs) and Beirut (S£175, with a stop in Tripoli).

Turkey It is supposedly possible to get a bus to Turkey, although they appear to be a little scarce. For information on services to Antakya (via Kassab), enquire at the office at 14 Ramadan St. You could also get a microbus to Kassab, and proceed with local transport or by hitching from the border to Antakya.

Microbus Microbuses to Baniyas (S£15, 45 minutes), Tartus (S£35, 1½ hours) and Homs (S£60) leave from a small lot next door to the Haroun Hotel.

The Basl bus company has regular microbuses to Aleppo for S£100 from a separate lot on 14 Ramadan St.

Yet another station near the stadium has microbuses and the odd minibus to Kassab (S£20, 1½ hours), Al-Haffeh (S£10, 40 minutes) and Jabla (S£11, 30 minutes).

Train The railway station is about a km east of Baghdad Ave. There are three daily departures for Aleppo (S£57/30, 1st/2nd class). The trip normally takes 3½ hours.

Service Taxi Service taxis to Beirut and Tripoli in Lebanon leave from a rank on 14 Ramadan St outside the Hotel Kaoukab al-Chark. The trip to Beirut costs S£500 per person.

Ferry A ferry departs every Wednesday at 4 pm for Alexandria (Egypt). It takes about three days and goes via Beirut (Lebanon). In summer it may well call in at Cyprus too, although this appears to be a less definite arrangement.

The cheapest possible ticket is an airline-style seat on the deck for US$140. No meals or drinks are included in that price. For US$100 more you can get a bed in a two berth cabin and basic meals. US$330 gets you a bed in a two berth *mumtaz* (1st class) cabin.

You can buy tickets at the Ali Dib (☎ 462617) agency on Baghdad Ave. The Shipping Agencies Company on Al-Jazaer St can also sell tickets. Book at least the day before and take your passport with you when you do so. You need to be at the port three hours before departure.

Getting Around

The Airport A taxi to the airport from Lattakia will cost about S£300.

Microbus Frequent local microbuses leave from a lot behind the school on 14 Ramadan St. Destinations include Ugarit (Ras Shamra) and Blue Beach, known to the locals as Shaati al-Azraq (S£5).

AROUND LATTAKIA

Blue Beach (Shaati al-Azraq)

The road to Ras Shamra also passes Blue Beach, what passes for Syria's premier coastal resort. It lies between the sports complex (built for the 1987 Mediterranean Games) and the Hotel Meridien. There are expensive bungalows set up along the beach and some effort is made to keep it cleared of garbage. The murky brown water, however, is none too inviting.

Out on a point, the multistorey Hotel Meridien sticks out like a sore thumb. Here the beach is a little better, but in high season you have to pay to use it. Th hotel has pedal boats and sailboards for hire.

Getting There & Away Catch the Ras Mediterranean Coast – Around Lattakia Shamra microbus and get off in front of the Côte d'Azur de Cham hotel.

Ras al-Bassit & Kassab

The black-sand beaches just south of the

Ugarit (Ras Shamra)

Although there's not so much to see today, Ugarit was once the most important city on the Mediterranean coast. It first came to prominence in the 3rd millennium BC, when it traded with Cyprus and Mesopotamia. Only in the 16th century BC, however, did the city enter its golden age as a centre for trade with Egypt, the Aegean Sea, Cyprus, Mesopotamia and the rest of Syria. Offerings were sent by the kings of Egypt to the famous Temple of Baal and Ugarit became a centre of learning. The good times were cut short when the city was destroyed by the Philistines, who invaded in about 1190 BC.

In the 13th century BC, the royal palace at Ugarit was one of the most imposing and famous edifices in western Asia. Initially a modest structure, it was in time enlarged to cover more than one hectare and featured courtyards, piped water, drainage and burial chambers. Similar features were also found in the houses of the well-to-do. At its peak, Ugarit was a wealthy city. One indication of the extent and durability of that wealth is the simple fact that the city was built of stone, allowing at least some of it to last to the present day.

What is widely accepted as being the earliest known alphabet was discovered in the clay tablet writings unearthed in the city's library. Later adapted by the Greeks and Romans, it was thus the ancestor of the modern European alphabets.

Excavation first began here in the late 1920s under French direction, and has continued with some interruptions to this day.

The tablets found here are among the most important source of information on early religion and life in Syria.

Ivory head excavated at Ugarit

1 Gate
2 Subsidiary Palaces
3 Royal Palace
4 Southern Palace
5 House of Alabasters
6 Houses of Rasap'abu & the Scholar
7 House of Rašap'abu
8 Temple of Baal
9 High Priest's House & Temple Library
10 Temple of Dagon
11 Southern Slope of Acropolis
12 Public Square

Excavation Area
Lower City
Acropolis
Southern City
Ugarit (Ras Shamra)
0 100 200 m

Now on display in museums in Lattakia, Aleppo and Damascus, as well as the Louvre in Paris, they contain various texts and myths of religious significance as well as dictionaries and lists of gods.

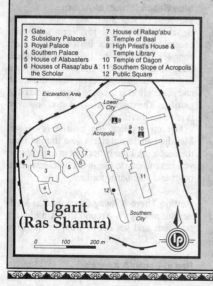

Things to See On the right of the track up to the ruins is the original entrance to the city, although now it looks more like a large drainage outlet. Once inside, you can gain an impression of the layout of the place from the low hill in the north-eastern quarter of the site that once served as Ugarit's acropolis. What you see stretched out below is a massive jumble of blocks with poorly defined streets and buildings. In the ruins there are vaulted tombs, wells and water channels. Water in fact played an important part in funerary rites. The dead had to have water near them, hence the elaborate wells and channels.

Two temples dominated the acropolis. One was dedicated to the storm god, Baal, the supreme deity for the Canaanites, Phoenicians and Aramaens. Baal was considered something apart from El, the father of all gods and creator of humankind according to Ugaritic belief. The second temple was dedicated to Dagon, the father of Baal and the god associated with the fertility of crops.

What little remains of the **Baal temple** is sited to the north-west of the acropolis, while the **Dagon temple**, of which only bits of the foundations can be made out, is about 50m further over to the east.

Ugarit's **royal palace** and related buildings were constructed in the west of the city, a short way south from where the present tourist entrance is located. Presenting itself now as something of a labyrinth, the main entrance in the north-western corner of the palace is marked by the bases of two pillars. Inside, the palace rooms are largely organised around a series of courtyards. On the east side of the complex the royal gardens once thrived. It was in storerooms of the palace that a good many of the precious Ugaritic archives were unearthed. The area between the palace and the acropolis was given over largely to private housing.

Gold bowl, Ugårit

The site is open from 9 am to 6 pm (4 pm in winter) daily, and entry costs S£200. Given that making out various elements of the site is not necessarily so easy, you might consider taking on a guide for S£100 to indicate the main points of interest.

The Mediterranean is just visible through the trees to the west. It has receded 100m or so since Ugarit's heyday. Don't try to walk directly through to the water as it's a military area and you're likely to get a less than friendly reception. However, if you follow the road back a bit, you'll find some quiet stretches of water and bits of beach, usually too liberally strewn with garbage to be greatly tempting. There are a few little shops where you can get something to drink.

Getting There & Away Local town microbuses make the 16 km trip to Ras Shamra, as Ugarit is known to the locals, every hour or so from Lattakia. Ask the driver where to get off for the *athaar* (ruins). It's easy to hitch back to Lattakia or flag down a microbus.

The road goes through some extremely fertile country full of orchards surrounded by high cypress hedges. Fruit stalls along the road sell apples and oranges in season. ■

Turkish frontier are probably the best of a pretty uninspiring lot along the Syrian coast. Jebel Aqra forms a dramatic backdrop and, if you're coming down the awful road from Kassab, the views are spectacular.

Outside the summer holiday period, the beach can be quite pleasant. There are not too many people around, the water is clean and so too, unusually enough, are the beaches. When the holiday crowds hit, get out.

Kassab itself is a popular mountain escape with Syrians, and is pleasing enough on the eye without being anything remarkable. What is doubtless true is that the route through here is among the most inviting ways into and out of Syria. There are a few hotels and snack places in Kassab should you need them.

Places to Stay & Eat Quite a few beach bungalows, cabins and 'chalets' are dotted along the beaches, but most are closed in the off season. There are also the usual snack places. You may want to stay in one of the hotels up in Kassab, but the only way to get down will be to negotiate with taxi drivers.

Getting There & Away In summer there are

one or two microbuses from Lattakia, but the service is unreliable, especially for the return trip, as there is no service back after about 4 pm. Otherwise, you can catch a microbus up through the mountains to Kassab (S£20, 1½ hours) and negotiate your way down to the beaches by service taxi.

Qala'at Salah ad-Din

Perched on a heavily wooded ridge 24 km east of Lattakia and made almost impregnable by the surrounding ravines, Saladin's Citadel (also known in Arabic as Qala'at Sahyun) is so called in memory of the Muslim commander's taking of the Crusader-held citadel in 1188 after the fall of Lattakia. Although it ranks behind the Crac des Chevaliers and Qala'at al-Marqab to the south, it is well worth a visit. Originally in Byzantine hands, it was taken by the Franks and expanded in the first half of the 12th century. Sultan Baibars brought it under Mameluke control in 1272.

The Crusaders' single most astounding feat of engineering was to clear an **artificial gorge** on the citadel's east side, through which the modern road now passes but which served at the time to cut the castle off from assault. The pillar of stone in the middle of the road helped prop up a drawbridge.

Today, the entrance is behind the high tower on the south-eastern side. Once inside you can see the remains of a pillared room that served as **stables**, and next to it a two storey **dungeon**, the main defensive structure. To the left of the entrance are the remains of **baths** and a **mosque** installed by the Muslims, and further down again what's left of a **Byzantine fort** and **chapel**. A ditch separates the main part of the castle from its lower, western half. The castle is closed on Tuesday and admission costs S£100.

Getting There & Away Take a microbus from Lattakia to Al-Haffeh (S£10, 40 minutes). From there it is about a seven km walk or hitch to the castle. Keep heading east along the main road out of town and follow the signs. Alternatively, haggle with a service taxi or with one of the *trezeenas*, the

The Savagery of the Crusades

The history of the Crusades began at Clermont-Ferrand, 27 November 1095. It was the plea of Pope Urban II to recapture the Holy Sepulchre in Jerusalem that resulted, some months later, in the embarkation of hundreds of thousands of people on the road to the Holy Land. Knights and peasants, even entire families set off, intending to carry the fight to the 'infidels' and to bring help to the Christians of the orient, most notably those in Syria and Palestine. For almost two centuries, from 1096 to 1291, the orient was the theatre for countless scenes of destruction, massacre and carnage in the name of Christ. All along the Crusader's route cities such as Nicea (modern Iznik), Antioch, Aleppo, Apamea, Damascus, Tripoli, Beirut, Kerak, and Jerusalem, weakened by their own rivalries and divisions, were exposed to the invaders' untempered violence.

The Crusaders were encamped before the walls of Antioch in October 1097. By this time, the massacre of the Jews of the Rhineland, and the pillaging and slaughter in Hungary and the Byzantine Empire were no longer a secret. Throughout the orient armies dissolved before the advancing Franks. The bravery of the Turks and the Saracens was ineffective in the face of the heavily armoured Crusader men and horses. When Antioch fell on 3 June 1098, the road to Jerusalem lay open and it seemed that nothing could stand in the way of the Crusader forces.

The atrocities inflicted on the population of Ma'aret an-Nu'aman in the Syrian interior, in December 1098, perhaps demonstrate the worst aspect of the Crusades. The town did not possess an army, only a town militia. The inhabitants fought bravely as the besieging army built towers of wood against the town walls. At one stage the defenders threw hives full of bees down upon their assailants in an attempt to repel them. However, surrender was the only option. But the promise of Bohemond, the new master of Antioch, to leave the population unharmed was not honoured. His troops forcefully invaded the town and put more than one hundred thousand people to the sword. One of the most gruesome episodes of the Crusades ensued; Raoul de Caen recorded in his chronicles that the bodies of the victims were then boiled and roasted before being eaten.

The taking of Jerusalem by the Crusaders, on 15 July 1099, was marked by the same excesses of savagery, and only a handful of Jewish and Muslim inhabitants escaped alive. The sacking of Jerusalem and its atrocities left the orient in shock. It was not until the end of the thirteenth century and the passage of seven crusades that the orient was again free of the yoke of the Crusaders. ■

odd-looking, locally assembled three wheeled 'vans'. They occasionally do a run to villages beyond the castle but are irregular and driven by sharks. Pay no more than S£20 per person. This is still outrageous but apparently what they hit the locals for, too.

Jabla

Only about half an hour south of Lattakia, the Phoenician settlement of Gabala was founded by the island state of Arwad. It is worth a quick look for its fairly dilapidated **Roman theatre**, a couple of hundred metres south of the microbus station, and perhaps more so for a stroll along the coast road.

There is a wonderful café perched over the rocks just past the two little fishing boat harbours as you head south. It is a perfect spot to have a coffee, smoke a nargileh and watch the sun go down over the Mediterranean. Up on the promenade you may strike a rare sight indeed – women in traditional dress also sitting around enjoying a nargileh!

Although a couple of cheap hotels huddle by the theatre, transport to Lattakia is so regular that staying here overnight seems hardly worth it. The microbus costs S£11.

BANIYAS

Lying south of Lattakia, about halfway to Tartus, Baniyas is a busy port town with a large oil refinery. The only reason to stop here, though, is to visit the old Crusader fort of Qala'at al-Marqab, six km south of the town.

Getting There & Away

Microbuses to and from Lattakia cost S£15 and take about an hour. Competition for a place on them can be fierce, especially in the mornings, and you have to pay for an assigned seat at a booth just to get on. The microbuses from Tartus take only half an hour and cost S£11.

QALA'AT AL-MARQAB

This citadel was originally a Muslim stronghold, possibly founded in 1062, and it commands almost limitless views of the Mediterranean to the west and surrounding valleys dropping away to the east and south. After falling into Crusader hands in the early 12th century, the fortifications were expanded. The main defensive building, the dungeon, is on the southern flank, as the gentler slopes made that point the castle's most vulnerable. After several attempts, Saladin gave up trying to take Marqab, which only fell to the Mamelukes from Egypt in 1285.

The walls and towers are the most impressive element of what remains today, and the interior of the citadel is gradually being overrun by the slow march of vegetation. The entrance now is through the **gate tower** in the west wall. After getting through the main gate (just push it open if 'nobody's home'), turn off to your right and, across what was the central courtyard, you will see a **chapel** with two fine doorways and frescoes. Keep heading south past the chapel to the cylindrical **dungeon** and, next door, a great **hall**. To the north and east (stretching off to the chapel's left) are the barely distinguishable remnants of **storerooms** and possibly dining and living quarters.

It is open from 9 am to 6 pm (4 pm in winter) daily except Tuesday, and entry is S£200.

Getting There & Away

Take a microbus (S£5) from Baniyas for Zaoube – it goes right past. You may have to wait a while for this, and hitching is your best bet on the way back.

TARTUS

Tartus, Syria's second port, is an easy-going – some might say dead, at least in the cooler months – town with what could be a reasonable beach if it weren't so liberally strewn with garbage. The compact remnants of the old city (known to the Crusaders as Tortosa) are a fascinating warren of old and new, as is the once-fortified island offshore, Arwad. Stench and rubbish seem to be a big theme here though, spoiling Arwad as well as the beach. Anyone game to pick through the junk lovingly ladled over the sand to go for a dip should note the occasional dribble of sewage into the sea. Even if the beach was

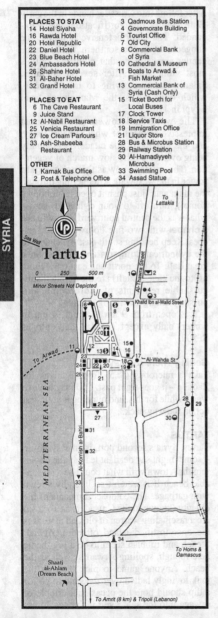

PLACES TO STAY
14 Hotel Siyaha
16 Rawda Hotel
20 Hotel Republic
22 Daniel Hotel
23 Blue Beach Hotel
24 Ambassadors Hotel
26 Shahine Hotel
31 Al-Baher Hotel
32 Grand Hotel

PLACES TO EAT
6 The Cave Restaurant
9 Juice Stand
12 Al-Nabil Restaurant
25 Venicia Restaurant
27 Ice Cream Parlours
33 Ash-Shabeeba Restaurant

OTHER
1 Karnak Bus Office
2 Post & Telephone Office
3 Qadmous Bus Station
4 Governorate Building
5 Tourist Office
7 Old City
8 Commercial Bank of Syria
10 Cathedral & Museum
11 Boats to Arwad & Fish Market
13 Commercial Bank of Syria (Cash Only)
15 Ticket Booth for Local Buses
17 Clock Tower
18 Service Taxis
19 Immigration Office
21 Liquor Store
28 Bus & Microbus Station
29 Railway Station
30 Al-Hamadiyyeh Microbus
33 Swimming Pool
34 Assad Statue

Tartus

Minor Streets Not Depicted

twinkling in pristine cleanliness, the jumbled strip of half finished bunker-style concrete housing and slums that form the backdrop to the sea is hardly conducive to fanciful Mediterranean day-dreaming. Women will feel most comfortable swimming as the local women do – fully clothed, however, some travellers wear one piece bathing suits. Bikinis would be inappropriate, and definitely should be avoided.

Just south of Tartus is the virtually untouched Phoenician site of Amrit, and not far inland the soaring, white Crusader dungeon of Safita. Tartus is also a good base from which to visit the beautifully preserved Crusader castle, the Crac des Chevaliers. Alternatively, you could visit the Crac en route from Tartus to Homs or vice versa, as long as you don't mind carting your gear around with you all day.

History

Tartus seems to have been first established as a service town for the island of Arados (later called Ruad, now called Arwad) and given the name Antarados. It was taken over by Alexander the Great and then rebuilt by Constantine in 346 AD and renamed Constantina.

A chapel devoted to the Virgin Mary was built and the town became a popular pilgrimage site during the Crusader period. It was then that it acquired the new name of Tortosa. The town first came into Crusader hands in 1102. Later that century, it became the seat of a bishop and the cathedral was constructed on the site of the ancient chapel.

In 1188, Saladin conquered all but the dungeon, the town's last redoubt. He eventually withdrew and the Knights Templar set about building the town and its defences up again. Only in 1291 did the Mamelukes force the Crusaders to flee to Cyprus. Another garrison managed to hang on to Arwad for a further 11 years.

Information

Tourist Office The tourist office is north of the cathedral and is open from 8 am to 2 pm daily except Friday. The staff have a few of the usual brochures, but are happy to help in whatever limited way they can.

Visa Extensions The immigration office for visa extensions is in a small street just behind the clock tower, and is open from 8 am to 2 pm Saturday to Thursday. There is nothing to distinguish the street entrance but a black and white sign and a Syrian flag overhead. The office is upstairs.

Post & Communications The post office is open from 8 am to 8 pm (2 pm on Friday). The telephone office, in the same building, is open until 10 pm.

Money The Commercial Bank of Syria has two branches: the main one, on a corner just up the road east of the tourist office, is open from 8 am to noon and changes cash or travellers' cheques; the other, between the port and the clock tower, supposedly opens from noon to 4 pm, but take this with a pinch of salt. It only changes cash.

Cathedral & Museum

Don't be put off by the rather austere exterior of the 12th century Cathedral of Our Lady of Tortosa, the interior is all graceful curves and arches and houses a good little museum. On this site, more or less, a chapel dedicated to the Virgin Mary is thought to have been destroyed as early as 367 AD. It is from that chapel that an altar and icon that became the object of pilgrimage supposedly survived to be incorporated into the cathedral.

From the outside it looks more like a fortress, and that is no coincidence, as its construction was conceived with its own defence in mind. The only decoration is the five-arched windows (which were only finished shortly before the Mamelukes took over the city in 1291) and the reconstructed doorway. The interior consists of a nave with aisles on either side. Fragments of earlier buildings have been incorporated into the construction; most obvious are the Corinthian-style capitals used in two pillars in the nave.

The second pillar on the left of the nave is built on top of a rectangular structure containing an arched passage. This is believed to have been the entrance to the original chapel where pilgrims made their devotions to the icon of the Virgin Mary, which the Crusaders took with them when they finally abandoned the city.

Items on display in the museum come from various sites including Ras Shamra, Arwad and Amrit. The sarcophagus in the central apse dates from the 2nd century AD, during the Roman era, as do the four to the left of the entrance. The headless statue in the nave is of Bacchus, the god of revelry. Left of the sarcophagus, in the apse, is a mural taken from the Crac des Chevaliers depicting Christ, Mary and St Simon.

The cathedral is supposedly open from 9 am to 6 pm (4 pm in winter) daily except Tuesday, although it has been known to open then too. Entry costs S£200.

Old City

If you head down to the waterfront, pretty well directly in front of the cathedral, you will see remains of the medieval town walls and ramparts. The area of the old city is small and still buzzing with the activity of its crowded inhabitants. New structures have been added to or blended in with the old, and the whole area is honeycombed with low archways, stairways seemingly leading nowhere, narrow lanes and tumbledown houses. It is, unlike so many medieval city centres in Europe cleaned up by modernity, to all intents and purposes the direct heir of its Crusader past, a living microcosm of a world long gone, unpolished for any passing visitors, although some limited excavation and restoration is being done. It's to be hoped that the restorations can strike the right balance between living town and museum.

Arwad

This small island, a few km south-west of Tartus, is a real gem. If only it were not so filthy! There are no cars or wide streets, only a maze of narrow lanes that twist and turn between the tightly packed buildings and, with each turn, reveal something new.

Founded by the Canaanites and at one stage occupied by the Egyptians, it has known a long and eventful history. In Phoenician times the island was a prosperous and powerful maritime state, with colonies on the mainland at Amrit, Baniyas and Jabla. It gradually declined in the 1st millennium BC and was of little importance by the time it became part of the Roman Empire. During the Crusades it assumed strategic importance and was the last Frankish outpost to fall to the Muslims, in 1302.

Today, Arwad is an interesting, somewhat claustrophobic place to wander around. Right next door to the cafés you can see fisherfolk mending their nets and building boats with a mixture of traditional methods and modern tools.

Little is left of the island's defensive walls, but two forts remain; the one on the highest point houses a small museum. Nothing is labelled but the attendants are eager to show off their English and guide you around. It's closed on Tuesday, and entry is S£200.

The stalls down by the boat harbour sell the most amazing array of tacky souvenirs, from shell-encrusted ashtrays to plastic toys. You can get an expensive cup of tea at the waterfront café, but if you want a more reasonably priced snack, wait until you stumble across one of the small shops in the tangle of lanes. It won't take too long, the whole island only measures 800 by 500m.

Small boats head out to the island every 15 minutes or so from the small fishing harbour. The return trip costs S£20, which you pay on the island, and takes about 20 minutes each way. The last boat leaves the island around sunset – don't get stranded as there is no accommodation.

Shaati al-Ahlam

For most of the year, it appears, little attempt is made to keep the so-called Dream Beach clean, making it anything but a dream. In fact, at times there seems to be more rubbish on it than on the beaches closer to town! At the southern end of town, it is a little more relaxed than Tartus and women should feel less inhibited about swimming here. You may have to pay a fee to use the beach.

There are bungalows, called chalets, for rent at about S£600 per day. They have three beds, bath and cooking facilities. The fancy *Shaati al-Ahlam Restaurant* is very upmarket and has live music in the evenings.

Places to Stay – bottom end

Once one of the best deals in Syria, the *Daniel Hotel* (☎ 220582) has for too long been living off its reputation. Quality of the rooms varies considerably, although they are generally reasonable. They come with private bath and tepid water. You will pay S£300/600 for singles/doubles, a little hefty for what you get, and breakfast is extra if you want it. There is a curfew at 11 pm.

Among the cheaper alternatives for those on a strict diet of rock-bottom hotels, the *Hotel Tourism & Resort* (☎ 221763) is about the best, especially if you snag one of the rooms with a balcony. It's further east on Al-Wahda St from the Daniel and is known in Arabic as Hotel Siyaha. You pay S£175/275 and hot water *may* be available. Rooms of a similar quality can be had at the *Hotel Republic* (☎ 222580) for the same price. The *Rawda Hotel* is in much the same league. Otherwise, there is a string of cheap little places north of the clock tower along Al-Thawra St.

Places to Stay – middle

The only other places start at about US$15 a single. The *Ambassadors Hotel* (☎ 220183) down on the waterfront (the entrance is in the backstreet) is enormous and has rooms with balconies overlooking the water for US$20/25. Rooms in the back can be had for less. Next door, the *Blue Beach* (☎ 222746) hotel offers similar rooms with a shower for US$15/22, and the proprietor speaks Spanish. Both have hot water, but apart from that and the views, offer little that the Daniel doesn't.

South down the beach and with much better rooms (US$18/25) is the *Al-Baher Hotel* (☎ 221687).

Then comes the *Grand Hotel* (☎ 225475),

where rooms cost US$40/45 and the only significant improvement is a TV and fridge. The *Shahine Hotel* (☎ 221703; fax 315002), back a bit from the beach, is newer and considerably better, with rooms costing US$34/38 plus taxes.

Places to Eat

The cheap restaurants and snack places are clustered around the clock tower and Al-Wahda St. You'll find a juice stand north of the clock tower on Khalid Ibn al-Walid St.

The small restaurant just behind the boat harbour, *Al-Nabil*, sells baked fish that is heavily spiced and salted. The fish is really quite good, but a meal with extras and a beer or two will set you back almost S£400. It also does more regular dishes (like chicken and kebabs), for about half the cost.

Along the waterfront are a few outdoor restaurants. The *Ash-Shabeeba Restaurant* at the southern end of Al-Kornish al-Bahri (the coastal road) is right on the beach, but seems to open during the summer months only.

Next to the Ambassador Hotel is the *Venicia Restaurant*, which serves up a strange version of a pizza on a thin, flaky base. It also does (surprise, surprise) things like kebabs, hummus and salad without fail. At about S£200 for a full meal with a drink or two, it's nothing great.

Another seafood joint is *The Cave*, nestled in below the old city walls on the seaward side. Food is not cheap and foreign beers are served at S£100 a bottle. Another bright restaurant with the usual favourites is the *Family Club*, below the Blue Beach Hotel on the waterfront.

Opposite the Shahine Hotel is a couple of good ice-cream parlours and a vaguely western-style snack bar.

Getting There & Away

Bus/Microbus The old bus and microbus station is about a 15 minute walk from the town centre and right in front of the railway station. Old buses and minibuses, and the newer, slicker microbuses leave from in and around the station when full. The trip to Lattakia by microbus costs S£35 and takes about 1½ hours; Baniyas is S£11 and 30 minutes away. There are also plenty of buses heading for Homs (S£23, 1½ hours) and Damascus (S£53, four hours). You can also get a microbus to Safita (S£8, 45 minutes) from here.

The Karnak office is across the road from the post office. There is a daily departure at 7 am for Tripoli (S£100) and Beirut (S£150), and another to Damascus (S£75).

The new Qadmous private bus station is about a block south next to the governorate building. Buses from here leave to a strict timetable and are among the best you'll find in Syria. The fare to Aleppo is S£115, to Hama, S£65, and S£110 to Damascus. Microbuses also leave from here (as well as the old station discussed earlier) for Lattakia and Baniyas.

Train The attendant insists the only train for Damascus leaves at 1.23 am and costs S£67 (1st class) or S£45 (2nd class). Another train leaves at about 4 am for Lattakia, where you must change for Aleppo.

Service Taxis Service taxis congregate around the clock tower. Demand is not high so you may have to wait quite a while for one to fill up. They charge way over the bus prices. Destinations include Damascus, Homs and Lattakia, as well as Beirut and Tripoli.

Getting Around

Although you're not likely to need to use them much, the local buses can make life a little easier. A ticket booth is located about 200m north of the clock tower. A pink ticket valid for four rides (punch a corner at a time) will cost S£10. From the stop just south of the clock tower buses head south to Shaati al-Ahlam in summer.

AROUND TARTUS

Amrit

Two quite odd-looking monuments, raised as long ago as the 6th century BC, dominate the mysterious ancient site of Amrit, which is eight km south of Tartus. Known later to the Greeks as Marathos and conquered by Alexander the Great in 333 BC, Amrit had fallen by the wayside of history by the time it was incorporated into the Roman Empire.

The so-called *meghazils* (spindles) stand in what was once a necropolis and, although no one is entirely sure how to explain the origins of this settlement, it appears that Phoenicians from Arwad made of the area a kind of satellite or religious zone. Both towers stand above underground funeral chambers – you'll need a torch (flashlight) to poke around them – and betray a curious mix of Hellenistic, Persian and even Egyptian influences in their decoration. About a km north lie the remains of a temple built to serve a cult centred on the springs here. The water that once filled the basin here was considered to have curative powers. Nearby, evidence of a stadium has been unearthed.

The sea sparkles invitingly to the west of the ancient site, but most of the land around here belongs to the armed forces. This may change, as plans are afoot to create a US$70 million tourist complex. As yet about the only evidence of this is a scarcely credible sign announcing its imminent appearance. Although it may pave the way for sun lovers to get onto largely untouched beaches, such a development will be a dubious addition to the area.

Getting There & Away Take the Al-Hamadiyyeh microbus (S£5) from near the old bus and railway stations and ask to be let off at the track leading to Amrit – mention you want the *athaar* (ruins). The track leads off towards the sea from the main road. After about 1.5 km you pass an army post (there are firing ranges around here). Some 200m further on you can see the temple remains in the distance off to the left. Another 20 minutes or so of walking brings you to the meghazils. To get back to Tartus, return to the main road and flag down a microbus.

Safita

This restful mountain town is dominated by the striking white *donjon* (dungeon), all that remains of the once-powerful Crusader era **Castel Blanc**. Known to locals simply as Al-Burj (The Tower), it was built and rebuilt several times by the Knights Templar as the result of earthquake damage, and fell shortly before the Crac des Chevaliers to Sultan Baibars in 1271. The fact that a hefty portion of the local populace is Christian suggests the presence of the Crusaders left a more profound mark than bricks and mortar.

From the chaotic central town intersection where you will be dropped by most microbuses, take the road leading uphill to the west. After about 200m you'll see the donjon ahead of you. Keep going until you note a cobbled lane off to the right that passes under the arched gate of what remains of the castle's defensive perimeter.

Two steep, cobbled lanes lead up to the donjon, and you enter from the western side. On this level there is a still functioning Orthodox church. Stairs in the south-west corner lead up to spacious living quarters. The simple vaulted ceiling and columns constitute one of the best examples of the Romanesque design you'll encounter in Syria. Another flight takes you to the roof, from where the tower was defended. To the south-east you can just make out the Crac (the two were thus linked in the Crusaders' chain of communications), and directly to the south the snowcapped peaks of northern Lebanon.

It's supposedly open from 8 am to 1 pm and 3 to 6 pm, but this is not to be taken too literally. Entrance is free, but the guardian deserves a small tip for his troubles.

Places to Stay & Eat Virtually on the town intersection, at the beginning of the road you take to reach the donjon, is possibly one of the worst dives in Syria. The *Hotel Siyaha* is a true fleapit, where a bed will cost you S£100.

The only other options are beyond the budget traveller. A few km south-east of the central square, where the buses terminate and the taxis hang about, is the *Hotel Burj Safita*, which offers decent singles/doubles/triples for US$18/22/25.

Even further out of the range of most mortals is the *Safita Cham Palace* (☎ 043-525980), unfortunately the most prominent building in the town next to the tower itself. Rooms cost US$125/160 plus taxes.

Quite a few travellers swear that you can organise to stay in a private home.

There are a few snack places in the middle of town, but the best of them is the little *Restaurant Bar* on the intersection. It is run by a Portuguese-speaking chap who spent a good chunk of his life in Brazil. He makes tasty snacks and charges very little for them. The restaurant next to the Castel serves the standard fare, beer and, best of all, marvellous views across the valleys and hills surrounding Safita. The comestibles are at rather inflated prices.

Getting There & Away The microbus from Tartus costs S£8 and takes about 45 minutes to wind its way up to Safita. It is possible to get here from Homs as well. There is a daily Karnak bus connection to Damascus via Homs.

Hosn Sulayman

A worthwhile excursion north of Safita will take you along some of the highest mountain ridges of the Jebel an-Nusariyah some 25 km distant to a remarkable and imposing testament to thousands of years of religious fervour. Exit the village of Hosn Sulayman and you are confronted by temple walls constructed of huge stone blocks, some of them as great as 10m by three metres!

Although evidence suggests the site has been home to temples of one religious persuasion or other since the time of Persian occupation of the Levant, what you see was largely erected under Roman domination in the 2nd century AD.

Four gates permit entry to the site, in the centre of which rises up the *cella*, the focal point of worship and offerings in the temple. The gates themselves preserve the most intact decoration, with columns, niches and inscriptions (the clearest of these can be observed above the east gate). The east and west gates display the same sculptural adornments. The figure of a bearded man stands above the lintel, while the same area on the inside is dominated by figures depicting two youths and a lion's head. As you pass through each gate, look up to see the outspread wings of an eagle.

Across the road are the less extensive ruins of what appears to be another temple compound, but little is known about its history or function.

Minibuses and microbuses (S£7) run at irregular intervals from Safita to the village of Hosn Sulayman, taking about 40 minutes. It is quite feasible to visit Safita and Hosn Sulayman as a combined day trip from Tartus, but the earlier you get started, the less likely your chances of getting stuck in Hosn Sulayman.

CRAC DES CHEVALIERS

The remarkably well-preserved Crac des Chevaliers (Castle of the Knights, or 'Qala'at al-Hosn') is one of Syria's prime attractions and should not be missed. Impervious to the onslaught of time, it cannot have looked a great deal different 800 years ago.

The fort is sited in the only significant break in the mountain range between Antakya (Turkey) and Beirut (Lebanon), a distance of some 250 km. Anyone who held this gap was virtually assured of authority over inland Syria by controlling the flow of goods and people from the ports through to the interior.

Even today, this gap is important and carries the major road link from Homs to Tartus, as well as the oil pipeline from the fields in the far east of the country to the terminal at Tartus.

The Crusaders built and expanded the fort over a period of 100 years from around 1150; when completed, it could house a garrison of 4000. Local basalt was used in early stages of construction, but subsequently limestone was also employed. After holding off a number of concerted attempts to take the fort, the Crusaders were finally forced to surrender to Sultan Baibars in 1271. He allowed them to march out of the castle on

Crac des Chevaliers: Things to See

The stronghold comprises two distinct parts: the outside wall with its 13 towers and **main entrance**; and the inside wall and central construction, which are built on a rocky platform. A moat dug out of the rock separates the two walls.

The main entrance (No 1 on the plan) leads to a gently sloping ramp with steps wide enough to allow the garrison's horses to ride up. The first tower on the left (2) was a guard room and, next to it, the long hall served as stables (3). The ramp (4) continues up to a point where it turns sharply to the right and leads to the inner fortress. The **tower** (5) at this point is massive, with a doorway leading out to the moat through a five metre thick wall. On the outer wall above the doorway are the figures of two lions facing each other, supposedly symbols of the English Crusader king, Richard the Lionheart.

The moat here is usually full of stagnant water. When the castle was occupied, this water was used to fill the **baths** (6) and water the horses. Near the baths is the easily missed and largely overgrown entrance to what was a secret passage into the Crac.

The cavernous room (7) on the southern edge of the moat (8) measures 60 by nine metres and the roof is totally unsupported. The **square tower** (9) bore the brunt of the attack in 1271 and was rebuilt by Sultan Baibars. The long room leads to the **tower** (10) in the south-west corner. Its central pillar, which supports the upper level of the tower, bears an inscription in Arabic recording Sultan Baibars' full title: 'Al-Malek az-Zaher Rukn ad-Dunya wad-Din Abu al-Fath Baibars' (the Manifest King, Pillar of the World and the Faith, Father of the Victory)!

Walking around between the two walls from the south-west tower, you reach the **Tower of the Daughter of the King** (11). You'll know you're inside the right place by the flies and stench of rotting rubbish piled up at the bottom. This tower is unusual in that it is wider than it is deep. On the façade are three rows of triple-pointed arches. A large projecting gallery, where rocks were hurled at assailants, is concealed in the face. The only danger visitors face today is the kitchen garbage nonchalantly hurled off the top of the tower from the café. The eastern face of this tower has a rear gate opening on to the moat.

Continue around and enter the inner fortress through the tower (12) at the top of the access ramp into an open courtyard (13). The **corridor** (14) on the western side of the yard is the most impressive structure in the Crac. Of the seven trusses facing the yard two are open doorways, while the other five each hold a pillar with delicate carvings.

The doors through the corridor lead to a large **vaulted hall** (15), which was probably a reception room. On the far side of this is a 120m long room (16) running the whole length of the western wall. A few old latrines (17) are still visible at the northern end. In the middle of the room are the remains of an **old oven** (18) measuring more than five metres in diameter. The room has been bricked up just behind it, but you can walk into the other half from the pillars room and see a well (19) and, right at the end, another oven in the wall.

The **pillars room** (20) has five rows of heavy squat pillars and it is vaulted with fist-sized stones. It has been suggested that it was used as a refectory. Rooms 21, 22 and 23 were used as warehouses. In room 22 are the remains of massive pottery oil jars and in 23 there's an old oil-mill, more oil jars and a well.

Back in the courtyard, the **chapel** (24) has a nave of three bays of vaults. It was converted to a mosque after the Muslim conquest and the minbar (pulpit) still remains. The staircase that obstructs the main door is a later addition and leads to the upper floors of the fortress.

One of the impressive 12th-century towers of Crac des Chevaliers

The upper floor of the Tower of the Daughter of the King (11) has been converted into a café selling tea, beer and snacks. From various vantage points on this level there are some magnificent views if the haze clears: the snowcapped peak of Kornet as-Saouda (3088m) in the Anti-Lebanon Range to the south and the valley of the Nahr al-Kabir (Big River) to the east. To the west you should also be able to make out the solitary pale figure of Safita's Castel Blanc.

For the best view of the Crac itself, walk along the road around to the right of the entrance and up to the small hill behind the south-west corner.

The castle is open from 9 am to 7 pm (5 pm in winter) daily (except public holidays), and entry costs S£200. A torch (flashlight) would be handy to explore some of its darker passages. Those passing through en route to Homs, Tartus or anywhere else should have little trouble leaving their packs at reception. ■

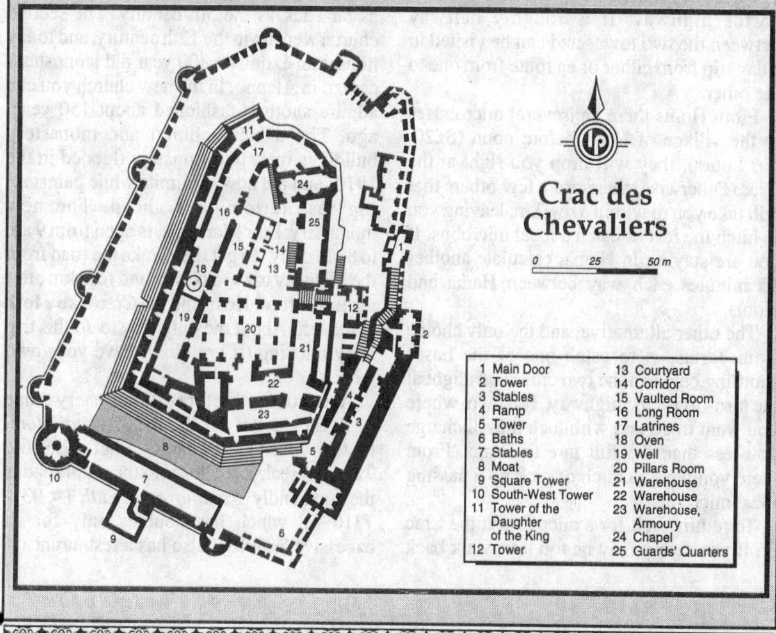

condition that they leave the country, but it seems they only went as far as Tartus and Tripoli. Additional towers were built by Baibars and the different Frankish and Arabic styles can be clearly distinguished.

Places to Stay & Eat

The *Restaurant La Table Ronde* (☎ 031-734280), about 100m off to the left of the main entrance, has basic rooms with three beds for S£500. You can also camp here (S£150 to pitch a tent and use the shower). Otherwise, the *Amar Tourist Resort* (☎ 031-733203), about four km down the road past the Crac, is a popular resort-style hotel with expensive rooms, pool and restaurant. It's only open in summer and a suite with two bedrooms and kitchenette costs S£1350. The only other possibility are the hotels on the road to St George's Monastery.

The Crac is an easy day trip from Tartus or Hama, which both offer better accommodation possibilities.

About the best value for food and drink is the *Restaurant La Table Ronde*. Or you could try the *Restaurant des Chevaliers*, opposite the Crac entrance. The café inside the castle is a shameless rip-off joint.

Getting There & Away

The Crac lies some 10 km north of the Homs-Tartus highway. It is roughly halfway between the two towns and can be visited in a day trip from either or en route from one to the other.

From Homs there are several microbuses to the village of Hosn before noon (S£20, 1½ hours); they will drop you right at the Crac. Otherwise, there are a few others that will take you to within a few km, leaving you to hitch the rest or catch a local microbus. If you are staying in Hama, calculate another 45 minutes each way between Hama and Homs.

The other alternative, and the only choice from Tartus, is to catch one of the buses shuttling between the two cities and alight at the turn-off on the highway. Tell them where you want to go and with luck they'll charge you less than the full fare to Homs. From there you have to hitch or pick up a passing local microbus.

To return, wait for a microbus at the Crac or, if you fear it may be too late, walk back down through the village and out to the road that leads to the Homs-Tartus motorway. You have a better chance of picking up passing traffic late in the day from here than from the Crac or village.

AROUND CRAC DES CHEVALIERS

St George's Monastery

The first Greek Catholic church on this site, in a valley to the west of the Crac, was built as far back as the 5th century. The second church went up in the 12th century, and today houses an exquisite 300 year old iconostasis carved in Aleppo. In the new church you can admire another, fashioned about 150 years ago. The ancient church and monastery buildings were unfortunately flooded in the 1970s and are now off limits while painstaking restoration goes ahead. The new monastery, Deir Mar Jirjis, is open from 9 am to 8 pm daily. To get there, take the road from the highway toward Nasira and four km after the turn-off for Hosn and the Crac take a fork to the left. About the only way to do this trip is by hitching (if you don't have your own wheels).

About two km before the monastery is one of Syria's better hotels, the *Al-Wadi Hotel* (☎ 031-730547). It charges a hefty US$60/72 with breakfast. Closer to the main road is the unfriendly *Funduq ar-Riyadh* (☎ 031-731095), which has doubles only for an excessive S£800. It also has a restaurant.

Orontes Valley

The Orontes River ('Nahr al-Assi' in Arabic – the Rebel River – because it flows from south to north) has its headwaters in the mountains of Lebanon near Baalbek. It enters Syria near Tell Nabi Mend, the Kadesh of ancient times where, in around 1300 BC, the Egyptians were beaten back by the Hittites in a bloody confrontation.

Just south of the city of Homs is a dam dating from the 2nd millennium BC. With some modern additions, it is known today as Lake Qattinah and supplies Homs with drinking water and irrigates some 200 sq km.

The river flows through the industrial city of Homs before reaching Hama, where the only obstruction to the flow are the ancient *norias* or water wheels. The Orontes used to flow north-west from Hama and seep away in the swamps of the plain of Al-Ghab, but those swamps have long been drained to form one of the most fertile plains in Syria, allowing the river to pursue its course northwards into Turkey, finally reaching the Mediterranean beyond Antakya.

HOMS

There's little of interest to see in Homs but it's a busy city with a lively air. It is also one of those crossroads that most travellers have to pass through at some stage. Roads head north to Hama, east to Palmyra and the Euphrates, south to Damascus and west to Tartus and the coast.

Homs, Syria's third largest city, is an industrial centre where half the country's total oil refining capacity is based. Superphosphates are produced here, there is a sugar refinery and also some light manufacturing.

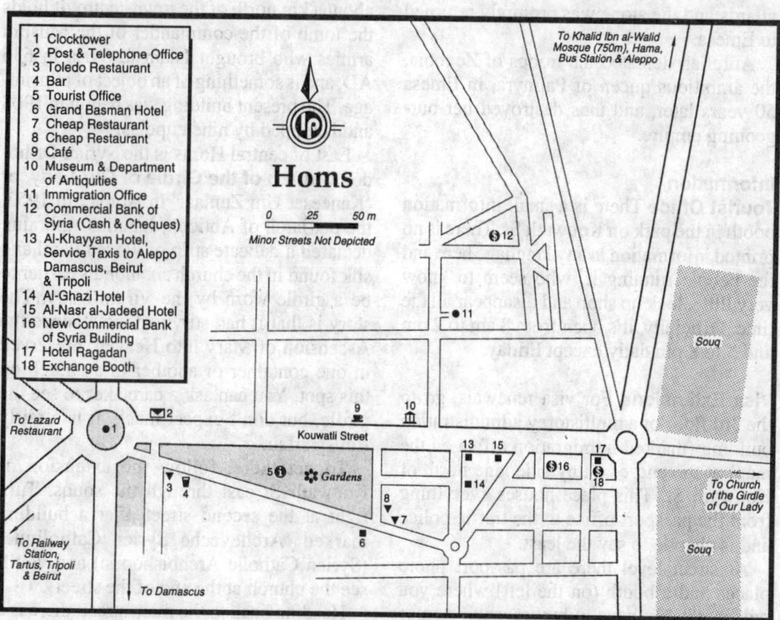

Despite its long history, almost nothing is left as a witness to its past. The few remaining items of interest only really justify a stop for travellers with time to kill. And although some see it as a base for visiting the Crac des Chevaliers, there is absolutely no reason not to opt for the more attractive Hama as a base for this and other excursions.

History

In ancient times, the city was known as Emesa and its people are mentioned among those who opposed the Roman conquest. In 194 AD, Emperor Septimius Severus married Julia Domna, who came from an Emesan family of priests.

His successor, Elagabalus, was proclaimed emperor in 218 AD and made a sun-god cult from Emesa the main official religion of Rome. The central object of this cult, a large, black conical stone, was even sent to Rome. By 222 AD the slightly eccentric Elagabalus had finally gone off his trolley. He was assassinated by Praetorian guards and the stone was promptly returned to Emesa.

Aurelian defeated the troops of Zenobia, the ambitious queen of Palmyra, in Emesa 50 years later, and thus destroyed her burgeoning empire.

Information

Tourist Office There is a small information booth in the park on Kouwatli St. There is no printed information in any language here and the people running it, who seem to know very little, lock up shop and disappear all the time. Officially, it's open from 8 am to 2 pm and 5 to 8 pm daily except Friday.

Visa Extensions For visa renewals, go to the 3rd floor of a multistorey administration building (marked immigration office on the map) at the end of a tiny side lane north of Kouwatli St. This place houses everything from the passport office to the traffic police and is chaotic to say the least.

At street level there are passport photo places and a booth (on the left) where you will inevitably have to buy revenue stamps for your visa extension forms. It's open from 8.30 am to 2 pm Saturday to Thursday.

Money A few blocks north of Kouwatli St is the main branch of the Commercial Bank of Syria, where you can change cash or travellers' cheques from 8 am to 12.30 pm daily except Friday. On Kouwatli St a big new branch was yet to open at the time of writing. Otherwise, there is an exchange booth close to the souqs that also takes cash and cheques and is open from 8 am to 8 pm (the guy here shuts for a few hours in the early afternoon for lunch).

Post The post and telephone office is near the clock tower roundabout at the western end of Kouwatli St, and is open daily from 8 am to 2 pm and 5 to 8 pm except Friday when it's open only from 8 am to 1pm.

Things to See

The only building of great note is the **Khalid Ibn al-Walid Mosque** on the Hama road about a km north of the town centre. It holds the tomb of the commander of the Muslim armies who brought Islam to Syria in 636 AD, and is something of an object of pilgrimage. The present building was begun in 1908 and is topped by nine cupolas.

East of central Homs is the Syrian Orthodox **Church of the Girdle of Our Lady**, or 'Kaneesat Um Zumaar' in Arabic. In 1953, the patriarch of Antioch, Ignatius Aphraim, declared a delicate strip of woven wool and silk found in the church six months earlier to be a girdle worn by the Virgin Mary. The story is that it had survived intact since the Ascension of Mary into Heaven, preserved in one container or another in a church on this spot. You can ask a caretaker to see the girdle, but don't expect much. It is a fairly flimsy affair.

To get there, follow the extension of Kouwatli St east through the souqs. Turn right at the second street after a building marked 'Archevêché Syrien Catholique' (Syrian Catholic Archbishopric) and you'll see the church at the end of the street.

Heading back to the main street, there is a

small Ottoman building in a lane off to the right called Beit Zahrani. A small **Museum of Popular Traditions & Culture** – you know, the type with the wax dummies – is housed here. It opens from 8 am to 2 pm, and entry costs S£100.

The city's main **museum** is housed in the Department of Antiquities building on Kouwatli St. You can see its rather lacklustre archaeological collection from 9 am to 6pm (4 pm in winter) daily except Tuesday, if you are prepared to shell out S£200.

The souq is unusually large and busy but, as it is all modern, it's no great shakes.

The citadel, in the south of the city, is a military zone and off limits. It is little more than an outsize mound anyway.

Places to Stay

The cheap hotels are on or around Kouwatli St between the tourist office and the souq. The best is the *Al-Nasr al-Jadeed Hotel* (☎ 227423). Its owner is a polite old guy who speaks English well and with whom you can have a long chat in the big lounge room. The entrance is in a side street off Kouwatli St and clean singles/doubles cost S£200/300. A hot shower can be cranked up in the corridor.

Around the next block off Kouwatli St, the *Al-Khayyam Hotel* (☎ 223959) has doubles only for S£300 but no hot water. Next door, the *Al-Ghazi Hotel* (☎ 222160) has gloomy rooms for S£200/300 and just as much hot water. Neither have anything to recommend them.

Across the road from the Khalid Ibn al-Walid Mosque is the *Az-Za'afran Hotel* (just 'Hotel' in English). With no hot water and at S£200 for one person, it has little to recommend it above the others. It is one of several such dives on this main drag.

For something a bit more 'up-market', the

SYRIA

The Sword of Allah

Although Arab raiding parties had been harrying local troops and villages in southern Syria for centuries, it was not until shortly after the Prophet's death that the first ever serious campaign beyond the Arabian peninsula took place. Some 10,000 warriors from numerous tribes rode into the Wadi Araba in 633, and by February 634 had surprised and wiped out the local Byzantine contingents. Constantinople had been caught on the hop – no serious threat had ever before emerged from the desert wastes of Arabia. They were not long to rebound however, sending an army south from Homs under a certain Theodorus, who looked set to turn the tide back.

Meanwhile, a keen commander by the name of Khalid Ibn al-Walid with an intrepid band of 500 hungry veterans had earlier begun, with the help of local tribes, Islam's first campaign outside Arabia – in Iraq. He was having quite a deal of success when Abu Bakr, the caliph, ordered him to head west. With fewer than 1000 men, he force marched for 20 days along a circuitous desert route to evade observation, appearing as if out of nowhere in the vicinity of Damascus. The cameleers had brought horses with them, which they were to use with great effect in battle. He immediately attacked local forces from the rear, sowing disorder and panic among Byzantine troops. In the next year he joined forces with the other Arab units and took overall command, occupying Bosra and Pella (and thus securing all of Palestine) before arriving again at the gates of Damascus. In September 635 the future political capital of the Muslim empire surrendered. Khalid employed the carrot, promising the inhabitants they would be in no way molested so long as they allowed his army in and thereafter paid the poll tax to which all non-Muslims were to be subjected. So attractive were the terms that a row of other Syrian cities quickly followed suit.

Theodorus came back for more, with an army of some 50,000, so Khalid went for broke. Temporarily abandoning most of his conquests, including Damascus, he marshalled all the men he could muster, perhaps 25,000, on the Yarmouk River. Months of skirmishes culminated in the great Battle of Yarmouk in August 636, in which Theodorus and his men were utterly routed. The Sword of Allah marched triumphantly up to the northern boundary of Syria with Byzantium (modern Turkey). The conquest, aided to some extent by the local people's favourable reception to the newcomers, was complete. Khalid's brilliant career, however, had come to an end. Caliph Abu Bakr's successor, Omar, apparently was not so taken with him, and appointed a rival as governor-general of the area, a ruling Khalid appears not to have contested. He now lies buried in Homs. ■

Grand Basman Hotel (☎ 235700) has rooms with bath and fan for US$15/22. The entrance is in the middle of a small shopping arcade. It's not bad, but as is so often the case with the lower end hotels charging dollars, it's well overpriced and tends to be a haunt for some dubious passing trade. The *Hotel Ragadan* (☎ 225211) on Kouwatli St charges the same and is nothing to write home about either.

Places to Eat

The *Toledo Restaurant*, set back a little from the gardens around the tourist information booth, serves a reasonable variety of stews, soups and rice dishes and a filling meal can easily be had for under S£200.

Other cheap restaurants are all in a group one block south of Kouwatli St and have the same old stuff – kebabs, chicken, felafel, hummus and salad.

Quite a distance west from the town centre is the recommended *Lazard Restaurant*, on Al-Hamra St near a roundabout. The street is marked on the free tourist map should you be of a mind to try it out.

On Kouwatli St there is a big shady café, formerly the *Gandool* and now called the *Majmu' ar-Rawda as-Siyahi* (something along the lines of Tourist Garden Association!), where you can sit down for a drink and nargileh, but there's no food.

Getting There & Away

Bus Homs is a busy transport hub serviced by Karnak, Pullman and microbuses.

The Karnak bus station is about two km north of the city centre. There are several daily buses to Damascus, the first at 8.15 am and the last at 6.30 pm. The trip costs S£50. Three buses run to Aleppo (calling at Hama) for S£60. There is a daily departure for Safita and another for Tartus – both cost S£30.

The regular bus station is next to the Karnak bus station and it's pretty busy. The old buses will take you to Damascus for S£27, while minibuses will do it for S£35 and modern microbuses for S£60. The old bus to Aleppo is S£30 and its minibus equivalent S£40. An old minibus will clatter to Hama in 40 minutes or so for S£10, or you can pay S£17 for the microbus.

For Palmyra, a private Pullman-style bus will cost S£90, which is actually the full fare to Deir ez-Zur.

Several microbuses do the trip to Qala'at al-Hosn (Crac des Chevaliers) for S£20.

Train The new railway station is a good half-hour walk from the centre. Take the street heading south-west of the clock tower until you merge with the main road (Tarablos St). At the second set of lights turn left down a side street (Al-Mahatta St) and head right to the end to the rather grandiose station building.

There are three departures a day south to Damascus (S£47/34, 1st/2nd class) and north to Aleppo (S£45/32). Two of the latter go on to Qamishle and all stops in between.

Service Taxi All the service taxis gather around the corner of the Al-Khayyam Hotel on Kouwatli St and run to Damascus, Aleppo, and Beirut and Tripoli (Lebanon).

HAMA

This is one of the more attractive towns in Syria with the Orontes River flowing through the centre, its banks lined with trees and gardens and the ancient, groaning norias. There's not an awful lot to see, but the town's peaceful atmosphere makes it a pleasant place to spend a few relaxing days. It is also a good base for excursions to the ruins of Apamea, Musyaf, Qala'at Sheisar and several other spots. You can even get to the Crac des Chevaliers via Homs and back in a day, far preferable to spending a night in Homs itself.

The people here are some of the most conservative in Syria and it is common to see smartly dressed women with their faces completely veiled in black. In contrast to this are the many peasant women in local costume of full-length black dresses boldly embroidered in bright reds and yellows, their unveiled faces often tattooed with traditional markings.

Hama is also an important industrial city,

and the bulk of Syria's iron and steel industry is centred here.

History

Although its history is not well known, Hama has occupied a position of importance for centuries. Excavations have revealed settlement as long ago as the New Stone Age.

During the reigns of David and Solomon (1000 to 922 BC), the Aramaean kingdom of Hamah (or Hamath) is known to have traded with Israel. Later occupied by the Assyrians, Hamah joined Damascus in a revolt against their occupiers in 853 BC, defeating the troops of Samalnasar. Under Sargon II, however, the Assyrians got their revenge in 720 BC and deported all the city's citizens. In the time of the Seleucids it was known as Epiphania after Epiphanes (Antiochus IV), and was called Emath during the early Christian era.

During the early years of the Crusades, Damascus, Aleppo (then divided) and the Franks all competed to win influence over Hama. Finally, under the tutelage of the Mamelukes, the Arab poet Abu al-Fida was made sultan of the city.

The most recent chapter in Hama's history

SYRIA

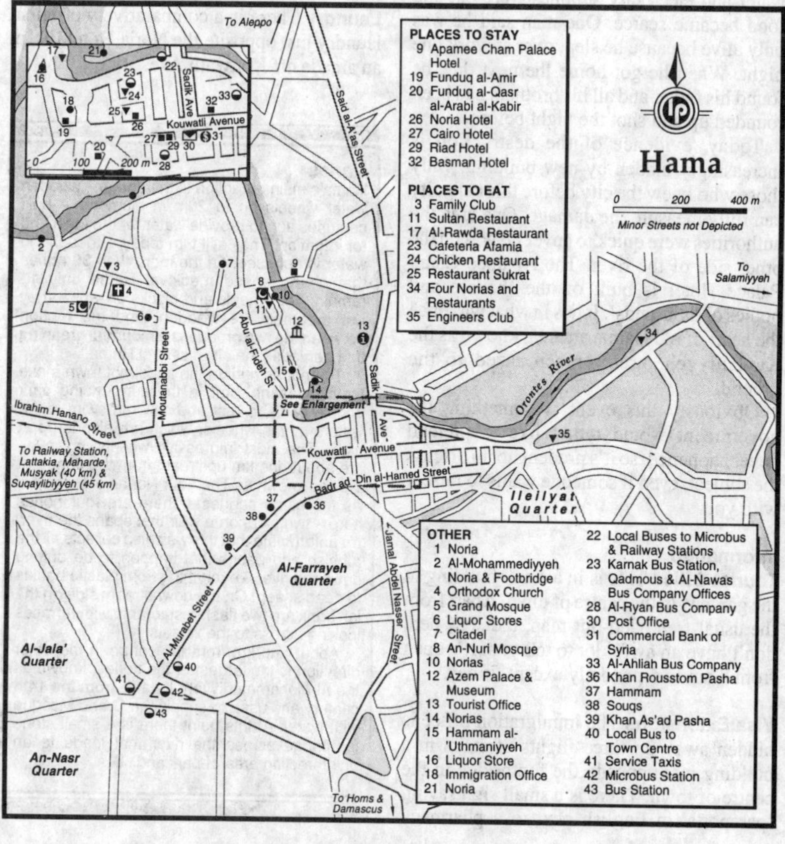

has been one of the country's saddest. For here the repressive nature of Assad's regime was brutally demonstrated in 1982. The details of what happened in that bloody February are hazy at best, but it appears that about 8000 troops moved in to quash a rebellion by armed members of the then outlawed Muslim Brotherhood – by all accounts an ill-conceived and unpopular uprising.

Townspeople willing to talk describe bombing attacks by the air force, tank assaults and fierce fighting. In all, up to 25,000 people may have died in fighting and as a result of mass executions and atrocities. As the city was sealed off for that month, water and electricity supplies were cut and food became scarce. One man said he was only alive because he slept over at work one night. When he got home the next day, he found his father and all his brothers had been rounded up and shot the night before.

Today, evidence of the destruction is increasingly hidden by new building. Only those who knew the city before this calamity can fully measure the damage. One area the authorities were quick to cover up was on the other side of the river. The Apamee Cham Palace Hotel is built on the 'houses and bodies of thousands'. It lies in what was once the heart of old Hama, an area, known as the Kaylaniyyeh, pretty much razed to the ground.

Obviously this event is something the government would rather like to pretend never happened, so it's prudent not to discuss the subject, even if someone wants to raise it with you.

Information

Tourist Office This is in a small building in the gardens in the centre of town. Apart from the usual free hand-out map, the staff here don't have an awful lot to tell you. It's open from 8 am to 5 pm daily except Friday.

Visa Extensions The immigration office is hidden away up three flights of stairs in a building just opposite the footbridge in the centre of town. There is a small sign saying 'passports' in English next to a pharmacy near the traffic island. The office is open from 8 am to 2 pm daily except Friday.

Money The Commercial Bank of Syria on Kouwatli Ave, next door to the post office, is open from 8.30 am to 12.30 pm. It accepts cash and travellers' cheques.

Post The main post office, open from 8 am to 6 pm (1 pm on Friday), is on the corner of Kouwatli Ave and the old Damascus-Aleppo highway (Sadik Ave). The posting box is an anonymous wooden box inside on the left. Behind it is a phone office, open from 8 am to noon and 5 to 7 pm daily.

Laundry There is a comparatively efficient laundry just opposite the Noria Hotel lift, in an arcade off Kouwatli Ave.

Norias

Hama's main attraction is the norias – wooden water wheels up to 20m in diameter – built centuries ago to provide water for the town and for irrigation. They still turn today, although the water is not used. Of the more than 30 norias that characterised medieval Hama only 17 remain. The wheels and blocks on which they are mounted are wooden, and the friction between the two produces a mournful groaning that pervades the air of central Hama.

The norias right in the middle of town make for a pleasant spot. In the surrounding park people come to rest and children swim in the waters by the wheels, which are also lit up at night. The most impressive wheels, however, are about one km upstream from the centre at a place known as The Four Norias of Bichriyat. As the name suggests, there are four norias here – two pairs on a weir that spans the river. It's unfortunate that this weir also collects all the rubbish and debris that happen to be drifting down the river – everything from plastic bottles to dead sheep. On the downstream side on the left bank are two flash restaurants with terraces looking across to the wheels.

About one km from the centre in the other direction is the largest of the norias, known as the Al-Mohammediyyeh. It dates from the 14th century and used to supply the Grand Mosque with water. At this point there is a small stone footbridge across the river that leads to an uninteresting area of parkland. ■

SYRIA

Citadel

For a good view over the city, walk up to the park on top of the citadel. Apart from a few unrecognisable fragments, nothing remains of the old fortress as all the stone was long ago carted off for use in other buildings. Danish archaeologists did extensive work on this tell and found evidence of continuous settlement since Neolithic times, particularly during the Iron Age.

The area has been landscaped and developed into a picnic and recreation area, with a café for those who don't bring their own.

Grand Mosque

The Grand Mosque, about 150m south of the Al-Mohammediyyeh noria, has been largely restored after its complete destruction during the 1982 uprising. Once the most striking of Hama's monuments, it was built by the Omayyads along the lines of their great mosque in Damascus. It had a similar history, too, having been converted from a church that itself had stood on the site of a pagan temple. What you see today, however faithfully the restorers seek to recreate its pre-1982 grandeur, is but a pale shadow of what has been lost.

Although the mosque is not on the city's free hand-out map, the tourist office staff are less coy about its existence than they used to be. This should not be interpreted as a cue for launching into a discussion of *why* it is in its present state.

Azem Palace & Museum

The museum is housed in the old Azem Palace, the residence of the governor, As'ad Pasha al-Azem, who ruled the town from 1742. The palace reminds its visitors of the more grandiose building of the same name in Damascus, which is hardly surprising, as the latter was built by the same man upon his transfer to Damascus.

The shady **courtyard** has various bits of ancient sculpture lying around, some bearing Arabic and Christian inscriptions. When the palace was extended in the late 18th century, this area became known as the *haramlik*, reserved for family and women. Stairs from here lead up to what is known as the **Royal Hall**, where it is supposed As'ad Pasha had his sleeping quarters. It took a pounding during the uprising but has largely been repaired. Opposite are three small rooms with some mannequins depicting scenes from local life.

Back on the ground floor, another door leads into a small museum containing artefacts discovered in the citadel. The most interesting of the exhibits is a 3rd century mosaic found near Hama. Historians have found its depiction of musicians a rich source of information on ancient instruments.

The haramlik was connected to the *salamlik* by the baths. The salamlik was reserved for men and guests and today offers little for the visitor. The top floor remains closed.

The museum is open from 9 am to 6 pm (4 pm in winter) daily except Tuesday. Entry is S£200.

An-Nuri Mosque

Just north of the palace is the An-Nuri Mosque, built by the Muslim commander Nureddin in the 12th century. The building is more interesting on the outside than the inside. The three norias here all have names: from east to west they are the Al-Kaylaniyyeh, the As-Sahuniyyeh and the Al-Ja'abariyyeh.

Caravanserais & Souqs

The two caravanserais (khans) are notable only for their stone entrances built in alternating colours. The Khan Rousstom Pasha, just south of the town centre on Al-Murabet St, was at one time an orphanage but is now being refurbished by the Ministry of Defence. Just what its future function will be remains unclear. Generally you cannot enter, although occasionally workers leave the main gate open and you can steal a glance.

The Khan As'ad Pasha, built in 1751 and further out of the centre near the souqs, is now a local area Ba'ath Party branch and off limits to nosy outsiders.

Much of the surrounding area is given over to Hama's souqs. While they may not be the most exciting you'll ever encounter, nevertheless they offer all the spectrum of sounds, sights and smells you could hope for from the traditional oriental market. It is a great place to go for a wander in the morning and, with little on offer for tourists, it is unlikely anyone will so much as say 'boo' to you.

Hammams

The Hammam al-'Uthmaniyyeh (Ottoman Turkish bath), south of the Azem Palace, is supposedly open from 8 am to noon and 7 to 11 pm daily for men, and from noon until 5 pm for women. Judging by the often firmly shut doors, this timetable is to be interpreted flexibly.

Less opulent but just as effective is the hammam next to the entrance to the gold souq on Al-Murabet Street.

Swimming

You can use the pool at the Apamee Cham Palace Hotel during summer for S£200 a day.

Organised Tours

The Noria, Cairo and Riad hotels can all organise transport for a day trip taking in several sights around Hama, including the Crac des Chevaliers. The itinerary can vary and, at S£500 or so per head, is no money-saver for the budget-conscious. It is a time-saver though, if that is important to you.

Places to Stay

As Syria slowly opens up to greater waves of European tour groups, Hama is waking up to the potential of tourism. Several hotels are experiencing a fever of expansion and more hotels are waiting on the drawing board for the green light.

Two of the best value-for-money places in Syria are right next to one another in Kouwatli Ave in Hama. The *Cairo Hotel* (☎ 237206; fax 511715) is spotlessly clean, has great showers and the friendly owner, Bader, speaks English and German. A bed in a shared room is S£175 (or S£150 if you don't want a shower) and doubles are S£350. If you don't mind having no shade to retreat to in the heat of summer, a bed on the roof will cost you S£100. The hotel is being expanded, and since Bader opened his new place across the road, the Cairo is now generally run by his nephew.

The *Riad Hotel* (☎ 239512) is in direct and not necessarily friendly competition with the Cairo, and is also being expanded and refurbished. A bed in a shared room will cost S£150. There is a variety of single and double rooms, some with ensuite bathroom, fridge and small B&W TV (for what that's worth). Singles/doubles will cost you up to S£350/450. It's pretty much a toss-up between the two – both ply you with complimentary tea on arrival, and organise excursions to the Crac des Chevaliers and several other attractions in the area for about S£500.

There's a couple of cheap flophouses where S£125 gets you a bed in a basic, noisy hotel that can only be recommended if you're in dire straits. The *Funduq al-Amir* at the end of Kouwatli Ave (actually on a lane called Hadat Abi Taleb) is upstairs and just has a green, black and red sign in Arabic above the door. Another is the *Funduq al-Qasr al-Arabi al-Kabir* ('Hotel' in English).

Bader of the Cairo Hotel has gone up-market with his new mid-range *Noria Hotel* (☎ /fax 511715). Singles/doubles here cost US$18/28 and are among the highest quality in this price bracket that you are likely to find in Syria. All have air-con, private bath and colour TV. There is a small restaurant and a roof terrace is planned.

Hama's only other mid-range hotel is the *Basman Hotel* (☎ 224838; fax 223910) on Kouwatli Ave opposite the Commercial Bank of Syria. Here you'll be paying US$18/25 for singles/doubles with fan, bath, satellite TV and balcony. It's quite scruffy and not nearly as good a deal as the Noria.

At the top of the range is the *Apamee Cham Palace Hotel* (☎ 227429; fax 233195), where singles/doubles will cost US$112/134. It's across the river from the An-Nuri Mosque.

Places to Eat

In the couple of blocks along Kouwatli Ave west of the Cairo Hotel are all the usual cheap kebab and chicken restaurants. There's about half a dozen of them here so if one doesn't have what you want, just try next door.

On a small street running from Kouwatli Ave to the river is a couple of *chicken restaurants* – the one nearer the river is good and has fans. The standard half chicken, salad and hummus is S£85.

The new *Restaurant Sukrat* is a bright little spot with good quality food. A full meal of the usual stuff will cost around S£200 without drinks (no alcohol).

The *Al-Rawda Restaurant* on the banks of the river has a fine setting overlooking the norias. The food is only average, the prices are not, and don't be surprised if the waiter deducts a tip for himself before giving you the change, not that there'll be much change from S£300 for a meal of kebabs, chips, salad and hummus. Occasionally, there is a band and dance performances.

For considerably better food in a pleasantly intimate location right next to a grand noria on the Orontes, head for the *Sultan Restaurant*, which you can reach by the low vaulted tunnel under the An-Nuri Mosque. There's no alcohol though. A meal should cost no more than S£200.

As mentioned earlier, there are two very pleasant but fairly up-market restaurants out by the Four Norias, which is in fact the name of one of them.

Locals out for a higher quality and wider range of food select either the *Engineers' Club* ('Nadi al-Mohandiseen') up in the wealthy Ileilyat quarter, or the *Family Club* ('Nadi al-'A'ili'), a block from the Orthodox church and actually run by it. The latter also opens a terrace in summer. The easiest thing to do is choose a variety of mezzeh. At the Family Club you will actually be presented with a menu in Arabic, on which you are meant to tick off which items you want – you may need to ask assistance with this! Both places serve alcohol and nargileh, and you may be looking at S£300 for a meal.

Although you can find it outside Hama, the halawat al-jibn is a not-too-sweet dessert speciality of the city. It is a cheese-based soft doughy delicacy drenched in honey or syrup and often topped with ice cream. A lot of places around Kouwatli Ave sell it; some sell nothing else.

Entertainment

For just a tea or coffee, and maybe a nargileh and a game of backgammon, you can't beat the outdoor café next to the Al-Rawda. It's set in a garden of shady eucalyptus trees and has views of the river and norias. It is a great place to escape the heat. Every so often a waiter will come around with a shiny silver coffee pot and very small cups; this is Arabic coffee, strongly flavoured with cardamom and quite bitter. It is drunk in tiny doses that you just knock back in one hit – a real heart-starter. When you've had enough, hand the cup back with a quick jiggle of the wrist. Bear in mind that this is not a free service – the guy serving it will expect a tip on your way out.

Getting There & Away

Bus/Minibus The old bus and minibus station is on the southern outskirts of town, about two km from the centre or half an hours' walk. You can catch a local bus from Kouwatli Ave for S£2. Regular minibuses go to Homs (S£10, half an hour), Suqaylibiyyeh (for Apamea, S£10), Salamiyyeh (S£7, 45 minutes), Musyaf (S£10), Maharde and other surrounding towns. Buses also serve Aleppo (S£25), Damascus (S£32, 2¾ hours) and Lattakia.

Microbus For quicker, more frequent service, microbuses depart from a separate station virtually across the road. They run to Homs (S£17), Suqaylibiyyeh (S£20) and Salamiyyeh (S£13).

Karnak & Luxury Bus Several companies, including Qadmous, Al-Nawras and the government-run Karnak have offices next door to one another in the centre of town near the river. Karnak's is in Cafeteria Afamia. It runs three daily buses to Damascus (S£60) and two a day to Beirut (S£150). The other two companies are more expensive and of a higher standard. Qadmous goes to Damascus at 5 pm (S£90), Aleppo at 11 pm (S£65), Lattakia four times a day and Tartus twice daily (S£65). The company also has six daily services to Beirut by bus (S£300) or microbus (S£250). Al-Nawras costs about the same and also runs buses to Raqqa (S£130), Qamishle (S£275) and Homs (S£20).

Two other companies, Al-Ahliah and Al-Ryan, also have offices close to the centre (refer to the Hama map) and offer similar services for equivalent rates.

Train The railway station is way out of town to the south-west. A local bus from Kouwatli Ave is S£2, and a service taxi about S£20. The new railway station is still being completed, so the area is a bit of a mess.

There are two daily trains to Damascus (S£57/40, 1st/2nd class; four hours). To Aleppo there are also two services (S£34/23; 2½ hours). At least one of these trains goes all the way to Qamishle.

Service Taxi Service taxis leave from near the microbus station.

Getting Around

The local buses may come in handy for getting to and from the bus and railway stations, both of which are uncomfortably far from the town centre. Buses leave from the corner of Kouwatli and Sadik Aves. Ask at the booth for the bus station or train (*'qitaar'*). You pay the S£2 fare on the bus.

To get into town from the bus station, the stop is about 200m to the north. It's not marked, but the people milling around will be a clue.

AROUND HAMA

Hama makes an ideal base for a series of side trips that could keep you occupied for days.

Apamea (Qala'at Al-Mudiq)

From Hama the Orontes River flows north-west and into the vast Al-Ghab depression, some 50 km away. Once a stagnant swamp, this low-lying area of some 40 sq km has, with World Bank help, been drained and irrigation ditches dug, turning it into one of the most fertile areas in Syria. Major crops are wheat, barley, sugar beet and a range of fruit trees.

In ancient times it is said that the Pharaoh Thutmose III came here to hunt elephants. A thousand years later Hannibal was here teaching the Syrians how to make use of elephants in war. On the eastern edge of this valley lie the ruins of the ancient city of Apamea ('Afamia' in Arabic), now known as Qala'at al-Mudiq.

Founded by Seleucus I in the 2nd century BC and named after his wife, the city became an important trading post and crossroads for the east. It was connected by road to Lattakia (Laodicea), which served it as a port. Seized by Pompey for the Romans in 64 BC, Apamea only entered upon its true golden era in the 2nd century AD, when much of the city was rebuilt after an earthquake in 115 AD. In its heyday, Apamea boasted a population of about 500,000 (120,000 free people) and was visited by many dignitaries, including Mark Antony, accompanied by Cleopatra, on his return from staging a campaign against the Armenians upon the Euphrates.

The city declined after the Roman era but again assumed importance during the Crusades when the Norman commander, Tancred, took possession of the city. The occupation was short-lived, however, and Nureddin won the city back 43 years later, in 1149.

The fortifications around the hilltop that dominates the valley are still standing after being restored following the earthquakes of 1157 and 1170.

Museum In the small village at the foot of the hill is a restored Ottoman caravanserai (khan) dating from the 18th century and used as a trading post on the route to Mecca from Constantinople. It is now a museum, and the floors of the vaulted rooms surrounding the

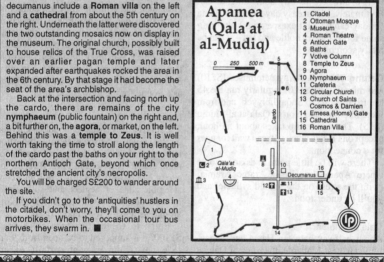

Apamea (Qala'at al-Mudiq): the Ruins

The main area of ruins is about 500m east of the village in a plain where the re-erected columns of the two km long *cardo* look quite incongruous amid wheat fields and thistles. The northern end was bounded by the Antioch Gate and the southern end by the Emesa (Homs) Gate. Several lesser cross-streets, or *decumani*, intersected the cardo. The columns themselves, originally erected in the 2nd century AD, bear unusual carved designs, mostly straight or twisted fluting. Even now, work continues to re-erect and restore columns along this magnificent thoroughfare.

Along the length of the cardo and the one surviving decumanus (which now serves as the modern access road to the site), the ground is littered with great chunks of rock that were once part of structures such as a temple, theatre, churches and shops. Many of these pieces are sculpted or have Greek inscriptions. The whole site covers a large area, and even in the small zone where the reconstruction has taken place, the excavations carried out since the 1930s by Belgian teams can still hardly be considered exhaustive. Glass fragments are everywhere and there must still be some fine pieces waiting to be unearthed.

As you approach the site from the village, the first significant ruins to appear belong to the **Roman theatre**, largely destroyed by earthquake and pilfering. It has a diameter of 135m, making it the largest in Syria and possibly throughout the entire Roman world. Just south of the intersection of the decumanus and cardo stand a largely destroyed circular church (erected in the 6th century under Justinian) on the right and, across the cardo, the church where the saints Cosmos and Damien were interred.

The remains at the eastern end of the decumanus include a **Roman villa** on the left and a **cathedral** from about the 5th century on the right. Underneath the latter were discovered the two outstanding mosaics now on display in the museum. The original church, possibly built to house relics of the True Cross, was raised over an earlier pagan temple and later expanded after earthquakes rocked the area in the 6th century. By that stage it had become the seat of the area's archbishop.

Back at the intersection and facing north up the cardo, there are remains of the city **nymphaeum** (public fountain) on the right and, a bit further on, the **agora**, or market, on the left. Behind this was a **temple to Zeus**. It is well worth taking the time to stroll along the length of the cardo past the baths on your right to the northern Antioch Gate, beyond which once stretched the ancient city's necropolis.

You will be charged S£200 to wander around the site.

If you didn't go to the 'antiquities' hustlers in the citadel, don't worry, they'll come to you on motorbikes. When the occasional tour bus arrives, they swarm in. ■

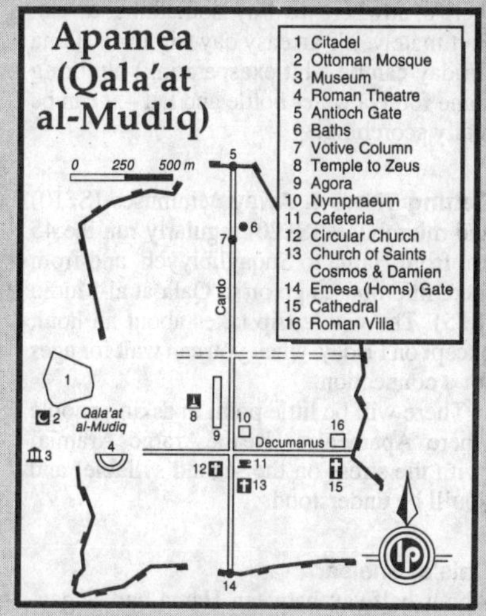

massive courtyard have been covered with the brilliant mosaics found in Apamea during excavations.

The most impressive, located in a room in the south-west corner of the khan, are two large mosaics found in cathedral ruins at the eastern end of the main east-west boulevard. A third one is being restored in Damascus and will also be transferred to the museum when work is complete.

Unfortunately, what labelling there is in Arabic. It's a real crime that there's nothing to stop visitors from just walking all over these priceless pieces. The museum is open from 9 am to 6 pm (4 pm in winter) daily except Tuesday; entry is S£100.

Fortifications The citadel on the hill is, typically, more impressive from the outside. It dates from the 13th century and occupies what had been the acropolis of the ancient city. Inside is the village of Qala'at al-Mudiq, where local hustlers will try to sell you glass and coins from the ruins. A few of the pieces are obviously old and most are just as obviously made in the local workshop, so if you're interested, it's a case of buyer beware. It's quite an unkempt, grimy little place – especially after rain.

Places to Stay & Eat There's nowhere to stay in Qala'at al-Mudiq and, apart from a cafeteria near the ticket booth and a couple of small general stores in the village below, there's nowhere to buy something to eat. Fortunately, it's an easy day trip from Hama (Friday can be a bit exasperating) but bring some food, a water bottle and hat – it can be really scorching.

Getting There & Away Minibuses (S£10) and microbuses (S£20) regularly run the 45 km from Hama to Suqaylibiyyeh, and from there microbuses go on to Qala'at al-Mudiq (S£5). The whole trip takes about an hour, except on Friday, when you can wait for ages for a connection.

There will be little point in asking people where 'Apamea' is. Use the Arabic 'Afamia' (with the stress on the second syllable) and you'll be understood.

Qala'at Sheisar

About halfway between Hama and Suqaylibiyyeh, near Maharde, the ruins of Qala'at Sheisar rise above the escarpment on the right and a small ruined noria groans away slowly by the river on the left. You can hop off the Hama-Suqaylibiyyeh microbus here to have a look at the castle, an Arab fortification dominating the right bank of the Orontes.

The castle was the base for opposition to the Crusaders during their occupation of Apamea and resisted all attempts to take it. Only the northern gate complex and the main defensive tower, or dungeon, are still reasonably well preserved.

It is also believed by some to be the site of the ancient town of Caesarea, although nothing is left to confirm this today.

If you end up hanging around this area, the exclusively Christian town of Maharde offers an uncommon nocturnal experience in its version of the Italian *passeggiata*. About a half dozen so-called cafeterias buzz in the early evening with a mixed crowd of men and women enjoying a coffee or beer until about 8 or 9 pm. Just the sight of both sexes (not a veil to be seen) apparently so freely mingling seems wholly out of place. Outside, the main drag fills with the town populace parading self-consciously up and down in a slow and deliberate fashion. It is clear men and women still keep some distance from one another, unless married or family, and for many it appears this is an opportunity to take a look at possible future life partners. Whatever the ins and outs of it, the scene is one not often repeated in other Syrian towns. If you want to eat a good meal, ask around for the *Restaurant Atlal*.

Musyaf

The solid castle in Musyaf, about 40 km west of Hama, was long the easternmost bastion in a string of castles held by the Ismaelis for more than a century from 1140. Built on the site of earlier forts, the structure is in a considerable state of neglect, but sufficiently intact to keep the castle buff happily poking around its innards for an hour or so.

Entry to the castle technically costs S£100. It is supposed to be open from 9 am to 6 pm (4 pm in winter) daily except Tuesday, but it's anybody's guess whether you'll find the caretaker around when you arrive. Minibuses to Hama and Homs cost S£10 and S£15 respectively, while microbuses cost S£18.50 and S£25.

Deir Soleib

Four km south of the Hama-Musyaf road lie the well preserved remains of a 6th century basilica, featuring three columned aisles, a completely intact apse and a baptistry in the

The Old Man of the Mountain

The Ismaelis were an extreme Muslim sect leaning towards the mystical, and little loved by orthodox Sunnis, by whom they found themselves regularly persecuted. Not surprisingly perhaps, since the doctrine of these followers of Ismael (the 8th century son of the sixth Imam) included murder as a means of removing obstacles to the propagation of their faith. Under their charismatic 12th century leader Sinan, known to the Europeans as the Old Man of the Mountain, the surrounding Muslims and Crusaders came to fear and respect the Ismaelis.

The Ismaeli Assassins, so called – according to one account – because they smoked hashish (an Arabic word from which 'assassin' is said to be derived) before embarking on their murderous exploits, attempted on a couple of occasions to kill both Nureddin and Saladin, two of Islam's principal champions against the Crusaders. Among the Christian rulers to end up on the wrong end of their poison-tipped swords was Raymond II of Tripoli, who bit the dust about 1150, and Conrad de Montferrat, king of Jerusalem, about 40 years later.

By the late 13th century, however, Sultan Baibars had not only all but finished-off the Crusader presence in the Levant, but taken the Ismaeli fortresses and stripped the group of any political importance. ■

southern annexe. About two km to the east lie ruins of another church. About the easiest way to get here is to pick up a Hama-Musyaf microbus and alight at the turn-off. From there it's about an hours' walk or you'll have to hitch.

Salamiyyeh & Qala'at ash-Shmemis

Perched atop what for all the world looks like an extinct volcano, the ruins of the 13th century Arab fort known as Qala'at ash-Shmemis are far more impressive at a distance than close up. About 32 km south-east of Hama on the road to Salamiyyeh, the castle lies in already arid territory, its position making it virtually impregnable. The transition to near desert takes place with dramatic speed as you move away from the sheltered greens of Hama and the Orontes.

The town of Salamiyyeh itself, three km further east, is a sleepy sort of backwater with a long history. Parts of the old defensive walls can still be seen, and the oldest parts of the central Ismaeli mosque date from the 16th century. A trap door near a marble sarcophagus said to contain the remains of Ismael (see Musyaf earlier in this chapter) once led to a tunnel that passed beyond the city walls – to be used in case of siege.

Minibuses (S£7) and microbuses (S£13) connect Hama regularly with Salamiyyeh. For the castle, ask to be let off shortly after it comes into view north of the road. It takes about half an hour to walk out to it.

Isriyeh

Of the ancient desert settlement of Seriana only the main temple remains which, apart from a missing roof, is largely in one piece. Dating from the 3rd century AD, the stone employed is the same as that used in much of the construction in Palmyra. Seriana was in fact an important way-station in the imperial Roman road network, with highways to Palmyra, Chalcis, Rasafeh and Homs (ancient Emesa) all meeting here.

Getting to Isriyeh can be a bit trying. From Salamiyyeh you could hire a service taxi for about S£600 one way. Otherwise, take a microbus the first 45 km north-east to Saan (S£10). From there you have another 45 km of piste to get behind you, and may still be obliged to deal with a service taxi for the remainder.

Qasr Ibn Wardan

One of the least visited sites in the area is also one of the most remarkable. Erected by the Byzantine emperor Justinian in the mid-6th century as part of a defensive line that included Rasafeh and Halabiyyeh on the Euphrates, Qasr Ibn Wardan was a combined military base, palace and church. Smaller in area than, say, Rasafeh, it is nevertheless striking for its grace, particularly the church. The basic form was square, the whole capped by a now disappeared dome and ringed by galleries on three sides. The fourth side is rounded off by the semi-circular and half-domed apse common to many early

Byzantine churches. The best preserved wall of the partly restored palace faces south. Made largely of basalt and brick, it is assumed to have been home to the local governor. The guardian here doesn't get many visitors and is a friendly chap.

Another 25 km of rough piste lead north-east to El-Anderine, another Byzantine settlement of which precious little remains today. The defensive settlement was dominated by a cathedral, but only a few pillars still stand.

SYRIA

Aleppo (Halab)

With a population nudging three million, Aleppo is Syria's second largest city. Since Roman times it has been an important trading centre between Asia and the Mediterranean, and the long presence of a strong corps of merchants from Europe (not to mention French occupation in the interwar mandate years) may go some way to accounting for the vaguely European feel of its more well-to-do areas, with their tree-lined boulevards, parks and up-market restaurants. Trading routes led to Aleppo from Istanbul, Mosul (in Iraq), Lattakia and Damascus. Under the French Mandate after WWI the city lost much of its remaining significance as a commercial centre, cut off as it was from southern Turkey, for which it had until then continued to serve as a trading outlet.

The sizable Christian population, comprised mainly of Armenian refugees from Turkey, contributes a unique atmosphere to the city. In certain quarters, you'll see as many signs in the condensed-looking script of Armenian as in the familiar 'shorthand' with which many equate Arabic. In a still more intriguing quirk of recent history, Aleppo has been a particular beneficiary of the crumbling of the USSR. A steady stream of traders from the former Soviet republics bustles through Aleppo on large-scale shopping sprees. Every night, the entrances of their favoured hotels buzz with activity as trucks are loaded up with the goods these people take home for resale. Some of them stay behind and ply a different trade – as in Turkey to the north, prostitutes from the once-great socialist empire do a thriving business here.

Its fascinating covered souqs, the citadel, museum and caravanserais all evoke ages long past, making the city a great place to spend a few days. The Church of St Simeon (Qala'at Samaan), the largest Christian building in the Middle East when it was built in the 4th century, and the ancient city of Ebla are just two of a treasure trove of little-visited archaeological jewels scattered across north-western Syria – nearly all of them within easy reach of Aleppo. Most of them date from Byzantine times and have come to be known collectively as the Dead Cities.

History

Texts from the ancient kingdom of Mari on the Euphrates show that Aleppo was already the centre of a powerful state as long ago as the 18th century BC, and the site may have been continuously inhabited for the past 8000 years. Its pre-eminent role in Syria came to an end with the Hittite invasions of the 17th and 16th centuries BC, and the city appears to have fallen into obscurity thereafter.

During the reign of the Seleucids, who arrived in the wake of Alexander the Great's campaign, it was given the name Beroea, and with the fall of Palmyra at the hands of the Romans, it became the major commercial link between the Mediterranean to the west and Asia to the east. The town was completely destroyed by the Persians in 611 AD and fell to the Muslims during their invasion in 637. The Byzantines overwhelmed the town in 961 and again in 968 but they could not take the citadel. Three disastrous earthquakes also shook the city in the 10th century and the town and fortress were subsequently rebuilt by Nureddin. In 1124 the Crusaders under Baldwin laid siege to the town.

After raids by the Mongols in 1260 and 1401, in which Aleppo was practically emptied of its population, the city finally came into the Ottoman Turkish orbit in 1517. It prospered greatly until another earthquake struck in 1822, killing over 60% of the inhabitants and wrecking many buildings, including the citadel.

As long as four centuries ago European merchants – particularly French, English and Venetian – had established themselves here and set up factories, but the flood of cheap

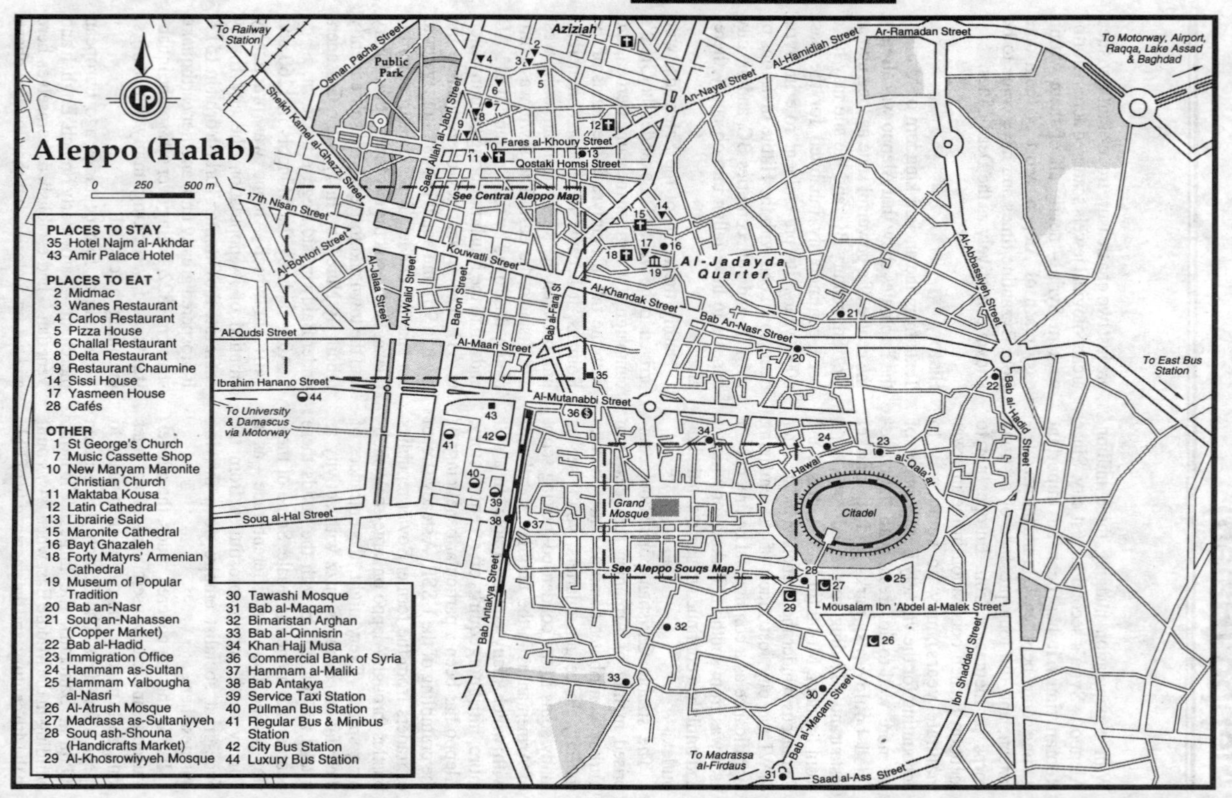

Aleppo (Halab)
0 250 500 m
PLACES TO STAY
35 Hotel Najm al-Akhdar
43 Amir Palace Hotel
PLACES TO EAT
2 Midmac
3 Wanes Restaurant
4 Carlos Restaurant
5 Pizza House
6 Challal Restaurant
8 Delta Restaurant
9 Restaurant Chaumine
14 Sissi House
17 Yasmeen House
28 Cafés
OTHER
1 St George's Church
7 Music Cassette Shop
10 New Maryam Maronite Christian Church
11 Maktaba Kousa
12 Latin Cathedral
13 Librairie Said
15 Maronite Cathedral
16 Bayt Ghazaleh
18 Forty Matyrs' Armenian Cathedral
19 Museum of Popular Tradition
20 Bab an-Nasr
21 Souq an-Nahassen (Copper Market)
22 Bab al-Hadid
23 Immigration Office
24 Hammam as-Sultan
25 Hammam Yalbougha al-Nasri
26 Al-Atrush Mosque
27 Madrassa as-Sultaniyyeh
28 Souq ash-Shouna (Handicrafts Market)
29 Al-Khosrowiyyeh Mosque
30 Tawashi Mosque
31 Bab al-Maqam
32 Bimaristan Arghan
33 Bab al-Qinnisrin
34 Khan Hajj Musa
36 Commercial Bank of Syria
37 Hammam al-Maliki
38 Bab Antakya
39 Service Taxi Station
40 Pullman Bus Station
41 Regular Bus & Minibus Station
42 City Bus Station
44 Luxury Bus Station
To Railway Station
To Motorway, Airport, Raqqa, Lake Assad & Baghdad
To East Bus Station
To University & Damascus via Motorway
To Madrassa al-Firdaus
Aziziah
Public Park
Osman Pacha Street
Sheikh Kamel al-Ghazzi Street
Saad Allah al-Jabri Street
Fares al-Khoury Street
Qostaki Homsi Street
See Central Aleppo Map
17th Nisan Street
Al-Bohtori Street
Al-Jalaa Street
Al-Walid Street
Baron Street
Kouwatli Street
Bab al-Faraj St
Al-Qudsi Street
Al-Maari Street
Ibrahim Hanano Street
Al-Mutanabbi Street
Souq al-Hal Street
Bab Antakya Street
An-Nayal Street
Al-Hamidiah Street
Ar-Ramadan Street
Al-Jadayda Quarter
Al-Khandak Street
Bab An-Nasr Street
Al-Abbassiyeh Street
Bab al-Hadid Street
Hawal
al-Qala'at
Citadel
Grand Mosque
See Aleppo Souqs Map
Mousalam Ibn 'Abdel al-Malek Street
Ibn Shaddad Street
Bab al-Maqam Street
Saad al-Ass Street

goods from Europe in the wake of the Industrial Revolution and the increasing use of alternative trading routes slowly killed off a lot of Aleppo's trade and manufacturing. Today the major local industries are silk-weaving and cotton-printing. Products from the surrounding area include wool, hides, dried fruits and, particularly, the pistachio nuts for which Aleppo is justly famous. And in the souqs of Aleppo, artisans still manufacture the famous Aleppo soap, a unique mix of olive and laurel oils.

Orientation

The centre of town and the area where the cheap hotels are clustered is a compact zone centred on Kouwatli and Baron Sts. A lot of the restaurants, the main museum and places to change money are here. About two km to the south-east is the citadel, and to the west of it, the souqs. North-east of the centre are the main Christian quarters, the majority of their inhabitants Armenians. Directly to the north, beyond the chic area around the main park (parched in summer but quite pleasant otherwise), is the poorest part of the city. To the west are the newer suburbs and university district.

Information

Tourist Office The tourist office, in the gardens opposite the National Museum, is next to useless, and doesn't seem to be staffed half the time. It is theoretically open from 8.30 am to 2 pm daily except Friday. It has a reasonable free map and little else. The tourist police are based here too.

Visa Extensions The immigration office for visa extensions is on the 2nd floor of a building just north of the citadel. You must bring *five* passport photos and processing takes a day, but you may be given an extension of up to two months. The office is open from 8 am to 1.30 pm.

Money Down on the corner of Kouwatli and Bab al-Faraj Sts is an exchange booth open daily except Friday from 8 am to 7.30 pm. You can change travellers' cheques as well as cash. For the latter transactions, most currencies (including Turkish lira) are accepted.

If you have any trouble with cheques, go to the Commercial Bank of Syria on Baron St north of Kouwatli St. There is a big sign in English – 'Branch No 2' – but the entrance is hidden away at the back of an arcade and the office is up on the 1st floor. It's open daily except Friday from 8.30 am to 1.30 pm, and changes cash as well. Note that you will probably be required to take (or at least show) the counterfoil receipts for your cheques, which you are normally meant to keep separate from the cheques. Patient and polite refusal has been known to wear the staff down on this point. There's another branch of the bank south of the town centre.

Post & Communications The main post office is the enormous building on the far side of the square opposite Kouwatli St. It's open every day from 8 am to 5 pm (and until 10 pm for telephones; the counter is off to the left). There is a fax service – you pay for time used as you would for a phone call.

If you've forgotten anything from postcards to envelopes, there are plenty of guys set up on the steps of the post office selling them.

The parcels office is around the corner to the left of the main entrance.

Bookshops About the best bookshop in town is the one in the Amir Palace Hotel. It has a fair range of books on Syria and a handful of novels in English and French. The Librairie Said, on the corner of Qostaki Homsi and Litani Sts, has a small selection of dusty old novels as well. The Cham Palace Hotel Bookshop (☎ 223 2300) has a good selection of paperbacks and books on Syria.

The odd copy of *Time* and similar magazines may turn up in the big hotel bookshops, but generally foreign newspapers are hard to come by – even the *Syria Times* hardly seems to make an appearance. You could also try the Maktaba Kousa (bookshop) on Qostaki Homsi St (sign in Arabic only).

SYRIA

Walking Tour

There are many interesting attractions to see in Aleppo. The following sights are suggested inclusions for a walking tour of the city.

Citadel

Rising up on a high mound at the eastern end of the souqs, the citadel dominates the city and was long the heart of its defences. It is surrounded by a moat, 20m deep and 30m wide, which was dug in the 12th century. The site had already been in use since at least the 10th century BC, when it hosted a temple, but it was probably the Seleucids who first fortified it.

To enter, you cross the bridge on the south side and pass through a 12th century gate, behind which is the massive fortified main entrance. Finely decorated on the outside, the inside is a succession of five right-angle turns, where three sets of solid steel-plated doors made a formidable barrier to any would-be occupiers. Some of the doors still remain and one of the lintels of the doorways has carvings of entwined dragons; another has a pair of lions. The main entrance area was actually reworked in the 16th century under the Mamelukes, after Aleppo had been freed from Mongol hands.

Just before you pass the last door into the interior of the citadel, a door to the right leads to the **armoury**. If you follow the path, which doglegs to the right and left, you'll see an entrance to your right leading to what is now called the **Byzantine Hall**. Double back and head up the stairs. Here you enter the **Royal Palace** built in 1230 by Malik (king) Al-Aziz Mohammed and largely destroyed 30 years later by the Mongols. You pass through what originally were the servants' quarters and an antechamber before entering the lavishly restored **throne room**, whose dominating feature is the intricately decorated wooden ceiling.

Two buildings inside the citadel survived pillage and an earthquake in 1822. Halfway up the main path on the left is the entrance to a small 12th century **mosque** attributed to Nureddin and one of several legendary burial places for the head of John the Baptist. It retains little of its original charm. At the northern end of the path, opposite what is now a café, is the 13th century **great mosque**, a rather grandiose title for a building of its humble dimensions. The café is housed in what was the *thukna* (barracks) of an Ottoman commander, Ibrahim Pasha. There is now also a small museum, but at S£100 to enter, it is hardly worth the effort.

The views from the walls are terrific and you get a good idea of just how big this city is. The citadel is open from 9 am to 6 pm daily except Tuesday. Entry is S£200, and this is one of the places where you're charged absurd amounts of money for the right to take photographs and video tape.

Grand Mosque

On the northern edge of the souqs is the Grand Mosque (also known as the Omayyad Mosque and Jami'a Zakariyyeh) with its remarkable minaret dating from 1090. Although it was constructed on what was probably the cemetery for the Christian cathedral across the lane and dates from early Islamic times, most of what remains of the mosque today is from the Mameluke period. The 47m high minaret is indeed the mosque's finest element, and in the opinion of some learned fellows the most stunning single piece of architecture in all Syria. Square-based, it rises up to the muezzin's gallery in five distinct levels, the top four of which are graced with different styles of blind arch.

Inside the mosque itself is a fine, 15th century carved wooden pulpit ('*minbar*') and behind the railing to the left of it is supposed to be the head of Zacharias, the father of John the Baptist, after whom the mosque is named.

The mosque is closed for refurbishing and restoration, and at the moment has a rather forlorn air of disuse and emptiness. However, if you bash on the west door, the keeper will let visitors have a wander around for S£25.

Madrassa Halawiyyeh

Opposite the mosque's western entrance, the

Madrassa Halawiyyeh stands on the site of what was once the 6th century Cathedral of St Helen. It is a rather scruffy place now, although the minbar is still particularly beautiful.

South of the Citadel

Virtually opposite the entrance to the citadel lies the **Madrassa as-Sultaniyyeh**, built in 1223 as madrassa and mausoleum for Sultan Az-Zahir Ghazi and his family. Inside, the most striking element is the mihrab, whose eye-catching ornamentation is achieved with multicoloured marble inlays.

Just across the road, the **Al-Khosrowiyyeh Mosque** was one the great Turkish architect Sinan's earliest works and about the first Ottoman-style mosque built in Aleppo, in 1537. A couple of blocks east rises an earlier mosque built in a quite different tradition. The **Al-Atrush Mosque**, erected in the first decade of the 15th century, lies fully in the Mameluke tradition of combining mosque and mausoleum, often begun before the ruler destined for its grave died. Aqbogha al-Atrush was governor of Aleppo, and when the mosque was constructed it was also designed to serve as the local district's main Friday mosque. Alternating colours in stone and lavish ornamentation of the exterior mark Mameluke monuments such as this apart from their more sobre Ayyubid predecessors and Ottoman successors.

From the Al-Atrush Mosque head down to Bab al-Maqam. Just after the first big intersection on the right is the **Tavashi Mosque**, built in the 14th century and remodelled in the 16th century. A good 10 to 15 minute walk out the gate and south-west will bring you through a cemetery to the **Madrassa al-Firdaus**, one of the great Ayyubid theological schools-cum-mausoleums. In this case Daifa Khatun, the wife of Saladin's son Az-Zahir Ghazi, financed construction, which ended in 1236. It is a rather massive building whose small entrance leads you into a courtyard, one side of which opens onto an iwan. The oratory is at the opposite end, with a noteworthy mihrab. Have a look too at the nearby and contemporary **Madrassa az-Zahiriyyeh**.

Museums

National Museum Aleppo's main museum, right in the middle of town, has a fine collection of artefacts from Mari (Tell Hariri), Ebla (Tell Mardikh), Ugarit (Ras Shamra) and Tell Brak. There are sculptures from Hama, and the black basalt statues at the entrance are from the temple-palace at Tell Halaf (a 9th century BC Hittite settlement in the north-east of Syria, near present-day Ras al-'Ain). Upstairs, the collections are mainly from the classical period and include Greek and Roman pottery, a lot of material from Palmyra, and Byzantine coins.

It is a fine museum and well worth the S£200 entrance fee. On sale at the entrance is a guidebook to the museum for another S£200. It is open from 9 am to 6 pm (4 pm in winter) daily except Tuesday.

Museum of Popular Tradition Tucked away in the former residence of an Ottoman official in the narrow Haret al-Yasmin (formerly the Souq as-Souf, or Wool Market), the museum contains the all-too familiar scenes of local life in bygone centuries and displays of clothing, tools, weapons, furniture and the like. The house has stood for 250 years, and from the top you can see across to the citadel in the south-east. Entrance is S£100 and it's open daily from 8 am to 2 pm except Tuesday.

To find the museum, turn left (north) from Al-Khandak St into the narrow lane that veers right and serves as a souq. The museum is on the left a few metres before the lane opens out onto a little square.

Christian Quarter

The area immediately surrounding the Museum of Popular Tradition is a Christian, mainly Armenian, quarter called Al-Jadayda, and a number of stately old homes (the museum is itself one) dating from the 17th and 18th centuries can be visited. Various people have the keys to these places. One is the museum attendant, another is the owner

Aleppo Souqs

The fabulous covered souqs are the city's main attraction. This labyrinth extends over several hectares and once under the vaulted stone ceiling, you're swallowed up in another world. All under one roof are the smells of cardamom and cloves from the spice stalls, the cries of the hawkers and barrow-pushers, the rows of carcasses hanging from the doorways in the meat souq, and the myriad stalls selling everything from rope to prayer mats. Parts of these markets date from the 13th century, but the bulk of the area is an Ottoman-era creation. Today, as ever, people from all walks of life and many different countries meander down its lanes, inspecting merchandise or just stopping for a friendly chat. Little here seems to have changed in hundreds of years, and Aleppo's markets have few rivals in the Middle East. More fascinating than what you find in Damascus, only Cairo's Khan al-Khalili competes.

A walk through the souqs could take all day, particularly if you accept some of the many invitations by the merchants to stop and drink tea. There's no obligation and generally little pressure to buy – this is just Syrian hospitality. While wandering around you may well find yourself latched onto by a young Syrian who wants to be your 'guide' and take you to the shop of his 'cousin'. They may be helpful for finding what you want, if you don't mind paying a little extra for their commission.

In among the souqs are several caravanserais, or khans. It was in the caravanserais that the bulk of the European commercial representatives were to be found, the first of whom to set up a trade bureau were the Venetians in 1548. Unfortunately, most are of limited interest because they are almost totally obscured by modern additions. It is worth noting their location, however, as several still boast portentously disposed gateways, sometimes seemingly located higgledy-piggledy in the tangle of souq lanes.

Before diving into the darkness, pop into the **Khan al-Wazir** (Minister's Khan), just north of the Grand Mosque. Built in 1682, it still has an interesting gateway, although inside it is not so inspiring. Nevertheless it transmits a good idea of the layout of the traditional khan. One single highly ornamental gateway leads into a quadrangle. The lower of the two storeys surrounding this courtyard served as warehouses while offices and sleeping quarters were found above. Not a whole lot has changed.

In the block east of the Grand Mosque is another caravanserai, the early 16th century **Khan as-Sabun**. Cluttered as it is, you stumble across the façade of the doorway at its southern end. Above the window is inscribed the basic Muslim profession of faith: 'There is no God but Allah, and Mohammed is his Prophet.' Jammed between the two khans is the rather oddly named **Al-Fustuq Mosque**, or Pistachio Mosque. Also worth a quick look is the **Hajj Musa Mosque** north across the road.

Penetrating the souqs proper, south of the Khan as-Sabun gate, you quickly find yourself in the heart of the gold and jewellery stands. The other most notable merchandise here is rugs. The area is known as the **Souq Istanbul al-Jadid**. Head a few metres further south until you hit what looks like the 'main street' – a slightly wider than usual alley. Turning westwards, you pass two more khans, although they are both so obscured by local shops and the like that you'd hardly know they were there. The first, **Khan an-Nahaseen**, now largely given over to footwear, housed the Venetian consul from the 16th to the 19th centuries, and in the 1930s his Belgian counterpart. Next up, the **Khan al-Jumruk** was built in 1574. It was designed to much the same plan as the Khan al-Wazir and served as the main headquarters of the French, Dutch and English merchants of the 16th and 17th centuries.

Further down the street is the **Al-Baramiyyeh Mosque**, built in the Turkish style at the end of the 16th century. Although quite large, its dimensions are hard to appreciate with all the clutter around it. Behind it down a lane are the pitifully neglected remains of what was once one of Nureddin's many beneficiary legacies, the **Maristan an-Nuri**, or hospital.

In considerably better nick is the **Bimaristan Arghan**, to the south-west of the Maristan an-Nuri down the road that leads to Bab al-Qinnisrin, one of the city gates. This mental hospital, built in 1354 in a converted private mansion, boasts a particularly attractive main doorway, through which you can wander (free) into the main courtyard. Three further smaller courtyards further in were used to take in and care for the mentally ill. Occasionally there are music performances here in the evening and even whirling dervishes. The **Bab al-Qinnisrin** itself, further down the road, is about the most impressive of the old city gates.

Bab al-Hadid, on the east side of what were the old city walls, is also fairly well preserved, while its western counterpart, **Bab Antakya** (the Antioch Gate), is all but completely hidden by the swarm of workshops and material around it. A couple of blocks north of the citadel is **Souq an-Nahaseen** (Copper Market), not far from Bab An-Nasr. The souqs are dead on Friday. ■

of a big souvenir shop on another small square about 200m north of the opening to Haret al-Yasmin by the museum. Otherwise, just ask around. You actually pass one of the houses, **Bayt Ghazaleh**, on the left as you walk up towards the shop.

The whole area is fascinating to wander around on a Sunday, when it's busy with the faithful of five Christian faiths thronging together. Along Haret al-Yasmin is the entrance to the **Forty Martyrs' Armenian Cathedral**. A little way to the north is the **Maronite Cathedral**, and squeezed between them are Latin (Roman Catholic), Greek Catholic and Syrian Orthodox churches.

Cultural Centre

Just behind the clock tower is a cultural centre, where there are occasional art and photographic exhibitions.

Hammams

Just to the south-east of the bridge to the citadel is the Hammam Yalbougha al-Nasri (☎ 623154). Originally constructed in 1491, it had been destroyed and rebuilt several times before the latest restoration, completed in 1985. The corridor leading in acts as a mini-museum. Noteworthy is the sun clock inside the dome above the reception area – three intricate designs mark out four o'clock, eight o'clock and 12 o'clock.

It will cost S£400 for as long as you want inside, full massage, sauna and baths, along with soap, towels and complimentary tea. Women only get to go on Tuesday, Thursday and Saturday from 10 am to 5 pm. It's open to men from 6 pm until midnight Tuesday, Thursday and Saturday, and from 10 am to midnight on all other days of the week.

It is something of a tourist stop, and there are other possibilities. Before the days of running water in all homes, Aleppo was covered in local hammams. Hammam as-Sultan is a more modest place used mostly by locals and is to the north of the citadel on As-Sayyaf

SYRIA

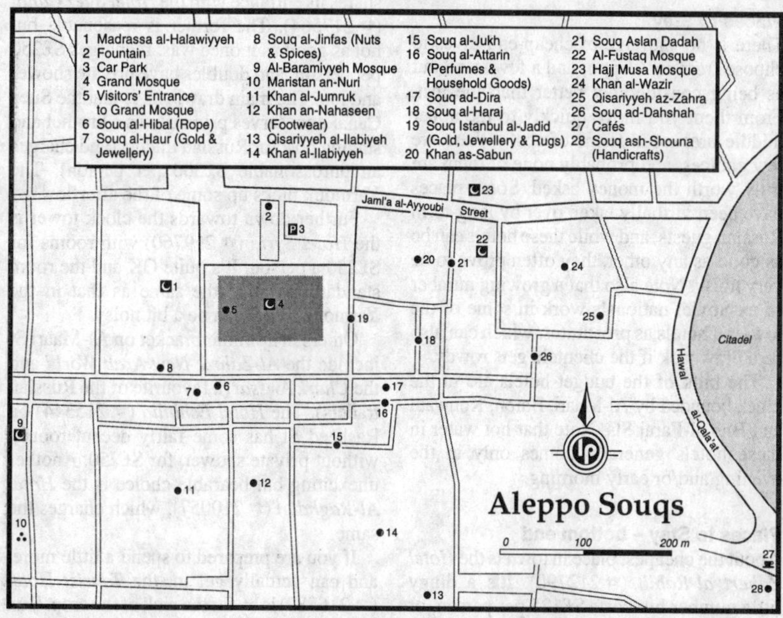

St. It's open to women during the day and to men at night. Another old Aleppo hammam that comes in about halfway between the above two in terms of quality and price is the Hammam al-Maliki, just inside Bab Antakya. It is open daily for women from 11 am to 6 pm and from 7 to 11 pm for men. For S£250 you get the massage, use of saunas and bathing, as well as a complimentary tea.

Swimming

People wanting to cool off with a simple swim can try the Basil al-Assad sports centre (☎ 666497), out west next to the Pullman Shahba Hotel. Men swim on Wednesday from 10 am to 2 pm and 3 to 6 pm and on Friday from 3 to 6 pm. Women get to use the pool on Monday from 10 am to 2 pm and 3 to 6 pm and on Thursday from 10 am to 2 pm. The other days are for families. The Cham Chahba Palace, also out in the west, charges S£400 a day to use its pool (summer only). Otherwise, take a nice cold shower!

Places to Stay

There is no shortage of cheap-end dives to choose from in Aleppo, and a few stand out as being considerably better than the rest. From them you move quickly to the upper middle bracket in terms of cost – there are few choices, and probably none of them are truly worth the money asked. Some places have been virtually taken over by long-term Russian guests, and while these hotels can be as good as any other, they often prove to be very noisy. Note also that a growing number of ex-Soviet nationals work in some of the low-end hotels as prostitutes, which can also be a drawback if the clientele gets rowdy.

The bulk of the budget hotels are in the block bounded by Al-Maari, Baron, Kouwatli and Bab al-Faraj Sts. Note that hot water in these hotels generally comes only in the evening and/or early morning.

Places to Stay – bottom end

About the cheapest place in town is the *Hotel Zahert al-Rabih* (☎ 212790). It's a dingy little number but costs S£125 per person, or S£75 on the roof. You get what you pay for. Better value if you can get a room on an upper floor looking onto the street and not out the back by the generator is the *Hotel Jamie al-Arabie* (☎ 220993). It charges S£150 per person. A popular choice with backpackers at this end of the scale is the *Hotel Kawkab al-Salam*, where simple but decent rooms contain beds at S£150 a throw. It has hot water and even satellite TV in the lounge. It's in a side street south of the clock tower. If you head east into the winding market streets, you'll find another good choice, the *Hotel Najem al-Akhdar* (☎ 239157). The friendly guy here charges S£200 per person for beds in clean doubles with private shower and toilet.

A hotel that comes well recommended is the clean and quiet *Hotel Al-Raoudah* (☎ 233896), on Al-Maari St. You pay S£500 for a double room with bath and balcony, or S£200 for a bed in other rooms.

There is a stack of cheap hotels on this street. The *Hotel Yarmouk* (☎ 217510) shares its entrance with the *Hotel Suez Canal* (☎ 217564). The former is reasonable but not as good as it once was. It charges S£250 per person, and doubles have private shower and loo. The main drawback is that the Suez Canal now serves primarily as a brothel and staging post for Russian traders (and charges an unreasonable S£300 per person). The Yarmouk picks up some of the afterflow.

Further down towards the clock tower is the *Hotel Syria* (☎ 219760) with rooms for S£250 a person. It's quite OK and the room standard is much the same as that in the Yarmouk, but it can be a bit noisy.

Others in a similar bracket on Al-Maari St include the *Al-Zahra, New Arab World* and the *Chark Awssat* (a favourite of the Russian traders). The *Hotel Eshbilia* (☎ 215344) on Rasheed St has some fairly decent rooms, without private shower, for S£250. Another unexciting but bearable choice is the *Hotel Al-Raghdan* (☎ 210057), which charges the same.

If you are prepared to spend a little more, and can actually get in, the *Tourist Hotel* (☎ 216583) is by far the pick of the crop. Run by the somewhat excentric Lebanese Madame Olga, immaculately kept rooms cost S£300 per person. They are worth every last pound. The piping-hot shower is spotless and is available all day.

Just down the road, the *Hotel Somar* (☎ 212198) is also fairly good, but wants US dollars. The charge of US$13 for a double works out about the same as at the Tourist, but the currency issue can be a pain. It is also often full.

This list of hotels is far from exhaustive, but you would be unlucky indeed to find the 'full' sign posted in all of them.

Places to Stay – middle

There's really only one place [...] range – the *Baron Hotel* (☎ 210880). It is as close as you will come in Syria to a hint of a long-gone era – stylish European travel to far-flung exotic places. It is run by the grandsons of the original 'baron' brothers. It's still a handsome building but if it's luxury you're after, forget it! Nothing much has changed since 1909 – the beds are old and squeaky (and rumoured by some expats to be populated with bedbugs), the walls need painting and the plumbing is antediluvian. For all that the place has character and, if you don't want

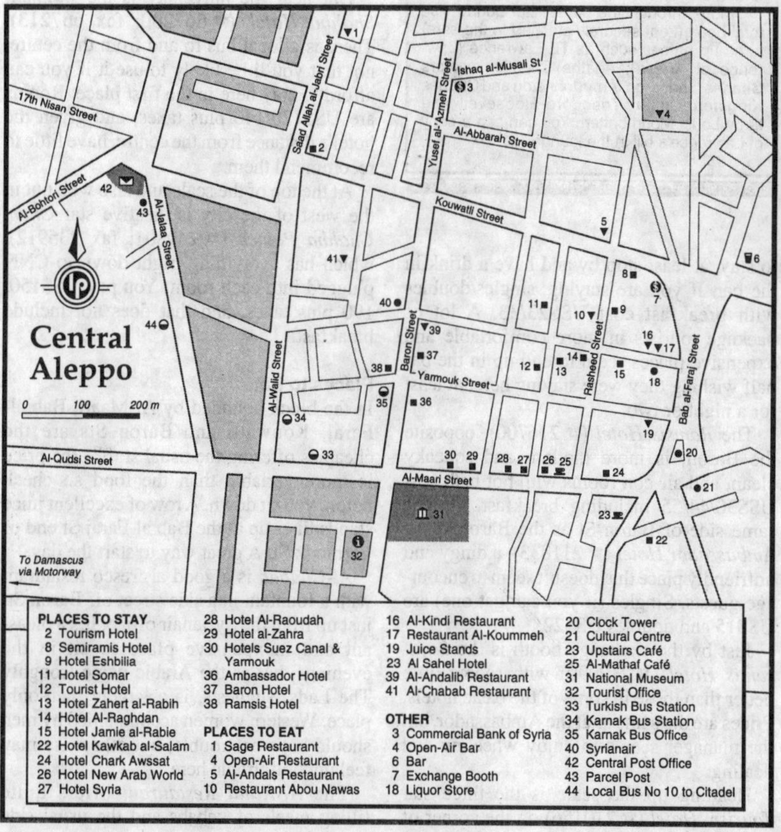

PLACES TO STAY
- 2 Tourism Hotel
- 8 Semiramis Hotel
- 9 Hotel Eshbilia
- 11 Hotel Somar
- 12 Tourist Hotel
- 13 Hotel Zahert al-Rabih
- 14 Hotel Al-Raghdan
- 15 Hotel Jamie al-Rabie
- 22 Hotel Kawkab al-Salam
- 24 Hotel Chark Awssat
- 26 Hotel New Arab World
- 27 Hotel Syria
- 28 Hotel Al-Raoudah
- 29 Hotel al-Zahra
- 30 Hotels Suez Canal & Yarmouk
- 36 Ambassador Hotel
- 37 Baron Hotel
- 38 Ramsis Hotel

PLACES TO EAT
- 1 Sage Restaurant
- 4 Open-Air Restaurant
- 5 Al-Andals Restaurant
- 10 Restaurant Abou Nawas
- 16 Al-Kindi Restaurant
- 17 Restaurant Al-Koummeh
- 19 Juice Stands
- 23 Al Sahel Hotel
- 39 Al-Andalib Restaurant
- 41 Al-Chabab Restaurant

OTHER
- 3 Commercial Bank of Syria
- 4 Open-Air Bar
- 6 Bar
- 7 Exchange Booth
- 18 Liquor Store
- 20 Clock Tower
- 21 Cultural Centre
- 23 Upstairs Café
- 25 Al-Mathaf Café
- 31 National Museum
- 32 Tourist Office
- 33 Turkish Bus Station
- 34 Karnak Bus Station
- 35 Karnak Bus Office
- 40 Syrianair
- 42 Central Post Office
- 43 Parcel Post
- 44 Local Bus No 10 to Citadel

SYRIA

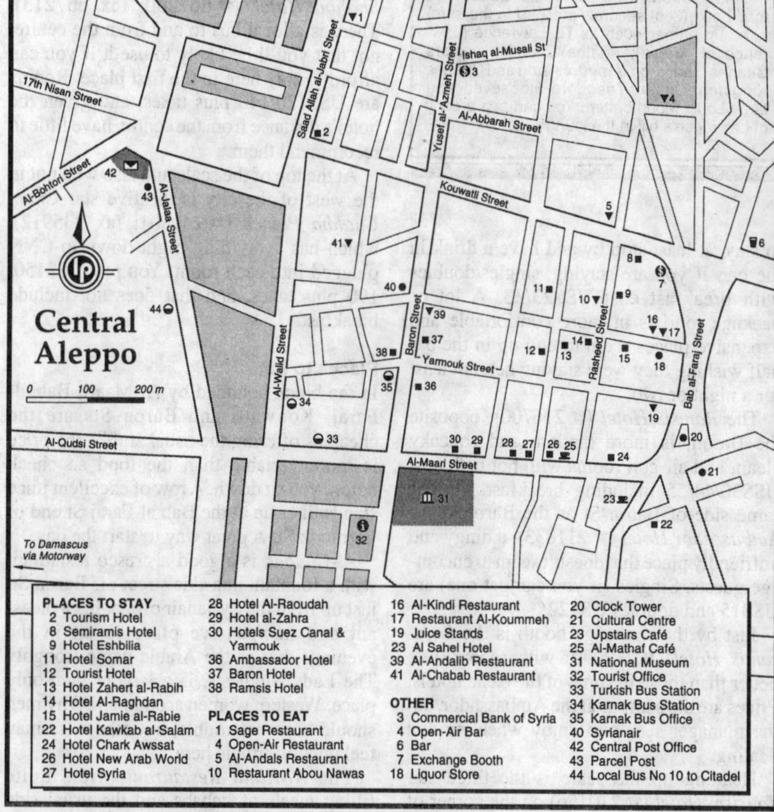

The Baron Hotel

Hardly on a par with the Raffles of this world, the Baron still retains some patchy charm. When it was built in 1909, the hotel was on the outskirts of town 'in gardens considered dangerous to venture into after dark'. The hotel was opened by two Armenian brothers and called the Baron because residents of Aleppo addressed the brothers as 'baron' (although some say the title meant little more than 'mister' in Armenian at the time).

The Baron quickly became noted as one of the premier hotels of the Middle East, helped by the fact that Aleppo was still a busy trading centre and staging post for travellers. The Orient Express used to terminate in Aleppo and the rich and famous travelling on it generally ended up in the Baron.

A look through the old leather-bound visitors' book (kept securely stashed in the safe) turns up names such as TE Lawrence (Lawrence of Arabia); Agatha Christie; aviators Charles Lindbergh, Amy Johnston and Charles Kingsford-Smith; Theodore Roosevelt and Lady Louis Mountbatten. You can see a copy of Lawrence's bill in the lounge. ■

to stay, at least stop by and have a drink in the bar. If you are staying, singles/doubles with breakfast cost US$23/33. A lot of package tourists in more comfortable and expensive places seem to end up in the bar half wishing they were staying here, at least for a night or two.

The *Ramsis Hotel* (☎ 216700), opposite the Baron, is more modern and squeaky clean, and air-con rooms with hot bath cost US$30/44/55 including breakfast. On the same side of Baron St as the Baron is the *Ambassador Hotel* (☎ 211833), a dingy and unfriendly place that doesn't seem to encourage guests. Singles (if you can get one) are US$15 and doubles US$22.

Just by the exchange booth is the *Semiramis Hotel* (☎ 219990) with rooms little better than those in some of the basic hotels. Prices are the same as at the Ambassador, but the manager seems to enjoy wheeling and dealing.

Heading up the scale is the three star *Tourism Hotel* (☎ 210156) on the corner of Kouwatli and Saad Allah al-Jabri Sts. Quite reasonable, if bland, rooms with TV, hot bath and air-con cost US$45/60/70. The upper floors are the best, although at the time of writing the lower ones were being renovated.

Places to Stay – top end

Just near the microbus and Pullman stations is the *Amir Palace* (☎ 214800). Pretty much a standard four star hotel, its principal advantage is its relative proximity to the places of interest compared with the other biggies. Singles/doubles go for a crazy US$90/140, plus 10% taxes, out of all proportion to the quality of rooms or service.

Out near the university is the *Pullman Shahba Hotel* (☎ 667200; fax 667213). There is a local bus to and from the centre, not that you'll be likely to use it if you can afford to stay here in the first place. Rooms are US$120/140 plus taxes, and given the hotel's distance from the centre, have little to recommend them.

At the top of the scale and also well out in the west of the city is the five star *Cham Chahba Palace* (☎ 249801; fax 235912), which has everything, right down to CNN plugged into each room. You pay US$150/190 plus taxes, and that does not include breakfast.

Places to Eat

In the block bounded by Al-Maari, Bab al-Faraj, Kouwatli and Baron Sts are the cheapies offering the usual stuff – the price is more variable than the food so check before you sit down. A row of excellent juice stands lines up at the Bab al-Faraj St end of Yarmouk St. A great way to start the day.

Al-Chabab is a good al fresco restaurant with a fountain in a side street off Baron St, just up from the Syrianair office. It's a pleasant and inexpensive place to sit in the evenings, but as the Arabic name (roughly The Lads) suggests, is a largely men-only place. Western women accompanied by men should have no trouble, but otherwise may feel uncomfortable here.

The *Al-Kindi Restaurant* offers quite filling meals of kebabs and the usual side orders for about S£120. There is quite a wide menu written in English. A bottle of Al-Chark beer costs S£40. Next door, the *Restaurant Al-Koummeh* has a good upstairs section and is in much the same league as the Al-Kindi. Across the road there is a liquor store (the sign simply reads 'Boissons', which is French for drinks).

Quite a decent upstairs place with tables for two on separate little balconies is the *Al-Andals* on Kouwatli St. It serves up a reasonable dish of meat, salad, hummus and something to drink for around S£150. It's a pleasant vantage point from which to contemplate the antics in the streets below and sip a slow beer.

For about the same price you can eat in the *Al-Andalib*, a few doors up from the Baron Hotel. It's a good place in the summer and a full meal with beer will cost about S£200.

A bright and comparatively recent arrival in central Aleppo is the *Restaurant Abou Nawas*. A full meal will cost about S£200, but alcohol isn't available.

A respectable meal in the restaurant at the *Tourism Hotel* will set you back about S£300, and although there is nothing wrong with the food, you're really just paying to be posh.

Expensive Restaurants For a better class of restaurant, you need to head to the chic part of town near the main park. After passing the Tourism Hotel you'll see the *Sage Restaurant*, a family place with decent food for around S£250 a person. A little more elegant is the *Restaurant Chaumine*, on Fares al-Khoury St, where you're looking at about S£300 per person.

More than half a dozen classy restaurants are crammed together on or near Georges and Mathilde Salem Sts, about level with the northern end of the park within the Aziziah district. *Wanes Restaurant* has a well established reputation as one of the best, but for a meal with wine expect little change from S£500. For something a bit cheaper and catering suspiciously to local aspirations at imitation western fast food, you could try a burger or pizza at *Midmac* – look for the yellow 'M'. Other restaurants on this street include *Challal* and *Carlos*. The latter dabbles in approximations of Chinese and Mexican cuisine. The nearby *Pizza House* even does home delivery! In the same class as Wanes is the *Delta Restaurant*, on Yusef Shulhat St.

If you have a little spare cash, make the effort to search out a couple of special places in the Armenian quarter. Two beautiful 17th century residences have been converted into fine restaurants. *Sissi House*, in Samira St, and *Yasmeen House* can be quite expensive, particularly for dinner, but the food is excellent. Try the stuffed courgettes, and at dinner time be prepared to part with around S£500.

For something a little different, there's an equally pricey *Italian restaurant* in the Pullman Shahba Hotel.

Quality sweet-teeth should try to get their hands on pastries and chocolates produced at the *Azrak* patisserie, 45 Yusef al-'Azmeh St. It has even opened a branch in Paris!

SYRIA

Entertainment

Cinema There is no shortage of cinemas, most of them showing rubbish so heavily censored that it is impossible to know what is going on. In fact, most of the slightly risqué stills used to entice the almost exclusively male customers belong to scenes removed from the film! Occasionally, though, a quite recent and decent flick seems to slip through the net, so keep your eyes peeled for the rare good one.

Nightclubs The centre of town is liberally sprinkled with an assortment of nightclubs. The number of drunk Syrian men spilling out of these sleazy joints makes the area one to be wary of late at night.

Bars If it's just a drink you're after, the outside terrace at the *Baron Hotel* takes a lot of beating, but it's only open in summer and the beer will cost you S£100. There is also a curious, gawdily lit little bar along Jibrail Dallal St.

Cafés There are a few cafés worth trying.

Opposite the entrance to the citadel you can linger over a shay and watch the world go by from the tables of two shady spots.

Back in the downtown area there's an upstairs café right by the clock tower. It has a view of the hectic intersection and the antics of the drivers and pedestrians are good entertainment. The entrance is in the side street, through the Al-Sahel Hotel. When everything else is closed, this place should still be going.

Another good café along the same lines, and great for smoking nargileh and playing dominos, is the *Al-Mathaf Café* along Al-Maari St.

While in the Armenian quarter (Al-Jadayda), keep your eyes open for the convivial little cafés hidden away in the interior courtyards.

SYRIA

Things to Buy

For a rundown on the kinds of articles you might like to track down as souvenirs, see Things to Buy in the Regional Facts for the Visitor chapter. Refer also to Souqs Area earlier in this chapter. Pressure to buy is pretty low key in Aleppo, but if you want to browse in comparative peace and quiet, check out **Souq ash-Shouna**, a regulated handicrafts market just behind the cafés on the south-western side of the citadel. Here you can take your time to inspect goods and quality with minimum fuss.

There's a reasonable place to replenish your supply of music cassettes across the road from the Delta Restaurant, north of the city centre.

Getting There & Away

Air Aleppo has an international airport with some connections to Turkey, Europe and other cities in the Middle East, although it is not easy to find a travel agent who will organise international flights to Aleppo. Syrianair has flights to Istanbul for US$166 (one way) and to Cairo for US$170.

Internally; there are daily flights to Damascus for S£602.

If you want to book international flights with other airlines, most foreign airline offices are on Baron St.

Bus/Minibus The station for regular old buses and minibuses, and more modern microbuses, to the north, west and south lies a couple of blocks behind the Amir Palace Hotel. For many destinations you actually have to buy tickets from a window. This supposedly ensures you a seat. Alternatively, you can hop on at the last moment and join the standing-room only squash. This is the cheapest, and generally slowest, transport you'll find.

Buses to Damascus take six hours (S£60), to Hama a bit over two hours (S£25) to Homs about three hours (S£30), and to Lattakia three to four hours (S£30, or S£40 on a minibus). Microbuses to Azaz (for Turkey) also leave regularly from here and cost S£10.

For destinations east of Aleppo it is easier to catch a Pullman or luxury bus. If you want to save every possible pound, you'll have to make your way to the east bus station for services to the east and south-east, which, appropriately enough, is on the eastern side of town. As it's about three km from the centre, the only sensible way to get there with luggage is by taxi, thus killing any saving you'd make over the Pullman bus.

Note also that if you arrive in Aleppo by microbus from the east, you'll end up at the east bus station and will have the long trek (or taxi ride) into the centre.

Karnak Bus The government-run Karnak bus office is on Baron St diagonally opposite the Baron Hotel. The buses leave from around the back, almost opposite the tourist office.

There are daily connections to Lattakia (S£50), Deir ez-Zur (S£90, 4½ hours), as well as Hama (S£45), Homs (S£60) and Damascus (S£100, five hours). There is also a service to Tripoli, in northern Lebanon (S£200). Book at least one day in advance.

Pullman Bus Directly south of the local city bus station behind the Amir Palace is a separate bus station from where private companies operate to most long-distance destinations. Different bays are allotted to various competing companies and you buy tickets before boarding.

Pullman buses are cheaper than Karnak but on a par in terms of quality (the trip to Deir ez-Zur, for instance, costs S£70) and more comfortable than the regular buses and minibuses. Also, they leave to a set timetable. Other fares include: Damascus (S£90); Hassake (S£80); Qamishle (S£90); Beirut (S£250) and Tripoli (S£200).

Luxury Bus For the top of the range in long-distance transport, you should head for another terminal west along Ibrahim Hanano St. Most of the new private companies, such as Qadmous, operate from here. On average, you'll pay S£150 for Damascus, S£100 for Homs, S£175 for Qamishle, S£85 for Raqqa, S£100 (microbus) for Lattakia and up to S£350 for Beirut (Lebanon).

Turkish Bus Buses leave from next to the Karnak bus station for Antakya (S£250) and Gaziantep (S£350). The former is the most used service, with departures at 6 am and 2 pm. You can also book a through ticket to other destinations, including Istanbul (S£1000, 24 hours). Book in one of the booths at the bus station or enquire at one of the nearby travel agencies. Check around though, as some ask a little more than others.

Train The railway station is just to the north of the big public park, about 15 minutes' walk from the downtown hotel area. Local trains run daily to Damascus, Lattakia, Deir ez-Zur and Qamishle in the north-east. The trip to Damascus costs S£85/57 in 1st/2nd class. A sleeper would cost S£325. The fares to Qamishle are S£132/87 and S£350 respectively.

Once a week there's a train from Aleppo to Istanbul. It takes forever (anything up to 48 hours) and costs S£530/430 in 1st/2nd class. There is no sleeper. It leaves Aleppo at 11.07 am on Saturday (winter) and Tuesday and Saturday at 2.14 pm in summer. For details on the trip from Istanbul to Aleppo see the Syria Getting There & Away chapter.

Service Taxi Next to the Pullman bus station is a service-taxi stand. This is the expensive but fairly quick way to go. Sample fares include (for the whole taxi): Hama (S£150); Damascus (S£400) and Beirut (S£700).

Car Rental Europcar has a desk at the Amir Palace Hotel. For other details, see the Syria Getting Around chapter.

Getting Around

All the sights of interest are in a compact area so getting around on foot poses no problems.

Bus You'll hardly need the local buses, and if you go to the bus station behind the Amir Palace it's all but impossible to get any sensible information. A ticket good for four rides (punch a corner each time) costs S£10 and can be bought on the bus. The No 10 runs past the post office out to the citadel.

Taxi Car buffs may like to ride in a regular taxi just for the hell of it. They are mostly enormous, lumbering old American limousines from the 1940s and 50s and have the usual assortment of lights and decorations inside – some light up like Christmas trees at night. The vintage, however, is beginning to change with the relaxation of car import laws. An average cross-town ride should cost no more than about S£20.

Some service taxis run set routes and pick up passengers for standard rates along the way, but it's difficult to tell them apart from the regular taxis which multiple hire, until you're in one and find you can't go to exactly your chosen destination.

Around Aleppo

The ruins and historical sites to the north, west and south of Aleppo have come to be known collectively as the Dead Cities. The area is crowded with the remnants of towns

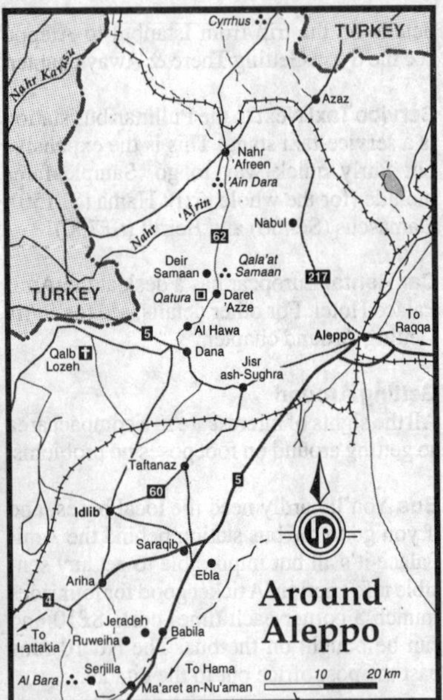

and monuments, many dating from early Byzantine Christianity. The majority are in such an advanced state of decay that they possess only limited interest for the passing traveller and some are hard to reach. For the expert or amateur historian, they represent a still largely unexplored archive in stone.

QALA'AT SAMAAN

This is the basilica of St Simeon, also known as St Simon of Stylites, who was one of Syria's most unusual early Christians. In the 5th century this shepherd from northern Syria had a revelation in a dream and joined a monastery. Finding monastic life insufficiently ascetic, he retreated to the barren hills.

In 423 he sat on top of a three metre pillar and went on to spend the next 36 years atop this and other taller pillars! For his last 30 years, the pillar was some 15m high. There was a railing around the top and an iron collar around his neck was chained to the pillar to stop him toppling off in the middle of the night. Rations were carried up a ladder by fellow monks and twice a week he celebrated mass on top.

Pilgrims started coming from as far away as Britain, hoping to see a miracle. St Simeon would preach to them daily from his perch, and shout back answers to their questions. He refused to talk to women, however, and even his mother was not allowed near the column.

After his death in 459, an enormous church was built around the famous pillar. It was unique in design in that it was four basilicas arranged in the shape of a cross, each opening onto a central octagonal yard covered by a dome. In the centre stood the sacred pillar. One basilica was used for worship; the other three housed the many pilgrims. It was finished in 490 and at the time was the largest church in the world. A monastery was built at the foot of the hill to house the clergy and a town with inns soon sprang up.

The church today is remarkably well preserved, with the arches of the octagonal yard still complete, along with much of the four basilicas. The pillar is in a sad state and is nothing more than a boulder on top of a platform. After St Simeon's death, pilgrims chipped away at it and took small fragments home as souvenirs of the holy place.

The views of the barren hills to the west are stunning and the ruins of the monastery can be seen down to the left at the foot of the hill in the village of Deir Samaan. People have taken up residence in the ruins but they don't mind if you wander around.

The site is open daily except Tuesday and entry is S£200. The ruins can be quite a popular spot with Syrians, and Lebanese up from Tripoli for a visit.

Getting There & Away

Microbuses from Aleppo leave every hour or so from the main central station for the one hour trip to the village of Daret 'Azze for S£10. About two-thirds of the way there you'll notice the 5th century Mushabbak basilica, isolated in an empty field to the left.

It is about eight km from Daret 'Azze to

Qala'at Samaan and if you can't be bothered waiting for a local microbus (S£10) it's a matter of negotiating with a local taxi driver, who will take you out there for S£100. Hitching is a reasonable possibility on weekends, when a lot of locals head out. Sometimes the minibus from Aleppo will take you the whole way – after all, they've got no timetable to stick to – but only for a substantial amount of money.

The last minibus from Daret 'Azze to Aleppo leaves at about 8 pm.

QATURA

About five km before Deir Samaan are the old Roman tombs at Qatura. They are about one km off the road to the west. The tombs are cut into the rock and it's easy to scramble up to them. The Greek inscriptions are still clearly visible.

'AIN DARA

A thousand years before Christ, a Hittite temple dedicated to the mountain god and the goddess Ishtar stood on an acropolis off the modern road that now leads north from Qala'at Samaan to the mainly Kurdish town of Nahr 'Afreen. The temple was destroyed in the 8th century BC, rebuilt and then gradually gave way to other constructions.

Excavations since the mid-50s have revealed the layout of the site and, most interestingly, some extraordinary basalt statues and reliefs, which litter the site. The single most impressive statue is a huge lion tipped over on its side.

As you climb the path up the side of the hill, a local chap (who is caretaker while archaeologists are absent) will probably greet you and do his best to show you around. However, readers report that the site has been closed while an enclosure is built around it to protect it against the elements. When open, entry costs S£100.

Getting There & Away

You can continue hitching from Deir Samaan towards 'Afreen (you may be able to pick up a local microbus for S£5), or catch a microbus from Aleppo direct to Nahr 'Afreen (S£13) and from there one of the irregular pick-ups to 'Ain Dara (S£10). It will drop you at the turn-off just before the village; you can see the acropolis in the distance. Follow the road around (about two km), or cut across the path and onion fields directly to the site.

CYRRHUS

Overlooking the Turkish border and deep in Kurdish territory is the 3rd century provincial town of Cyrrhus (Nabi Houri, or Prophet Cyrrhus, to the locals). Little is left of the town today, which once held a strategic position for troops of the Roman Empire. From the dusty town of Azaz (a windy, putrid little dump) the road takes you through cheerful countryside, dotted by wheat fields and olive groves, across two 3rd century **Roman bridges** on the Sabun River and past a Roman-era **mausoleum**. This pyramid-capped monument has survived well, partly because it was preserved by local Muslims as a holy site. Here you branch right off the road to the ruins.

The easiest to distinguish is the **amphitheatre**. Of the town walls, colonnaded street and basilica in the north of the town, not a lot remains, but it is quite fun to scramble up through the ruins past the theatre to the Arab **citadel** at the top, from where you have sweeping views. You can be virtually guaranteed of having this particular place to yourself.

Getting There & Away

Microbuses run from Aleppo to Azaz (S£10), from where you have no real choice but to bargain with one of the taxis. Do not be surprised to be hit for as much as S£800 for the ride there and back. You can try to hitch, but there is precious little traffic on this road. The same taxis also run people to the Turkish border for S£100 (for the car, not per person). You could try to rent a minibus or microbus at the Aleppo bus station for the day to do Cyrrhus and Qala'at Samaan. This would probably cost about S£1000 – not so bad if you have a big enough group.

By the way, the microbus drivers to Azaz from Aleppo will ask as much as S£100 to take you right to the border – an offer that should be refused.

EBLA

About 60 km south of Aleppo, just off the modern highway to Hama, lay the ancient city of Ebla (Tell Mardikh), where more than 15,000 clay tablets in a Sumerian dialect have been unearthed, providing a wealth of information on everything from economics to local administration and dictionaries of other tongues. However, only a small portion of the cuneiform secrets have as yet been unlocked.

The Italian teams that have been excavating the site since 1964 have discovered that it was one of the most powerful city-states in Syria in the late 3rd millennium BC (known as the Early High Syrian period), but was sacked before the close of the millennium, probably by Sargon of Akkad. In its heyday, Ebla probably controlled most of north-western Syria and it again rose for a relatively brief period from about 1900 to 1750 BC, before being destroyed in 1600 BC by Hittite invaders. Troops of the First Crusade passed by thousands of years later, when it was known as Mardic Hamlet.

The site lies over a rise about one km beyond the village of Tell Mardikh. You buy your ticket (S£100) outside the small museum dedicated to the story of the excavations and discoveries of Ebla, and then continue along the road and over the rise. The shallow remains of the city lie before you, dominated by the limestone tell (artificial hill) that once formed the core of the city's fortress. Before you go clambering all over the site, note that it is strictly forbidden to do precisely that. Stick to the ill-defined trails around the edge of the excavations.

When standing atop the former citadel you have a 360 degree view over the expanse of the whole city – or what is left of it. Once enclosed by a defensive wall pierced by four gates, the best preserved of which is the Middle Bronze Age one on the south side of the city, you now command views across wide plains all around. The most interesting ruins for the casual visitor are probably those labelled 'Palace G', just west of the acropolis, which display remains of a royal staircase, walls and columned halls. The famous archives unearthed by Professor Matthiae's team were stored in the southern part of this administrative district. Professor Matthiae continues to work here, and is confident of more astounding finds in the future.

Getting There & Away

Take any Hama-bound microbus, or to be sure of not paying the full fare for Hama, one of the less frequent ones to Ma'aret an-Nu'aman, and get off at the turn-off. You shouldn't have to pay more than S£17. From there it is a 40 minute walk to the site. Local microbuses may give you a ride, but will ask silly sums of money. From the turn-off to the village of Tell Mardikh should not be more than S£5, and from there it's just one km.

JERADEH & RUWEIHA

A rewarding day trip from Aleppo (which could feasibly be combined with a stop at Ebla) would see you exploring two little-visited Dead Cities about 10 km north of Ma'aret an-Nu'aman. From Aleppo (or the Ebla turn-off), pick up a minibus for Ma'aret an-Nu'aman and ask to be let off at Babila, seven km to the north. From here it's a three km hike to Jeradeh, which lies to the north-west.

The extensive remains of **noble houses** and a 5th century Byzantine cathedral are overshadowed by the six storey watchtower. Some of the simple geometric designs on column capitals and lintels is vaguely reminiscent of Visigothic work done in Spain (the other extreme of the Mediterranean) at about the same time. About the only interruption you'll have here will come from the odd local who is more curious about you than you are about the ruins.

Hit the road again and follow it for another 2½ or so km across a barren lunar landscape to reach the even more striking, scattered remains of Ruweiha. The most imposing building here is the 6th century **Church of Bissos**, now home to a local family. Its transverse arches are thought to be among the oldest of their kind. Just outside, the domed mausoleum housing the body of Bissos (possibly a bishop) has since found its echo in similar designs throughout the Arab world. Few people live among the ruins now, although the occasional family gets up here for a Friday picnic. It is a marvellous place to explore and again you may well be the object of quite a bit of local attention.

MA'ARET AN-NU'AMAN

This lively little market town is nothing special in itself, but if you want to get some idea of how many of the buildings of the Dead Cities were decorated, the **mosaic collection** housed in a 16th century Ottoman khan is well worth a visit. Most of the mosaics covered the floors of the more important or luxurious buildings and private houses of this string of 5th and 6th century Byzantine towns. Not quite as old is the lovingly executed mosaic of Assad, which takes pride of place facing the entrance. The museum is about 50 metres to the north of the bus station, on the right side of a large square. It is open daily except Tuesday and entry costs S£200.

Further north and off to the right is the **Grand Mosque**, whose 12th century minaret was rebuilt after an earthquake in 1170. From the mosque, head away to the right of the square and north for a few hundred metres – where the street opens out you'll see the sad remains of a medieval **citadel**, which now serve as cheap accommodation for a few families. All up, it's about one km from the mosque.

Getting There & Away

Every hour or so a minibus leaves Aleppo (S£17, one hour), passing the Ebla turn-off on the way. The bigger old lumbering buses also do this run (S£13).

AL-BARA (AL-KAFR)

About 20 km west of Ma'aret an-Nu'aman is just one of many sets of ruins belonging to the Dead Cities. In the late 5th century it was one of the most important centres of wine production in the region, and today boasts remains of at least five **churches** among ruins that cover six sq km. Small plots are still intensively worked in among the ancient buildings. The land is good and olives, grapes and apricots thrive here.

The most striking structures are the **pyramid tombs**, of which there are two. Just ask the locals in the modern town which path to take to the brooding grey basalt ruins (you can see them from the town) and head out. Take plenty of water and food as there's not much to be had in the town, although you will stand out so much that an invitation to tea is more than likely.

Getting There & Away

The road from Ma'aret an-Nu'aman is bad and you'll have to negotiate with a *trezeena* driver to get a lift to the modern village. It's easier to get a microbus from Aleppo to Ariha (S£15, one hour) and then another minibus to Al-Bara (S£10, 30 minutes). Friday is always a bad time to try this kind of trip by public transport, as there's little about.

SERJILLA

Equally, if not more, interesting than what you find at Al-Bara are the remains of the obviously once prosperous Serjilla. The outstanding building here is the **baths**. Now stripped of the mosaics that once decorated it, the remains are quite austere, but the mere

Al-Ma'ari the Poet

Born in 973 in Ma'aret an-Nu'aman, Abu al-'Ala al-Ma'ari was among the last of the great classic Arab poets. Left blind as a small child after a smallpox attack, he gradually gained himself a reputation for his cutting commentary of the anarchic society around him. In 1009 he travelled to Baghdad to broaden his education, and by the time he returned home almost two years later, he had become a vegetarian and something of a recluse. It was in this period, however, that some of his greatest work was done, and it has even been claimed that his seriously sceptical approach had an influence on Dante when he wrote the *Divine Comedy* three centuries later. ■

existence of Christian-era baths is itself a source of curiosity. Virtually next door lies an *andron*, or men's meeting place, and further east a small church. Spreading away from this core are substantial leftovers of private houses and villas.

QALB LOZEH

One of the best preserved examples of Syrian-Byzantine ecclesiastical architecture, the church of Qalb Lozeh predates Saint Simeon by perhaps only a few decades. The entrance to this church, flanked by two three-storey towers, its walls, not to mention the semicircular apse are almost completely intact today. Even some stone slabs of the roof have still been retained, but the once-impressive arch between the towers has, unfortunately, been lost. The simple elegance of the structure and clean lines of the columns around the apse and classical decoration make this church a clear precursor to the Romanesque style that would later dominate, in its various forms, the breadth of European church-building.

Qalb Lozeh lies a short way south of the main road from Aleppo to the Turkish border and Antakya.

The Desert

The Damascus-Aleppo highway marks roughly the division between the cultivable land to the west and the barren desert spreading eastward all the way to the Euphrates.

The wide fringe of the desert gets sufficient rain to maintain grazing land for sheep and goats, and the people who live in this area traditionally built beehive-shaped houses as protection against the extreme heat. You can see these houses on the road from Homs to Palmyra, in the area south of Lake Assad and around Aleppo, but increasingly concrete is taking over as the main building material and the standard anonymous housing typical of much of the Middle East is asserting itself.

The desert proper extends south-east from Palmyra into Jordan and Iraq. Its Arabic name is Badiyyat ash-Sham and it is also known as the Syrian Desert. Rather than the seas of shifting sands that so excite the movie-inspired imagination, this desert consists of more prosaic stony plains stretching to the horizon. Rain is extremely irregular and it is not uncommon for two or three years to pass between falls.

Dotting this desert are the oases – the main one is Palmyra – that once served as way-stations for the caravans en route between the Mediterranean and Mesopotamia.

PALMYRA

Known to the locals as Tadmor (its ancient Semitic name), Palmyra is Syria's prime attraction and one of the world's great historical sites. If you're only going to see one thing in Syria, make it Palmyra. Even if you have seen enough ruins to last you a lifetime

SYRIA

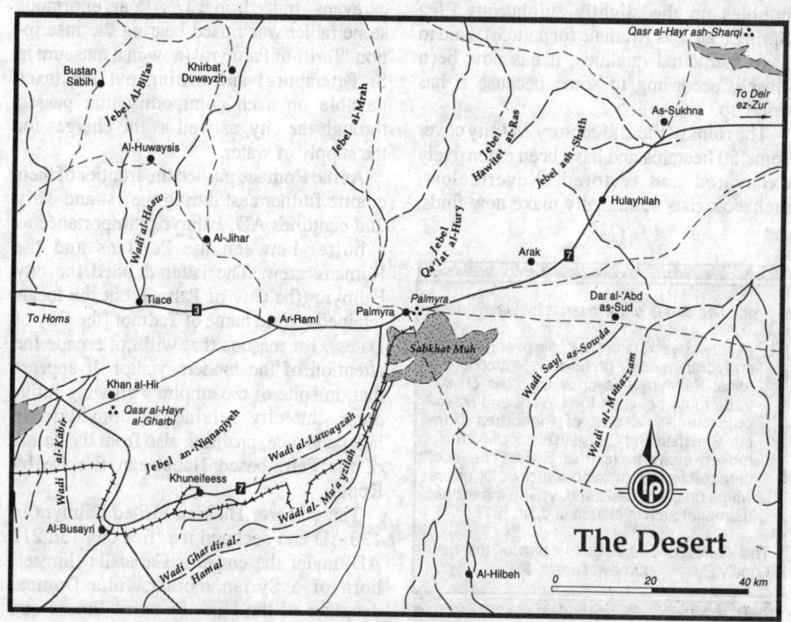

and the thought of more is enough to make you groan, Palmyra really is something special.

Although the days when you could expect to have all the splendour of this place to yourself have passed, the flow of tourists has yet to reach such proportions as to rob you of its magic. For much of the year you can still wander around the ruins pretty much by yourself, especially if you choose to get up early in the morning. Nevertheless, Palmyra *is* increasingly conscious of itself as a tourist destination. New hotels are springing up, and some bright spark has struck upon the idea of selling dates to visitors. A whole row of vendors has set up shop near the tourist office, and if they could sell you whole plantations of dates they probably would!

The oasis is really in the middle of nowhere – 160 km from the Orontes River to the west and 225 km from the Euphrates to the east. This is the very end of the Anti-Lebanon Mountains, and the final fold of the range forms a basin at the edge of which bubbles up the slightly sulphurous Efca Spring ('*efca*' is Aramaic for source). Said to have medicinal qualities, it has now been closed, according to some because it has dried up.

The ruins of the 2nd century AD city cover some 50 hectares and have been extensively excavated and restored. Nevertheless, archaeologists continually make new finds. In 1994 for instance, a team of Belgian archaeologists stumbled across some Roman tombs south-east of the Temple of Bel. The new town is rapidly growing around the ruins, spreading out with especial speed towards the west, and now counts more than 40,000 inhabitants. Nearby is an air-force base, and the sight of fighters screaming over the ancient ruins (thankfully, they don't come in too low) in training runs is curious to say the least.

Tucked well out of sight to the west of the old and new cities is a high-security prison with a grim reputation.

From *The Gates of Damascus* by Lieve Joris:

> At sunset a soft pink glow falls over Palmyra, and Ibrahim and I go for a walk among the ruins. Palmyra was once an oasis on the trade route between the Levant and Mesopotamia – it's one of the cities from pre-Christian and Christian history which are tucked away in Islamic Syria. The cool breeze blowing through the rows of pillars whips up the desert sand, veiling the distant triumphal arch in clouds of dust.

The *Gates of Damascus* is part of the new Lonely Planet Journeys series. ■

History

Tadmor is mentioned in tablets as far back as the 19th century BC, and from an early moment was an indispensable staging post for caravans travelling from the Mediterranean to the countries of the Gulf. It was also an important link on the old Silk Route from China and India to Europe and the city prospered greatly by levying heavy tolls on the caravans. Indeed, in 137 AD an enormous stone tablet was raised bearing the inscription 'Tariff of Palmyra' (now in a museum in St Petersburg) and setting out the taxes payable on each commodity that passed through the city, as well as the charges for the supply of water.

As the Romans pushed the frontier of their empire further east during the 1st and early 2nd centuries AD, Palmyra's importance as a buffer between the Persians and the Romans grew. The latter dubbed the city Palmyra (the City of Palms), but the locals retained the old name of Tadmor (the City of Dates), for reasons that will not escape the attention of the modern visitor. It appears that, in spite of the empire's growing influence, the city retained a considerable independence, profiting also from the defeat of the Petra-based Nabataean Empire by Rome.

The emperor Hadrian visited Palmyra in 130 AD and declared it a 'free city'. In 212 AD, under the emperor Caracalla (himself born of a Syrian mother, Julia Domna, daughter of the High Priest of Emesa and wife of Emperor Septimius Severus), it became a Roman colony. In this way, its citizens obtained equal rights with those of Rome and exemption from paying imperial taxes. During this period the great colonnaded street was enlarged, temples were built and the citizens grew extremely wealthy on the caravan trade – some even owned ships sailing in the Arabian Gulf.

The colony gradually evolved into a kingdom ruled by Odenathus, a brilliant military leader who had earned the respect and trust of Rome. In 256 the emperor Valerian bestowed upon him the title of 'Corrector of the East' and put all Roman forces in the region under his command.

The city's downfall began when Odenathus was assassinated in 267 in suspicious circumstances. His second wife, Zenobia (of Greek and Arabic descent) took over in the name of their young son, Vabalathus, who claimed the titles of his father, but Rome was not keen to recognise them. Zenobia was suspected of involvement in her husband's death, but it was never proved.

With her sights set on Rome, Zenobia declared complete independence and had coins minted in Alexandria bearing her image and that of her son, who assumed the title of Augustus. The emperor Aurelian, who had been prepared to negotiate, couldn't stomach such a show of open defiance and after defeating her forces at Antioch and Emesa (Homs) in 271, he besieged Palmyra itself. Zenobia was defiant to the last and instead of accepting the generous surrender terms offered by Aurelian, made a dash on a camel through the encircling Roman forces. She headed for Persia to appeal for military aid, only to be captured by the Roman cavalry at the Euphrates. The city then surrendered and got off pretty lightly with only a fine for its insurrection.

Zenobia was carted off to Rome in 272 as Aurelian's trophy and paraded in the streets, bound in gold chains. She spent the rest of her days in Rome, some say in a villa provided by the emperor, although others claim she chose to fast to death rather than remain captive.

Whatever became of her, it was the end of Palmyra's prosperity and its most colourful figure. The emperor Aurelian wrote the following of Zenobia.

> Those who say I have only conquered a woman do not know what that woman was, nor how lightning were her decisions, how persevering she was in her plans, how resolute with her soldiers. ■

The city itself was destroyed by Aurelian in 273 following another rebellion, when the inhabitants massacred the 600 archers that were stationed there. Aurelian's troops were particularly brutal, slaughtering Palmyra's residents and torching the city.

Palmyra was never able to recover its former glory and became a Roman outpost. The emperor Diocletian later fortified it as one in a line of fortresses marking the eastern boundary of the Roman Empire. Justinian rebuilt the city's defences in the 6th century but by this stage it had lost all its wealth and declined steadily with the drop in caravan traffic.

The city fell to the Muslims in 634 and was largely destroyed by a devastating earthquake in 1089. It seems that a Jewish colony existed there in the 12th century but the city had passed into legend by then.

In 1678 it was rediscovered by two English merchants living in Aleppo and the tales of Odenathus and Zenobia fascinated Europe, mainly because nobody had any idea that this once-important city had even existed.

Excavations began in 1924. Until then, Arab villagers had lived in the courtyard of the Temple of Bel (or Baal), from which they were now removed to the fledgling new town. Restoration has seen the number of standing columns go from 150 in the 1950s to more than 300 now. Some of the earlier restoration work, particularly noticeable on the *tetrapylon* (four groups of four pillars), was crudely executed.

The Beautiful Desert Rebel

Claiming to be descended from Cleopatra, Zenobia was a woman of exceptional ability and ambition. Fluent in Greek, Latin, Aramaic and Egyptian, she effectively turned Palmyra into an independent empire, wresting control of Egypt from Rome and marching deep into Asia Minor. The 18th century traveller, Edward Gibbon, said of her in *The Decline & Fall of the Roman Empire*:

> She equalled in beauty her ancestor Cleopatra and far surpassed that princess in chastity and valour. Zenobia was esteemed the most lovely as well as the most heroic of her sex. She was of dark complexion. Her teeth were of a pearly whiteness and her large black eyes sparkled with an uncommon fire, tempered by the most attractive sweetness. Her voice was strong and harmonious. Her manly understanding was strengthened and adorned by study.

She was also a ruler with a sense of humour. A merchant was to be punished for overcharging and was summoned to the theatre to appear in front of the queen and the public audience. The merchant stood alone in the arena and shook with fear, thinking that a wild beast was to be set upon him. When the beast was released the crowd roared with laughter – the merchant turned around to be confronted by a chicken. ■

Ancient coin bearing the head of Zenobia

SYRIA

Today, the unhurried traveller could easily spend a couple of days wandering around the main site, the funerary towers, and the 17th century Arab castle on the hill.

Information

Tourist Office Open from 8 am to 2 pm and 5 to 7 pm (4 to 6 pm in winter), the tourist office is about halfway between the town and the site proper.

Money There is no bank or exchange office in Palmyra, so you'll need to bring all you need or look around, discreetly, for someone willing to change money on the black market – this is not terribly difficult. Failing that, it is possible to change at the Palmyra Cham Palace Hotel at not terribly favourable rates.

Post The post office is a very laid-back place with flexible opening hours – don't count on it being open much after 2 pm. There are a couple of card phones in front of the main entrance, but the whole area is blocked off after 2 pm.

The Ruins

Tempting though it may be to think of Palmyra as simply another Roman city, it is in fact anything but. Its layout does not follow classic Roman town planning at all, although Roman and Greek influences are obvious. Despite the power of its neighbours (whether Roman, Persian or Parthian) Palmyra retained a distinct culture and expression in its own language, a dialect of Aramaic.

You could easily spend a lot of money visiting everything in Palmyra – the sum total of entry to all museums, the funerary towers and Temple of Bel would come to S£600, plus whatever you pay arranging a lift out to the funerary towers (see Funerary Towers for details). Those on a tight budget should make the Temple of Bel their first priority, followed by the main museum.

Temple of Bel The temple stands in a massive courtyard some 200m sq. Originally this courtyard was surrounded by a 15m high wall but only the northern side is original, the rest being of Arab construction. The western wall, which contains the entrance and a small souvenir shop, was built out of fragments of the temple when it was fortified. A double colonnade used to run around three sides of the interior while the fourth (western) had a single row of columns much taller than the others. Some of these can be seen to the right and left of the entrance.

Just to the left of the entrance inside the courtyard is a passage that enters the temple from outside the wall and gradually slopes up to the level of the courtyard. This is where sacrificial animals were brought into the precincts. In front of the shrine are the ruins of a banquet hall. The podium of the sacrificial altar is on the left, and the remains of another platform on the right, possibly used for religious purification ceremonies.

The shrine itself is unusual in design in that the entrance is in one of the sides rather than at the ends, and is offset from the centre. Inside, the shrine has porticoes at either end, with ceilings cut from single blocks of stone.

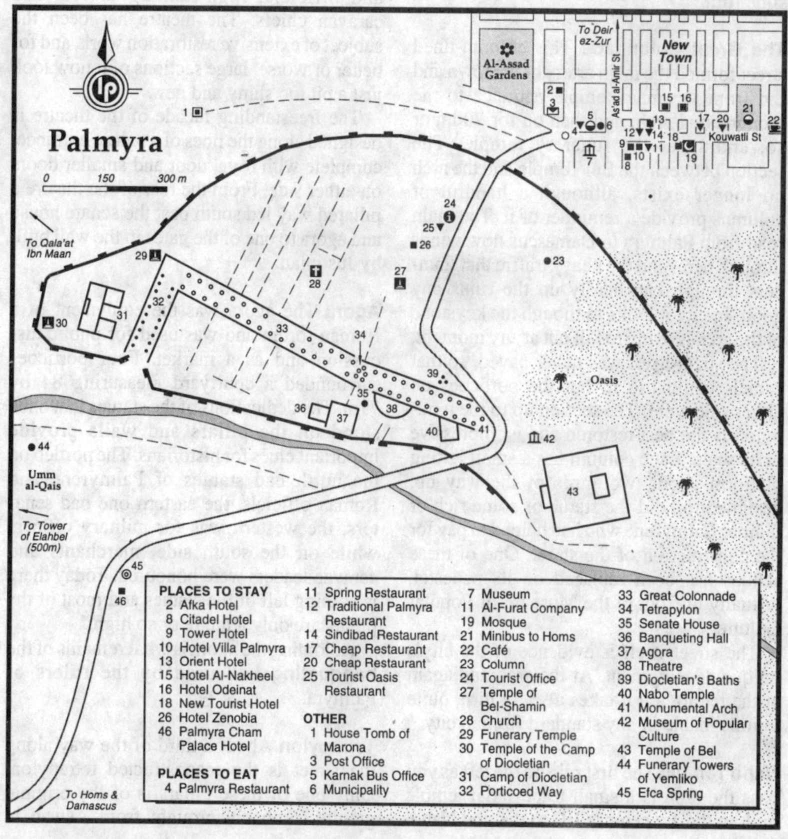

The northern one is highly decorated and the ceiling has a rosette. Dominating the centre is a cupola featuring a bust of Jupiter and signs of the zodiac. The stepped ramp leading to the southern portico suggests that it may have contained a portable idol used in processions.

Around the back of the shrine is a pile of old railway tracks that were used to remove trolleys of rubble during the original excavations. The temple enclosure is open daily from 8 am to 1 pm and 4 to 6 pm (8 am to 4 pm in winter). Entry is S£200.

There is a selection of books available here on Syria and Palmyra, and there's even slide film.

The Great Colonnade This column-lined street formed the main artery of the town and ran from the main temple entrance to the monumental arch, and then on for 700m or so, ending at the funerary temple. The section between the Bel Temple and the arch no longer exists, although a handful of columns provide a reminder of it. The main road from Palmyra to Damascus now winds through here, and the heavy traffic that thunders through can hardly do the ruins any good. In fact it looks as though the keystone of the arch is ready to fall out at any moment.

The street itself was never paved, so that camels could use it, but the porticoes on either side were. The section up to the tetrapylon is the best restored and is impressive in its scale. Each column has a small jutting platform about two-thirds of the way up, designed to hold the statue of some rich or famous Palmyrene who had helped to pay for the construction of the street. One of these statues has been replaced on its pedestal, virtually in front of the Museum of Popular Culture.

The street itself is evidence of the city's unique development. At the arch and again at the tetrapylon it takes a slight turn, quite unimaginable in any standard Roman city.

Nabo Temple The first ruin on the left as you pass the arch is a small trapezoidal temple built in the 1st century BC to the god Nabo. It seems that the temple underwent a few changes, as some of the construction stretched into the 3rd century AD.

Diocletian's Baths Next up on the right, but pretty much indistinguishable, is the site of baths built by Diocletian.

Theatre The theatre is on the south side of the street between two arches in the colonnade. Beneath the platforms on many of the columns are inscriptions with names for the statues that once stood there. It seems the statues were of prominent people such as emperors, princes of Palmyra, magistrates and officials, high-ranking priests and caravan chiefs. The theatre has been the subject of extensive restoration work, and for better or worse, large sections of it now look just a bit too shiny and new.

The freestanding façade of the theatre is designed along the lines of a palace entrance, complete with royal door and smaller doors on either side. From the rear of the theatre a pillared way led south past the senate house and agora to one of the gates in the wall built by Justinian.

Agora The agora was the equivalent of a Roman forum and was used for public discussion and as a market. Four porticoes surrounded a courtyard measuring 84 by 71m. The dedications of the statues that once stood on the pillars and walls provide important clues for historians. The portico on the north had statues of Palmyrene and Roman officials, the eastern one had senators, the western was for military officers while on the south side, merchants and caravan leaders were honoured. Today there is nothing left of the statues and most of the pillars are only a metre or so high.

Adjoining the agora is what remains of the **banqueting hall** used by the rulers of Palmyra.

Tetrapylon About a third of the way along the street is the reconstructed tetrapylon. Only one of these pillars is of the original granite (probably brought from Aswan in

Egypt). The rest are just coloured concrete and look pretty terrible – a result of some rather hasty and amateurish reconstruction.

Each of the four groups of pillars supports 150,000 kg of solid cornice. A statue used to stand between the pillars on each of the four pedestals, one of them of Zenobia herself. Unfortunately, no vestiges of the latter have ever been found.

This monument marks a major intersection of the old city. From here the main street continues north-west, and another smaller pillared street leads south-west to the agora.

Funerary Temple The main street continues for another 500m and ends in the impressive, reconstructed portico of the funerary temple, dating from the 3rd century. This was the main residential section of town and streets can be seen leading off to both sides.

Camp of Diocletian South of the funerary temple along the porticoed way, the area around the Camp of Diocletian is littered with fallen stones and the intricacy of the carvings can be seen at close quarters.

It is believed Diocletian built this camp on the site of what had been the Palace of Zenobia, but excavation so far has been unable to prove it. The camp, erected after the destruction of the city by Aurelian, lay near what was the Damascus Gate, which gave on to a 2nd century colonnaded street that supposedly linked Emesa (Homs) and the Euphrates.

Temple of Bel-Shamin Dedicated to the god of storms and fertilising rains, this small shrine stands near the Zenobia Hotel. Bel-Shamin was a Phoenician god, not unlike Bel a master of sun and moon, but only really gained popularity in Palmyra when Roman influence was at its height.

Although it is permanently closed, the six columns of the vestibule have platforms for statues and bear inscriptions. The one on the far left has an inscription in Greek and Palmyrene, dated 131 AD, praising the secretary of the city for his generosity during the visit of 'the divine Hadrian' and for footing the bill for the temple's construction. A branch road led to the temple from the tetrapylon.

Funerary Towers of Yemliko & Elahbel These lie to the south of the city wall at the foot of the hill of Umm al-Qais. The whole area forms what has come to be known as the Valley of the Tombs and is littered with tombs of varying types and ages. The oldest of them are the square-based towers that contained coffins in niches on up to five levels. The interior was often decorated with cornices and friezes.

The two best preserved and partly restored towers are kept locked and can only be visited in groups and accompanied by a guide from the museum. Nearest to the line marking what was the city wall is a series known as the Towers of Yemliko. The tallest of these is the most interesting and worth exploring. Behind them, the Umm al-Qais hillock makes a wonderful vantage point for surveying the whole Palmyrene scene.

SYRIA

Dating from the 3rd century, this funerary sculpture can be seen in the area known as the Valley of the Tombs.

Scramble back down the hill and follow the track down the valley to the west. After about 500m you reach the best of the towers, that of Elahbel. Built in 103 AD, it has four storeys and could purportedly accommodate up to 300 sarcophagi. On the way to the Tower of Elahbel you'll note the much excavated Tomb 36, about which there is a detailed display in the main museum.

Visiting the towers can be a bit of a pain. A museum attendant with keys is prepared to go out there four times a day (details posted at the museum), and tickets cost S£100. You are supposed to bargain with a local driver to take a group of people out – this should not cost more than S£200 and, given that you can walk out in less than half an hour, is a real pain. Your friendly museum attendant, however, will not budge unless you have organised the vehicle – a local form of state-assisted private enterprise. Given that you can walk out and peer in by yourself, you'll have to decide whether climbing about inside the towers is worth the rigmarole. For those without a special interest in this sort of thing and a tight budget, it certainly is not.

Qala'at Ibn Maan

To the west the dominant feature is the Arab castle, Qala'at Ibn Maan, built in the 17th century by Fakr ad-Din the Maanite. You can't miss it, just jump the wall and head uphill. It is surrounded by a moat, and a footbridge across it has been made passably safe. It is well worth scrambling up the hill to get in, for although the castle is not in a wonderful state of repair, the views over Palmyra and the surrounding desert are magic. It's best to go up in the late afternoon when the sun is behind you and the shadows are long. Townspeople will happily drive you up (an asphalted road winds up behind the castle to within spitting distance of the entrance) for an exorbitant fee if you don't fancy the climb.

Once inside, the old guardian will try to extract hefty tips from you, but at the time of writing a visit was still technically free. This could change at any time – it might be worth asking at the tourist office before heading up if there is an official entry charge. Opening hours depend largely on whim, but it's roughly 9 am to dusk.

Museum

The museum has an excellent array of statuary from Palmyra, most in surprisingly good condition considering they have been buried in the sand for a thousand years. Among the most outstanding is a statue of the goddess Allat, associated with the Greek Athena and found by a Polish team in 1975. A couple of dead Palmyrenes are on display, looking a little worse for wear. Also interesting is a handful of Palmyrene mosaics and bits of Byzantine-era glassware. Tomb 36 in the Valley of the Tombs has been rather thoroughly examined by German-Syrian teams, and some of their drawings and conclusions are on display in the museum. The descriptions of the displays are in English, which is unusual for Syrian museums.

You will also find fairly detailed explanations of the Palmyrene language, which had 22 letters and remained the main tongue of the region until the arrival of Islam, from which time it was gradually usurped by Arabic. The upper level of the museum is closed.

The museum is on the edge of the new town and open daily, except Tuesday, from 8 am to 1 pm and 4 to 6 pm (2 to 4 pm in winter). The entrance fee is S£200.

Museum of Popular Culture

The whitewashed building with the air of a Beau Geste fort, just by the Temple of Bel, houses the Museum of Popular Culture. It contains the usual scenes from Arab life, recreated using mannequins, but is better than most. The guardian may even play you a tune on the traditional Bedouin single-string *rababa*.

There is a lot of interesting information posted up about the Bedouin tribal system – the catch is it's all in French. The museum is officially open daily except Tuesday from 8.30 am to 2.30 pm, but it may open up if you hang around outside these hours. Entry is S£100.

Efca Spring

Just past the Palmyra Cham Palace, on the way into town, is the Efca Spring. Tourist office tales that the spring has simply dried up seem unlikely, but it is no longer possible to visit this grotto, which had been used for bathing since Roman times.

Festival

Since 1993, Palmyra has been the scene of an annual popular folk music festival. Largely aimed at tourists, it takes place over three or four days towards the end of April. The inaugural event was attended almost exclusively by local Bedouin, but the show looks set to go on.

The Countess of Andurain

Countess Marga d'Andurain was born in Bayonne on 28 May 1893 in a bourgeois family and began challenging the establishment from a very young age. She seemed to revel in her reputation as an adventuress and from the first day of her arrival in Palmyra she referred to herself as 'the child of this strange earth'. Calling herself the reincarnation of the Queen Zenobia (see the boxed story called 'The Beautiful Desert Rebel'), she soon decided to take over the management of the Hotel Zenobia. The hotel was internationally famous for its refinement, its elegance, its view of the ruins and for the irresistible charm of its hostess.

Her life never ceased to be full of excitement and controversy – the amicable separation from her husband Pierre d'Andurain and the suicide of her new partner (intelligence officer) Jeffrey Sinclair was followed by her incredible journey to Mecca disguised as a poor Bedouin. The Countess wanted to be the first Christian to enter the religious capital of Islam. She achieved this feat, but not without causing another scandal. She found herself imprisoned in Jeddah and on her return to Palmyra was condemned to death. But following the enactment of a sham hanging she fled into the desert, and was later implicated in the suspected murder of her second husband. The assassination in mysterious circumstances of Pierre d'Andurain, who she remarried, effectively ended her life in Syria. In Europe, the start of WWI was imminent, and the Countess left Palmyra for new adventures in occupied Paris. She died in Tangier in November 1948. ■

Places to Stay

At one time, about the only place you could find a bed in Palmyra was the *New Tourist Hotel* (☎ 910333). Since then, things at this hotel haven't changed much, and basic singles/doubles cost S£200/325. A bed in a shared room is S£150. There is a hot communal shower and some rooms have their own (cold) bath. It's basic but OK. The mosque is nearby, so you will be subjected to the early morning call to prayer.

The *Citadel Hotel* (☎ 910537) has a couple of simple rooms that seem popular with backpackers. It charges the same prices as the New Tourist. The dingiest place around is the *Afka Hotel* (☎ 220386), where the owners will try to charge S£200 per bed or up to S£300 for a single. Avoid this place if you can.

Marginally better than all of these is the *Hotel Odeinat* (☎ 911067). It generally charges S£300/500 but it is worth making the effort to bargain if possible. That's about it for the real cheapies.

Of the middle bracket places, the *Hotel Al-Nakheel* (☎ 910744) has comfortable rooms with private bathroom and heating in winter for S£700/1200. Also decent is the recently refurbished *Orient Hotel* (☎ 910 131), known as Funduq ash-Sharq in Arabic. This hotel is clean and quiet, and the rooms have good bathrooms and effective heating in winter. Rooms cost US$15/25 – virtually the same as at the Al-Nakheel but hard currency only is accepted by the Algerian owner.

Close by, in the main street, is the *Tower Hotel* (☎ 910116; fax 910273). It's OK, with a nice lounge on the 1st floor, and also charges US$15/25.

Since late 1991, the *Hotel Zenobia* (☎ 910 107; fax 912407) out by the ruins has been in the hands of new owners – the Damascus-based tourism company Orient Tours. The hotel originally dates from the French Mandate, but little evidence of that bygone era remains. Singles/doubles/triples cost US$55/66/76 in high season and US$42/51/59 in the off season, which can be paid with Visa, MasterCard and American

Express credit cards. For S£200, you can pitch a tent out the back and grab a hot shower.

The *Hotel Villa Palmyra* (☎ 910156; fax 912554) has rather bland rooms with ensuite bath and air-con for an outlandish US$60/70 plus 10% taxes.

By the Efca Spring, some three km from the new part of town on the road to Damascus, is the *Palmyra Cham Palace Hotel* (☎ 237000) with five star prices and facilities (although it has been criticised by a couple of travellers). Singles/doubles cost US$160/190. Access to the swimming pool costs S£200 a day for non-guests of the hotel.

Places to Eat

Everyone seems to agree that the best place to eat in Palmyra is the *Traditional Palmyra Restaurant.* For S£150 you can have a hearty meal and be plied unfailingly with tea. It does a great soup for S£50.

Next door, the *Sindibad Restaurant* is not nearly as inviting, but it does sell overpriced beer (S£60 a bottle). Both places also do breakfast menus (fried eggs, toast, jam, juice and coffee or tea). For a still pricier beer (S£75) you could head up the road to the *Palmyra Restaurant*, which does rather ordinary food.

The *Afka Restaurant* is about as inviting as the hotel in the same building. You would normally only enter the *Spring Restaurant* to get a bus ticket to Damascus or Deir ez-Zur, but you can have a serve of kebabs for S£35 if you want.

The *Al-Khayyam Restaurant*, out by the tourist office, is in much the same fly-blown league and a meal of the usual stuff will cost about S£150.

There are a few cheap restaurants also as far down as the town square. A half chicken and the usual trimmings should not cost more than about S£100.

For a more expensive meal, you can choose between the *Zenobia* and *Cham Palace* hotel restaurants. For ambience you're better off at the former, where there's also a somewhat expensive bar.

Next door to the mosque is the local tea shop where you can sit and watch the world go by. The much trumpeted Assad Gardens supposedly sport a café, but there's precious little evidence of it.

Getting There & Away

Bus/Minibus The government-run Karnak bus company has all but folded here, with a daily departure for Damascus (S£90) via Homs (S£50).

Al-Furat Tours has set up shop in the Spring Restaurant. It has several daily departures to Damascus (S£100) and Deir ez-Zur (S£90).

Otherwise, you can try to jump on any of the buses regularly passing through en route between Damascus and Deir ez-Zur (and beyond). For Deir ez-Zur, the best bet is to wait at one of the restaurants on the Deir ez-Zur highway (head north about 1½ km up Assad al-Amir St, the highway forms a T-junction about 200m past the last tree). The Damas Tour company is ensconced in the Sahara Restaurant out here, and offers regular runs to Damascus, Deir ez-Zur, Hassake (S£160) and Qamishle (S£225).

For Damascus, you can also wait near the Karnak office. You need to energetically flag buses down if you do it this way. An old-style bus passing through Palmyra will cost S£75 to Deir ez-Zur.

Several minibuses and microbuses leave for Homs (S£50) from the main square when full.

QASR AL-HAYR ASH-SHARQI

If you have some spare cash, a worthwhile excursion is to head 120 km north-east of Palmyra into the desert to see one of the most isolated and startling monuments to Omayyad Muslim rule in the 8th century. The Qasr al-Hayr ash-Sharqi falls into the category of 'desert castles', such as those that can be fairly easily visited in Jordan (see the East of Amman chapter), but is much grander.

The palace held a strategic position, commanding desert routes into Mesopotamia. As support from the nomadic Arab tribes (of which they themselves were a part) was one of the main Omayyad strengths, it is no coincidence that they made their presence felt in the desert steppes.

The palace complex and rich gardens, once supplied by an underground spring about 30 km away, covered a rough square with 16-km sides. Built by Hisham around 730, the palace long outlived its Omayyad creators. Harun ar-Rashid, perhaps the best known of the Abbasid rulers, made it one of his residences, and evidence has suggested that it was only finally abandoned in the 14th century.

The partly restored walls of one of the main enclosures, with their mighty defensive towers, are the most impressive remaining sign of what was once a sumptuous anomaly in the harsh desert. The ruins to the west belong to what may well have been a khan. In the south-eastern corner are remnants of a mosque – the column with stairs inside between the two areas was a minaret. The remains of baths are to be found just to the north of the main walls. Traces of the old perimeter wall can just be made out to the south, and in fact border the best track leading here from the highway.

This castle has a counterpart west of Palmyra, Qasr al-Hayr al-Gharbi, but little of interest remains on that site (its impressive façade has been superimposed over that of the National Museum in Damascus).

Getting There & Away

The only way to get out here is by private transport. A planned asphalted road will, if it's ever laid, considerably facilitate the trip, but until then a 4WD is, although not essential, probably the best idea for the last part of the ride (about 35 km from the town of As-Sukhna, which is just off the Palmyra-Deir ez-Zur highway). You could probably manage it in Renault 4 or something similar (the higher the chassis the better). A local driver or guide, at least from As-Sukhna, is indispensable. In the unlikely event that it has rained in the previous days (it does happen), it is best not to attempt it – getting bogged in the desert is few people's idea of fun.

You can arrange with a local to go from Palmyra. Prices start at S£2000 for the car and you'll be doing well to get them below S£1500. Take plenty of water and some food with you. Unless you end up in one of the few Bedouin houses scattered around the desert (none of them very close to the site) for a cup of tea, it can be a thirsty way to spend the day, especially if your driver or guide gets lost in the labyrinth of tracks left in the desert by Bedouin pick-ups!

The Euphrates River

The Euphrates River ('Al-Furat' in Arabic) starts out high in the mountains of eastern Anatolia in Turkey and winds through the north-east of Syria into Iraq, finally emptying into the Shatt al-Arab waterway and the Persian Gulf – a total distance of more than 2400 km. Like a cool green ribbon, it makes a change to see some water and fertile land after all the steppes and desert of the interior.

One of the few tributaries of the Euphrates, the Kabur, flows down through north-eastern Syria to join it below Deir ez-Zur. These two rivers make it possible to irrigate and work the land, and the cotton produced in this area has become an important source of income for the country.

The Jezira (literally 'island'), bounded loosely by the Kabur and, further east, the Tigris (which just touches Syria on its way from Turkey into Iraq), constitutes some of

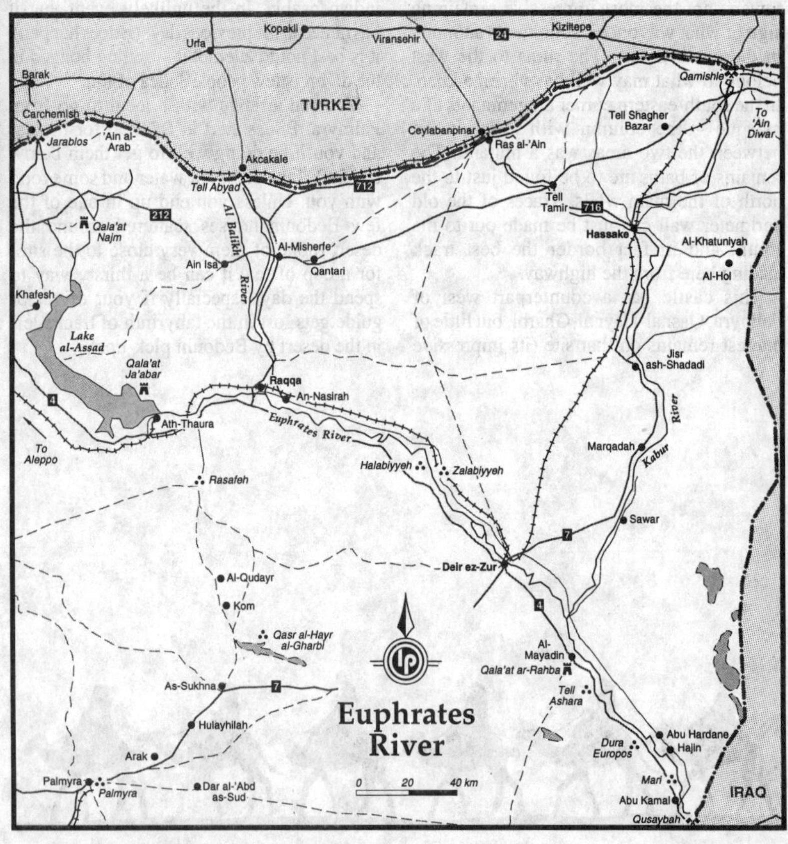

the richest land in the country. Locals say the best of it is to be found in the strip just south of the Turkish border, mostly in Kurdish territory. Cotton and wheat are the two big crops.

Oilfields at Qaratchok in the far north-eastern corner of the country produced oil for nearly three decades, but only low-grade stuff that had to be mixed with better imported oil for refining. Big high-grade oil finds around Deir ez-Zur in the 1980s changed all that. Production from the area, which stood at zero in the early 80s, has plateaued at nearly 400,000 barrels a day, two-thirds of the country's total. National and foreign companies are searching for yet more reserves, as there are fears this small-scale oil bonanza may already have peaked.

LAKE AL-ASSAD

By the time the Euphrates enters Syria at Jarablos (once the capital of the Hittite Empire) it is already a mighty river. To harness that power for irrigation and hydro-electricity production, one of the Assad regime's most ambitious plans, to dam the Euphrates, went into effect in the 1960s.

Work began at Tabaqah in 1963 and the reservoir started to fill in 1973. Now that it's full, it stretches for some 60 km. The dam is Syria's pride and joy and the electricity produced was supposed to make the country self-sufficient. The flow of the Euphrates has however been reduced by the construction of the Ataturk dam in Turkey, and Syria and Iraq are concerned that the Turks may at any time decide to regulate the flow for political reasons. The decision by Istanbul in late 1995 to proceed with construction of a further dam, the Birecik dam, has only served to heighten the two Arab countries' worst fears. Syria has protested to the UN Security Council and other international groups that Turkey is reneging on water-sharing arrangements and also violating international law. The Turks deny all claims of having thus far used their position to reduce the flow of the river, attributing any slowing down to natural causes.

The lack of water in the river has been a disappointment, but by the late 1980s the regular power cuts that had long been a daily reality across the country had been all but eliminated. Other non-hydroelectric projects appear for the moment to have secured Syria's power needs and cuts are the exception rather than the rule.

The dormitory town of Ath-Thaura (the Revolution) was built at Tabaqah to accommodate dam workers and peasants who had to be relocated because of the rising water levels. Not only were villages inundated, but also some sites of historical and archaeological importance. With aid from UNESCO and other foreign missions, these were investigated, documented and, where possible, moved to higher ground. The 27m high minaret of the Maskana Mosque and the 18m high minaret from Abu Harayra were both segmented and transported, the latter to the centre of Ath-Thaura.

QALA'AT NAJM

The northernmost citadel/castle of its kind along the Euphrates in Syria, Qala'at Najm, which has been partly restored, has sweeping vistas of the river. Originally built under Nureddin in the 12th century, it was later reconstructed under Saladin. It commands a natural defence position over the Euphrates plain, and the views out across what was once a strategic crossing point are alone worth some effort.

Watch out for the warden – he or his son will soon get wind of your presence and invite you in for a friendly cup of tea in their house at the foot of the castle. The hand will then be out for a friendly piece of baksheesh.

Getting There & Away

Take a bus for 'Ain al-Arab from the East bus station in Aleppo (S£30, two hours) and get off at the village of Haya Kabir (tell people on board where you want to go). You may be able to get an 'Ain al-Arab bus from the station behind the Amir Palace Hotel too. From Haya Kabir it is 15 km to the castle, and hitching is the only way.

The earlier you get going the better, as there is not a lot of traffic on this dead-end trail. The road passes through rolling wheat fields that form a cool green carpet in spring. It appears there are no buses at all to 'Ain al-Arab on Fridays.

QALA'AT JA'ABAR & ATH-THAURA

An impressive sight from a distance, this citadel built entirely of bricks in classic Mesopotamian style does not add up to all that much once you're inside. It is situated on a spit of land connected to the bank of Lake al-Assad, about 15 km north of Ath-Thaura. Before the lake was built, the original castle had rested on a rocky perch since before the arrival of Islam, and had then been rebuilt by Nureddin and altered by the Mamelukes. The castle makes a great backdrop for a day by the lake, and on Friday this is an extremely popular spot with Syrians. It's a great place for a picnic. It is also ideal for a swim, unless you are a woman, in which case it could be decidedly uncomfortable.

You will have to pass through Ath-Thaura to get to the citadel, and it may be worth a quick visit anyway to have a look at the dam. The town itself, however, has nothing at all to recommend it and is a confusing place to get around when searching for the right road to the citadel or anywhere else. Even the buses don't seem to terminate in the same place. Ask about and you shall, eventually, work it out.

Getting There & Away

Without your own car, it can be a pain to get to. You'll have to go via Ath-Thaura, either coming from Raqqa (S£23 by microbus) or Aleppo (S£50 by bus). Raqqa is the much closer base; from Aleppo it can be a long and hassle-filled day. From the centre of Ath-Thaura, you have to head out towards the north of town and try to hitch across the dam ('*as-sidd*'). The turn-off for the citadel is a few km further on to the left. From here it is about 10 km.

Friday is a good day to hitch across the dam, as the place is crawling with day-trippers. If you want peace and quiet on the other days, be prepared for longer waits, or negotiate with a local driver to take you out (expect to pay about S£200).

Note that there are few, if any, buses or microbuses from Ath-Thaura anywhere after about 4 pm.

RAQQA

From 796 to 808 AD, the city of Raqqa (then Ar-Rafika) reached its apex as the Abbasid caliph, Harun ar-Rashid, made it his summer residence. The area around the city had been the site of numerous cities that had come and gone in the preceding millennia, including that founded by the Seleucids, Nikephorion (sometimes attributed by legend to Alexander the Great). After the Mongol invasion in 1260, Ar-Rafika virtually ceased to exist. It is only since the end of WWII that it has again come to life and become an important Euphrates basin commercial centre.

Things to See & Do

Practically nothing of the city's old glory has been preserved, but there are a few exceptions. The partly restored **Bab Baghdad**, Raqqa's only remaining city gate, lies about a 10-minute walk to the east of the clock tower, a central landmark when you arrive in the city. The old **Abbasid city wall**, restored at some points to a height of five metres, runs north from the gate past the **Qasr al-Binaat** (Daughters' Palace), which served as a residence under the Ayyubids.

To the north-west are the remains of the old **grand mosque**, built during the reign of the Abbasid caliph Al-Mansur in the 8th century and reconstructed in 1165 by Nureddin. It is slowly being replaced by an Iranian-financed monstrosity behind the Bab Baghdad, although given the lack of progress in building, it is tempting to think someone has run out of money. A small **museum**, halfway between the Bab Baghdad and the clock tower, has some interesting artefacts from excavation sites in the area, worked on since the 1920s. The displays transmit a reasonable impression of the archaeological richness of the area around Raqqa. The museum is open daily except

Tuesday from 9 am to 6 pm (4 pm in winter), and entry costs S£100.

Every day but Friday, a livestock market impressive for its size is held early in the morning about two km north of Bab Baghdad. Follow the city wall to the end and ask for the *'souq ad-dawab'*.

Places to Stay

There are a few hotels around the clock tower, all of them amazingly expensive. The *Hotel Tourism*, east of the clock tower on Al-Quwatly St, charges S£300/450 singles/doubles for spacious, clean but rather bare rooms. The rooms have their own cold shower. Better is the *Ammar Hotel* (☎ 222612), which charges an equally hefty S£350/500 for singles/doubles. It is clean, has hot showers and is perfectly all right. Don't accept the kind offers of coffee or tea – they'll only be added to the bill at double the normal price. Some travellers warn they have been charged US dollars here.

Places to Eat

The *Al-Rasheed Restaurant* on King Faisal (Al-Malek Faisal) St is about the best Raqqa has to offer, and in warmer weather is ideal with its garden dining area. Otherwise, the *Al-Waha Restaurant* on Ath-Thaura St is not bad either. A set meal known as wajabeh, including soup, rice and stew, costs S£100 – a post prandial tea is thrown in too.

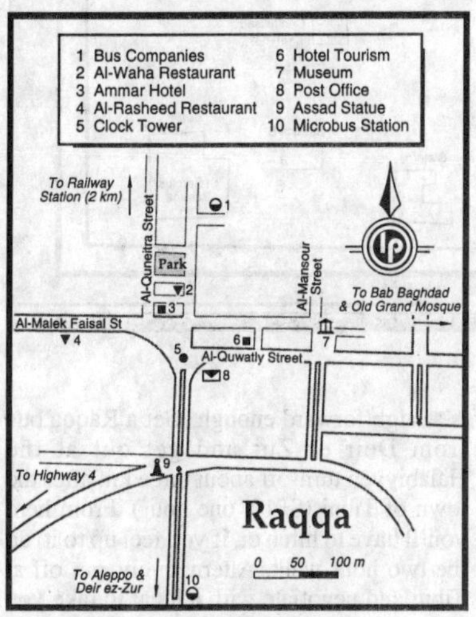

Getting There & Away

Bus The area around Ath-Thaura St is swarming with bus companies eager to whisk you off wherever you want to go. Fares vary depending on the quality of the bus. A trip to Damascus can cost up to S£225. The fare to Aleppo on a good bus is S£85 and you could even go direct to Beirut for S£325.

Microbus From the microbus station, about 200m south of the clock tower (on the road leading out of town), there are regular microbuses west to Al-Mansura (S£11.50), Ath-Thaura (S£23) and Aleppo (S£75, three hours).

Train The railway station lies about two km north of the clock tower – head up Al-Quneitra St and its continuation, Al-Tahrir St. There are two trains a day to Aleppo, at 10.30 am and 3 pm (S£55/37 in 1st/2nd class), one of which goes on to Damascus, and two to Deir ez-Zur (S£38/27) and on to the end of the line at Qamishle.

HALABIYYEH & ZALABIYYEH

Halabiyyeh was founded by Zenobia, the rebellious Palmyrene leader, in the years immediately preceding her fall in 272. It was later re-fortified under emperor Justinian, and it is mainly the result of his work that survives today.

The fortress town was part of the Roman Empire's eastern defensive line against the Persians, who took it in 610 AD. The walls are largely intact, and there are remnants of the citadel, basilicas, baths, a forum and the north and south gates. The present road follows the course of the old colonnaded street.

Across the river and further south is the much less intact forward stronghold of the main fort, Zalabiyyeh. In summer, the Euphrates is sometimes passable between

Rasafeh

This startling walled city lies in the middle of nowhere, and rises up out of the featureless desert as you approach it. Possibly inhabited in Assyrian times, Diocletian established a fort here as part of a defensive line against the Sassanian Persians (or Sassanids) late in the 3rd century AD. A desert road led through Rasafeh from the Euphrates and south to Palmyra, a trail that can be followed today with a 4WD and guide or adequate orienteering skills. About this time a cult to the local martyr St Sergius began to take hold, so that by the 5th century the place had been expanded and an impressive basilica had been raised.

A century later, Emperor Justinian further expanded the centre's defences against Persian assault, but in the end the real threat emerged from another quarter – the Muslim Arab invasion of the 630s. The city was eventually taken over by the Omayyad caliph, Hisham, who built a palatial summer residence here. The Abbasids completely destroyed the residence some years after Hisham's death in 743 and thereafter the city fell into ruin. The Mongols finished the job when they swept across northern Syria in the 13th century.

The walls, enclosing a quadrangle measuring 550 by 400m, are virtually all complete. As you enter by the northern gate, you are confronted by the immensity of the place, mostly bare now save for the churches inside. Little excavation has yet been done here. You can walk along the complex defensive perimeter before exploring the site.

Three churches remain standing. The grandest is the partially restored **St Sergius basilica**. The wide central nave is flanked by two aisles, from which it is separated by a series of sweeping arches each resting on pillars and a pair of less ambitious arch and column combinations. This and the two other churches date from the 6th century. In the south-western corner of the complex lie huge underground **cisterns** (watch your step) that could keep a large garrison supplied with water through long sieges.

Speaking of water, there is nobody at the site selling the stuff, or anything else for that matter, so bring food and water with you – it gets stinking hot in summer.

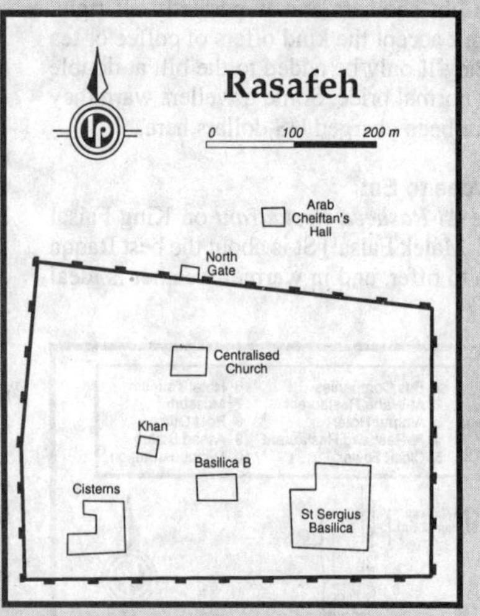

Getting There & Away It requires a little patience to get to Rasafeh as transport is infrequent. Catch a microbus from Raqqa to Al-Mansura (S£11.50, 20 minutes) – that's the easy bit. Now it's just a matter of waiting at the signposted turn-off for a pick-up to take you the 35 km to the ruins for about S£20. Wait a while – one will turn up eventually. If you're impatient, you can ask one of the pick-up drivers lounging around here to take you there and back for some extraordinary sums – S£200 would not be unusual. The difference seems to be an I'm-going-out-of-my-way-for-you fee. ■

the town and the fort, which is what made Zalabiyyeh necessary.

Getting There & Away

Neither Halabiyyeh or Zalabiyyeh is easy to get to. Halabiyyeh is the more interesting of the two, and at least the first stage of this hike is straightforward enough. Get a Raqqa bus from Deir ez-Zur and get out at the Halabiyyeh turn-off about three km after the town of Tibni (S£10, one hour). From here you'll have to hitch or, if you feel up to it, do the two hour walk. Alternatively, get off at Tibni and negotiate with a local to take you out there – this could cost you up to S£500 for the round trip.

For Zalabiyyeh, the hardest bit is getting back. Ask for Zalabiyyeh at the Deir ez-Zur microbus station. The trip takes 1½ hours to the turn-off and costs S£15. From there it's a half-hour walk west. There aren't many buses plying the right bank of the Euphrates, and that's what makes the return trip a pain. If you're here in the afternoon, you'll just have to sit it out and hope for a passing truck.

The railway line passes by Zalabiyyeh, and you could follow it north a couple of km to a small station and wait for a train – locals swear they actually stop here.

DEIR EZ-ZUR

A crossroads for travellers in eastern Syria, Deir ez-Zur is a pleasant little riverside town on the Euphrates. Roads fan out north-east to Qamishle and Turkey; south-east to Mari, Abu Kamal (or Albu Kamal) and Iraq; south-west to Damascus via Palmyra; and north-west to Raqqa and Aleppo.

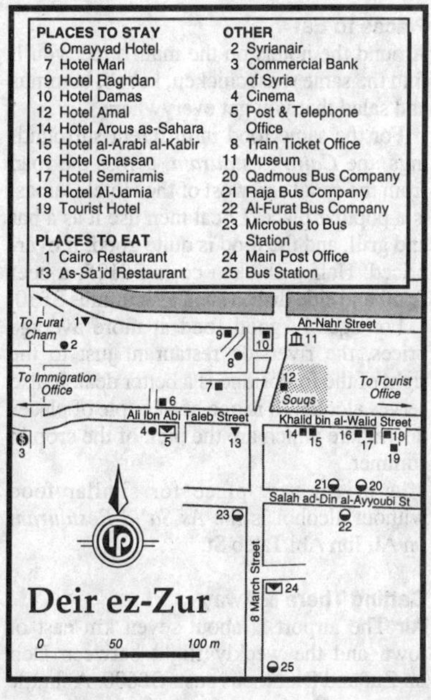

Deir ez-Zur ('Deir' to the locals) became something of a boom town in the early 1990s with the discovery of high-grade oil in the surrounding area, which now accounts for two-thirds of the country's total production. The town has expanded rapidly as a result, but there are fears now that production has already plateaued, casting doubt over just how long the bonanza will last.

There's not much to see in the town, but a stroll along the riverbank, particularly at sunset, is a popular activity. What flows through the town centre is actually a tributary canal. To get to the main body of the river, cross the canal and head north straight on to the suspension bridge, which is only for pedestrians and bicycles. On the other side of the bridge is a small recreation ground where you can swim with the locals.

The main north-south axis running from the river through the square and on up past the new post office to the microbus station is called 8 March St. The main east-west axis runs through the square and is called Khalid bin al-Walid St, becoming Ali Ibn Abi Taleb St west of the square.

Information

Tourist Office This is in a side street right off Khalid bin al-Walid St, about 10 minutes' walk east of the square. It's not much use, but the staff are friendly. It's open from 9 am to 2 pm daily except Friday.

Visa Extensions To get to the big immigration and passports building, continue 500m west of the bank, turn left at the roundabout and left again and it's just on the corner. It is open from 8 am to 1.30 pm and issues extensions on the same day, but it seems to take *all* day.

Money The Commercial Bank of Syria is about 15 minutes' walk west of the square on Ali Ibn Abi Taleb St. It's open from 8.30 am to 12.30 pm. You can also change money at the Furat Cham hotel.

Post The big new post office, halfway between the square and the microbus station on 8 March St, opens daily from 8 am to 8 pm (to 1 pm on Friday). There's another one west along Ali Ibn Abi Taleb St, a few hundred metres before the bank.

Museum
Deir ez-Zur's fairly crummy archaeological museum is for the dedicated and cashed up only. It houses an eclectic smattering of odds and sods ranging from Roman times through to 18th century Islamic items, including a few weapons and some minor finds from Mari. Perhaps most interesting is a room dedicated to artefacts from Tell Sheikh Hamad on the Kabur River. This was the site of the Assyrian city of Dur Katlimmu, which dates from 1300 BC and was later replaced by a partly Romanised Parthian settlement. German and Syrian teams have been working on the site since 1978. Unfortunately, most of the explanations are in German and Arabic, with just the odd label in English. The museum is near the canal on 8 March St, and opens daily except Tuesday from 8 am to 2 pm and 3 to 6 pm. Entry is a staggering S£200.

SYRIA

Places to Stay – bottom end
If you can get a room with a balcony overlooking the canal, the very basic *Hotel Damas* (☎ 221481) is probably the best bet at this end of the scale. It's on the corner of 8 March St. Singles/doubles cost S£200/325, while a bed in a shared room costs S£150, including hot shower.

The *Hotel Amal* (☎ 222245), in among the noisy souqs on the square, is a dump where rooms cost S£200/250 and some quite remarkable odours waft out of the loos. East of the square, along Khalid bin al-Walid St, are several pretty crummy places, including the *Ghassan*, *Semiramis* and the *Hotel al-Arabi al-Kabir* (☎ 222070). The latter is possibly a little cleaner and brighter than the Damas, but without the views. You pay S£150 for a bed in a shared room or S£300/350 for doubles/triples.

The *Hotel Arous as-Sahara* is very basic, but beds are cheap at S£100 a go.

Places to Stay – middle & top end
Just around the corner from the Damas is the *Hotel Raghdan* (☎ 222053), which has acceptable if overpriced rooms for US$16/26. A couple of blocks back from the canal and little further west, the *Hotel Mari* (☎ 224340; fax 221657), is a newer and more comfortable hotel. If you have the extra money, it is better value than the Raghdan at US$24/39.

For those who have loads of money, you can rub shoulders with foreign oil-company employees at the *Furat Cham* (☎ 225418; fax 225950), five km out of town along the river. Singles/doubles go for US$160/190. You can use the pool for S£200 a day. Otherwise, there's the brand spanking new *Hotel Concord* (☎ 225411; fax 224272) with rooms for US$130/160 plus 10% taxes – and minus the probable 25% discount you should enquire about.

Places to Eat
Around the hotels on the main street you'll find the same roast chicken, kebab, hummus and salad that you get everywhere.

For the same food in different surroundings, the *Cairo Restaurant*, across the road from the canal and west of the Hotel Damas, is a popular place. Local men use it as a bar and grill, and the food is quite good, if overpriced. Half a chicken costs S£125, a beer S£50 and side dishes such as hummus S£30.

For equally good food at more average prices, the riverside restaurant just to the right of the footbridge is a better deal. It also serves alcohol. It is one of a couple of places down here which are the pick of the crop in summer.

A bright new place for similar food without alcohol is the *As-Sa'id Restaurant* on Ali Ibn Abi Taleb St.

Getting There & Away
Air The airport is about seven km east of town and the weekly flight between Deir ez-Zur and Damascus costs S£600. A shuttle

bus runs from the Syrianair office, a block north of the bank.

Bus/Minibus The bus station is a couple of km south of town, towards the end of 8 March St. There's a local shuttle-bus service from a stop about five minutes' walk south of the square, on the right-hand side, for S£2.

Old buses leave regularly for Damascus (S£106) via Palmyra, Aleppo (S£70), Homs (S£75), Hassake in the north-east (S£75) and on to Qamishle on the Turkish border (S£125). The minibus to Abu Kamal costs only S£30, but is agonisingly slow.

Microbus There's an hourly microbus to Raqqa (S£60, two hours) and plenty of microbuses south to Abu Kamal (S£50).

Luxury Bus Several private companies operate big comfortable buses to most main destinations in Syria from their offices on Salah ad-Din al-Ayyoubi St. The companies include Qadmous, Raja and Al-Furat, and although timetabling varies considerably, prices tend to be similar. Qadmous is about the best, with services to Damascus costing S£150, and to Aleppo S£135.

Train The railway station is across the river to the north of town, about three km from the centre. If you feel like a half-hour walk to get there, cross the footbridge, continue to the T-junction and turn right. The alternative is to catch one of the yellow shuttle buses which run from the railway booking office to the railway station for S£5. These only run when a train is due to leave. The booking office itself is open from 9 am to 1 pm and 4 to 8 pm.

Trains to Aleppo leave at 8.45 am and 2.15 pm (S£87/58 in 1st/2nd class). The 8.45 am train goes right through to Damascus (S£153/103, S£500 in a couchette). Several trains run to Hassake and on to Qamishle (S£60/40), but the bus trip is much more interesting as it follows the heavily cultivated region alongside the Kabur River, passing along through a series of mud-brick villages.

SOUTH OF DEIR EZ-ZUR

The route south-east of Deir ez-Zur follows the Euphrates down to the closed Iraqi border, and is dotted with sites of archaeological and historical interest. The impatient traveller with a car could visit the lot and be back in Deir ez-Zur for dinner in the same day. With a very early start, it might just be possible to do the same with a combination of microbuses and hitching.

Qala'at ar-Rahba

The 13th century defensive citadel of Qala'at ar-Rahba, which was finally abandoned after the battles between Mongol invaders and the Mamelukes subsided, is a few km south of the town of Mayadin. You can see it in the distance (it's about four km west of the main road) shortly after leaving Mayadin.

Like many castles it is more impressive from the outside than in, but the views of the desert to the west, and the Euphrates and occasional oilfield to the east, are breathtaking. Take the Abu Kamal bus and ask the driver where to get off, and hitch or walk out (about an hour).

Tell Ashara

Just 17 km south of Mayadin is the sleepy village of Ashara. Three sites that date back to the early centuries AD are being excavated by Italian teams, but there is little of real interest here. An old mud-brick mosque, with only a fragile eight-storey minaret surviving, is the main item of note. Most of the area under excavation overlooks or lies near the Euphrates. Again, from Deir ez-Zur you need to get the Abu Kamal bus – or pick one up on the way – and ask where to be let off.

Mari*

The ruins of Mari (Tell Hariri), an important Mesopotamian city dating back some 5000 years, are about 10 km north of Abu Kamal. Although fascinating for their age and the single greatest key serving to unlock the door on Mesopotamia's ancient past, the mud-brick ruins do not grab the neophyte's imagination as much as you might hope.

The most famous of Mari's ancient Syrian

Dura Europos

For the uninitiated, the extensive, largely Hellenistic/Roman fortress city of Dura Europos is by far the most intriguing site to visit on the road from Deir ez-Zur to Abu Kamal. Based on earlier settlements, the Seleucids founded Europos here in around 280 BC. The town also retained the ancient Assyrian name of Dura (wall or fort), and is now known to locals as Tell Salhiye. The desert plateau abruptly ends in a wall of cliffs dropping 90m into the Euphrates here, making the location an ideal site for a defensive installation.

In 128 BC the city fell to the Parthians and remained in their hands (although under the growing influence of Palmyra) until the Romans succeeded in integrating it into their defensive system in 165 AD. As the threat from Persia to Roman pre-eminence grew, so did the importance of Dura Europos. It is reputed for its religious tolerance, seemingly confirmed by the presence of a church, synagogue (now in the National Museum in Damascus) and other Greek, Roman and Mesopotamian temples side by side.

The Sassanian Persians (or Sassanids) seized control of the site in 256 AD, and from then on its fortunes declined. French and Syrian archaeologists continue to work on the site.

Ruins The western wall stands out in the stony desert two km east of the main road, its most imposing element the **Palmyra Gate**. You'll have to deal with a gun-toting guardian here, who is likely to want a tip for allowing you into the site. Just inside the wall was a church to the right and a synagogue to the left. The road leading towards the river from the gate passed first Roman **baths** on the right, a **khan** on the left and then the site of the Greek **agora**.

Opposite this are the sites (little remains) of three temples dedicated to Artemis, Atargatis and the Two Gads. The original Greek temple to Artemis was replaced by the Parthians with a building along more oriental lines, characterised by an internal courtyard surrounded by an assortment of irregular rooms. These were added to over the years, and even included what appears like a small theatre for religious gatherings. In the block next door, the temple dedicated to Atargatis was built along similar lines. Precious little remains of the temple of the Two Gads, where a variety of gods were worshipped.

At the north-western end of the city the Romans installed themselves, building barracks, baths, a small amphitheatre and a couple of small temples, one to Zeus Dolichenus. Immediately west of the **citadel**, which commands extraordinary views over the Euphrates Valley, the Romans placed their **Palace of the Dux**, built around a colonnaded courtyard of which nothing much remains.

Getting There & Away Any microbus between Abu Kamal and Deir ez-Zur will drop you on the highway. Just walk straight out, you can't possibly miss it. ■

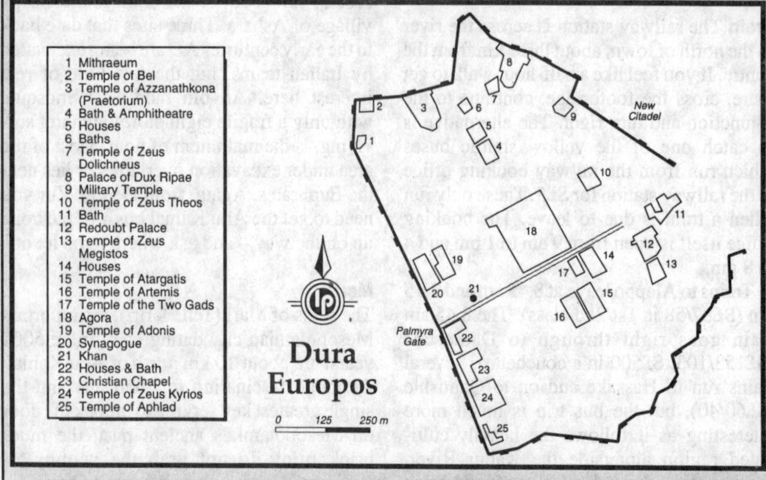

SYRIA

leaders, and about the last of its independent ones, was Zimrilim, who reigned in the 18th century BC and controlled the most important of the trade routes across Syria into Mesopotamia, making his city-state the object of several attacks. The **Royal Palace of Zimrilim** was enormous, measuring 200 by 120m with more than 300 rooms. Today sheltered from the elements by a modern protective roof, the palace remains the main point of interest of the whole site. The city was finally destroyed in 1758 BC by the Babylonians under Hammurabi. Before this, Mari had not only been a major commercial centre but also an artistic hothouse, as the many fragments of ceramics and wall paintings (now mostly in the Louvre and Damascus and Aleppo museums) discovered since 1933 amply attest.

Large chunks of pottery lie scattered around all over the place, but most of the good stuff is on display in the museums in Aleppo, Damascus and the Louvre in Paris. Excavations begun in 1933, financed largely by the French, revealed two palaces (including Zimrilim's), five temples and the remains of a **ziggurat**, a kind of pyramidal tower peculiar to Mesopotamia and usually surmounted by a temple. Perhaps more importantly, a great many archives in Babylonian – some 25,000 clay tablets – were also discovered, providing valuable insights into the history and workings of this ancient city-state. French teams continue to work at the site.

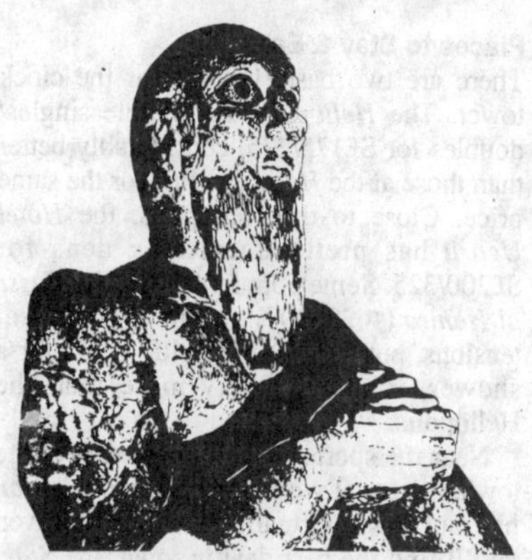

The god Hur-Shamagan, one of the fascinating finds in the excavations at the 5000 year old Mesopotamian city of Mari.

Although attributed to Zimrilim, the Royal Palace had been around for hundreds of years by the time he came to the throne. Comprising a maze of almost 300 rooms disposed around two great courtyards, it was protected by earthen ramparts. Interpretations of what each room was used for vary. For instance, the room immediately south of the central courtyard is seen by some as a throne room, by others as a sacred hall dedicated to a water goddess. It appears the area to the north-west of the central courtyard served as the royal living quarters, with baths located immediately to the right (directly north of the central courtyard).

Just to the south-east of the palace complex are the ziggurat and several temples. A temple to Ishtar stood to the west of the palace. You will be charged S£200 to enter the site.

Getting There & Away There is a microbus from Abu Kamal that goes right by Mari. It leaves from a side street east of the square and takes about half an hour by a circuitous route (S£10). Alternatively if you are coming from Deir ez-Zur, buses will drop you at the turn-off from the highway. From this same spot it is normally possible to hitch a ride or pick up a passing microbus for the return trip to Deir ez-Zur.

Abu Kamal

Abu Kamal (also known as Aibu Kamal) is a frontier town 140 km south-east of Deir ez-Zur, close to the Iraqi border. This border has been closed for some years because of Syria's support for Iran in the first Gulf war, and its subsequent participation in the anti-Iraq coalition after Baghdad's invasion of Kuwait in 1990. The frontier is about 10 km out of town.

Places to Stay & Eat There only appears to be one cheap hotel in the centre – the

Jumhuriyyeh (there is no sign in English), in a side street two blocks south of the square in Alrifi St (off Baghdad St). Ask around. It has pretty awful doubles for S£300 and cold water only. There are a few cafés and cheap eateries around the square.

Getting There & Away Most buses and microbuses leave from the main square or nearby. The microbuses to Deir ez-Zur leave to a set timetable and cost S£50. They are a better deal than the older, slower minibuses that leave only when full and charge S£30.

The microbus for Mari leaves from a side street east of the square (S£10, 30 minutes).

Some bus companies have their offices on Baghdad St, the main drag through town that passes by the square. Al-Furat is one of them, and it has three buses a day to Damascus (S£185), two to Aleppo (S£150) and one to Homs (S£160). The Al-Halab company runs cheaper, older buses from the square.

The North-East

Bordered by Turkey and Iraq, there are no major monuments or sites in the north-eastern corner of the country, but this does not mean it is empty of attractions. Perhaps the greatest is the chance to meet the Kurds, a people without a state, who have yet to give up their struggle. Only about one million of a total of some 20 million Kurds live in Syria. The rest are spread across south-eastern Turkey, northern Iraq and north-western Iran.

The area between the Kabur and Tigris rivers is also known as the Jezira and is an increasingly rich agricultural zone, helped along by underground aquifers and the irrigation schemes born of the Lake al-Assad project on the Euphrates to the west. The heavy crude oilfields right up in the north-east corner have paled into insignificance beside the fields around Deir ez-Zur.

The numerous tells (artificial hills) dotted around the place are a sign that it has been inhabited since the 3rd millennium BC, its mainstay the wheat and cotton crops that still predominate. They are increasingly attracting archaeological teams, and although there is generally precious little for the uninitiated to see, you can visit the sites so long as you respect the teams' work. They are generally present in the spring and summer. **Tell Brak**, 45 km north of Hassake, was excavated under the direction of one Max Mallowan, Agatha Christie's husband. Since 1992 a Franco-Syrian team has been digging at **Tell Beydar**, 35 km north-west of Hassake. Some of the tablets found there are on display in the museum at Deir ez-Zur.

HASSAKE

The capital of the *muhafaza* (governorate) of the same name, Hassake doesn't offer the visitor an awful lot to do, but it's not a bad base from which to explore the area, unless you're planning on entering Turkey here, in which case you may as well push on to Qamishle. The main drag is Fares al-Khouri St, which ends at the statue of Assad. From the statue, Jamal Abdel Nasser St leads to the central square and clock tower. There is a Commercial Bank of Syria on this road and it opens daily except Friday from 8.30 am to 12.30 pm. You can change cash and cheques. Hassake's telephone code is 052.

Places to Stay & Eat

There are two basic hotels near the clock tower. The *Heliopolis* has simple singles/doubles for S£175/275, considerably better than those at the *Hotel Ramsis*, for the same price. Close to the Heliopolis, the *Hotel Ugarit* has pretty unenticing dens for S£200/325. Some 50m farther on, the *Cassr al-Hamra* (☎ 226307) may have grand pretensions, but at US$18/22 plus US$2 for a shower, it offers barely more than the Heliopolis.

Near the sports ground in the east of the town, the equally overpriced *Hotel Boustan* has shut down. Virtually next door, however, you'll find the best deal in town, the *Stars Hotel* (☎ 313250) with doubles for US$22 and singles at whatever price you can negotiate. The *Hotel Sanabel* (☎ 224283) has singles starting at US$12 and doubles ending at US$30. It's OK, but avoid the windowless rooms.

There are a few of the usual places to eat around the centre, mostly run by Iraqi Christians from the nearby refugee camp at Al-Hol. The *Karnak Restaurant*, in Hafez al-Assad St, offers copious quantities of the usual stuff for around S£200 per person, and it has a garden too.

Getting There & Away

Bus The more expensive luxury buses to Damascus cost S£250 and take about seven hours. Companies like Hatab operate such services from Jamal Abdel Nasser St. The trip to Deir ez-Zur takes just over two hours and costs S£75. Al Salam buses serve Aleppo (S£150, four hours) and Homs (S£250).

Microbus The station for destinations like Qamishle, Deir ez-Zur and Ras al-'Ain is about two km north of the town centre. You can catch a shuttle there from a side street just east of the clock tower for S£5.

Train To get to the railway station, walk about 50m north along Fares al-Khouri St and turn left. The railway station is at the end of the street – about 10 minutes' walk. There are at least two departures a day for Qamishle (S£30/24 in 1st/2nd class). There are up to three departures a day for Deir ez-Zur, Raqqa and Aleppo, but only one continues (direct) to Damascus.

Service Taxi The service-taxi station is just south of the bridge on the left-hand side.

Getting Around

If you want to inspect Tell Beydar, take a Derbassieh microbus (S£20). Hiring a taxi to yourself would cost you S£700 round trip. For Tell Brak, pick up a Qamishle bus and get out at the turn-off for the village. From the village it's about two km.

RAS AL-'AIN

There's not an awful lot to this largely Kurdish town on the Turkish border (you cannot cross here), but the chances are high you'll be invited to eat and stay with the locals. Don't be surprised if the subject of conversation turns to politics. The Kurds are not much more pleased with their position in Syria than elsewhere, and discretion may be the better part of valour when chatting. In summer, the attraction is the restaurant in the main park (near the road to Hassake), where they set the tables in the shin-deep water from nearby sulphur springs. You cool your heels as you eat!

Three km away is **Tell Halaf**, the site of an ancient northern Mesopotamian settlement discovered in 1899 by Baron Max von Oppenheim, a Prussian engineer overseeing the construction of the much trumpeted Berlin-Baghdad railway. Although plenty more artefacts are said by locals to be buried here, you'll see nothing other than a bald artificial hill. The bulk of what has been found so far can be seen in the museum in Aleppo, including the giant basalt statues at its entrance.

Getting There & Away

The microbus from Hassake, about 75 km away, takes about 1½ hours and costs S£45. It seems no public transport returns in the afternoon, especially on Friday and holidays; other than this you should be OK until 4 pm.

QAMISHLE

Situated at a crossing point on the Turkish border in the north-east, Qamishle is full of Kurds and Turks and the cheaper hotels will sometimes quote prices in Turkish lire rather than Syrian pounds.

There is nothing to see in Qamishle, but the mix of people makes it an intriguing spot nonetheless. Because of its proximity to the border, you should be prepared for passport checks at the hotels (even during the night), and when getting on or off buses or trains. The Turkish border is only about one km from the centre of Qamishle – a 15 minute walk.

The telephone code for Qamishle is 053.

Places to Stay & Eat

About 100m south of the microbus station is the town's top establishment, the two star *Hotel Semiramis* (☎ 053-421185), which charges foreigners US$15/22/24 for clean rooms with fan. Expatriate workers in the oilfields often stay here.

Just around the corner is the *Chahba Hotel*, which is nothing to write home about and asks S£100 a bed (women must take a double). The upstairs terrace is OK.

The *Mamar*, a block south, is better value, although a tad more expensive at S£300/400 for singles/doubles. The rooms with balconies are quite good and there's hot water.

The cheapest and lousiest is the *Omayad Hotel*, in a side street across from the Semiramis. A bed here costs S£100, although you may find yourself being charged for a double.

In Al-Wahida St, which crosses the northern end of the main drag, the *Hadaya Hotel* (☎ 420141) is not exactly the friendliest place on earth, and the dollar rooms aren't anything special either at US$15/22.

Across from the Chahba is a quite pleasant restaurant with an outdoor section. A good meal of kebabs and the usual side orders will cost about S£200.

Getting There & Away

Air The airport is about two km south of town. Take a taxi or any Hassake-bound bus. The Syrianair office is just off the main street, two blocks south of the Semiramis. There are three flights a week to Damascus (S£900). There may be one to Aleppo, but no-one seems to be sure.

Bus Several Pullman and more expensive private companies operate buses from Qamishle to most major destinations. The better buses run from a station opposite the Gabriel Restaurant. The trip to Damascus takes up to 10 hours and costs around S£340, depending on the company. For Aleppo, reckon on at least five hours and S£175. More rickety buses do the same trips from another station ('*garage*') and cost as little as S£150 and S£90 respectively.

Microbus The microbus station is on the main street, 100m north of the Semiramis. There are departures for Hassake, Ras al-'Ain and Al-Malkyer in the east.

Train The railway station is, typically, a long way from the centre, and you'll have to catch a taxi there.

There is, however, a booking office in the centre, virtually opposite the Chahba Hotel. It's open from 8.30 am to 3 pm and 4.30 to 6 pm.

Up to three trains go as far as Aleppo (S£132/87 in 1st/2nd class, S£350 for a sleeper), and one or two proceed all the way to Damascus (S£198/132 and S£740 respectively). The Damascus train, calling at all stops along the line, can take from 16 to 19 hours.

'AIN DIWAR

In the extreme north-east corner of the country is an impressive medieval bridge over the Tigris. Unfortunately, relations between Turkey and Syria are not brilliant, and a Syrian border garrison may stop you from getting out to it – they say because the Turkish border troops tend to shoot first and ask questions later. You may have guessed that there is no crossing here.

There are great views from the plateau (which may be as far as you can safely get) which overlooks the Tigris, north-east to the snowcapped mountains of southern Turkey, and east to Jebel Zakho in Iraq (some locals call it Jebel Barzani, after one of the rebel Kurdish leaders there). On a clear day, you might just make out mountains in Iran through the gap between Jebel Zakho and the Turkish ranges.

Getting There & Away

If you want to try your luck, take a microbus from Qamishle to Al-Malkyer (S£45, about two hours). From there, negotiate with one of the kids to take you out on a motorbike, or just hitch. Bear in mind that there is not much traffic on this last stretch of road.

Health Appendix

Travel health depends on your pre-departure preparations, your day-to-day health care while travelling and how you handle any medical problem or emergency that develops. While the list of potential dangers can seem quite frightening, with a little luck, some basic precautions and adequate information few travellers experience more than upset stomachs.

Travel Health Guides

There are a number of books on travel health:

Staying Healthy in Asia, Africa & Latin America, Dirk Schroeder, Moon Publications. Probably the best all-round guide to carry, as it's compact but very detailed and well organised.

Travellers' Health, Dr Richard Dawood, Oxford University Press. Comprehensive, easy to read, authoritative and also highly recommended, although it's rather large to lug around.

Where There is No Doctor, David Werner, Hesperian Foundation. A very detailed guide intended for someone going to work in an undeveloped country, rather than for the average traveller.

Travel with Children, Maureen Wheeler, Lonely Planet Publications. Includes basic advice on travel health for younger children.

Pre-Departure Preparations

Health Insurance A travel insurance policy to cover theft, loss and medical problems is a wise idea. There are a wide variety of policies and your travel agent will have recommendations. The international student travel policies handled by STA or other student travel organisations are usually good value. Some policies offer lower and higher medical expenses options, but the higher one is chiefly for countries, like the USA, that have extremely high medical costs. Check the small print:

- Some policies specifically exclude 'dangerous activities' which can include scuba diving, motorcycling, even trekking. If such activities are on your agenda you don't want that sort of policy.
- You may prefer a policy which pays doctors or hospitals direct rather than you having to pay on the spot and claim later. If you have to claim later make sure you keep all documentation. Some policies ask you to call back (reverse charges) to a centre in your home country where an immediate assessment of your problem is made.
- Check if the policy covers ambulances or an emergency flight home. If you have to stretch out you will need two seats and somebody has to pay for them!

Medical Kit A small, straightforward medical kit is a wise thing to carry. A possible kit list includes:

- Aspirin or Panadol – for pain or fever
- Antihistamine (such as Benadryl) – useful as a decongestant for colds, allergies, to ease the itch from insect bites or stings or to help prevent motion sickness
- Antibiotics – useful if you're travelling well off the beaten track, but they must be prescribed and you should carry the prescription with you
- Kaolin preparation (Pepto-Bismol), Imodium or Lomotil – for stomach upsets
- Rehydration mixture – for treatment of severe diarrhoea, this is particularly important if travelling with children
- Antiseptic, Mercurochrome and antibiotic powder or similar 'dry' spray – for cuts and grazes
- Calamine lotion – to ease irritation from bites or stings
- Bandages and Band-aids – for minor injuries
- Scissors, tweezers and a thermometer (note that mercury thermometers are prohibited by airlines)
- Insect repellent, sunscreen, suntan lotion, chap stick and water purification tablets
- A couple of syringes, in case you need injections in an area where you are not sure about the state of medical hygiene. Ask your doctor for a note explaining why they are being carried

Ideally antibiotics should be administered only under medical supervision and should never be taken indiscriminately. Overuse of antibiotics can weaken your body's ability to deal with infections naturally and can reduce the drug's efficacy on a future occasion. Take only the recommended dose at the prescribed intervals and continue using the antibiotic for the prescribed period, even if the illness seems to be cured earlier. Antibiotics are quite specific to the infections they can treat. Stop immediately if there are any serious reactions and don't use it at all if you are unsure if you have the correct one.

The medical services in both countries are well developed in the larger towns and cities and many of the doctors have been trained overseas and speak English. Your embassy will usually be able to recommend a reliable doctor or hospital if the need arises. For minor complaints, pharmacies can usually supply what you need, although you will probably have to use sign language in out-of-the-way places. Drugs normally sold only on prescription in the west are available over the counter in Syria, and to a lesser extent in Jordan. That said, the price of antibiotics in Jordan can be outrageous, so you may want to bring a supply with you. Always check the expiry date of drugs, and be aware that some drugs no longer recommended or even banned in the west are still being dispensed in Jordan and Syria.

Health Preparations Make sure you're healthy before you start travelling. If you are embarking on a long trip make sure your teeth are OK; if you find yourself in need of a dentist in either Jordan or Syria, the preferable option is to head for either Amman or Damascus and get a recommendation from your consulate.

If you wear glasses take a spare pair and your prescription. Losing your glasses can be a real problem, although in many places you can get new spectacles made up quickly, cheaply and competently.

If you require a particular medication take an adequate supply, as it may not be available locally. Take the prescription, with the generic rather than the brand name (which may not be locally available), as it will make getting replacements easier. It's wise to have the prescription with you to show you legally use the medication – it's surprising how often over-the-counter drugs from one place are illegal without a prescription or even banned in another.

It's advisable to take a decent supply of any contraceptives you may use with you. Even condoms are difficult to come by in Syria and Jordan. About the easiest countries in the area to get a hold of contraceptives are Israel and the bigger cities of Turkey.

Immunisations No inoculations are required for entry to Jordan or Syria, unless you're coming from a disease-affected area, but it's a good idea to have preventive shots for polio, tetanus and typhoid. Most travellers from western countries will have been immunised against these diseases during childhood but your doctor may still recommend booster shots. The period of protection offered by vaccinations differs widely and some are contraindicated if you are pregnant.

If you are coming from an infected area such as sub-Saharan Africa, a yellow fever vaccination is required. All vaccinations should be recorded in a duly stamped International Health Card (available from your physician or government health department). Apart from the shots mentioned, you may need further inoculations if you plan to travel beyond Jordan and Syria, particularly to Egypt and further into Africa. Plan ahead for your vaccinations: some require an initial shot followed by a booster, and some should not be given together. Seek medical advice at least six weeks prior to travel.

Smallpox has been wiped out worldwide, so immunisation is no longer necessary.

In some countries immunisations are available from airport or government health centres. Travel agents or airline offices will tell you where. The possible list of vaccinations includes:

Cholera Protection is not very effective. The vaccine only lasts six months and is contraindicated for pregnancy. The occasional outbreak of cholera still does occur in Syria, so keep your eyes and ears open. A good sign is a notable absence of salad, especially parsley, being served in restaurant meals. (Cholera can be transmitted via the water that salad greens are washed in.)

Hepatitis Type A hepatitis is the most common travel-acquired illness and can be prevented by vaccination. Protection can be provided in two ways – with the antibody Gamma globulin or a vaccine called Havrix 1440.

Havrix 1440 provides long-term immunity (possibly more than 10 years) after an initial injection and a booster within a year. It may be more expensive than gamma globulin but certainly has many advantages, including the length of protection and ease of administration. The vaccination takes about three weeks to provide satisfactory protection.

Gamma globulin is a ready-made antibody that has proven very successful in reducing the chances of hepatitis infection. Because it may interfere with the development of immunity, it should not be given until at least 10 days after administration of the last vaccine needed; it should also be given as close as possible to departure because of its relatively short-lived protection period of six months.

Persons who should receive a hepatitis B vaccination include anyone who anticipates contact with blood or other bodily secretions, either as a health-care worker or through sexual contact with the local population, particularly those who intend to stay in the country for a long time.

Tetanus & Diptheria Boosters are necessary every 10 years and protection is highly recommended.

Typhoid Protection lasts from one to five years and is useful if you are travelling for long periods in rural, tropical areas. You may get some side effects such as pain at the injection site, fever, headache and a general unwell feeling. A single-dose injectable vaccine, Typhim Vi, has few side effects, but is more expensive.

Basic Rules

Care in what you eat and drink is the most important health rule. Stomach upsets are the most likely travel health problem (between 30% and 50% of travellers in a two-week stay experience this) but the majority of these upsets will be relatively minor. Don't become paranoid – trying the local food is part of the experience of travel, after all.

Food & Water Tap water in the major towns is safe to drink, but if your stomach is a bit delicate or you find yourself in out-of-the-way places where you cannot be sure of water quality, bottled water is widely available. If you have just come from Turkey or Egypt and survived you shouldn't have any trouble here. Make sure when buying bottled water that the seal is unbroken or you may be paying for plain old tap water. If bottled water is unavailable, the locally made soft drinks are fine.

When it comes to food, there is an old colonial adage that says: 'If you can cook it, boil it or peel it you can eat it...otherwise forget it'. Never eat unwashed fruit or vegetables and steer clear of stalls where the food doesn't look fresh. When eating in restaurants, cooked vegetables are safest, but generally the salads are OK too. Vegetables that need to be treated with the greatest caution are the leafy variety. This means lettuce (again, nine times out of 10 it's not a problem) and parsley.

Contaminated food and water can give you all sorts of weird and not-so-wonderful diseases such as hepatitis A, typhoid, cholera, dysentery, giardia and polio but you can minimise the risks of catching any of them by being selective about where and what you eat and by exercising meticulous care with your personal hygiene. Always wash your hands before eating (restaurants provide a basin for this purpose) and, needless to say, after using the toilet.

Milk and cream should be avoided in Syria. Having said that, the banana and milk fruit drinks available at juice stands are hard to resist and *usually* seem to cause no major problems. Jordan has its own dairy industry and its products are pasteurised. Yoghurt is always OK and some people swear by it if you have a dose of the shits. Ice cream in

Syria rarely contains dairy products, so it is OK unless your stomach is having problems coping with the water.

Meat is always all right to eat as long as it is thoroughly cooked. In stews it's never a problem but when you are buying *shawarma* – lamb cooked on a vertical spit, usually on the street – go for one that looks overdone rather than underdone. The more meat there is on the spit, the better it is likely to be. If nothing else, that is a sure sign that it hasn't been sitting around all day.

Water Purification The simplest way of purifying water is to boil it thoroughly. Technically this means boiling for 10 minutes, something which happens very rarely! Remember that at high altitudes water boils at a lower temperature, so germs are less likely to be killed.

Simple filtering will not remove all dangerous organisms, so if you cannot boil water it should be treated chemically. Chlorine tablets (Puritabs, Steritabs or other brand names) will kill many but not all pathogens. Iodine is very effective in purifying water and is available in tablet form (such as Potable Aqua), but follow the directions carefully and remember that too much iodine can be harmful.

If you can't find tablets, tincture of iodine (2%) or iodine crystals can be used. Two drops of tincture of iodine per litre or quart of clear water is the recommended dosage; the treated water should be left to stand for 30 minutes before drinking. Iodine crystals can also be used to purify water but this is a more complicated process, as you have to first prepare a saturated iodine solution. Iodine loses its effectiveness if exposed to air or damp so keep it in a tightly sealed container. Flavoured powder will disguise the taste of treated water and is a good idea if you are travelling with children.

Nutrition If your food is poor or limited in availability, if you're travelling hard and fast and therefore missing meals, or if you simply lose your appetite, you can soon start to lose weight and place your health at risk.

Make sure your diet is well balanced. Eggs, beans, lentils and nuts are all safe ways to get protein. Fruit you can peel (bananas, oranges or mandarines for example) is always safe and a good source of vitamins. Try to eat plenty of grains (rice) and bread. Remember that although food is generally safer if it is cooked well, overcooked food loses much of its nutritional value. If your diet isn't well balanced or if your food intake is insufficient, it's a good idea to take vitamin and iron pills.

In hot climates make sure you drink enough – don't rely on feeling thirsty to indicate when you should drink. Not needing to urinate or very dark yellow urine is a danger sign. Always carry a water bottle with you on long trips. Excessive sweating can lead to loss of salt and therefore muscle cramping. Salt tablets are not a good idea as a preventative, but in places where salt is not used much adding salt to food can help.

Everyday Health A normal body temperature is 98.6°F or 37°C; more than 2°C (4°F) higher is a 'high' fever. A normal adult pulse rate is 60 to 100 per minute (children 80 to 100, babies 100 to 140). You should know how to take a temperature and a pulse rate. As a general rule the pulse increases about 20 beats per minute for each 1°C (2°F) rise in fever.

Respiration (breathing) rate is also an indicator of illness. Count the number of breaths per minute: between 12 and 20 is normal for adults and older children (up to 30 for younger children, 40 for babies). People with a high fever or serious respiratory illness (like pneumonia) breathe more quickly than normal. More than 40 shallow breaths a minute usually means pneumonia.

Many health problems can be avoided by taking care of yourself. Wash your hands frequently – it's quite easy to contaminate your own food. Clean your teeth with purified water rather than straight from the tap. Avoid climatic extremes: keep out of the sun when it's hot, dress warmly when it's cold. Avoid potential diseases by dressing sensibly. You can avoid insect bites by covering bare skin when insects are around, by screening windows or beds or by using insect repellents. Seek local advice: if you're told the water is unsafe for whatever reason, don't go in. In situations where there is no information, discretion is the better part of valour.

Medical Problems & Treatment

Self-diagnosis and treatment can be risky, so wherever possible seek qualified help. Although we do give drug dosages in this section, they are for emergency use only. Medical advice should be sought where possible before administering any drugs.

An embassy or consulate can usually recommend a good place to go for such advice. So can five star hotels, although they often recommend doctors with five star prices. (This is when that medical insurance really comes in handy!) In some places standards of medical attention are so low that for some ailments the best advice is to get on a plane and go somewhere else.

Environmental Hazards

It gets stinking hot during the summer in Jordan and Syria and you should take care to protect yourself. Wear a hat, keep plenty of sunscreen handy and, when it's practical, keep out of the sun altogether during the real heat of the day.

Sunburn Working on your tan is not always the best idea, particularly in the desert where you can get badly burned quickly. Use strong sunscreen on unprotected parts of the body, and preferably do as the locals do and keep covered up.

Remember that too much sunlight, whether its direct or reflected (glare) can damage your eyes. If your plans include being near water, sand or snow, then good sunglasses are doubly important. Good quality sunglasses are treated to filter out ultraviolet radiation, but poor quality sunglasses provide limited filtering, allowing more ultraviolet light to be adsorbed than if no sunglasses were worn at all. Excessive ultraviolet light will damage the surface structures and lens of the eye.

Prickly Heat Prickly heat is an itchy rash caused by excessive perspiration trapped under the skin. It usually strikes people who have just arrived in a hot climate and whose pores have not yet opened sufficiently to cope with greater sweating. Keeping cool by bathing often, using a mild talcum powder or even resorting to air-conditioning may help until you acclimatise.

Heat Exhaustion Dehydration or salt deficiency can cause heat exhaustion. Take time to acclimatise to high temperatures and make sure you get sufficient liquids. Salt deficiency is characterised by fatigue, lethargy, headaches, giddiness and muscle cramps, and in this case salt tablets may help. Vomiting or diarrhoea can deplete your liquid and salt levels.

Anhydrotic heat exhaustion, caused by an inability to sweat, is quite rare. Unlike the other forms of heat exhaustion, it is likely to strike people who have been in a hot climate for some time rather than newcomers. You will stay cooler by covering up with light, cotton clothes that trap perspiration against your skin than by wearing brief clothes.

Heat Stroke This serious and sometimes fatal, condition can occur if the body's heat-regulating mechanism breaks down and the body temperature rises to dangerous levels. Long, continuous periods of exposure to high temperatures can leave you vulnerable to heat stroke. You should avoid excessive alcohol or strenuous activity when you first arrive in a hot climate.

The symptoms are feeling unwell, little or no sweating and a high body temperature (39°C to 41°C). Where sweating has ceased, the skin becomes flushed and red. Severe, throbbing headaches and lack of coordination will also occur, and the sufferer may be confused or aggressive. Eventually the victim will become delirious or convulse. Hospitalisation is essential, but meanwhile get patients out of the sun, remove their clothing, cover them with a wet sheet or towel and fan continually.

Fungal Infections Hot weather fungal infections are most likely to occur on the scalp, between the toes or fingers (athlete's foot), in the groin (jock itch or crotch rot) and on the body (ringworm). You get ringworm (a fungal infection, not a worm) from infected animals or by walking on damp areas, like shower floors.

To prevent fungal infections wear loose, comfortable clothes, avoid artificial fibres, wash frequently and dry carefully. If you do get an infection, wash the infected area daily with a disinfectant or medicated soap and water, and rinse and dry well. Apply an antifungal powder like the widely available Tinaderm. Try to expose the infected area to air or sunlight as much as possible and wash all towels and underwear in hot water as well as changing them often.

Motion Sickness Eating lightly before and during a trip will reduce the chances of motion sickness. If you are prone to motion sickness try to find a place that minimises disturbance – near the wing on aircraft, close to midships on boats, near the centre on buses. Fresh air usually helps, reading or cigarette smoke doesn't. Commercial anti-motion-sickness preparations, which can cause drowsiness, have to be taken before the trip commences; when you're feeling sick it's too late. Ginger (available in capsule form) and peppermint (including mint-flavoured sweets) are natural preventatives.

Jet Lag Jet lag is experienced when a person travels by air across more than three time zones (each time zone usually represents a one hour time difference). It occurs because many of the functions of the human body (such as temperature, pulse rate and emptying of the bladder and bowels) are regulated by internal 24 hour cycles called circadian rhythms. When we travel long distances rapidly, our bodies take time to adjust to the 'new time' of our destination, and we may experience fatigue, disorientation, insomnia, anxiety, impaired concentration and loss of appetite. These effects will usually be gone within three days of arrival, but there are ways of minimising the impact of jet lag:

- Rest for a couple of days prior to departure; try to avoid late nights and last-minute dashes for travellers' cheques, passport etc.
- Try to select flight schedules that minimise sleep deprivation; arriving late in the day means you can go to sleep soon after you arrive. For very long flights, try to organise a stopover.
- Avoid excessive eating (which bloats the stomach) and alcohol (which causes dehydration) during the flight. Instead, drink plenty of non-carbonated, nonalcoholic drinks such as fruit juice or water.
- Avoid smoking, as this reduces the amount of oxygen in the aeroplane cabin even further and causes greater fatigue.
- Make yourself comfortable by wearing loose-fitting clothes and perhaps bringing an eye mask and ear plugs to help you sleep.

Infectious Diseases

Diarrhoea A change of water, food or climate can all cause the runs; diarrhoea caused by contaminated food or water is more serious. Despite all your precautions you may still have a mild bout of travellers' diarrhoea but a few rushed toilet trips with no other symptoms is not indicative of a serious problem. Moderate diarrhoea, involving half-a-dozen loose movements in a day, is more of a nuisance. Dehydration is the main danger with any diarrhoea, particularly for children where dehydration can occur quite quickly. Fluid replacement remains the mainstay of management. Weak black tea with a little sugar, soda water, or soft drinks allowed to go flat and diluted 50% with water are all good. With severe diarrhoea a rehydrating solution is necessary to replace minerals and salts. Commercially available oral rehydration salts (ORS) are very useful; add the contents of one sachet to a litre of boiled or bottled water. In an emergency you can make up a solution of eight teaspoons of sugar to a litre of boiled water and provide salted cracker biscuits at the same time. You should stick to a bland diet as you recover.

Lomotil or Imodium can be used to bring

relief from the symptoms, although they do not actually cure the problem. Only use these drugs if absolutely necessary – for example, if you *must* travel. For children under 12 years, Lomotil and Imodium are not recommended. Under all circumstances fluid replacement is the most important thing to remember. Do not use these drugs if the person has a high fever or is severely dehydrated.

In certain situations antibiotics may be indicated:

- Watery diarrhoea with blood and mucus (gut-paralysing drugs like Imodium or Lomotil should be avoided in this situation)
- Watery diarrhoea with fever and lethargy
- Persistent diarrhoea for more than five days
- Severe diarrhoea, if it is logistically difficult to stay in one place

The recommended drugs (adults only) would be either norfloxacin 400 mg twice daily for three days or ciprofloxacin 500 mg twice daily for three days.

The drug bismuth subsalicylate has also been used successfully. It is not available in some countries. The dosage for adults is two tablets or 30 ml and for children it is one tablet or 10 ml. This dose can be repeated every 30 minutes to one hour, with no more than eight doses in a 24 hour period.

The drug of choice in children would be co-trimoxazole (Bactrim, Septrin, Resprim) with dosage dependent on weight. A three day course is also given.

Ampicillin has been recommended in the past and may still be an alternative.

Giardiasis The parasite causing this intestinal disorder is present in contaminated water. The symptoms are stomach cramps, nausea, a bloated stomach, watery, foul-smelling diarrhoea and frequent gas. Giardiasis can appear several weeks after you have been exposed to the parasite. The symptoms may disappear for a few days and then return; this can go on for several weeks. Tinidazole, known as Fasigyn, or metronidazole (Flagyl) are the recommended drugs for treatment. Either can be used in a single treatment dose. Antibiotics are of no use.

Dysentery This serious illness is caused by contaminated food or water and is characterised by severe diarrhoea, often with blood or mucus in the stool. There are two kinds of dysentery. Bacillary dysentery is characterised by a high fever and rapid onset; headache, vomiting and stomach pains are also symptoms. It generally does not last longer than a week, but it is highly contagious.

Amoebic dysentery is often more gradual in the onset of symptoms, with cramping abdominal pain and vomiting less likely; fever may not be present. It is not a self-limiting disease: it will persist until treated and can recur and cause long-term health problems.

A stool test is necessary to diagnose which kind of dysentery you have, so you should seek medical help urgently. In case of an emergency the drugs norfloxacin or ciprofloxacin can be used as presumptive treatment for bacillary dysentery, and metronidazole (Flagyl) for amoebic dysentery.

For bacillary dysentery, norfloxacin 400 mg twice daily for seven days or ciprofloxacin 500 mg twice daily for seven days are the recommended dosages.

If you're unable to find either of these drugs then a useful alternative is co-trimoxazole 160/800 mg (Bactrim, Septrin, Resprim) twice daily for seven days. This is a sulpha drug and must not be used by people with a known sulpha allergy. In the case of children the drug co-trimoxazole is a reasonable first-line treatment.

For amoebic dysentery, the recommended adult dosage of metronidazole (Flagyl) is one 750 mg to 800 mg capsule three times daily for five days. Children aged between eight and 12 years should have half the adult dose; the dosage for younger children is one-third the adult dose.

An alternative to Flagyl is Fasigyn, taken as a two gram daily dose for three days. Alcohol must be avoided during treatment and for 48 hours afterwards.

Cholera Outbreaks of cholera do occasionally occur in Syria, but vaccinations are not very effective. The bacteria responsible for this disease are waterborne, so attention to the rules of eating and drinking should protect the traveller. The disease is characterised by a sudden onset of acute diarrhoea with 'rice water' stools, vomiting, muscular cramps, and extreme weakness. You need medical help – but treat for dehydration, which can be extreme, and if there is an appreciable delay in getting to hospital then begin taking tetracycline. The adult dose is 250 mg four times daily. It is not recommended for children aged eight years or under nor for pregnant women. An alternative drug is Ampicillin (not suitable for people allergic to penicillin). Remember that while antibiotics might kill the bacteria, it is a toxin produced by the bacteria which causes the massive fluid loss. Fluid replacement is by far the most important aspect of treatment.

Viral Gastroenteritis This is caused not by bacteria but, as the name suggests, by a virus. It is characterised by stomach cramps, diarrhoea, and sometimes by vomiting and/or a slight fever. All you can do is rest and drink lots of fluids.

Hepatitis Hepatitis is a general term for inflammation of the liver. There are many causes of this condition: drugs, alcohol and infections are but a few.

The discovery of new strains of viral hepatitis has led to a virtual alphabet soup, with hepatitis A, B, C, D, E and a rumoured G. These letters identify specific agents that cause viral hepatitis. Viral hepatitis is an infection of the liver, which can lead to jaundice (yellow skin), fever, lethargy and digestive problems. It can have no symptoms at all, with the infected person not knowing that they have the disease. Travellers shouldn't be too paranoid about this apparent proliferation of hepatitis strains; hep C, D, E and G are fairly rare (so far) and following the same precautions as for A and B should be all that's necessary to avoid them.

Viral hepatitis can be divided into two groups on the basis of how it is spread. The first route of transmission is via contaminated food and water (leading to hepatitis A and E) and the second route is via blood and bodily fluids (which results in hepatitis B, C and D).

Hepatitis A This is a common disease in Jordan and Syria. Most people in developing countries are infected as children; they often don't develop symptoms, but do develop life-long immunity. The disease poses a real threat to the traveller, as people are unlikely to have been exposed to hepatitis A in developed countries.

The symptoms are fever, chills, headache, fatigue, feelings of weakness and aches and pains, followed by loss of appetite, nausea, vomiting, abdominal pain, dark urine, light-coloured faeces, jaundiced skin and the whites of the eyes may turn yellow. You should seek medical advice, but in general there is not much you can do apart from resting, drinking lots of fluids, eating lightly and avoiding fatty foods. People who have had hepatitis must forego alcohol for six months after the illness, as hepatitis attacks the liver and it needs that amount of time to recover.

Routes of transmission are via contaminated water, shellfish contaminated by sewerage, or foodstuffs sold by food handlers with poor standards of hygiene. Taking care with what you eat and drink can go a long way towards preventing this disease. But this is a very infectious virus, so if there is any risk of exposure, additional protection is highly recommended.

Hepatitis B This is also a common disease, with almost 300 million chronic carriers in the world. Hepatitis B, which used to be called serum hepatitis, is spread through contact with infected blood, blood products or bodily fluids, for example through sexual contact, blood transfusions and unsterilised needles, or via small breaks in the skin. Other risk situations include having a shave or tattoo in a local shop, or having your body

HEALTH

pierced. The symptoms of type B are much the same as type A except that they are more severe and may lead to irreparable liver damage or even liver cancer. Although there is no treatment for hepatitis B, a cheap and effective vaccine is available; the only problem is that for long-lasting cover you need a six-month course. The immunisation schedule requires two injections at least a month apart followed by a third dose five months after the second.

Hepatitis C This is another recently defined virus that seems to lead to liver disease more rapidly than hepatitis B. The virus is spread by contact with blood – usually via contaminated transfusions or shared needles. Avoiding these is the only means of prevention, as there is no available vaccine.

Hepatitis D Often referred to as the 'Delta' virus, this infection only occurs in chronic carriers of hepatitis B. It is transmitted by blood and bodily fluids. Again there is no vaccine, so avoidance is the best prevention. The risk to travellers is certainly limited.

Hepatitis E Little is yet known of this recently discovered virus. It appears to be rather common in developing countries, generally causing mild hepatitis, although it can be very serious in pregnant women. Care with water supplies is the only current prevention, as there are no specific vaccines for this type of hepatitis. At present it doesn't appear to be too great a risk for travellers.

Typhoid Typhoid fever is another gut infection that travels the faecal-oral route – that is, contaminated water and food are responsible. Vaccination against typhoid is not totally effective and it is one of the most dangerous infections, so medical help must be sought.

In its early stages typhoid resembles many other illnesses: sufferers may feel like they have a bad cold or flu on the way, as early symptoms are a headache, a sore throat, and a fever which rises a little each day until it is around 40°C or more. The victim's pulse is often slow relative to the degree of fever present and gets slower as the fever rises – unlike a normal fever where the pulse increases. There may also be vomiting, diarrhoea or constipation.

In the second week the high fever and slow pulse continue and a few pink spots may appear on the body; trembling, delirium, weakness, weight loss and dehydration are other symptoms. If there are no further complications, the fever and other symptoms will slowly diminish during the third week. However you must get medical help before this because pneumonia (acute infection of the lungs) or peritonitis (perforated bowel) are common complications, and because typhoid is very infectious.

The fever should be treated by keeping the victim cool and dehydration should also be watched for.

The drug of choice is ciprofloxacin at a dose of one gram daily for 14 days. It is quite expensive and may not be available. The alternative, chloramphenicol, has been the mainstay of treatment for many years. In many countries it is still the recommended antibiotic but there are fewer side effects with Ampicillin. The adult dosage is two 250 mg capsules, four times a day. Children aged between eight and 12 years should have half of the adult dose; younger children should have one-third of the adult dose.

People who are allergic to penicillin should not be given Ampicillin.

Worms These parasites are most common in rural, tropical areas and a stool test when you return home is not a bad idea. They can be present on unwashed vegetables or in undercooked meat and you can pick them up through your skin by walking in bare feet. Infestations may not show up for some time, and although they are generally not serious, if left untreated they can cause severe health problems. A stool test is necessary to pinpoint the problem and medication is often available over the counter.

Tetanus This potentially fatal disease is found in undeveloped tropical areas. It is difficult to treat but is preventable with immunisation. Tetanus occurs when a wound becomes infected by a germ that lives in soil and in the faeces of horses and other animals, so clean all cuts, punctures or animal bites. Tetanus is known as lockjaw, and the first symptom may be discomfort in swallowing, or stiffening of the jaw and neck; this is followed by painful convulsions of the jaw and whole body.

Rabies Rabies is a fatal viral infection found in many countries and is caused by a bite or scratch by an infected animal. Dogs are a noted carrier. Any bite, scratch or even lick from a mammal should be cleaned immediately and thoroughly. Scrub with soap and running water, and then clean with an alcohol solution. If there is any possibility that the animal is infected medical help should be sought immediately to prevent the onset of symptoms and death. Even if the animal is not rabid, all bites should be treated seriously as they can become infected or can result in tetanus. A rabies vaccination is now available and should be considered if you are in a high-risk category – eg, if you intend to explore caves (bat bites could be dangerous) or work with animals.

Bilharzia Bilharzia, or schistosomiasis, is present in Syria. It is carried in water by minute worms. The larvae infect certain varieties of freshwater snails found in rivers, streams, lakes and particularly behind dams. The worms multiply and are eventually discharged into the water surrounding the snails. They attach themselves to your intestines or bladder, where they produce large numbers of eggs. The worm enters through the skin, and the first symptom may be a tingling and sometimes a light rash around the area where it entered. Weeks later, when the worm is busy producing eggs, a high fever may develop. A general feeling of being unwell may be the first symptom; once the disease is established abdominal pain and blood in the urine are other signs. The infection often causes no symptoms until the disease is well established (several months to years after exposure) and damage to internal organs irreversible.

Avoiding swimming or bathing in fresh water where bilharzia is present is the main method of preventing the disease. Even deep water can be infected. If you do get wet, dry off quickly and dry your clothes as well. Seek medical attention if you have been exposed to the disease even if you don't have symptoms and tell the doctor your suspicions, as bilharzia in the early stages can be confused with malaria or typhoid. If you cannot get medical help immediately, praziquantel (Biltricide) is the recommended treatment. The recommended dosage is 40 mg/kg in divided doses over one day. Niridazole is an alternative drug.

Diphtheria Diphtheria can be a skin infection or a more dangerous throat infection. Treatment must be given under close medical supervision. It is spread by contaminated dust contacting the skin or by the inhalation of infected cough or sneeze droplets. Frequent washing and keeping the skin dry will help prevent skin infection. A vaccination is available to prevent the throat infection.

Sexually Transmitted Diseases Sexual contact with an infected sexual partner spreads these diseases. While abstinence is the only 100% preventative, using condoms is also effective. Gonorrhoea, herpes and syphilis are the most common of these diseases; sores, blisters or rashes around the genitals, discharges or pain when urinating are common symptoms. In some STDs, such as wart virus or chlamydia, symptoms may be less marked or not observed at all in women. Syphilis symptoms eventually disappear completely but the disease continues and can cause severe problems in later years. The treatment of gonorrhoea and syphilis is by antibiotics.

There are numerous other sexually transmitted diseases, for most of which effective treatment is available. However, there is no cure for herpes and there is also currently no cure for AIDS.

HIV/AIDS HIV, the Human Immunodeficiency Virus, may develop into AIDS, Acquired Immune Deficiency Syndrome. HIV is not a major problem in Jordan and Syria, but this does not mean you should not take the usual precautions. Any exposure to blood, blood products or bodily fluids may put the individual at risk. In many developing countries transmission is predominantly through sexual activity between heterosexuals. This is quite a different situation from industrialised countries where transmission is mostly through contact between homosexual or bisexual males, or via contaminated needles shared by IV drug users. Apart from abstinence, the most effective preventative is always to practise safe sex using condoms. It is impossible to detect the HIV-positive status of an otherwise healthy-looking person without a blood test.

HIV/AIDS can also be spread through infected blood transfusions; some developing countries cannot afford to screen blood for transfusions. It can also be spread by dirty needles – vaccinations, acupuncture, tattooing and ear or nose piercing can potentially be as dangerous as intravenous drug use if the equipment is not clean. If you do need an injection, ask to see the syringe unwrapped in front of you, or better still, take a needle and syringe pack with you overseas – it is a cheap insurance package against infection with HIV.

Fear of HIV infection should never preclude treatment for serious medical conditions. Although there may be a risk of infection, it is very small indeed.

Insect-Borne Diseases

Malaria Malaria in the desert? Surprising as it may seem, there is a small risk of catching malaria in Syria. The World Health Organisation reports that it no longer occurs in Jordan. Doctors generally do not recommend anti-malarial tablets to people travelling in the region, but they are recommended if you intend to spend a while along the Euphrates River in the north of Syria. The disease is spread by mosquitoes which, fortunately, are few in number. Also, unlike in many places, the strains of malaria here are not resistant to chloroquine. The period of highest risk is from May to October. Mosquitoes appear after dusk. Avoid getting bitten by covering bare skin and using an insect repellent.

Typhus Typhus is spread by ticks, mites or lice. It begins with fever, chills, headache and muscle pains followed a few days later by a body rash. There is often a large painful sore at the site of the bite and nearby lymph nodes are swollen and painful. Typhus is uncommon in travellers, but can be treated under medical supervision.

Tick typhus is spread by ticks. Scrub typhus is spread by mites that feed on infected rodents and exists mainly in Asia and the Pacific Islands. Seek local advice on areas where ticks pose a danger and always check your skin carefully for ticks after walking in a danger area such as a tropical forest. A strong insect repellent can help, and serious walkers in tick areas should consider having their boots and trousers impregnated with benzyl benzoate and dibutylphthalate.

Bugs, Bites & Stings

Cuts & Scratches Skin punctures can easily become infected in hot climates and may be difficult to heal. Treat any cut with an antiseptic and, where possible, avoid bandages and Band-aids, which can keep wounds wet. Dive instructors will discourage walking on the coral along Jordan's Red Sea coast, but if you must, wear shoes – coral cuts are notoriously slow to heal as the coral injects a weak venom into the wound.

Bites & Stings Trekkers in desert areas should keep an eye out for scorpions, which often shelter in shoes and the like and pack a powerful sting. Snake bites are also a possibility. Wrap the bitten limb tightly, immobilise it with a splint and seek medical help (if possible with the dead snake). Use of tourniquets and sucking out the poison have now been comprehensively discredited.

Scorpions Scorpion stings are a serious

cause of illness and occasional deaths in Jordan and Syria. Shake shoes, clothing and towels before use. Inspect bedding and don't put hands or feet in crevices in dwellings where they may be lurking. A sting usually produces redness and swelling of the skin, but there may be no visible reaction. Pain is common, and tingling or numbness may occur. At this stage, cold compresses on the bite, and pain relief, such as paracetamol are called for. If the skin sensations start to spread from the sting site (eg along the limb) then immediate medical attention is required.

Jellyfish In the Red Sea, jellyfish are a common problem. Local advice is the best way of avoiding contact with these sea creatures which have stinging tentacles. Stings from most jellyfish are simply rather painful. Dousing in vinegar will de-activate any stingers which have not 'fired'. Calamine lotion, antihistamines and analgesics may reduce the reaction and relieve the pain.

Bedbugs & Lice Bedbugs live in various places, but particularly in dirty mattresses and bedding. Spots of blood on bedclothes or on the wall around the bed can be read as a suggestion to find another hotel. Bedbugs leave itchy bites in neat rows. Calamine lotion may help.

All lice cause itching and discomfort. They make themselves at home in your hair (head lice), your clothing (body lice) or in your pubic hair (crabs). You catch lice through direct contact with infected people or by sharing combs, clothing and the like. A powder or shampoo treatment will kill the lice and infected clothing should then be washed in very hot water.

HEALTH

Women's Health

Gynaecological Problems Poor diet, lowered resistance due to using antibiotics for stomach upsets and even contraceptive pills can lead to vaginal infections when travelling in hot climates. Keeping the genital area clean, and wearing skirts or loose-fitting trousers and cotton underwear will help one to prevent infections.

Yeast infections, characterised by a rash, itch and discharge, can be treated with a vinegar or even lemon-juice douche, or with yoghurt. Nystatin suppositories are the usual medical prescription.

Trichomonas is a more serious infection; symptoms are a discharge and a burning sensation when urinating. Male sexual partners must also be treated, and if the use of a vinegar-water douche is not effective medical attention should be sought. Flagyl is the prescribed drug.

Pregnancy Most miscarriages occur during the first three months of pregnancy, so this is the most risky time to travel. The last three months should also be spent within reasonable distance of good medical care, as quite serious problems can develop at this time.

Pregnant women should avoid all unnecessary medication, but vaccinations and malarial prophylactics should still be taken where possible. Additional care should be taken to prevent illness and particular attention should be paid to diet and nutrition.

Glossary

This glossary is mostly a list of Arabic (a) and French (f) words commonly used in Jordan and Syria. It also contains some words of other linguistic derivation.

'abaaya (a) – woman's full-length black robe
Abbasids – Baghdad-based successor dynasty to the Omayyads, which lasted from 750 until the sack of Baghdad by the Mongols in 1258. By that time, the Abassid caliphs had lost much of their power, although in the first three centuries of their rule, Arabic and Islamic culture flourished. The Abbasid caliphate was maintained in Cairo until 1517 after the sacking of Baghdad, but had no power.
al-matar (a) – airport
al-Medina al-riyadiyya (a) – sports complex
andron (a) – men's meeting place
as-sidd (a) – dam
Ayyubids – the dynasty founded by Salah ad-Din (Saladin) in Egypt in 1169. He was largely responsible for uniting the fractious Muslims in the fight against the Crusaders, and the retaking of Jerusalem and most of the Crusaders' other possessions.

bab (abwab) (a) – gate
bayt (a) – house
bayt ash sha'ar (a) – goat hair tent
benzin (a) – regular petrol
burj (a) – tower

caliph 'successor' – the Muslim rulers who succeeded Mohammed were religious and secular rulers at once, whose power reached its apogee under the early Abbasids. As the power of this dynasty declined, numerous others sprang up in the disintegrating Muslim world, and the caliphate lost importance. It remained the highest authority in the Muslim world, but increasingly in name only.
caravanserai – large inn enclosing a courtyard, providing accommodation and a marketplace for caravans
centraal (f) – telephone office

deir (a) – monastery
donjon (f) – dungeon
duwaar (a) – circle

garage – commonly used term for bus and service taxi stations in Syria (from French)

Hajj (a) – the pilgrimage to Mecca
Hajji (a) – one who has made the Hajj to Mecca
hammam (a) – Turkish-style bathhouse with sauna and massage. It can also mean an ordinary bath, and is often used to refer to the toilet.
hijab (a) – woman's head scarf

imam (a) – religious leader
iwan – (a) vaulted hall, opening onto a central court, usually in the madrassa of a mosque

jalabiyyeh (a) – man's full-length robe
jazira (a) – island
jebel (a) – hill or mountain

khan (a) – see caravanserai
khususi (a) – special
khutba (a) – sermon
kibla (a) – direction of Mecca

madrassa (a) – theological college that is part of a non-congregational mosque; also a school
Mamelukes – 'slaves'. This Turkish slave and soldier class rose to power in Egypt and ruled it and later Syria from 1250 to the coming of the Ottoman Turks in 1517. Their reign was characterised by seemingly unending blood-letting and intrigue for the succession.
mashad (a) – ablution hall
mazout (a) – diesel

medina (a) – city
meecro – microbus (local dialect from French)
midan (a) – town or city square (see also saha)
mihrab (a) – niche in the wall of a mosque that indicates the direction of Mecca
minbar (a) – pulpit in a mosque
muezzin (a) – mosque official who, from the minaret, calls the faithful to prayer five times a day
muhafaza(t) (a) – governorate(s)
mukhabarat (a) – secret police
mumtaz (a) – super petrol/1st class (eg on trains); literally 'excellent'

narjileh (a) – water pipes used to smoke tobacco (also spelled nargileh and Arjileh)
noria – wooden water wheels, built centuries ago

Omayyads – first great dynasty of Arab Muslim rulers, based in Damascus, which lasted from 661 to 750 AD

qasr (a) – castle or palace; used generically in reference to a series of buildings that were erected, mostly in the 8th century, across the desert in southern Syria and Jordan by Omayyad rulers

rababah (a) – traditional single string Bedouin instrument
ras (a) – headland; also head

saha (a) – town or city square (see also midan)
servees – service taxi (local dialect from French)
sharq al-awsat (a) – Middle East
sheikh (a) – officer of the mosque
sidd (a) – dam
siq (a) – gorge
souq (a) – market

tawaabi' (a) – postage stamps
tell (a) – artificial hill
temenos (a) – courtyard
tetrapylon – four groups of four pillars
thukna (a) – barracks
trezeena – three wheeled motorised cart (local dialect from French)

wadi (a) – valley formed by watercourse which is often dry except after heavy rainfall

Index

ABBREVIATIONS

Jor – Jordan
Syr – Syria

MAPS

TEXT

Map references are in **bold** type

THANKS

Thanks to the following people and many travellers from all over the world who took the time and trouble to write to us about their experiences in Jordan and Syria:

Barry Aitken, Katharine Barnes, Susan Bauer, Nick Bayley, Eric Beauchemin, Sven Behrendt, Chris & Bev Bennett, Asa Berggren, Robert Best, Helmut Bock, Anne Marie Bohlers, Les Bonwell, Martinette Boonekamp, David Borenstein, Fraser Borwick, Tanya Bosch, Steve Bougerolle, Xavier Bourgeat, Carsten Brandt, Mary Bredin, Gerard Brockhoff, Charles Brown, W W Brown, Glen O Brown, Richard Brunning, Michael Bussiere, Danny Byrne, Helen & Chris Cahill, Chris Caley, Robin Carlisle, Lawrence Cavedon, E Christopher, David Churchman, Mark Conrod, Jeanne Conte, G A Cowper, John Cox, Russell Crumrine, Eleanor Culley , Paolo dalla Zonca, Michael Dalo, Rene David, Trudi Davies, Jane C Davis, Rosario de Paz, Fiona Dent, Ingo Dewald-Werner, Doug Dewar, Ben Dipple, Paul & Shiela Doherty, Betty Donald, Susan & Ian Dunn, Elizabeth Durham, Jo Eades, Rachel Edwards, Katharina Eger, Lisette Eijermans, Ushi Engel, Tony Esler, Jenn Feray, Anthony Field, John Field, Stephen Fischer, Roland Fohn, R Frank, Keith Fraser-Smith, Martin Frissel, James Gallantry, Heidi Gayer, Dean George, P Gibbs, Ruth Glassnock, Matthias Gockler, Jo Goldby , Mac Gollifes, Karen Goodison, Jill Goulder, J Llorens Granollers, M Gregoire, Dave Griffiths, Alison Groves, D M Halford, Annette Hamilton, Miss C J Hamilton, Narrelle Harris, Peter Hartung, Michael Harvey, J Hawker, Rosemary Haywood, Jonathan Hibbs, Gary Hickman, Steven & Michael Hill, Kevin Hill, David Hodge, Lynda Hoevland, Lambert Hogenhout, Andrew & Jane Homer, Dr & Mrs Horner, Philipp Hufschmid, Mark Ignativ, M Jackson, Michael Jacobson, Joyce James, Elisabetta Jankovic, Ton Janusch, F Jensen, Stephen Job, Margaret Johnson, Jenny Jones, Lambert Karel, Denis Kearney, Len Keating, Anne-Kathrin Keinath, Nick Kenrick, Matthias Klein, Jolanda Kortehaas, J Kortelaas, Dimitri Kotzamanis, Tim Kretzer, Janet Kupfer, Duncan Lamb, Jeri Lang , Edwin Latter, Lynne Leatherdale, Ka Fai Lee, Stephen-Andrew Lee, Ray Lister, Amber Lloyd, Serena Love, Eimear Lovelle, Graham Lowe, Andrew Lowton, Dawn Mackie, L A Mackie, Paul Macro, A Magrys, M E Mahon, Bronwen Manby, Dorothy Mares, Beth Matsuto, Anthony McCarter, Christine McGowan, Warren Meneely, Dr Mess, Dr Ade Miller, Mark Milton, Tsevi Minster, Alex Monier-Williams, Liz Montague, Nick Moody, Nick Morgan, Jason Morris, Robert Moss, Andy Mudd, Christoph Mueller, Michael Nedeff, Erik Neilsen, Arlynn Nellhaus, Anna Norris, Yaser Al Olabi, Roderick Oates, Phil Offer, Alberto Padova, Norman Parker, Silke Pasker, Frank Pedley, Didia Person, C Pierrot, H Pietka, A J Pinion, Rene Platell, Anja Pleit, Dr Istvan Pokoradi, Mr G A Poole, Michele Provinciael, Jens Pusch, Shiela Read, Mr & Mrs Renty-Huys, Jean Robinson, Rachel Robinson, O Rogge, David Ross, Gavin Rummery, F Russell, H H Saffery, Sarah Sanders-Davies, Robert Sandham, Nigel Sarbutts, R Schulze-Honighaus, John Sear, Robin Sherwen, Jim Shimwell, T Sidey, Laurent Siklossy, Stephanie Sim, Sandra Simmons, Chris Smart, C Smith, Janet Smith, Alessandra Sonnati, Albert Spykman, Paul Starkey, Peter Stein, Kay Stern, Claire Stewart, David Stone, Reinhard Storiko, Maria Svensson, Roisin & Andre Tambour, Gavin Tanguay, Jennifer Thayer, Terry Thomas, Henry Thompson, Valentine Tixier, Susan Tod, Dave Tootall, Gerhard Topfer, Jason & Louise Travis, Kevin Troy, G L A Tuck, Mr & Mrs R Turner, Mark Turpin, Markus Ulrich, P W Valentine, Magda van Korlaar, H van der Kop, Torger Vedeler, Stuart Veitch, George Vrontos, Sin Wai Man, Cam Walker, Sue Watts, Sheila Webb, Stella Wegman, Bjorn Weidner, Paul Werne, Jane & Andrew Wilkie, Reginald Williams, Paul & Liz Williamson, Simon & Lizzi Winn, Shelley Wolbrink-van der Berg, Jennifer Woo, C H & W B Yee and Ian Young.

Turkish

bugün - TODAY
bilet - TICKET

please - lütfen
thankyou - teşekkur edirim

water - su

0 - sıfır
1 - bir
2 - iki
3 - üç
4 - dört
5 - beş
6 - altı
7 - yedi
8 - sekiz
9 - dokuz
10 - on
20 - yirmi
30 - otuz
40 - kırk
50 - elli
60 - altmış
70 - yetmiş
80 - seksen
90 - doksan
100 - yüz

1000 - bin

LONELY PLANET JOURNEYS

JOURNEYS is a unique collection of travellers' tales – published by the company that understands travel better than anyone else. It is a series for anyone who has ever experienced – or dreamed of – the magical moment when they encountered a strange culture or saw a place for the first time. They are tales to read while you're planning a trip, while you're on the road or while you're in an armchair, in front of a fire.

JOURNEYS books will catch the spirit of a place, illuminate a culture, recount a crazy adventure, or introduce a fascinating way of life. They will always entertain, and always enrich the experience of travel.

THE GATES OF DAMASCUS

Lieve Joris

Translated by Sam Garrett

This best-selling book is a beautifully drawn portrait of day-to-day life in modern Syria. Through her intimate contact with local people, Lieve Joris draws us into the fascinating world that lies behind the gates of Damascus. Hala's husband is a political prisoner, jailed for his opposition to the Assad regime; through the author's friendship with Hala we see how Syrian politics impacts on the lives of ordinary people.

Lieve Joris, who was born in Belgium, is one of Europe's foremost travel writers. In addition to an award-winning book on Hungary, she has published widely-acclaimed accounts of her journeys to the Middle East and Africa. *The Gates of Damascus* is her fifth book.

'Expands the boundaries of travel writing' – Times Literary Supplement

KINGDOM OF THE FILM STARS
Journey into Jordan

Annie Caulfield

Kingdom of the Film Stars is a travel book and a love story. With honesty and humour, Annie Caulfield writes of travelling in Jordan and falling in love with a Bedouin. Her book offers fascinating insights into the country – from the traditional tent life of nomadic tribes to the first woman MP's battle with fundamentalist colleagues. *Kingdom of the Film Stars* unpicks some of the tight-woven Western myths about the Arab world, presenting cultural and political issues within the intimate framework of a compelling love story.

Annie Caulfield is an award-winning journalist and playwright. She lives in London and has travelled widely in the Middle East.

Other Journeys titles:

FULL CIRCLE: A South American Journey by Luis Sepúlveda (translated by Chris Andrews)

IN RAJASTHAN by Royina Grewal

ISLANDS IN THE CLOUDS: Travels in the Highlands of New Guinea by Isabella Tree

LOST JAPAN by Alex Kerr

SEAN & DAVID'S LONG DRIVE by Sean Condon

SHOPPING FOR BUDDHAS by Jeff Greenwald

LONELY PLANET TRAVEL ATLASES

Lonely Planet has long been famous for the number and quality of its guidebook maps. Now we've gone one step further and in conjunction with Steinhart Katzir Publishers produced a handy companion series: Lonely Planet travel atlases – maps of a country produced in book form.

Unlike other maps, which look good but lead travellers astray, our travel atlases have been researched on the road by Lonely Planet's experienced team of writers. All details are carefully checked to ensure the atlas corresponds with the equivalent Lonely Planet guidebook.

The handy atlas format means no holes, wrinkles, torn sections or constant folding and unfolding. These atlases can survive long periods on the road, unlike cumbersome fold-out maps. The comprehensive index ensures easy reference.

- full-colour throughout
- maps researched and checked by Lonely Planet authors
- place names correspond with Lonely Planet guidebooks – no confusing spelling differences
- legend and travelling information in English, French, German, Japanese and Spanish
- size: 230 x 160 mm

Available now:
Chile & Easter Island; Egypt; India & Bangladesh; Israel & the Palestinian Territories; Jordan, Syria & Lebanon; Laos; Thailand; Vietnam; Zimbabwe, Botswana & Namibia

---

LONELY PLANET TV SERIES & VIDEOS

Lonely Planet travel guides have been brought to life on television screens around the world. Like our guides, the programmes are based on the joy of independent travel, and look honestly at some of the most exciting, picturesque and frustrating places in the world. Each show is presented by one of three travellers from Australia, England or the USA and combines an innovative mixture of video, Super-8 film, atmospheric soundscapes and original music.

Videos of each episode – containing additional footage not shown on television – are available from good book and video shops, but the availability of individual videos varies with regional screening schedules.

Video destinations include: Alaska; Australia (Southeast); Brazil; Ecuador & the Galápagos Islands; Indonesia; Israel & the Sinai Desert; Japan; La Ruta Maya (Yucatán, Guatemala & Belize); Morocco; North India (Varanasi to the Himalaya); Pacific Islands; Vietnam; Zimbabwe, Botswana & Namibia.

Coming soon: The Arctic (Norway & Finland); Baja California; Chile & Easter Island; China (Southeast); Costa Rica; East Africa (Tanzania & Zanzibar); Great Barrier Reef (Australia); Jamaica; Papua New Guinea; the Rockies (USA); Syria & Jordan; Turkey.

The Lonely Planet TV series is produced by:
Pilot Productions
Duke of Sussex Studios
44 Uxbridge St
London W8 7TG UK

Lonely Planet videos are distributed by:
IVN Communications Inc
2246 Camino Ramon
California 94583, USA

107 Power Road, Chiswick
London W4 5PL UK

Music from the TV series is available on CD & cassette.
For ordering information contact your nearest Lonely Planet office.

PLANET TALK

Lonely Planet's FREE quarterly newsletter

We love hearing from you and think you'd like to hear from us.

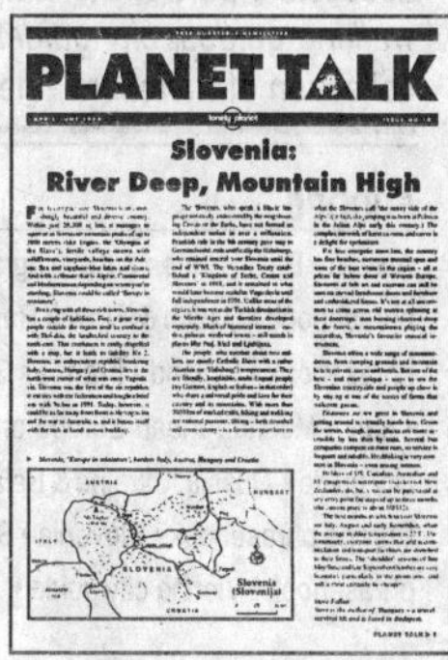

When... is the right time to see reindeer in Finland?
Where... can you hear the best palm-wine music in Ghana?
How... do you get from Asunción to Areguá by steam train?
What... is the best way to see India?

For the answer to these and many other questions read PLANET TALK.

Every issue is packed with up-to-date travel news and advice including:

- a letter from Lonely Planet co-founders Tony and Maureen Wheeler
- go behind the scenes on the road with a Lonely Planet author
- feature article on an important and topical travel issue
- a selection of recent letters from travellers
- details on forthcoming Lonely Planet promotions
- complete list of Lonely Planet products

To join our mailing list contact any Lonely Planet office.

Also available: Lonely Planet T-shirts. 100% heavyweight cotton.

LONELY PLANET ONLINE

Get the latest travel information before you leave or while you're on the road

Whether you've just begun planning your next trip, or you're chasing down specific info on currency regulations or visa requirements, check out the Lonely Planet World Wide Web site for up-to-the-minute travel information.

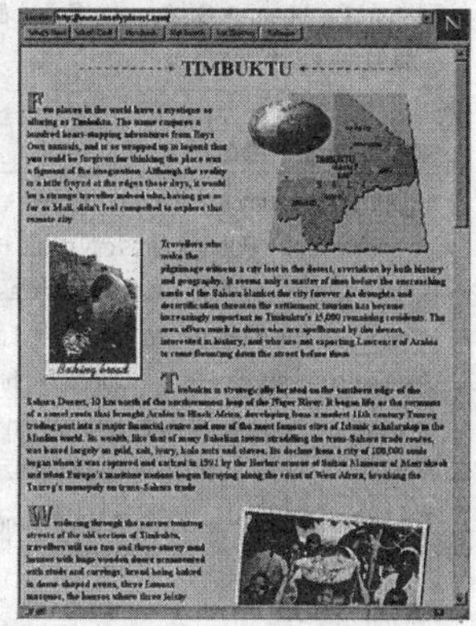

As well as travel profiles of your favourite destinations (including interactive maps and full-colour photos), you'll find current reports from our army of researchers and other travellers, updates on health and visas, travel advisories, and the ecological and political issues you need to be aware of as you travel.

There's an online travellers' forum (the Thorn Tree) where you can share your experiences of life on the road, meet travel companions and ask other travellers for their recommendations and advice. We also have plenty of links to other Web sites useful to independent travellers.

With tens of thousands of visitors a month, the Lonely Planet Web site is one of the most popular on the Internet and has won a number of awards including GNN's Best of the Net travel award.

http://www.lonelyplanet.com

LONELY PLANET PRODUCTS

Lonely Planet is known worldwide for publishing practical, reliable and no-nonsense travel information in our guides and on our web site. The Lonely Planet list covers just about every accessible part of the world. Currently there are eight series: *travel guides, shoestring guides, walking guides, city guides, phrasebooks, audio packs, travel atlases* and *Journeys* – a unique collection of travellers' tales.

EUROPE

Austria • Baltic States & Kaliningrad • Baltic States phrasebook • Britain • Central Europe on a shoestring • Central Europe phrasebook • Czech & Slovak Republics • Denmark • Dublin city guide • Eastern Europe on a shoestring • Eastern Europe phrasebook • Finland • France • Greece • Greek phrasebook • Hungary • Iceland, Greenland & the Faroe Islands • Ireland • Italy • Mediterranean Europe on a shoestring • Mediterranean Europe phrasebook • Paris city guide • Poland • Prague city guide • Russia, Ukraine & Belarus • Russian phrasebook • Scandinavian & Baltic Europe on a shoestring • Scandinavian Europe phrasebook • Slovenia • St Petersburg city guide • Switzerland • Trekking in Greece • Trekking in Spain • Ukrainian phrasebook • Vienna city guide • Walking in Switzerland • Western Europe on a shoestring • Western Europe phrasebook

NORTH AMERICA

Alaska • Backpacking in Alaska • Baja California • California & Nevada • Canada • Florida • Hawaii • Honolulu city guide • Los Angeles city guide • Mexico • Miami city guide • New England • New Orleans city guide • Pacific Northwest USA • Rocky Mountain States • San Francisco city guide • Southwest USA • USA phrasebook

CENTRAL AMERICA & THE CARIBBEAN

Central America on a shoestring • Costa Rica • Cuba • Eastern Caribbean • Guatemala, Belize & Yucatán: La Ruta Maya • Jamaica

SOUTH AMERICA

Argentina, Uruguay & Paraguay • Bolivia • Brazil • Brazilian phrasebook • Buenos Aires city guide • Chile & Easter Island • Chile & Easter Island travel atlas • Colombia • Ecuador & the Galápagos Islands • Latin American Spanish phrasebook • Peru • Quechua phrasebook • Rio de Janeiro city guide • South America on a shoestring • Trekking in the Patagonian Andes • Venezuela

Travel Literature: Full Circle: A South American Journey

ANTARCTICA

Antarctica

ISLANDS OF THE INDIAN OCEAN

Madagascar & Comoros • Maldives & Islands of the East Indian Ocean • Mauritius, Réunion & Seychelles

AFRICA

Arabic (Moroccan) phrasebook • Africa on a shoestring • Cape Town city guide • Central Africa • East Africa • Egypt • Egypt travel atlas • Ethiopian (Amharic) phrasebook • Kenya • Morocco • North Africa • South Africa, Lesotho & Swaziland • Swahili phrasebook • Trekking in East Africa • West Africa • Zimbabwe, Botswana & Namibia • Zimbabwe, Botswana & Namibia travel atlas

ALSO AVAILABLE:

Travel with Children • Traveller's Tales

MAIL ORDER

Lonely Planet products are distributed worldwide.They are also available by mail order from Lonely Planet, so if you have difficulty finding a title please write to us. North American and South American residents should write to Embarcadero West, 155 Filbert St, Suite 251, Oakland CA 94607, USA; European and African residents should write to 10 Barley Mow Passage, Chiswick, London W4 4PH; and residents of other countries to PO Box 617, Hawthorn, Victoria 3122, Australia.

NORTH-EAST ASIA

Beijing city guide • Cantonese phrasebook • China • Hong Kong, Macau & Canton • Hong Kong city guide • Japan • Japanese phrasebook • Japanese audio pack • Korea • Korean phrasebook • Mandarin phrasebook • Mongolia • Mongolian phrasebook • North-East Asia on a shoestring • Seoul city guide • Taiwan • Tibet • Tibet phrasebook • Tokyo city guide

Travel Literature: Lost Japan

MIDDLE EAST & CENTRAL ASIA

Arab Gulf States • Arabic (Egyptian) phrasebook • Central Asia • Iran • Israel & the Palestinian Territories • Israel & the Palestinian Territories travel atlas • Jordan & Syria • Jordan, Syria & Lebanon travel atlas • Middle East • Turkey • Turkish phrasebook • Trekking in Turkey • Yemen

Travel Literature: The Gates of Damascus • Kingdom of the Film Stars: Journey into Jordan

INDIAN SUBCONTINENT

Bangladesh • Bengali phrasebook • Delhi city guide • Hindi/Urdu phrasebook • India • India & Bangladesh travel atlas • Indian Himalaya • Karakoram Highway • Nepal • Nepali phrasebook • Pakistan • Rajasthan • Sri Lanka • Sri Lanka phrasebook • Trekking in the Indian Himalaya • Trekking in the Karakoram & Hindukush • Trekking in the Nepal Himalaya

Travel Literature: In Rajasthan • Shopping for Buddhas

SOUTH-EAST ASIA

Bali & Lombok • Bangkok city guide • Burmese phrasebook • Cambodia • Ho Chi Minh city guide • Indonesia • Indonesian phrasebook • Indonesian audio pack • Jakarta city guide • Java • Laos • Lao phrasebook • Laos travel atlas • Malay phrasebook • Malaysia, Singapore & Brunei • Myanmar (Burma) • Philippines • Pilipino phrasebook • Singapore city guide • South-East Asia on a shoestring • Thailand • Thailand travel atlas • Thai phrasebook • Thai audio pack • Thai Hill Tribes phrasebook • Vietnam • Vietnamese phrasebook • Vietnam travel atlas

AUSTRALIA & THE PACIFIC

Australia • Australian phrasebook • Bushwalking in Australia • Bushwalking in Papua New Guinea • Fiji • Fijian phrasebook • Islands of Australia's Great Barrier Reef • Melbourne city guide • Micronesia • New Caledonia • New South Wales & the ACT • New Zealand • Northern Territory • Outback Australia • Papua New Guinea • Papua New Guinea phrasebook • Queensland • Rarotonga & the Cook Islands • Samoa • Solomon Islands • South Australia • Sydney city guide • Tahiti & French Polynesia • Tasmania • Tonga • Tramping in New Zealand • Vanuatu • Victoria • Western Australia

Travel Literature: Islands in the Clouds • Sean & David's Long Drive

THE LONELY PLANET STORY

Lonely Planet published its first book in 1973 in response to the numerous 'How did you do it?' questions Maureen and Tony Wheeler were asked after driving, bussing, hitching, sailing and railing their way from England to Australia.

Written at a kitchen table and hand collated, trimmed and stapled, *Across Asia on the Cheap* became an instant local bestseller, inspiring thoughts of another book.

Eighteen months in South-East Asia resulted in their second guide, *South-East Asia on a shoestring*, which they put together in a backstreet Chinese hotel in Singapore in 1975. The 'yellow bible', as it quickly became known to backpackers around the world, soon became *the* guide to the region. It has sold well over half a million copies and is now in its 8th edition, still retaining its familiar yellow cover.

Today there are over 180 titles, including travel guides, walking guides, language kits & phrasebooks, travel atlases and travel literature. The company is one of the largest travel publishers in the world. Although Lonely Planet initially specialised in guides to Asia, we now cover most regions of the world, including the Pacific, North America, South America, Africa, the Middle East and Europe.

The emphasis continues to be on travel for independent travellers. Tony and Maureen still travel for several months of each year and play an active part in the writing, updating and quality control of Lonely Planet's guides.

They have been joined by over 70 authors and 170 staff at our offices in Melbourne (Australia), Oakland (USA), London (UK) and Paris (France). Travellers themselves also make a valuable contribution to the guides through the feedback we receive in thousands of letters each year.

The people at Lonely Planet strongly believe that travellers can make a positive contribution to the countries they visit, both through their appreciation of the countries' culture, wildlife and natural features, and through the money they spend. In addition, the company makes a direct contribution to the countries and regions it covers. Since 1986 a percentage of the income from each book has been donated to ventures such as famine relief in Africa; aid projects in India; agricultural projects in Central America; Greenpeace's efforts to halt French nuclear testing in the Pacific; and Amnesty International.

'I hope we send the people out with the right attitude about travel. You realise when you travel that there are so many different perspectives about the world, so we hope these books will make people more interested in what they see. These are guidebooks, but you can't really guide people. All you can do is point them in the right direction.'

– Tony Wheeler

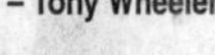

LONELY PLANET PUBLICATIONS

Australia
PO Box 617, Hawthorn 3122, Victoria
tel: (03) 9819 1877 fax: (03) 9819 6459
e-mail: talk2us@lonelyplanet.com.au

USA
Embarcadero West, 155 Filbert St, Suite 251,
Oakland, CA 94607
tel: (510) 893 8555 TOLL FREE: 800 275-8555
fax: (510) 893 8563
e-mail: info@lonelyplanet.com

UK
10 Barley Mow Passage, Chiswick,
London W4 4PH
tel: (0181) 742 3161 fax: (0181) 742 2772
e-mail: 100413.3551@compuserve.com

France:
71 bis rue du Cardinal Lemoine, 75005 Paris
tel: 1 44 32 06 20 fax: 1 46 34 72 55
e-mail: 100560.415@compuserve.com

World Wide Web: http://www.lonelyplanet.com